DR. AMBEDKAR: LIFE AND MISSION

To,
Dear Jack
'your are my love'
I felt in my life you
are a my great friend.

from Vinod.

Dr. Bhimrao Ramji Ambedkar
14th April 1891 — 6th December 1956

Dr. AMBEDKAR
LIFE AND MISSION

DHANANJAY KEER

Popular
prakashan
www.popularprakashan.com

Published by
Harsha Bhatkal
for Popular Prakashan Pvt. Ltd.
301, Mahalaxmi Chambers
22, Bhulabhai Desai Road
Mumbai 400 026
www.popularprakashan.com

© 2009, Dr. Suneet Keer
First Published 1954
Revised Second Edition 1962
Third Edition 1971
Reprinted 1981, 1987, 1990
Reprinted 1991, 1992, 1994, 1995
Reprinted 2004
Fourth Edition 2009
Reprinted 2016
Fifth Edition 2016

(4436)
ISBN : 978-81-7991-877-7

Cover and Design : Satish Bhavsar
Cover photo and letter on back cover courtesy: Vijay Survade

Printed by
India Printing Works
42, G.D. Ambekar Marg
Wadala, Mumbai - 400 031

To

R.D. *alias* APPASHEB TINAKAR

PUBLISHER'S NOTE

'NIRMALA SADANAND SERIES' is being published under Popular Prakashan imprint to commemorate Nirmala (1924-2011) and Sadanand Bhatkal (1922-2011), who along with G.R. Bhatkal (1896- 1972) laid the foundation of Popular Book Depot (established in 1924) and its publishing division Popular Prakashan.

Sadanand was the president of the Federation of Publishers and Booksellers Associations in India and put Indian publishing on the world map. He edited a three-volume Marathi 'Encyclopaedia of Marathi Literature', the first of its kind. Apart from their sterling contribution to the book world, particularly as editors of the Journal *Indian Publisher & Bookseller* (1950-1985), they played a leading role in community and cultural work. Before 1947, they had both participated in India's freedom movement.

Keer's biography of Mahatma Jotirao Phooley was brought out with important additions as the first book in the series. Dr. Babasaheb Ambedkar was first published by the author in 1954 and is now being reissued.

Dhananjay Keer (b.1913), the foremost biographer in India, had the privilege of personal dialogue with the protagonists when he wrote on Vinayak Damodar Savarkar(1883-1966)and Bhimrao Ambedkar (1888-1956). When Dr. Ambedkar expressed regret at his not being able to write a biography of Mahatma Phooley, whom he considered his Guru, Keer promised to take up this task.

Keer's biographies have enabled scholars from different parts of India, not familiar with Marathi, to explore sources not hitherto available to them. Keer's biographies of Mahatma Jotirao Phooley, Chhatrapati Shahu Maharaj and Dr Babasaheb Ambedkar complete the trilogy, that played an important role in rewriting social history of India just as his works on Bal Gangadhar Tilak, Mahatma Gandhi and Veer Savarkar have provided a different perspective on the political history of modern India.

All these biographies are being reissued to mark the birth centenary of Dhananjay Keer.

Mumbai
November 11, 2014

PREFACE TO THE THIRD EDITION

I am extremely happy to present the third edition of the complete biography of Dr. B. R. Ambedkar which has been termed a monumental and immortal biography. The favourable reception accorded to the original biography by leading Indian and foreign papers and by eminent persons has encouraged me to bring it up-to-date. I have incorporated new facts and new information collected by me, at the appropriate places in historical sequence. This additional matter reveals the opinion of Dr. Ambedkar on the work and mission of Marathi saint-poets, gives his views on the main features of the Constitution and relates the tragic event in his life in the death of his infant son.

I acknowledge my debt of gratitude to S. N. Shivtarkar and Shankarrao Wadvalkar for providing me with some material for the first edition of the book and to Vasantrao Chitre, Naval Bhathena, S. S. Rege, and N. C. Rattu for providing me with some material for the second edition. I am grateful to the readers and reviewers and publishers who provided me with a unique opportunity of offering this definitive biography. My thanks are also due to the printers for the interest they take in my work.

BHAGESHWAR BHUVAN   **DHANANJAY KEER**
DILIP GUPTE ROAD
MAHIM
BOMBAY 16
March 27,1971

PREFACE TO THE FIRST EDITION

It is my pleasure and privilege in present the first full-length, up-to-date and authentic biography of this great Indian scholar and statesman, leader and liberator and the Chief Architect of the Constitution of India. Having won her political independence, India now needs to be refashioned into a social and economic democracy; and the life of no other political leader constitutes this message than the life of Dr. Ambedkar. Although his life, with all his sacrifices, struggles and scholarship, is chiefly devoted to liberating six crores of people from their age-long bondage and is a new era in the lives of those suppressed people, it is no less a glorious fight for ushering in India a social and economic democracy.

This book is a study of the history of this great man in which I have endeavoured to cast a gripping light on his words and deeds and the motives from which they sprang. I have limned him as he is.

Ambedkar has played the part of destiny in the liberation of suppressed humanity in India. So India must learn to understand his life, character and mission and know him as he is and not as he is distorted by his enemies or deified by his devotees. In order to help readers see the development of his mind and understand the bitterness and violence with which he attacked the old views and values that had defaced a part of humanity in this land, I have traced the events and facts in their proper context and perspective and dealt with the views of his great contemporaries with whom he came into clash. In doing so I have not the remotest idea of belittling their greatness. Every great man has his minor foibles and flaws and when he moves and struggles in a particular field, he comes into conflict with the great ones in that field.

This biography is important from another point of view. Thought-provoking and provocative, this life is highly instructive to everyone who yearns for human dignity and equality in human relations in society. Besides, it provides a most inspiring example of what a man can achieve by his indomitable perseverance and great self-denial, even under the most depressing and destitute circumstances. It provides also a lesson that one should rely upon one's own efforts in life rather than depend upon the help and patronage of others. Ambedkar's eternal search for knowledge, his incredible industry and his unflinching aim with which he raised himself from dust to doyen, from the life of a social leper to the position of a constitution-maker, and his heroic struggles for raising the down-trodden to human dignity will constitute a golden chapter in the history of this nation and in the history of human freedom as well.

I am deeply indebted to Dr. Ambedkar for the interviews he granted me and for clearing some points in relation to some events. I acknowledge with gratitude the kindness of my friends in reading the manuscript and the proofs, and also the encouragement my benefactors gave me at every stage in the production of the book.

My grateful thanks are due to those who have supplied me with the material. I acknowledge gratefully my debt to all the authors, journals and publishers from whose books or publications I have drawn excerpts. Thanks are due to the India Printing Works for their prompt and exquisite execution of the work.

Mahim, Bombay   DHANANJAY KEER
May 16,1954

CONTENTS

CHAPTER 1

TWENTY-FIVE HUNDRED YEARS

AMBEDKAR hailed from a poor family belonging to one of the Hindu untouchable communities in India. The Untouchables comprised a number of distinct groups which form the lowest strata of Hindu society, and were condemned as Untouchables by the caste Hindus through centuries untold. Before the Indian Constitution abolishing untouchability was adopted in 1950, untouchable classes were 'divided into three categories— Untouchables, Unapproachables and Unseeables. They numbered about sixty million out of three hundred million Hindus. That is to say, very nearly twenty per cent of Hindustan was untouchable. In short, every fifth Hindu, man, woman and child was an Untouchable.

The Untouchables had different names in different parts of the country. They were called Outcastes, Untouchables, Pariahs, Panchamas, Atishudras, Avarnas, Antyajas and Namashudras. Their social disabilities were specific and severe and numerous. Their touch, shadow and even voice were deemed by the caste Hindus to be polluting. So they had to clear the way at the approach of a caste Hindu. They were forbidden to keep certain domestic animals, to use certain metals for ornaments; were obliged to wear a particular type of dress, to eat a particular type of food, to use a particular type of footwear and were forced to occupy the dirty, dingy and unhygienic outskirts of villages and towns for habitation where they lived in dark, insanitary and miserable smoky shanties or cottages. The dress of the male consisted of a turban, a staff in the hand, a rough blanket on the shoulder and a piece of loin cloth. The women. wore bodices and rough sarees barely reaching the knees.

These untouchable Hindus were denied the use of public wells, and were condemned to drink any filthy after they could find. Their children were not admitted to schools attended by the caste Hindu children. Though they worshipped the gods of Hindus observed the same festivals, the Hindu temples were closed to

1

them. Barbers and washermen refused to render them service. The caste Hindus, who fondly threw sugar to ants and reared dogs and other domestic pets and welcomed persons of other religions to their houses, refused to give, a drop of water to the Untouchables or to show them an iota of sympathy. These untouchable Hindus were treated by the caste Hindus as sub-humans, less than men, worse than beasts. This picture is still true of villages and small towns. Cities have now mostly overcome this prejudice.

Their miseries did not end at this. As they were illiterate, ill-treated and untouchable for ages, all public services including police and military forces were closed to them. Naturally they followed hereditary occupations. Some of them plied trades of a lower and degrading order such as those of street-sweepers, scavengers and shoemakers. Some skinned carcasses, tanned hides and skins, worked in bamboos and cane and mowed grass. Others who were more fortunate tilled the land as tenants, worked as labourers in fields, a great number of them subsisted on food or grain given to them as village servants and also at carrion. Thus being deprived of social, religious and civic rights, they had no chance of bettering their conditions; and so these untouchable Hindus lived the life of a 'bygone and dead age, dragging on their miserable existence in insufficient accommodation, insanitary surroundings and social segregation. In short, they were born in debt and perished in debt. They were born Untouchables, they lived as Untouchables and they died as Untouchables.

II

The origin of untouchability is an enigma to modern history. But it is generally held that it is a perverted outcome of the caste system. The Vedic Aryans knew no caste system. As time went on, the Aryans divided themselves for different occupations on the basis of division of labour and according to aptitude, liking and capacity of the individual. Those who took to learning were called Brahmins, those who undertook governance were classified as Kshatriyas, those who resorted to trade were termed Vaishyas, and those who served the foregoing three classes were known as Shudras.

Dr. Ambedkar (1918)

With fellow students and a group of Professors
at the London School of Economics and Political Science

A young and confident
Dr. Babasaheb Ambedkar

Second Round Table Conference, London (1931)
British Prime Minister Ramsay McDonald, Gandhiji,
Pandit Madan Mohan Malviya, B. Mukundrao Jaikar,
Sir Tej Bahadur Sapru, Dr. Ambedkar (looking back)

Pillar dedicated to the memory of
the Revolutionaries at Mahad

With fellow workers of Samaj Samata Sangh (9 June, 1929)

Outside Yerawada Jail, after Poona Pact
From left : B. Mukundrao Jaikar, Sir Tej Bahadur Sapru,
Dr.Ambedkar, Dr. P. G. Solanki, Rao Bahadur, R. Srinivasan,
Munnuswamy Pillai, Ganesh Akaji Gavai

With family members:
From left: Yashwantarao (son), Dr. Ambedkar, Ramabai (wife),
Lakshmibai (sister), Mukundrao (nephew) and family pet Tobby

At Government Law College with fellow professors (1928-29)
Sitting from left: Prof. A. A. Aadarkar, Prof. G. S. C. Brown,
Principal A. A. Fedgie, Prof. T. N. Walawakar, Prof. A. B. Vaidya, and Dr. Ambedkar
Standing from left: Prof. S. B. Jathar, Prof. M. S. Vakil, Prof. N. C. H. Kaiji,
Prof. L. F. Rodriques, Registrar R. P. Karve

Marriage celebration organised by Samaj Samata Sangh (29 June, 1929)
Right side of bridegroom - Lakshmibai & Ramabai
Left side of the bride – Purohit Sundarrao Vaidya
Behind – Dr. Ambedkar, Rao Bahadur Bole, Dr. P. G. Solanki,
Shivtarkar, Chitre, Kadrekar, Govind Adrekar, Pradhan

First session of All India Dalit Samaj (19-20 July, 1942)

Labour Minister Dr. Ambedkar and
labour leader N. M. Joshi, Jamnadas Mehta,
Govt. official Dwarkanath Pradhan and others

Going to give evidence to the Mission led
by Sir Stafford Cripps

Members of the Constituent Assembly of free India
Sitting from left: N. Madhavrao, Syed Sadullah,
Dr. Ambedkar (President), Aladi Krishnaswami Iyer, Sir Benegal Narsinh Rao
Standing: Executive officers

Dr. Ambedkar going to Birla House
to have last glimpse of Gandhiji (1948)

Dr. Ambedkar
with his second wife
Dr. Savita (1948)

Dr. Rajendra Prasad, the first President of independent India with the ministers
Sitting from left: Dr. Ambedkar, Rafi Ahmad Kidwai, Sardar Baldev Singh,
Dr. Maulana Abul Kalam Azad, Pandit Jawaharlal Nehru, Dr. Rajendra Prasad,
Sardar Vallabhbhai Patel, John Mathai, Jagjeevan Ram, Rajkumari Amrit Kaur,
Dr. Shyama Prasad Mukherji
Standing from right: Dr. Keskar, Satya Narain Singh, K. Santhanam, Jairam Das Daulatram,
K.C. Niyogi, N.V Gadgil, N. Goplaswamy Aiyengar, Mohanlal Saxena, R.R. Diwakar, Khurshid Lal

Dr. Ambedkar addressing the meeting at Ambedkar Bhavan,
Delhi on the occasion of Buddha Jayanti

Dr. Ambedkar taking oath
as first Law Minister of independent India (8th May, 1950)

A honoarary degree of Law
(Doctor of Law (L.L.D.))
conferred by
Columbia University (1952)

Inspecting the building construction work
at the college of People's Education Society, Aurangabad

Dr. Ambedkar inaugurating
the All India Sai Devotees Conference (1954)

Inaugurating the Buddha Vihar and installing the Buddha idol at Dehu Road (1954)

Dr. Ambedkar and Mai Ambedkar
getting initiated into Buddhism (14th October, 1956)

Initiation Ceremony for Buddhism at Nagpur (14th October, 1956)

The huge crowd gathered for the Initiation ceremony for Buddhism

Dr. Ambedkar speaking, the next day after the initiation ceremony
at the same venue (15th October 1955)

Dr. Ambedkar being honoured by the Nagpur Municipality

At the World Buddhist Conference held
at Kathmandu (20th October, 1956)
(Above and Below)

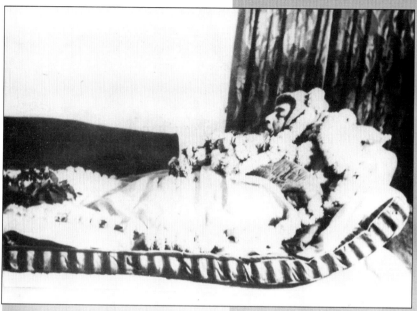

The last glimpse of Dr. Ambedkar (6th December 1956)

Pandit Jawaharlal Nehru paying his last respects

The huge mass of humanity gathered to bid farewell to their beloved leader

But in actual practice this original principle of division of labour did not sustain itself long, so much so that even a most ignorant, vile and fallen Brahmin continued to be regarded as someone next to God whereas man from the lowest-class, however high his qualifications, was condemned forever as a Shudra. The result was that the original four divisions became watertight compartments, and degenerated later into the present caste system. In this way the four Varnas came to stay as four castes, and the present tyrannous caste system became the reverse, the negation of its original meaning and purpose. Thereafter different professions, barriers of provinces, varying ways of living and diet, different superstitions and customs, broke up the main four castes and further led to the creation of over three thousand sub-castes.

There is a view that the Aryans adopted this system to preclude the possibility of racial mixture with the original dwellers in India. As they did not accept the Aryan suzerainty, they led forays on their conquerors, kidnapped their children and women, and harassed them by looting. In course of time they were reduced to a servile status, their arrivals in and departures from the villages were regulated, unpleasant duties and insufferable disabilities were imposed upon them, and in the end they were condemned as Untouchables.

Yet a third theory holds that these Untouchables originally were Broken Men[1] and then the followers of Buddhism. In their fallen days they did not assimilate themselves with the Vedic Hindus, or give up beef-eating, and so they were degraded and segregated as " Untouchables ".

But did this disruptive system go unchallenged? Absolutely not. Several worthy sons of India have made from generation to generation energetic attempts to free Hindu society from this evil system which has degraded, segregated and devitalised it. Five hundred years before the birth of Christ, the kingly, mighty and rational Buddha rocked this system to its foundations for a considerable period and even initiated the Untouchables into his religion. In the eleventh century Ramanuja, who had an untouchable disciple, threw open to the Untouchables the monastries and temples which he had founded and built. Basav,

---

1. Borale. Dr. P. T., *Segregation and Desrgregation in India, A Socio-Legal Study*, pp. 62-63.

who was a minister of a Karnatak king, tried in his own way to pull down this system. In the succeeding centuries saints like Chakradhar, Ramananda, Kabir, Chaitanya, Eknath, Tukaram, Rohidas and Chokhamela succeeded to a great extent in establishing equality in matters of their Bhakti cult.

Then followed the waves of the socio-religious revival inaugurated by Ram Mohan Roy and his lieutenants. But the most vital role was played by Mahatma Phooley who started in Poona, in 1848, the first school in India for the Untouchables. Although insulted, ridiculed and ousted by reactionaries and relatives, Phooley and his saintly wife nobly and unflinchingly served the cause of the Untouchables and strove for the education and emancipation of the Untouchables. Shashidhar Bandopadhyaya from Bengal, too, served this cause. Among the Indian Princes it was Shri Sayajirao Gaekwad of Baroda who started schools for the Untouchables in 1833. But in those days his State had to depend upon Muslim teachers for the growth of those schools, for caste Hindu teachers would not accept the posts of teachers in those schools.[2]

The Untouchables in Maharashtra, too, showed signs of a stirring from their age-long slumber. Their leader, Gopal Baba Walangkar, who was a follower of Mahatma Phooley and a bold propagandist, strove to remove the stain of untouchability and to convince the caste Hindus of their inhuman behaviour. The virile and valiant Dayananda made great efforts towards the abolition of untouchability. In the extreme south Col. Olcott was about to start his school for the Untouchables.

Ill

The attitude of the British rulers, who had just abolished slavery in their own land, towards these age-long sufferers in Hindustan, was quite indifferent. Frankly, theirs was an imperialistic alien rule and their neutral role in respect of the Untouchables was in effect a negative support to the caste Hindu oppressors. The Britishers were a shrewd race. After the fall of the Mahratta Empire they set about stabilising their newly acquired Empire in a manner so as to drain the people slowly, fleece them safely, and exploit them softly and methodically. Statesmanly

---

2.   *Maharashtriya Dnyana Kosh*, Part VII, p. 644.

enough, they first took up the cause of the Brahmins who had
suffered tremendously by the change of Government. For
enlivening their hearts the Bombay Government began to educate
them in order to enable them to be useful in the service of the new
Government.[3]

In those days literature was the privileged treasure and
education was the monopoly of the Brahmins. They were things
forbidden to other caste Hindus. Such was the power and awe
exercised by the Brahmins that even the Maharaja of Satara had
to take his lessons at night.[4] The Government opened a Sanskrit
school in Poona, in 1821. But abominable and violent as was the
Brahmin opposition to the education of these castes, the Brahmin
teachers not only opposed vehemently the new move sponsored by
the new Government to admit other caste Hindus to the Sanskrit
school but a majority of them also tendered their resignations.[5]
However, schools for other caste Hindus were provided by and by,
and may it be said to the credit of the British Government that the
non Brahmins and Backward Class Hindus advanced gradually
in education and in Government service as never before.

If this was the plight of other caste Hindus, what must have
been the condition of the Untouchables? They were not in the
picture at all. They were miles behind in the sphere of education.
As the new Government was careful not to antagonise the
Brahmins by educating the lower classes and especially the
Untouchables, it always sidetracked the issue as far as possible.
Besides, in those times the teachers, inspectors and officers were
all Brahmins who would not bear the idea of mass education.

The Christian missionaries fully exploited this situation.
They took up the cause of the education of lower classes as also of
the Untouchables; of course, with an ulterior motive, and began
to disseminate education among them. By their tact, kindliness and
ready help the missionaries ingratiated themselves with the lower
classes as well as with the Untouchables, so much so that a strong
feeling grew upon these classes that foreigners were preferable to
the Brahmins.

---

3.   Report of the Board of Education for the year 1840-41, p. 24.
4.   Latthe, A.B., *Memoirs of His Highness Shri Shahu Maharaj of Kolhapur,* p. 135.
5.   Vaidya. D.G, *Narayan Ganesh Chandavarkar* (Marathi), pp. 61-62.

Despite this culpable opposition, the problem of the education of the Untouchables was rearing its head now and then before the new rulers. It was brought to the forefront by one incident in 1856. The Head of the Government school at Dharwar refused admission to an untouchable boy. The question came up before the Bombay Government for consideration. At last, in 1858, Government announced that it reserved the right of refusing its support "to any partially aided school in which the benefits of education are withheld from any class of persons on account of caste and race" and also that "all schools maintained at the sole cost of Government shall be open to all classes of its subjects without distinction."[6] But this directive could not be effective enough to check the mentality of the caste Hindus for a long time to come. Their representatives branded the efforts made towards the education of the Untouchables as a groundless agitation caused by sentimental English officials and unpractical native reformers.[7]

IV

Not less colossal and conflicting were the problems in the political and social fields of Maharashtra. The eighteen-nineties had seen the trampling march of a tremendous epoch in Maharashtra. It was a period of strong, powerful as well as propelling influences. A socio-political revival had set in. Those were the flaming days of social reformers and eager political agitation. The revolt of Wasudeo Balwant Phadke had subsided into tranquillity. The main problems that confronted the leaders along with the political backwardness were the caste system, untouchability, child marriage, widow re-marriage and emancipation of women. A bitter controversy raged over the question whether or not the social reforms should take precedence over the political reforms. The partisans in the controversy were men of highest ability, men of noblest vision, men of supreme courage, men of power and learning.

The British statesmen and editors advocated with sedulous care total cessation of political activities and advised the Indian leaders to direct their energies first to removing the anomalies in

---

6.   Ghurye, Dr. G.S., Caste and Class in India, p. 166,

7.   Bhagat, M.G, The Untouchable Classes of Maharashtra, pp. 31-32.

the social system. Their only object at heart was that the Indians should anyhow bypass the political agitation. But the situation was viewed by the Indian leaders quite differently. They led simultaneously both the movements, political as well as social. The foremost among them was the glowing and mighty Ranade who conceived a vast broadening of the social foundations. Agarkar, who was a man of intellect and force of character, envisaged a profound reshaping of the national, social and individual values. Dr. Bhandarkar, a man of great learning and broader vision, actively propagated the view of the social reformers.

On the side of the political reformers was the commanding, aggressive and erudite personality of Tilak. He then led the orthodox section of the people, who, with a subtle motive of bypassing the social reforms, shouted that the political grievances,, constituted the common platform and nation's first necessity. Telang, an eminent judge and an erudite personality, was of opinion that the social reform running along the line of least resistance should be undertaken simultaneously with the political work. Both the analyses were not far from truth. But the social reformers' analysis was more realistic and honest while the approach of most of the political reformers was practical but at the same time evasive. For most of them opposed the social reformers not because they could not have removed the social ills along with the political, but these social Tories feared that the social and religious disabilities and inequality, if removed, would jeopardise their own prestige, privileges and position in the Hindu society. So they bitterly opposed every move sponsored to give Hindu society a real and sound foundation.

The Indian National Congress had been founded some seven years earlier. Its sessions, however, ended in appeals to the British Government for at least Indianising the Governmental administrative posts and Councils.

This was the intellectual, social and political situation in Maharashtra and India on the eve of the birth of Dr. Bhimrao Ramji Ambedkar.

❑❑❑

CHAPTER 2

CHILDHOOD AND YOUTH

THE AMBEDKARS come from Konkan, a region which provided India with great brains and great fighters, men like Tilak, Karve and Paranjpye. Ambedkar's ancestral village is Ambavade, five miles off Mandangad, a small town in the Ratnagiri District. The family was of some consequence in that village. It enjoyed the honour of keeping the palanquin of the village goddess and naturally the yearly festival was a great occasion for the family to attract the attention of the whole village.[1] Ambedkar's grandfather Maloji Sakpal came of a good Mahar family. Of all the untouchable communities in the fold of Hindu society the Mahars are the most robust, adaptable, intelligent, fighting, brave, virile and leading community. Keenly sensitive to their inferior position, they are conscious of their slavery. It is held by some that the Mahars were the original inhabitants of Maharashtra, which, they say, was a Mahar Rashtra! Yet the origin of the word Mahar is said to be Maha-Ari, the great enemy! The Mahars were the first to come in contact with the Europeans in India. They then formed a part of the Bombay Army of the East India Company just as the Dusads of Bihar and the Pariahs of Madras manned the armies of the Company in those provinces.

Maloji Sakpal also was a retired military man. Of his children two survived. One was Ramji, the father of the hero of this biography, and the other was a daughter named Mira.

The family belonged to the devotional Kabir school of thought. This Bhakti school of thought found consolation in the human attributes like compassion, benevolence and resignation to God. These devotees sought and found moral and spiritual food in Lord Krishna or Shri Rama. But the most humanising and broadening effect upon their mind was that the followers of this Bhakti school had abolished the rigidity of the caste system, as Kabir, the founder of the school, had roundly condemned it.

1. Editorial in the *Janata*, 7 January 1933.

This was one of the reasons why some Untouchable families turned to the Kabir cult. To the followers of Kabir anybody who worshipped God belonged to God irrespective of caste and birth. So sincere and true was their belief that they sang with their master.

"Jat pant puchhe na koi,
Har ko bhaje so harka hoi!"

Ramji Sakpal had fourteen children. The hero of this biography was the fourteenth child born to this man from a very dutiful wife. Pious and gentle, she was a very self-respecting woman.

A story is associated with the birth of the hero of this biography. It is as strange and significant as the one that is connected with the symbolic interpretation of the dreams dreamt by the mother of the Great Gautama Buddha when he was in the pre-natal stage. It tells that one of the uncles of Ramji Sakpal who had turned sanyasin—a term for a hermit—some years later in his grand old age came in the company of some hermits upon Mhow in Central India where Ramji Sakpal resided with his family. One of the women from his family, who was on her way to the river for washing purposes, happened to pass by the group of hermits among whom was the old relative. She at once recognised him. Ramji Sakpal ran to him and entreated him to bless his house with a visit. But as the sanyasin had renounced the world he would not come. However, he conferred on Ramji Sakpal a boon that a boy would be born in the family who would leave his mark on history. Entranced with the belief, Ramji Sakpal and his wife intensified their religious observances. The boon took effect at Mhow, on April 14, 1891, in the birth of a boy who was named Bhim and who became really a picturesque figure in the history of Hindustan.

Bhim's mother, Bhimabai, came of the Murbadkars, an untouchable Hindu family. They were a rich family from the village of Murbad in the Thana District of Bombay State. Fair by complexion, she had a broad forehead, curly hair, round glowing eyes and a short nose. Her father and her six uncles were all Subhedar Majors in the Army. They also belonged to the Kabir cult and discussed hotly and keenly the philosophy of Kabir and theology at troupes.

Bhim was hardly two years old when his father retired from military service and came down to Dapoli in Konkan from Central India. He was put to school at Dapoli when he was five years old. There he began his primary education along with his elder brother. Subhedar Ramji Sakpal could not stay long at Dapoli. He moved to Bombay and secured a job in the military quarters at Satara.

Soon after their arrival at Satara, a great misfortune befell the family. Bhimabai, a self-respecting and self-reliant and religious soul, gave up her spirit. The *samadhi** of Bhimabai is at Satara. At the death of Bhim's mother, who died when he was about six, only three sons and two daughters survived out of fourteen children. Balaram was the eldest, Anandrao was the second, then followed two daughters Manjula and Tulsi and the youngest was Bhim, who in later life humorously called himself *Chaudave Ratna* which signified 'a sound thrashing'. The daughters were married and they looked after their brothers turn by turn. Besides Ramji's sister, Mirabai, was there to take care of the family. She was a smart, short and hunchbacked woman and had a good knowledge of the practical world. Bhim, being the Benjamin in the house, claimed the special care and attention of his aunt, and as was natural the motherless youngest child Bhim became her favourite.

Ramji Sakpal lived a very industrious and intensely religious life. Stout, impressive, generous and voluble, he was a devotee. He offered prayers and devotions to God morning and evening. The children joined in his devotions. The sweet devotional lyrics and spiritual hymns of devotion flowed from his mouth like water from a fountain. It was a very rigid observance and a slight deviation from it on the part of the children incurred his displeasure. It was at times easy to evade or hurry through the hymns in the morning under the show and bustle of study but in the evening it was a very stern affair! Then the chain of sweet songs of God would go on in a choir.[2] This compulsory routine continued till their father's death.

---

*   A stone or a monument over the place where a great man or woman is cremated.

2.   Hudlikar, Prof. Satyabodh, The *Navayug's Ambedkar Special Number,* 13 April, 1947.

Bhim's father read and recited to his children the great national epics, the Ramayana and the Mahabharata, the two unfailing sources of divine inspiration, the motive force, which have nurtured and moulded the lives of great men in India in every generation, Ramji Sakpal sang also the spiritual songs from the Marathi saint poets like Moropant, Mukteshwar and Tukaram. His children derived immense benefits from these songs. Constant recitals, recitations and exposition of these songs helped develop a taste in his children, and provided them with a certain toning and command of the language in their early age. At Mhow the family resided in military quarters. The stern military discipline required every household to put out light at certain hour. Engrossed in the songs and hymns, Ramji Sakpal would sit far into the night, singing them slowly and softly with the doors and windows of his apartments closed.

Bhim's father was not merely after the spiritual development of his children. He cared also for the worldly betterment of his sons. He was a full-fledged teacher trained at the Normal School then established by Government for turning out teachers to impart education in Government schools. It may be noted that education was then compulsory for the children as well as both male and female relations of the military servants. For fourteen years Ramji Sakpal served as headmaster in the military school and had attained the rank of Subhedar-Major in the 2nd Grenadiers. But lie was known as Subhedar Ramji.

From his unfailing recitations and songs and their exposition Ramji Sakpal had obtained a mastery of the Marathi language and could easily teach his pupils and children how to use the appropriate words. He had also studied English and could teach his sons translation books with ease and confidence. Arithmetic was another subject to his liking. For the benefit of his sons he had a ready notebook which served as a key to the Arithmetic by Gopal Krishna Gokhale.

Ramji Sakpal's one outstanding characteristic was that he was a confirmed teetotaller and never touched meat. He was also a sport. In his youth he was a good cricketer and played football well. Cheerful and courageous in society, he took keen interest in religious and theological discussions. A friend and admirer of Mahatma Phooley, this industrious man always took great interest in the social problems of his day which concerned the fate of his community. When in 1892 the Government of India issued orders banning the recruitment of the Mahars in the Indian Army, Subhedar Ramji Sakpal took a leading part in protesting against these unjust orders and approached the ever-helping Ranade to draft a petition appealing to the Government of India to rescind the unjust orders. A few years later, Bhim came across a copy of this petition in the bundle of his father's old papers. In his old age Ramji Sakpal had interviewed the British Governor of Bombay and appealed to him to throw open the proposed buildings under the scheme of Development to the Untouchables. Such a family tree was bound to bear fruit of enduring sweetness. No wonder then that Bhim derived from his father his painstaking spirit, his forceful mental energy and the intense interest in the welfare of his society.

II

At Satara, Bhim completed his primary education and began his high school career along with his elder brother. During his school days Bhim realised quickly though painfully what the stigma of untouchability meant. One summer day he and his elder brother with his little nephew set out to meet their father who worked as a cashier at Goregaon. They got in at Padali Railway station and travelled upto Masur. As their father did not receive their letter in time he did not turn up at the station. After waiting for long weary hours, they could with difficulty persuade the station master, who was a caste Hindu, to secure them a bullock cart, and started for Goregaon.

Hardly had the cart gone a few yards when the god-fearing caste Hindu cartman, to his wrath, came to know that the well-dressed boys in his cart were the accursed Untouchables! In a fit of rage he threw them out on the road as one overturns the dustbins; for he felt they had polluted his wooden cart and destroyed the purity of his domestic animals! But the boys soothed the cartman's anger by paying double the fare and Bhim's elder brother drove the cart, the cartman following the cart on foot. From the evening till midnight the boys travelled with their mouths parched with thirst; but nowhere could they get drinking water on the way. Every time people either pointed to the filthy water or asked them to go away. This was the first rude and shattering shock to the budding mind of Bhim. That day he knew that he belonged to a family that was untouchable, degraded to drink and eat filthy things.[3] A few days later this impression became confirmed. Mad with thirst, one day, Bhim was drinking water stealthily at a public watercourse. He was discovered and was beaten black and blue.

Yet another shock awaited the growing mind and understanding of Bhim. It was indeed a touching scene when Bhim came to know that his hair defiled the purity of the razor of the barber who regarded even the buffalo-shaving as a better and holier affair than tonsuring a human being who was his co-religionist and his countryman. So Bhim's sisters cut the brothers' hair.

What an indelible impression these cruel disabilities must have made upon Bhim's young mind that was so strong, so sensitive and yet so resolute. Under the pressure of all sorts of such disabilities and maltreatment attendant on the birth of an untouchable and humble rank, Bhim was cultivating a spirit of patience in the school of experience. It is said that letters cut into the bark of a young tree grow with age. All such insulting refusals and ill-treatment must have engendered in him a burning hatred for Hinduism. It was thus in his boyhood that Bhim experienced at the hands of his co-religionists the galling humiliations and the inhuman treatment under which his whole community had been labouring for untold ages.

A boy is the man in miniature, and a few anecdotes from his boyhood light up the character of Bhim. He was pugnacious, resourceful and fearless. He could defy anybody and anything that dictated rules of conduct and discipline. Nobody could forbid him to do a thing without a challenge or reaction. One day, in soaking rains he went to school because his classmate challenged him to go to the school without an umbrella. He took up the gauntlet and walked, like the invincible general in Napoleon, to the school despite the cold, chilling torrents of rains. His shirt and the loin cloth called the dhoti—for this was his dress during his childhood—were dripping. The class teacher by name Pendse,

---

3. Ambedkar's speech, the *Janata*, 20 November 1937.

who was a Brahmin, was moved at the sight, and he at once asked
his son to take Bhim to his residence, to give him a hot bath and a
piece of cloth to wear and to hang up his wet clothes to dry. For a
short while the obstinate boy was happy over the success of getting
an off-day! His pleasure, however, soon rolled into tears as he was
brought into the class and made to sit half-naked!

There was another Brahmin teacher in the High School.
His surname was Ambedkar. Obliging and humane, he was a
very irregular teacher. He loved Bhim very much. He dropped
daily a part of his meal—boiled rice, bread and vegetables— into
the hands of Bhim during the recess. This teacher has left his
impress on the life of his pupil. The original surname of Bhim's
father was Sakpal. It was a family name. Bhim drew his surname
Ambavadekar from his native village Ambavade, as
Maharashtrian surnames are often derived from the names of
the ancestral villages. The teacher took so much fancy to the boy
that he even changed his surname from Ambavadekar to his own
surname Ambedkar in the school records. During the school hours
this teacher spent his time in a peculiar way, He worked as an
accountant in a tobacco shop nearby the school and committed
his class to the care of a grown-up Muslim student during his
absence. Yet he was very careful in making good the loss in the
study of the children. At the time of annual inspection he stood
behind the inspector and covertly showed his students the
answers to arithmetical problems.

Ambedkar gratefully remembered this teacher who kindly
treated him during his school days. Later in life, when he was
on the eve of departure for the first session of the Round Table
Conference, Ambedkar received a letter of hearty congratulations
from this teacher, which he had treasured with pride and
pleasure. Well has it been said that one good word can warm
three winters.

Despite these oases of warmth, there was all around a
scorching desert. Bhim and his brother were usually made to
squat in a corner of the class on a piece of gunny cloth which
they carried to school. The teachers would not touch their
notebooks, nor did some of them even ask them to recite poems
or put questions to them for fear of being polluted! When these

two boys felt thirsty in the school they turned their mouths upward and then somebody would kindly pour drinking water into their mouths as if through a funnel !

But was Bhim progressing well in his studies? So far he had little or no love for his studies. He had full freedom to indulge in all sorts of hobbies and fancies, and gardening had so much fascinated his mind that he spent every pie he could lay his hand upon purchasing new plants. Fed up with this, he took to tending cattle and rearing goats. He was rarely to be found at home. On one occasion "I actually did some *hamal* work at Satara station. My aunt terribly felt humiliated at this conduct of mine, but she loved me so much that she had no heart to punish me."

When Bhim was nine, reading in standard II, M.G. Ranade breathed his last in 1901, in Poona, Speaking about it at the death anniversary of Ranade after forty years, Bhim, who rose in the nation as Dr. Ambedkar, told his audience in Poona that he got a holiday, but he then did not know who Ranade was and what he had done. Student Bhim had a holiday and was glad.

Some time before this, Bhim's father had changed his mind and married a second time, although he had intended at first not to marry and put his children under a step-mother. Bhim did not like the idea of another woman taking the place of his mother, and he hated her for wearing his mother's ornaments. Bhim now decided that he must not depend upon his father for maintenance and must earn his own bread. He had heard from his sisters that boys from Satara had found jobs in mills in Bombay, and he, therefore, decided to be a winding boy in a Bombay mill.

But how was he to get the money to go to Bombay ? He thought out a plan to steal the purse of his dear aunt in whose company he slept on the floor. "For three successive nights I tried to remove the purse tucked up at the waist of my aunt, but without success. On the fourth night I did get hold of the purse, but to my disappointment I found only half an anna in it. And in half an anna, of course, I could not go to Bombay. The four nights' experience was so nerve-racking that I gave up the idea of collecting money in this shameful manner and I came to another

decision—a decision that gave an entirely different turn to my
life. I decided that I must give up my truant habits, that I must
study hard and get through my examinations as fast as possible,
so that I might earn my own livelihood and be independent of
my father."[4] From that day he gave up all his irregular habits
and activities and became so diligent in his studies that his
teachers, who were at first disappointed in him, now advised his
father to give him the best possible education.

III

Then another change came over the Ambedkar family.
Subhedar Ramji moved his children to Bombay. The family lived
in a small room in a chawl called the Dabak chawl at Lower
Parel. It was situated in the labour area with an environment of
the underworld. His daughters had been already married and
they also resided in Bombay. He got his sons admitted to the
Maratha High School. By now Bhim had made much progress in
his studies. Under his father Bhim did the Howard's English
Reader and the three famous translation books by Tarkhadkar.
Bhim was well grounded in translation exercises, and he had
now attained knowledge of English better than most of his
classmates. This particular method of translation adopted by his
father, he gratefully once observed, made him ransack his
memory for equivalent terms, increased his vocabulary and laid
the foundation on which he could subsequently build up his fame
as a front-rank author of India.

Bhim, like Tilak and Savarkar, developed in his youth a
passion for reading. His desire to possess books was insatiable.
Instead of studying class books he showed keen interest in
reading other books. All scholar-politicians and scholar-
statesmen lay the foundation of their future eminence and
leadership in their early life by application to their studies. A
wide reading, deep knowledge and historic perspective bestow
upon their growing lives a certain prestige and toning. They do
not care much for the rank in the class-room while they are
building the repository of knowledge on which stands their future
eminence in the country. Here one factor is to be remembered

---

4.   Ambedkar speech, the *Bombay Soiling*, 20 January 1942.

that access to literature was easy and instinctively propelling in the case of Tilak and Savarkar, they being Brahmins, but diametrically opposite was the case of Bhim due to untouchability and illiterate surroundings. Though a man of ordinary means and little influence, Bhim's father ungrudgingly supplied him with new books, borrowing money from his two married daughters on most of the occasions and at times even pawning their ornaments, which he had given them as marriage gifts and redeeming them after he received his monthly pension which was a meagre sum of rupees fifty. It was his ardent desire that his son should become a man of letters and light. Naturally he saw every day that his son applied himself to his study with patient industry. This made him a little stern disciplinarian, often casting a feeling of boredom on his son.

After a few months, Bhim was sent to the Elphinstone High School which was until lately one of the leading High Schools in Bombay. Bhim now studied hard. He lived in the same one-room tenement in the old chawl at Parel. There was no chance for the provision of a study, and the possibility of employing a tutor was beyond a dream. The small room was full of domestic articles and utensils. It was smoky and crowded. Firewood was stored above head and also in one corner, and in the other corner was the fireplace. The room served as a kitchen, a parlour, a lying-in room, a study—all in one!

The Subhedar solved the problem of his son's study in his own way. He asked his son to go to bed early. Bhim slept on a quill. Near his head lay a grindstone huddled into the wall and a she-goat panted below his legs. His father sat up all night till two in the morning, and, awakening his son for study, he retired. Bhim studied till early morning, now and then turning in his bed before a flickering kerosene oil-lamp which had no glass cover to serve as a chimney. After having a little sleep in the morning, he took his bath and went to school.

It is reasonable to suppose that he could have studied in this High School without enduring humiliations. But although it was a Government institute, the atmosphere in the school was not free from casteism. There were the same prejudices and the same hatreds. The school was a miniature reflection of the vast insulting world outside. One day it so happened that the class

teacher called upon Bhim to come to the blackboard to solve an
example. Instantaneously there was an uproar in the class. The
caste Hindu children used to keep their tiffin-boxes behind the
blackboard. Since they feared that their food would be polluted by
Bhim's presence near the board, they dashed to the blackboard and
hurled their tiffin-boxes aside before Bhim could reach and touch
the blackboard. This crackling sound of the tiffin-boxes was not
less piercing than the croaking voices of the children's parents at
home and in the streets at the Untouchables. One of the teachers
tried, as was their wont, to discourage Bhim by saying that it was
useless for him to receive instruction. This jarring and teasing
discouragement irritated Bhim much, and one day, rising in auger,
he asked the teacher to mind his own business ![5]

Bhim ate his meals at school. The meal consisted of some
pieces of bread and vegetables and was left at his school by a
workman who had his job in the Fort area. Bhim's residence being
in a labour locality he was in constant touch with the labour life
which was full of hardships. Sometimes he had opportunities of
observing the conditions of the labour class when he carried the
tiffin-carriers of some of his relatives to the mills. As a school
boy, he had his lighter moments. Sometimes he played cricket
and football and often led the teams. In sports the defeats often
turned into broils. In this environment three years glided by.
Bhim now marched forward in his academic studies. By dint of
study and application he got through his examination every year.

Yet the school life of Bhim was to receive its unkindest cut.
The cut was too deep which all his life afterwards he remembered
with strongest aversion. During his High School days both Bhim's
elder brother and he were not allowed to take up Sanskrit as the
second language. It was the key to the study of the *Vedas* which
were neither to be heard nor to be read by the Shudras and the
Atishudras—the Untouchables. Hindu leaders like Tilak, who
were popular among the orthodox sections, defined a Hindu as
one who had faith in the Vedas, but the pity of it was that seventy
per cent of the Hindus were forbidden to study, much less to
listen to the *Vedas*! Yet these very leaders read with appreciative
and gesticulating looks and studied as never before the treatises
on the *Vedas* by foreigners who belonged to different religions!

5. Shivtarkar, S.N., the *Janata*, 14 April 1934.

Poor Bhim and his brother were torn asunder from Sanskrit by the Brahmin teachers as was also done in the case of Dr. M. R. Jayakar in his school days and were compelled to take Persian against their will. This was another pill of poison that was rammed down the unwilling throats of the two Hindu boys by the defenders of Hinduism! Had these so called defenders of Hinduism fought with the aggressive forces of other religions with the same degree of bigotry and fanaticism, they would have at least not been humiliated in their own land!

In after years Ambedkar studied Sanskrit partly by himself and sometimes with the help of some pandits and himself became a pandit. In his opinion Persian stands no comparison with Sanskrit as the latter, observes he, is the golden treasure of epics, the cradle of grammar, politics and philosophy and the home of logic, dramas and criticism.[6]

Notwithstanding the ills and intolerable insults inflicted by narrow-minded bigots, and stimulated by his father to endeavour at rising to a high position in life and encouraged by broadminded men, Bhim prosecuted his studies and at last passed the Matriculation Examination in 1907 from Elphinstone High School. As the Subhedar could not keep the elder son Anandrao at school, he had some time ago left the school to seek a job, and they both decided to concentrate their efforts on Bhim's education. Bhim obtained 282 out of 750 marks, his highest score being in the Persian language. This scoring of average number of marks is not uncommon in case of ambitious boys whose minds are absorbed in subjects other than the texts and who become great in their future lives.

But this was surely an uncommon achievement for an Untouchable, The event was, therefore, celebrated by his community. They called a meeting in Bombay to honour Bhimrao under the presidentship of S. K. Bole, who was a well-known social reformer. At this meeting was present a well-known Marathi author and social reformer, Krishnaji Arjun Keluskar. He was an assistant teacher at Wilson High School and had come across Bhimrao at a garden where both of them spent their evenings in reading. Charmed with the studious habits of young

6. Hudlikar. Prof. Satyaboth, The *Navayug—Ambedkar Special Number,* 13 April 1947.

Bhimrao, he took a fancy for him, lent him books and presented him with a copy of his new book, *Life of Gautama Buddha!* Keluskar spoke at the meeting in praise of Bhimrao's commendable achievement. After the meeting was over, Keluskar inquired of Subhedar Ramji Sakpal whether his son was going forward to the university in higher studies. In reply the Subhedar said that although his distressed circumstances could not permit him to do so, he was determined to send his son for higher education.

IV

A short time after his success in the Matriculation Examination, came off the marriage of Bhimrao. In those days early marriage was a rule. Several other men of distinction, who were born in the latter part of the nineteenth century, were married after their success in this examination. There seems no reason other than the custom that drove Subhedar Ramji to the thought of his son's marriage. And in deference to the wish of his father Bhimrao prepared himself for the event. It seems Ramji Sakpal was thinking for some days past of the marriage of his son. He had disapproved of some girls. Once he had approved of a girl, but soon afterwards changed his mind, And for setting aside that betrothal the Subhedar had to pay a fine of rupees five to his caste Panchayat. The place where Bhimrao's marriage took place was a strange one. It was the open shed of the Byculla Market in Bombay. After the day's market was over, at night the bridegroom and his men lodged in one spacious corner of the open shed, and the other corner was occupied by the bride and her relatives. Small gutters of dirty water flowed underneath their feet. The little stone-platforms in the market served them as benches, and the whole market place served as a marriage hall!

The marriage took place with due ceremony and jollity, and the people quitted the place in the morning before the arrival of the fisherwomen. Bhimrao was then hardly seventeen and his girl wife, Rami, was nine years old. She was renamed Ramabai. She was a sober and good girl. She came of a good, but poor family, being the second daughter of her deceased father who worked as a porter at Dapoli. His name was Bhiku Walangkar.

By now the problem of the Untouchables had gradually made a headway. From among the Untouchables had emerged in Maharashtra a leader by name Shivram Janba Ramble. It was he who had the unique distinction of convening the first conference of Untouchables in India. He edited a Monthly called *Somavanshiya Mitra* at Poona and sent a memorandum in 1910 to the British Government appealing to them to enlighten and elevate the Untouchables "by allowing them to remain as followers of their own ancestral faith".

At this time another stalwart rose from the Maratha community. It was Karmaveer V. R. Shinde. After completing his studies in Sociology and the comparative study of religion at Oxford University, he gained first-hand knowledge of the work of the social institutions run for the elevation of the lower classes in England. On his return to India, this patriotic social reformer toured India and with the support of Sir Narayan Ganesh Chandavarkar started in 1906 the Depressed Classes Mission of India. This was the first organised attempt for the uplift of the Untouchables. Soon after branches of the D.C. Mission sprang up in some of the important cities in India. The Servants of India Society of Gokhale, too, sympathised with the cause of the Untouchables.

Encouraged by the noble ambition of his father, Bhimrao Ambedkar joined Elphinstone College in Bombay. For an Untouchable it was a new experience and a new life and an unprecedented opportunity. He began his studies in right earnest; but owing to ill-health he lost one year. After he, passed the Inter Arts Examination his father ran out of funds and here Keluskar ran to his succour. Keluskar lost no time to wait upon the Maharaja of Baroda. He reminded the Maharaja of the announcement which he had made a few days earlier at a Townhall meeting in Bombay, promising help to any worthy Untouchable in the prosecution of higher studies. Sayajirao Gaekwad was a ruler who practised what he preached. He welcomed the opportunity. Accordingly Bhimrao was given audience. The great benefactor asked him some questions. Satisfied with his answers, he granted a scholarship of rupees twenty-five per mensem. Thus Keluskar proved to be a real teacher. By the significant present he made to his disciple he indirectly spurred him to attack the tyranny of the caste system, and by securing him a scholarship he enlightened his path and added ballast to his brains.

In his college days Prof. Muller of Elphinstone College lent Bhimrao a hand. He lent him books and gave him clothes, but, it seems, no professor in India could capture his mind. Moreover, the insulting environment and pitiable sights of the down-trodden must have added to his restlessness. The college hotelkeeper who was a Brahmin would not give him tea or water.

Bhimrao Ambedkar studied now with a view to passing the examination. But reading was the greatest joy of his life. It was directed to some purpose in life. It was his aim to arm himself with every possible missile, make himself master of a repository of knowledge and develop the power of his mind to prepare himself for the higher attainments and the new life that was to open the portals and possibilities of a great career.

About this time Subhedar Ramji moved into the Improvement Trust Chawl No. 1 at Parel, Bombay. There the family occupied on the second floor two rooms Nos. 50 and 51, one opposite the other. Room No. 50 was used as both a study and a parlour and the other was used for household purposes. Bhimrao Ambedkar studied in this room and his father sat outside watching. As the final examination drew near, he concentrated his mind on his studies and passed his B.A. Examination in 1912. A. B. Gajendragadkar, who in after life happened to be the Principal of Siddharth College founded by Ambedkar in Bombay, topped the list of the successful candidates.

It was during this period that the rights of the Indian citizens were totally suppressed by the British Government. Freedom of discussion and meeting was slowly extinguished; complaints, protests and appeals made in regard to these rights were denounced as seditious murmurings; and champions of these rights and freedom were denounced by Government as sedition mongers. This gave rise to a whirlwind of discontent and volcanic political unrest that was roaring forth with unprecedented vigour. This state of repression must have agitated the strong currents of Bhimrao Ambedkar's mind. Tilak's provocative deportation to Mandalay, Savarkar brothers' revengeful transportation to the Andamans, imprisonment of several other leaders and editors, and the deaths of some of the patriotic youths on the gallows smote the bottom of Maharashtra so violently that after the deportation of Tilak and transportation of Savarkar a period of deluge reigned over Maharashtra.

The repercussions of these events were seen on Ambedkar's patriotic mind later when he wrote his famous historic thesis, *The Evolution of Provincial Finance in British India.* Stating that power seldom commits suicide of its own accord, the patriot in Ambedkar describes in it how the British Government resorted to repressive measures during this period and indicts the British administration in India in these words: "Not satisfied with the aid of power with which the Executive was endowed by the provisions of the Criminal and Penal Codes to anticipate offences by preventing acts, it besmeared the Indian Statute Book with a set of repressive laws hardly paralleled in any other parts of the world."[7] He condemns the then ruling bureaucracy as conservative, repressive, irresponsible, and observes that it poured its money on services and not on education and industry. He tells us that the Indian Press Act of 1910 put a complete muzzle on the Press, the right of public meeting was suppressed in the same measure and with the same sternness as was the right to personal freedom and the right to freedom of discussion. Few front rank authors of whole times described this period of Indian history as pithily as Bhimrao Ambedkar has done.

Bhimrao Ambedkar's reactions to the Morley-Minto Reforms are noteworthy. Tracing the growth of constitutionalism at different stages such as the Act of 1853, the Act of 1861 the Act of 1892 and the Act of 1909, he relates in his foregoing thesis that there had been always an ingenious attempt made by the British Government to make the legislature independent and at the same time to muzzle it. He further observes that the reason why the Indian Parliamentary system was but an empty form is to be found in the fact that it was a Parliamentary system without a Parliamentary Executive and in which the legislature could neither make nor unmake the Executive. The Executive in India did not do certain things most conducive to progress, Ambedkar goes on, it was because by reason of its being impersonal and

---

7. pp. 198.

also by reason of its character, motives and interests it could not sympathise with the living forces operating in the Indian Society. It was not charged with its wants, its pains, its carvings and its desires, was inimical to its aspirations, did not advance Education, disfavoured Swadeshi and snapped at anything that smacked of nationalism. This was because all these things went against its grain.[8] This was Bhimrao Ambedkar's verdict on the British bureaucracy in India.

After his graduation, Bhimrao Ambedkar took service in Baroda, the State of his benefactor, despite his father's repeated disapprovals. He was appointed to the post of a lieutenant in the Baroda State Forces. This acceptance of a post on the part of Bhimrao Ambedkar might be a shrewd step probably taken with the full knowledge of the unbearable situation that might have come in the smooth working of Bhimrao as a Government official in British India where offices were mostly manned by the orthodox Hindu upper classes.

Bhimrao Ambedkar served in the Baroda State for about fifteen days in January 1913 when he received a telegram informing him that his father was seriously ill in Bombay. He left Baroda immediately to look after the health of his father. On his way home he got down at Surat station to buy sweetmeats for his father and lost his train. Next day when he reached Bombay he stood aghast at the sight of his sinking father. The sinking but searching eyes of the dying man moved on to his darling son upon whom he had revolved his thoughts, his hopes, and his existence. He moved his feeble hand over his son's back and the next moment death-rattle was in his throat. His eyes dosed and his legs and hands became motionless. He breathed his last. So great was the outburst of Bhimrao's sorrow that words of consolation failed to soothe his heart and his loud lamentations drowned the wails of the members of his family. It was February 2, 1913, the saddest day in Bhimrao Ambedkar's life.

Thus passed away an Untouchable, Subhedar Ramji Maloji, who was to the end of his life industrious, abstemious, devotional and aspiring. He died ripe in age but poor in wealth, for he had   .

---

8.   pp. 196-97.

run into debt; but was exemplary in character and unconscious of his great legacy to his clan, country and humanity. Having infused in his son a strength of will to resist worldly temptations and a depth of spirituality very seldom found in his son's contemporaries, he left him behind to fight the battle of life and to break the world to his way.

CHAPTER 3

SELF-DEVELOPMENT

BHIMRAO AMBEDKAR was now left to stand on his own feet. His insatiable thirst for knowledge and the spur of ambition made him restless. He was now in no mood to return to his job in Baroda. His short stay there had been unhappy. At last another chance came his way in June 1913. The Maharaja of Baroda, at this juncture, thought of sending some students to the U.S.A. for higher studies at Columbia University. Bhimrao narrated his whole story to the Maharaja in his palace in Bombay. He advised him to apply for one of the scholarships which his State had advertised. He did so, and the Maharaja decided to send Bhimrao along with three other students for higher education. Bhimrao was called to Baroda. On June 4, 1913, he signed an, agreement before the Deputy Minister for Education of the Baroda State, agreeing to devote his time to studying the prescribed subjects and to serve for ten years the Baroda State after the completion of his studies.

This was a unique opportunity for an Indian and an event of enormous magnitude for an Untouchable. And, indeed, it was an epoch-making event! An Untouchable, an abominable Mahar, going to a foreign land to cultivate the best, the enduring and the ennobling influence and imbibe the spirit of the age! Among the first-rate Indian political leaders Ambedkar was the first to receive instruction in the land of Lincoln and Booker T. Washington. Of course, the Socialist leader, Jayprakash Narayan, may be the other to study in South America in the early thirties.

Ambedkar arrived in New York in the third week of July 1913. For a week he stayed at the Hartley Hall, a dormitory of the University. He did not like the food as a majority of the dishes were ill-cooked and consisted of beef. So he shifted to a Cosmopolitan Club at 554 West, 114 Street, where some of the Indian students lived. Thereafter he stayed at Livingstone Hall

26

Dormitory with Naval Bhathena, a Parsi student, who formed a lifelong friendship with him.

Life in America, a foreign land, was a unique and moving experience in life that Ambedkar met with in New York. There, in company with other students and colleagues he could move freely. He could read, he could write, he could walk, he could bathe and he could rest with a status of equality. Meals at regular hours, eating on a table cloth, and napkin! To him life at Columbia University was a revelation. It was a new world. It enlarged his mental horizon. A new kind of existence began. His life gleamed with a new meaning!

In that fresh atmosphere he wrote a letter to one of the friends of his father in which one sees the working of his mind. In it he observed that he was one of those who earnestly desired the well-being of the down-trodden community, that he liked to see many more men of the latter's reforming spirit in the community and then he cited the immortal lines of Shakespeare impressing upon his mind to seize every opportunity to further the cause of the community. The lines were:

"There is a tide in the affairs of men,
    Which, taken at the flood, leads on to fortune."

He then comes out with a diagnosis of the ills of his community and suggests a remedy in which one finds the seeds of the great spirit of the Saviour. "We must now," he proceeds in the same letter, "entirely give up the idea that parents give birth—'Janma'— to the child and not destiny—'Karma'. They can mould the destiny of the children ; and if we but follow this principle, be sure that we shall soon see better days and our progress will be greatly accelerated if male education is pursued side by side with the female education the fruits of which you can very well see verified in your own daughter." "Let your mission,"concludes the young man of twenty, "therefore be to educate and preach the idea of education to those at least who are near to and in close contact with you."[1]

These are the seeds of the future self-respect, self-help movement, the revolt against the philosophy of helplessness which makes the ignorant people resign themselves to their fate

---

1. Khairmode, C.B., *Dr. B.R. Ambedkar (Marathi*—upto 1923), pp. 66-67.

and accept their position as a divine dispensation. The lines from Shakespeare suggests caution and watchfulness to utilize every opportunity and also the spirit of resilience.

Imbued with those thoughts and visions, Ambedkar knew well that without the asset of name or influence he was to make his way in life. He could attain it by developing his native worth. For that tremendous work was necessary. For a while his mind was diverted, but he soon woke up to his responsibilities and resolved to engage in his studies with great diligence and thoroughness. There was no time for pleasant idleness, or for the fill of enjoyment of the University life habitual with the sons of rich men. The thought of going to the theatre did not cross his mind, nor did he spend his time in strolling, nor did he loiter in sightseeing in the city of New York. He had a vigorous. appetite, but appeased it with a cup of coffee, two muffins and a single meat or fish dish, which cost him one dollar and ten cents. Out of his stipend he had to remit some money every month, and so he had to keep down his expenses. His college colleagues related afterwards with pride how Ambedkar seized every possible hour for his study for which he said he had been given a life's opportunity. His aim was now not only to be a holder of the highest university degrees but also to be the master of science, politics, sociology, economics. In India he had obtained his B.A. degree with the English and Persian languages ; but now he took up Political Science, Moral Philosophy. Anthropology; Sociology and Economics as the subjects for his study.

The one professor that he was enamoured of was Edwin R.A. Seligman. He was a friend of Lala Lajpat Rai who was introduced to Seligman by Sidney Webb. Ambedkar took to Seligman as a duck takes to water and ran after the professor from class to class with his special permission to attend his classes. This professor, who was fond of dogearing the pages of the book in hand while teaching, taught well and guided his students with affection, and thus produced a lasting effect upon Ambedkar. When asked by Ambedkar as to the methods of research, he advised him to go on earnestly so that he might evolve his own method.

Thus started the *Dnyana Yadnya*. For eighteen hours a day went on the endless digging for knowledge and this continued for months together. At last after two long years of toil, success came with tremendous gusto. Ambedkar obtained his M.A. degree in 1915 for his thesis "Ancient Indian Commerce". He also read a paper on "Castes in India, Their Mechanism, Genesis and Development" before the Anthropology Seminar of Dr. Goldenweiser in May 1916. Therein he observes that endogamy is the essence of castes. According to him, a caste is an enclosed class and it existed before Manu whom he describes as an audacious person and a dare-devil. He adds that Manu simply codfied the existing caste rules. He concludes that caste in the singular number is an unreality; caste exists only in plural number.[2]

This was the first rung of the ladder of success. The second was reached not long afterwards. Ambedkar was working simultaneously on another thesis. It was the "National Dividend of India—A Historic and Analytical Study". After long hours of concentration and hard labour devoted to the research, he completed this thesis. It was accepted by the Columbia University in the second week of June 1916. Eight years after this Messrs. P.S. King & Son, Ltd., London, published an extension of this thesis under the title, *The Evolution of Provincial Finance in British India*. Ambedkar then submitted the required number of copies of the thesis to the University, and Columbia University officially awarded him the degree of Doctor of Philosophy for this dissertation.

His success in the academic world was so brilliant that he was heartily felicitated at a special dinner given in his honour by the students and professors belonging to the faculty of Arts. Young Americans whose forefathers had struggled for the abolition of slavery of the Negroes were celebrating the success of a young man who had the will and mission of Lincoln and the labour of Booker T. Washington.

The book was dedicated to His Highness Shri Sayajirao Gaekwad, Maharaja of Baroda, as a token of "my gratitude to his help in the matter of my education". The original thesis was revised and brought up-to-date by including a review of the Montagu-Chelmsford Reforms with a particular reference to finance. The work opens with an introduction by Edwin R.A.

2. The *Indian Antiquity*, May 1917, pp. 81-95.

Seligman who taught Ambedkar the first lesson in public finance.
Observing that the problem discussd by Ambedkar in his
excellent dissertation was one that was arousing a growing
interest in all parts of the world, the professor remarked:
"Nowhere to my knowledge, has such a detailed study of the
underlying principles been made." In this thesis Ambedkar traces
the growth of the financial arrangements from the Act of 1833
under the imperial system. The chapters on Budget are very
valuable in their educative and illustrative aspects with regard
to the nature and enlargement of the Provincial Finances. From
chapters X to XII the book becomes eloquent, interesting and
powerful in its appeal. The style of the professor becomes one
with the soul of the patriot and Ambedkar bitterly exposes the
British bureaucracy, denounces the designs and objects of the
imperial system and also lashes out at all the reactionary forces
in the country.

In the thesis Ambedkar admits that there was some
advancement in material progress, but observes that no people
in the world can long remain content with the benefits of peace
and order, for they are not dumb brutes. He adds that everybody
knows that the whole policy of India was dictated by the interests
of the English industries and English manufacturers. He
concludes that in every country there have been downtrodden
communities suffering from social oppressions and social
injustice, and yet no country has had to be without political power
on that account.

This famous book became a companion of the Member of
the Indian Legislative Councils and the Central Assembly at the
time of budget discussions during the British regime, a ready
reference for men in authority and a guide to students of
economics. Shortly after the publication of this book, Ambedkar
was called to give evidence before the Royal Commission on
Indian Currency. It must have been a matter of great pleasure
to Ambedkar to see every Member of the Commission holding
the book in his hand.

Ambedkar's insatiable thirst for books remained for ever
unquenched. He spent his leisure in roaming and browsing
through the second-hand book-stalls in the city. In New York he
purchased about two thousand old books with the joy of a
bibliophile and entrusted the boxes containing the books to the

care of a friend to take them to India. Somehow this trust proved to be somewhat misplaced; since later in India he got only some and not all of these books.

While in America, Ambedkar's mind must have been deeply impressed with two things. The first was the Constitution of the U.S.A. and more so the fourteenth Amendment to that Constitution which declares the freedom of Negroes. The second was the life of Booker T. Washington whose death occurred in 1915. He was a great reformer and educator, of the Negro race in America and was the founder and President of the Tuskegee Institute which disseminated among ihe Negroes the doctrine of education of the head, heart and hand, and thus broke the shackles of bondage which had crushed the Negroes for ages physically, mentally and spiritually.

After a very successful career at Columbia University, Ambedkar turned his attention to London, the great international centre of learning, where the talents of every kind had the fullest scope for development. He left America in June 1916 and reached London after a few days.

The First World War was not yet over. As Ambedkar came from America where the Gadar Party led by Lala Har Dayal was carrying on propaganda to arouse the Indians in America to go to India and drive out the Britishers, on his arrival Ambedkar's person, clothes, boots and luggage were minutely searched by the British secret police officers, thinking that he also belonged to the Indian Revolutionary Party. The fact was that Lala Lajpat Rai, who was in those days in New York and was a close friend of Ambedkar's professor, Edwin R.A. Seligman, could not succeed in winning Ambedkar to join the political, if not the revolutionary, movement for the freedom of India. Apart from all other reasons, Ambedkar told the great leader of India that he was a student and he must complete his studies without betraying the sacred trust of the Maharaja who had given him an opportunity in his life.

Immediately Ambedkar got himself admitted in October 1916 to the Grays Inn for Law and for the study of Economics to the London School of Economics and Political Science. He had persuaded the Maharaja of Baroda to grant him permission for pursuing his studies in London. His studies in Economics now were far advanced. So the London professors allowed him to prepare for the D.Sc. He started to work on a thesis. But in the meanwhile he was informed that the period of scholarship was over, and therefore he was called back to India by the Dewan of Baroda.

This was an unsufferable setback, and although Ambedkar was following his motto 'hard study and spare diet' to complete his studies, he was obliged to leave them in the middle. Yet his longing for completing his studies was so irresistible that helpless as he was he thought of returning to India, but made up his mind to come over to London again after making some provision for studies in London. To that end he secured permission from London University through the benevolent recommendation of his professor, Prof. Edwin Cannan, to resume his studies within a period not exceeding four years from October 1917. Ambedkar, then, insured his luggage which consisted mostly of books and entrusted it to Messrs. Thomas Cook & Son to be sent over to Bombay.

He boarded a train at Boulogne on July 27, and reaching Marseilles, he embarked the s.s. *Kaiser-i-Hind*. War destruction was at its meridian. It was very dangerous to travel in the midst of the terror of bombs and submarines. And it so happened that about this time a steamer was torpedoed in the Mediterranean Sea. When this dreadful news reached Ambedkar's family, all the members of the family were plunged into deep sorrow. Cablegrams were exchanged, and they heaved a sigh of relief when they came to know that Bhimrao was travelling in the *s.s. Kaiser-i-Hind* and the steamer that fell a victim to the enemy submarine carried his luggage only.

II

Ambedkar reached Bombay on August 21, 1917, *via* Colombo. The British Government was then facing a grave crisis. It was depressed by the war reverses, pressed by the Indian Home Rule movement and oppressed by the Indian revolutionary forces. In order to pacify them and to strengthen Britain's resources, Montagu, the then Secretary of State for India, made on August 20, 1917, the famous declaration in the House of Commons of Britain's "policy of gradual development of self-governing institutions with a view to progressive realisation of responsible Government in India as an integral part of the British Empire".

Montagu, thereafter, came to India to study the different shades of political opinion. All sorts of organisations, all sorts of interests, all sorts of demands gushed forth. With earnest appeals all and sundry placed their grievances before him in November and December 1917. Among them appeared for the first time in the political history of India the representatives of the Untouchables. Being fresh from foreign lands, Ambedkar was then a mere nobody in Indian politics.

Among those institutions which represented the Untouchables was the Punchama Kalvi Abhivarthi-Abhimana Sanga, a Madras Presidency Untouchables Association. It deprecated any political change and appealed to Government to save them from the yoke of the Brahmins whose struggle for greater share in the administration of Government they likened to the struggle of a cobra that seeks guardianship of young frogs. The Madras Adi-Dravida Jana Sarigha, representing 6,000,000 aborigines, made a vigorous protest against the caste Hindus who hated them as lepers and denied them any chance of betterment in their life. There was also a strong representation from the organisation of the Untouchables from Bengal. Sir N.G. Chandavarkar interviewed Montagu on behalf of the Depressed Classes Mission.

Immediately after Ambedkar's arrival in Bombay, a meeting was called by Sambhaji Waghmare and others to felicitate him on his great achievement in the academic world. Rao Bahadur Chunilal Setalvad, the then Chief Presidency Magistrate of Bombay, presided. Ambedkar, however, did not attend the meeting. A feeling of embarrassment and a modest estimate of his own merits must have weighed upon his mind. After the meeting was over, some of the speakers and admirers went straight to the humble residence of Ambedkar and showered their felicitations upon the reserved and ascetic man.

In conformity with the agreement, Ambedkar decided to leave for Baroda. He had no money to go to Baroda. But fortunately for him Messrs. Thomas Cook & Son paid him damages for his luggage. Ambedkar received the payment with mixed feelings. He was sad because he had lost his valuable collection of books which he had collected in New York and London, and was glad because he would give part of the money

to his wife for household expenses and use the balance for his
railway fare. He went to Baroda in the middle of September.
The Maharaja of Baroda had ordered his men to see him at the
station. But who would go to receive a Mahar? So there was none
to guide him. The news that a Mahar youth was to come to Baroda
had spread in the city. No hotel or hostel accepted Ambedkar
and his eldest brother who had accompanied him. At last they
took shelter in a Parsee inn. Ambedkar stayed in that inn
incognito!

According to the bond, Ambedkar was to serve the Baroda
State for ten years. The Maharaja wanted to appoint Ambedkar
Finance Minister after his gaining some experience in the
administration of different departments. So he was immediately
appointed Military Secretary to the Maharaja. But there too his
birth as an Untouchable turned everything turtle. He was treated
by his staff and peons as a leper. The poor illiterate peons thought
it sinful to hand over office papers and files to him. They flung
the bundles of files and hurled papers at his desk. They rolled
the mats when he got up to go. Drinking water was not available
to him in office. This mortifying amosphere drove him to seek
refuge in the public library. And his immediate officer allowed
him to do so when there was no work on his table.

But the climax of humiliations was reached when one
day a party of Parsees armed with lathis called on Ambedkar
and asked him who he was. He said that he was a Hindu.
"You arrant knave, you are the despicable untouchable we
know", were the angry words of the Parsees. They asked him
what he meant by defiling the hostel reserved for their
community, and ordered him to vacate instantly. Ambedkar
pulled himself together and quietly asked for eight hours'
leave to do so. No Hindu, no Muslim would give him shelter
in the city. He sent a note to the Maharaja, who referred him
to the Diwan, and the Diwan expressed his inability to do
anything in the matter. Tired, hungry and fagged out, he sat
under a tree and burst into a flood of tears.[3] The sky above
was his shelter and the ground below, his floor! Although he
was a man of learning and a thousand times superior to those
creatures who wallowed in the mire of ignorance, superstitions
and evil customs, he realised now that even with his personal

---

3.   Ambedkar's speech, *The Janata*, 23 May 1930.

attainment he could not soften the prejudices of the caste Hindus. He was terribly grieved.

So in a helpless mood, in deep gloom and utterly disgusted with the insulting environments, Ambedkar returned in the middle of November 1917 to Bombay. Again through Keluskar, who had been instrumental in securing him opportunities so far, he tried to bring to the notice of Shri Sayajirao Gaekwad the insufferable treatment meted out to him; but to no purpose. Keluskar tried to make some sort of arrangements with a professor at Baroda who was supposed to be a gentleman of progressive leanings. He agreed at first to accept Ambedkar as a paid guest, but in the end trembled like a lamb before his flaming orthodox wife, and withdrew his support. When Ambedkar reached Baroda station at the instance of Keluskar, he received a note from the professor requesting Ambedkar not to come to his house as he said his wife was hostile to the proposal. Ambedkar returned again from Baroda station. Thus he bade farewell to the State of his benefactor!

On his arrival in Bombay, he found his step-mother very seriously ill. She died after a few days. Ambedkar performed her obsequies though her turbulent nature had almost alienated the family.

The Indian National Congress was now growing conscious of the existence of the Depressed Classes. Wedded to constitutional political agitation, it considered, up till now, this problem as being beyond their domain and deliberations. But now its sudden love for the Depressed Classes emanated from an ulterior motive of winning their support for the Congress-League Scheme in which premium was put on the separate identity of the Muslims, but no notice was taken of the existence of the Untouchables.

To consider the Congress-League demands the Depressed Classes held two Conferences in November 1917, in Bombay. The first one was held at the behest of Sir Narayan Ganesh Chandavarkar. By one resolution this Conference appealed to Government to protect the interests of the Untouchables by granting the Depressed Classes the right to elect their own representatives to the legislatures in proportion to their population and by another it supported the Congress-League

Scheme, asking the Congress in turn to pass a resolution at its ensuing session impressing upon the caste Hindus the necessity, the justice and righteousness of removing all disabilities imposed upon the Depressed Classes in the name of custom and religion.

The other Conference, which was held a few days after this, opposed the transfer of power to the caste Hindus and appealed to Government to grant them the right to choose their own representatives.

Ambedkar was in mourning when the first Conference met. Besides there was no possibility of his attending the Congress-sponsored Conference of the Untouchables; and although tne aims of the second Conference were akin to his, he was not in a mood to participate in it.

In accordance with the demands of the first Untouchable Conference mentioned above, the Congress at its annual session held at Calcutta, in December 1917, passed a resolution as a return gift to the Untouchables who had declared their support to the Congress-League Scheme.

It will be interesting to record here Ambedkar's reactions to the Congress-League Scheme. The Scheme, observes Ambedkar, did not ask that the Legislatures should have the power to make or unmake an Executive as it pleases. "The Scheme was unsound," he concludes, "because in it the Executive and the Legislatures derived their mandates from and were responsible to different powers."[4]

Three months after the above-cited Calcutta resolution of the Congress respecting the Untouchables, an event of great significance took place. The Depressed Classes Mission Society of India held its First All-India Depressed Classes Conference on March 23 and 24, 1918, in Bombay. On this occasion the most deserving personality, His Highness the Maharaja Sayajirao Gaekwad of Baroda, presided over the Conference. It was attended by prominent Indian celebrities such as Vithalbhai Patel, M. R. Jaykar, Bepin Chandra Pal and others. Messages from Dr. Harold H. Mann, Sir Rabindranath Tagore, Shri Shankaracharya of Dwarka, Dr. Kurtakoti of Karveer, were received. The Chairman of the Reception Committee, Sir Narayan

---

4.   *The Evolution of Provincial Finance in British India*, pp. 207.

Ganesh Chandavarkar said that they had met for the purpose of appealing to the conscience of the country, awakening its reason, its heart and asking the whole of India to remove the blot of untouchability. The Maharaja said that the ignorant prejudices and class fanaticism could not forever withstand the pressure of scientific thought and forces of social regeneration which were remoulding the outlook and temper of thousands of our countrymen.

Tilak, Khaparde and A.V. Thakkar also attended the proceedings of the Conference on the second day. Supporting a resolution, Tilak said that if God were to tolerate untouchability he would not recognise him as God at all and added that he did not deny that in some old days the autocracy of the Brahmins created that usage. He concluded his speech by declaring that untouchability was a disease and it must be removed; that it was a matter of social usage and it must change.[5] At the conclusion of the Conference there came out an All-India Anti-Untouchability Manifesto signed by all prominent leaders to the effect that they would not observe untouchability in their everyday affairs. Tilak, however, did not sign it, it is said, on account of pressure from his followers.[6] Karmaveer V.R. Shinde was the organiser of this Conference.

III

Reserved and sceptical of the movement started by the caste Hindus for the uplift of the Untouchables, Ambedkar did not associate himself with this Conference. He was fundamentally opposed to it. He was watching and waiting for the right opportunity to draw on his enormous resources of energy and brains. First he must have a footing, a position. To achieve it there was now no alternative for him but to earn his living independently. Law was before his mind. It would serve him as a means of livelihood and would act as a powerful attraction to his people. But his studies at the Grays Inn in London were incomplete. He had an unsuppressed longing to complete his studies in London. He had made up his mind to fight his way out. Through the good offices of a Parsee gentleman he became a

---

5. *The All-India Anti-Untouchability Movement*, p. 22.
6. *Maharashtriya Dnyana Kosh*. Vol. VII, p. 647.

tutor to two students. Simultaneously he started a business firm offering advice to the dealers in the Stocks and Shares. It promised a good income. But soon it became known to all dealers that its proprietor was an Untouchable, and he had to close it down. For some time he looked after the correspondence and accounts of a Parsee gentleman.

Yet the mind was busy with the ideas of intellectual conquest. About the time he wrote a review article on Bertrand Russell's book *Reconstruction of Society* in *The Journal of the Indian Economic Society*. Describing it as a war book, he observed that Russell was right in believing that war could not be banished by rationalistic appeals alone but by positive life of impulses and passions antagonistic to those that led to war. Russell was against war; but not for quietism. According to Russell activity led to growth; quietism was another name for death. Force was energy which must be used constitutively to achieve anything, and not destructively as violence. Ambedkar was afraid that Indians might read in Russell's book a justification for their philosophic bias for the doctrine of non-violence. In the end Ambedkar added that Russell deserved full credit for having emphasized the psychic basis of social life. Social reconstruction depended upon the right understanding of the relations of individuals in society—a problem which had eluded the grasp of many sociologists.

Ambedkar also reprinted his paper on *Castes in India* in a book form and contributed a thought-provoking paper on 'Small-Holdings in India and their Remedies'. This subject was then being discussed by experts who held the view that the enlargement and consolidation of the small and scattered holdings would improve the condition of agriculture in India. Criticising the Baroda Committee's report and the views of other experts, Ambedkar concluded: "It can be laid down without fear of challenge that industrialization will foster and facilitate the enlargement of holdings, though it may not bring about consolidation. It is an incontrovertible fact that so long as there is premium on land, consolidation will not be easy. Industrialisation must precede consolidation."[7]

With all this intellectual ballast, the ship of Ambedkar's life was not sailing smoothly, While he was in such a depressing

---

7. *The Journal of the Indian Economics Society*, Vol. I, No. III.

state of mind, he heard the news that a vacancy had occurred in
Sydenham College of Commerce and Economics, Bombay. He
applied for the post of professorship. He wrote, a letter to Lord
Sydenham, former Governor of Bombay, who was his London
acquaintance, requesting him to recommend him to the
Government of Bombay for the post of professorship in Sydenham
College. All arrangements and his interview also turned well,
and Government appointed him professor of political economy
in Sydenham College. He accepted the post in November 1918,
on a temporary basis as his sole object in accepting the post was
to accumulate sufficient funds to enable him to go to London to
complete his studies in Law and Economics.

At first the students in Sydenham College did not take this
new professor seriously. What could an Untouchable teach the
caste Hindu students and others from advanced societies? They
knew not what happened when a man stood before them with
sincerity and serious study behind him. By and by Ambedkar's
deep study, exhaustive exposition and thoughtful style gripped
the minds of his students. The young professor with his fine dress,
his profound studies, his serious glowing eyes became well known
in the circle of students of economics and as a result students
from other colleges also attended his classes with special
permission. The notes and other material which he had collected
for preparing his lectures, it is said, were vast enough for the
production of an exhaustive work on Economics. But his success
as a professor could not mitigate the evils of untouchability in
the holy atmosphere of the place of learning. Some Gujarati
professors objected to his drinking water from the pot reserved
for the professorial staff.

Professorship was, however, a means and not an end in itself
to Ambedkar. The wanton insults and humiliations were goading
him to go to the root of the trouble. So gradually he began to feel
the pulse of the Untouchables and was silently contacting and
tapping all the centres of the sympathisers with their cause. He
was trying to infuse life into the dead cells and fanning the live
ones into a glow.

It was with this end in view that Ambedkar encouraged the
Rohidas Vidyavardhak Samaj to felicitate P. Balu on his great
achievement in cricket. Ambedkar took great pains to make that
function a success. As a student, Ambedkar looked at the solid

fame of the untouchable bowler with pride. Immediately afterwards, he tried for P. Balu's elevation to the membership of the Bombay Municipal Corporation and got one seat added to the original one apportioned to the Untouchables.

In Maharashtra, at this juncture, another Maratha Prince of broad humanity and uncompromising courage appeared on the scene, and took deep interest in the removal of untouchability and in the welfare of the Depressed Classes. This illustrious Prince was His Highness the Maharaja of Kolhapur. Shri Shahu Maharaj did his utmost to promote education, among the lower classes, to eradicate the prejudices and barriers created by the caste system and to emancipate the lower classes from the tyrannous priesthood and unjust dominance of the Brahmins. He encouraged the Untouchables in every possible way. He appointed them to posts on his personal establishment; he granted them *sanads* to practise as lawyers; he took meals with them in public. He provided untouchable students with free education, free lodging and boarding. The honour of being his State elephant-driver was also accorded to an Untouchable.

About this time the Southborough Committee, dealing with the franchise in the light of the Montagu-Chelmsford Reforms, examined representatives of different interests and communities. Karmaveer Shinde and Ambedkar were called upon to give evidence before them. Ambedkar demanded separate electorate and reserved seats for the Depressed Classes in proportion to their population. What views he held on the demand for Home Rule can be guessed from a letter which he wrote then to *The Times of India*, Bombay, under a *nom de plume*. He said that before demanding Home Rule it was the duty of the advanced classes to put the Lower and Depressed Classes on social equality who belonged to the same religion, followed the same customs, lived within the same borders, with the same aspirations for Liberty and Home Rule. For everybody recognised, he observed, that Home Rule was as much the birthright of a Brahmin as that of a Mahar. The first duty, therefore, of the advanced classes was to educate, enlighten and elevate them. Unless and until that attitude was adopted, the day on which India would have Home Rule was distant.[8]

---

8.   The *Times of India*, 16 January 1919.

It was in 1919 that Ambedkar came in closer contact with the Maharaja of Kolhapur through Dattoba Powar. Ambedkar secured from the Maharaja some help for the fortnightly paper which he proposed to start. He started it on January 31, 1920, under the title *Mook Nayak*, Leader of the Dumb, Although Ambedkar was not its official editor, he was the man behind it and it was his mouthpiece. How violent and unfavourable were the times can be seen from the fact that the Kesari refused even to announce its publication although solicited to do so as a paid advertisement![9]. And this happened when Tilak was yet alive!

In the first issue of the *Mook Nayak* Ambedkar brilliantly propounded the aim of the paper in a very simple, convincing and forceful language. He wrote that India was a home of inequality. Hindu society, he observed, was just like a tower which had several storeys without a ladder or an entrance. One was to die in the storey in which one was born. Hindu society, he continued, consisted of three parts: the Brahmins, the non-Brahmins and the Untouchables. He pitied the souls of those persons who said that according to their philosophy there existed god in animals as well as in animate things and yet treated their co-religionists as Untouchables! He lamented that not the spread of knowledge and literacy but accumulation and monopoly was the aim of the Brahmins. In his view the backwardness of the non-Brahmins was due to lack of education and power. In order to save the Depressed Classes from perpetual slavery, poverty and ignorance, herculean efforts must be made, he asserted, to awaken them to their disabilities.

In another article the *Mook Nayak* asserted that it was not enough for India to be an independent country. She must rise as a good State guaranteeing equal status in matters religious, social, economic and political, to all classes, offering every man an opportunity to rise in the scale of life and creating conditions favourable to his advancement. There did not exist such a despicable man, who, continued the voice in the article, would object to the statement that if the Brahmins were justified in their attack upon and opposition to the unjust power of the British Government, the Depressed Classes were justified a hundred times more so in their opposition to the rulership of the Brahmins in case the transfer of power took place. The article

9. The *Bahiskrit Bharat*, 20 May 1927.

asserted that if the protection of the Britishers were withdrawn, those who did not condescend to look at the Untouchables would trample upon them. In another article Ambedkar stated that the Swaraj wherein there were no fundamental rights guaranteed for the Depressed Classes, would not be a Swaraj to them. It would be a new slavery for them.

Ambedkar was not then prepared for an all-out attack upon Hindu society. He was working as a professor in a Government college and besides his armoury was not yet full with weapons.

On March 21, 1920, Ambedkar presided over a conference of the Untouchables at Mangaon in the Kolhupur State. It was attended by Shri Shahu Maharaj himself. Speaking at the Conference, the Maharaja declared in a prophetic vein: "You have found your saviour in Ambedkar. I am confident that he will break your shackles. Not only that, a time will come when, so whispers my conscience, Ambedkar will shine as a front-rank leader of all-India fame and appeal."[10] The conference ended in holding an intercaste dinner attended by His Highness the Maharaja, the State officials, the Jahagirdars and others in company with the Untouchables headed by Ambedkar.

Another important conference in which Ambedkar's voice echoed was held in the last week of May 1920, at Nagpur. This was the first All-India Conference convened by Untouchables and was presided over by no less a personality than Shri Shahu Maharaj of Kolhapur. About this time Karmaveer Shinde suggested on behalf of his Depressed Classes Mission that the representatives of the Untouchables should be selected by the Members of the Legislative Council, and not by Government or by the institutions belonging to the Untouchables. He had deputed his men to Nagpur to get his point of view accepted by this Conference. Ambedkar, who boiled at this gross insult, made a fighting speech resenting the attitude taken by Shinde, and the Conference by a special resolution protested against such a step being taken by Government.[11] It was during this debate that Ambedkar's skill and presence of mind as a debater and his ability as a prospective leader were seen to a remarkable degree. It was here that Ambedkar won his first victory in public life.

Ambedkar held that howsoever the caste Hindus worked

10. Shivtarkar, S.N., The *Janata* Special Number, April 1933.
11. *Ibid.*

hard for the welfare of the Untouchables they did not know their mind. That was why he was fundamentally opposed to any organisation started by the caste Hindus for the uplift of Depressed Classes. This Nagpur Conference gave him an opportunity of turning the eyes of the Untouchables from the Depressed Classes Mission. At the conclusion of the Conference, Ambedkar made an attempt in the direction of consolidating the forces of the Depressed Classes. In the Central Provinces the Mahar community had eighteen sub-castes. He called the leaders of the community together and gave a dinner in which they all participated. It should be noted that with great persuasion Ambedkar could get all the sub-castes of the Mahar community and not all the Untouchable communities to dine together. It was not possible yet to make all the communities belonging to the Untouchables participate in an Intercaste dinner!

The affection and admiration of the Maharaja of Kolhapur for Ambedkar grew, and one day the Maharaja's sudden appearance at his residence embarrassed him. He hurriedly put on his clothes and welcomed the Maharaja to his study.

IV

Although, as a professor, Ambedkar drew a handsome salary, he lived very frugally. He lived in the same two rooms one opposite the other in the Improvement Trust Chawl at Parel in the labour area. He gave a fixed portion of his salary to his wife for running the household. Dutiful, self-respecting, silent, resolute, pious and given to self-denial, Ramabai, his wife, almost spent her early life in struggles and yet lived in peace and harmony, taking care of the family of her husband's deceased brother. At times she could not help being sensitive and stubborn in matters of religious observances which were rigid and rigorous.

While Ambedkar was in America, this saintly woman lived in a state of extreme destitution but without a whisper of grumbling, her eyes turned towards God for the safety and prosperity of her husband. When her husband had left for America she was pregnant. She gave birth to a son, but that son, Ramesh, died in infancy. After her husband's return, she bore a son. He was named Gangadhar. He also died in infancy. She had now her only son Yashwant whose health caused her anxiety.

Yet she lived as sparingly as she could, kept herself from her husband's study, gave him no news of any illness in the family and saw that nobody disturbed him in his studies. Through the efforts of her husband she now learnt a little reading and writing. It has been a peculiar charm with lives of great Indians that they had simple and good wives. Like Tilak, Gandhi and Savarkar, Ambedkar, too, was blessed with a great and good wife.

At last, the young professor saved some money, got some help from the Maharaja of Kolhapur, took a loan of Rs. 5,000 from his friend Mr. Naval Bhathena, and again left for London in July 1920 to complete his studies in Law and Economics. The tranquil support his pious and patient wife afforded was no less valuable. His wife was again left to pass days in struggles looking after her little son, Yashwant and the family of the elder brother of her husband.

Meanwhile, the Baroda officials in their flaming zeal to guard the interests of the Maharaja and to control the finances of the State, took extraordinary pains in insisting on the repayment of the scholarship by Ambedkar. They wrote to the Sydenham College authorities, the Bombay Provincial educational authorities and N. M. Joshi, a reputed labour leader of Bombay, in the matter of recovery of the money which they now styled a loan. It seems the Maharaja was not kept in touch with this matter and although he himself passed remarks on the papers of the case that the money was expended on education and as such the question of recovery did not arise at all, those in charge of the State affairs were racking for a considerable period, their envious brains for an opportunity to take legal action against Ambedkar. At long last, however, came a final rebuff from the ruler, and the Council had to abandon in 1932 the idea of harassing their scholar ward.

On his arrival in London, Ambedkar resumed his studies in Economics from September 1920 at the London School of Economics and Political Science and also kept terms for the Bar at the Grays Inn. He now turned his attention to the London Museum where the relics of saintly and scientific thoughts are preserved, where the ruins of the antique world are displayed and where Karl Marx, Mazzini, Lenin and Savarkar had dug for knowledge and digested it. In the Museum Ambedkar pored over books whenever possible, often from 8 a.m. to 5 p.m.

Time was an important factor with him. To save both money and time he would go without a lunch. He had then taken his lodgings at a semi-boarding house conducted by a lady. Asnodkar from Bombay also stayed with the same family as a paying guest. The keeper of the boarding-house was a harsh and terrible lady. The breakfast she offered her boarders consisted of a piece of fish, a cup of tea, a piece of bread with a sprinkling of jam. Cramming this stinted little stuff, Ambedkar ran to the Museum in the early morning and was almost the first man to enter it. Then commenced his daily reading in the British Museum for hours together without any break or rest. So intense was his reading and so much engrossed was he in it that he was always hunted out by the watchman in the evening, he being the last man to leave the Museum every day, with his pockets bulging with notes, his face pale, tired and slimy.

Ambedkar's research work did not confine itself to the Museum alone. He also read several volumes and old reports in the India Office Library, in the London University Library and in other city Libraries noted for books on economics, and took down voluminous notes on the subject of his thesis.

This tremendous laborious day-time work was followed by an evening walk in the open air for about half an hour and then dinner at the house of the same lady. It consisted of a cup of bovril to be relished with some biscuits and a little butter. The recollection of this ruthless thrift in his regimen evoked a few years later a severe remark from Ambedkar. He said to Prabhakar Padhye: "The landlady was a terrible woman. I am always praying for her soul; but I am sure she will go to perdition."[12]

After this the second round of reading began at his residence. About ten at night the fire in the stomach seemed to suppress the fire in the head and made Ambedkar wriggle. He was mad with hunger. An Indian acquaintance of his had made him a present of a bundle of thin crisp Indian wafers called *papad*. He secured a thin tin plate to fry those crisp wafers. A cup of tea and four pieces of *papad* would partly appease the intensity of his hunger. Then again the endless reading, the *Dnyana yadnya*.

---

12. Padhye, Prabhakar : *Prakshatil Vyakti* (Marathi), p. 30.

It would go on till early morning when his roommate Asnodkar, who after enjoying sound sleep, woke up by chance, and could see Ambedkar still studying with intense absorption. With sympathy in his eyes he sincerely requested Ambedkar to retire. But the scholar replied softly that his poverty and want of time required him to finish his studies as early as possible and hence the dogged and ceaseless persistence.

Now and then Ambedkar turned to his friend, Mr. Naval Bhathena, for help. He responded splendidly and on one such occasion the scholar wrote with a moving touch to Bhathena: "Believe me, I extremely regret to see you bothered on my account. I fully realise that the worries which I have thrown on you are more than even the thickest friend can bear. I only hope that my constant asking for something or other does not break your back, and alienate you from me the only and dear friend of mine." He pressed Bhathena for a sum of Rs. 2,000 as he desired to buy German exchange in advance which was then very low but was likely to look up after some days.

Benjamin Franklin, who entered life as a very poor boy and concluded as an eminent man, said that success in life depended on two things—Industry and Frugality. Ambedkar lived so sparingly that he subsisted on a small sum of eight pounds a month and he was clearer in head and healthier in body ! He hardly spent on dress, rarely on fares and trudged along from one place to another in the great metropolis. No money or time for restaurants, no feasts, excursions or the theatre! Few lives in history illustrate so eloquently how one should build up one's future and personality, how difficulties arouse the powers of a great man. Long hours of hard labour, intense hardships and high thinking alone have crowned with success the great men of the world.

Yet in his struggle for academic eminence, Ambedkar had not forgotten the real aim in life. A great man develops not for enjoyment but for action. On his arrival in London he had seen Montagu, the then Secretary of State for India, and Mr. Vithalbhai Patel who then happened to be in London, and had talks with them in respect of the grievances of the Untouchables in India.

Although Ambedkar was away from India for these long toilsome years, he was keeping himself well-informed about the centres of the Depressed Classes that were working for the uplift of the Untouchables in India. He often guided from London S.N. Shivtarkar, who stood by him for over twenty years in his great war against untouchability, to put the movement on the right path. He took great interest in the conduct of the *Mook Nayak* and often showed anxiety for its threatened existence. In one of his letters home he observes that it is very painful for the founder of a newspaper to break away from it. The duty must be performed; let the efforts be successful or not; let the work be appreciated by the ignorant or not. When a man's sincerity of purpose and capacity are proved, he adds, even his enemies come to respect him.

On another occasion he says that it is not a sin to crave for honour. But if honour does not come your way, you should not give up your struggle in despair. Your resilience should not desert you if you are ungratefully ignored or denied the credit you deserve. He then cites his own case and points out to the new year's editorial in the *Mook Nayak* wherein the editor beamed with self-praise and ignored its founder Ambedkar. Still he says that he was satisfied that the paper was running and doing service to the Untouchables. In every letter he emphasized the need for unity among all the numerous untouchable castes as their combined efforts, he said, would go a long way to solve their problem.

This was his repeated advice. In those days Ambedkar, as all great leaders do in the early part of their career, used to take deep interest in the sorrows and joys of his colleagues, and their personal difficulties. Often he inquired after the health of the senior leaders of his community like D.D. Gholap, and condoled with those who lost their relatives. One thing caused him anxiety. It was the education of his son and his nephew. He wrote to Shivtarkar about it, asking him to engage a tutor to look after their studies.

In those days it seems he was reading Marathi plays. He constantly reminded Shivtarkar to send some excellent Marathi dramas by Maharashtra's leading playwright, Gadkari. Another book he asked for from London was *Ricardo's Works* by McCulloch. It was a rare book. He wrote to S.N. Shivtarkar to go to a certain second-hand bookstall in Bombay, in which he had seen the book a few months earlier! Ambedkar's fine suit had impelled the shrewd shopkeeper to raise the price of the old tattered book.

During his stay in London Ambedkar normally kept good health but it seems from one of his letters that he was ill in October 1922. The news was not to be given out, and Shivtarkar suppressed the news from Ambedkar's family lest it should make his embarrassed wife still more anxious about her husband.

The political scenes in India were changing with dramatic suddenness. A short while after Ambedkar's arrival in London, India mourned the saddest death of her great son, Lokmanya Tilak. In the wake of this misfortune, surged up and spread the politics and influence of the Gandhian movement. Ambedkar described these times, a few years later, as "the dark age of India".

There was nothing revolutionary in the field of the removal of untouchability in those days except that Gandhi, who, while collecting the Tilak Swaraj Fund, had made the removal of untouchability one of the important planks of the Congress propaganda, now refused to spend on it beyond a meagre amount out of one crore of rupees. Owing to want of sympathy and sincerity, the Congress Working Committee also had resolved, after some months of incubation, that the problem of the uplift of the Untouchables should be left to the Hindu Mahasabha as it was thought that the Hindu Mahasabha alone was concerned with the problem.

The Act of 1919 recognised for the first time in Indian history the existence of the Depressed Classes. Among the fourteen non-official Members nominated by the Governor-General to the Central Legislative Assembly one was the representative of the Depressed Classes. In the Provincial Legislatures the Depressed Classes were represented by four nominations in the Central Provinces, two in Bombay, two in Bihar and one each in Bengal and the United Provinces. In Madras ten Members were nominated to represent nine specified Depressed Classes.

Days rolled by. Ambedkar's tremendous research work was gradually coming to an end. One thesis was completed. It was the "Provincial Decentralization of Imperial Finance in British

India". For this he was awarded the degree of Master of Science in June 1921. In October 1922 he completed his famous thesis, *The Problem of the Rupee*, and submitted it to the University of London. About the same time he was called to the Bar. He could not take his bar examination earlier as he was working unflaggingly on his thesis; moreover, the law books promised by some student were not made available to him.

Meanwhile, as his studies were nearing completion, he was thinking of joining another world-famous academic centre in Europe. He had been to Germany for about a month from the middle of April to the middle of May 1922 to make arrangements for his admission to Bonn University and returned to London. On submitting his thesis to London University, he went to study at Bonn University. Hardly was he there for a quarter of the year, when in March 1923 he was called back to London by his professor Edwin Cannan as the terse exposition in his thesis had given offence to the British imperialist examiners who asked him to rewrite his thesis without changing his conclusions. This was not, however, the first time that Ambedkar's writing had caused a furore in the academic world of London. A few days earlier he had read a paper on 'Responsibilities of a Responsible Government in India' before the Students' Union. It had caused a stir in the academic world, and Ambedkar was suspected to be an Indian revolutionary; even Prof. Harold J, Laski, then teaching at the London School of Science, opining that the thoughts expressed in the paper were frankly of a revolutionary nature.

But now he could not extend his stay in London to rewrite his thesis. His financial resources had almost run out. What little money he had saved after living a life of utmost want he had spent on books. In India his family, too, was hard up. So with his thoughts centred on his thesis he had to return to Bombay in April 1923. A few days after, he re-submitted his thesis, *The Problem of the Rupee*, from Bombay. The examiners accepted it and to his great joy he was at last awarded the degree of Doctor of Science. A long laborious industry, iron will and conquering intellect won at last a great victory!

The amplification of this thesis was published by Messrs, P.S. King & Son Ltd., London, in December 1923. The author dedicated this great work to the memory of his father and mother as a token of "my abiding gratitude for the sacrifices they made and the enlightenment they showed in the matter of my education." The book was introduced to the public by his great teacher Edwin Cannan. Although he disagreed with-a good deal of Ambedkar's criticism in the book, he was glad to note that the author hit some nails very squarely on the head; and this great celebrity in the world of economics paid a glowing tribute to Ambedkar for his 'stimulating freshness in his views and reasons'.

In this work Ambedkar reveals how in the final settlement of the currency problem the relationship of the rupee to the pound was manipulated to the greater profit of the Britishers, and how it inflicted crushing hardships on the Indian people as a whole.

Ambedkar was now a Barrister reinforced by a London Doctorate in Science, an American Doctorate in Philosophy and studies at Bonn University. He was thus well equipped as a lawyer and an authority to challenge the scholars of economics and sociology in India, and to storm the Indian citadel.

□□□

CHAPTER 4

MAN OF THE HOUR

AMBEDKAR now decided to practise law which would provide him opportunities, means and leisure to devote himself to the aim of his life, the uplift of the Untouchables. He had no money to obtain a *Sanad*. And once again the difficulty was got over by Mr. Naval Bhathena, his friend and benefactor, who gave him the money. With that money the Doctor got his *Sanad* and started life as a Barrister in June 1923. The thorns of untouchability, the colour of his skin, the inexperienced legal mind and the unhelpful surroundings in Courts turned his path into an uphill task. But he was not disappointed. Excellence in pursuit, he knew, is achieved by laborious application. He knew it from his boyhood, and he was bent upon attaining it in this sphere as well.

Ambedkar joined the Appellate Side of the Bombay Bar as success in practice on the Original Side depended more upon one's influence with the solicitors than upon one's ability. In those days it was the general impression that briefing European barristers was more impressive before the English judges, as their skin sometimes shone better than their arguments. Moreover, Ambedkar's path was beset with difficulties from all sides. The solicitors would not condescend to have any sort of business dealings with him on the ground of untouchability, and therefore he had to content himself with whatever work he got in the mofussil till he could light his own path to the front benches in the High Court. All famous legal luminaries in their early career had to cool their heels likewise.

By now the outer influences and inner forces had brought about a visible change in the mental and moral outlook of the Depressed Classes. The spread of education, the development of communications, modes of travelling and the spirit of nationalism had gradually begun to act as effective correctives to the prejudicial ideas of untouchability.

The rise of the textile industry, which improved the economic condition of labour during World War I, helped the Depressed Classes, too, to some extent along with other working classes, and stimulated them to activities for the betterment of their own conditions. On top of it all came the currents of democratic ideals generated by the inevitable forces of World War I and gave an impetus to the social reforms movement all the world over. They caused ripples of restlessness also in the minds of the Untouchables in India. The spirit of self-assertion was manifesting itself in the thoughts and actions of those classes. It always so happens when an enslaved class begins to regain its consciousness and rejuvenates its thinking power. The law of social reforms is that they come speedily not from the efforts of philanthropists, but from the organised self-assertion on the part of the sufferers themselves.

About this time, in the reformed Legislative Council of Bombay the representatives of the lower classes took active interest in the promotion of the welfare of the Depressed Classes. D.D. Gholap, who was the first nominated representative of the Untouchables in the Bombay Legislative Council, moved a resolution recommending to the Government to make primary education compulsory in order to bring it within the reach of the Depressed Classes. He then asked a volley of questions regarding the insufficiency of water supply to Mahars in villages and about the provision of new primary schools for boys of the Depressed Classes, and inquired of the Government whether it intended to establish special hostels for the Depressed Class girls. Another Member of the Council, Anandrao Surve, interpellated Government whether it was a fact that in the Thana District members of the Depressed Classes were not admitted into public conveyances.

But the most important resolution was the one moved by S.K. Bole which the Bombay Legislative Council adopted on August 4, 1923. This remarkable, patient and discreet social reformer, who had courageously overcome the threats of excommunication by the Bhandari Community for having taken an active part in an intercaste dinner with the Arya Samajists as early as 1906, took a bold stand for promoting the interests of the Depressed Classes. Moving the resolution, Bole said that untouchability was a great stigma on the good name of India and added: "We resent the segregation policy of the South African Colonies and therefore we must set our house in order. It is in our interests and in the interests of the country that the Depressed Classes should be given better treatment."

Bole then sounded a warning that if they did not improve their lot the Untouchables would some day resort to satyagraha. His resolution cried for a new departure, a turning over of an epoch in the caste Hindu attitude towards their brethren, and a strong action on the part of the Government. Said the famous Bole resolution: "The Council recommends that the Untouchable Classes be allowed to use all public watering-places, wells and dharmashalas which are built and maintained out of public funds or administered by bodies appointed by Government or created by statute, as well as public schools, courts, offices and dispensaries." The Depressed Classes of Bombay were so much overwhelmed with feelings of gratitude that they held a congratulatory meeting in Bole's honour under the presidentship of J. Addyman, M.L.C., and awarded him a gold medal for his signal services to their cause.

As a result of this resolution, the Bombay Government issued the following directive to the Heads of all Departments on September 11, 1923: "In pursuance of the foregoing Council resolution, the Government of Bombay are pleased to direct that all Heads of offices should give effect to the resolution so far as it relates to the public places and institutions belonging to and maintained by Government. The Collectors should be requested to advise the local public bodies in their jurisdiction to consider the desirability of accepting the recommendation made in the resolution so far as it relates to them." The Chairman of the Bombay Improvement Trust, and the Municipal Commissioner for the City of Bombay also were requested to take similar steps with the consent of the trustees and the Corporation respectively for giving effect to the resolution with regard to the places under their control.

There was another notable proclamation made concerning the Depressed Classes at the end of the year 1923. Maulana Mahomed Ali, stimulated by the cringing co-operation of Mahatma Gandhi with the Indian Muslims in their insistence on the rights of the Khilafat, and inflated with pride at being bracketed with Gandhi, was led to express a rapacious desire from the Presidential Chair of the Indian National Congress, which boasted of its secular approach to all national problems, to divide the Hindu untouchables equally between the Muslims and the Hindus. These savage wishes entertained by Gandhi's God-fearing Muslim colleagues, were often faithfully blustered out in the holy presence of Gandhi without even causing a ripple of demur or displeasure on his face. Presiding at a meeting called to present an address to Gandhi at Madras, Yakub Hussein once openly enjoined upon the Musalmans the duty of converting all the Untouchables in India to Islam![1]

II

The year 1924 was one of the most eventful years in Indian history. It witnessed the release of three great forces in the social field in India. After undergoing a hellish jail life over twelve years in the Andamans, Veer Savarkar was released and interned in Ratnagiri on January 6, 1924, from Yeravda Jail where he had been brought a few days before being interned. Gandhi was also released on February 11, 1924, on health grounds from the same jail after suffering jail life for nearly two years consequent on the debacle of his Khilafat-Swaraj movement. In their helplessness both Savarkar and Gandhi wanted to make the most of the situation. Both took a plunge into the social field. Savarkar started his work in April 1924 for the consolidation of Hindu society—which work was known as Hindu Sanghatan—and invariably for the uplift of the Depressed Classes for whose welfare and rights he had been fighting ever since his transportation to the Andamans. Gandhi applied his methods and herculean energy to the amelioration of the Depressed Classes.

Ambedkar also prepared himself in March 1924 to launch his social movement for the uplift of the Untouchables. To achieve his objective he convened a meeting on March 9, 1924, at the Damodar Hall, Bombay, to consider the desirability of establishing a central institution for removing difficulties of the Untouchables and placing their grievances before Government. After much discussion and debate, it was resolved that an

---

1. *Young India*, 8 September 1920.

institution be established and accordingly it was founded on July 20, 1924 under the title 'Bahishkrit Hitakarini Sabha', and was registered under Act XXI of 1860. Its activities were confined to the Presidency of Bombay and its head office was situated at Damodar Hall, Bombay 12. The aims and objects of the Sabha were as under :

(a) To promote the spread of education among the Depressed Classes by opening Hostels or by employing such other means as may seem necessary or desirable.

(b) To promote the spread of culture among the Depressed Classes by opening libraries, social centres and classes or study circles.

(c) To advance and improve the economic condition of the Depressed Classes by starting Industrial and Agricultural Schools.

(d) To represent the grievances of the Depressed Classes.[2]

The President of the Bahishkrit Hitakarini Sabha was Sir Chimanlal Harilal Setalvad, L.L.D., and its Vice-Presidents were Meyer Nissim, J.P.; Rustomji Jinwala, Solicitor; G. K. Nariman, Dr. R.P. Paranjpye, Dr. V.P. Chavan and B.G. Kher, Solicitor, who fifteen years later became the first Prime Minister of the Bombay Province. The Chairman of the managing committee was Ambedkar, its Secretary was S.N. Shivtarkar and its Treasurer, N.T. Jadhav.

This Central Organisation devoted itself to raising the Depressed Classes from their down-trodden condition to a status of social and political equality with others in Indian society and to promoting their economic interests. It thus fulfilled in a way the need expressed in a resolution at the Second Bombay Provincial Conference which was held at Barsi in Sholapur District by the Depressed Classes in the early part of the year 1924.

While clarifying its position and casting light on its composition, this Sabha said in its first annual report that the object in taking up the majority of workers from the Depressed Classes on its Committees and Boards was that it believed that no substantial progress could be made by any institution, nor could its aims be realised unless its members and workers were chosen from amongst the people suffering from similar

---

2. Bahishkrit Hitakarini Sabha. Rules of Constitution, p. 1.

grievances. The success of an organisation, observed the report, depended from the sincerity of its constituents and their devotion to its aims and programme. But although ample scope was thus provided for the workers of the Depressed Classes, promoters of the institution held that its huge programme could not be carried out without the sympathy and support of the upper classes. It was suicidal, it observed, in the interest of the Depressed Classes to refuse donations from those classes.

But why was Ambedkar channelling a new path? There were indeed several institutions and organisations in the social field devoted to the uplift of the Depressed Classes. There were some that aimed at reforming the society. But Ambedkar made a distinction between social reforms in the sense of the reforms of the Hindu family and social reforms in the sense of the reorganization and reconstruction of Hindu society. According to him the social reform movement inaugurated by reformers like Ranade and his Social Conference related to re-marriage of widows, women's rights to property, education of women, child marriages and other matters while the latter type related to the abolition of the caste system and reconstruction of Hindu society on the basis of equality. The Social Conference was, no doubt, a body that aimed at vitalising the conscience of Hindu society, but the orbit of its activities did not cross the borders of the upper class Hindus. The Social Conference consisted of enlightened high caste Hindus who either did not feel the necessity for agitating for the abolition of caste system or had not courage enough to fulfil the enormous uphill task. Fundamentally, they strove for the removal of all the evils prevailing in Hindu society and its reorganization; but they began at the top and not from the bottom.

The sponsors of the Prarthana Samaj and the promoters of the Brahmo Samaj did their bit in the field on the basis of humanitarianism. Princes like Chhatrapati Shahu and Sayajirao Gaekwad and leaders like Karmaveer Shinde toiled untiringly for the uplift of the Untouchables. Apart from those that had made the problem their cult and profession, there was in the past a goodly crowd of fashionable reformers, showy rationalists and wordy humanitarians who expressed lip sympathy in chaste diction for the Depressed Classes in order to please and show off their radical views to their ruling imperial bosses and the enlightened world. Not that the noble services and the lifelong efforts of the foregoing galaxy of reformers were less energetic and effective. The galaxy of earlier patriots, princes. reformers, humanitarians, Mahatmas and rationalists diagnosed the disease in their own way and prescribed for it, but in vain. The disease was in the stomach and often the medicine was applied by the reformers to the head. Few of them provided for the education of the Depressed Classes, many fondled them, some partook food with them, others helped them to reform their concept of living, dwelling and dress while some taught them how to bathe.

Despite these high-souled services to the cause, none could stir in the heart of these suppressed people an emotion of confidence, hope and aspiration for their own salvation, A feeling of dependency, a sense of guardianship and an impression of patronage had grown among them. The Untouchables knew this; but could not express the difference between help and self-help. Self-help is the best help. That was their basic want.

The conservative feeling in the country was at this juncture as unmoved as a rock. Only the conscience of the more political-minded Hindus was tweaked when they were reminded by the rival Muslim politicians that more than one-third of the total Hindu population was not accepted by the Hindus as part and parcel of their community, was denied the ministration by Brahmin priests and excluded from Hindu temples. So indifferent and callous was the attitude of the vast masses of caste Hindus to the problem that they thought that the fate of these suppressed untouchable Hindus was to be determined at their leisure and pleasure!

That is why the Hindu Mahasabha as also the Arya Samajists could not succeed much in their work of consolidation of Hindu society. In spite of the fact that the Hindu Mahasabha had passed in 1923 a resolution appealing to the Hindus to throw open temples, schools and other public places to the untouchable Hindus, its achievement was not a solid one due to lack of efforts. In fairness to the Hindu Sabha leaders it must be said that they undertook a mission which the conservative minds of the vast masses of the Hindus looked on with disfavour. Further, a majority of the active and patriotic Hindu workers were engaged in the fight with foreign rule. And a fight with a foreign rule always evokes the silent, secret and, at times, open sympathy and support of a people than does the fight for a social reform. Naturally the task of the Hindu Sabha leaders was rather difficult. So they could not win the support of

the masses for a Campaign which stood opposed to their
superstitions and traditions.

But the chief cause of their failure lay in the fact that some
of their first-rate leaders were incurably orthodox at heart and
were careful not to mix with the reformers except when it suited
their ends. And the result was that their professed ideal of
unifying all Hindus on a footing of equality remained distant.
Their intention was good, but its execution was worse. Their
resolutions carried more gestures than active struggle for
breaking the shackles that bound the Depressed Classes. So their
contribution to the annihilation of Untouchability, although
decidedly greater than that of any other party, was not equal to
their vociferous claims. Politically vigorous, valiant and watchful,
socially most of them wished to whitewash a decayed house. They
forgot the truth that whitewashing does not save a dilapidated
house. You must pull it down and build a new. Their apathy and
indifference was so much cold that even Swami Shraddhananda
had to resign from their camp. No wonder then that the world
Press described the Hindu Mahasabha organization crowded with
such conservative reformers as orthodox and reactionary, in spite
of its being led by great leaders like Shraddhananda, Parmanand
and later by Savarkar.

The attitude of the Congress leaders towards this problem
was woefully harmful. In their honest zeal to establish the
Muslim claims to the Khilafat, the Congress leaders thought of
the existence, importance and lives of the Indian Muslims only.
Their standard of measure for history, politics, social life,
nationalism and patriotism was only one and that was the
satisfaction of the Muslim parochialism and fanaticism. So they
not only did not care to know whether or not the Depressed
Classes suffered any disabilities, but also did not care to note
that the Depressed Classes were converted to Islam or
Christianity by force or fraud. They did not follow Gandhi's
movement for the uplift of Untouchables. The Congress had held
till then over forty sessions in the country, but it did not care
whether the Depressed Classes in their own country could get
water to drink or not. It was more concerned with the religious
questions of the Muslims and their Khilafat. The Congress
remained unconcerned with this problem because it benefited
the Hindus alone!

III

And as related above, these three forces, Gandhi, Savarkar and Ambedkar began to operate for the uplift of the Untouchables. Gandhi believed in the caste system and the four varnas! It was his aim to keep the castes intact and raise the Depressed Classes to the status of a fifth caste by removing the stigma of untouchability. As a humanist, his efforts stemmed from his genuine sympathy for the suppressed people under the sun, and as the Depressed Classes were the worst sufferers at the hands of the caste Hindus in India he took up their cause so far as the caste Hindus were concerned. He was all the while cautious not to hurt the susceptibilities of his orthodox capitalist admirers who were the prop of his movement. It was not his purpose to refashion or to reorganize Hindu society. As a world teacher in the making, he never cared to raise his little finger against the threatened conversion of these ignorant, dumb millions to the Muslim or Christian fold. Besides, the method of Gandhi's organization was more propagandistic than effective. At best, therefore, Gandhi was a reformer while Savarkar and Ambedkar were social revolutionaries. A reformer rebuilds the old structure. A revolutionary blows up the old building and builds a new one.

Savarkar's stand was nationalistic, realistic and revolutionary in its outlook as well as in action inasmuch as he aimed at moulding the different castes of the Hindus into a casteless Hindu society in which all Hindus would be socially, economically and politically equal. It was his aim to establish a powerful State on the invincible foundation of oneness and unity of the Hindus. But interned as he was in Ratnagiri District, the impact, the revolutionary aspect and urge of his movement could not do much outside that district beyond capturing the minds of rationalists and men of progressive views.

The case of Ambedkar was quite different. He sprang from amongst the Untouchables themselves. He was a leader who thought as they thought and felt as they felt. He knew how to win their unselfish and unbounded love. Over a decade he had observed, experienced and studied their utter privations, the appalling penury of their lives and their unclean habits. He boiled at their degraded condition and gave vent to their pent-up passions, their mind and their stifled self. Now before them appeared a leader on the scene who had seen much, suffered much, had also studied much. He had built up an invincible personality with his phenomenal energy and with the vast erudition he attained at the three world-famous universities as also with his supreme moral courage. He was a man who regarded the woes and miseries of those classes as a personal humiliation, and therefore he had taken a vow to make self-respecting citizens out of those virtual slaves.

Ambedkar hated the sense of dependency and abhorred the feeling of patronage of the caste Hindu reformers. He held in utter contempt the organizations and movements that prospered or were reared in the name of the Depressed Classes wherein Untouchables were treasured for functional occasions. Ambedkar was a believer in the divine principle that self-help is the best help. He diagnosed the disease correctly. He knew from history that injustice is not removed till the sufferer himself does away with it by his own exertions and actions. As long as the conscience of a slave does not burn with hatred for his slavery, there is no hope for his salvation. "Tell the slave he is a slave and he will revolt" was the slogan raised by Ambedkar. He exhorted the Untouchables to fight for self-elevation. Self-help, self-elevation and self-respect was the symbol on the standard he unfurled. It was the trident with which he goaded his people to action.

The new leader of the Untouchables talked to them in a very caustic manner. He remonstrated with them in a tone, in a vein that was at once teasing, carping and goading. He cried out: " My heart breaks to see the pitiable sight of your faces and to hear your sad voices. You have been groaning from time immemorial and yet you are not ashamed to hug your helplessness as an inevitability. Why did you not perish in the prenatal stage instead? Why do you worsen and sadden the picture of the sorrows, poverty, slavery and burdens of the world with your deplorable, despicable and detestable miserable life? You had better die and relieve this world if you cannot rise to a new life and if you cannot rejuvenate yourselves. As a matter of fact it is your birth-right to get food, shelter and clothing in this land in equal proportion with every individual high or low. If you believe in living a respectable life, you believe in self-help which is the best help!" The spate of his burning speeches like these began to have a telling effect upon their minds and to rouse them against their slavery.

Ambedkar did not join the movement for the political independence of the country. This he did with full knowledge. Those who were deprived of their political rights by the foreign rule were busy wresting them from foreign rulers, because the exit of British rule from India meant the automatic rise of their supremacy in India. The new leader of the Untouchables had no faith in their wordy cry for democracy and independence- His study of Indian history had taught him that benevolent kings and magnificent kingdoms had flourished in the land, but his people were always treated like lepers. The Untouchables, who were segregated, had no civic, religious and political rights. It was now Ambedkar's aim to create those rights, to prepare his people's heads, hearts and hands to secure Man's rights, and to make them real men, real countrymen out of sixty million virtual slaves. He knew that he would have to fight with the caste Hindus and to deal with the British Government in respect of political rights. He, however, realised that hatred of British rule would be inviting double enmity on his people. So he thought it prudent to co-operate with British rule so far as its co-operation would enable him to secure those rights.

It was indeed the noblest mission of his life that aimed at adding to the nation's strength, health, wealth, honour and culture by relieving these dumb millions who crawled in the dust with hunger and thirst in their eyes and perished in hovels and dunghills. Was this not a noble aim to rejuvenate the gaping Hinduism, to lighten its future, to save it from eclipse, to restore its honour, and to wipe off the stain that had spoiled the pages of its history for the last twenty-five hundred years ? Ambedkar gave a clarion call to the Untouchables, and at the same time sounded a warning to the indifferent, callous, caste-ridden Hindus. Gandhi's appeal was directed to the hearts of the caste Hindus; Savarkar's appeal moved their intellect and pricked their conscience! But Ambedkar's appeal to the Untouchables, like that of the Shakespearean characters, moved from heart outwards while that of other reformers went from skin inwards, never touching the hearts of the Depressed Classes. This was the difference between Ambedkar's attitude and that of the other social reformers.

IV

With the birth of the Bahishkrit Hitakarini Sabha dawned the age of self respect. The Sabha began to find its feet. It started, on January 4, 1925, a hostel at Sholapur for High School students belonging to the Depressed Classes. The Sabha bore the expenses incurred by the students on clothes, stationery and boarding. The Sholapur Municipality sanctioned a grant of rupees forty towards the maintenance of the hostel. Jivappa Subha Aydale a councillor from an untoucnable caste, looked after the management of the hostel.

The Sabha started also an institution for the Depressed Class students with a view to inculcating a liking for knowledge and learning and a love for social service into the minds of the students. Under the direction of the Sabha the students conducted a monthly magazine named Sarasvati Vilas. There were, in addition, a free reading room in Bombay and a Mahar Hockey Club, started in the hope of persuading the Untouchables to set their faces against gambling, drinking and other vices, and unhealthy ways of recreations.

The Depressed Classes were now being attracted to Ambedkar's personality. The first public meeting, he once recalled, held some days after his arrival from London as a bar-at-law, was not attended by any member of the Depressed Classes excepting the organizers themselves. Some persons were sitting on the doorsteps of the houses surrounding the meeting place; a few smoking and others chatting in the corners. Unsupported by the Press and unaided by any purse, he moved through the hamlets, villages and towns to stir up his people, stinging them into protests and driving them to revolt. He attended and guided the first Provincial Depressed Classes Conference held at Nipani in the Bombay Presidency. He presided over the First Conference of Untouchables at Malwan in Ratnagiri District in April 1925. From Malwan he went to Goa at the pressing request of an admirer. Shivtarkar was with him. They visited some places in Goa and returned to Bombay.

The Royal Commission on Indian Currency and Finance examined Dr. Ambedkar on December 15, 1925, in the light of the statement submitted by him to the Commission. He emphatically stated that the Gold Exchange Standard could not be continued with any advantages to India, for it had not the native stability of the Gold Standard.

But the most outstanding event of the year concerning the struggle of the Depressed Classes was the satyagraha or the passive resistance sponsored by Ramaswami Naicker, a non-Brahmin leader, at Vaikam in the Travancore State for vindicating the rights of the Untouchables to use a certain road to which they were forbidden entry. Its moral pressure and the spirit of righteous assertion had a tremendous effect, and the orthodox Hindus, for a while, regained their civic sense and sanity, and the road was thrown open to the Untouchables.

Another incident took place at this time. It shook both sensible touchables and self-respecting Untouchables. In March 1926 an Untouchable by name Murgesan entered a Hindu temple in Madras despite the customary ban on the Untouchables. He was discovered, arrested and convicted on a charge of defiling the Hindu temple.

Ambedkar was watching these developments very carefully. He referred to the Vaikam struggle, a few months later, very touchingly in one of his editorials, on the eye of the Mahad satyagraha. These were notable events. Coming events cast their shadows before!

Ambedkar's message of self-elevation was gathering force in its appeals. In April of the same year he visited Jejuri. There was a meeting at which he suggested that the Untouchables should seek some land for colonisation. Upon this one of the speakers replied that if they failed to abolish Untouchability they would act up to the wishes of their leader. The idea of colonisation was indeed astounding. But it shows also to what extent the leader himself was distressed and disgusted with the environment in the country.

Ambedkar was now gaining a foothold as a lawyer. During this year Ambedkar was engaged in a very important lawsuit. Some Brahmins from Poona had filed a suit against three non-Brahmin leaders K.B. Bagde, Keshavrao Jedhe and Dinkarrao Javalkar. They were charged with libelling the Brahmin community as they had published a pamphlet declaring that the

Brahmins had ruined India. On the prosecution side was L.B.
Bhopatkar, a great lawyer from Poona. The case came up before
the Sessions Judge for hearing. Ambedkar argued his case very
ably, put up a very eloquent defence and won the case in October
1920. The victory was resounding, both socially and individually,
for the clients and the Doctor. As a barrister he was now rising
gradually. He was slowly emerging from the back benches with
much credit in the High Court in spite of indifferent atmosphere.

The spasms of social revolution were stirring the society. In
spite of the Bole resolution a good number of Local Boards and
Municipalities did not appear as yet to grant the Depressed Classes
their civic rights. If at all they had passed some resolutions favouring
them with the use of public wells, tanks, schools, hospitals and
dharmashalas, it meant nothing more than mere gestures. There
was no genuine desire on their part to meet the needs of the
Depressed Classes. As the previous resolution had thus remained
a dead letter, Bole moved another resolution in the Bombay
Legislative Council on August 5, 1926, recommending to
Government not to give any grant to those Municipalities and Local
Boards which refused to give effect to the resolution on the subject
passed by the Council three years earlier.

While the resolution was on the *lapis*, most of the Hindu
Members agreed to the principle. One Member asked the House
not to put the resolution into action as he feared that it would
have to face a storm of opposition outside. But there came forward
Noor Mohomed of Hyderabad District (Sind) who stingingly
taunted the non-Brahmin Members of the House that they tried
to get all their rights from the Brahmin community but refused
to do bare justice to their lower classes, and he grew prophetic
in an insinuating tone: "I think the day will not be distant when
the people, who are placed by the tyranny of the higher classes
into the lower grade of Society, even at the present time, will
find themselves driven to the other religious folds. There will be
then no reason at all for Hindu society to complain that
Mohammedan or Christian missionaries are inducing members
of the Depressed Classes to change the religion of their birth."

This was the picture of Hindu society depicted by a Muslim.
It was real yet unpleasant, piercing yet perilous. The picture in
the Provincial Legislative Council and the scenes in other parts
of the country show how the currents of rejuvenation of Hindu

society were at grips with the orthodox and reactionary forces. Ambedkar had to make his way by overcoming these forces of reaction. It was a task which required a man of superb courage, invincible faith and supernatural energy to fulfil it!

V

There is always a fall in the barometer before a storm breaks out. Ambedkar was passing his days in the same Improvement Trust Chawl. These B.I.T. Chawls are big three-storeyed buildings each containing about eighty one-room tenements. They possess no modern conveniences, each floor having a pair of lavatories and a pair of taps for bathing, washing and cleaning cooking utencils. Most of the tenants were millhands belonging to the Depressed Classes.

Ambedkar's office was in a small room in a nearby building owned by the Social Service League, Bombay. Men of authority and eminence came to meet him at his residence. When they came to see him without appointments, they often found the leader of the Untouchables without his full dress. In that case the interviews took place at his office in the veranda on the armless benches. Everything was simple and bare in the room. One day a meeting called by a Municipal Officer to inaugurate the scheme for compulsory primary education was going on in the chawl in front of Ambedkar's office. Just then the Muslim leader, Maulana Shaukat Ali, came to meet him. He asked the Muslim leader with a smile to accommodate his huge body into the crowd till the meeting was over. And most willingly the Muslim leader did so.

While performing these multifarious duties as a public man and a lawyer, Ambedkar had some chances to engage himself in the academic field or to be a nominated Member of the Legislative Council or a Member of the Bombay Municipal Corporation. About this time the post of the Principal of Sydenham College, Bombay, fell vacant. Although probably there was no candidate in the Province better qualified than Ambedkar, who had once acted as a professor in the same college, even a man of so progressive views as Dr. R.P. Paranjpye, the then Member for Education, could not find it possible to appoint Ambedkar to the

post. Keluskar saw Paranjpye at Mahabaleshwar in this
connection, but he prevaricated as he could not find his way to
make the appointment. Paranjpye then offered him a
professorship in Elphinstone College, Bombay; but the Doctor
refused to accept it. He immediately wrote back, to Keluskar
saying that he was firm in his resolve to dedicate himself to a
life of service to his people and did not want to take up any job in
future that would hinder his social work.[3] He had, however,
accepted a part-time post of a lecturer since June 1925 in the
Batliboi's Accountancy Training Institute where he taught
Mercantile Law. He served this Institute till the end of March
1928.

It was during this period that Ambedkar's wife bore him a
son. He was named Rajratna whom he loved dearly. Before the birth
of this son, Ramabai had given birth to a daughter, but she passed
away in her infancy. Her name was Indu. Ramabai's health had
now begun to deteriorate. She was, therefore, sent away with her
two sons Yeshwant and Rajratna for a change of air.

But unfortunately Ambedkar lost his dearest son Rajratna
somewhere in July 1926. He was so much plunged in grief that
he would not part with the dead body; and for days together he
would not enter the room wherein his son had breathed his last.
His friend Dattoba Powar condoled with him upon the loss of his
son. Expressing his terrible grief to Dattoba Powar he said in
his reply dated the 16th August 1926, "There is no use pretending
that I and my wife have recovered from the shock of our son's
death and I do not think that we ever shall. We have in all buried
four precious children, three sons and a daughter, all sprightly,
auspicious and handsome children. The thought of this is
sufficiently crushing, let alone the future which would have been
theirs if they had lived. We are living no doubt in the sense that
days are passing over us as does the cloud. With the loss of our
kids the salt of our life is gone and as the Bible says: 'Ye are the
salt of the earth; if it leaveth the earth wherewith shall it be
salted?' I feel the truth of this every moment in my almost vacant
and empty life. My last boy was a wonderful boy the like of whom
I have seldom seen. With his passing away life to me is a garden

---

3.   The *Janata* Special Number, April 1933.

full of weeds. But enough of this. I am too overcome to write any more. With best regards of a broken man. Yours in grief."

Times were not so favourable yet. At times despondency overcame Ambedkar's stubborn mind. A sense of helplessness descended on his heart. Hours rolled by in gnawing thoughts and deep meditation, his mind being in quest of new light. With loin-cloth on he often sat motionless for hours together in a chair in his study, looking to the blue bowl of the sky outside and slept on a bed of a couple of bare benches.

He had acquired strength of mind, knowledge of almost all sciences and scriptures. Like a yogin he was now spending his days in penance and austerities, immersed in silent contemplation. Think of the pangs of an unrecognised Napoleon. But the dawn of action was singing at his door. Men who move the world always surmount disheartening difficulties with their power of perseverance. So did Ambedkar.

Men of Depressed Classes, needy and harassed, came from far and near in search of the poor men's barrister. Deeply grieved at their sad plight, he heard their grievances with an undisturbed mind, gave them legal advice free, and fought out their cases with great sincerity and industry, with nominal or no charges. He showed utmost geniality in those days towards his people. He treated them with care and cordiality. The poor people were struck with a sense of overwhelming gratitude by his simplicity and sincerity.

While the family was away, one day two men from a district place came to Bombay on some private business. They wanted to consult the Doctor and at the same time were in need of lodging. Naturally they sojourned at his residence. The Doctor was alone in the house. One of the guests recalls gratefully how the leader took bread and tea along with them before he left for the Court. And in the evening, on their return to the leader's residence, they found to their surprise their leader waiting for their company at the dinner which he had himself prepared. Their eyes beamed with gratitude and astonishment.

This man of great learning was also an expert at cooking. The taciturn man whose presence filled the visitor with awe, whose mannerism was inscrutable, whose personality was domineering, was not expected ordinarily to do such a turn to the lowest of the low. But what of leadership, empires were built upon the warmth of the hearts of great men. The most important attribute of a great leader, next to spotless sincerity, is the possession of an ever-flowing heart towards his men who are ready to do or die at his command. Those who preserve these qualities preserve their leadership; those who discard or shed it are dislodged in course of time.

□□□

CHAPTER 5

UP AGAINST SLAVERY

THE new year opened with a meeting at the Koregaon War Memorial held by the Depressed Classes. This year prominent leaders of the Depressed Classes attended the ceremony. Ambedkar addressed the meeting at the Memorial and told the audience that hundreds of fighters from their community had fought on the side of the Britishers who ungratefully later dubbed them a non-military community. He, however, said that their fighting on the side of the Britishers was not a matter of pride. Since the caste Hindus treated them as Untouchables and a despicable lot, they had no means of livelihood, and in the last resort they joined the British forces. In the end, he asked his people to agitate against this policy and compel Government to remove the ban on their military career.

About this time the Governor of Bombay nominated Ambedkar to the Bombay Legislative Council. The Bombay Depressed Class teachers called a meeting on February 2, 1927, and decided to celebrate this event by presenting a purse to their leader. Accordingly, two months later, on April 19, a meeting was held in Damodar Hall at Parel, Bombay, under the presidentship of S.B. Pendurkar, a Municipal educational supervisor, who took deep interest in the spread of education among the lower classes. On the occasion of presenting the purse to the leader, Pendurkar told the audience that he was confident that Ambedkar would discharge his heavy responsibilities efficiently, and he appealed to the Depressed Classes to make his mission a success by sharing the responsibility on their own part. Ambedkar thanked the Depressed Class teachers for their grateful appreciation of his work and donated the purse to the Bahishkrit Hitakarini Sabha.

The sun of self-respect had now arisen in the sky, and the clouds of oppression had begun to flit away. The Depressed Classes began to look up. And we now come to a momentous event in the life of Ambedkar. That event was a march on Mahad. This

had its origin in the important resolution of the Bombay
Legislative Council moved by Bole and adopted by the Bombay
Government. In pursuance of the Bole resolution passed in 1923
and reaffirmed with a slight change in 1926, the Mahad
Municipality had thrown open the Chowdar Tank to the
Untouchables. However, the resolution of the Municipality
remained a mere gesture in that the Untouchables had not
exercised their right owing to the hostility of the caste Hindus.

It was, therefore, decided by the Kolaba District Depressed
Classes to hold a Conference at Mahad on March 19 and 20, 1927.
The leaders of the Conference had notified Ambedkar the date
of the Conference in the first week of the previous month.
Arrangements for the Conference were made with care by Suren-
dranath Tipnis, Subhedar Savadkar and Anantrao Chitre. For
the past two months workers and leaders had trodden hills and
dales in the vicinity and had roused the Depressed Classes to
the importance of the Conference. As a result boys of fifteen to
old men of seventy from far and near plodded distances of over
hundred miles with bundles containing pieces of bread hanging
from their shoulders and reached Mahad. About ten thousand
delegates, workers and leaders of the Depressed Classes from
almost all the districts of Maharashtra and Gujarat attended
the Conference.

Every care had been taken, every convenience was provided,
and every means was adopted to make the Conference a success.
Water worth rupees forty was purchased from the caste Hindus
to satisfy the needs of the Conference, for water was not available
to the Untouchables at the place of the Conference. The
Conference commenced at noon in a pandal named after the local
deity Veereshwar.

Ambedkar rose to deliver his presidential address to the
half-clad, embarrassed, earnest men and women and began it in
his simple, short and forceful sentences. With a strange agitation
in his voice he described the conditions of Dapoli where he had
received the first rudiments of education and said that one was
attracted to the place where one passed one's childhood and the
beautiful scenery surrounding it deepened one's love for such a
place. He recalled the days of his childhood and said: "There was
a time when we, who are condemned as Untouchables, were much

advanced, much ahead in education compared with communities other than the advanced classes. This part of the country was then pulsating with the action and authority of our people."

With great earnestness he then delivered a message to his people which echoed throughout the hills, dales and villages of Maharashtra. Declaring that the demilitarisation was one of the causes of their downfall, he said: "The military offered us unique opportunities of raising our standard of life and proving our merit and intellect, courage and brilliance as army officers. In those days Untouchables could also be headmasters of military schools and compulsory primary education in the military camps was very effective and wholesome." "It is nothing less than a betrayal and a treachery," he went on, "on the part of the British to have closed the doors of the army to the Untouchables who had helped them establish the Indian Empire while their home Government was at grips with the French during the Napoleonic War."

Then in an inspiring tone he said: "No lasting progress can be achieved unless we put ourselves through a three-fold process of purification. We must improve the general tone of our demeanour, re-tone our pronunciations and revitalise our thoughts. I, therefore, ask you now to take a vow from this moment to renounce eating carrion. It is high time that we rooted out from our mind the ideas of highness and lowness among ourselves. Make an unflinching resolve not to eat the thrown-out crumbs. We will attain self-elevation only if we learn self-help, regain our self-respect, and gain self-knowledge." He further urged his people to agitate against the Government ban on their entry into the Army, Navy and Police, and impressed upon them the importance of entering 'Government services and of education. Turning to the question of Mahars, he tweaked their self-respect by telling them that it was utterly disgraceful to sell their human rights for a few crumbs of bread, and appealed to them fervently to do away with the humiliating, enslaving traditions, to abandon their Vatans and seek forest lands for agricultural pursuits. In conclusion he said in a moving tone: "There will be no difference between parents and animals if they will not desire to see their children in a better position than their own."

The Conference passed resolutions on important subjects. By one resolution the Conference appealed to the caste Hindus to help the Untouchables secure their civic rights, to employ them in services, offer food to untouchable students, and bury their dead animals themselves. Lastly, it appealed to Government to prohibit the Untouchables by special laws from eating carrion, enforce prohibition, provide them with free and compulsory primary education, give aid to the Depressed Classes hostels and make the 'Bole Resolution' a living reality by enjoining upon the local bodies, if necessary, to proclaim section 144 of Indian Criminal Procedure Code at their places, for its enforcement.

II

On the first day, a few caste Hindu spokesmen, local as well as outsiders, made speeches justifying the rights of the Depressed Classes and promised them help. The Subjects Committee, which met that night, decided, after taking the sense of the leaders of the upper classes who attended the Conference, that the Conference should go in a body to the Chowdar Tank and help the Depressed Classes to establish their right to take water. Next morning the Conference called upon two caste Hindu spokesmen to support the resolution regarding the duties and responsibilities of the caste Hindus. Excluding the clause regarding inter-caste marriage, they both supported the resolution. In pursuance of the resolution of the Mahad Municipality which in 1924 had declared to have thrown open its Tank to the Depressed Classes, it was now decided to take water from the Tank and establish the right of the Untouchables. The delegates accordingly began to march peacefully in a body to the Chowdar Tank to assert their right of taking water from the Tank.

And now the momentous event, great in its magnitude and far-reaching in its consequences, was taking place. Anti-slavery, anti-caste, anti-priest, Ambedkar, who represented the awakened spirit of the Untouchable Hindus, was marching towards the Tank from which the Muslims and Christians took water along with the so-called touchable Hindus, but from which the Untouchable Hindus, who worshipped the Hindu gods, stuck to the same Hindu religion through ages past, were, although their throats parched with thirst, not allowed to take even a drop of water. There never was such a thrilling spectacle in the whole history of the suppressed people when the down-trodden who had groaned under the heels of injustice, through ages rose to assert their human, civic rights. A virile and aggressive champion of social revolution, Ambedkar was marching with an army of men to attack all the so-called venerable accepted customs. He was establishing new social levels and new status and was remaking and reshaping Hindustan, the Sick Man of the World! Those ten thousand people who followed their great leader in a file of fours represented the pent-up might of a "suppressed people surged up to surface with an intensity, a force unequalled in ages gone by.

Political marches are moving and colourful. But Ambedkar's march was more difficult and more risky. It was on a socio-religious system imposed ruthlessly and upheld religiously by a vast society upon its weaker and helpless constituent, a society based on fantastic, antiquated, unjust and inhuman laws that bolted out, throttled and bled millions of the Depressed Classes from time immemorial. The agitation in a slave country for political independence and political marches is, to a great extent, easier; for the mass of people sympathise overtly or covertly with the rising forces in the nation. The people may sprinkle the roads of their political liberators with rose water. But reverse is the fate of those who launch a ruthless attack to liberate society from its ills, superstitions, out-worn traditions and evil customs; for their action, their move and their drive are against the belief of the whole society of whom the majority are always conservative, unwilling to part with old customs and traditions that are dear to their hearts.

Ambedkar was now exorcizing the spirit of despair from the minds of the dumb millions who had been forced to live the lives of sub-human beings. Here was a liberator preaching them the grand universal law that liberty is never received as a gift; it has to be fought for. Self-elevation is not achieved by the blessing of others but only by one's own struggle and deed. Those inert, dormant masses lacked courage and needed a vision and a mission. Ambedkar was now inspiring them to do battle for their human rights. He was driving them to action by acting himself. And action is the governing characteristic of all makers of History. Ambedkar was displaying energy by his own action; rousing their

faith by showing faith. The cause he espoused was now moving
through the thick and thin of a battle.

Thus, led for the first time in their history by a great leader
of their own, the Untouchables were marching to vindicate their
rights. They all displayed discipline, energy and enthusiasm. The
march wended its way through the streets of Mahad and
terminated at the Chowdar Tank. Ambedkar himself was now
standing on the verge of the Tank, Enlightened among the
enlightened, the equal of any erudite man on earth, a Hindu of
noble aspirations, yet unable even to take water from a public
watercourse or to read in a public library in Hindustan, the land
of his birth and faith, was now defying the arrogance of the
tyrants, exposing the baseness of a people who boasted that their
religion treated even animals with forbearance, but who treated
their co-religionists worse than cats and dogs.

Ambedkar took water from the Tank and drank it. The vast
multitude of men followed suit and vindicated their right. The
processionists then returned peacefully to the pandal. Ruskin
says that doing is a great thing. Carlyle says that the end of
man is action. One action of such a magnitude at the proper time
does more good than a series of vocal, vociferous and empty
resolutions passed year in and year out!

Two hours after this event, some evil-minded caste Hindus
raised a false rumour that the Untouchables were also planning
to enter the temple of Veereshwar. At this a large crowd of riffraff
armed with bamboo sticks collected at street corners. All orthodox
Mahad was up in arms and the whole town at once became a
surging mass of rowdies. They said that their religion was in
danger, and strangely enough they clamoured that their God,
too, was in danger of being polluted! Their hearts fluttered, their
hands shivered, and their faces were ablaze with anger at this
humiliating challenge. Those chosen men of God did not feel
lowered in the scale of life when the Muslims, who condemned
them as Kaffirs and some of whom broke their idols and
performed cow slaughter, shared with them the waters of the
Tank. Their bravadoes died off in their throats when the
Christians, who believed that religious truth outside the Biblical
revelation was a work of the devil, too, took water along with
them from the same Tank. But their gods were polluted, their
houses came under the shadow of heavenly calamity and they

seemed to lose face in the estimation of the world when these untouchable Hindus, their own brethren who were the worshippers of their own Gods, Rama and Krishna, took water from that Tank!

But this rationalist view was anathema to the orthodox Hindus at Mahad. Enraged at this misconstrued outrage on their religion and at the thought of defilement of the temple of Veereshwar, the caste Hindus dashed into the pandal of the Depressed Classes Conference. Many of the delegates were at that time scattered in small groups in the city. Some were busy packing, and a few were taking their meals before dispersing for their villages. The majority of the delegates had by now left the town. The rowdies pounced upon the delegates in the pandal, knocked down their food in the dust, pounded the utensils, and belaboured some before they knew what had happened. There was utter confusion in the pandal. Up till now the orthodox had lost their conscience. They now showed signs of losing their senses !

Untouchable children, women and delegates, who were strolling in the streets of Mahad, were frightened at the sudden sweep of this event. Stray individuals amongst them were beaten. They had to run into Muslim houses for shelter. The local Mamlatdar and the Police Inspector, who failed to check the rowdies, saw Ambedkar in this matter at four o'clock in the evening at the Travellers' Bungalow where Ambedkar and his party were staying during the days of the Conference. "You control others, I will control my people," said Ambedkar to the officers, and he hurried to the scene with two or three of his lieutenants. In the street a batch of rowdies mobbed him, but he calmly tried to soothe them by telling that there was no desire nor any plan on their part to enter the temple. He went ahead, saw things for himself and returned to the Bungalow. Up to this moment about twenty persons from the Untouchables were seriously wounded. A doctor was sent for. He came. He jeered at them for their "ill-timed" adventure and dressed their wounds!

The rowdies then began patrolling the main streets and assaulting members of the Depressed Classes who were in stray batches on the way to their villages. But the most reprehensible part of their conduct was that they sent messages to their henchmen to punish the delegates of the Conference in their respective villages. In obedience to this mandate assaults were committed on a number of Mahar men and women either before or after they had reached their villages.

Meanwhile, this news of the brutal attack on the delegates spread like wild fire. When Ambedkar returned to the Bungalow, he saw about a hundred men impatiently awaiting his orders, their eyes literally blazing with fire and their hands itching for retaliation and revenge. Their leader, however, appealed for peace and discipline. There was hushed silence for a while. A word of provocation from Ambedkar would have turned Mahad into a pool of blood and destruction. The number of delegates still lingering in the town, in the pandal and in the Bungalow together could have easily outnumbered the hooligans, and battered down their skulls. Hundreds among the Untouchables were men who had seen, fought, and moved actively in the theatres and battles of the First World War,

But discipline was wonderfully maintained at the behest of their leader. They set their faces against the aggressors. Their struggle was non-violent and constitutional. They did not dream of breaking the law. Thus a more serious riot was averted. At nightfall all the delegates left for their respective villages. Ambedkar with his lieutenant, Anantrao Chitre, left the Bungalow as it was booked by a Government officer from that evening, and took up his residence in the police station rooms. He completed his inquiry into the riot and returned to Bombay on 23rd March.

Policemen appeared on the scene after the storm was over. They arrested some of the orthodox rowdies as trespassers. Out of the nine orthodox Hindu heroes, five, who were found to be most valorous, were, afterwards on June 6, 1927, sentenced by the District Magistrate to four months' rigorous imprisonment. Ambedkar was not far from truth when he remarked that had not the chief officers in the District been non-Hindus, justice would not have been administered impartially to the Untouchables. Under Peshwa rule, he said, he would have been trampled to death by an elephant. And it was the Peshwa rule under which Untouchables were not allowed to enter the city of Poona during certain hours by day-time, and when they were admitted at other times they had to walk in the city with earthen pots hanging from their necks to spit into.[1]

III

Thus ended the first big, open Conference of the Depressed Classes in Maharashtra and their first public attempt to assert their civic rights. This Conference was a great and momentous event, the opening of an epoch in the history of Hindustan. It was an event which changed both Ambedkar's personal life and the current of social and national reorganization. It was as significant in the history of India as were the proclamation of the partition of Bengal, Tilak's role at the Surat Congress, the first bonfire of foreign doth made by Savarkar, Khudiram Bose's bomb at Muzaffarpur, Gandhi's Dandi March of 1930 and Subhash Bose's war of liberation of 1943.

It is very interesting to note from the viewpoint of history that both the Indian political and the socio-religious revolution had their origin in Maharashtra.

Under the leadership of their saviour, the down-trodden, the dehumanised and dumb millions opened a new chapter in the annals of India. They not only voiced their age-long grievances but also took on themselves energetically to mitigate them. They now summoned up courage and showed the right spirit in standing boldly and shaking off the dust from their feet; faces and future.

The struggle inaugurated by their educated leaders gripped their minds and enkindled the flame of self-respect and self-elevation. They now smarted under the insults and humiliations inflicted upon them at Mahad. They applied their minds to self-improvement and self-culture as never before. As a result of this Conference, the Untouchables gave up eating carrion, skinning carcasses, and stopped begging for crumbs.

They realised the importance of organization and active struggle. Although some Hindus admitted the justice of their cause and their right to take water from public watercourses, they now well knew that it was not illegal to take water from public watercourses and that Government punished those who

1. Ghurye, Dr. G. S. *Caste and Class in India*, p. 11.

opposed their enjoying civic rights. Thus the struggle at
Mahad pushed the destiny to the Depressed Classes ahead
by fifty years.

When Ambedkar returned to Bombay, he found the members
of his family in a distressed state of mind. His elder brother, in a
semi-drunken mood but with a sincere heart, remonstrated with
Ambedkar. He asked the younger brother to mind his own
profession and not to create such dangerous encounters by his
social activities. He reviled all the caste Hindu colleagues of his
brother. Ambedkar muttered a few words in his brother's
presence ; but when he was gone he said that he knew what
things were better for him and beneficial to the society! But the
worst sufferer was Ambedkar's wife. She had not taken a wink
of sleep for two days and was writhing in her bed. When she saw
her husband back in Bombay she heaved a sigh of relief and said
her grateful prayers to God!

The offended orthodox Hindus now sharpened the daws of
the social boycott. Confirmed zealots and purblind bigots from
tha orthodox and reactionary camp forbade the Untouchables to
take their rounds in the villages and dislodged them from their
lands. They refused to sell them corn and picked quarrels with
them under this or that pretext, and prosecuted and jailed quite
a number of them.

For months the wave of protest against the unjust, shameful
and inhuman conduct of the Mahad caste Hindus swept Hindustan.
The topic became an important news-item all over India.

A bitter controversy raged. It evoked fierce hatred in the
minds of the orthodox and reactionaries. In Maharashtra
newspapers arrayed themselves in two camps. Some
denounced this bold step on the part of the Depressed Classes,
some took shelter under the law, a few shed crocodile tears
saying what took place in the city at the end of the Conference
was not good and others congratulated the Untouchable
Hindus on their courageous act in vindicating their right.
Public meetings urged the Government of India to look into
the matter, condemned the shameful act on the part of the
orthodox Hindus of Mahad, congratulated the Depressed
Classes and their leader Ambedkar, and appealed to the
Bombay Government to bring the 'Bole Resolution' into effect
and punish the wrong-doers, trespassers and law-breakers.

Such meetings were held in Bombay, in villages, in all taluka towns and cities in the Province. At one such meeting held in Poona to denounce the shameful act, L.B. Bhopatkar said that a day would dawn in his lifetime when untouchability would disappear from the fate of the land and be a matter of history.

The one leader who fearlessly and whole-heartedly supported, Ambedkar's struggle was Savarkar. Reiterating his views, he said that untouchability must be condemned and abolished not only as the need of the hour but also as the command of true religion; not only as a policy or as an act of expediency but also a matter of justice; not only as a matter of obligation but also as a service to humanity. He said that the notion of purifying oneself with animal urine was more ridiculous and despicable than the notion of defilement at the human touch. He, therefore, upheld the satyagraha of the Untouchables at Mahad and declared that the pious and bounden duty of the Hindu world at large was to restore full human rights to their co-religionists.

And what happened to the Chowdar Tank that was declared to have been desecrated by the touch of untouchable Hindus? The orthodox and reactionary Hindus called a meeting at the temple of Veereshwar to consider the question of the purification of the tank. They had a remedy for purifying any damned and polluted earthly thing. To them a mixture of cow-dung, cow-urine, curd and water was the potent remedy for all manner of pollution. Accordingly water in one hundred and eight earthern pots was taken out from the tank. These pots full of curd, cow-dung, milk and cow-urine were dipped in the tank in the midst of air-rending *Mantras* uttered by Brahmin priests, the elect. It was then declared that water was purified for the use of the caste Hindus. Of course Muhammadans and Christians had nothing to do with the act or process of purification. For, in their eyes human touch did not pollute water. They used the water of the tank as before without any interruption.

But it will be stating an extreme view if it is said that every touchable Hindu at Mahad was opposed to the claims of the, untouchable Hindus. Few caste Hindu leaders like Bapurao Joshi stood the wrath of the orthodox for years for having shown active sympathy with the Depressed Classes, and some caste Hindus helplessly simmered at the perverse attitude of the orthodox reactionaries. Dissenting views, no doubt, were expressed but these were of no consequence. The orthodox Hindu is a strange fossil of humanity. To him blind irrational tradition is greater than truth. Time and tide have no effect upon his mind!

IV

Ambedkar had to face now a flood of criticism. So he felt the need for a mouthpiece as never before. To represent the correct view and the ideal and to voice the grievances of his party, a newspaper is an inevitable necessity for a real leader in these days. A leader without a paper is like a bird without wings. So Ambedkar started his fortnightly Marathi paper, *Bahishkrit Bharat* on April 3, 1927, in Bombay. Explaining the aim of the journal, he observed that he had taken to the profession of a lawyer because he felt that one's attempt at conducting a newspaper for the welfare of the people, should always be backed up by an independent profession for one's personal livelihood. Long before he had realised that financial independence facilitated the work of a public worker. It was true that the financial condition of newspaper concerns in India was not then good and is not still so.

Justifying the need for a mouthpiece for the Depressed Classes, Ambedkar said that in the ensuing political reforms, which he expected to be effected by 1930, if the Untouchables failed to secure representation in proportion to their population, they would be doomed. He further warned them that in fact their condition would be worse than it already was under the Montagu-Chelmsford Reforms. To guard against this the Depressed Classes must be kept well informed about the happenings in the land and their grievances, views and reactions must be placed before Government and the people.

Ambedkar now began to explain his views, define his aims and reply to the critics of his movement through the new journal. He said that the temples and watercourses should be open to the Untouchables because the Untouchables were Hindus. He wrote editorial after editorial in his short, crisp and fearless style, asking Government to bring into force the 'Bole resolution' and not to trust the good sense of the local bodies for its implementation as they were dominated by persons who were narrow-minded, old-fashioned, orthodox, reactionaries and antagonistic to the interests of the Depressed Classes. He also appealed through his paper to the Government to punish the wrong-doers and trespassers who opposed the execution of the above-cited resolution.

To those critics who contended that the Untouchables were denied those rights because they ate carcasses and beef, he asked why some of the untouchable communities who never touched meat were, thrown into the untouchable category and why the beef-eating Muslims and Christians were regarded as touchables by them. Some said that the Tank was not a public property. Ambedkar hit back by saying that everything that was meant for the use of the public and controlled or conducted by Government or semi-Government institutions was public property whether it was used by some sections of the people or not. There were some who trampled the rights of the Untouchables under foot and yet asked the British Government in the name of democracy to conduct Government in accordance with public opinion. Ambedkar asked this set of people whether those words—justice and democracy—lay in their mouths!

There were some Hindus who shrewdly cloaked their cowardice and failed to do justice to the Depressed Classes in these matters by saying that the people were not prepared for such a radical change in the society. Ambedkar flung their arguments back by asking them why they clamoured for the independence of the country when the people as a whole were neither prepared for it nor deserved it. One in a hundred, he said, understood the significance of national independence and even then Tilak rose for their deliverance. They criticised Ambedkar because he drove the Untouchables to adopt a militant policy. But what was he to do when the rights and self-respect of a whole people were daily crushed under the fierce power of religion? If Tilak had been born amongst the Untouchables, Ambedkar proceeded, he would not have raised the slogan "Swaraj is my birthright", but he would have raised the slogan; "Annihilation of Untouchability is my birthright."[2] Ambedkar's

---

2. The *Bahishkrit Bharat*, Editorial, 29 July 1927.

reading of Tilak is unchallengeable. A man of Tilak's cast, volcanic force, iron will and boundless sell-respect would have undoubtedly applied the dynamo of his resourceful brains to shell the strongholds of orthodoxy had he been born an Untouchable. He would have nurtured and inspired all social revolutionary youths as he nursed and inspired the young political revolutionaries, to shell the barriers of untouchability.

There were some who raised violent protests against the insulting treatment meted out to the Indians in South Africa and to the Indian students in Britain, and at the same time denied human rights to their countrymen and co-religionists in India. Ambedkar exposed their inconsistent attitude, selfishness, shamelessness and held them to ridicule!

Lastly, Ambedkar made a powerful appeal to all leaders and the public at large, who favoured abolition of untouchability, to transform their sympathies into practicality and bring the reform into reality in their day-to-day life. It was sheer cruelty, he declared, to say that because the injustice had been extended across centuries, it should be borne for some time more. Only a cave-man, he added, could defend his sins in that way. It was his earnest appeal, therefore, to thoughtful men to act up to their views and vows.

Ambedkar, the social revolutionary, knew well that the problem of untouchability did not depend for its solution so much on the spread of education or on the rational appeal as on the abolition of the privileges, selfishness and the peculiar frame of mind of the high caste Hindus. He, therefore, urged the Depressed Classes to act in as forcible a way as to let the caste Hindus know that to observe untouchability was a risk as dangerous as to bear live coals on their tongues. These caste Hindus, he said, would not understand paper resolutions, or appeals made at conferences and would not realise the magnitude of their sins until they felt it unsafe to treat them as Untouchables. So he asked them to keep before their mind the struggle between the Hindus and the Muslims and said that it was a struggle for cultural predominance. The balance of power was, he asserted, in their hands and therefore he asked them to utilise their forces advantageously for the advancement of their own social and political rights.

"Lost rights are never regained," Ambedkar observed, "by begging, and by appeals to the conscience of the usurpers, but by relentless struggle." "Goats are used for sacrificial offerings and not lions," he concluded.

V

The proceedings of the new Legislative Council commenced on February 18, 1927. Ambedkar and Dr. Solanki, the nominated Members for the Depressed Classes, were present. Ambedkar made his maiden speech in the Bombay Council on the Budget on February 24, 1927. At the outset he regretted that there was no scope for effective criticism as out of rupees 15½ crores, the total revenue of the Province, about rupees 9½ crores was being levied by the Executive without the consent of the Council. He further observed that the essential requirement of the revenue system was that it should be reliable. He opined that the Budget was inequitable and indefensible from the standpoint of the tax-payer.

Ambedkar then explained how the difference in the method of levying the land revenue and the income-tax worsened the lot of the poor farmer who was required to pay the tax at the same rate whether he was an owner of one acre of land or a Jahagirdar or an Inamdar, whether there was a failure of crops or an abundance of crops. He said that the land revenue was a proportionate and not a progressive tax as it should have been. As regards the income-tax, he said that under the system no person was called upon to pay it if he had not earned any income during the year. "Again under the income-tax," proceeded he, "holders of income below a certain minimum are exempted from levy. But under the land revenue the tax is remorselessly collected from every one, be he rich or poor."

Turning to the problem of prohibition, he observed, "Mr. President, Government has accepted the policy of prohibition and has adopted certain measures for carrying out the policy to fruition. But it has not done so. The first of such measures is rationing." In the end he hoped that Government was really earnest in its desire for providing compulsory education and medical relief, for freeing people from the habit of drink and for providing all the amenities of life. It was the first speech of Ambedkar but so impressive, so illuminating and so stimulating! It manifested a sympathetic heart, a fearless critic, a deep study befitting a spokesman of the dumb and downtrodden.

On March 10 Ambedkar again made a speech in the Council
on the prohibition policy of Government and said that the
increase in the manufacture of illicit liquor in the country was
entirely due to the high tariff on country liquor. It is a matter of
opinion why Ambedkar, who was so intent upon the enforcement
of prohibition, was less enthusiastic about this issue in his
election manifesto of 1952. Whether the growing volume of illicit
liquor or the impracticability which led to the worsening of the
financial position of the State and an increase in the burden of
taxation on the people had thrown him on the opposite side,
although he supported prohibition in principle, is a debatable
point. The main reason why he looked askance at it can be seen
from the latter part of his foregoing speech in the Council. He
said: "I feel, Sir, the problem of prohibition whether you will be
able to carry it out to a successful end or not, entirely depends
upon the financial solution of the question, upon how we will
manage to make good the loss we are bound to incur as a result
of our new excise policy." How true, how practical and how abiding
these observations were!

During the debate on the Budget, Ambedkar spoke also on
the provisions for Education when he said that Government was
making very slow progress in the matter of education of children,
and added: "Education is something which ought to be brought
within the reach of every one. The policy of the Department
therefore ought to be to make higher education as cheap to the
lower classes as it can possibly be made." So he appealed to
Government to give favoured treatment to the backward classes.
He argued: "If all these communities are to be brought to the
level of equality, then the only remedy is to adopt the principle
of inequality and to give favoured treatment to those who are
below the level." People who lay emphasis on the principle of
equality in all things conveniently forget that numbers five and
ten if multiplied by two, a common factor, yield the product ten
and twenty respectively and not twenty in both the cases. That
is why Ambedkar held that equality meant raising the level of
the lower classes to the level of the higher classes.

As regards the agency which imparts education, he said, in
an editorial, a few days after this speech, that no real progress
could be made in education if education was entrusted to the
teachers coming from the Brahmin community whose minds

conceived an abhorrence for the lower classes and who showed callous disregard for the intellectual uplift of any other class, treated human beings worse than dogs and never treated them with equality or kindliness. He declared that teachers were the charioteers of the nation and there was no question more important from the standpoint of social reform than the selection of proper persons in this teaching profession. Those who drummed into the ears of the backward class students that they were born to do odd jobs like their forefathers, that they belonged to low categories, and that education was a thing meant for a particular class, should not be, observed Ambedkar, entrusted with this noble, national, human, enlightening work. What Ambedkar drove at was that Government would be able to achieve genuine progress by weeding out self-centred and nation-destroying agencies. Consolidation and progress of the nation, he added, would be stronger on such a broader base.

VI

Just then the tercentenary birthday celebrations of the great liberator of Hindustan, Shivaji the Great, were performed in 1927, all over Maharashtra. During the celebration Ambedkar was invited to preside over a meeting at Badlapur in Kolaba District. With his lieutenants Shivtarkar and Deorao Naik. Ambedkar went to Badlapur where he was cordially received by Palaye Shastri, his Brahmin host, who had extended this unique invitation to the leader of the Untouchables in consultation with the people in the neighbouring villages. Speaking at the meeting, Ambedkar ably and vigorously dwelt upon Shivaji's different facets of life such as his achievements, character and policy. Then he asked his audience numbering about five thousand to think over the causes that led to the downfall of the empire founded by Shivaji. He himself attributed the causes of its downfall to the invidious inequality in the social field and to the hatred for Peshwa rule.[3]

On May 8, 1927, Ambedkar was congratulated at Khara Abraham on his being nominated to the Bombay Legislative Council. Bhimbhai Desai, M.L.C., presided over the function.

---

3. The *Bahishkrit Bharat*, 20 May 1927.

The question of temple entry was now agitating the minds of the reformers. In the month of June 1927 it was announced in some of the Bombay newspaper that the new temple built at Thakurdwar in Bombay was open to all Hindus since its inception. This was confirmed by workers interested in this movement; so Ambedkar fixed up an appointment on phone with the secretary of the head of the temple, and went there with Shivtarkar. A mischievous man saw this and he incited the people in the locality to drive Ambedkar out of the temple. Ambedkar was mobbed and heckled. Had not Ambedkar dealt with the situation firmly and told the bigors and fanatics that since the call from the head of the temple had brought them there, they would not leave the place unless the man in charge asked them to quit it. But the mob would not listen.[4] The Secretary, who was terrorised into submission, cancelled the interview, the head of the temple went back on his word and afterwards even purified with ceremonies the temple 'defiled' by the feet of Ambedkar.

In the third week of July 1927, Ambedkar addressed a very important meeting at the Mangwada in Poona. V. M. Navale, editor of the *Deenbandhu*, presided. Some leaders like Subhedar Ghatge, Rajbhoj, K.M. Jadhav, Anandaswami from Berar. Aryasevak Ogale and others attended the meeting. An important feature of the meeting was, that Ambedkar in a fighting speech refuted all the charges levelled against him by a section of the Chamar Community who accused him of partiality. Detailing and dwelling upon his work in the hostels at Nasik and Jalgaon, which were open to all sections of the untouchable students, his efforts in installing P. Balu in the Bombay Corporation, the rearing up of a Mang boy at his own residence and his all-section dinner in conferences, he averred that his movement aimed at the uplift of the whole suppressed people. He asked the Chamars whether it was not proper on their part to send able representatives to the Legislative Council irrespective of castes to defend their interests. He added that it was the good fortune of the Mahar community that a man like him was born amongst them, and told the Chamars that he was willing to give his place to the worthiest leader from their community if one came forward to serve the cause.

---

4. The *Bahishkrit Bharat,* 1 July 1927.

And then turning to the other side of the question, he warned the Depressed Classes not to be stooges in the hands of interested groups who wanted to use them against the non-Brahmins with a view to counterbalancing their forces. He urged them not to believe those Hindu Sanghatanists who were wooing them because of the rising menace of the Muslim pressure. Citing his own example how a Brahmin hotel-keeper in Bombay refused to give him tea in a cup and offered it to him in a glass, he warned them that education alone would not solve their problem. Nothing could he achieved, he said, if they did not adopt an aggressive attitude and prove by their thought, words and deeds that they would not now tolerate insult and disabilities any further. With a fervent appeal he concluded his speech urging the Depressed Classes to wrest the right of drinking water at public water-courses, and force their entry into public temples. That was the immediate programme for the Depressed Classes, he announced.

In the last week of the month, a Bill intended to organise the University of Bombay into a better teaching University was introduced in the Council. One of the defects, it was said, from which the University suffered ever since its inception, was that it was primarily constituted as an organizing body. Criticising this, Ambedkar said: "I, therefore, submit, Sir, that the best method would not be to separate the colleges from the University as has been done now but to make a synthesis in which the University and the colleges would be partners on terms of equality and would be participating in promoting together the cultural progress of both undergraduate and postgraduate studies." He added that the recommendations of the Sadler Commission in this behalf would be far more effective than the recommendations of the Bombay University Committee.

With regard to the composition of the Senate, Ambedkar supported the view that the Backward and Depressed Classes should have representation on the Senate of Bombay University, and said it was surprising that those who throve on communalism, should oppose the demands. It was a dig at K.M. Munshi who, Ambedkar said, in his manifesto to the graduates of the University had asked the voters to support him on the plea of 'Gujarat was for Gujaratis'. Munshi flared up at this and shot back that the statement was absolutely incorrect. Ambedkar answered back that it was absolutely correct and added that politicians were men with very short memories. The next moment Ambedkar said that the Hindus and Muslims were communal in their attitude towards each other. This provoked sounds of 'sorry', cries of 'noes' and shouts of 'challenge'. Ambedkar retorted that it was all hypocrisy and he refused to believe in the 'noes'.

Besides showing keen interest in the major legislation affecting the whole Province, Ambedkar was very watchful about the welfare of the Depressed Classes. Even at the news of the faintest injustice done to them he took up cudgels in their behalf. He interpellated about the non-appointments of deserving members of the Depressed Classes to higher posts in Government services, asked Government whether there was any selection board for selecting candidates for clerical posts, inquired about the strength of the Depressed Classes in the public services, and asked Government about the judgment of a magistrate who according to him gave two different judgments on the same point.

He also requested Government to give for each village information regarding the total population, number of Mahars, the remuneration they got from Inam lands, Baluta and Government salary, and the total remuneration they got from all services. Government replied thut the labour involved in collecting this information would be enormous and so not feasible. On one occasion he had a passage-at-arms with the Home Member, J. E. B. Hotson. Ambedkar asked Government whether there was any rule prohibiting the enlistment of the Depressed Classes in the police constabulary force of the Presidency. The Home Member said that there was no such rule. Upon this Ambedkar asked him why the Commissioner of Police for the City of Bombay then refused to appoint Depressed Class members in the police constabulary if there was no restriction. Hotson was cornered. With a serious face he replied: "This opens a very large subject. I can only say that there are practical difficulties which are known to every Member of the House which stood in the more extensive enlistment of these classes in the police. There is no prohibition against it."

□□□

CHAPTER 6

DECLARATION OF INDEPENDENCE

THE news of the so-called purification of the Chowdar Tank lacerated the hearts of the Depressed Classes, and so deep was the wound on Ambedkar's heart that he grew indignant and decided to launch a satyagraha struggle for the vindication of his people's rights. Some feared that this 'impatient' remedy was worse than the disease. Ambedkar, in a mood of righteous indignation, replied that mere spread of education and exposition of the scriptures would not be able to root out that agelong disease. The disease, he said, was deep-rooted and merely dressing it with bandages of knowledge or ingenuous schemes would not cure it. Deadly diseases required drastic remedies.

The non-Brahmin leaders of Maharashtra, Javalkar and Jedhe declared their whole-hearted support for the proposed struggle on condition that all the Brahmins should be weeded out from it, that the struggle should be non-violent and that it should be staged on a mass scale after convening a conference at Mahad in this connection. Ambedkar replied that the view that all Brahmins were the enemies of the Untouchables was erroneous. What he hated was the men who were possessed with the spirit of Brahminism—tle idea of high-caste and low-caste—which implanted the idea of pollution from human beings and implanted social privileges and inequality. He said that a non-Brahmin filled with such ideas of highness and lowness, was as repellant to him as a Brahmin free from this spirit and sense of these privileges and unjust power, was welcome to him.

Accordingly, it was announced on June 26, 1927, in the *Bahishkrit Bharat* that those members of the Depressed Classes who wanted to wash out the stigma of pollution attached to their whole class by the Mahad Hindus by their act of purification of the Tank, and who wanted to denounce the act of assaults committed on their representatives for having taken water from the Chowdar Tank, should enlist themselves at the office of the Bahishkrit Hitakarini Sabha in Bombay. It was declared that the satyagraha struggle was to be launched under the auspices of the said institution.

The question now, observed Ambedkar, was whether religion was meant for men or men for religion. The Depressed Classes would die for that religion which took care of them, but they would not care for the religion which did not care for them. "The question whether we belong to Hindu religion or not," declared he, "is to be decided by us once for all." According to him, the Brahmins were the keynote in the social harmonium. If that note was not in proper tune, the whole society would be in disorder. To clean the unclean, to raise the fallen, and to elevate the Untouchables to a status of social equality was the real meaning of culture, he added.

Meantime, the Mahad Municipality revoked on August 4, 1927, its resolution of 1924 under which it had declared the Chowdar Tank open to the Depressed Classes. Ambedkar accepted the challenge and on September 11, at a public meeting in Damodar Hall, Bombay, a committee was formed to devise ways and means to make the struggle for re-establishing the right of the Depressed Classes to the Mahad Tank a success, and to fix the dates and details. Four days afterwards the committee met at Ambedkar's office and announced December 25 and 26, 1927, as the dates for offering the satyagraha.

Describing the nature of the struggle they were to launch, Ambedkar said that success in an undertaking depended upon the means as much upon the justness of the cause. If the end was good, there would not be much anxiety about its success because truth always succeeds in the end. Dwelling upon the various aspects of truth and the struggle for winning a just end, he observed that a satyagrahi must possess boundless self-confidence which was generated in its turn from the conviction that the end sought was good and just, and therefore the satyagrahi must know what was right and good. Any action that unified the people was good. Where there was unity there was a good cause. He ascribed the origin of this philosophy to the *Geeta*, the main theme of which was satyagraha. He cited examples from the *Geeta* because, he said, it was acceptable to both the Touchables and the Untouchables.[1] According to Ambedkar, fight, whether violent or non-violent, was just if the end sought was

---

1. *The Bahishkrit Bharat*, Editorial, 27 November 1927.

good. If the end sought was just, the insistence on its achievement and the fight for it must be equally just. If the end was unjust and unfair, then insistence on its achievement must be unjust. But the justness of an end did not change, he observed, with the means employed for its achievement; the justness of an end did not vary with the employment of different means as does a verb change with its subject.

In his view Arjun, the Bharatiya warrior, was justified in resorting to arms in defence of a just cause. It was not possible to observe at all times and on all occasions the grand principle. "Non-violence is the most proper law"; otherwise, he added, man could not stir even his eyelid for fear of killing the germs in the air, or eat fruits, or drink water, or breathe the air, or cut the grass or trees. "The man who comes to kill you, or to outrage the modesty of a woman, or sets fire to another's house, or commits theft and is killed while struggling to escape,"observed Ambedkar, "dies by his own sins as all aggressors and wicked men do". "If wounding one's feelings is violence," he said, "Gandhi's satyagraha is also based on violence." "Truly speaking," he concluded, "the law should be non-violence wherever possible; violence whenever necessary."

Coming to the proposed struggle, Ambedkar said that there was a possibility that the launching of Satyagraha was likely to lead to disturbances. In that event, he expected the Government to help those who were exercising their just rights. But what if the Government put a ban on the proposed satyagraha? He said that in that case the satyagrahis would have to defy the ban and court imprisonment. Those who realised this, he added, should take part in the struggle. Emphasizing his point, he said that untouchability was such an abominable stain that it would not matter much even if some lives were sacrificed to wash it out. "Dragging on life somehow or to live like a crow for a thousand years is not the only and worthy way to live in this world. Life can be ennobled and immortalised by sacrificing it for a lasting good such as the cause of truth, a vow, honour or country. For the protection of human rights several great men have immolated themselves at the altar of duty. Better to die in the prime of youth for a great cause than to live like an oak and do nothing."

In the end he warned Government that if it prevented the Depressed Classes from exercising their legitimate rights, the matter would be referred to the League of Nations. If the caste Hindus hampered their struggle, it would be explicitly clear to the whole world that Hinduism was a stonewall, and it was futile to embrace it; and the Untouchables would have to look to another religion for shelter.

The proposed satyagraha evoked a gale of bitter criticism and a storm of wild denunciations from caste Hindu institutions and newspapers which attributed motives to Ambedkar. Had he been enamoured of conversion, he answered, he would have instantly solved the question for himself. But since the Depressed Classes wanted to remain in the Hindu fold, they were fighting for equality and civic rights. "If you say your religion is our religion, then your rights and ours must be equal. But is this the case ? If not, on what grounds do you say that we must remain in the Hindu fold in spite of your kicks and rebuffs?" "The religion which discriminates between two followers is partial," he thundered, "and the religion which treats crores of its adherents worse than dogs and criminals and inflicts upon them insufferable disabilities is no religion at all. Religion is not the appellation for such an unjust order. Religion and Slavery are incompatible."

Ambedkar defined religion as something that offered you prosperity or elevation first in this world and then salvation; the former should be the first article of faith of every religion. "Untouchability shuts all doors of opportunities for betterment in life to the Untouchables. It does not offer an Untouchable any opportunity to move freely in society; it compels him to live in dungeons and seclusion; it prevents him from educating himself and from following a profession of his choice," observed Ambedkar. "Who has seen the world after death or salvation? On top of it all," continued he "it is mischievously propagated by Hindu scriptures that by serving the upper three classes the Shudras attain salvation. Untouchability is another appellation for slavery. No race can be raised by destroying its self-respect. So, if you really want to uplift the Untouchables, you must treat them in the social order as free citizens, free to carve out their destiny."

"Untouchability has ruined the Untouchables, the Hindus and ultimately the nation as well. If the Depressed Classes gained their self-respect and freedom, they would contribute not only to their own progress and prosperity but by their industry, intellect and courage would contribute also to the strength and prosperity of the nation. If the tremendous energy the Untouchables are at present required to fritter away in combating the stigma of untouchability had been saved them, it would have been applied by them to the promotion of education and development of economic resources of the nation as a whole. They would not have been required to embrace another religion for getting themselves called human beings," he added. That the cause which the Depressed Classes were determined to espouse was not only human and for their own good but also national; it was a great contribution to Hinduism itself, he concluded.

II

It was during these days that Lokamanya Tilak's son, Shridharpant, came in contact with Ambedkar. He was a friend and admirer of Ambedkar. He was a promoter of social reforms. In September 1927 he invited a choir of untouchable boy-singers to a function in Tilak's famous Gaikwad Wada in spite of the opposition of the Trustees of the *Kesari*. He was publicly congratulated by the Depressed Classes of Poona on the courageous step he took in the interest of social reform.

Ambedkar now bent his energies to galvanising the younger generation into activity. On October 2, 1927, he presided over a Conference of the Depressed Class students in Poona. This was a move to bring all the intellectual forces from the Depressed Classes into closer touch with Ambedkar's ideology and personality. The educated men could have an opportunity of having a glimpse of the man who promised them relief from grinding poverty, from stark ignorance and to win them human rights. Flags and bunting decorated the Ahalyashram; volunteer corps gave a guard of honour to their leader and saviour. Among the speakers were Shridharpant Tilak, Solanki and P. N. Rajbhoj. Ambedkar, in his address to the Conference, emphasized the important point that much depended upon how the Depressed Class students performed their duties and discharged their responsibilities. Their role in life was of tremendous consequence and was bound to contribute to the progress and destiny of the Depressed Classes. He hoped that the Depressed Class women would also contribute to the progress of the community if, after performing their household duties faithfully, they snatched some time from their daily life and devoted it to the uplift of their fellowmen.

Ambedkar then attended, on an invitation from Shridharpant Tilak, a tea-party at Tilak's Gaikwad Wada. It was unfortunate that such a promising youth should have put an end to his life, a few months later, in a tragic way. A few hours before the tragedy Shridharpant had written a letter to his friend Ambedkar.

During the same month Ambedkar presided over a send-off meeting in honour of Dr. Harold H. Mann, retiring Director of Agriculture, Bombay, on an invitation from S. J. Ramble, the Poona Depressed Class leader. The function took place at the Government Hostel, Poona. Concluding his speech at this function, Ambedkar told the audience that Dr. Mann had been a source of help to him in many ways, and so he expressed grateful thanks for his good help. In his speech Dr. Mann advised the Mahars to work under such able leaders as Dr. Ambedkar.

Ambedkar's movement was now gathering force and was attracting disciples, followers and sympathisers. The leaders now invested members of the Depressed Classes through the Samata Sangh with the sacred thread which according to the Hindu scriptures only the upper classes were entitled to wear. Most of such revolutionary activities were carried out through this Social Equality Society which was composed of men from all communities. On behalf of this Society every member had to invite the co-members of the Society to dinner, so that the distinction of degradation attached to the castes might be totally wiped out.

On November 4, 1927, a function took place at Damodar Hall in Bombay. The Depressed Classes Institute entertained at a party Mardy Jones, a Labour M.P. from U.K., who was then on a visit to India. Jones said that he was pained to see the tragic dehumanised condition of a people who numbered more than the total population of Scotland, Ireland and England. Jones concluded by expressing the hope that the great man of learning and energy the Untouchables had produced would soon deliver them from bondage.[2]

Simultaneously with the preparation for the Mahad struggle was coming to a head the issue of temple entry at Amraoti. For the previous three months this struggle was boiling, and the trustees of the Ambadevi temple were served with a notice by the promoters of the temple entry movement. Their reply came on August 21 that it was not possible for them to break off traditional customs and to allow the Depressed Classes to enter the temple. Thereupon leaders like Dr. Panjabrao Deshmukh, other promoters of the temple entry movement in Berar, and G.A. Gavai, a leader of the Untouchables, held a meeting at Amraoti to discuss the issue. A compromise was suggested, but ultimately it broke down. The vanguard of the movement, therefore, decided to hold a conference to take a final decision as to the struggle. Accordingly, on November 13, 1927, a conference of the promoters of temple entry movement was held at Indra Bhuvan Theatre, in Amraoti, over which Ambedkar was invited to preside. A vast crowd surged up at noon to receive the leader of the Untouchables at the station. The proceedings of the Conference commenced in great excitement. Among those present were Tikade, Bar-at-Law; Chaubal, pleader; K. B. Deshmukh, Deorao Naik, D. V. Pradhan and R.D. Kowly. Dr. Panjabrao Deshmukh made an introductory speech, traced the developments leading up to the Conference, and proposed the name of Ambedkar to the Presidential Chair. Nanasahib Amritkar seconded the proposal.

Ambedkar then rose to deliver his address amidst tumultuous applause. He said that the image of God in the temple should be accessible to all who wanted to worship it, without any discrimination, binding or condition. Recalling how the Hindus denounced the South African Government for throwing Indians into separate compartments, he proceeded: "The most important point we want to emphasize is not the satisfaction you get from the worship of the image of God, but the plain fact that a temple is not defiled by the presence of an Untouchable, nor is the purity of the image affected by it. That is why we oppose the idea of separate temples for us and insist on entering the existing ones."

---

2. *The Bahishkrit Bharat*, 27 November 1927.

Coming to the legal side of the question, he said that although it was a fact that the temples were not built with the aid of the Untouchables, they must be open to them for the simple reason that the temples belonged to all Hindus and were for the benefit of Hinduism. Even though in certain cases a temple was a private property, it was meant for the use of all Hindus; and since they called them untouchable Hindus, they were entitled to entry into the temples to worship the deity. He then turned to the cultural side of the question and said eloquently: "Hindutva belongs as much to the untouchable Hindus as to the touchable Hindus. To the growth and glory of this Hindutva contribution had been made by Untouchables like Valmiki, the seer of the *Vyadhageeta*, Chokhamela and Rohidas as much as by Brahmins like Vashishta. Kshatriyas like Krishna, Vaishyas like Harsha and Shudras like Tukaram." "The heroes like Sidnak Mahar, who fought for the protection of the Hindus, were innumerable. The temple built in the name of Hindutva, the growth and prosperity of which was achieved gradually with the sacrifice of touchable and untouchable Hindus, must be open to all the Hindus irrespective of caste."

He further said that if they accepted this fact, there was no use telling the Untouchables that they were not entitled to that right because they had not used it in the past, inasmuch as they could not prevent a man from going along a certain road because for years together in the past he had not used it. What was true in the case of roads, was also true of temples and public watercourses, he concluded.

The next day the Conference resolved to postpone the satyagraha to a future date, not later than three months, at the instance of G.S. Khaparde, a Member of the Council of State and Chairman of the Ambadevi Temple Committee. The Conference concluded its proceedings in acclamations to Ambedkar. Before his departure Ambedkar was invited by Chavan, editor of *Maharashtra Kesari* and K. B. Deshmukh to a tea-party.

One more thing about this Conference remains to be noted. It had stopped its proceedings on the morning of November 14, as a mark of respect to the memory of the death of Ambedkar's brother, Balasaheb. The sad news was conveyed to him by a telegram.

Ambedkar's brother, Balasaheb, was a stout, fearless, genial and vigorous figure. A voracious reader and a charming speaker, he had moved through an eventful career that was his own creation. A military band player, a musician, and a clerk, in the Bombay Municipality, he had varied experience in life. He lost his two wives and his only son, and leaving behind a daughter, he died in his fifty-fifth year, six months prior to his retirement. During Ambedkar's second stay in London Balaram had developed himself into a volatile leader of the Untouchables. Although his deceased brother's somewhat dissolute conduct had loosened the brotherly tie, on his arrival in Bombay from Amraoti, Ambedkar expressed publicly his thanks to those who had attended the funeral of his brother.

III

The day of the proposed Conference and the satyagraha at Mahad was drawing near. Mahad began to stir again. The opponents of the struggle held a meeting on November 27, 1927, at the Veereshwar Temple to formulate a plan to flout the attempts of Ambedkar and the Depressed Classes to take water from the Chowdar Tank. But owing to the presence of the sympathisers of the Depressed Classes the meeting ended in pandemonium. Some Poona Hindu leaders tried to dissuade the caste Hindus from opposing the struggle, but to no purpose.

The District Magistrate visited Mahad on December 7, and the leaders of both the sides discussed the question with him. He asked the caste Hindus to have recourse to law and refused to issue an order prohibiting the Untouchables from taking water from the Chowdar Tank. The leaders of the orthodox section,, therefore, filed a suit against Ambedkar, Shivtarkar and Krishnaji S. Kadam and Ganya Malu Chambhar of Mahad— leaders of the Depressed Classes—on December 12, 1927, in the Civil Court at Mahad and asked for the issue of a temporary injunction. The Court issued a temporary injunction on December 14, against the defendants pending the decision of the suit. Accordingly notices were served on Ambedkar, Shivtarkar and Krishnaji S. Kadam, prohibiting them and all the Depressed Classes or on their behalf these three leaders from going to the Chowdar Tank or from taking water from the Tank until further orders. The orthodox and reactionary forces shrewdly enough forced on Ambedkar a fight on two fronts. On the one side was standing an indifferent foreign Government and on the other was the caste Hindu section headed by the orthodox Brahmins.

Elaborate preparations for holding the Conference were made. As no Hindu landlord allowed the use of his land for the pandal, a site for the Conference was secured with great difficulty from a Muslim. As the local merchants refused to have any dealings with the men connected with the Conference, the Reception Committee had to purchase corn and other materials from outside, sufficient to last for ten days. Anantrao Chitre managed the work very efficiently. To Subhedar Ghatge was entrusted the food arrangement and maintenance of order and discipline. All the chief Government Executives of the District gathered at Mahad on December 19. Police were posted on all sides of the Chowdar Tank. Delegates and spectators began to pour in Mahad from December 21. The District Magistrate visited their camp every day to dissuade the delegates from the proposed satyagraha.

With a batch of two hundred delegates and leaders, Ambedkar left Bombay on the morning of December 24. The next day they got down at noon at Dasgaon, five miles off Mahad. There, with anxious faces, an army of 3,000 satyagrahis awaited their leader. When they saw their leader, they greeted him with tumultuous applause.

After the reception, the Police Superintendent handed over a letter from the District Magistrate to Ambedkar, requesting him to see the District Magistrate at his Mahad office without loss of time. Ambedkar, with one of his lieutenants, Sahasrabudhe, hurried to his office. The District Magistrate in a swift and soft tone advised, argued and pressed for the postponement of the struggle; but the leader did not see eye to eye with the Chief Executive of the District. It was, however, agreed that he should be given an opportunity to address the Conference. In the meanwhile, the procession of the delegates had left Dasgaon and, accompanied by police officers, it reached Mahad at half past two in the afternoon, singing songs which were punctuated by sky-rending slogans. The vast crowd entered the pandal amidst shouts of 'Shivaji Maharaj ki Jai'. In the pandal proverbs hanging from pillars displayed inspiring immortal truths. In front of the gate there was a pit.

After his interview with the District Magistrate, Ambedkar hastened to the pandal and had his lunch in the company of his common followers. He refused to have any special food.

The Conference commenced its proceedings at four-thirty in the evening. Messages from several prominent persons wishing the satyagraha success were read out. Then the leader rose to address the Conference amidst deafening cheers, shouts and slogans raised by a mammoth gathering of fifteen thousand people. A majority of them had no clothes to their backs. Their old turbans were torn, their chins were unshaven; but their sunburnt faces shone with a peculiar enthusiasm and hope. The vast audience calmed down, and Ambedkar began his speech in a low, dignified but forceful voice. He said: "At the outset let me tell those who oppose us that we did not perish because we could not drink water from this Chowdar Tank. We now want to go to the Tank only to prove that, like others, we are also human beings."

"This Conference," he continued, "has been called to inaugurate an era of equality in this land." He then drew a parallel incident from the history of France when the French representatives had met at Versailles and issued a manifesto of human rights, preaching revolt against social, religious and political privileges and declaring that all men were born equal and died as equals. Ambedkar avowed that it was the ultimate aim of politics to maintain and protect those human rights and added: "Removal of untouchability and inter-caste dinners alone will not put an end to our ills. All departments of services such as courts, military, police and commerce, should be thrown open to us." Concluding his speech, he said: "Hindu society should be reorganised on two main principles—equality and absence of casteism."

The first resolution passed was the declaration of human rights. India was the most pitiable and eloquent example, declared the Conference, of how a nation's fall was brought about by the prevalence of injustice, religious stupor, political backwardness and economic insufficiency. The Conference added that the way out of these evils was the adoption of the principle

that all men were born equal and continued to be so till death.
The Conference repudiated the authority of all the ancient and
modern Hindu scriptures that teemed with the doctrines of social
inequality, and reiterated its opposition to applying these
scriptures to the present social order. The resolution was moved
by Shivtarkar and was seconded by Bhaurao Gaikwad, N. T.
Jadhav and Mrs. Gangubai Savant.

Then came the major and bitter attack on the Hindu
reactionaries. The Conference declared that the *Manusmriti*
which directed molten lead to be poured into the ears of such
Shudras as would hear or read the *Vedas*, and which decried the
Shudras, stunted their growth, impaired their self-respect, and
perpetuated their social, economic, religious and political slavery,
be publicly burnt. On this resolution fiery speeches were made
by Sahasrabudhe, Rajbhoj and Thorat. The *Manusmriti*, the most
revered work of the caste Hindus, and the most hated work by
the Depressed Classes, was thus ruthlessly condemned. The
Manusmriti governs the law and life of the Hindus. Although
compiled over one thousand and five hundred years ago, and
although times are changed, it is considered by the orthodox to
be good, all-pervading and omniscient even to this day.

Yet those who ruthlessly applied the doctrines of the
Manusmriti to the non-Brahmins and the Atishudras
contravened all its laws themselves and still boasted of their
superiority. The Brahmins are forbidden by the *Manusmriti* to
trade in chemicals, liquids, coloured cloth, flowers, perfumery
and arms. Yet no Brahmin loses his high and undefiled prestige
in society even if he runs cloth-shops, medical pharmacies,
dairies, hotels, perfumery and cutlery shops. Even Tilak, who
had sponsored a textile mill, never upheld the right of the non-
Brahmins to Vedic forms of worship, or the study of the *Vedas* by
the non-Brahmins!

Sahasrabudha, the mover of the foregoing resolution on the
Manusmriti, condemning the holy scripture outright, said that
it was a symbol of inequality, cruelty and injustice from the point
of view of the Depressed Classes. All the speakers spoke of it
with exceptional bitterness and roundly denounced its precepts.
It was a furious onslaught on the scriptures. The wrath of the
Conference did not stop at verbal condemnation. At nine o'clock
that night the *Manusmriti* was placed on a pyre, in a specially

dug pit, in front of the pandal, and was ceremoniously burnt at the hands of untouchable hermits!

This explosive deed rocked all the charlatans, pundits, Acharyas and Shankaracharyas in India, and for a while, it spread a nervous brain-wave over such leaders as Bhaskarrao Jadhav, the bitterest enemy of Brahminism, who exclaimed that it was too outlandish an attack on the sacred Hindu scriptures which contained more good than evil.

One of the greatest iconoclasts for all times, Ambedkar was hammering out the false gods from their outworn sanctuaries. This act was one of the greatest sacrilegious blows ever since the days of Luther upon the egoistic bigots, custom-mongers and no-changers on earth. December 25, 1927, is, therefore, a red letter day in the annals of India as it was on tins day that Ambedkar burnt the old *Smriti* and demanded a new one in order to reshape the Hindu code governing the life of so vast a people. Mahad thus became the Wittenberg of India.

The third resolution passed by the Conference demanded that Hindu society be reduced to one class only, and by the fourth it demanded that the present priestly profession be turned into a democratic institution, allowing even one who desired to have an opportunity to become a priest.

When the next morning the Conference resumed proceedings. Ambedkar moved the resolution on the proposed satyagraha. In the course of his speech be impressed upon the delegates the magnitude of their proposed action and the bitter consequences that would ensue from the struggle. He advised them not to carry staffs in their hands, and asked every one to observe rigid discipline. He added that every satyagrahi would have to court imprisonment and in that event he must not tender an apology or beg for a release. He proceeded: "My heart leaps with joy to see that you are prepared for launching this attack in vindication of your rights and honour. I have no doubt about it. But, all the same, it would be proper on your part to accord approval to this proposed fight after giving a deep thought to the trials and tribulations you would be involved in its trail. Remember that nothing valuable in this world is achieved except by great efforts." Twelve leaders supported the plea for satyagraha, and four spoke against it.

Summing up, Ambedkar said that there were a few dissentient voices; but the overwhelming majority were for satyagraha. He then observed: " Mind you, do not leap into the fire because I tell you to do so. Do it, if you are fully convinced of the justice of your cause. We want men who will annihilate untouchability even by immolating themselves. If your decision remains firm even after listening to the address of the Collector, you should not hesitate to launch the satyagraha."

It was now noon and at this juncture the famous non-Brahmin leaders of Maharashtra, Jedhe and Javalkar, came to Mahad from Bombay and entered the pandal. Ambedkar asked them to put their views before the Conference. They, too, supported the righteous cause of the Depressed Classes, asking them to fight under the leadership of the great man of learning and ability, and added that he would surely relieve them from their slavery. The Conference then adjourned at half past one in the afternoon.

IV

Meanwhile, twenty workers were asked to register the names of delegates who were willing to join the satyagraha. Within an hour over 4,000 delegates registered their names for the struggle, and a vast multitude still cried out for registration, every one saying that he would not show his face in his village without capturing the Tank, or courting imprisonment in the attempt.

The District Magistrate was then informed about the sense of the Conference, and as agreed he came to address the Conference. The Collector and District Magistrate said: "According to the resolution of the Bombay Legislative Council, public tanks, schools and roads are open to all. But twelve persons have filed a suit saying that the Tank is a private property. You should, therefore, await the decision of the court. You know that those who assaulted you last time were punished. If you break the law, you will also suffer the same fate. As a friend, I advise you not to precipitate this issue till the decision of the court is out."

Then Javalkar rose and read the declaration of the Marathas supporting the satyagraha, but appealed for its postponement. Subhedar Ghatge, too, spoke on the same lines. The Collector was then led by Ambedkar out of the pandal. Till seven in the evening speaker after speaker supported the launching of satyagraha, and those who uttered discordant notes were booed and heckled. Ambedkar again adjourned the discussion till the next morning.

At night the chief men gathered together, held discussions and decided to postpone the struggle in view of the case pending before the court, but it was also decided to march in procession winding its course around the tank. Accordingly, this decision was notified to the District Magistrate. On the morning of December 27, Ambedkar rose to withdraw the first resolution on the struggle and to move another resolution amidst breathless silence, asking the Conference to postpone the struggle. He was on the horns of a dilemma. It was now the psychological moment to curb the enthusiasm of the delegates and pin it down. He tactfully began to deal with the critical situation. He said in an appealing tone to the delegates, who had by now grown restless and frantic: "You are a brave people. The people who are prepared to lay down their lives for the vindication of their just rights are sure to prosper. But the moment now has come when you should think twice before you strike the blow." "You know well that the satyagraha movement started by Gandhi," he proceeded, " was backed up by the people as it was against a foreign domination. Our struggle is against the mass of caste Hindus and naturally we have little support from outside. Taking these facts into consideration, I feel, we should not antagonise the Government and put it on the side of our opposition. It is not beneficial either."

"Do not suppose," asserted the leader, "that if you postpone the issue humiliation will be its concomitant. As regards my position, I assure you I am prepared to face the three-fold danger—breaking of an order, being charged with a breach of rules governing the conduct of a lawyer and the possibility of imprisonment." "My brothers," he softly concluded, "you rest assured that a postponement of this struggle will not mean that we have given up the struggle. The fight will go on till we establish our claims to this Tank."

There was a sudden lull, a feeling of nervous tension in the minds of the delegates. A wave of bitter disappointment swept over the Conference, and some of them in the innermost recesses of their hearts even fluttered at the retreat of their leader. Yet there was no alternative but to render implicit obedience to their leader's call.

The Conference agreed. The delegates immediately formed themselves into a procession and started. The Bombay volunteer corps was at the head. At intervals volunteers with slogans, boards and placards were pacing slowly. The procession reached the Tank and took its round. And what were the caste Hindus doing? The streets were deserted. They had shut their houses and the orthodox Hindus were wriggling with excruciating venom in their hearts. After an hour and a half, the procession returned to the pandal about noon without any mishap.

In the evening Ambedkar addressed a meeting at the Chamar quarters in Mahad and asked the Chamars whether they wanted to live with self-respect or to live like pet animals in gilt cages. The Chamars are a business community dealing in shoes and sandals. Though an untouchable community, they are in closer touch with the caste Hindus. They are a small minority. For every fifty Mahars there is one Chamar in Maharashtra.

At 10 p.m. the Conference wound up its proceedings by expressing its gratitude to the Reception Committee and thanking the delegates and its sympathisers. Immediately after conclusion of the Conference, Ambedkar addressed a meeting of about three thousand women of the Depressed Classes, the first meeting of its kind in modern India. This was also a unique occasion when the women folk of the Depressed Classes showed signs of a stirring. Ambedkar spoke to them in a simple homely manner. He said: "Never regard yourselves as Untouchables. Live a clean life. Dress yourselves like the touchable ladies. Never mind if your dress if full of patches, but see that it is clean. None can restrict your freedom in the choice of your garments and in the use of the metal for your ornaments. Attend more to the cultivation of the mind and the spirit of self-help."

Then with a little fall in his voice he said: "But do not feed in any case your spouse and sons if they are drunkards. Send your children to schools. Education is as necessary for females as it is for males. If you know how to read and write, there would be much progress. As you are, so your children will be. Mould their lives in a virtuous way, for sons should be such as would make a mark in this world." And to the surprise of all the women left early in the morning with a wonderful change in the fashion of their sarees as ordained by their great leader, guide and uncrowned king.

Thus the Mahad struggle ended. With its conclusion India closed an epoch. The end of the epoch was sounded by Ambedkar's declaration of human rights of equality and by the Indian National Congress, which at its Madras session, during ihc same week, declared "the goal of the Indian people to be complete National Independence." The first declaration related to social independence, and the second to political- independence. It was a good and great coincidence, a sign of India's conscious efforts at a revaluation of social and political equality!

V

The Mahad struggle had a far-reaching effect upon the Untouchables. It exercised a tremendous influence upon the Government and gave a rude shock to the orthodox section of the Hindus. The awakening and the spirit of self-assertion among the Depressed Classes had now grown too strong to be curbed or suppressed. Representatives from different districts who had attended this conference now realised that it was possible for them to organise resistance, to challenge the injustice they were smarting under. They realised that they were not alone; their brothers from other districts were ready to respond to their brotherly call in times of danger. Government now realised that these people were of some consequence and so it began to pay more attention to their grievances.

But the outstanding gain was that the name and fame of Ambedkar spread far and wide. His leadership of the Depressed Classes was now almost an established and undeniable fact. The world of his influence grew and Ambedkar became a name to conjure with in the Depressed Class world. Mahad proved that Ambedkar was a statesman as well as a savant, a man of study as well as a man of action. In him there were life and literature happily blended.

The bonfire of the *Manusmriti* calls for some comment. Ambedkar himself revealed afterwards that it was not made for the sake of mere hatred. The *Manusmriti* has been indeed the charter of rights for the caste Hindus and at the same time a Bible of slavery for the Untouchables. While speaking of this event later in 1938, in an interview with T.V, Parvate, a front-rank journalist, Ambedkar said: "The bonfire of *Manusmriti* was quite intentional. It was a very cautious and drastic step, but was taken with a view to forcing the attention of caste Hindus. At intervals such drastic remedies are a necessity. If you do not knock at the door, none opens it. It is not that all the parts of the *Manusmriti* are condemnable, that it does not contain good principles and that Manu himself was not a sociologist and was a mere fool. We made a bonfire of it because we view it as a symbol of injustice under which we have been crushed across centuries. Because of its teachings we have been ground down under despicable poverty, and so we made the dash, staked all, took our lives in our hands and performed the deed."[3]

This is a parallel with the first bonfire in India which Savarkar made of the foreign clothes in 1906 is a symbol of foreign rule and exploitation of a people in whom discontent was growing. The object and effect of Ambedkar's deed, too, was to show discontent in and hatred of slavery. He attacked the *Manusmriti* as it was a symbol of unjust social laws. It is very interesting to note here the attitude of these two giant rationalists from Maharashtra towards Hindu scriptures. Both Savarkar and Ambedkar were social revolutionaries. Both were rationalists. Both were iconoclasts. But there was a slight difference in their attitude towards the ancient scriptures.

The bonfire of *Manusmriti* put the hair of almost all Hindu reformers on its end. The social reformers recoiled with horror from Savarkar's caustic attack upon their beliefs, holy works, and scriptures, and his caustic essay on the cow wherein he enjoined upon the Hindus to eat even beef in a state of national emergency! The burning of *Manusmriti* and asking the Hindus to eat beef were both horrible outlandish blows upon the orthodox, tradition-mongers and sanatani reformers. But Savarkar differed a little from Ambedkar in his attack on Hindu scriptures. In his rational approach Savarkar appealed to the Hindus to test all their ancient works on the touchstone of Science and to follow fearlessly what

---

3.   Parvate, *T.V., Mee Ghetaleya Mulakhati* (Marathi). pp. 58-59.

contributed to the good of the nation, and to eschew what hampered their growth, prosperity and consolidation. Naturally Savarkar was not prepared to apply the code of Manu to the Depressed Class Hindus and Hindu women.

But Ambedkar, who was the symbol of a suppressed people who suffered throughout ages, smashed and hammered out the scriptures with the violence of a Voltaire, while Savarkar whose forefathers never felt the pinch of the caste system, swept the outworn scriptures into a corner as historical and cultural monuments for record and research, and looked at them with the eye of a historian and possibly with gratitude. What Ambedkar did to these scriptures Savarkar would have done with equal violence, and what Savarkar wrote Ambedkar would have asserted with equal force had they been born in the opposite communities.

Yet the last word on the Mahad episode is not said. At the conclusion of the Conference, Ambedkar and his party went to see in the neighbourhood of Mahad the excavations supposed to have dated from the time of Lord Buddha. Moved at the sight of those figures, he described to his party how the disciples of Buddha in those times remained bachelors, embraced poverty and served society selflessly. He advised his party, with a note of reverence, not to occupy the seats at the place as they might have been the seats of Buddhist priests.

The party then set out to see the sacred place of the Hindus of Modern India. It was the capital Fort of Shivaji the Great, the Saviour of the Hindus in modern times, who is regarded as the symbol of liberty, the source of self-respect and the fount of an immortal inspiration. When Ambedkar was on his way to this place, all was not well in the neighbourhood. The members of antagonism fanned by the subtle enemies were glowing with revenge. Those who could not thwart the Mahad struggle were smarting under a feeling of bitterness. It was rumoured that caste Hindus lay in ambush to attack the leader of the Depressed Classes. Suspecting foul play against their leader, the Depressed Class men sent messages to their people in the neighbouring dales. The Untouchables quickly responded to the call and gathered at the foot of the Fort at night. At nightfall Ambedkar and his party made their first halt on their way at the village Nate.

Early next morning, the party climbed the Fort Raigad. Ambedkar was moved at the sight of the place which was once a stirring and living centre of Hindustan. The scattered, deserted, moth-eaten relics of a magnificent empire, the imposing portals ever gaping wide, the scattered pillars, the stately palaces and the invisible historic figures must have unrolled to the visitors the stories of the vivid past! At night the party sojourned in the Fort. Tired and fatigued, they soon fell asleep. At dead of night somebody sprinkled water from outside over the party who were fast asleep in one of the apartments of the dilapidated Fort. There were dim voices. All the visitors stood pale and petrified. The men below whispered to them to be on their guard. But the party did not know who they were. Night wore on and morning came. The men turned out to be their protectors. Their devotion was boundless. Their caution was timely. Fortunately their leader and his party came to no harm. So great was their joy at his safety that the untouchable women folk, did humble obeisance in all filial love to their saviour and gratefully thanked heavens for his safety.

But what happened to the claim of the Untouchables on the Chowdar Tank? It assumed the form of a long-drawn fight in the Court. Ambedkar himself fought out the suit in the Lower Civil Courts for nearly three years.

CHAPTER 7

THE MORNING STAR

THE Depressed Classes were now searching with new light for the scattered sources of their spiritual and historic inspiration. Early in January 1928, a meeting was convened by the Depressed Classes at Trymbak, near Nasik, which is a place of pilgrimage of the Hindus, to consider a proposal for building a temple in the name of their great saint, Chokhamela. Ambedkar was specially invited to preside over the meeting. The meeting, after a full discussion, decided that the real memorial of the saint consisted in devoting themselves with unflagging energy rather to the removal of the blot of untouchability than to the erection of a temple. The fact was that firstly, Ambedkar was in the innermost recesses of his heart against the idea of separate temples; secondly, the building expenses would have been a financial burden; and thirdly, Ambedkar was more of a utilitarian than an idol worshipper.

It was Ambedkar's view that the saint-poets of Maharashtra (1300-1600) belonging to Bhagavat Dharma did not preach directly against the caste system which stood for the domination of one caste over others, for social inequality and social injustice. The efforts of these saint-poets were directed to establishing equality, not between a Brahmin as an individual and a Shudra as an individual, but between a Brahmin and a Shudra devotee of God. In this struggle the saints succeeded, and the Brahmins had to accept the superiority of the devotee irrespective of caste.

"Yet from the view point of the annihilation of caste", Ambedkar stated, "the struggle of the saints did not have any effect on society. The value of man is axiomatic, self-evident; it does not come to him as the result of the gilding of Bhakti. The saints did not struggle to establish this point. On the contrary, their struggle had a very unhealthy effect on the Depressed Classes. It provided the Brahmins with an excuse to silence them by telling that they would be respected if they also attained the status of Chokhamela". As the followers of different cults of

Bhakti were themselves filled with caste prejudices. Ambedkar proceeded, they not only turned a blind eye to their message of equality, justice and humanitarianism, but also described their incredible miracles with utmost exaggeration.

As regards the cult of Ramdas, he said that his followers were notorious for their caste prejudices since its inception, and their founder himself was obsessed with the ideas of Brahmin superiority. According to Ramdas, even a fallen Brahmin was superior to men of other castes in heaven and on earth; nay, a Brahmin was one to whom even the gods made an obeisance.

At this juncture the proposed marriage of Sir Tukojirao Holkar with Miss Miller, an American lady, had become a controversial issue between the orthodox and progressive groups all over Maharashtra. The Dhangar community to which the Maharaja belonged was divided in its opinion on the marriage. Its members, therefore, met in conference to decide the issue. Ambedkar and Bole were invited to attend and guide the Conference which was held at Baramati, in March 1928. Both the leaders supported the Maharaja as did other progressive groups. The Conference upheld the decision of the Maharaja. Whether Ambedkar's support was for the conversion of the lady to the much-hated Hinduism or for the idea of non-endogamy is, however, not known.

The same night the Depressed Classes of Baramati took the occasion of his visit to accord him a reception under the presidentship of Bole. They showered praises on their leader and felicitated M.K. Jadhav on his being the first untouchable Hindu to be appointed to the post of a deputy collector. His elevation was the fruition of Ambedkar's ceaseless demand for appointments of able men from amongst the Depressed Classes to higher posts in Government offices. To that end, on one occasion, he crossed swords with the British Governor, Sir Leslie Wilson. The British Governor had called him to the Government House and expressed surprise at and disapproval of the criticism of Government policy made by him as a nominated Member. Ambedkar at once replied that he said in the Council what was right in his opinion and added fearlessly that Wilson's Government had, in fact, done nothing to promote the interests of the Depressed Classes and, for that matter, even qualified and able men from amongst them were not selected for higher posts. Ambedkar pointed out Jadhav's application as a case in point. This impressed the decision of the Government, and there was a change in the attitude of the Government towards the employment of Depressed Class candidates. It was an example of the truism that no door is opened till it is knocked.

In the Legislative Council Ambedkar never lost an opportunity to fight for the amelioration of the condition of the poor. When an important Bill proposing maternity benefits for women labourers was introduced in the House, he showed intensity of feeling for the cause of the poor. Supporting the Bill in a very vigorous speech, the Doctor said: "And I believe, therefore, sir, that it is in the interest of the nation that the mother ought to get a certain amount of rest during the prenatal period and also subsequently, and this Bill is based entirely on that principle." Although Ambedkar was of the opinion that the burden of this expenditure should be borne by Government, he said it was not altogether wrong if the Bill sought to impose the liability under the existing circumstances on the employer who employed women labour, being cheaper and more profitable.

But the most important Bill in which he showed an undivided interest was introduced by Ambedkar himself. It was the Bill to amend the Bombay Hereditary Offices Act, 1874. He introduced it on March 19, 1928.

According to this Hereditary Offices Act, the Mahars, the holders of the posts, were required to slave all day and night; and in the absence of a Mahar servant, his father or any other member of his family was impressed into the Government service. And for this hard, arduous and ceaseless work they got each a piece of land called Watan, some corn from the villagers and a paltry pittance varying from annas two to a rupee and a half per mensem. The result was that the Mahars had grown lethargic. They had lost the stimulus in life; they had lost their self-respect, and their ambition and ability were perpetually, tied down to these trifling menial jobs. In order to break these shackles of serfdom Ambedkar introduced this Bill.

Before introducing the Bill, Ambedkar had acquainted his community with the contents and objects of the proposed Bill. Several meetings and conferences were held ardently at taluka and district towns, during the preceding year to discuss the issues

involved in the Bill, to resolve doubts and to remove misunder-
standings created in the minds of the ignorant community by
interested groups.

A big meeting of 5,000 Watandar Mahars was held at
Kamathipura, Bombay, on November 5, 1927, under the
presidentship of Rao Bahadur S. K. Bole. A conference was held
by the Nasik District Watandars on November 13, 1927. Another
big meeting of 3,000 Watandar Mahars was held at Jalgaon where
Ambedkar explained to them the principles and provisions of
his proposed Bill.

A tremendous agitation had been thus made before the
introduction of the Bill in the Legislative Council by the leader.
Moving the Bill on August 3, 1928, Ambedkar observed that the
Mahars were treated as maids of all work of all Government
Departments at any hour of the day and night for a paltry
pittance. He then described their utter penury and said that the
sources of their income were mainly two. "The first source was
the Inam lands and the second was what is called *baluta*, the
collection of grain made by the Watandar Mahars from the
villages." Bringing to the notice of the House that those lands
were given to those Mahars by the ancient emperors of the
country, he continued that the Government had neither increased
the extent of the land, nor paid a moment's attention to the
remuneration of these people although prices had increased, the
cost of living had gone up, every Government servant had been
given an increase in salary and their population had increased
enormously. The land assigned to them was divided and
subdivided to such an extent that the income these people got
from the Watan lands was absolutely not worthy of being taken
into consideration.

He, therefore, appealed to the House: "That, I submit, sir,
is an atrocious system, a system which has no justice in it
whatsoever. If the Government desires that these people should
work for it, it is absolutely necessary that the Government should
take upon its shoulder the responsibility of paying these Mahars.
It ought not vicariously to throw off this burden in a most careless
way upon a third party, the ryot; but that is exactly what is
happening under the system."

Ambedkar, therefore, proposed that the Watan lands should
be given to the holders of those posts at the full rate of

assessment, and they should be relieved from the obligation to serve. According to him 60,000 Mahars were assigned those Watans, but one-third of the number would be sufficient. They should be paid from the revenue derived from the assessment levied on the lands of the Mahars, and from the *baluta*, which the village population would have to bear for paying the cost of the watch and ward. Thus there would be no additional burden on the Government treasury.

"Sir, if the Government have got,"Ambedkar proceeded, "the nerve, the courage and the sympathy for these classes (teachers and talatis) to bring forward financial measures to remunerate their services, why should not Government have the same nerve, the same courage and the same sympathy in the case of these Mahars?" "I do not understand, sir," he went on, "why Government should continue to be a party to a system. which enthrals and enslaves a class of his Majesty's subjects. I submit, sir, that either on the legal ground or on the moral ground, and I say, on the financial ground the principle I have enumerated in section 4 of my Bill is just and equitable."

Ambedkar, in an emotional touch, declared in the House that the Mahars were determined to have the Bill passed, and threatened Government with a general strike and also with his resignation if the House did not pass it, as he was convinced that the principles of the Bill were very essential for the welfare of the Mahars and that the Watans were the greatest hindrances in their advancement. And hoping that the Council would unanimously pass this Bill, he concluded, "with these words I move the first reading of the Bill".[1]

This two-hour speech was so forcible, straight-forward and eloquent that all the Members heard it in complete silence. After a preliminary discussion, on August 4, Ambedkar moved that the Bill be referred to a Select Committee consisting of twenty-three Members of the House. It was to report on the Bill by the beginning of June 1929. The fate of the Bill was tragic. The Select Committee changed its body beyond recognition. The friction came over the question of *baluta* which Ambedkar proposed to convert into a money cess and over the Committee's opinion that the Watan lands should not be given over to the Watandars on

---

1. Bombay Legislative Council Debates, Vol. XXIII, Part XI, pp. 708-21.

payment of the full assessment on their lands but should be given
on half the proceeds of the lands. Almost all representatives of
the privileged and orthodox sections showed the cold shoulder
to this Bill and few sided with Government. The Muslim Members
opposed the Bill as they were displeased with Ambedkar for his
having violently attacked[2] and exposed their anti-national
designs in the special report he had submitted some months
before to the Simon Commission, as explained in the following
pages. At long last, on July 24, 1929, Ambedkar rose and said:
"Sir, I beg to withdraw the Bill." A quarter of a century-has rolled
by, and the miserable condition of the Mahars remains unchanged
and uncared for.

II

In order to ease the troubled situation in India, the British
Government decided to re-examine and revise the Act of 1919.
So it announced the appointment of the Indian Statutory
Commision better known as the Simon Commission after Sir John
Simon, its chairman. The Commission consisted of two Peers and
four Commoners to work under Sir John Simon, who was a great
Parliamentarian, and it was declared that the proposals framed
in the light of this Commission's recommendations would be
submitted to a Joint Select Committee at Westminster before
which Indian witnesses would be examined.

The Simon Commission came on its first visit, and landed at
Bombay on February 3, 1928, to commence the work of
re-examination of the Indian problem as declared in the Act of
1919. Its non-Indian character offered an affront to almost all
Indian parties. The Congress Party decided to boycott the
Commission at every stage and in every form. So, on its arrival,
the Simon Commission was greeted with black flags, curses and
placards with the slogan "Go back, Simon!" Congressmen staged
hostile demonstrations on a nation-wide scale, and the police had
to open fire at some places. This black welcome was also extended
later to the Commission during its second visit in the winter of
1928-29.

Meanwhile, the All Parties Conference convened by the
Congress Party met in February and later in May 1928, and
appointed a Committee under Pandit Motilal Nehru to draft a

---

2. *The Bahishkrit Bharat*, editorial, 16 August 1929.

Swaraj Constitution for India. The Nehru Committee worked from June to August 1928 and drafted a Constitution.

This was the first Indian attempt at constitution-making. It mainly aimed at closing the Muslim breach. As regards the Depressed or Suppressed Classes, the Nehru Report said: "In our suggestions for the constitution we have not made any special provision for the representation of the 'depressed' classes in the legislatures. This could only be done by way of special electorates or by nomination." But as these two methods were considered harmful and unsound, the Committee said that they were not going to extend either principle. They observed that their Declaration of Rights would be a panacea for all the ills affecting the Depressed Classes.[3] The attitude of the Congress Party towards the problem of the Untouchables will be clearer when one notices that the Congress Working Committee issued invitations to all prominent Muslim, Parsi, Christian, Sikh, Anglo-Indian organisations and even the non-Brahmin institutions and the Dravida Mahajana Sabha, but not to the Depressed Classes Institute led by Ambedkar or for that matter any Depressed Class Institution. It may be recalled that ten years before this Ambedkar had given evidence before the Southborough Commission.

At this juncture Ambedkar accepted an appointment as an acting professor at the Government Law College, Bombay, from June 1928. Amidst the struggle for the liberation of his people, the heated controversies, the fleeting visits to different towns and villages to attend meetings and conferences, he could hardly find sufficient time to make headway in his profession as a lawyer. A leader of the downtrodden, a man of great learning, and an editor of his Party organ, he found very little time to accept briefs. So for making both ends meet he had to accept the post.

To co-operate with the Simon Commission the Central Government appointed a committee for all British India, and every Legislative Council elected its Provincial Committee to work with the Simon Commission. On the Bombay Provincial Committee was selected Ambedkar along with other Members by the Bombay Legislative Council on August 3, 1928.

The proceedings and tours of the Simon Commission lit up the Indian political firmament, and along with other forces it

---

3. All Parties Conference Report, 1928, pp. 59-60.

brought to the front the force, intellect and vitality of Ambedkar. By now he was sufficiently known in the college for his fiery, fearless and outspoken views. As Ambedkar was cooperating with the Simon Commission, he was dubbed a British stooge, a Judas, a ghoul and a traitor. One day when he entered the morning class in the college, the law students boycotted his class; and one ardent student-patriot denounced him for his association with the Simon Commission. Needless to say, the incident flashed next day across the pages of all newspapers!

Eighteen Depressed Class Associations gave evidence before the Commission and placed their memoranda before it. Sixteen of them pleaded for separate electorates for the Depressed Classes. On behalf of the Bahishkrit Hitakarini Sabha Ambedkar submitted a memorandum to the Simon Commission demanding joint electorates with reservation of seats for the Depressed Classes.[4] The memorandum complained that those in charge of the nation's affairs always forgot the dumb millions and added that under the Act of 1919 grave injustice was done to the Depressed Classes who constituted one-fifth of the population of British India. The Bahishkrit Hitakarini Sabha demanded 22 out of 140 seats in the Bombay Legislative Council, vehemently opposed the principle of nomination, and insisted upon the extension of the principle of election to the Depressed Classes. It said that they needed political education, and as ministership was a very important privilege, they must find a place in the cabinet.

In addition to these demands for adequate representation, the Sabha felt a need for the inclusion of clauses in the coming constitution of the country, laying down education of the Depressed Classes to be the first charge on the Revenue of the Provinces, and according the right of the Depressed Classes to recruitment in the Army, Navy and Police.

The B.H. Sabha further cautioned the Simon Commission against being lured into forming a better opinion of the Hindu majority from its best instances and quoted instances of atrocities, maltreatment and oppression under which life was made impossible for the Depressed Classes socially, economically and religiously. The B.H. Sabha, however, expressed its confidence in

---

4.   Indian Statutory Commission, Vol. XVI, pp. 37-47.

sane Hindu leadership when it observed in its memorandum:
"Nobody among the Depressed Classes doubts that there would
be great and universal happiness under the Government of a good
Hindu." But the fact, it observed, was that laws and institutions
required to be adapted not to good men but bad.

The Madras Central Adi-Dravida Mahajana Sabha
demanded nomination for the Depressed Classes. The Bombay
Provincial non-Brahmin Party in its memorandum recommended
separate electorates and reserved seats for the Depressed
Classes. The Muslim League reiterated its demands for
separation of Sind, creation of a new Province in the N.-W.F.,
separate electorates for Muslims and residuary powers for the
Provinces in a federal constitution.

On October 23, 1928, the Simon Commission, the Central
Committee and the Bombay Provincial Committee examined
Ambedkar in Poona. The whole Committee had before them the
memorandum submitted by the B.H. Sabha and the memorandum
submitted by the Depressed India Association. At the outset Sir
John Simon asked Ambedkar a number of questions about the
population of the Depressed Classes in the Presidency. Then Sir
Hari Sing Gour asked Ambedkar the following pertinent questions:[5]

Q. Dr. Ambedkar, would you regard "Depressed Classes" and
Untouchables as synonymous terms?

Ans. Yes.

Q. In asking for special representation for the Depressed
Classes you confine yourself to the Untouchables?

Ans. Yes.

Q. You say that some aboriginals are not untouchables?

Ans. In some parts they may be. I do not propose to speak on
their behalf.

Then the following questions and answers were exchanged
between the Committee and Ambedkar:

Q. Taking that figure, what is it that you want to represent
as the proper way in which the constitution of India and
more particularly the constitution of the Bombay
Presidency should deal with these people?

Ans. The first thing I would like to submit is that we claim
that we must be treated as a distinct minority, separate

---

5. Indian Statutory Commission. Vol. XVI, pp. 52-57.

from the Hindu community; a distinct, independent minority. Secondly, I should like to submit that the Depressed Classes minority needs far greater political protection than any other minority in British India for the simple reason that it is educationally very backward, that it is economically very poor, socially enslaved and suffers from certain grave political disabilities from which no other community suffers. We claim reserved seats if accompanied by adult franchise.

Q. And if there is no adult franchise?

Ans. Then we would ask for separate electorates.

Q. You are particularly anxious to get appointments in the public services. Why is that so?

Ans. I wish to say emphatically that in many cases the law is administered to the disadvantage of the Depressed Class man.

Q. Can you give me a strict definition of the Depressed Classes?

Ans. Castes which cause pollution.

Q. Do intermarriages take place between the Mahar and Mang castes?

Ans. No, the caste Hindus have spread their poison to the rest.

Q. Do they dine together?

Ans. Yes, now-a-days.

Q. Would you class the Depressed Classes as real Hindus?

Ans. I do not care for the nomenclature. It does not matter whether I call myself a Hindu or a non-Hindu as long as I am outside the pale of Hinduism.

Q. If you were outside the pale of Hinduism you would not be subject to Hindu Law. . . . . . . Then by what law could you be governed?

Ans. We are governed by Hindu Law.

As regards the efforts of the Hindu social reformers, Ambedkar said that they were speeches on the platform.

During these days Ambedkar could find very little time for his legal practice. Whenever he accepted a brief he diligently toiled for the success of his clients, though at times he seemed to be in a hurry to wind up his arguments in the court, and to leave early for some urgent political discussion or social work. But he never let down his clients. An example will bear out the truth of this remark. He had to argue in a murder case at the Thana Sessions Court as defence counsel on the very day when he was to give evidence before the Simon Commission at Poona. The case was very important as his clients were to be saved from the gallows. At the same time he could not forego the opportunity of giving evidence before the Simon Commission on behalf of his people. So he pleaded to the District Judge to allow him as a special favour to argue his case first though legally he would be called upon to reply to the arguments of the prosecution after the address of the Crown Counsel. The Judge agreed. And arguing his case ably, Ambedkar left for Poona, and his interview with the Simon Commission took place as said above. And so much confident was Ambedkar of his success that most of the accused were acquitted in that case.

Ambedkar was always watchful about the civic rights of the Depressed Classes, and he never missed an opportunity for educating his people to assert them even in the face of danger. Such an opportunity offered itself to them in Bombay, in September 1928, during the Ganesh Festival when the tussle arose between the reformist Hindus and the orthodox section over the question whether all Hindus had a right to worship the image of god Ganapati at a public place. But it was through the efforts and threats of Ambedkar, his social equality League and social reformers like Bole that the question was settled amicably, and the untouchable Hindus secured their right of worshipping the deity in the pandal.

Another activity that engaged Ambedkar's thoughts about this time was the first textile workers' strike in Bombay which brought the working of mills to a standstill for over six months involving 1,50,000 workers. The millowners had introduced a new system in the mills whereby one worker was required to work on three looms. So they resorted to retrenchment. The millhands resented this innovation and the new system The Girni Kamgar Mahamandal, one of the chief labour unions in Bombay, fanned the resentment and the strike began. During the strike workers belonging to the Depressed Classes were the worst sufferers; and they, the poorest of the poor, desired to be relieved of the gnawing trouble.

Ambedkar for his own part did not favour the strike. The fact that during the last eighty years of existence of the textile

mills the Depressed Classes were not allowed to work in any
profitable departments like weaving was troubling his mind. No
labour organisation had so far cared to remove this blot and
serious hindrance to the welfare of the Untouchables in the
textile industry. Besides, in Ambedkar's view communism and
strike were inseparable twins. He knew that the labour
movement was developing a new outlook and shedding its old
garb. His view therefore was that the labour movement did not
aim so much at the economic welfare of the labourers as at
political revolution. The weapon of strike was utilised for political
ends. This, in fact, worsened the economic condition of the
Depressed Classes. So Ambedkar was thinking of an independent
line of action.

The way out for the Depressed Class workers was to join
work. Mr. Frederick Stones, the manager of the group of E.D.
Sassoon Mills, encouraged Ambedkar to ask his men to call off
the strike and resume work. The latter took a courageous stand
with the help of Bole, who was one of the pioneer leaders in the
labour movement of Bombay, and moved through the dangerous
zones of the strike area. Ambedkar was living in the underworld
of Bombay for a decade, and so he knew the powers and
weaknesses of the labourers. Protected by a chosen party of
daredevils, he strove to bring his men back to work and in the
end succeeded to a great extent.

Those were the days of tension and bitter feelings. The
headquarters of the Trade Unions was in the vicinity of his office
and residence. He passed by the embittered crowds of workers
who used to sit on pavements. When he walked to and from his
residence for taking his meal, a select group of his men followed
and guarded him. One day, while returning from his residence
to his office he asked his men why they dogged his steps. They
remained quiet. Their eyes spoke of their devotion. But like the
Buddha, he said to them: "Stop this nonsense. Don't risk your
lives for me. Who would avert my death? There is no necessity
for taking such a great precaution." Yet the protection continued.

It may be recalled here that the evidence of Ambedkar before
the Simon Commission as detailed in the foregoing pages was
given during the strain of this strike. The British Labour leader,
Major Attlee, who later became the Prime Minister of Britain,
was a Member of the Simon Commission. Attlee asked Ambedkar

some pertinent questions in the course of the Doctor's examination. It is worthwhile to note here the exchange of views between them pertaining to the labour problem :[6]

Attlee : Are the members of the Depressed Classes working in industry, in cotton mills and so on?

Ambedkar : All of them. The Depressed Class men are all labourers.

Attlee : You have not got my point. I am talking of industry. You have members of the Depressed Classes who work in villages, for the most part in certain occupations. But are there large numbers of the Depressed Classes engaged in industry?

Ambedkar : A very large number.

Attlee : Do they cease in any degree to be Untouchables?

Ambedkar : No. The Depressed Class man is entirely left out of the Weaving Department, the most paying department He can only enter departments like the throstle department and others.

Attlee : Why?

Ambedkar : On account of untouchability.

Ill

The work of the Simon Commission continued till the winter. The Provincial Committees were also drafting their own reports. The Committee appointed by the Bombay Legislative Council to co-operate with the Simon Commission, after hearing both official and non-official evidence relating to the constitutional problem, submitted later their report on May 7, 1929. The report said that they were in full sympathy with the demand for separation of Sind, but for financial reasons, they said, it was impracticable. As for the separation of Karnatak, they observed that the demand was not a strong one. They suggested 10 reserved seats for the Depressed Classes with joint electorates and 33 per cent of elected seats out of 140 seats to the Muslims with separate electorates.

---

6. Indian Statutory Commission, Vol. XVI. p. 56.

Ambedkar, who fundamentally differed with the Committee, did not sign that report and submitted a separate Report[7] containing his own views and recommendations on May 17, 1929. Referring to the demand for the separation of Karnatak, he said he was opposed to the separation of Karnatak from the Bombay Presidency because "the principle of one language one province is too large to be given effect to in practice. The number of provinces that will have to be carved out if the principle is to be carried to its logical conclusion shows in my opinion its unworkability" "For I am of the opinion," declared the patriot in Ambedkar, "that the most vital need of the day is to create among the mass of the people the sense of a common nationality, the feeling not that they are Indians first and Hindus, Mohammedans or Sindhis and Kanarese afterwards, but that they are Indians first and Indians last. If that be the ideal then it follows that nothing should be done which will harden local patriotism and group consciousness."

As regards the separation of Sind which had assumed tremendous significance in those days, he said it was a sectional demand, a part of a large scheme designed to make the communal majority of the Muslims a political majority in five provinces. "The scheme," he warned the nation, "is neither so innocent nor so bootless as it appears on the surface." He asserted that the motive that lay behind the scheme was undoubtedly a dreadful one involving the maintenance of justice and peace by retaliation and had stemmed from the principle that the best way of keeping peace was to be prepared for war. To support his conclusions he quoted the address delivered to the Muslim League Session at Calcutta by the Gandhian nationalist Muslim leader, Maulana Azad, in which the Muslim leader said: "There would be nine Hindu Provinces as against five Muslim Provinces and whatever treatment Hindus accorded to the Muslims in the nine provinces, Muslims would accord the same treatment to the Hindus in the five provinces. Was not this a great gain? Was not a new weapon gained for the assertion of Muslim rights?" This is a search light on the Gandhian nationalist Muslim leaders.

Ambedkar then dealt with the Muslim demand for separate electorates. He described how different people in Europe lived under a common Government in proximity of each other without

---

7.   Indian Statutory Commission, Vol. III, Appendix D, pp. 87-156.

objecting to a common electorate. He observed: "It does not seem to be sufficiently known that India is not the only country where the Mohammedans are in a minority. There are other countries in which they occupy the same position. In Albania, the Mohammedans form a very large community. In Bulgaria, Greece and Romania they form a minority and in Yugoslavia and Russia they form a large majority. Have the Mohammedan communities there insisted upon the necessity of separate communal electorates? As all students of political history are aware, the Mohammedans in these countries have managed without the benefit of separate electorates; nay, they have managed without any definite ratio of representation assured to them. The Mohammedan case in India, therefore, overshoots the mark in my opinion and fails to carry conviction." The communal representation, he said, was so fundamentally wrong that to give in to sentiment in its case would be to perpetuate an evil.

Ambedkar further said: "Although I am for securing special representation for certain classes, I am against their represen-tation through separate electorates. Territorial electorates and separate electorates are the two extremes which must be avoided in any scheme of representation that may be devised for the introduction of a democratic form of Government in this undemo-cratic country. The golden mean is the system of joint electorates with reserved seats. Less than that would be insufficient, more than that would defeat the ends of good Government."

The report, viewed in the context of principles, theories and personalities then prevailing, was as rationalistic as it was patriotic. It had both a balance and a ballast. When it was published, it derived spontaneous eulogy from Ambedkar's inveterate foes, obstinate critics and the hostile press. Ambedkar was found overnight to be a great politician, a great patriot, a diamond in the abysmal coal-mine of the Untouchables, a statesman of rare gift. Like a meteor and a mentor, he emerged as one of the great political minds of his generation. Thus this Report bound him to the active destinies of his country! It will be a sure guide to historians.

❑❑❑

CHAPTER 8

LAND, LABOUR, EDUCATION

ALTHOUGH circumstances demanded the major portion of Ambedkar's efforts, energy and talents in the struggle for securing the constitutional and legislative rights for his people, he was always conscious of the backwardness of his people in education, which was the strongest need and the greatest weapon to forge their progress. So he tried every possible means to disseminate education among his people. He started two hostels in the beginning of June 1928, and closing down the Bahishkrit Hitakarini Sabha on June 14, 1928, he established the Depressed Classes Education Society to organise the school education of his community on a sound basis. He appealed to the Bombay Government to help the Depressed Classes Education Society in its work of providing hostels for the benefit of students of the Depressed Classes, who were unable to bear the burden of High School education.

Government approved of a scheme on October 8, 1928, and the Governor declared that he would sanction a scheme for five hostels for the special benefit of Secondary school students belonging to the Depressed Classes.

Ambedkar's Education Society was a recognised institution under the Charitable Society's Registration Act XXI of 1861. It was governed by a Board of Trustees which had for its Members Meyer Nissim, Shankar Sayenna Parsha, Dr. Purushottam Solanki and Ambedkar, and was assisted by an Advisory Board consisting of nineteen Members. Ambedkar himself was the General Secretary, and Shivtarkar, the Secretary and Treasurer. These Members were very sincere persons surcharged with the ideas and energy of their leader. Naturally their efforts and sincerity instilled confidence in Government; so it entrusted this Society with the management of the proposed five new hostels involving a grant of Rs. 9,000 per annum.

The Government grant-in-aid was, however, insufficient to meet the expenses. So Ambedkar had to collect donations from different quarters. He approached generous-minded public, enlightened local bodies, charitable institutions and magnanimous personalities for help. Presidents of some District Local Boards and Municipalities showed active sympathy for this deserving cause by reducing fees for the Depressed Class students, granting free land for building hostels and in such other ways.

The Society provided students with boarding and lodging and with funds enough to meet the students' other requirements in the schools. The caste Hindu institutions were indifferent to this problem. So the pressing need drove Ambedkar to the Muslims. He tapped some Muslim quarters. In one such appeal to the Muslim quarters he wrote to the managing trustees of a Charity Fund in July 1929, giving details about his institution and said that the aim of the Education Society was to do all that was possible to spread education among the Depressed Classes of the Bombay Presidency. He also approached Parsee Charitable Institutions. A few months later, in his application to the Secretary of the N. M. Wadia Charities he wrote: "The Society has found it considerably difficult to collect this amount from the Depressed Classes on account of their poverty or from the high class Hindus on account of their apathy, if not antipathy, towards the Depressed Classes. In fact the Society has run into debt for keeping the hostels."

The Society found it very difficult to house its boarders. No caste Hindu landlord would easily let his house for the purpose, and in case he did so it was at a very high rent and that too as a favour. Always worried with this problem, Ambedkar had to make personal appeals to different Members of the local bodies and prominent men in the Districts. Appeals flowed unceasingly. To one Member, whom Ambedkar desired to help the Society to procure aid to the hostel from a District Local Board, he said: "Elevation of the Depressed Classes is recognised to be the cause of all the enlightened people in the country." To another Member whom he prevailed upon to attend a certain meeting of the District Local Board when the problem of education of the Depressed Classes was to come up for discussion, he wrote in a very appealing tone: "The cause is the cause of the Depressed Classes, and in that sense it is your cause as much as it is mine; and I need hardly press you to keep yourself alive to it."

When the leaders of enslaved humanity rise to lift up their race, those who resort to the political side of the movement arouse hatred of slavery and fan the slaves' passion against their oppressors; but the leaders, who are of reformative zeal, bend inward and preach the doctrine of education of the head, heart and hand. Booker T. Washington, the founder of the Tuskegee Institution and leader of the Negro race, laid more stress on the practical education and economic development than on the right of vote. He, too, took advantage of the benevolence, sympathies and practical help from other races. He attached more importance to the education and economic development of the Negroes. Here in India, owing to the rising leadership of Ambedkar in the domain of politics, his attention was for some days diverted from the education of the Depressed Classes. The reason was perhaps that there was something in Ambedkar that motivated him, like Napoleon Bonaparte, to astonish and electrify his great contemporaries and to show that he was an equal of those who ranked the highest on earth. To such an ambitious nature politics is a more congenial field than a social one.

Moreover, Ambedkar had his own diagnosis of the Indian situation. The jobs in the lower categories of services and military that were demanded by Ambedkar for the Depressed Classes were not enough to raise them in the scale of life. Ambedkar knew well that the more the education, the more the chances for progress and the easier the opportunities for his people. But since he thought that by investing his people with political equality and political power the problem of their education would be automatically solved through Governmental efforts and agencies, he devoted his time and talent more to securing political rights than to securing educational uplift.

The problem of education of the Untouchables was beset with difficulty from one more side. In spite of Government directive in the matter of admission, children of the Depressed Classes were refused admission to schools. Ambedkar had to fight out the issue in schools. Karmaveer Shinde and Veer Savarkar also were struggling to secure the right of the Depressed Classes of Maharashtra to have their children educated along with the caste Hindu children and were successful to a great extent.

II

In the first week of February, Ambedkar presided over a vast meeting at Valpakhadi, Bombay, which was attended by Maharashtrian and Gujarati Depressed Classes. In the course of his speech he exhorted them to struggle hard to gain material relief and comfort in this world, to attain equal status with other human societies under the sun, and to absolve the Hindu Society of a great sin.

As Professor of Law, the impression he made on his students was lasting and enthralling. Deep, devoted and endowed with a vast knowledge on the subject, he taught his classes constitutional law in a thought-provoking manner His term of office, however, terminated at the end of March 1929. For the next four years the Doctor-professor was drawn into the vortex of politics and was occupied with the discussion on the constitutional reforms for India which were hammered on the anvil of the Round Table Conference and the Joint Committee.

During the second and third quarters of 1929, Ambedkar attended and guided a number of conferences. In April 1929 he was invited to preside over the Ratnagiri District Conference at Chiplun. Great efforts had to be made for securing a site for the Conference pandal. Fear lurked in the minds of the orthodox Hindus that there would be a repetition of the Mahad incident, and the untouchable Hindus might pollute their wells if the Conference was held in their town. So they closed their wells with great care and caution as if there were an enemy raid. Ambedkar and his party put up for two days at the Dak Bungalow in Chiplun.

Men of progressive leanings like Vinayakrao Barve and B. G. Khatu, two local pleaders, attended the Conference. Omswami Ragji welcomed the delegates and stressed the necessity for a broader outlook on the part of the caste Hindus. In his Presidential address to the Conference Ambedkar said: "You must abolish your slavery yourselves. It is disgraceful to live at the cost of one's self-respect. Self-respect is a most vital factor in life. Without it man is a mere cipher. To live worthily with self-respect one has to overcome difficulties. It is out of hard and ceaseless struggle alone that one derives strength, confidence and recognition." He then referred to the land system of Konkan called Khoti, which sucked their blood, and promised them to strive his utmost for the abolition of that system. Telling them that he was prepared to go through any ordeal for their good, he declared: "My life was threatened if I came here to wake you up to the causes of your misery and shame. Man is mortal. Every one is to die some day or other. But one must resolve to lay down one's life in enriching the noble ideals of self-respect and in bettering human life. We are not slaves. We are a warrior clan. Nothing is more disgraceful for a brave man than to live a life devoid of self-respect and without love for the country."

He then suggested that his people should migrate to some better and distant lands, if they wished to be relieved of the oppression at the hands of caste Hindus and Hindu landlords. He said he would try to secure them land for cultivation in Sind and in the Indore State. He cited the examples of their Muslim neighbours, who went to Africa and returned to Konkan as rich men. The idea of migration to Sind must have occurred to Ambedkar when he visited Sind to survey, in company with other councillors, the Sukkur barrage which was expected to turn thousands of acres of the desert land into a fertile agricultural region. His new contract with the Maharaja of Indore must have made him hopeful of securing some land for the Untouchables.

At, the conclusion of the Conference, sacred threads were distributed among the delegates. Deorao Naik, a Brahmin colleague of Ambedkar, acted as an Acharya and invested about 6,000 delegates with the sacred threads amid the singing of Vedic hymns.

At night Ambedkar was cordially invited by Vinayakrao Barve to dinner. He attended it saying that one should participate in such an inter-caste dinner not because one attained salvation when one dined in company with the Brahmins, but because such dinners smoothened social intercourse and fostered the principle of equality.

The next day Ambedkar presided over an Agricultural Conference at the same place. Delivering his address, he told the people that he had now come to believe that the purpose of his life was to struggle for the welfare of the downtrodden. He said that he came of a poor family and had lived among the poor in an Improvement Trust Chawl in Bombay. "I know your grievances," Ambedkar continued, "the Khoti system is sucking your blood. This system of land tenure must be abolished. Its abolition will bring you peace and progress. In order to achieve your goal you must keep the agitation going on. India is likely to attain full control of its destines in the coming four or five years. At that time you must take particular care to send to the Legislatures the right type of men as your representatives who would devoutly struggle for the abolition of this Khoti system."

On his return from Chiplun to Bombay, Ambedkar again set on foot his movement against the textile strike sponsored by the Girni Kamgar Union in obedience to whose call the textile workers of Bombay had resolved to go on strike. Undeterred by the great fiasco in its first attempt, the left wing of the communists compelled the mill workers in Bombay to resort to strike a second time from April 26, 1929. The cause of this discontent lay in the replacement of a number of workers in the mills as a result of the previous strike. Ambedkar, who believed in the workers right to strike, said that the weapon of strike should be used sparingly and to the advantage of the workers, and not for political objectives of the communist leaders. With his characteristic boldness he reiterated his view that the communists were impelled to resort to a strike more with political objectives than with the object of bettering the lot of the workers.

Ambedkar's opposition to the communist-inspired strike was greater than ever because of the fact that the communist leaders had never raised their voice against the prohibitive barriers that kept the Depressed Class workers away from the lucrative departments in the Mill industry on account of untouchability. The second reason why he was not in favour of the strike was that the condition of the Depressed Class workers had been already worsened by the previous strike with the result that the creditors' and the money-lenders' grip was more tightened on their necks and honour. Ambedkar, therefore, declared that it was their right to resort to strike with a view to bettering their conditions. There should be a change for the better, he continued, but it should be effected without doing any further harm to the interests of the workers. The disease should be cured without impairing the condition of the patient, he concluded.[1]

---

1. *The Bahishkrit Bharat*, 31 May 1929.

Ambedkar, with two other labour leaders, R. R. Bakhale and Shyamrao Parulekar, carried a very extensive propaganda to counteract the propaganda of the Girni Kamgar Union. The Textile Labour Union called a meeting of workers on April 29, 1929, at the Damodar Hall, Bombay. Ambedkar presided over the meeting which concluded after passing a resolution against launching the strike.

While this labour conflict was going on, Ambedkar addressed a big Conference at Chitegaon. In his address he told his people that education was not the only factor that counted in keeping up one's self-respect. If one's achievement in the academic world had been sufficient to evoke due respect for oneself, he, and others like him, would not have been ill-treated by men of learning and authority in society. He made a fervent appeal to the delegates to get over the obstacles that beset their path and remove the stigma of untouchability from their life.

Yet another important Conference was awaiting Ambedkar's guidance at Jalgaon. It was convened by the Depressed Classes of Central Provinces and Berar on May 29, 1929. Though Ambedkar was very busy with the strike affairs in Bombay, he snatched some time to preside over the Conference. It was at this Conference that a resolution was passed stressing the need for embracing some other religion in the event of continued disregard for their condition by the caste Hindus. In this concluding speech Ambedkar told the Conference bluntly that it was quite impossible for them to get their disabilities removed by remaining in the Hindu fold. So he advised such of them as could endure no longer the pangs of poverty, misery and disabilities, to embrace some other religion for the betterment of their lot and honour, if their disabilities were not removed by the caste Hindus before a prescribed date. The next day Ambedkar returned to Bombay as the strike situation demanded his presence in Bombay

The feeler, however, was not taken seriously by the Jalgaon Hindus. They thought it was a ruse aimed at bargaining for more civic rights by working on the feelings of the caste Hindus in a puerile manner. But the time limit expired, and about twelve Mahars embraced Islam in the first week of June 1929. This put the sanatani reformers to consternation. Their eyes opened to the realities and reason for some time. Those who held that the stigma of pollution disappeared with the death of a Mahar were moved to throw open two wells to the Depressed Classes without delay or demur. Ambedkar said that it was a belated step and not a spontaneous gesture and therefore did not flatter the caste Hindus. He further observed that had Hindu society shown a sense of justice, equality and humanity, they would not have allowed matters to come to such a pass. But thanks, he exclaimed, to the pressure of Muslim and Christian religions, the Depressed Classes were deriving some benefits.

These conferences gave a fillip to Ambedkar's movement. The Depressed Classes adopted more drastic measures in their internal boycott of the defaulters of their vows. As they refused to carry away dead animals and wore the sacred threads, the high caste Hindus harassed them in every possible way. In response to their complaints and grievances, at a public meeting in Bombay, under the Presidentship of Bole, Ambedkar sounded a warning to the oppressors against harassing the Depressed Classes.

A controversy raged over the activities of the Social Equality League conducted by Ambedkar and his friends. Those who were perturbed by its broad and revolutionary ideal bitterly criticised the institution. In a detailed reply to the criticism Ambedkar observed that the man who practised what he preached was worthy of reverence. But a good principle never suffered because some men holding it did not show the requisite courage to practise it. Yet there were some who said that inequality would never disappear from the face of the earth. Ambedkar asked them why they preached morality to the people when immorality had prevailed at all times and in all climes. He expressed his confirmed view that the principle of social equality is the cornerstone of a stable society. To establish society on a sound foundation of morality it is necessary to apply to all the component parts of the society the principle of equality in all fields, religious, social, political and economic, he added.

In the month of September Ambedkar went to Ratnagiri in connection with a murder trial at the Sessions Court. Savarkar seized this opportunity and extended to Ambedkar an invitation signed by hundreds of citizens to address a meeting. At the

Vithoba temple, a very important centre where battles for social reforms had been fought and won by Savarkarites. The reactionaries ran for an injunction. The question became the talk of the town. Just then Ambedkar received a wire from Bombay demanding his presence, and Ratnagiri lost an opportunity of vitriolic and valuable speeches on one platform by India's two great revolutionaries.

This year again Ambedkar fought for the right of worshipping the image of Ganapati at a public place, in Bombay. The President of the Dadar Sarvajanik Ganesh Festival informed the Social Equality League that the Committee had now revoked their last year's decision; and so no untouchable Hindu would be allowed in or near the room where the image was to be installed. The atmosphere became tense on the morning of the image installation day. The organisers of the festival had taken the utmost precaution, called the police, and posted hooligans in the pandal. About 1,000 untouchable Hindus collected outside the pandal demanding admission. Ambedkar, Bole and other local leaders appeared on the scene. With difficulty Ambedkar prevailed upon the huge crowd to keep calm and opened negotiations with the orthodox leader, Dr. Javle. The leader of the Untouchables pleaded for ordinary human rights. The talks seemed to prove unavailing and the situation grew threatening. At last when the orthodox leaders saw that every minute the crowd was pressing in, they revised their decision at three in the afternoon, and the Untouchables marched in with triumph and rejoicings.

Ill

The leader of the Depressed Classes was now busy with the proceedings of the Starte Committee appointed by the Bombay Government following a resolution by Dr. P.G. Solanki, to inquire into the education, economic and social condition of the Depressed Classes (Untouchables) and Aboriginal Tribes of the Presidency, and to recommend measures for their uplift. A.V. Thakkar, better known as Thakkar Bappa, was on this Committee with Ambedkar and Solanki. As a Member of the Committee, Ambedkar visited Belgaum, Khandesh and Nasik Districts. Although a Member of the Committee, Ambedkar himself experienced insulting treatment during his tours. The headmaster of a Primary Local Board School did not allow him to enter the class-rooms. On a complaint from a guardian, Ambedkar had paid this visit to that school to see why that boy was not allowed to sit in the class and why he was made to sit in the verandah. The second incident happened when the Members of the Committee were touring East Khandesh.

At Chalisgaon, his people gave Ambedkar a reception and wanted to take him to their locality. But all the tonga-drivers refused to carry the untouchable leader. As a compromise, a tonga-driver allowed an Untouchable to drive the tonga. But he being unaccustomed to the work of a driver, the horse bolted, and Ambedkar was thrown on the stone pavement severely injured. Writing about it a month later, Ambedkar said: "The tonga in which I was travelling on October 23, 1929, overturned and I was thrown out. Owing to this accident one of the bones of my right foot was fractured. As a result of this fracture I was confined to bed till the last week of December and though I am in a position to move about I cannot do so without the help of a stick."[2]

The Starte Committee later, in March 1930, submitted its report in which it said that although the Depressed Classes observed Hindu rites, laws and festivals, they were obliged to live in a state of isolation which prevented social osmosis and resulted in servility. The Committee observed that common schools would facilitate their schooling, and recommended an increase in scholarships and hostels for the Depressed Class students attending secondary schools; provision of scholarships for Industrial training of apprentices in Mills and Railway workshops, and a scholarship for studying abroad in Engineering works; and the appointment of a special officer to look after these arrangements.

The Committee further recommended due representation on village co-operative societies, a Money-lenders' Act and Provident Fund for the Municipal conservancy staff. It recommended that the Depressed Class members be recruited to Police and Military services and that provision be made for their housing accommodation in the cities. The Committee opined that deforested lands and waste lands be made over to the

---

2. Ambedkar's letter dated 8 December 1920 to the Director of Public Instruction, Poona.

Depressed Classes, and the Sukkur barrage scheme be utilised for their amelioration.

Although, for a while, the accident had made Ambedkar unfit for outdoor work, he was not idle. One of the chief attributes of greatness is indefatigable energy. He wrote a brilliant article on the abolition of priesthood. A Parsee gentleman had written a very pungent article against Parsee priests in the *Bombay Chronicle* in October 1929, stressing the need for an association the prime object of which would be the abolition of priesthood as a caste.

Supporting the move in his article entitled " Wanted an Anti-Priest Craft Association", Ambedkar wrote in the *Bombay Chronicle*[3] that the Hindu priestly classes stood in no way superior ethically, educationally or otherwise to the average member of Parsee priesthood. "The counts in the indictment," he proceeded, "against the hereditary Hindu priests are numerous and appalling. He is a clog on the wheel of civilisation. Man is born, becomes the father of a family and then in time dies. All along the priest shadows him like an evil genius."

Ambedkar described the officiating Brahmin as a miserable specimen of humanity and further said: "He practises the sham of being a middleman between the unseen powers and the helpless man and makes a living by it." "Be it an occasion of joy like a wedding or of sorrow like death," he went on, "it is equally availed of by the priests, many of whom pray, as one of the Parsee correspondents has excellently shown, in order to be able to prey on their victims." And quoting the appropriate remarks of the Parsee writer who said that a dead Parsee was economically a heavier burden on the poor family than a living one, Ambedkar concluded his article by appealing to the enlightened Hindus, Mohammedans and Christians to initiate means for ridding India of the evil of priestcraft, and hoping that they would join that heroic and noble task of cleansing priesthood, the weight of which they were certainly far less fitted to bear than the Parsee brethren.

About this time the Poona Depressed Class leaders Shivram Janba Kamble and Rajbhoj, in consultation with some Poona caste Hindu leaders like V. V. Sathe, Deshdas Ranade, G.N. Kanitkar, Keshavrao Jedhe and N.V. Gadgil—who later became

---

3. The *Bombay Chronicle*, 8 November 1929.

a Minister for Works and Mines in the first Cabinet of Free India—launched satyagraha in the second week of October to establish the Depressed Classes right of worshipping the deity in the famous temple of Parvati in Poona. The opponents of temple entry movement raised threatening cries and pelted the satyagrahis with stones with a result that Gadgil, Ranade and some Aryasamaj leaders were bruised, and Rajbhoj was severely injured and was taken to hospital.

Public meetings were held, and a strong protest was voiced against the conduct of the orthodox Hindus towards the satya-grahis. Ambedkar was busy with the proceedings of the State Committee, and because the Movement was dominated by caste Hindu leaders he must have kept aloof. Yet at a meeting in Bombay he made a very stirring speech in which he said that it was not only the duty of the Depressed Classes in Bombay to lend their whole-hearted support to the Poona Depressed Classes in their fight for elementary human rights, but also to give financial help and to prepare themselves to go to Poona in batches to strengthen the satyagraha, if need be. Ambedkar said he could not help deprecating the mentality of those, who put in the plea: "wait for some time and await the change of heart on the part of the touchables". The Indian National Congress, he observed, had given an ultimatum to the British Parliament to grant Dominion Status by 31st December 1929. "Is there then," retorted Ambedkar "any sense in asking the Depressed Classes to wait any longer in establishing an ordinary human right to enter a place of worship?" In the end he declared that a similiar agitation would be launched by him in Bombay; and he, as the President of the Samata Sangh, would see that it was brought to a successful termination.

The Poona satyagraha was not, however, the first of its kind. Savarkar had launched such a movement in Ratnagiri, and similar struggles were launched at Karwar, Amraoti, Munshigunj, and Khulna in Bengal. The Poona satyagraha was resumed, but it was withdrawn as the temple was kept closed. Ambedkar did not abandon the idea of launching a struggle on this issue.

☐☐☐

CHAPTER 9

BEFORE THE BAR OF WORLD OPINION

In the history of India the year 1930 was a year of action and reaction. It brought forth a new line of thinking and a new angle of approach; new measures of repression and new methods of rapprochement. Better still, it was the age of satyagraha. It was in this year that Mahatma Gandhi as the generalissimo of the Congress inaugurated his great movement for the liberation of the country on March 12, 1930, and transformed the whole country into a theatre of passive resistance, vast crowds facing battalions of mounted police, rounds of firing and terms of jail life.

Ten days before the Dandi March of Gandhi, Ambedkar, the father of Indian social unrest, launched his temple entry movement at Nasik. Preparations for this movement had been going on for over three months. Ambedkar was guiding, inspiring and organising it from Bombay through his letters and lieutenants. The Depressed Classes at Nasik had formed a Satyagraha Committee and through its Secretary, Bhaurao Gaikwad, informed the Trustees of the famous Kalaram Temple that they would launch satyagraha, if the Trustees did not throw the temple open to the untouchable Hindus before a particular date. Simultaneously, a clarion call was issued to the Depressed Classes to come to Nasik to assert their right of worshipping Shree Rama in the said temple. In response to this call of the Satyagraha Committee, about 15,000 volunteers and representatives assembled in a specially erected pandal in the Depressed Classes locality at Nasik. Notable among those present were Deorao Naik, Rajbhoj, Pradhan, Shivtarkar, Patitpavandas and B.G. Kher.

At last the day of action dawned. It was Sunday, March 2. 1930. In the morning at ten, a Conference was held under the presidentship of Ambedkar in the pandal to consider, the situation and adopt ways and means for launching the satyagraha. At noon the Conference adjourned and again met at half past one.

At three in the afternoon, the congregation divided itself into batches of four extending itself over a mile-long procession. It was the biggest procession in the history of Nasik. At the head played a band after the military style redolent of the association of many of the Depressed Class members with military life. Then followed a batch of scouts. Behind them walked about 500 women satyagrahis showing a revolutionary change in their outlook; and they were followed by a multitude of processionists enthused with an exalted spirit, but walking with a full sense of discipline, order and determination. As soon as the procession came up to the eastern gate of the temple, the District Magistrate, the Police Superintendent and the City Magistrate moved towards the gate of the temple. As all the gates of the temple were closed, the processionists proceeded to the Godawari Ghat. There the procession transformed itself into a meeting.

At eleven o'clock that night the leaders again discussed the issue in all its aspects and decided to launch a non-violent struggle before the gates of the temple. This historic struggle thus commenced on the morning of March 3, 1930. The first batch of 125 men and 25 women was posted at the four gates of the temple, and over 8,000 enlisted satyagrahis were awaiting their turn. But the gates of the temple were closed and barricaded. While the satyagrahis squatted at the entrance, chanting hymns and singing bhajans, crowds of Untouchables numbering over 3,000 gathered in their vicinity; but the police were on the alert and kept them on the move. A strong force of armed police was posted at each gate. Two First Class Magistrates were on duty at the place since early morning to meet any emergency. Reynalds, the Police Superintendent, had shifted his office to a tent pitched right in front of the temple.

The touchables, too, were precluded from entering the temple as the gates remained closed, and their leaders were deliberating behind closed doors to find a way out of the impasse. A difficult situation would have developed had the gates been opened to the caste Hindus.

At night, a public meeting of the citizens of Nasik was held under the presidentship of Dr. Kurtakoti, the Shankaracharya, but it ended in pandemonium due to the predominance of the orthodox people. The sanatanists by now had got panicky and rowdy. They pelted the meeting with stones and shoes. It was felt that even Rama himself would be thrown aside, if he were to tell the orthodox Hindus to throw open the temple to the Untouchables!

The satyagraha struggle continued for about a month. April 9 dawned. It was the day of the chariot procession of the image of Rama. A compromise was patched up between the caste Hindus and the Untouchables. It was decided that strong men from both sides should draw the chariot. Thousands of people assembled at noon near the main gate of the temple to see the sight. Ambedkar, with his choice gymnasts, stood near the gate. But before they could touch the chariot, they were engaged in broils by the riotous element of the caste Hindus, and the caste Hindus ran away with the chariot, as secretly planned, through a street, narrow, thorny and inconvenient on either side, and the mouth of which was guarded by armed police. A daring Bhandari youth by name Kadrekar broke the cordon of the armed police who were awaiting orders to fire, and in a moment crowds of Untouchables pursued the chariot amidst showers of stones and captured it. Dangerously wounded, Kadrekar fell down in a pool of blood. Ambedkar was protected by his men. and as the umbrellas that protected his person were shattered, he, too, received minor injuries. There was free fighting between groups of Untouchables and caste Hindus all over the city.

This satyagraha provoked considerable ill-feeling in the minds of the orthodox Hindus throughout the District. As a result of this tension children of the Untouchables were thrown out of schools, roads were closed to them, and necessaries of life were denied to them in the market because they claimed equal rights with all other Hindus. Untouchables in several villages were maltreated. Despite these sufferings, the struggle at Nasik was carried on. Attempts were being made to persuade both the parties to reach a compromise. Dr. Moonje and Dr. Kurtakoti, the Shankaracharya, were trying to reach a settlement. The great multi-millionaire Birla also saw Ambedkar in Bombay in the middle of April 1930. But so firm was the resolve of the Depressed Classes that orthodox Hindus had to keep the famous temple closed for a whole year, and the agitation continued right up to the end of October 1935.

II

While this Nasik satyagraha was going on, the Depressed Class leaders were thinking of holding an all-India Congress immediately after the publication of the report of the Simon Commission. Accordingly, a Reception Committee was formed in Nagpur under the chairmanship of K. G. Nadgooli. The Committee decided, in consultation with Kamble, the 'Poona leader', to hold the Depressed Classes Congress at Nagpur under the presidentship of Ambedkar, and it also unanimously decided to depute him to London as the representative of the Depressed Classes for the Round Table Conference.

At long last, the report of the Simon Commission came out in May 1930. The Commission disregarded the meaning and aim of Indian nationalism and its forces. It deliberately ignored the Indian view. It recommended a continuation of separate electorates in Indian elections for want of any agreed pact among the Indian political parties. It was the opinion of the Commission that the Nehru Report was not an agreed solution.

It allocated 150 seats to the Hindus including the Depressed Classes out of a total of 250 in the Central Legislature, i.e. 60 per cent. They also proposed for the Depressed Classes joint electorates with reservation of seats; but no candidate of the Depressed Classes was to be allowed to stand for election unless his fitness was certified by the Governor of the Province.

Busy with multifarious activities, Ambedkar did not show much interest in the day-to-day legislative work. During the February-March session of the Bombay Legislative Council, he attended it only for five days. The Nasik struggle had engaged his mind. Only one interpellation stood in his name on the Council Agenda and that was about the grants-in-aid to Secondary Schools. In the middle of May 1930, the Patro Committee appointed by the All-Party Conference met in Bombay. Ambedkar was invited to attend its meeting, which he did. The Committee, however, failed to reach an agreement on the Hindu-Muslim question and on the minorities problem.

Ambedkar attended the July-August session of the Bombay Legislative Council upto July 19, 1930, but did not participate in the Council proceedings. He avoided any commitment being made prior to the Nagpur Depressed Classes Congress regarding the demand put forward by the Indian National Congress or the British denial to it.

As arranged, the first session of the Depressed Classes Congress was held at Nagpur on August 8, 1930, under the presidentship of Ambedkar. In the course of his presidential address Ambedkar declared that it was possible for the people of India to become one united self-governing community. If Yugoslavia, Estonia, Czechoslovakia, Hungary, Latvia, Lithuania and Russia with all their differences in race, creed, language and culture, could function as united self-governing communities, he said, there was no reason why India could not. But he affirmed that the diversity of conditions and peoples prevalent in India must be taken into account while framing the constitution for a self-governing India. He expressed great concern at the probability of caste-ridden Hindu oligarchy being granted unrestricted power.

No country, he observed, was good enough to rule another, and it was equally true that no class was good enough to rule over another. As the fundamental principle of the modern democratic state was the recognition of the value of the individual and the belief was that each individual had but one life, full opportunity should be accorded to each to attain his maximum development in that life. But the living and operative faith, he pointed out, of the oligarchy in India was against this ideal. It was also an erroneous belief to think that the social and the political were two separate compartments of human conduct, having no interaction between them. The Indian aristocracy which was clamouring for power had been responsible for the continuance of the curse of untouchability under which six crores of people were denied elementary human rights and the benefits of civilization and culture; and an equally large population of aboriginal and hill tribes were left to roam in a nomadic and barbaric state.

Ambedkar, therefore, demanded adequate safeguards for the down-trodden Untouchables in the Constitution and pleaded for direct representation in the Councils commensurate with the strength of the Depressed Class community.

Coming to the recommendations of the Simon Commission as affecting the Depressed Classes, President Ambedkar

denounced the proviso that authorised the Governor to certify
the fitness of a candidate and to select even a non-Depressed-
Class member to represent the Depressed Classes, and
thundered: "This is nothing else than nomination pure and
simple. If he chooses only one candidate in a constituency, there
is no election." Ambedkar, therefore, exhorted his people:
"Demand the right to elect our own representatives of our choice,
untrammelled by any condition or limitation whatsoever. We are
certainly the best judges of our interests, and we must not allow
even the Governor to assume the authority to determine what is
good for us."

Ambedkar then referred to the Indian demand for freedom
and declared: "The ideal of Dominion Status seems to me
superior, for it has in it the substance of independence without
the attendant risks involved in complete independence."

As regards the Civil Disobedience Movement, then launched
by Gandhi, with his magnificent colourful Dandi March and
which had resulted in the incarceration of thousands of Indians,
Ambedkar said that he was opposed to it because it was extremely
inopportune.

The Civil Disobedience Movement was a movement of mass
action; its essence was coercion; it was a method of stampede,
which, he said, if carried out on a sufficiently large scale, was
bound to end in a revolt. A revolution—bloody or bloodless, made
no difference—was a method of change which was most uncertain
in its issue and in which the danger of confusion and disaster in
the process was very great. Revolutions were often inevitable.
All the same they must not forget the vast difference that
separated a revolution from real social change. A revolution
transferred political power from one party to another, or one
nation to another. The Depressed Classes should not be satisfied
with an empty change. The transfer of power must be
accompanied by such distribution of power that the result would
be a real social change in the relative strength of the forces
operating in society.

But did the leader of the Depressed Classes of India spare
the British Government at Nagpur? No. Like Ranade, he
regarded the advent of the British in India as providential, and
responsible for the intellectual awakening and the concept of
liberty, equality and fraternity. It made the Indians feel the

shame of the social customs and moral code and forced upon them the revaluation of its social values, besides giving a, common system of Law and a common system of Government. Yet he boldly described the British Government in India as the costliest Government in the world, and he asked his people whether there was any parallel to the poverty of the Indian people in any part of the world. "In the first quarter of the 19th century when British Rule in India had become an established fact, there were five famines with an estimated loss of 1,000,000 lives. During the second quarter there were six famines with a recorded loss of life of 5,000,000. And during the last quarter of the century what do you find? Eighteen famines with an estimated mortality, which reached the awful total between 15,000,000 and 26,000,000." In plain terms, he asserted, the cause of this chronic poverty was the deliberate policy pursued by the British Government in the conduct of the Government of this country, and although he paid his meed of praise to the British Government in India for maintaining law and order, he said: "But we cannot forget that people, including the Depressed Classes, do not live on law and order; what they live on is bread and butter."

Ambedkar, therefore, warned his people that all their wrongs could not be righted as long as the British Government remained in power. "It is only in a Swaraj constitution," he observed, "that you stand any chance of getting political power in your hands without which you cannot bring salvation to our people. Do not be obsessed by the past. Do not be swayed by fear or favour from any quarter in making your own decision. Consult your best interests and I am sure you will accept Swaraj as your goal."

Ambedkar further said that the Congress did not prescribe the removal of untouchability as a franchise for its membership; nor did Gandhi set out on a crusade against untouchability; nor did he fast for a charitable feeling between the Untouchables and the caste Hindus. The safety of the Depressed Classes lay in being independent of the Government and the Congress. "We must shape," he declared, "our course ourselves and by ourselves." They should ventilate their grievances through a central organisation. For ages they had remained dumb. They could not, with justice, blame the Government or the reformers for their condition.

Ambedkar added that the Congress was a national movement and not a political party. He had no doubt that when the time for test came, many a Congressman would be in the camp of the classes and not of the masses.

Although Ambedkar insisted upon the necessity of securing political power, he said: "But I must take this opportunity to emphasize that political power cannot be a panacea for the ills of the Depressed Classes. Their salvation lies in their social elevation. They must cleanse their evil habits. They must improve their bad ways of living. By a change of their mode of life they must be made fit for respect and friendship. They must be educated. Mere knowledge of the three R's is insufficient for the great height many of them must reach in order that the whole community may along with them rise in the general estimation. There is a great necessity to disturb their pathetic contentment and to instil into them that divine discontent which is the spring of all elevation."

Concluding his speech, Ambedkar said that the movement "will result in the emancipation of our people and the establishment of such a state of society in this country of ours in which one man will have one value in all domains of life, political, social and economic."

This declaration of political independence was a definite departure from the old policy, a landmark in the history of the movement carried on by Untouchables. In its early stage the leaders of the movement appealed to the British Government not to grant political independence to the country. After the advent of Ambedkar's leadership, they struggled and fought for social equality and political rights, and in 1930 they declared their belief in political independence! Another memorable statement made by Ambedkar at this Congress was that he told his audience that he would not abjure Hindu religion whatever might be the hardships inflicted upon him by the caste Hindus.

Seeing that Ambedkar had turned against the Government, some of the newspapers appreciated this change in his attitude. The *Kesari*, one of the leading newspapers in Maharashtra, taunted Ambedkar by quoting Caesar's remark, 'and you too, Brutus?'[1] It was characteristic of Ambedkar that he emitted both heat and light in his speech. Bitterness never clouded his vision

---

1. *The Kesari*, 30 August 1930.

when he spoke of the Indian problem in the context of British imperialism or world affairs. Didactic, drastic and anxious while dissecting political and social problems, his patriotic heart never stopped its throbs. Shortly after the Nagpur Congress, Ambedkar fell ill, and in his unconscious state he spoke about the fate of his people. The fever abated and he soon recovered.

III

As declared, the British Government convened a Round Table Conference in London consisting of the representatives of India, the British Government and the British Political parties to frame a constitution for India with a view to satisfying the demands of the people of India.

The Round Table Conference consisted of eighty-nine Members, out of which sixteen were representatives of the three British parties, fifty-three Indian Members of the delegation representing various interests except the non-co-operating Congress, and twenty of the Indian States. Amongst the invitees were thirteen eminent Hindu liberal leaders including Sir Tej Bahadur Sapru, M. R. Jayakar, Sir Chimanlal Setalvad, Srinivas Sastri and C. Y. Chintamani. Representing the Muslims, were H.H. the Aga Khan, Sir Muhamed Shafi, Mohomed Ali Jinnah, and Fazlul Huq, while Sardar Ujjal Singh represented the Sikhs, Dr. B.S. Moonje, the Hindu Mahasabha, K.T. Paul, the Indian Christians. Rulers of Alwar, Baroda, Bhopal, Bikaner, Kashmir, Patiala and Sir Akbar Hydari, Sir C. P. Ramaswamy Aiyar, Sir Mirza Ismail represented the Indian States. Sir A.P. Patro and Bhaskarrao V. Jadhav represented other interests; Ambedkar and Rao Bahadur Srinivasan represented the Depressed Classes.

Ambedkar received the invitation to the Round Table Conference through the Viceroy on September 6, 1930. The Round Table Conference was indeed a great event in the history of both India and England. But to the Untouchables in particular it was an epoch-making event in their history; for, it was at this Conference that they were being invested along with other Indians with the right to be consulted in the framing of the constitution for India. Their voice was to echo for the first time in the history of two thousand years, and more so in the governance of their Motherland.

On the eve of Ambedkar's departure for England, he was given a grand send-off by the Untouchables in Bombay, who presented him with a purse and an address on October 2, 1930, as a token of their abiding gratitude for his selfless services to their cause. The President of the meeting Dr. Solanki, and other speakers, like Bole, were all praise for Ambedkar's high mental and moral qualities.

Replying to the address, Dr. Ambedkar said what little he had achieved, had been done with the co-operation of his numerous workers and colleagues. He praised the work and sincere help of Dr. Solanki in the Legislative Council, and, styling Deorao Naik his right hand, added that he would guide the movement on proper lines in his absence. He gratefully thanked Shankarrao S. Parsha, who had expended large sums on his movement, and declared that a fortnightly paper named *The Janata*, the People, would soon be published in place of his old Fortnightly, the *Bahishkrit Bharat*—the Excluded India.

As regards the Round Table Conference, Ambedkar said it was definitely advantageous from the point of view of the Depressed Classes. He further said that all parties including the Depressed Classes had resolved that the goal of India was Swaraj. The difference had arisen over the pattern of the constitution and the rights of the minorities under the constitution. The cardinal question was whether those powers were to be vested in the hands of a small minority or divided equally among all classes. "As regards myself", continued Ambedkar, "I will demand what is rightful for my people, and I will certainly uphold the demand for Swaraj."In the end he promised his people that he would meet the leaders and representatives of Germany, Russia, Japan and America and acquaint them with the problem of the suppressed Indians, and, if possible, he would place their problem even before the League of Nations. He concluded his speech with a warning to his lieutenants and his people to keep themselves aloof from internal quarrels; otherwise the greed for leadership would weaken their strength, worsen their position and mar their goal.

Ambedkar left Bombay for London on October 4, 1930, by the *s.s. Viceroy of India.* The atmosphere in the country was not congenial to his departure. The whole country was in a turmoil.

Congressmen hated, abused and cursed those leaders who co-operated with the British Government in solving the Indian problem in their own honest way. The situation was so tense and fraught with danger that Ambedkar wrote from Aden, on October 8, to Shivtarkar, his secretary and trusted lieutenant, that he was very anxious for their safety. He warned them to be on their guard in their walks and talks and to avoid all work at night. He asked him to lock the office of the party with an iron bar across it and to watch the movements of a certain Depressed Class leader in Bombay who was at loggerheads with their organization.

Ambedkar further wrote to Shivtarkar to teach his son Yeshwant how to deal with the bank affairs, asked him to see and remind a certain officer in the matter of jobs for two of his men, and advised him to intimate him at Marseilles about any hostile attack by Congressmen or if his men were involved in any skirmish with Congress volunteers.

Indeed, the times were unfavourable to any leader who was opposed to the ways of the Indian National Congress. The left wing of the Congress was impatient of the Liberal leaders who believed in maturity and gradualness in matters political. Not only that, according to some of the Congressmen patriotism itself was confined exclusively to the membership of the Congress organization. They, therefore, stigmatised all those who co-operated with the Britishers at the time of the Round Table Conference as softies, lackeys, stooges of the British Empire and traitors to the cause of India. And Subhas Bose's attack on Ambedkar that "Ambedkar had had his leadership thrust upon him by a benign British Government because his services were necessary to embarrass the nationalist leaders"[2] was no better than this verbal flamboyance. It was characteristic of Congressmen that they acted upon the principle of non-violence where the Britishers and the Muslims were concerned, and behaved with inveterate hatred and violence where other Indian parties were concerned. So the Congress newspapers vented their wrath and showered words of abuse seldom on the Muslim delegates, sometimes on Moonje, Sapru and Jayakar, but always on Ambedkar. Sir Tej Bahadur Sapru and Dr. Moonje, in their

2. Bose, S.C., *The Indian Struggle*, p. 41.

speeches before the Round Table Conference, described this 1930 movement atmosphere very graphically.

On board ship one thing made Ambedkar's voyage very unhappy. He had left the keys of his trunks at home and had to break the lock of one of the trunks to get another suit. The sea was not rough. On his arrival in London, on October 18, 1930, he temporarily lodged at 8, Chesterfield Gardens, Mayfair, London, W.I. and thereafter asked his men to write to him care of Thomas Cook & Son, Berkeley Street, London, W.I. On October 28, he received the keys and other things from home.

Ambedkar found the political atmosphere in England much sympathetically inclined to the problem of the Depressed Classes. On his arrival, he immediately began to contact Britain's important political party bosses in connection with the problem of the Depressed Classes. Yet he was anxious to know by cable from India about the new list of the members nominated to the Bombay Legislative Council and about the judgment of the Court on the Chowdar Tank Case.

IV

The curtain was raised on November 12, 1930. Keen interest was evinced by the British public in the opening of the Round Table Conference. Approaches to the House of Lords, the avenue of the Conference, were thronged by spectators. His Majesty the King-Emperor appeared. Inaugurating the Conference, he said: "More than once the Sovereign has summoned historic assemblies on the soil of India, but never before have British and Indian statesmen and Rulers of Indian States met, as you now meet, in one place round one table, to discuss the future system of Government for India and seek agreement for the guidance of my Parliament as to the foundations upon which it must stand." The King-Emperor concluded by expressing a hope: "May your names go down to history as those of men who served India well". After the King-Emperor had withdrawn from the House, Ramsay MacDonald was unanimously elected Chairman of the Round Table Conference. A labour leader and author of *The Government of India*, he expressed Britain's determination to solve the Indian problem, and said that they were at the birth of a new history.

The Round Table Conference was not a Constituent Assembly entrusted with the work of drafting a Constitution. It was a gathering of Indian and British statesmen who were not to take decisions by votes. The sense of the Conference on the main issues which came up before it for consideration was to be ascertained and noted.

The venue of the Conference thereafter shifted to St. James' Palace. During the course of a general discussion which took place from 17th November to 21st November, Sapru, Jayakar, Moonje, Jinnah, the Maharaja of Bikaner and Ambedkar made very sincere and impressive speeches. In his lucid and appealing style the guide, friend and philosopher of the Conference, Sir Tej Bahadur Sapru, said: "India wants and is determined to achieve, a status of equality—equality with all the three members of the British Commonwealth—an equality which will give it a Government not merely responsive to, but responsible to the popular voice."

The Maharaja of Bikaner identified himself and the princely order with the aspirations of British India and declared that the Princes were prepared to federate of their own free will with self-governing Federal British India. This was a surprise to all. This declaration of Federation was also endorsed by the Maharaja of Patiala and the Nawab of Bhopal.

The Muslim Members welcomed an All-India Federation; but with great vigour they pressed for a status for the North-West Province equal to that of the other Provincial units of British India and for the creation of a separate province of Sind.

Jayakar, in his deep and sweet flow of speech, asked for a declaration of Dominion Status, and added: "If you give India Dominion Status today, in the course of a few months the cry of independence will die of itself. If, on the other hand, we return empty-handed from our labours in the Conference, it will be the surest way of raising in volume and in intensity this demand for independence."

Dr. Moonje, following the Maharaja of Patiala, refuted all the arguments of Lord Peel and told the Conference how the British Government had crushed Indian shipping, cotton and other industries. He added that the British belief that they would put down the national movement of Civil Disobedience by a display of force was erroneous; the time had passed.

N.M. Joshi pleaded for more rights for the labourers in the new constitution. Sir Mirza said that the future constitution should be based on federal basis. Sir C.P. Ramaswami Iyer opined that the future constitution should be worth living under. Then, after two or three speakers, rose a man, stout, sober and confident, with scintillating eyes and tight lips. Arisen from the lowest rung to the height by dint of his mental and moral force alone, he sat there in the assembly of the princes and potentates, legal celebrities and great brains representing great thrones, jahagirs, institutions and interests. He represented the poorest of India's poor who were half-fed, half-nude and dumb! What would he say now? How would he say it? There was in the Assembly the prince who had financed his education. There was one amongst them who was his teacher in the school. All eyes were riverted upon the speaker. He was not the least agitated. He knew his mind; he knew what to say and how to say it. Except the Premier MacDonald and Joshi none from that august Assembly had seen poverty in its crudest and ugliest form. There were highlights in the Conference, pandits and litterateurs, but he was the only leader who had attained the highest degree in the academic world, the Doctorate in Science. This man was Dr. Ambedkar, the leader of the suppressed humanity in India.

At the outset, Ambedkar declared that in speaking before the Conference, he was placing the viewpoint of one-fifth of the total population of British India—a population as large ,as the population of England or France—which was reduced to a position worse than that of a serf or a slave. He then declared to the surprise of all that the Untouchables in India were also for replacing the existing Government by a Government of the people, for the people and by the people. He said that this change in the attitude of the Untouchables to British rule in India was surprising and a momentous phenomenon. And justifying his stand, he observed with a rise in his voice and a glow in his eyes: "When we compare our present position with the one which it was our lot to bear in Indian society of pre-British days, we find that, instead of marching on, we are marking time. Before the British, we were in the loathsome condition due to our untouchability. Has the British Government done anything to remove it? Before the British, we could not draw water from the village well. Has the British Government secured us the right to

the well? Before the British, we could not enter the temple? Can
we enter now? Before the British, we were denied entry into the
Police Force. Does the British Government admit us into the
force? Before the British, we were not allowed to serve in the
Military. Is that career now open to us? To none of these questions
can we give an affirmative answer. Our wrongs have remained
as open sores and they have not been righted, although 150 years
of British rule have rolled away."

"Of what good is such a Government to anybody?" he asked
the Conference. At this the British representatives looked at one
another. There was a stir among the Indian representatives. "It
was a Government," continued Ambedkar, "which did realize that
the capitalists were denying the workers a living wage and decent
conditions of work and which did realize that the landlords were
squeezing the masses dry, and yet it did not remove social evils
that blighted the lives of the down-trodden classes for several
years. Although it had", he proceeded, "the legal powers to remove
these evils, it did not amend the existing code of social and
economic life, because it was afraid that its intervention would
give rise to resistance." He, therefore, declared: "We must have
a Government in which the men in power will give their
undivided allegiance to the best interests of the country. We must
have a Government in which men in power, knowing where
obedience will end and resistance will begin, will not be afraid
to amend the social and economic code of life which the dictates
of justice and expediency so urgently call for."

Ambedkar upheld the demand for Dominion Status, but
expressed doubts as to whether the Depressed Classes would
be heir to it unless the political machinery for the new
constitution was of a special make. While making that
constitution, it should be noted, he observed, that the Indian
society which was formed with an ascending scale of reverence
and a descending scale of contempt and was a gradation of
castes, gave no scope for the growth of the sentiment of
equality and fraternity, and the intelligentsia which came of
the upper strata and conducted political movements had not
shed its narrow particularism of castes. Hence he asserted:
"We feel nobody can remove our grievances as well as we can,
and we cannot remove them unless we get political powers in

our own hands. I am afraid the Depressed Classes have waited too long for time to work its miracle!"

Referring to the Indian deadlock, he recalled the memorable words of Edmund Burke whom he called the greatest teacher of political philosophy that "the use of force is but temporary" Concluding his brilliant speech, he sounded a great warning to the British Government and to those who were engaged in the "battle of wits" in the Conference: "I am afraid it is not sufficiently realized that in the present temper of the country, no constitution will be workable which is not acceptable to the majority of the people. The time when you were to choose and India was to accept is gone, never to return. Let the consent of the people and not the accident of logic be the touchstone of your new constitution, if you desire that it should be worked."[3]

The fearless tone and the bold criticism in the speech had a wonderful effect upon the Conference. The frankness and fearlessness with which Ambedkar lucidly put the facts before the Conference impressed the delegates immensely, and they congratulated him on his brilliant speech. It created a good impression upon the British Premier. The *Indian Daily Mail* described this speech as one of the finest bits of oratory during the whole Conference. One man in the Conference was extremely pleased with his speech. He returned to his kingly residence full of admiration, satisfaction and high appreciation; and with joyful tears in his eyes, he told his princely wife that their efforts and the money they had spent on the speaker of the day were all realised. It was an achievement, a glorious success! This admirer was nobody else than His Highness the Maharaja of Baroda who invited Ambedkar to a special dinner given by him in London to his choice friends. It was a strange freak of destiny that Gaekwad and Ambedkar should meet after years of estrangement in a melodramatic situation.

The effect of this powerful speech of Ambedkar was tremendous on the newspapers also. The English newspapers and pressmen devoted their attention to the leader of the Depressed Classes and English statesmen, like Lord Sydenham, O'Dwyer and others, who had bitterly criticized Ambedkar's Nagpur speech in the *Spectator*, were now

---

3. Indian Round Table Conference, 1930-31, Proceedings, pp. 123-29.

thoroughly convinced that Ambedkar was a nationalist; and so they began to whisper that he also was one of the revolutionary leaders of India. Some of the English statesmen confidentially asked A. B. Latthe whether Ambedkar belonged to the revolutionary camp. And this inquiry on the part of the British statesmen was not unexpected. It may be recalled how the British secret police had taken a full search of Ambedkar when he landed in Britain, in 1917 from America.

During the early period of the Conference, there was an attempt made by the Liberal leaders, Sapru, Sastri and Setalvad, to read, an agreement with the Muslim delegates on the communal question. The Hindu delegates held meetings at the residence of Sir Cowasji Jehangir under the Chairmanship of Sastri to discuss the possibility of a compromise with the Muslim delegates. Moonje and Jayakar expressed the view that such a settlement would be possible after the grant of Dominion Status. The Liberal leaders, Jayakar, Moonje and Ambedkar held parleys with the Nawab of Bhopal, the Aga Khan, Jinnah and others at the residence of the Nawab of Bhopal, but the talks broke down over the Muslim demand for separation of Sind which was solidly opposed by Moonje and Jayakar. Besides, the Muslim leaders were not prepared to grant the same proportion of reserved seats to the Hindus and Sikhs in Muslim majority Provinces as they asked for themselves in other Provinces.

After the general discussion in the plenary session, the Conference appointed nine sub committees and Dr. Ambedkar found himself a Member of almost all the important sub-committees but the Federal Structure Committee. He served on the Minorities Sub-Committee, the Provincial Sub-Committee and the Services Sub-Committee with the great luminaries from India and England. In the course of the discussion on the report of the Provincial Sub-Committee, Ambedkar supported Chintamani's view that it was absolutely unnecessary and undesirable to have a Second Chamber in any province in India.

While the report of the Defence Committee was being discussed, Ambedkar pleaded that the recruitment to the Army should be open to all Indians consistently with the considerations of efficiency and the possession of the necessary qualifications.

The most important work Ambedkar did to achieve his goal was the preparation of the Declaration of Fundamental Rights safeguarding the cultural, religious and economic rights of the Depressed Classes. He prepared the scheme with great labour and statesmanship, and submitted it to the Minorities Sub-Committee for being included in the future constitution of India. The title of the scheme was: 'A Scheme of Political Safeguards for the Protection of the Depressed Classes in the Future Constitution of a self-governing India.'

The Declaration of Fundamental Rights said that the Depressed Classes must be given the right of equal citizenship in common with other citizens of the State, abolishing untouchablity and any other penalty, disadvantage, disability or discrimination in law, should be stopped. It demanded adequate representation in the Legislatures and a right to elect their own men as their representatives by separate electorates; due and adequate representation of the Depressed Classes in the services, establishment of a Public Service Commission to undertake the recruitment and control of the services.

Ambedkar despatched some copies of this Declaration of Fundamental Rights to his followers in India, asked them to hold meetings in different cities in support of the demands presented to the Minorities Sub-Committee by the Depressed Class representatives, and instructed them to send copies of the resolutions to Ramsay MacDonald, stating that those demands were the irreducible minimum for willing co-operation of the Depressed Classes; otherwise they would not consent to any constitution for self-government. Accordingly, a number of wires poured into the office of the British Premier from all parts of India.

One point about the deliberations of the Round Table Conference that was not then sufficiently known in India was that while these discussions were being held on the rights of the minorities, Dr. Moonje and Dr. Ambedkar had arrived at a compromise in regard to the rights of the Depressed Classes. It was announced by both the leaders to American and other journalists that there was no cause now left for the Depressed Classes to quarrel with the caste Hindus.

The general opinion was that the Liberal and Labour leaders were inwardly not inclined to favour the communal greed of the Muslims. Newspapers like the *Daily Herald* expressed their disapproval of the Muslim attitude to the Indian problem. The Muslims in their turn were not favouring the Untouchables' cause; for they feared that the caste Hindus and the Untouchable Hindus would any day become a united force and oppose their demands jointly.

The British Premier tried in his own way to bring the Indian delegates to a frame of mind for a settlement. The Premier's daughter gave a party to choice delegates. The Maharaja of Baroda, Ambedkar, Sir Mirza Ismail, Jinnah, Tambe and few others attended it. The British Premier took some of the delegates to his country home at Chequers. They had a talk there relating to the Indian problem, but there, too, they could not come to a settlement.

The Minorities Sub-Committee submitted its report to the Conference. The last paragraph of that report recorded that "the Minorities and Depressed Classes were definite in their assertion that they could not consent to any self-governing constitution of India unless their demands were met in a reasonable manner".

Like Joshi, Jadhav and Paul, Ambedkar dissented from the proposals of the Franchise Sub-Committee as in their opinion the proposals were inadequate, and they pleaded for immediate introduction of adult franchise. In the written speech, which he could not make for want of time, Ambedkar warned the British Government that it would be betraying the Depressed Classes if by limiting the franchise the Labour Government left them to the mercy of those who had taken no interest in their welfare.

V

Such was his sincerity and devotion to the problem and to the welfare of his people that Ambedkar worked day and night, sought interviews, gave interviews, supplied information, and even addressed a meeting of some Members of the British

Parliament to acquaint them fully with the problem of the Untouchables. He took every opportunity of contributing articles to foreign journals, of issuing statements to the foreign press and of addressing meetings in London with the sole object of exposing the intolerable humiliations and unbelievable sufferings under which the Depressed Classes were groaming in India for ages. In appeal after appeal to the Press he said that the cause of the Untouchables in India needed the support of the enlightened world. He, therefore, urged that it was the sacred duty of the people at large to help the solution of their problem on the basis of humanity!

The result was that the world came to know for the first time that the fate of the Untouchables in India was worse than that of the Negroes in America. The appeal moved some of the British leaders and consequently a deputation consisting of some Members of the British Parliament such as Miss Eleanor, Miss Ellen, Norman Angel and a few others, waited on Lord Sankey and pleaded for investing the Depressed Classes with franchise, and for removing their disabilities. Lord Sankey promised that in the proposed political set-up they would be placed with the other classes and masses of India. Some of the British papers, however, were hostile to Ambedkar because "I do not oppose the move for Dominion Status"[4]. He said that he, too, did not mind their indifference or opposition to his cause.

Ambedkar's profound study, great industry and conquering intellect created a tremendous impression upon the delegates and the British statesmen. He inspired respect as well as hatred in different circles. The *Sunday Chronicle*, at a later stage, paying a glowing tribute to Ambedkar about his work, said: "At heart a true nationalist, he had to put up a stern fight against the persuasive coquetry of the British diehards who are anxious to win him over to their side and at the same time his task was made more difficult by his anxiety to retain his brother delegate Rao Bahadur Srinivasan, within the nationalist fold. At the Chesterfield Gardens, time and again, he explained that Sir Tej Bahadur was giving more to the Princes in the process of give and take. But he admitted that Sir Tej had to manoeuvre through a very difficult situation."

---

4. Ambedkar's letter, 19 December 1930.

The *Indian Daily Mail* reporter observed: "Ambedkar
pointed out that he had a mandate to see that no responsible
Government was established, unless it was at the same time,
accompanied by a truly representative Government. He voiced a
fear that the proposed form of Government would be one of the
masses by the classes and his protest found much echoing
sympathy in the Labour and Liberal Parties of Great Britain."

In his otherwise very busy programme, the scholar in
Ambedkar snatched some time to enter some second-hand
bookstalls to purchase rare books. Three boxes full of books were
sent to India with V. M. Pawar, the old Labour leader of Bombay,
and the fourth was ready to be sent with his colleague Srinivasan.
Ambedkar wanted to meet some Russian leaders and so he wrote
to Shivtarkar to remind R.R. Bakhale, the famous Bombay labour
leader, to send the addresses of the Russian leaders. He had a
mind to go to the U.S.A. also to acquaint the Americans with the
problem of the Untouchables in India. But it seems he could not
find time to do so. It was in London that Ambedkar received the
news of the victory of his people over the orthodox in the Mahad
Tank case at the Mahad Sub-judge's Court and that of his
nomination to the Bombay Legislative Council.

Another thing he was pleased with, at this juncture, was
that as directed by him, Ambedkar's lieutenants, Deorao Naik
and Kadrekar, started a new fortnightly paper called the
Janata— the people. There is a strange evolution of Ambedkar's
role in the social as well as political sphere of India. His first
paper was named the *Mook Nayak*—the leader of the dumb, the
second was called the *Bahishkrit Bharat*—the Excluded India.
The third was *Equality* and the fourth was the *Janata*—the
People. The leader of the dumb made a stir and described the
sufferings of the outcastes. In the third stage he gave expression
to their aspirations for equality, and in the fourth he expressed
the desire of his people for assimilation into Hindu Society on
the basis of equality, liberty and fraternity. Ambedkar was
grateful to his lieutenants, Naik and Kadrekar, and wrote a letter
to Deorao Naik, appreciating their courage and service in
standing by the cause of the Untouchables and in merging
themselves completely into the emotions, hardships and
aspirations of the down-trodden millions.

After recording the reports of the different Sub-Committees, the Round Table Conference adjourned on January 19, 1931. This was followed by a debate on India in the House of Commons. During the course of the debate, one voice echoed the grievances of the Depressed Classes. It was Issac Foot who was a man of broader sympathies. Referring to the disabilities of the Untouchables, he said: "If we do not establish safeguards for their projection, their blood may cry out against us. If I had any advice to give to future Governors, it will be 'Let your main concern be for these people.' They may be defenceless now, but one day they will be strong. As there is justice upon the earth, there is no bank that can keep back for ever the accumulated sufferings of these people. The real test of the progress of India twenty years hence will be 'what have you done for these people'?" This speech was an eloquent tribute to Ambedkar's ceaseless work in London.

Before leaving London, Ambedkar expressed his opinion on the work of the Round Table Conference in a letter to his secretary Shivtarkar that although he was in two minds as to the outcome of the Conference, he was confident that it had laid the foundation of the self government of India. Viewed in this light the Conference was a success. Yet viewed from another angle, he observed that the foundation had more of sand than mortar.[5] Hence the foundation, was not strong enough. But so far as the rights of the Depressed Classes were concerned, it was a tremendous success, he added.

The notable contribution of this session of the Round Table Conference to Indian political thought was the evolution of the conception of a United India. Another solid outcome was the definite emergence of the Depressed Classes in the political picture of India, and more important was the brilliant and moving exposition of their insufferable conditions by Ambedkar before the bar of world opinion. Owing to disagreement on the question of seats, which the different communities sought to secure in the proposed legislatures, and on the system of election whether separate or joint electorates with reserved seats should be employed, the Conference was adjourned. Besides, it must have been thought that taking any vital decision at that time was like

---

5.   Ambedkar's letter 21 January 1931.

reckoning without hosts; for Congress, the major political party of India, had not participated in the proceedings.

Ambedkar left for India, embarking at Marseilles on February 13, 1931.

VI

Ambedkar arrived in Bombay on February 27, 1931. He was enthusiastically received at Ballard Pier by a battalion of Ambedkar Seva Dal led by Shankarrao Wadvalkar. In a Press interview, Ambedkar said that the Round Table Conference was a triumph of statesmanship and although there were defects which were not of vital character in the proposed constitution they could be removed. He, however, resented the restricted franchise. He added that if Gandhi failed them in their efforts to secure political power for the common man and woman, he would not hesitate to call Gandhi's act as the greatest betrayal of trust. He further said that the grant of political power depended upon the solution of the minority problem and concluded by expressing his satisfaction that in the future constitution of India the place of the Depressed Classes was secure and their disabilities would be non-existent.

In India the political situation was undergoing a rapid change. In accordance with the suggestions made in the British Premier's final speech before the Round Table Conference, the Viceroy, within a week of the termination of the Round Table Conference, released the Congress leaders on January 26; and Gandhi, after days of protracted negotiations, made a pact with the Viceroy Lord Irwin on March 5, 1931, at Delhi, abandoning Civil Disobedience Movement and promising to attend the second session of the Round Table Conference.

On his arrival, for three or four days, Ambedkar gave interviews, had cordial talks with his friends and colleagues, and a day or two thereafter addressed a vast meeting of his people at Parel, Bombay. He told them that their support and agitation had enabled him to wrest something for them. He, therefore, exhorted them to keep up the struggle. Next day Ambedkar took his seat in the Bombay Legislative Council and attended the session till the middle of March 1931. At this juncture a crisis developed in Nasik.

It was decided by the Depressed Class leaders headed by Bhaurao Gaikwad to revive the agitation for the temple entry, which was suspended in 1930, on an assurance from Dr. Moonje, who had promised them to set up a committee to decide the issue. But as nothing was done for months together, they decided to renew the agitation. Ambedkar, along with his Bombay colleagues, went to Nasik by the Nagpur Mail on March 14. They took up their lodgings at the bungalow of a Muslim gentleman named Zakeria Maniar. Ambedkar made a stirring speech at a meeting in Nasik, arousing his people's feelings to a pitch of enthusiasm and ended by laying stress on the value of discipline and non-violent struggle. Dinkarrao Javalkar, who was released from jail a day or two before, also cheered the Untouchables with hope and courage. Immediately Ambedkar left Nasik for Bombay, for he had to attend the hearing of the Chirner Firing Case on Monday, March 16, 1931, at Thana. At Nasik, on Sunday, at noon a procession of the Untouchables passed off, and at its turning point stones were thrown at the processionists by orthodox groups. It is to be noted that the President of the District Congress sided with the reactionaries as did the Nasik Municipality. Another thing worth mentioning is that the Congress, at its Karachi session, made a declaration by one of its resolutions that it regarded strict neutrality in matters religious. A little before this session, Gandhi had declared during his stay in Bombay that he would fight for the temple entry after freedom was won. This was a directive, clear-cut and expressive.

Returning to Bombay from Nasik, Ambedkar attended the Sessions Court at Thana. There he was to defend four accused out of forty-seven patriots involved in the famous Chirner Firing case. The case had arisen out of the Congress Jungle satyagraha which was launched at Chirner, a small village near Panvel, on September 25, 1930, and the consequential firing in which the Mamlatdar and some other persons were killed. Being a case of Government against the people, it had very wide repercussions; and its proceedings were watched with intense and close interest by the people all over India. As the case was very important in the history of Maharashtra, though perhaps unknown to the Congress historian Dr. Pattabhi Sitaramaya, eminent lawyers from Maharashtra were briefed to conduct the case before the

Sessions Judge, Sanjana. The Defence Counsel comprised the
famous old Tilakite, R.P. Karandikar, Dr. Ambedkar, K. N.
Dharap, Rege and others.

The Court was busy with the case, during the summer
vacation. Ambedkar cross-examined the witnesses closely and
intelligently and became the object of admiration to the vast
patriotic-minded countrymen. His boldness in standing against
the Government that had selected him to represent the Depressed
Classes at the Round Table Conference was much appreciated
by the people. On one occasion Ambedkar's interruption caused
laughter in the court. It was when the Prosecution asked a
witness whether the latter identified accused No. 15 by his face
or on account of the scars on his nose. Ambedkar exclaimed:
"What, is not his nose on his face?"

On Tuesday, June 20, Ambedkar put forward his arguments
in a very thought-provoking and convincing manner before the
Court in defence of accused Nos. 8, 9 and 10, and brought out
the points which were in favour of the accused. Lastly, he
reviewed the case very courageously from a different angle. He
looked at the Judge and Jury and said in an earnest appeal:
"The case has assumed peculiar complexion. It has come to be
regarded as a case of the people versus the Government. The
issue involved is the stability of the Government as against the
liberty of the people. A jury trial is intended in order that there
may be no prejudice to the liberties of the people. I would appeal
to the gentlemen on the jury to regard the rights and liberties of
the people far more important than the stability of the
Government.

The end of the most complicated and long-drawn trial came,
and the Judge delivered his judgment on July 2, 1931 convicting
twenty-nine accused with different terms of sentences and
acquitting the remaining seventeen.

Meantime, Ambedkar had convened a Leaders' Conference
in Bombay, which met in the Gokhale Education Society's Hall
at Parel, on April 19, 1931. All prominent Depressed Class leaders
from Bengal, C.P. Madras and Maharashtra attended and N.
Shivraj presided. Ambedkar submitted a report of the work which
he had done at the Round Table Conference. The report was
gratefully endorsed by the Conference amidst thunderous

applause. The Conference appealed to Government to nominate the representatives of the Depressed Classes on the Federal Structure Committee, to grant adequate representation to the Depressed Classes at the next Round Table Conference, and demanded that the representatives of the Depressed Classes be provided with ministerial responsibilities in the future cabinets of the Provinces. It also expressed its deep debt of gratitude to the delegates who fought bravely for the Depressed Classes at the Round Table Conference and to Issac Foot, Lord Reading, Lord Peel and Sir Tej Bahadur Sapru for having helped the cause of the Depressed Classes.

There was some tumult and uproar outside the hall in the street. An attempt to cause disturbance in the proceedings was made by some disgruntled men who styled themselves as nationalists. But their attempt was foiled by the disciplined volunteers of Ambedkar Seva Dal. The rout was so complete that the leader of the trouble-makers, Deorukhkar, had at last to run into Ambedkar's car entreating Babasaheb to save his life. The volunteers who pursued him in heat smashed the hood of their leader's car. Ambedkar, however, sheltered his malevolent opponent.

CHAPTER 10

WAR WITH GANDHI

JUST then the Government of Bombay announced that the Police Department was thrown open for recruitment to the Depressed Classes. Ambedkar's ceaseless efforts now began to bear fruit. Although it was a small opening, it meant much, economically and fundamentally. Ambedkar was now a force to reckon with. The agitation he had sponsored, the work he did in India, and the prestige he attained at the Round Table Conference were bringing sufficient pressure upon Government to change its attitude to the Depressed Classes.

There was now a visible change in the attitude of the Congressmen to the political problem of the country. Addressing a meeting at Madras, Jawaharlal Nehru said that Congressmen had never branded the delegates to the Round Table Conference as traitors. What they had said was that they were not people's representatives. Another important change was that Gandhi showed resilience enough to negotiate the terms of his participation in the proceedings of the next session of the Round Table Conference.

In June the Untouchables of Trichur, in the Cochin State, sought Ambedkar's advice whether they should participate in any Congress move for the temple entry. Ambedkar advised them not to depend upon Congress help as it would not redound to their credit, and added that they should win their freedom by their own efforts.

It was at this time that M. N. Roy, who, under the pseudonym, Dr. Mohamud, was feeling the pulse of Indian leaders, met Ambedkar at his office in Bombay. They discussed Indian politics; but Ambedkar found that Dr, Mohamud had not thought over the problem of the Untouchables. After the interview, Ambedkar told D.V. Pradhan with whom the visitor had come that the visitor seemed to be a Bengali leader and was not a Muslim leader from the U.P. as he posed to be. A fortnight later Dr. Mohamud was arrested as M. N. Roy.

Congressmen gave at this juncture another proof of their policy of tolerance and truth for outsiders and hatred and intolerance for non-Congressmen and non-Muslim leaders! Ambedkar paid a visit to Ahmedabad to look into the arrangements of the new Boarding which he had started for untouchable students. At the station the Congressmen of Ahmedabad greeted him with black flags.

Just at this time the names of the delegates to the second session of the Round Table Conference were announced in the third week of July. Ambedkar, Sastri, Sapru, Jayakar, Setalvad, Malaviya, Sarojini Naidu, Gandhi, Mirza Ismail, Jinnah, Ramaswami Mudaliar and others were invited to attend the Conference in London. Ambedkar was purposely dropped out from the Federal Structure Committee at the first session of the Round Table Conference, His patriotic mind and his fearless advocacy for the common man and democracy had given the Britishers an offence. But this time he was selected on the Federal Structure Committee, which was vitally connected with the drafting of the new constitution for India,

Congratulations were showered from all quarters of India and even from England on Ambedkar. Newspapers from the opposite camp also began to appreciate his patriotism, his love for democracy and his anxiety for the welfare of the common man. The *Kolaba Samachar*, district paper of note, which was hostile to him in matters of social reforms, expressed a debt of gratitude to Ambedkar for the patriotic service he had rendered to the country in the Chirner Trial. It recalled his services at the time of the visit of the Simon Commission and at the first session of the Round Table Conference; and it added that Ambedkar was a true patriot and would fight to break the shackles of the country and help others do so at the second session of the Round Table Conference.

The *Indian Daily Mail*, congratulating the Doctor upon his nomination to the Federal Structure Committee, paid a glowing tribute to Ambedkar. It said: "He is a patriot and is vitally interested in securing self-government. In the future discussions, which will centre on the franchise of the Senate and the Federal Assembly, this brilliant representative of the Depressed Classes is certain to play a most important part."

The *Sunday Chronicle*, the *Kesari*, and several other news-papers expressed satisfaction at the nomination of Ambedkar. Congratulating the Doctor and N.M. Joshi, the Journal of the Servants of India Society observed: "Being drawn from the humble ranks of the society, one representing the labour classes and the other the Depressed Classes, they are necessarily strangers to 'high politics' as they are understood in this country. They have the simple faith of the simple folk whose cause they have espoused, and they will not be deterred by the superior smile of the eminent personages surrounding them, from insisting on the literal application of certain principles which they have been taught to hold as inviolable." A little before this the London representative of the *Free Press Journal*, a leading nationalist daily in Bombay, in his reply to Miss Mayo had eulogised the services which Ambedkar had rendered at the first session of the Round Table Conference, and said that Ambedkar was a fearless, independent and patriotic-minded leader whose fearlessness was unbearable to both Hindus and Muslims, and that his opening speech at the first session of the Round Table Conference was the best speech in the whole proceedings of the Conference.

It was not decided as yet whether Gandhi would attend the Round Table Conference. Naturally all eyes were focussed on Manibhuvan at the Malabar Hill in Bombay, owing to the mysterious suspense created by Gandhi's stagecraft and state craft. In the bustle and hurry Gandhi wanted to sound Ambedkar as to his demands. So Gandhi wrote to Ambedkar on August 6, 1931, informing him that he would come to see the latter at eight o'clock that night if Ambedkar could spare the time. Gandhi added that he would gladly come over to Ambedkar's residence, if it was inconvenient to Ambedkar to come to him. Ambedkar had just arrived from Sangli, and was running a temperature. He wrote in reply that he would himself go to Gandhi at eight o'clock that night. But in the evening the temperature soared to 106; so Ambedkar sent a message that he would come after the fever abated.

Ambedkar went to meet Gandhi on August 14, at Manibhuvan, at two in the afternoon. A batch of his lieutenants, Deorao Naik, Shivtarkar, Pradhan, Bhaurao Gaikwad and Kadrekar, accompanied him. When Ambedkar was shown in to the third floor, Gandhi was busy talking with his partymen and eating some fruits. The Doctor and his party bowed to Gandhi and sat on a blanket.

In the characteristic way which Gandhi observed in dealing
with non-Muslim and non-European leaders and representatives,
he did not look at first for a while at Ambedkar and kept chatting
with Miss Slade and others, Ambedkar's men now feared that a
little more indifference on the part of Gandhi and a collision
would follow. Just then Gandhi turned to Ambedkar whom he
saw for the first time, and, after formal questions, he switched
on to the main topic.

Gandhi : Well, Doctor, what have you to say in the
matter?

Ambedkar : You called me to hear your views. Please tell
me what you have to say. Or you may please
ask me some questions and I shall answer.

Gandhi : (*with a staring look at Ambedkar*); I
understand that you have got some
grievances against me and the Congress. I
may tell you that I have been thinking ovei
the problem of Untouchables ever since my
school days—when you were not even born.
You may perhaps be knowing what enormous
amount of efforts I had put in to incorporate
this problem in the programme of the
Congress and make it a plank of the Congress
platform. The Congress leaders opposed it on
the plea that it was a religious and social
question and as such it should not be mixed
with political ones. This is not all. The
Congress has spent not less than rupees
twenty lakhs on the uplift of the Untouchables. And it is really surprising that men like
you should offer opposition to me and to the
Congress. If you have to say anything to
justify your stand, you are free to do so.

Ambedkar : It is true, Mahatmaji, that you started to think
about the problem of Untouchables before I was
born. All old and elderly persons always like to
emphasize the point of age. It is also true that
because of you the Congress Party gave
recognition to the problem. But let me tell you
frankly that Congress did nothing beyond giving
formal recognition to this problem. You say the

Congress spent more than rupees twenty lakhs on the uplift of the Untouchables. I say it was all waste. With such a backing I could have effected an astounding change in the outlook and economic conditions of my people. And in that event it would have been imperative for you to see me long before. But I tell you that the Congress is not sincere about its professions. Had it been sincere, it would have surely made the removal of untouchability a condition, like the wearing of khaddar, for becoming a member of the Congress. No person who did not employ untouchable women or men in his house, or rear up an untouchable student or take food at home with an untouchable student at least once a week should have been allowed to be a member of the Congress. Had there been such a condition, you could have avoided the ridiculous sight where the President of the District Congress Committee was seen opposing the temple entry of the Untouchables !

You might say that Congress wanted strength and therefore it was unwise to lay down such a condition. Then my point is that Congress cares more for strength than for principles. This is my charge against you and the Congress. You say the British Government does not show a change of heart. I also say that the Hindus have not shown a change of heart in regard to our problem, and so long as they remain adamant we would believe neither the Congress nor the Hindus. We believe in self-help and self-respect. We are not prepared to have faith in great leaders and Mahatmas. Let me be brutally frank about it. History tells that Mahatmas, like fleeting phantoms, raise dust, but raise no level. Why should the Congressmen oppose our movement and dub me a traitor?

Ambedkar now grew animated. His face flushed and eyes glowed. He paused for a moment and then continued in a bitter, indignant tone.

Ambedkar : Gandhiji, I have no homeland.

Gandhi : (*taken aback and cutting him short*): You have
got a homeland, and from the reports that
have reached me of your work at the Round
Table Conference, I know you are a patriot of
sterling worth.

Ambedkar : You say I have got a homeland, but still I
repeat that I am without it. How can I call
this land my own homeland and this religion
my own wherein we are treated worse than
cats and dogs, wherein we cannot get water
to drink ? No self-respecting Untouchable
worth the name will be proud of this land.
The injustice and sufferings inflicted upon us
by this land are so enormous that if know-
ingly or unknowingly we fall a prey to
disloyalty to this country, the responsibility
for that act would be solely hers. I do not feel
sorry for being branded as a traitor; for the
responsibilities of our action lie with the land
that dubs me a traitor. If at all I have
rendered any national service as you say,
helpful or beneficial, to the patriotic cause of
this country, it is due to my unsullied
conscience and not due to any patriotic
feelings in me. If in my endeavour to secure
human rights for my people, who have been
trampled upon in this country for ages, I do
any disservice to this country, it would not
be a sin; and if any harm does not come to
this country through my action, it may be due
to my conscience. Owing to the promptings
of my conscience I have been striving to win
human rights for my people without meaning
or doing any harm to this country.

The atmosphere turned grim. Faces changed colour. Gandhi
was growing restless. He wanted to give a turn to Ambedkar's
talk. Just then Ambedkar asked him the most pertinent question
which was the object of the interview.

Ambedkar : Everybody knows that the Muslims and the
Sikhs are socially, politically and

economically more advanced than the Untouchables. The first session of the Round Table Conference has given political recognition to the Muslim demands and has recommended political safeguards for them. The Congress has agreed to their demands. The first session has also given recognition to the political rights of the Depressed Classes and has recommended for them political safeguards and adequate representation. According to us that is beneficial to the Depressed Classes. What is your opinion?

Gandhiji: I am against the political separation of the Untouchables from the Hindus. That would be absolutely suicidal.

Ambedkar: (*Rising*) : I thank you for your frank opinion. It is good that I know now where we stand as regards this vital problem. I take leave of you.[1]

Ambedkar left the hall, his face beaming with a fiery resolve to fight out the issue with all his might and to win human rights for his down-trodden people.

The interview thus ended in a grim atmosphere. Gandhi was the boss of Indian politics, the dictator, the uncrowned king of the Indian masses, who were dazed and electrified by his dynamic actions. To answer Gandhi back was to incur permanent displeasure and to create undying bitterness. And that too a Hindu leader doing it was a thing beyond Gandhi's imagination! But the die was cast. The spark of opposition was ignited. The interview sounded the beginning of a war between Gandhi and Ambedkar.

It is, however, surprising to note here that Gandhi thought that Ambedkar was not a Harijan. Till he went to London he thought he was some Brahmin who took deep interest in Harijans and therefore talked in temperately.[2]

II

At night, at a send-off meeting in the Sir Cowasji Jehangir Hall, Ambedkar made a very stirring speech before the Depressed

---

1. The Navayug–Ambedkar Special Number, 13 April 1947.
2. Navajivan Publishing House. *The Diary of Mahadeo Desai*, Vol. I, p. 52.

Class women. He said: "If you stand by your resolve to extirpate your slavery root and branch and undergo all trials and tribulations for it, the credit and success of my being able to discharge the onerous task, will be yours." Immediately he addressed in the same hall another meeting attended by the Depressed Class men. In a moving speech he told his people that their boundless love was a great inspiration to him. As regards the Round Table Conference, he said: "In a Conference of one hundred and twenty-five Members we are two; but rest assured that we will move heaven and earth for the sake of your welfare. I had a talk with Gandhi this afternoon. At present he cannot do anything to promote your interests. We must stand on our own feet and fight as best we can for our rights. So carry on your agitation and organize your forces. Power and prestige will come to you through struggle."

The next day was Saturday, August 15, 1931. Almost all the Round Table Conference delegates were to sail for London by the *s.s. Mooltan*. The Ballard Pier at Bombay presented a picturesque appearance on the day. From princes to paupers all sorts of people were present at the Pier. Friends, admirers, followers and devotees assembled to wish *bon voyage* to their Princes and heroes. One leader who received a great ovation as soon as he got down from the car was Dr. Ambedkar. Over two thousand volunteers had collected on the road outside and greeted, him as he arrived at the Mole Station with shouts of "Ambedkar ki jai" and "Long live Ambedkar ".

On board ship Ambedkar came across Sir Prabhashankar Pattani, who asked him about the outcome of the latter's interview with Gandhi. Sir Prabhashankar told Ambedkar that as he had left the hall in the middle of the interview, he was not in the know of its outcome or end. Ambedkar, who got the clue from the strange note in the voice of the Knight, asked him why he had left the hall in the middle. The Knight said bitingly that according to Hindu scriptures a gentleman should quit the place where a detractor reviled a good man, if the hearer could not cut out the tongue of the detractor on the spot. Ambedkar was all the more tickled by the growing insensible temper of the Knight and, without any sign of irritation on his face, asked him what punishment was prescribed by Pattani's Hindu scriptures for a rank hypocrite and an abject flatterer. At this crack of the whip

Pattani got wild and asked Ambedkar what he meant by such a brutal attack. Ambedkar replied that he meant what the Knight understood and added that Gandhi should be freed from the grip of abject flatterers like him. The Police Commissioner, Wilson, intervened, and a further scene was averted. The Knight must have left a wiser man. Indeed, the world would be no less benefited, if all its great men turn introspective and get them-selves rid of the flattering unctions of men surrounding them!

Sapru, Jayakar and Iyengar were leaving by the same steamer, In an interview they said that they would try to see that Gandhi and Malaviya came to the Round Table Conference. Sarojini Naidu and Malaviya, who were to go by the same steamer, cancelled their passages, as Gandhi had not yet decided about his departure. In the interview which Ambedkar gave on the steamer he referred to Gandhi's refusal to go to the Round Table Conference and said it was the height of folly to place the interests of Bardoli above those of India, "to bother about petty grievances and to be unmindful of bigger problem the settlement of which will enable him to exercise control over those very officers is a thing which I cannot understand."

Ambedkar was now deeply thinking of Gandhi's decision to oppose his demands. So he sent a message to his people in India through his secretary to hold meetings to denounce the attitude of Gandhi towards their claims. From Suez he wrote another letter to Shivtarkar asking him to send copies of the Memorandum which he had submitted to the Minorities Sub-Committee of the first session of the Round Table Conference. He also asked him to send with Rao Bahadur R. Srinivasan the leather bag which he had left behind.

On the steamer, Jayakar, the Maharaja of Rewa and other leaders expressed their satisfaction at the imposing sight of the Samata Seva Dal of the Depressed Classes. Shaukat Ali was glad; Dr. Moonje was pleased and even expressed his hidden joy that in spite of the failure of the Hindu Mahasabha to raise such a disciplined volunteer corps, there was one organization of the untouchable Hindus to stand face to face with the Muslim volunteers! Moonje even congratulated Ambedkar on his being the leader of the Untouchables, who were conscious enough to know Ambedkar's services to their cause, and added that they were not indifferent and ungrateful, like the caste Hindus, who knew not their benefactors!

On reaching London on August 29, Ambedkar was down with influenza and suffered terribly from vomiting and diarrhoea. The illness sapped his energy, so much so that he wrote to Shivtarkar that his health was on the brink of a crisis. From Monday, September 7, he began to feel better but weakness still lingered. All the time he advised Shivtarkar not to utter a word about his illness to his wife. One thing weighed on his mind. Defeated at the Mahad Sub-judge's Court, the orthodox Hindus had appealed to the District Court at Thana. and the judgment of the District Judge at Thana was due. He asked Shivtarkar to inform him about it as soon as it was delivered.

In the meanwhile, Gandhi, Vallabhbhai Patel. Jawaharlal Nehru and Sir Prabhashankar Pattani met the Viceroy at Simla where the differences were patched up, and Gandhi left for Bombay to catch the earliest steamer to go to London. Gandhi. along with Sarojini Naidu, Pandit Malaviya, and his parry, sailed for England on August 29, and reached London on September 12, 1931.

Ill

The second session of the Round Table Conference commenced on September 7. This time the personnel of the Conference was enlarged by including a few more delegates such as Sir Muhamed Iqbal, the Muslim League President; Dr. S.K. Dutta, the Christian representative; G.D. Birla, the great financier; Pandit Malaviya, a sanatani reformer; Sarojini Naidu, the Nightingale of India; and Sir Ali Imam. The outstanding feature of this session was the presence of Gandhi's enigmatic personality. The first session of the R.T.C. was ' Hamlet' without the Prince of Denmark!

Shortly before the Conference met, a change had come over Britain. The Labour Government was replaced by a National Government, the Prime Minister, Ramsay MacDonald, remaining in the saddle as before. The Secretary of State for India, Wedgwood Benn, was replaced by Sir Samuel Hoare. Conservative leaders like Churchill vehemently opposed the proposed transfer of power to India.

The main work of the Round Table Conference was to be done in the Federal Structure Committee and the Minorities Committee. The Conference was to re-examine and amplify the reports prepared by the corresponding Committees of the first session of the Round Table Conference. Mahatma Gandhi made

his first speech in the Conference on September 15, 1931, in the
Federal Structure Committee. He claimed that the Congress
represented all Indian interests and classes. He told the
Conference that the Congress represented the Muslims because
it had Muslims as Presidents and Muslims as members of its
Working Committee. It represented the Depressed Classes
because removal of untouchability was a plank on the political
platform of the Congress. Gandhi told the Princes that Congress
stood for States also inasmuch as "even now the Congress had
endeavoured to serve the Princes of India by refraining from
any interference in their domestic and internal affairs". The
Congress represented women, Gandhi observed, because
Congress had Dr. Annie Besant and Sarojini Naidu as Presidents.
And because he was the sole representative of the Congress, it
followed that he was the sole representative of the Indian nation!

Ambedkar sensed from this speech of Gandhi in what direction
the wind was blowing. Ambedkar made his first speech in the Federal
Structure Committee on the same day. He told the Princes that the
Federal Structure Committee could not blindly give to the States
what they wanted. This put the Maharaja of Bikaner on his legs,
and he replied that nor could the States sign a blank cheque either.
Ambedkar, emphasizing his point, said that before a State was
allowed to join the Federation, it must prove that it had the necessary
resources and the capacity to give its citizens a civilized life, and
the main condition laid down by Ambedkar was that the States'
representatives to the Federal Assembly should be chosen by election
and not by nomination. It was his confirmed opinion that nomination
made the Executive irresponsible to the Legislature giving a false
appearance to the outside world that the Legislature was working
normally on the basis of a majority rule. He added that the principle
of nomination was against the principle of responsible Government.
As regards the demand of the landlords for special representation,
he said that they should not be given special representation as they
sided with the orthodox, and thereby defeated the ends of freedom
and progress. Obviously, this was the first and best speech made in
defence of the rights of the States' people.

These strong views gave a shock to the Princely Order, the
landlords and their benefactors, who favoured the view of the
Princes that their representatives to the Federal Assembly should
be selected by nomination. The result was that every speaker
devoted some part or other of his speech to refuting or supporting

Ambedkar's speech as a majority of them thought that his views were radical and revolutionary.

The next day Gandhi expressed his views that the Round Table Conference delegates were not the chosen ones of the nation, but chosen ones of the British Government. Not that Gandhi was not aware of this before his departure to London. But he now began to twit the delegates. Regarding Ambedkar's views on States' representation on the Federal Legislatures, Gandhi said that while his sympathies were, broadly speaking, with Ambedkar, his reason was wholly with Gavin Jones and Sir Sultan Ahmed, who echoed the views of the Princely Order. Gandhi favoured the proposal for Federation, but supported the standpoint of the Princes as against the States' people, saying: " Here we have no right, in my humble way, to say to the States what they should do and what they shall not do!"

Gandhi then turned to the pivotal problem that was haunting the delegates. He referred to the problem of special representation claimed by the different communities, and said: "The Congress has reconciled itself to special treatment of the Hindu-Muslim-Sikh tangle. There are sound historical reasons for it, but the Congress will not extend that doctrine in any shape or form. I listened to the list of special interests. So far as the Untouchables are concerned, I have not yet quite grasped what Dr. Ambedkar has to say, but of course, the Congress will share the onus with Dr. Ambedkar of representing the interests of the Untouchables. The interests of the Untouchables are as dear to the Congress as the interests of any other body or of any other individual throughout the length and breadth of India. Therefore, I would most strongly resist any further special representation."

This was nothing but a declaration of war, Ambedkar observed, by Gandhi and by the Congress against the Untouchables. "With this declaration by Mr. Gandhi," he added, "I knew what Mr. Gandhi would do in the Minorities Committee which was the main forum for the discussion of this question."

On September 18 Ambedkar rose and asked Gandhi in the Federal Structure Committee whether the views placed by Gandhi regarding the Federal Legislature and the formation of the Federal Executive were his own or those of the Congress. When Diwan Bahadur Ramaswami Mudaliar stated that the public servants, who constituted the Political Department, were as conscientious and fair as any other body of public servants anywhere in India or outside, Ambedkar at once asked him why then he wanted responsible Government at all if that was so. In his speech Pandit Malaviya pleaded for patience and courtesy to be shown to the Princes and observed that had Government utilized all resources and spent sufficient money on promoting primary education among the people, he was sure the words Depressed Classes would have been a matter of history by that time. Ambedkar at once pointed out his own case and laid that in spite of his education he was still an Untouchable. In the course of his speech Sir Akbar Hydari, while replying to Dr. Ambedkar, said: "Speeches like those of Ambedkar, if I may say so, do not sufficiently appreciate the realities of the situation." Upon this Ambedkar answered back: "I have never been guilty of not appreciating realities."

While discussing the formation of the Federal Constitution, nobody referred to the time-limit for initiation of Federation. It was Ambedkar who lifted the veil by saying: "I do not know that there would be any British Indian who would like to put the establishment of responsible Government in cold storage until the Princes make up their minds to enter into the Federal Government of India."

During these discussions in the Federal Structure Committee there were flashes, exchanges of views, reviews of the constitutional history of the world and ideas about Free India. Ambedkar's speeches on those topics were full of information, interest and valuable suggestions. The politician, the barrister, the constitutionalist, the professor, the defender of the down-trodden millions and the friend of the States people profoundly impressed the Conference with different facets of his erudition.

By now the third week of September 1931 was over. The Minorities Committee was to commence its work on September 28, On the eve of this session, Gandhi's son, Devdas Gandhi, saw Ambedkar at his residence, and an interview was fixed between Gandhi and Ambedkar at the residence of Sarojini Naidu between 9 and 12 p.m. Accordingly, Ambedkar saw Gandhi and placed his cards on the table. But Gandhi did not open his mind and said that he would consent to Ambedkar's demands if others agreed.

The Minorities Committee met for the first time on September 28, 1931. The Premier admitted that the problem of minorities in India had baffled them all. He observed that some of the delegates had suggested that Government should arbitrate as the delegates themselves had failed to agree, but he opined that the arbitration would probably be unacceptable to some of them. Upon this the Aga Khan said that Mahatma Gandhi was going to see the Muslim delegates that night and so he asked for an adjournment. Seconding the Aga Khan, Malaviya wished that the general discussion might stand over.

Ambedkar was in the know of the secret talks that were going on between the Muslim leaders and Gandhi regarding the Hindu-Muslim agreement. So referring to the motion for adjournment, he said: "As far as the Depressed Classes are concerned, we have already presented our case to the Minorities Sub-Committee last time. The only thing which remains for me to do is to put before this Committee a short statement suggesting the quantum of representation which we want in different Legislatures."

He himself had heard with great pleasure, Ambedkar continued, that further negotiations were going to take place for the settlement of the communal issue. He further observed: "But I would like to make this matter absolutely plain at the start. Those who are negotiating ought to understand that they are not plenipotentiaries at all; that whatever may be the representative character of Mr. Gandhi or the Congress people, they certainly are not in a position to bind us—certainly not. I say that most emphatically in this meeting." And concluding his speech with a warning, he said: "I want to say most emphatically that whoever claims weightage and whoever is willing to give that weightage he must not give it — he cannot give it — out of my share." Upon this the Chairman, MacDonald, said: "Dr. Ambedkar's position has been made absolutely dear, in bis usual splendid way. He has left no doubt at all about it."[3]

IV

On October 1 Mahatma Gandhi again asked for a week's adjournment. He told the Committee that he was being closeted with Muslim leaders of various groups. At this Dr. Ambedkar got up and said that he did not wish to create any difficulty in arriving at such a settlement, but wanted to know

---

3. Proceedings of Federal Structure Committee & Minorities Committee, p. 527.

whether or not the Depressed Classes would be represented on that formal committee. Gandhi replied in the affirmative. Ambedkar thanked Gandhi for this, and turning to the delegates, explained: "Mahatma Gandhi told us on the first day that he spoke in the Federal Structure Committee that as a representative of the Indian National Congress he was not prepared to give political recognition to any community other than the Muslims and the Sikhs. He was not prepared to recognize the Anglo-Indians, the Depressed Classes and the Indian Christians. I do not think that I am doing any violence to etiquette, by stating in this Committee that when I had the pleasure of meeting Mahatma Gandhi a week ago and of discussing the question of the Depressed Classes with him and when we, as Members of the other minorities, had the chance of talking with him yesterday in his office, he told us in quite plain terms that the attitude that he had taken in the Federal Structure Committee was his full and well-considered attitude."

Ambedkar, then, thundered that if the Depressed Classes were not going to be recognized in the future constitution of India, as was done by the Minorities Sub-Committee during the first session of the Round Table Conference, he would neither join that particular Committee nor whole-heartedly support the proposition for adjournment. Sir Herbert Carr, Dr. Dutt and others welcomed the adjournment.

The discussions between Gandhi and the Muslim leaders went on for a week. The newspapers declared that the discussions had reached an encouraging stage. It was reported that Gandhi had conceded to the Muslims their fourteen points, accepted that the residuary powers be vested in federating provinces, allowed the Muslims majority in the Punjab and in Bengal, and had offered the Muslims a blank cheque. The talks, however, failed on the Sikh-Muslim question.

On October 8 Gandhi announced, with deep sorrow to the Minorities Committee, his utter failure in securing an agreed solution of the communal question through informal conversations amongst and with the representatives of different groups. He said that the causes of failure were inherent in the composition of the Indian Delegation, and that they were almost all not the elected representatives of the parties or groups whom they were presumed to represent, nor were those whose presence was absolutely necessary for an agreed solution. He, therefore, moved for an adjournment of the meeting *sine die*. Ambedkar took up the challenge and stood to reply to Gandhi. He said that Gandhi was guilty of a breach of understanding according to which it was agreed the previous night that none of the delegates was to make any speech or any comment that would cause exasperation.

Ambedkar's vitriolic tone began to rise. He thundered: "What disturbs me, after hearing Mr. Gandhi, is that instead of confining himself to his proposition, namely, that the Minorities Committee should be adjourned *sine die*, he started casting reflections upon the representatives of the different communities who are sitting round this Table. He said that the delegates were the nominees of Government, and that they did not represent the views of their respective communities for whom they stood. We cannot deny the allegation that we are nominees of the Government, but, speaking for myself, I have not the slightest doubt that even if the Depressed Classes of India were given the chance of electing their representatives to this Conference, I would, all the same, find a place here. I say, therefore, that whether I am a nominee or not, I fully represent the claims of my community. Let no man be under any mistaken impression as regards that."

"The Mahatma has been claiming," Ambedkar proceeded "that the Congress stands for the Depressed Classes, and that the Congress represents the Depressed Classes more than I or my colleagues can do. To that claim I can only say that it is one of the many false claims which irresponsible people keep on making, although the persons concerned with regard to those claims have been invariably denying them."[4] Ambedkar thereupon showed how he had received from the farthest untouchable corner of India—from the places which he had never visited and from the men he had never seen—telegrams supporting the stand taken by him. He then told the Committee that either the Committee should solve the problem or the British Government should undertake its solution. In his utter disappointment and fear he said that the Depressed Classes were not anxious about the transfer of power under the present circumstances, but if the Government wanted to transfer power,

---

4. Proceedings of Federal Structure Committee & Minorities Committee, p. 534.

it should be accompanied by such conditions and by such provisions that the power should not find itself into the hands of a clique, into the hands of the oligarchy, or into the hands of a group of people whether Mohammedans or Hindus; the solution should be such that the power should be shared by all communities in their respective proportions.

The Prime Minister appealed to the Delegates not to attribute causes to any method by which they had been elected or to their own personal shortcomings. He asked them to face the facts and asked them whether the problem existed in India or not. The speech of the Premier was rather pungent in tone and some called it ingrate, full of bitter sideshafts against Gandhi.

Ambedkar's vigorous propaganda did not stop here. He wrote from London, on October 12, a letter to The Times of India throwing light on the whole episode. "We are, however, reliably informed," he wrote, "that in carrying his negotiations with our Muslim friends, Mr. Gandhi demanded that as one of the conditions for his accepting their fourteen points, they should oppose the claims of the Depressed Classes, and the smaller minorities." "To say in public," Ambedkar observed with his caustic ruthlessness, "I will agree if all others agree, and then to set out to work in private to prevent others from so agreeing by buying off those who are willing to agree, is, in our opinion, a piece of conduct unbecoming a Mahatma and to be expected only from an inveterate opponent of the Depressed Classes. Mr. Gandhi is not only not playing the part of a friend of the Depressed Classes, but he is not even playing the part of an honest foe."

In his letter home Ambedkar foretold that the Round Table Conference would end in a fiasco, and in his opinion Gandhi was responsible for that failure. According to Ambedkar, Gandhi's partiality, discriminating conduct in solving the problem of the minorities, his equivocal manner of dealing, his absolute disregard for the other representatives, the insults he inflicted upon them—all these qualities did not help Gandhi to solve the problem tactfully. Ambedkar further observed that Gandhi's diabolical way of playing one community against another was now quite clear! His undemocratic mental set-up, Ambedkar concluded, had given a rude shock to a man like Harold Laski, and Congress leaders, like Vithalbhai Patel, were murmuring disapproval of Gandhi's mishandling the situation!

Gandhi's hostility to the demands put forth by Ambedkar had wide repercussions and reaction in the quarters of the Untouchables all over India. The All-India Depressed Classes Conference, under the presidentship of Rao Bahadur M. C. Rajah, at its Gurgaon session, declared that Gandhi was misrepresenting the case of the Untouchables, and strongly denounced the claim made by Gandhi that the Congress had been taking care of the Untouchables from the beginning and had championed the cause of the Untouchables. "I say," said Rajah, the President of the Conference, "that these statements are untrue."

The Conference supported the demands put forth by Ambedkar and declared that no constitution would be acceptable to the Depressed Classes which did not include in it the system of separate electorates for the Depressed-Classes. Messages requesting Ambedkar not to put faith in Gandhi and in the Congress were sent to Ambedkar in hundreds by the Depressed Class leaders and associations from all parts of India, and by public meetings and conferences held at Tinnevelly, Robertson (Madras), Lyallpur, Karnal, Chidambaram, Calicut, Banaras, Kolhapur, Yeotmal. Nagpur, Chanda, Kanpur, Kamptee, Belgaum, Dharwar, Nasik, Hubli, Ahmedabad, Tuticorin, Colombo and at several other places.

These vociferous cablegrams demonstrated who was the real representative of the Depressed Classes. Gandhi, no doubt, received a few cables, but they were insufficient to meet the queries which Gandhi was pestered with in his talks and discourses at different places in London. Such was the powerful effect of Ambedkar's fighting propaganda that Gandhi was really nonplussed, and his assumed guardianship of the Untouchables lay exposed !

This exposure became more pronounced at this juncture by the temple entry movement launched by the Depressed Classes in India, at Nasik and at Guruvayur. The revival of satyagraha at Nasik gained a tremendous momentum. Five thousand volunteers poured in Nasik. Ambedkar's devoted lieutenant, Bhaurao Gaikwad, Depressed Class leaders like Rankhambe,

Patitpavandas and trusted lieutenant Deorao Naik, fought out
the struggle, exposing the orthodox Hindus and the pretended
sincerity of the Hindu leaders in their true perspective. The
shame was so carping that Dr. Moonje appealed from London to
the Hindus not to deny these civic and religious rights to their
kith and kin at their own peril. The gates of the Kalarara Temple
were closed as was done during the previous satyagraha.

Ambedkar was happy over this timely support from his
people in exposing the caste Hindu behaviour. He sent a message
to his people from London in which he observed: "As anticipated
by you, I did get a letter from the Commissioner, Central Division,
asking me to advise you people to stop the Nasik satyagraha. I
have not replied to him but I am going to do so by this mail. I am
going to tell him that we cannot stop. So you may tell our people
to go on. We must not take our orders from the Government just
as we must not take them from the orthodox Hindus." "We have
trusted," the message went on, "the Government long enough to
remove untouchability. But it has not lifted its finger to do
anything in the matter and it has no right to ask us to stop. We
must take the burden on our shoulders and do what we can to
free ourselves from this curse at any cost."[5]

The Nasik satyagraha was carried on with unique
enthusiasm and determination. Mass meetings were held, and
big processions were taken out. Several volunteers and leaders
were arrested. They bravely courted imprisonment and faced jail.
The news in the *London Times* about these arrests and the
developments of the satyagraha added to the weight of
Ambedkar's say.

After the clash with Gandhi, Ambedkar took part in the
discussions on the Fiscal system which was adumbrated by the
Sub-Committee for the Federal Government. He made a very
thought-provoking and illuminating speech on the composition
of the Federal Court in which Jinnah, Jayakar, Lord Sankey and
Lord Lothian, too, took much interest, and he was asked to clarify
some of his points.

In spite of this heavy work, Ambedkar was very busy giving
private interviews and explanations, issuing statements and

---

5.   The Times of India, 4 November 1931.

counter-statements and making speeches at different institutions in London in support of his stand at the Round Table Conference. His speech at the Institution of International Affairs proved very effective in demolishing Gandhi's platform. Those who were puzzled by Gandhi's extreme opposition to the demands of the Depressed Classes ran to Ambedkar to seek clarification of his stand. Miss Muriel Lester, with whom Gandhi was staying, saw Ambedkar who explained his standpoint to her. A common friend of Ambedkar and Gandhi invited both the leaders to tea and tried to reconcile them. Ambedkar admitted that Gandhi had done work for the uplift of the Untouchables in his humanitarian way and was striving to abolish untouchability; but they differed fundamentally on the question.

By the end of October 1931, elections were held in Britain and the Tories came into power. As regards the defeat of the Labour Government, Ambedkar said that their programme was too scientific to be understood by the labourer and average Britisher. In one of his letters Ambedkar said that the Depressed Class leaders who supported Gandhi did not understand that. Gandhi was opposed not only to the special electorate but also to the special representation for the Depressed Classes; otherwise the problem would have been solved long before.

While the session was going on, His Majesty the King-Emperor gave a reception to the Indian Delegates on November 5. It was arranged that a few Members should speak at the party. Gandhi was present bareheaded. He was clad in his customary loin-cloth and wore sandals. The King-Emperor asked Ambedkar about the condition of the Untouchables in India, and when he heard the harrowing tales from Ambedkar who narrated them with his flowing heart, eloquent eyes and scintillating face, he shuddered. The King-Emperor then inquired of Ambedkar cordially about his father and the place of his education, and how he had achieved academic eminence.

V

Ambedkar's was indeed a ruthless attack on Gandhi. Imagine what amount of strain Gandhi must have required to check the limitless flood of the wrath provoked in his human heart, the heart of a man who had developed his will-power to the nth degree. The Mahatma had attained an inscrutable mastery over his tongue, time and temper. When such a man looses the flood of his wrath, the enemy cannot but be drowned under its sway. Gandhi, with his ascetic mind and khadi apparel, stood exposed before the august Assembly by a man comparatively younger in age, but full of irreverent audacity, and who spoke with a cultivated ferocity and the fervour of an iconoclast.

The inordinate ambition of a giant clashed with the insatiable ambition in the young iconoclast. One was at the height of his power and splendour while the other was shining with his meteoric lustre. The will-power of the old man was proverbial whereas that of the young man was phenomenal. Both loved religion and believed in it. But to Mahatma Gandhi religion was politics whereas to Babasaheb Ambedkar true religion was the foundation of society and was essential to life and progress of society. And they both were, in the words of Pope, too fond to rule alone, and could bear, like the Turk, no brother near the throne. The Mahatma admired his rival's learning, respected the great powers of his brains and mind, and yet showed little sympathy with his policy. Ambedkar acknowledged the great powers of Gandhi and his humanitarian services to the Untouchables; but said that Mahatmas, like fleeting phantoms, raised dust, but raised no level! Gandhi and Ambedkar were temperamentally what Vashistha and Vishwamitra or Voltaire and Rousseau were to each other! Gandhi, who was one of the greatest men under the sun, was innocent of political science and principles of sociology whereas Ambedkar was a doyen of constitutionalists and a student of sociology.

The Mahatma said that he was the natural guardian of the Untouchables whereas Ambedkar said he was the natural leader of the Depressed Glasses. The Mahatma's leadership of the Depressed Classes was sentimental and assumed. The leaderhip of Babasaheb Ambedkar was natural, actual and practical. The young man challenged the imperial authority of the boss of Indian politics, and the boss of Indian politics tried to isolate and stifle him. The impregnable ego of the Mahatma outshone his unfathomable political craftiness. The pardonable pride in Ambedkar rivalled with his hatred.

The mighty shadow of the Mahatma lay across the world. The mighty man in Ambedkar was exposing man's inhumanity to man, and the ruthless strokes of his hammer resounded throughout the world. The Mahatma, who was accustomed to flattery and panegyrics in India, was now facing the practical world, eminent statesmen and fearless brains. There he was unassisted by the Indian press and was out of the circle of his devotees whereas Ambedkar was rising and shining in the world by overpowering the opposition sponsored by a commercialised press. Unaided by party caucuses, party funds, he was rising solely on the strength of his unbending will-power, phenomenal energy, heroic courage and great brains. With his conquering intellect he was strong enough to face a rationalist or a revolutionary, a Mahatma or a Messiah.

Describing this fight between Gandhi and Ambedkar, Glorney Bolton observes: "Day after day Dr. Ambedkar came into greater prominence. He spoke for the Untouchables and every speech on the welfare of India—whether from a conservative or a socialist platform—would contain a reference to the tragic plight of the Untouchables. It was a sentimental rather than a practical concern. Gandhi, by representing the Untouchables, would have drawn eulogies from almost every pulpit in England, but now Dr. Ambedkar had destroyed his platform. At first Mohammedans seemed to enjoy the discomfiture, but in time every delegate was wishing that Dr. Ambedkar would show Gandhi the courtesy to which his personal eminence certainly entitled him."[6]

A campaign of unbridled ferocity was let loose immediately by the so called Indian national press against Ambedkar. His statement that he was not anxious about the transfer of power was condemned as one voiced without a blush. They said that Ambedkar had cast restraint and decency to the winds.

Ambedkar now became the most hated man in India. He was stigmatized as an uncivil, insolent, inordinately rude man, devoid of human consideration. He was represented as a devil, was cursed as a public nuisance number one and was damned as a reactionary, a stooge of the British Government, a traitor to the country and a destroyer of Hinduism. At this time a fellow-passenger told T. A. Raman, a well-known Indian journalist, that if he ever murdered anybody it would be Dr. Ambedkar. Raman

---

6. Bolton, Glorney, *The Tragedy of Gandhi*, pp. 266-67.

observed that he had heard more unkind things said of Ambedkar than of any other ten men in the country.[7] Describing this terrific attack made by his opponents, a few years later, Ambedkar, with a fierce look, said to Edward Thompson: "In fact, I am not only hide-bound! I am skin-flint"[8]

They thus filled his cup of bitterness. But foreign journalists viewed the fight a little differently. One American observer wrote: "Gandhi's voice is only one against many. They may be small fry and the Mahatma may be speaking on behalf of a most influential organization. To my mind the Mahatma should have brought a strong contingent of representatives of the nationalist sections of the great minorities. Then they would have been able to speak in reply to such people as are criticising him today."

Similar opinion was expressed by Sir Chimanlal Harilal Setalvad in his *Recollections and Reflections*. But who was there in the Congress to represent the Depressed Classes? Rajah had denounced Gandhi and the Congress, and the other Depressed Class leaders in the Congress fold were not even fit to hold a candle to Ambedkar.

Another political observer in London stated in his report to a Congress journal that even the Muslims showed an extraordinary deference to Mahatma Gandhi, but the learned Doctor was inordinately rude to Gandhi and showed lack of human consideration, and he added that Ambedkar could let loose his rancour there because it would not have been possible for Ambedkar to do so in India. The political observer had the misfortune not to come across a man of mission. He had seen but not studied Ambedkar.

Ambedkar hit back his hostile critics by hammering their idol Gandhi in a ruthless manner whenever the opportunity offered itself. His attacks on Gandhi had the violence of Voltaire, Marx and Lenin with which they had attacked their opponents. Some years later Ambedkar described in his unmistakable terms the role which Gandhi played during the R.T.C.: "Unfortunately, the Congress chose Mr. Gandhi as its representative. A worse person could not have been chosen to guide India's destiny. As a

7. *The Illustrated Weekly of India*, 14 June 1936.
8. Thompson, Edward, *Enlist India for Freedom!*, p. 75.

unifying force he was a failure. Mr. Gandhi presents himself as a man full of humility. But his behaviour at the Round Table Conference showed that in the flush of victory Mr. Gandhi could be very petty-minded. As a result of his successful compromise with the Government just before he came, Mr. Gandhi treated the whole non-Congress delegation with contempt. He insulted them whenever an occasion furnished him with an excuse by openly telling them that they were nobodies and that he alone, as the delegate of the Congress, represented the country. Instead of unifying the delegation, Mr. Gandhi widened the breach. From the point of view of knowledge, Mr. Gandhi proved himself to be a very ill equipped person. On the many constitutional and communal questions with which the Conference was confronted, Mr. Gandhi had many platitudes to utter but. no views or suggestions of a constructive character to offer."[9]

Gokhale, the Guru of Gandhi, had predicted this. He said that when the history of political negotiations and parleys was written Gandhi would go down as a great failure.

Ambedkar's interpretation that the Muslims dropped Gandhi's proposal because they refused to betray the other minorities was, however, not a historically correct assessment. It was the unwritten policy of the Muslim leaders to drag the Hindu leaders to a certain line of agreement and then to turn to British Government for more concessions; for they knew that it was the British Government that had the power to give. Secondly, how can a shrewd man refuse others the right of asking a certain favour for which he himself begs? The Muslims moved heaven and earth to get separate electorates. They were shrewd enough not to refuse the same benefit to smaller minorities. A divided Hindu society was to their advantage, politically and socially; so they showed Ambedkar lip sympathy and nothing more.

And was it just and fair on the part of the Congress leaders and press to depict a man of Ambedkar's independence, integrity and service as a traitor? Because he was not with Gandhi, was he against the country? How can so strong, so vigorous, so stubborn a man play second fiddle to any man howsoever great? Two stars keep not their motion in one sphere. Congressmen led

9. Ambedkar, Dr. B. R., *What Congress And Gandhi Have Done To The Untouchables*, p. 55.

the people to believe that it was their party alone that wanted
independence. But the fact was that they, too, were very late in
that field to make the bid. It was Veer Savarkar and his
revolutionary party that first declared absolute political
independence of India as their goal. All parties wanted
independence. But the demand was put forth according to the
temperament of the party. Ambedkar, too, wanted it and had
declared it to be the goal of his Party. He had clearly said at
several conferences and at the first session of the Round Table
Conference that the fate of the Depressed Classes would improve
only in a free India. But he feared that the reins of Government
would fall into the hands of the majority which was hostile and
inimical to the interests and welfare of the Depressed Classes.
So sometimes his enthusiasm for that demand dwindled.

But the conflict which raged in Ambedkar's mind can be
best understood when historians will record one more incident
that casts a bright light on his mind. When Ambedkar saw that
his speeches were being used by the English statesmen against
the Hindus to support Muslim demands, he secretly submitted,
it is learnt from a circle close to him, a Memorandum to Ramsay
MacDonald defending the interests of the Hindus as against the
Muslims.

VI

But if at all justice was on any side in this controversy, it
was on Ambedkar's side. During the long history of kings and
dynasties in India, no one from the ruling classes had ever
thought of relieving the Untouchables from their age-long slavery.
To raise the dumb crawling millions to the status of human
beings. the caste Hindus had never, in the capacity of rulers,
made any laws. What Ambedkar did in London was to present
the tragic fate of his people in the most caustic language, which,
was very natural for a positive and powerful man of his
temperament.

The caste Hindus suffered political bondage, but Ambedkar's
people suffered social as well as political slavery in the land.
Social and political sufferers are bound to utter caustic
denunciation of their oppressors. If political slavery of one

hundred and fifty years could justify extreme methods and violent means against the British Government, the Untouchables were a thousand times justified in lashing with scathing hatred the spokesman of their oppressors and the system of the oppression. What good and gentle way can a people socially suppressed for two thousand years, speak of the leaders of the society which treated them in an inhuman way? What good could they expect from their oppressors if they were to be invested again with full political power? What should they speak of the people, who, while receiving kicks from foreigners, never felt ashamed to kick their poor helpless brothers wickedly? Had they any moral right to blame the leaders of the Depressed Classes for the caustic denunciation when they themselves conceded to the more progressive communities special safeguards and special rights on "historic grounds" and refused the same to those who were the real down-trodden in the country?

The leaders of the caste Hindus were fighting for their political independence, but it was the mighty task of Ambedkar to bring the Untouchables to the level of human beings. It was a psychological moment that comes only once in an age! Was he to lose it? Ambedkar saw it at the Round Table Conference and pounced upon it. For, had there been no representative like Ambedkar, who would have cared to bring the Untouchables in the political picture of India? Those who were fighting for political independence were equipped with resources of wealth, position and strength to fight for their advancement. But Ambedkar was fighting for the rights of those people whose minds, views, hearts, emotions and aspirations were trampled upon in this land for ages past. His was a nobler goal, a nobler task, a mightier endeavour, more momentous than the task of winning political independence. In his success lay the success, strength and safety of Indian Democracy and the Indian Nation as a whole.

It was sheer insolence, outrage and egotism on the part of the touchable leaders to attempt to thrust their leadership upon the politically-conscious Untouchables and to say that they would deliver the goods. For, oppressors never become saviours. It was a good sign, the dawn of the salvation of the Depressed Classes, that their saviour had sprung from amongst them and inspired them with courage to fight for their salvation as best they could. That the leader of such a dumb class could show such a courageous grip over political problems and an ability in judging constitutional problems was in itself a great asset and the sign of a new-age. Thus Ambedkar's efforts were directed to the lasting good of Hindu society as a whole and especially of the Depressed Classes. It was the sacred duty of those who professed liberty, equality and fraternity, to back his demands and concede to him "reserved seats and joint electorates". But the spokesmen of the Congress, instead of backing his demands, opposed him and yielded to the very demands made by Muslim leaders, who stood for an unjust, aggressive, and ulterior motive.

In short, Ambedkar was on the horns of a dilemma. Had he opposed the British statesmen and taken sides with Gandhi, he would not have gained anything for his people from the Britishers; and Gandhi would not have given his people anything more than words of blessings and hollow platitudes. Naturally the way out for Ambedkar was to side with the Britishers and secure recognition to his cause and sanction for his demands. The second alternative was to side with Gandhi and to get special representation with joint electorates. But the Mahatma was deadly against it. Had Gandhi shown this much insight, he could have averted this disaster !

To return. The last meeting of the Minorities Committee took place when leading representatives of the Muslims, the Depressed Classes, a section of the Christians, Europeans and Anglo-Indians jointly submitted a Memorandum, stating the general principles and special claims of the Muslims, the Depressed Classes, Christians, Anglo-Indians and Europeans. It stated: "No person shall, by reason of his origin, religion, caste or creed, be prejudiced in any way in regard to public employment, office of power or honour or with regard to enjoyment of his civic rights and the exercise of any trade or calling."

The Memorandum also demanded recruitment of the Depressed Classes to public services, Military and Police services, extension of the Punjab Land Alienation Act to the Untouchables in the Punjab, right of appeal for the Depressed Classes to the

Governor or Governor-General for redress of any prejudicial action or neglect of interest by any executive authority.

Besides this Memorandum, Ambedkar and Srinivasan put a supplementary Memorandum, asking for special representation for the Depressed Classes in all Provincial Legislatures and in the Central Assembly in proportion to their population in India. They demanded separate electorates, but added that if the system of joint electorates was to exist with reserved seats, it should take place only after a referendum but that also not until after twenty years. Their last demand was for a change of nomenclature namely, that they should be called "non-caste Hindus", "Protestant Hindus", or "non-conformist Hindus" instead of Depressed Classes.[10]

When Gandhi saw this Minorities Pact which conferred on the Depressed Classes separate electorates, he was terribly enraged and he thundered in the Minorities Committee: "I would like to repeat what I have said before, that, while the Congress will always accept any solution that may be acceptable to the Hindus, the Mussalmans and the Sikhs, it will be no party to special reservation or special electorates for any other Minorities." He then described the claims advanced on behalf of the Untouchables as the unkindest cut of all and the perpetual bar sinister, and added that if there was any referendum of the Untouchables he would top the poll. In the course of his fighting speech he said that he had regard for Ambedkar's ability, but added that Ambedkar's bitter experiences in life had warped his judgment.

"I am speaking with a due sense of responsibility when I say," Gandhi proceeded in his broadside against Ambedkar, "it is not a proper claim which is registered by Dr. Ambedkar, when he seeks to speak for the whole of the Untouchables in India. It will create a division in Hinduism which I cannot possibly look forward to with any satisfaction whatsoever. I do not mind the Untouchables being converted to Islam or Christianity. I should tolerate that but I cannot possibly tolerate what is in store for Hinduism if there are these two divisions set up in every village. Those who speak of political rights of the Untouchables do not

---

10. Proceedings of Federal Structure Committee & Minorities Committee, pp. 563-64.

know India and do not know how Indian society is today
constructed. Therefore, I want to say with all the emphasis that
I can command that if I was the only person to resist this thing
I will resist it with my life."

Ambedkar did not reply to Gandhi who had felt the insult
too carpingly and come down to measuring his strength of
popularity with that of Ambedkar amongst the Untouchables.
The telegrams, the meetings, and the conferences of the
Untouchables throughout India, which had voiced protests
against Gandhi, would have staggered any opponent, but still
Gandhi went on in his own way. Gandhi could have clinched the
issue by accepting joint electorates with reserved seats for the
Depressed Classes. But he was not prepared to conciliate with
Ambedkar while he surrendered totally to the Muslims and
allowed the head of the Muslim camel of separate electorates
and separate provinces into the tent of the constitution. Had he
used persuasiveness to argue Ambedkar into a spirit of
compromise, Ambedkars brains and guns would have been a
positive help in demolishing the fortress of Muslim communalists.

Another thing Gandhi revealed in the course of his speech
was that he did not care if the Untouchables were converted to
Christianity or Islam. In fact never did he care to voice even a
feeble protest against it. Because of this attitude of Gandhi, he
laid himself bare to the charge of non-Congress Hindu leaders
that his aim in life was to be the fusion of Paigamber, Buddha
and Christ. Had he uttered a word of protest against the
conversion of Hindus, his critics asserted, he would have come
into collision with the Muslims and Christians, and the colour of
his Mahatmaship would have evaporated like a dream.

When the British Premier saw that there was no unanimous
solution to the Minorities problem, he asked all the Members of
the Minorities Committee to sign a requisition authorising him
to settle the communal problem and to pledge themselves to
accept his decision. Gandhi signed this pledge along with other
Members. Ambedkar did not sign this requisition as he believed
in the justice of his demands. The Prime Minister then adjourned
the Conference on December 1. Just before this requisition,

Ambedkar had a talk with Gandhi at the residence of Sir Mirza Ismail. Gandhi suggested a novel method to win the support of Ambedkar. He said that if the Untouchable candidates failed in the general election held on the basis of joint electorates without reservation of seats, the Depressed Classes should prove their *bona fides* in a Court of Law. Gandhi sometimes showed a knack of speaking absurd things with distinction, and Ambedkar therefore laughed heartily at the novel but meaningless idea.

While Ambedkar was in London, he was made a J.P. by the Bombay Government and on this event even Congress-minded men like N. S. Kajrolkat congratulated him. Ambedkar informed Shivtarkar that he would leave London for America on December 5, and return to India in a month. He added that he was sending with Srinivasan thirty-two boxes containing books. Accordingly, he left for New York to meet his old professors and, it was said, for a little rest.

Gandhi left for India and reached Bombay, on December 28, 1931. A few days before this, the *Free Press Journal*, Bombay, had announced that the Depressed Classes from all other parts of the country were coming to Bombay to show their faith in Gandhi. Thereupon Shivtarkar, Secretary of the Depressed Classes Institute, threatened the Secretary of the Bombay Provincial Congress Committee that as a counterblast they would resort to a hostile demonstration against Gandhi. He issued a charge-sheet against Gandhi and the Congress, stating that Gandhi's hostility to their demands at the Round Table Conference was most unreasonable, obstinate, inexplicable and ridiculously fanatical. S. K. Patil, the then Secretary of the Bombay Provincial Congress Committee, wrote in a reply a very polite letter to Shivtarkar, saying that the reception was nothing but an expression of love, loyalty and reverence they felt and expressed.

The tension, however, did not ease. On the early night of December 27, Congress volunteers gathered at the Mole Station. A vast procession of about eight thousand male and female members of the Depressed Classes marched to the Mole Station

at half past two in the morning. The cold night wore off. At last
Mahatma Gandhi got down at six in the morning. The Depressed
Class people staged a black flag demonstration against him, and
then there ensued a free fight, exchanging stones, lathis,
brickbats and sodawater bottles, acclaiming and decrying the
arrival of the apostle of non-violence to the Homeland! This was
indeed uncharitable, but charity must begin at home. Congress
leaders and journals were the fathers of unchari-
tableness and intolerance towards their political opponents. They
had preached hymns of hatred against the leader of the
Depressed Classes. They had decried him as a British stooge
and a serpent in the grass, a traitor and a Charvak! Congressmen
had showed black flags at Ahmedabad to Ambedkar. This was a
return gift!

CHAPTER 11

TRUCE

AMBEDKAR returned to London on Sunday, January 4, 1932. He left London, and embarking at Marseilles, on January 15, reached Bombay on January 29. On board were the British Members of the Franchise Committee, appointed by British Premier, of which Ambedkar was also a Member. As usual Ambedkar's purchases were with him. They were twenty-four boxes of new books.

Ambedkar was to land at six o'clock in the morning. A huge crowd of his followers and admirers had been awaiting his arrival since early dawn. Some leaders of the Depressed Classes including P. Balu and Kajrolkar, though politically inclined to Gandhi, garlanded and greeted him on the deck.

Ambedkar and his fellow-passenger, Maulana Shaukat Ali, landed at the Mole station. The Muslim leader and the Depressed Class leader were received amidst a burst of cheering. Addressing the huge crowds of the Muslims and the Depressed Classes, the Muslim leader said that every man must have an undeviating faith in his cause, and he appreciated the courage shown by Ambedkar in fighting for his cause. Shaukat Ali and Ambedkar were then taken out in procession which terminated at Byculla.

To the Depressed Classes Ambedkar now became a symbol of strength, hope and ambition. It was now proved that he could not be suppressed. He had ably led the Untouchables to the end of an epoch. The dead cells of the Depressed Classes were filled with new energy, new blood and new inspiration. That energy, vision, and consciousness would hold on in spite of difficulties and dangers.

The same evening, at a mass meeting at Parel, Bombay, Ambedkar was presented with an address on behalf of one hundred and fourteen institutions. Impressed with the abiding love and gratitude of his people, he stood' embarrassed and motionless for a moment before the vast gathering. After a pause

he declared to the vast audience that whatever services he could
render were the summation of the co-operation of all the workers
and the unflinching backing of his people. He said that no leader
was by himself responsible for the fulfilment or failure of a
mission; so he asked them to continue the struggle. As for his
own self, he said, after all, he was a human being and it was
human to err. He might have been at times partial, but that
should be excused, he added.

"I am described as a traitor by Congressmen," he observed,
"because I opposed Gandhi. I am not at all perturbed by this
charge. It is baseless, false and malicious. But it was a great
shock to the world that Gandhi himself should have sponsored
violent opposition to the breaking of your shackles. I am confident
that the future generations of Hindus will appreciate my services
when they study the history of the Round Table Conference." He
also disclosed how he happened to see Gandhi four or five times
in London, how Gandhi went secretly to the Aga Khan with a
copy of the Holy Koran in his hand and asked the Muslim leader
to withdraw his support to the Depressed Classes, and how the
Aga Khan had refused to do so.[1] Lastly, he appealed to his people
not to deify him as he hated deification. At the conclusion of the
meeting, he honoured the Nasik heroes who had been by then
released from jails.

The address of welcome given to Ambedkar on this occasion
by the Depressed Class people, said: "You have, indeed, proved
to the hilt our claim for equality of status and treatment, and,
but for the valiant fight you put on our behalf, our claims would
have been ignored. You have done all that is humanly possible
in safeguarding our rights and we are sure to stand, as a result
of your endeavour in London, on an equal footing with all other
major communities in India in the near future." The address
concluded: "The sense of responsibility and the present outlook
of our community, which is now out to assert its rights all over
the country, is, it will not be an exaggeration to say, but the fruit
of your exclusive efforts and guidance."

Ambedkar immediately left for Delhi to take part in the
proceedings of the Franchise Committee headed by Lord Lothian.
On his way to Delhi, he was enthusiastically received at every

---

1. The *Janata*, 30 January 1932.

station by the Depressed Classes; especially the functions held at Nasik, Igatpuri, Deolali, Manmad, Bhusaval and Jhansi stations were colourful and imposing.

In the early days of February the Franchise Committee visited Bihar. The Depressed Classes greeted Ambedkar with great enthusiasm at every place. The Committee then moved to Calcutta via Patna. Depressed Class leaders of his persuasion, while giving evidence before the Franchise Committee, supported the scheme of separate electorates as they feared that in the system of joint electorates with reserved seats the candidates of the Depressed Classes would be at the mercy of the majority of electorates, and in order to win their votes they would have to pander to their prejudices, or there would be every possibility of the seats being occupied by the stooges of the majority community. It was observed by many leaders of the Depressed Classes that if the joint electorates were to work successfully, that pre-supposed broad-mindedness on the part of the majority community. It was their view that such a favourable atmosphere did not exist then.

Now another trouble brewed for Ambedkar. Dr. Moonje made a pact with M. C. Rajah on the basis of reserved seats and joint electorates. Rajah submitted to the British Premier his memorandum telegraphically giving details of his pact with Dr. Moonje. This pact put Ambedkar in an awkward position. It may be recalled that it was Rajah who had cabled to Ambedkar and supported his demand for separate electorates, saying that Gandhi evidently did not know their woes, and therefore he had tried to force joint electorates down the unwilling throats of the Depressed Classes. Originally, the Rajah Party stood for joint electorates with reserved seats. But he changed sides. Rajah was the only Depressed Class Member in the Central Assembly, and he was not invited to the Round Table Conference. Perhaps grieved at this omission from the Round Table Conference, or greatly perturbed by Gandhi's professed claim to represent the Depressed Classes, he had dropped the idea of joint electorates and insisted on separate electorates. And now he reverted to the original demand. Ambedkar too changed sides. He had in his report to the Simon Commission demanded joint electorates and reserved seats, and vehemently criticised the demand of the

Muslims for separate electorates. But Gandhi's determined opposition to the demand of the Untouchables for reserved seats worsened the situation, and Ambedkar switched over to separate electorates, putting forth separate electorates as a united demand of the Untouchables.

The Franchise Committee met at the Viceregal Lodge. Ambedkar, on behalf of the Depressed Class, pleaded for the incorporation in the Indian Penal Code or in the future constitution, of a punishment for the instigation or promotion of boycott against the Depressed Classes which prevented them from the free enjoyment of the fundamental rights. The Franchise Committee accepted the suggestion.

On February 28, 1932, Arabedkar was accorded a colourful reception at Madras by a huge gathering of 10,000 men belonging to the Depressed Classes. Muslims, Christians and non-Brahmins also participated in the reception. The chairman of the Depressed Class Army Service presided. Almost all Depressed Class Institutions in the Southern India such as the Depressed Class Army Services Institution, Madras Provincial Depressed Classes Federation, the Presidents of Adi-dravida Malayalam Sabha, Adi-Andhra Mahasabha, Arundhateya Mahasabha, Kerala Depressed Classes Association, and the Labour Union unanimously presented Ambedkar with an address. At the meeting Ambedkar revealed Rajah's somersault from separate electorates to 'joint electorates with reserved seats'. He said that Rajah should not have made any commitment before the Kamtee session of the All-India Depressed Classes Congress was held. He, therefore, exhorted the Untouchables to capture political power, to be on their guard against any verbal and rosy promises, and urged them to believe only those leaders who had experienced their woes. In the end he asked them to keep before their eyes the fate of the touchable leaders like Gautama Buddha and Ramanuja who had struggled to better their condition and to remove the stain of untouchability.

When the news of the Rajah-Moonje pact was out, the Bengal and Assam Depressed Class leaders denounced Rajah for his swing to the system of joint electorates with reserved seats, and supported the demands put forth by Ambedkar. M. B. Malik. M.LA., President, Bengal Depressed Class Association; the

President, U.P. Adi-Hindu Association; the President, All-Assam Depressed Class Association; the President, Adi-Dharma Mandal, Punjab; the President, Depressed Class Aid Society, Delhi; all denounced Rajah and endorsed the demands put forth by Ambedkar. Ambedkar was congratulated by the Ratnagiri Hindu Sabha on his brilliant advocacy of the claims of the Untouchables. This was an unmistakable appreciation of Ambedkar's work by Veer Savarkar.

About this time the Bombay Government instituted a Committee consisting of Symington, I.C.S., and Zakeria Maniyar, to inquire into the condition of the Depressed Classes in the Nasik District. One of the chapters of the report revealed that in that District there were as many as eleven hundred District Local Board wells from which the Untouchables were not allowed to draw water in spite of the Government Resolution of 1923. It was in the same month that the Nasik satyagraha entered its third stage, and its leaders, Bhaurao Gaikwad and Rankhambe, were arrested. News about their arrest was wired to Ambedkar the same day, April 14; but Ambedkar said that he was almost dejected, and tired under the pressure of work and events. Unfavourable times worried him terribly. The extreme opposition of Chintamani, Bakhale and Tambe, the Hindu Members of the Franchise Committee, to the demand of the Depressed Classes for separate electorates had created bad blood between them and Ambedkar. They were not even on speaking terms with Ambedkar. Amid such tense atmosphere Ambedkar informed his secretary that he was sorry he could not deal with two situations at the same time. He was of the opinion that the problem of political rights was more important than the problem of temple entry; and therefore it was unwise and dangerous to deviate from that work to which he had devoted himself heart and soul.

In a letter written from Simla, Ambedkar said that it was very imperative to see the British Premier in London before the latter gave his decision on the communal issue. He, therefore, asked his trusted lieutenants to see whether it was possible to collect money for the proposed voyage without disclosing the reasons. He had also written to the Aga Khan, who was then in London, seeking his advice in the matter and asking him about the possibility and possible date of the Premier's decision on the communal issue. In another letter written during the same week, Ambedkar poured his disgust upon the Hindu Members of the

Franchise Committee and said that he hated their frame of mind which allowed them to be self-centred and aggressive inside their own camp and cowardly and yielding outside. He wrote that he was utterly disgusted with their selfish and thoughtless attitude and that he would try to keep himself away from Hindu society. He was working under mental and physical pressure. In addition, he was suffering from diarrhoea.

In April the Bengal Namashudra Association held its 14th Annual Session at the Albert Institute Hall, Calcutta, under the presidentship of Dr. Kalicharan Mandal. The Session unanimously endorsed Ambedkar's demands, denounced the newspapers which unjustly criticized Ambedkar's stand, and declared that the Congress attitude to their problem was unsympathetic and impractical.

The Franchise Committee finished its business on May 1, 1932 ; but, as Lord Lothian desired to have some discussion with him on some vital points, Ambedkar stayed for a day or two more. The Franchise Committee drafted its report giving detailed proposals on which to face the revision of Franchise, and distribution and demarcation of the constituencies for the new legislatures, Central and Provincial. As Ambedkar differed from the Hindu Members of the Committee, he submitted to the Committee a separate note. One of the most important decisions of the Committee was on the exact definition of the term Depressed Classes. The Indian Legislature Committee in its decision in 1916, Sir Henry Sharp, the Educational Commissioner under the Government of India, and the Southborough Franchise Committee had all grouped the Depressed Classes with the aboriginals or Hill Tribes, Criminals or with others, but now the Lothian Franchise Committee said that they were of the opinion that the term should be applied only to those who were untouchables. This was clearly Ambedkar's victory as he had insisted in his note to the Committee that the test of untouchability "must be applied in its notional sense as untouchability in its literal sense has ceased to obtain."

II

Ambedkar returned from Simla to Bombay on May 4, 1932. Immediately, on May 6, he left Bombay by Calcutta Mail to attend the All-India Depressed Classes Congress at Kamtee near

Nagpur. The Congress had been postponed to this date to suit Ambedkar's convenience. On his way he was greeted throughout that night by enthusiastic crowds of Untouchables at all the railway stations from Kasara to Nagpur.

The train steamed in at nine in the morning, and Nagpur station echoed with cries of 'Long Live Ambedkar'. A rousing reception was accorded to Ambedkar on the platform by a vast crowd of 5,000 people. Sakhare received Ambedkar and other leaders on the platform. There a handful persons who favoured the Rajah-Moonje Pact tried to greet Ambedkar with black flags. But they were hurled out of the station. The City Magistrate and the Police Superintendent were present at the station for the maintenance of peace and order.

The Congress pandal was decorated and was huge enough to accommodate 15,000 persons. The dais was a very big rostrum. As most of the Depressed Class leaders from the four corners of India had gathered to take a vital decision, the atmosphere was charged with tense feeling and excitement. It was very surprising that such a vast gathering of the Depressed Class delegates should assemble despite their poverty. It was said that some leaders of the Congress and Hindu Mahasabha had arranged for the railway fare of the supporters of the Rajah-Moonje Pact, but it seemed that this arrangement could not inspire confidence in the Depressed Class leaders. Another significant fact about the Depressed Classes Congress was that it was held at a place which was supposed to be the stronghold of Dr. Moonje, and the supporters of the Rajah-Moonje Pact. In order to have a complete picture of the situation, it may be recalled here that immediately after the announcement of the Rajah-Moonje Pact in one of his letters to Gavai who was the General Secretary of the All-India Depressed Classes Association, Ambedkar had, under great provocation, given him a threat of "breach between us and war amongst ourselves" if his organization advocated the system of joint electorates and reserved seats. It was reported then that Gavai had made a protest to Lord Lothian against this intimidation!

On the evening of May 7, the proceedings of the Congress commenced. About two hundred messages, supporting the demand for separate electorates as adumbrated in the Minorities

Pact, repudiating the Rajah-Moonje Pact and wishing this Congress success, were read out. The General Secretary of the Buddha Mahasabha sent a message of good wishes and asked the Depressed Classes to embrace Buddhism. At 6 p.m. when the Chairman of the Reception Committee rose to read his address of welcome, Rajbhoj, who favoured Rajah-Moonje Pact, and who became afterwards the General Secretary of the All-India Scheduled Castes Federation led by Ambedkar, stood up to ask some questions. He was advised to wait till the President took the chair. There were shouts of 'Make him sit down, drive him out', and Rajbhoj had to leave the pandal. Discipline and organization make or unmake political leaders. Ambedkar's party was then well organized and it maintained rigid discipline. Poor Rajbhoj and his supporters had no such organised backing.

Hardas, the Chairman, then traced the history of the Depressed Classes Congress and, emphasizing the need for unity among the Depressed Classes, remarked: "With separate electorate we will swim or sink." In a two-hour address Muniswami Pillay, defining the aspirations of the Depressed Classes, expressed dissatisfaction at the conduct of the Government, especially for not taking a sufficient number of delegates and asked Government to invite at least two more delegates from the Depressed Classes.

The next day when the open session commenced, Rajbhoj rose again to oppose. This gave rise to uproar, minor scuffles and loud denunciations. The City Magistrate rescued Rajbhoj and sent him to hospital. The Depressed Classes Congress adopted twelve resolutions. It declared that its considered opinion was that the Minorities Pact contained the irreducible minimum demands of the Depressed Classes. It repudiated the Rajah-Moonje Pact as, according to its delegates, it was detrimental to the interests of the Depressed Classes; and it appreciated the magnificent services of Ambedkar and Rao Bahadur Srinivasan they had rendered at the Round Table Conference. The Congress of the Depressed Classes thus concluded by declaring that it stood by Ambedkar and the Minorities Pact.

After the Kamtee Congress, Ambedkar visited Poona, Sholapur and Nipani, where he addressed meetings of the Depressed Classes. Of these visits the visit to Poona was very important. He reached Poona in the evening of May 21, 1932. There he was taken out in procession. The motor car in which Ambedkar was seated flew a big saffron flag, popularly called the geruwa flag, with the symbol OM inscribed on it. The huge procession went on raising anti-orthodox slogans and reached the open space at the Ahalyashram. There he was given an address of welcome under the presidentship of A.B. Latthe. Latthe revealed to the audience how in London British statesmen and high officials secretly inquired of him whether or not Ambedkar belonged to the Revolutionary Party of India. Latthe added that it was quite disgraceful on the part of the so-called nationalist press to depict a great man like Ambedkar as a traitor. Latthe, who, it is said, had once offered Ambedkar the principalship of the Arts College at Kolhapnr, recalled an occasion when he had asked Ambedkar about his success as a lawyer. He told the audience that Ambedkar's reply was that according to him success in life meant success in raising the Depressed Classes to the status of human beings. Latthe concluded by declaring that since Ambedkar was striving for the amelioration of the downtrodden humanity in India, his services to India were in themselves a great contribution to India and to the world as well.[2]

Replying to the address, Ambedkar said: "At present I am the most hated man in Hindu India. I am represented as a traitor, I am denounced as an enemy of the Hindus, I am cursed as a destroyer of Hinduism, and branded as the greatest enemy of the country. But believe me when I say that, when after some days the dust settles down and a review of the proceedings of the Round Table Conference is dispassionately taken by future historians, the future generations of the Hindus will acclaim my services to the nation. If they do not recognise, well I would not care for their disapprobation." "My great satisfaction," he concluded with a serene face, "is that the Depressed Classes have implicit faith in my work and undivided devotion to the mission for which I stand. It is my solemn vow to die in the service and cause of those down-trodden people among whom I was born, I was brought up and I am living. I would not budge an inch from my righteous cause, or care for the violent arid disparaging criticism by my detractors."

---

2. The *Janata*, 25 June 1932.

On May 26 Ambedkar left for England to see the British Prime Minister and other Cabinet Ministers before the decision on the communal issue was announced. He left by the Italian steamer, *s.s. Conte Rosso.* The news about his departure was kept a closely guarded secret as he had enjoined upon his men not to divulge it to anybody. Still a representative of the *Bombay Chronicle* screwed it out of some source and cast a revealing light upon Ambedkar's new move. Ambedkar travelled first class, carried very little luggage, and expected to return by the end of August 1932.

It was true that the sudden change in Rajah's attitude worried Ambedkar much, and the Lothian Committee's findings also were not much favourable to him. He thought that this was the moment which came once in an age. He therefore resolved to do his utmost and to stake his all. He was confident that his presence in London would add weight to his demands. In the letters written home, on his way to London, he expressed poignant anxiety for the safety of his Press which, he feared, the thoughtless caste Hindus from the Congress camp might burn down. He instructed Shivtarkar to procure a new room and to remove the boxes of new books or to keep them in safety elsewhere. All the while the thought of the safety of his books haunted his mind.

Ambedkar reached London on June 7, 1932. In a week he saw every big British official and all Cabinet Ministers in connection with his mission and pleaded his case with heart and soul. He presented to the British Cabinet a representation consisting of twenty-two typed pages. But he could not say anything just then about the outcome of his efforts. He said that discussions were held and decisions were taken at a very high level; and it was in the air that the Depressed Classes in the Provinces of Bombay, Madras and C.P. would get separate electorates. By June 14 he had done everything possible to achieve his end and wanted to return. But, as some of his supporters wished him to prolong his stay, he decided to stay for a month more for convalescing in a German Sanatorium conducted by Dr. Moller at Dresden, so that he could run to London if necessary. Ambedkar was in need of money. The indefinite period of his stay was causing him worry in matters of health and expense. So he asked Shivtarkar to make some arrangements for a remittance, if possible.

There was a rumour in the Indian circles in London, that Dr. Moonje was to go to London and Rajah was to accompany him. Ambedkar hated Rajah for throwing him into a quandary. He therefore asked his men in Bombay to give Rajah a black send-off if he left for London from Bombay. He said in his letter that he was dead sure that his followers must have thwarted Rajah's attempt to hold a conference in Bombay. And, in fact, the Conference which the Rajah Party held with great difficulty in Bombay, at this juncture, was routed when one of Ambedkar's followers died and in all fifty men were injured. In utter contempt for Rajah, Ambedkar said that Rajah was not so important a figure as to deserve serious consideration; still he was nervously anxious to frustrate Rajah's attempt on all fronts!

In the midst of these feverish activities, Ambedkar did not forget his nephew and his son or neglect their education. He wrote from Dresden inquiring about the progress of these boys in their studies. Great men are so much absorbed in their own activities and aims that they cannot pay individual attention to the development of their children. Their wives and children live as though they were moving in a bewildering blaze of limelight cast by the deeds and activities of their chief men. And that is why great men look like great peaks of mountains with deep and dark narrow glens on either side.

By the middle of July, Ambedkar recovered his health, left Dresden, and stayed for a week in Berlin which was then witnessing the emergence of Hitler. From Berlin he wrote that he would travel to Vienna and catch the steamer *Gange* at Venice. But this time, he said, he should not be worried with the formalities of a reception and welcome. Such is human nature. One pines for what one has not got. When Ambedkar left for foreign lands, during his student days, no one took note of his departure and arrival. But since the days of the Round Table Conference his departure and arrival had been made the occasions for public send-offs and receptions by thousands of his devotees as well as by pressmen.

III

Ambedkar arrived in Bombay on August 17. Only three days before the British Premier had given his Award on the communal issue in India. According to this Award, the Depressed Classes were granted separate seats in the Provincial Assemblies and the right of double vote under which they were to elect their own representatives and to vote also in the general constituencies.

The next day, after his arrival, Ambedkar wrote a very important letter to Sir Samuel Hoare asking him to clear the meaning of the last part of the paragraph nine of the Award as there was some doubt about it among some of the members of the Depressed Classes. He further wrote that it was impossible for him to make the Depressed Classes accept the Award with the proviso attached to it, and concluded his letter by saying that "pending the arrival of your reply I will try to hold the storm of indignation that is bursting over my head from the Depressed Classes from all parts of India from bursting in public".

The Communal Award perpetuated divisions among the Indians. It, so to say, politically balkanized India. It gave separate electorates to the Muslims, Sikhs, Europeans and Christians. The main object of the Award, in the words of the *Bombay Chronicle*, was to turn the national majority of the Hindus into a minority.[3] It was, therefore, condemned by all persons and the Press.

Yet the Communal Award was developing into a great political crisis in which Ambedkar would be dangerously involved. Back to India, Gandhi was arrested on January 4. Gandhi had not given up his fight for tying the untouchable Hindus to the caste Hindus in politics. In early March, he informed the British Cabinet from Yeravda Jail that he would resist with his life the separation of the untouchable Hindus from the caste Hindus. And when the Communal Award, was declared, granting separate electorates to the Untouchables, he declared his resolve to fast unto death if the separate electorates for the Depressed Classes were not abolished. Yet on principle, he had no word to say

---

3. The *Bombay Chronicle*, 18 August 1932.

against separate electorates being conceded to the Christians, Muslims and Sikhs.

On one more count Gandhi's resort to a fast unto death against the grant of separate electorates to the Depressed Classes was not justifiable either. As a matter of fact, he was a signatory to the requisition made to the British Premier at the time of the last meeting of the Minorities Committee, empowering the Premier to arbitrate in the matter of the final solution to the communal problem. So Gandhi was bound by his word. But politically frustrated, he declared the fast to rivet the attention of the world on India in general and to frustrate Ambedkar's attempt at securing separate electorates in particular. The governing and undying characteristic of Mahatma Gandhi was action. All his power emanated from his endless action. Action had made him what he was. Even in jail he would not sit a silent witness to any declaration affecting vitally the destinies of India. The politician in Gandhi was now appealing to the Hindus in the name of nationalism and in the name of patriotism to unite and to consolidate. And apparently it was a good stand!

As was natural, Gandhi's announcement threw the country into a state of consternation. Public appeals were made to Gandhi and the Government, statements were issued to the Press, and prayers were offered. Leaders like Dr. Rajendra Prasad said that Hinduism was on its trial. There was confusion and nervous strain in all Hindu circles; not because the caste Hindus and their leaders felt ashamed of their cruelty to the Depressed Classes, but because the life of their political hero, their political liberator, was at stake. The traditional tragic trend in the character of the Hindus got the upper hand, and they got panicky.

Pandit Malaviya declared from Simla his intention to hold a conference of Hindu leaders in Bombay, on September 19, to resolve the deadlock and save the life of the Mahatma, and informed Ambedkar about it by wire. For, to save the life of the Mahatma it was necessary to alter the British Premier's Award, and to amend it was necessary to get the approval of Ambedkar who had wrested these privileges for the Depressed Classes. Naturally, all eyes turned to Ambedkar as a man of the moment. It was a cruel irony of fate that the leaders and the Press that had refused to recognise Ambedkar as the leader of the Depressed

Classes were now compelled to recognise his leadership of and spokesmanship for the Depressed Classes. He now became the cynosure of the whole country.

Ambedkar knew the significance and magnitude of the crisis arisen out of Gandhi's fast unto death. Gandhi had hurled a most dangerous and fatal weapon at him. He prepared himself for repelling the weapon. He had an interview with the Governor of Bombay in Poona. He must have tried to read Government's reaction to the crisis. On the eve of the conference of the Hindu leaders, Ambedkar issued a statement to the Press in which he said: "So far as I am concerned, I am willing to consider everything, though I am not willing to allow the rights of the Depressed Classes to be curtailed in any way. It is no use holding a conference in a vacuum or discussing things without any specific data." He frankly related this to a deputation of the Depressed Classes from Ahmedabad, and also in his interview with the Indian multi-millionaire, Seth Walchand Hirachand. He told them that Gandhi could have discussed his proposal with the British Premier; since he was not putting forth any proposal, he alone was to blame.

Visitors, leaders and friends began to call upon Ambedkar. One of such early visitors was Thakkar who had served with him on the Starte Committee. He came to talk the matter over. Ambedkar to whom time was knowledge and a precious thing said that he was very busy studying an important criminal case and therefore asked Thakkar how much time he would require. Thakkar replied that he would require an hour or so. Ambedkar said that he would give five minutes. Thakkar asked for more. The interview ended with an algebraic brevity, and Ambedkar went in. Such a curt, blunt brevity many a time does more harm than good to the cause and career of a statesman. Thakkar, however, saw Ambedkar again the next day.

A furious campaign was launched against Ambedkar. He was again called a monster, a traitor and a hireling. B. G. Horniman wrote a furious article in the *Bombay Chronicle* on the eye of the Bombay Conference, saying that Ambedkar could not talk as if he had the Depressed Classes in the hollow of his hand. He added angrily that the Doctor had to reckon with his countrymen and should not therefore stick up to his superior aloofness as though he were in a position to dictate to the country. The adopted patriot warned Ambedkar that the man who assumed a proud and solitary position in a crisis of that kind was apt to find his solitariness become permanent.

Ambedkar was calm and collected. He issued another statement, on the eve of the conference, recalling Gandhi's declaration at the Round Table Conference that the problem of the Depressed Classes was of comparatively little importance, an appendix to the book of India's Constitution. "It would have been justifiable," he observed, "if Mr. Gandhi had resorted to this extreme step for obtaining independence for the country on which he was so insistent all through the Round Table Conference debates." "It is also a painful surprise," he went on, "that Mr. Gandhi should have singled out special representation for the Depressed Classes in the Communal Award as an excuse for his self-immolation. Separate electorates are granted not only to the Depressed Classes but to the Indian Christians, Anglo-Indians and Europeans as well as to Mohammedans and the Sikhs."

Ambedkar further said that if separate electorates to the Mohammedans and Sikhs did not split up the nation, Hindu society could not be said to be split up if the Depressed Classes were given separate electorates. Concluding his statement, Ambedkar said in his vitriolic vein: "The Mahatma is not an immortal person, nor the Congress, assuming that it is not a malevolent force and is not to have an abiding existence. There have been many Mahatmas in India whose sole object was to remove Untouchability and to elevate and absorb the Depressed Classes, but every one of them has failed in his mission. Mahatmas have come and Mahatmas have gone. But the Untouchables have remained as Untouchables."

The Mahatma, with his saintly decorum, was a man of the world and acted as such whenever his statecraft or ideology had to deal with the non-Muslims and Britishers. As an expert, he knew his art well. He knew what would have happened to his fast unto death, had he entered upon one aimed at wresting independence from the hands of the Britishers, or had he started one to force the Muslims to drop separate electorates. Nor did he enter upon a fast unto death for the abolition of untouchability. Ambedkar knew this bent of Gandhi and hit him hard.

The declaration of the fast unto death made the people learn more about the condition of the Untouchables and opened their eyes for a while to the passions that were seething in the bosom of the Untouchables. The people, the Press and patriots were roused to a realisation that there was a blot on their society. There was an endless talk about Ambedkar in every political party, in every social circle and in every religious institution. He was flooded with telegrams and letters, some threatening his life, some appealing to his conscience, and some supporting his stand.

IV

As declared, the conference of the Hindu leaders was held amidst this tense situation at the spacious Hall of the Indian Merchants' Chamber on September 19, 1932, under the presidentship of Pandit Madan Mohan Malaviya. Ambedkar and Dr. Solanki were seated just near the President's chair. Rajah and Dr. Moonje came to the Hall arm-in-arm. Among those present were Manu Subedar, Sir Chimanlal Harilal Setalvad, Walchand Hirachand, Dr. Rajendra Prasad, Kamala Nehru, Sapru, Choithram Gidwani, Thakkar, Dr. Deshmukh, Dr. Savarkar, Aney, K. Natarajan, P. Baloo and others. Seth Walchand Hirachand suggested to Malaviya that he should call upon Ambedkar to speak first. In a calm and firm voice Ambedkar told the conference that it was very sad that Gandhi should have started his fast against the interests of the Depressed Classes. It was very proper, he said, that every man should try to save the precious life of Gandhi, but in the absence of any alternative proposal from Gandhi there seemed to be no way out. He, therefore, asked them to secure Gandhi's alternative proposal and said that he would be then in a position to proceed with the discussion. "But one thing is decided. To save Gandhi's life I would not be a party to any proposals that would be against the interests of my people," he added. At this some leaders shuddered, and a few received a palpitating shock!

The Hindu Leaders' Conference then adjourned and met at noon the next day, September 20, in order to hear the Deputation that had waited upon Gandhi at Yeravda jail. Sir Chunilal, the leader of the Deputation, told the Conference that Gandhi had no personal objection to the reservation of seats for the Depressed Classes. Thereupon Ambedkar was requested to say something on the point at issue. Telling the Conference that he was placed on the horns of a dilemma, he said: "It has fallen to my lot to be the villain of the piece. But I tell you I shall not deter from my pious duty, and betray the just and legitimate interests of my people even if you hang me on the nearest lamp-post in the street. You better appeal to Gandhi to postpone his fast about a week and then seek for the solution of the problem." This was again a great shock to the Conference! His serene face and serious glowing eyes seemed to speak: "You ideologues, pundits and patriots, if you cannot treat us as your own, you have no right either to thrust joint electorates on us or to pin us down to your creed!"

The Conference then adjourned till two in the afternoon, next day, the 21st September. But immediately the leading members of the Conference went to Birla House and there Sir Tej Bahadur Sapru evolved a scheme of Primary and Secondary elections for the reserved seats. According to it the Depressed Classes themselves were to select for every seat a panel of not less than three candidates and then out of those three chosen candidates one was to be selected by the joint electorate of the caste Hindus and the Depressed Classes. Thereupon Ambedkar said that he would consult his colleagues and come back within two hours with his proposal. One of the colleagues whose advice he sought in time of crisis and on all important occasions was P. G. Kanekar, a man of sound judgment and great learning. After consultation with his colleagues, Ambedkar returned at night and told them he would accept the proposal, but demanded a much number of seats than the British Prime Minister's Award had given them. The leaders accepted his suggestion; and Jayakar, Sapru, Birla, Rajagopalachari and Dr. Rajendra Prasad left for Poona by the midnight train on Tuesday.

On the early morning of Wednesday, September 21, they saw Gandhi in the office room of Yeravda Jail at seven o' clock. Gandhi said he would consider the proposal and let them know. On September 21 Gandhi was removed at noon to the countryard just near the entrance of Yeravda Jail, and Sardar Patel and

Gandhi's Secretary Pyarelal were allowed to sit near his cot. At noon Sapru telephoned to Ambedkar from Poona asking him to come to Poona immediately. Ambedkar left by the midnight train. On the same day Rajah and Malaviya, too, left Bombay for Poona.

On Thursday morning, Gandhi had a talk with Dr. Rajendra Prasad and Rajagopalachari and said he did not like that election to some of the reserved seats should be both by primary and secondary election system and to some only by joint electorates. He said the primary and secondary election system should be applied to all seats alike. This was related to Ambedkar at the National Hotel. Again the atmosphere became heated. Some of the leaders suggested that in the meanwhile they should send a cable to the British Premier requesting him to cancel the separate electorates for the Depressed Classes. But Ambedkar stoutly and pointedly told them that he would be prepared to lose separate electorates which the British Premier had invested them with, provided he was given a concrete picture of the substitutes and added that he was not a man to run after a mirage. The atmosphere of dullness gave place to grim despair. At noon Jayakar, Sapru and Malaviya saw Gandhi in the jail. They were followed by P. Baloo and Rajah, who promised Gandhi that they would secure an agreement that would satisfy him.

Late in the evening Ambedkar, accompanied by Jayakar, Birla, Chunilal Mehta and Rajagopalachari, went to meet Gandhi in the jail. It was the gravest political crisis. When the party entered the prison court, Gandhi was lying on a white iron-cot with a jail mattress on it, under the thick shade of a low mango tree, and Sardar Patel and Sarojini Naidu sat near Gandhi. Near the cot were bottles of water, sodabicarb and salt.

When Ambedkar approached the cot, there was an echoless silence and a breathless eagerness. Would the entangling silence move Ambedkar? Jayakar had foretold that Ambedkar's intransigence would collapse when he saw Gandhi. Would the entrancing sadness in the atmosphere deepen by the twilight inveigle Ambedkar? Ambedkar was now in the presence of the enveloping pesonality of Gandhi who had cast his spell on powerful men and drowned them in the flood of his magnetic mysticism. Amidst the fierce whirlwind raging outside the jail and the entangling silence prevailing inside, Ambedkar was calm

and collected. A lesser man would have been buried alive in such
a cyclone of happenings. Ambedkar loved his people more than
his life and cared more for the happiness of his people than for
his own. Essentially a man of good heart, he would have burst
into tears at the moving sight. But the agelong sufferings,
humiliations and hardships under which his people had groaned
were keeping his eyes and heart under the pressure of his head.
Besides, Ambedkar, as is typical of all great Maharashtrian
leaders, kept his mind and nerve unaffected in the crisis. The
history of Maharashtra is replete with such instances.
Ambedkar had taken his political life in his hands and was
facing the storm.

This was another phase of the war that had started on
August 14, 1931. The iconoclast and revolutionary was again
facing the greatest man of action under the sun, the greatest
mystic and magnetic personality of his age, the riddle of the
twentieth century moulded into a marvellous alchemy by the
qualities of a *Bania*—a man of the world, a Barrister—a man
of legal acumen and a *Bairagi*—a hermit. When two such
minds come into collision, they are bound to spurt out fire,
and to raise hurricanes. This was happening in India outside
Yeravda Jail.

Gandhi was weak. He lay in his bed. The talk began. Sapru
related to Gandhi the whole story. Malaviya put the Hindu point
of view. Then in a soft, slow flow Ambedkar began. He said in a
low voice: "Mahatmaji, you have been very unfair to us." "It is
always my lot to appear to be unfair," replied Gandhi. "I cannot
help it." Then Ambedkar explained the whole situation and his
viewpoints. The sober Biblical language had its visible effect upon
Gandhi, He was convinced of the justice of Ambedkar's demands.
At length Gandhi replied: "You have my fullest sympathy. I am
with you. Doctor, in most of the things you say. But you say you
are interested in my life." "Yes, Mahatmaji, in the hope that if
you would devote solely to the cause of my people, you would
become our hero too," said Ambedkar in reply. "Well, then, if it is
so, then you know what you have got to do to save it. Do it and
save my life. I know you do not want to forego what your people
have been granted by the Award. I accept your panel system,
but you should remove one anomaly from it. You should apply

the panel system to all the seats. You are untouchable by birth and I am by adoption. We must be one and indivisible. I am prepared to give my life to avert the disruption of the Hindu community."

Ambedkar accepted Gandhi's suggestion. The interview ended, and the leaders started to settle other details regarding the number of men in the panel, number of total seats in the provincial assemblies, duration of the primary system, duration of the reserved seats and distribution of posts.

Friday, the 23rd September, dawned. For hours hot discussions raged over the number of candidates required to make the panel. Then there was the question of seats. Ambedkar demanded 197 seats in the Provincial Assemblies and the leaders reduced the number to 126. Negotiations dragged on. Hours rushed by. After ten hours of discussion, some points were referred to Gandhi and he upheld Ambedkar's points. But still the negotiations seemed to break down on the question of duration of primary election and referendum to decide the duration of reserved seats. Ambedkar said that the system of primary election should terminate at the end of ten years; but he insisted that the question of reserved seats should be settled by referendum of the Depressed Classes at the end of further fifteen years. The leaders' opinion was that the evil of reserved seats and separation would be perpetuated by making its removal dependent upon the will of the Depressed Classes. Ambedkar's insistent demand for a referendum at the end of twenty-five years created a furore among the caste Hindu circles. Ambedkar frankly told them that he refused to believe that untouchability would be no more in the next twenty years or so, and therefore he said that faced with the sword of Damocles, the caste Hindus would be compelled to change their inhuman attitude to the Untouchables.

It was now four in the evening. News came in that Gandhi's health had taken a serious turn, and he was fast losing strength. Gandhi's son, Devdas Gandhi, with tears in his eyes, described the condition of his father to Ambedkar and entreated him not to hold over the agreement by pressing for a referendum. At last it was decided to refer this matter to Gandhi. Ambedkar with selected leaders saw Gandhi in the jail at nine o'clock that night.

Gandhi approved of the idea of referendum, but said it should take place after five years. Gandhi's voice had now sunk to a whisper. The jail Doctors intervened and stopped further conversation. The leaves of the mango tree above refused to move. It was a breathless silence. The visitors had to return. Ambedkar was not prepared to give up his point. His will-power was on the strain. Letters threatening his life came in showers. Murderous looks were cast at him in the street, and some of the leaders insanely reviled him behind his back.

Friday night grimly witnessed all things in suspense. On Saturday morning discussions were resumed. The question of the total number of seats was decided by granting 148 seats to the Depressed Classes in the Provincial Assemblies, and it was also decided that 10 per cent of the seats of the Hindus from British India in the Central Assembly should be given to the Depressed Classes. And then discussion was held for hours on the question of referendum which baffled the solution as before. As nobody would agree to Ambedkar's demand, he thought it proper to see Gandhi once again in the matter. So, accompanied by Dr. Solanki and Rajagopalachari, he went to Gandhi. Gandhi told Ambedkar that his logic was irrefutable; but he said mere statutory guarantee would not root out the disease. He, therefore, entreated Ambedkar to give a last chance to Hinduism to make a voluntary expiation for its sinful past and added that there should be a. referendum but not at the end of any period longer than five years. "Five years or my life," said Gandhi with a tone of finality.

Returning to the place of discussion, Ambedkar said that he was not prepared to yield on the point of the period of referendum which should be, he averred, not less than ten years. After an hour or so they decided to make the agreement without the condition of referendum attached to it! Rajagopalachari explained it to Gandhi in the jail at three in the afternoon. Gandhi said it was excellent and gave his consent. Rajagopalachari returned post-haste to 1, Ramkrishna Bhandarkar Road. Shivlal Motilal's Bungalow, and amidst rejoicings announced that Gandhi had blessed the agreement. It took them no time to draft the agreement. Amidst an atmosphere of joviality, freshness and chat, the agreement was signed at five in the evening on

Saturday, 24th September, and it went down to history as the
Poona Pact. On behalf of the Depressed Classes, Ambedkar signed
it, and on behalf of the caste Hindus, Pandit Madan Mohan
Malaviya signed it. The other signatories were Jayakar, Sapru,
G. D. Birla, Rajagopalachari, Dr. Rajendra Prasad, Rao Bahadur
Srinivasan, M. C. Rajah, Devdas Gandhi, Biswas, Rajbhoj, P.
Baloo, Gavai, Thakkar, Solanki, C. V. Mehta, Bakhale and Kamat.
More signatures were added to the list in Bombay.

Rajagopalachari was so much overjoyed that he exchanged
his fountain-pen with Ambedkar.

V

Immediately the contents of the Pact were cabled to the
British Cabinet, wired to the Viceroy, and also handed over to
the Secretary of the Bombay Governor by each party separately,
and next morning the leaders returned to Bombay to ratify the
Pact. At 2 p.m. the leaders held a meeting at the Indian
Merchants' Chamber Hall. Presiding over the meeting, Malaviya
declared that no one should be regarded as untouchable by reason
of his birth and appealed to Hindus to make,the idea of
untouchability disappear from the land. Mathuradas Vasanji
moved the resolution ratifying the Pact and Sapru supported it.
With a full-throated tribute to Ambedkar, Sapru congratulated
him on his valiant fight for the cause which he represented and
added that Ambedkar promised to be a good fighter in the future
life of the country.[4]

When Ambedkar rose to support the resolution, a
thunderous applause greeted him. Ambedkar said that what had
happened the previous day was beyond his dream. After a
tremendous stuggle and confusion, they had found the solution.
He said no man was ever placed in such a dilemma as he was.
There was the life of tbe greatest man of India to be saved, and
on the other side the interests of the down-trodden community
were to be safeguarded. But at last, he said, with the co-operation
of Gandhi, Sapru and Rajagopalachari they could arrive at the
solution. "My only regret is, "he added, " why did not Mahatmaji

---

4.   Pyarelal, *The Epic Fast*, p. 186.

take this attitude at the Round Table Conference ? If he had shown the same consideration to my point of view then, it would not have been necessary for him to go through this ordeal."[5]

Concluding his speech, be earnestly appealed to the caste Hindus to abide by the Pact and trusted that they would look upon the document as sacrosanct and work in an honourable spirit.

The British Government announced on September 26, that it would recommend to Parliament the endorsement of the Poona Pact. In the evening prayers were said in the Prison yard. Kasturba then handed Gandhi orange juice, and he broke his fast about half-past five amidst a gathering of some two hundred disciples and admirers, poet Tagore, Sarojini Naidu, Sardar Patel and Swarup Rani Nehru being conspicuous.

The Poona Pact thus vibrated the whole country and had repercussions throughout the world. It proved once more that Ambedkar whom in pre-Poona Pact days the Congress leaders and the press refused to recognise as the leader of the Depressed Classes, came out as the accredited leader of the Depressed Classes all over India. In the new arrangement both the sides had to lose something. The caste Hindus had to grant 148 seats instead of 71. The Depressed Classes lost their chance of bending the caste Hindu leaders to their will as the Depressed Classes were under the Award entitled to elect their own representatives to the Assemblies separately, and besides they were to vote in general constituencies with the caste Hindus in electing the caste Hindu representatives. Now the caste Hindus got the power to elect the representatives of the Depressed Classes. By a resolution at its Delhi Session on September 26, the Hindu Mahasabha also ratified it. But then one wonders why Dr. Ambedkar opposed the Rajah-Moonje Pact which was less troublesome and more straightforward. Was it because the offer came from a good-hearted but powerless Party ?

The third thing that was proved was that whenever the Mahatma in Gandhi got the upper hand of the politician in Gandhi, he performed the marvel of making simple things

5. Ibid, p. 189.

complex and complicated! At the Round Table Conference the
Mahatma in Gandhi dominated the politician in him; and the
Mahatma shook the world, but the politician failed. At Yeravda
the politician in Gandhi became successful and the Mahatma
was defeated! So effective and crushing was the victory of Gandhi
that he deprived Ambedkar of all the life-saving weapons and
made him a powerless man as did Indra in the case of Karna.
Ambedkar was justified in saying that had Gandhi shown enough
resilience at the Round Table Conference in the matter of the
problem of the Depressed Classes, the Mahatma would not have
been required to go through the ordeal. The ordeal was of
Gandhi's own making.

The Poona Pact closed an epoch. But did the war which had
been declared at Manibhuvan on August 14, 1931, rome to an
end? Or was it a second battle and the war was to continue even
after the truce ?

                                                      ☐☐☐

CHAPTER 12

THE REAL PATH

As a result of the Pact, the caste Hindu leaders seemed to have taken readily to the temple entry movement. In the early twenties Gandhi was not in favour of temple entry of the Untouchables and was also against inter-dining. Prominent Congressmen had opposed this movement.

During the days of Gandhi's fast, some temples were reported to have been thrown open to the Untouchables. The figures were romantic, but the facts were sad. Ambedkar said that dilapidated, haunted and non-existent temples were listed to extend support and sympathy to the Mahatma. And even this small list contained almost no names from Gujarat, the home province of Gandhi, which was then, and is now, socially as rigid and reactionary as before!

The struggle for temple entry launched by Ambedkar at Nasik, in March 1930, and at Guruvayur by Kelappan in November 1931, had been neglected so far by Congressmen. Kelappan went on a fast from September 21, 1932, declaring that he would not stop it till the doors of the temple at Guruvayur were thrown open to the Untouchables. But he suspended his fast for three months, on receipt of a telegraphic assurance from Gandhi saying that he would go on a fast with Kelappan from January 1, 1933, if the doors of the temple were not thrown open to the Untouchables. As Kelappan was a great asset to the Untouchables in Malabar, Ambedkar sent him a message that his life was more valuable than the entry of the Untouchables into that temple.

But Ambedkar, who had vigorously launched a movement in his own way at Nasik for temple entry, now swiftly changed the rudder of the ship of his movement. He urged his people to devote their energies to gaining political power. Addressing a meeting at Worli, in Bombay, on September 28, 1932, Ambedkar said: "The object of the temple entry movement is good. But you should care more for your material good than for spiritual food.

You do not get food to eat, clothes to wear, opportunities of educating your children, and medical help for want of money. You should, therefore, be watchful of the political gains, and you must develop your strength and struggle for gaining material advancement in life." It was at this meeting that he made a fervent appeal for a building fund to erect a central building to house the headquarters of the movement.

Ambedkar reiterated the same views when he addressed a meeting at Bellasis Road, in Bombay, in the second week of October 1932. He vividly described to his people how hard they had made their struggle for existence by hankering after ideas about the unseen happiness in the other world rather than concentrating their minds on the material forces in this world. In a heart-rending appeal he said that because people neglected the material needs of life and grew indifferent to the knowledge that enabled them to secure them, the country remained backward and her progress came to a standstill. "The appearance of Tulsi leaves around your neck," he continued, "will not relieve you from the clutches of the money lenders. Because you sing songs of Rama, you will not get a concession in rent from the landlords. You will not get salaries at the end of the month because you make pilgrimages every year to Pandharpur. Because the major part of the society is absorbed in these worthless mysteries of life, superstitions and mysticism, the intelligent and self-centred people get ample scope and opportunities to carry out their anti-social designs." "I, therefore, appeal to you," he concluded, "to act and utilise what little political power is coming into your hands. If you are indifferent and do not try to use it properly, your worries will have no end. Fear lurks in my mind that the slavery which we are fighting out may overtake us again. Will this awakening of ours be short-lived? "

Ambedkar had a brief in a very important murder case at Sawantwadi. The trial was to take place at Sawantwadi on September 19, 1932. but owing to Gandhi's fast he could not go to Sawantwadi, and so the hearing of the case was postponed to October 19. On his way to Sawantwadi, Ambedkar saw Gandhi in Yeravda Jail. Discussing the personnel of the Anti-Untouchability League with Gandhi, he suggested that there

should be a majority of the Untouchables on its different
committees. He stressed the need for a special census and told
Gandhi that there was a visible slackness in the movement for
the uplift of the Depressed Classes, and expressed his opinion
that the activities of the Anti-Untouchability League should be
mainly directed to the economic, educational and social
improvement of the Depressed Classes rather than to the
problems of temple entry and inter-dining.

On his return from Sawantwadi to Bombay, he was
presented with an address, on October 28, 1932, by the Rushi
Samaj at the Sir Cowasji Jehangir Hall. There he warned his
people not to get themselves lost in the temple entry movement
and inter-dining. He told them that the problem of bread and
butter would not be solved by it. "The sooner you remove the
foolish belief that your miseries were pre-ordained, the better.
The thought that your poverty is an inevitability, and is inborn
and inseparable is entirely erroneous. Abandon this line of
thought of considering yourselves to be slaves," he added. Another
address was given to him on November 4, on the eve of his
departure to London for the third session of the Round Table
Conference. He was honoured this time by the Gujarati Meghwal
community. The address evoked unending blessings on their
chosen leader and wished him a long and prosperous life.

Ambedkar left for England on November 7, 1932. In an
interview, at the time of his departure, he said that the
establishment of Provincial Autonomy without responsibility at
the Centre would be unwise and that he disliked the idea of
Central responsibility for British India being made dependent
upon an All-India Federation. As regards the Civil Disobedience
Movement of Gandhi, he opined that it was not a rebellion as it
could not oust the British Bureaucracy.

A man of enormous strength, master of himself and lord of
his people, Ambedkar was now, after crossing swords with the
greatest political leader of India, in the best of his spirits. He
liked the Italian liner, *Victoria*, very much for her speed, her
shape; and her well furnished accommodation and modern
equipment were an attraction to him. The Indian ocean was calm
and looked like a limitless glittering glass cover. The Red Sea

also was comparatively cool; otherwise it was an ordeal to cross the Red Sea at that time of the year, he said.

In his letters home he further said that he was very much restless at the tumultuous send-off given every time by vast crowds. He added that his frame of mind was quite suited to democracy, but he was smothered by these crowdy, noisy and undemocratic displays which smacked of hero-worship. He said that his heart craved for loneliness and a calm and quiet atmosphere, and that nobody had a better claim to such a retired life than he. If the law, he observed, that peace followed trouble was true, he should have enjoyed retired life long before by virtue of his strenuous and ceaseless struggle. But he well knew that that rule of life was not applicable to his life. He was destined to have a busy and noisy time to the end of his life. It was sheer love of duty that had bent him to this inevitability, and he hoped that the sincerity of purpose and love of duty would inspire him always with courage to perform the supreme task ably.

II

On board ship many important passengers talked about the Poona Pact and about Gandhi's fast that had rocked the Indian world. The fast had impressed them tremendously. One of the European passengers, pointing to Ambedkar, said to his friend: "This is the young man who is writing new pages of Indian history!"

While discussing the political problem with the other delegates on board ship, Ambedkar was shocked to know how the British officials and statesmen had planned to deprive the Depressed Classes of representation in the Central Assembly. They had hatched this plan on the plea that the problem of the Depressed Classes was the concern of the Provincial Governments and so their quota of representation in the Central Assembly was to be lavished on the Muslims and Europeans. Ambedkar felt a thrill of joy when he saw the designs of the British officials and statesmen flouted by the Poona Pact which gave them 18 per cent of the Hindu seats in the Central Assembly. He also learnt that some of

the delegates were inclined to accept whatever reforms the
British offered. Upon this Ambedkar said that India would
not gain more than what the Simon Commission offered,
unless something unexpected happened.

Ambedkar was suffering from a slight pain in his leg. He
could not enjoy a fast walk on the deck as he had done on the
last occasion. However, he spent his time reading a life of
Napoleon, his favourite historical figure, by Prof. Sloane, and
Gandhi's statements issued from Yeravda Jail regarding the
Harijan Movement. Referring to these statements, Ambedkar
said in his letters to his colleagues that there were signs that
Gandhi was coming round to their views; but he added that
Gandhi's mental frame had not reached a stage that welcomed
or encouraged inter-dining and inter-marriage. He expressed the
view that Gandhi should not go on a fast, for he thought that
Gandhi would die in vain.

Commenting upon these statements of Gandhi, Ambedkar
wrote a letter to Thakkar, the General Secretary of the Anti-
Untouchability League, from Port Said, on November 14, 1932,
on his way to London. This letter was described as the most
valuable document which laid before the Hindu Social workers
some constructive suggestions in the matter of annihilation of
untouchability, not in his usual provocative and vitriolic spirit,
but in a practical, just and unchallengeable way. In it Ambedkar
observed: "The touchables and Untouchables cannot be held
together by law, certainly not by any electoral law substituting
joint electorate for separate electorate. The only thing that can
hold them together is love." "The salvation of the Depressed
Classes," he went on, "will come only when the caste Hindu
is made to think and is forced to feel that he must alter
his ways. I want a revolution in the mentality of the
caste Hindus."

He, therefore, asked the Anti-Untouchability League to
launch a campaign all over India to secure the Depressed Classes
the enjoyment of their civic rights such as taking water from
village wells, admission into village schools and to village chowki,
and the use of the public causeways. This would, he believed,
bring about a social revolution in Hindu society.

"If this campaign for civic rights is to be successful," he proceeded, "the League will require an army of workers in the rural parts, who will encourage the Depressed Classes to fight for their rights and who will help them in any legal proceedings. It is true that this programme involves social disturbance and a violent struggle. But I do not think that it can be avoided. Adopting the line of least resistance will be ineffective in the matter of uprooting untouchability."

"For that you must create," he asserted, "a crisis by direct action against the customary code of conduct of the caste Hindus. The crisis will compel the caste Hindu to think, and once he begins to think he will be more ready to change than he is otherwise likely to be. The great defect in the policy of least resistance and silent infiltration of rational ideas lies in this that they do not produce a crisis. The direct action in respect of the Chowdar Tank at Mahad, the Kalaram Temple at Nasik and the Guruvayur Temple in Malabar have done in a few days what million days of preaching by reformers would never have done."

He pointed out that much of the poverty and misery of the Depressed Classes was due to the absence of equality of opportunity in all the departments of work and service. He asked the Anti-Untouchability League to fight for the removal of that discrimination against the Depressed Classes. He further asked the League to engage full-time workers from the Depressed Classes for that work. Since they came from the class of sufferers, they would serve the cause better and more sincerely than the fair-weather friends of the problem. He concluded his famous letter by quoting Tolstoy who said, "Only those who love can serve", and by saying that mercenary workers would not serve the purpose.

While the steamer was crossing the Mediterranean Sea, it rolled terribly. Ambedkar longed for the day when steamers would travel undisturbed by any storm. He said that it was not impossible for human brains to build such steamers.

In one of his letters written at this stage of the voyage he said that he had no knack of making friends. This was partly because his face gave a stern and grave appearance, and partly because he loved the company of books more than the company of men and was most of the time engrossed in thinking. Still on board ship he could make friends with the Prince of Jath and formed a good opinion of K. V. Godbole, the gentle and polite Dewan of the Phaltan State.

Ambedkar was all praise for the attractive and splendid Hall at Geneva. To him it was beauty incarnate, and he paid his meed of praise to Benito Mussolini whose sense of beauty was responsible for that great piece of architecture.

On reaching London, Ambedkar found that the joint Meeting of the third session of the Round Table Conference had commenced on the 17th November. This time the delegation was smaller and Congressmen were conspiciously absent. The sight of a division among the delegate, made Ambedkar very unhappy. He was sorry to observe that the Muslim delegates, even after securing almost all of their demands contained in their fourteen-point memorandum, were still not co-operating with the other Indian groups in the demand for responsible Government at the Centre. He was more than ever convinced that the Muslims were acting as a said separate bloc and that the Hindu delegates were proverbialy, divided among themselves and were, therefore, powerless.

Another mark of the character of the Muslim mind he was surprised to note was that the Muslim leaders were not only self-centred but also narrow-minded and regressive in their social attitude. Ambedkar drew the inevitable conclusion that it was unsafe to count on their support with regard to the demands of the Depressed Classes. He then described how Ghuznavi received a telegraph from the orthodox Hindus of Bengal seeking the Muslim support in opposing the movement for temple entry and entreating the Muslim delegates to voice their grievances. Ambedkar declared that the appeal of the orthodox Hindus to the Muslims to protect their religion was a grave warning to all Indian reformers. The leader of the Depressed Classes was of the opinion that, like the Hindu orthodox, the Indian Muslim was a strange being. To the Indian Muslim, social reorganisation was anathema. Ambedkar also wrote that Indian Muslims would be benefited if they took a leaf out of Kemal's book. He added that he himself had great respect for the great leader of Turkey while the Indian leaders like Shaukat Ali had no respect for

Kemal Pasha and Amanulla because both Kemal and Amanulla were progressive in their outlook.

The proceedings of the third session of the Round Table Conference went according to its programme. The chief business before the third session was to supplement the work so far accomplished at the previous sessions by filling some details and gaps left out, and to decide the composition of the Central Government in the light of the reports of the Lothian, the Percy and the Davidson Committees. It was declared that adult franchise was impracticable under the existing conditions, that the franchise should be extended, and that a portion of the women population should be enfranchised. The Princes had lost their enthusiasm his time, and they were marking time. In respect of the Depressed Classes it was decided that provision be made to enfranchise a larger portion of the Depressed Classes.

III

Ambedkar worked on the Commercial Safeguards Committee. A memorandum signed by eight delegates, namely Ambedkar, Jayakar, Sir Cowasji Jehangir, Joshi, Kelkar, Sapru, Nanakchand, and N. N. Sircar was submitted to the Conference, asking it to remove the discriminating legislation and appealing to the Premier that there should be some small clause incorporated in the constitution, abolishing privileges based on incident of birth, caste or religion.

In the second week of December 1932, Ambedkar wrote in a letter home from the Imperial Hotel that nobody showed interest in the proceedings of the Round Table Conference. The British people, too, being anxious about the settlement of their debts to the U.S.A., were unmindful of the Conference, Amidst such grim surroundings India's future did not look bright to Ambedkar, as there was no chance of gaining a responsible and real Government for India. Ambedkar further said that details about the structure of Federation were placed before the Conference, but no date of its inauguration was ever mentioned. He lamented that the Muslim and States' representatives betrayed indifference to the immediate grant of Indian demand for Responsible Government at the Centre, and naturally the

divided men, he observed, would not be able to bring anything
to India.

At last the Conference ended its work on December 24, 1932,
amidst depressing world conditions and amidst the intransigence
of the Muslim delegates, and their indifference to the goal of
India. Ambedkar immediately left for India.

By now the temple entry movement had made a stir on
the platform and in the Press. The Mahatma's threat of
sympathetic fast with Kelappan had exposed several black
sheep in the Mahatma's own camp. That the caste Hindu
leaders had come to a rough and hasty agreement at Poona
out of blind affection for Gandhi became clear. The movement
was gradually spending itself. The Zamorin refused to throw
open the temple at Guruvayur to the Untouchables; and this
Zamorin was a Hindu prince in whose ceremonial functions
the Muslims enjoyed some rights.

Gandhi then suggested that if a referendum in the Ponnani
Taluka decided by majority against the entry of the Untouchables
into the Guruvayur temple, he would refrain from his proposed
fast. The majority decided in favour of the temple entry. Still the
Zamorin would not yield. About the same time Ranga Iyer
presented for introduction in the Central Assembly The
Untouchability Abolition Bill. Similar Bills were presented for
introduction by Rajah, Gayaprasad Singh and B. C. Mitra in the
Central Assembly, and a resolution was moved later by Bole in
the Bombay Legislative Council in the same matter.

At this Gandhi extended the time-limit for entering upon
the fast and declared that he would not commence the fast on
January 1, 1933, but would await the decision of the Governor-
General. But if Gandhi was the uncrowned King of the land, and
his word was law, why should there be this fuss? So said the
Ambedkarites.

Ambedkar returned to Bombay by the *Gange* on January
23, 1933. Along with him was Sir Purshottamdas Thakurdas.
On landing, he was given an enthusiastic reception by the Samata
Dal. In an interview to the representative of *The Times of India*,
Bombay, he reiterated his view that the grant of responsible
government to British India should not be made dependent on

the eagerness or otherwise of the Princes to join an All-India Federation.

When asked about his reaction to the temple entry Bills, he expressed concern at the rumours which said that the Viceroy was not likely to give permission immediately to the introduction of these Bills in the Central Assembly and the Madras Legislative Council. He further said that Gandhi should not stake his life on the question of temple entry and added that the Viceroy should not stifle discussion in the legislatures. He should use the power of his veto if he thought the legislation as passed was beyond the dictates of the people.

At the Ballard Pier, Ambedkar received a telegram from Gandhi asking him to see the latter in Yeravda Jail. Ambedkar wired back to Gandhi that he would see him on his return from Delhi. The next day Ambedkar received a wire from Dr. Ba Maw of Rangoon which said: "Burma anti-separatist leaders proceeding to Delhi next week to meet Indian leaders during the Assembly session. They are anxious to discuss Burma constitutional situation with you and other leaders. We, therefore, request you to meet the deputation in Delhi on 4th and 5th February. Kindly wire your Delhi address to enable us to get in touch with you there. Reply U Chit Hlaing, 80, Hermitage Rd,, Rangoon,—U Chit Hlaing and Dr. Ba Maw." Several congratulatory messages were received in Ambedkar's office from all quarters of the country. One of them was from the Thiya Yuvajan Samaj of Ernakulam, congratulating their great leader gratefully on the bold fight he gave at the Round Table Conference for the rights and liberties of the Depressed Classes and the people of the Native States.

Immediately the Doctor left Bombay for Delhi to attend the informal meeting of delegates to the Round Table Conference convened by the Viceroy. After his return from Delhi, he wired to Gandhi that he would be able to see him on the 4th February. Gandhi informed Ambedkar by wire on February 3: "Wire just received tomorrow 12-30 will suit—Gandhi." It is clear that Ambedkar could not meet the Burma delegation in Delhi as he wanted to see Gandhi in Yeravda Jail on February 4, 1933.

Accompanied by S. N. Shivtarkar, Dolas, Upasham, Kowly, Ghorpade and Keshavrao Jedhe, Ambedkar entered

Yeravda Jail at 12-30, on February 4. In a happy mood Gandhi got up and welcomed the visitors. After a while, the conversation turned to the question of temple entry. Gandhi requested Ambedkar to lend his support to Dr. Subbarayan's Bill and that of Ranga Iyer. Ambedkar flatly refused to have anything to do with Subbarayan's Bill, since the Bill did not condemn untouchability as a sin. It only said that if a referendum favoured the temple entry, temples should be thrown open to the Depressed Classes, but said nothing of their right to worship the deity in the temples.

He told Gandhi that the Depressed Classes did not want to be Shudras in the order of the caste system and added that he honestly could not call himself a Hindu. Why, he asked, he should be proud of that religion which condemned him to a degraded position. If that system was to continue, he had no use of the benefits of the temple entry.

Gandhi said that according to him the caste system was not a bad system. He continued: "Let the touchable Hindus have an opportunity to expiate their sins and purify Hinduism. Do not be indifferent to this question. Sanatanists and Government would take advantage of this. If this reformation takes place, the Untouchables would rise in society."

Ambedkar differed from Gandhi. He was convinced that if the Untouchables made progress is the economic, educational and political fields, temple entry would follow automatically.

He stressed the same point in his message given to the first number of *Harijan* started by Gandhi on February 11, 1933, to propagate the cause of the 'Untouchables. In the message Ambedkar said: "The out-caste is a by-product of the caste system. There will be outcastes as long as there are castes. Nothing can emancipate the outcaste except the destruction of caste system. Nothing can help Hindus and ensure their survival in the coming struggle except the purging of Hindu faith of this odious and vicious dogma." In reply Gandhi said that many educated Hindus held this view; but he was not able to share it.

IV

On his return from Poona, Ambedkar joined the Bombay Legislative Council's debates. He made a vitriolic speech supporting an amendment which aimed at incorporating a proviso in the Village Panchayat Bill enabling the Collector to appoint representatives of the Muslims and the Depressed Classes, it they were not on the village Bench.

Replying to the charges, Ambedkar observed: "Sir, India is not Europe. England is not India. England does not know caste system. We do. Consequently the political arrangements that may suit England can never suit us. Let us recognise the fact. I want a system in which I will have not only a right to go to the ballot box, but also the right to have a body of people belonging to my own class inside the House, who will not only discuss matters but take part in deciding issues. I say, therefore, that communal representation is not a vicious thing; it is not a poison; it is the best arrangement that can be made for the safety and security of the different classes in this country. I do not call it a disfiguring of the constitution."

One Member said: "Decoration !"

Dr. Ambedkar: "It is a decoration of the constitution."

Referring to the opposition point as to why they should admit the principle of communal representation in respect of the judiciary, he said that; the judiciary had decided cases, more often than not, with a communal bias and had in such cases prostituted and abused its position. He then cited cases in which the parties were Brahmins and non-Brahmins.

This speech caused a stir in the Council and in the Press, and the next day Members fulminated against the wholesale condemnation of the judiciary. Explaining his stand to the House, Ambedkar said that he did not mean a wholesale condemnation of the judiciary, or to single out any particular community for special condemnation. And the matter ended.

On February 12, 1933, Ambedkar issued his famous statement on the temple entry Bills and movement, and sent a copy to "Dear Mahatmaji" in Yeravda Jail. Referring to Ranga

Iyer's Bill, Ambedkar said that the Untouchables were not inclined to support it because the Bill was based on the principle of majority and did not regard untouchability as a sin. They said that the majority was opposed to temple entry. "Sin and immorality," Ambedkar went on, "cannot become tolerable because a majority is addicted to them or because the majority chooses to practise them. If untouchability is a sinful and immoral custom, in the view of the Depressed Classes it must be destroyed without any hesitation even if it was acceptable to the majority. This is the way in which all customs are dealt with by courts of law, if they find them to be immoral and against public policy. This is exactly what the Bill does not do."

"Looking to the problem from the materialistic point of view," Ambedkar observed, "the surest way for their salvation lies in higher education, higher employment and better ways of earning a living. Once they become well placed in the scale of social life, they would become respectable; and once they become respectable the religious outlook of the orthodox towards them is sure to undergo a change and even if this does not happen it can do no injury to their material interest." There was also the point of self-respect. He said that just as the Hindus did not beg for admission into clubs and social resorts run by Europeans who said "Dogs and Indians are not allowed," so also the Untouchables did not beg for admission into temples where the boards said. "All Hindus and all animals including dogs are admitted—only Untouchables are not admitted". He asserted that all what they said to the caste Hindus was: "To open or not to open temples is a question for you to consider and not for me to agitate. If you think it is bad manners not to respect the sacredness of human personality, open your temples and be a gentleman. If you rather be a Hindu than be a gentleman, then shut the doors and damn your self. For I do not care to come."

Ambedkar, then, stated that if temple entry was not the final goal, and was a step in the direction of the final goal, they might be inclined to support it just as the Indians wanted to accept for India political reforms, if the Dominion Status for India was accepted by Britain as the goal.

The Untouchables were determined not to tolerate a religion which tried to defend social inequality. "If Hindu religion is to be their religion, it must become a religion of social equality. Then it must recognise them as nationals and not aliens. If Hindu religion is to be the religion of social equality, then an amendment of its code to provide temple entry is not enough. What is required is to purge it of the doctrine of Chaturvarnya. This is the root cause of all inequality and is also the parent of the caste system and untouchability which are merely other forms of inequality. Unless it is done, the Depressed Classes will reject not only the temple entry but also the Hindu faith. For to accept the temple entry and be content with it, is to compromise with evil, and to barter away the sacredness of human personality that dwells in them."

He concluded his statement by asking a pertinent question to Gandhi: "If I accept the temple entry now and agitate for the abolition of Chaturvarnya and caste system, on what side Gandhi would be. If he will be in the opposite camp, I cannot be in his camp now."

Almost all the Depressed Class leaders of Ambedkar's persuasion, endorsed the views of their leader. Srinivasan, Premrai and Malik upheld the views of their leader.

Gandhi issued a statement in reply in which he stated: "I am a Hindu, not merely because I am born in the Hindu fold, but I am one by conviction and choice. There is no superiority or inferiority in the Hinduism of my conception. But when Dr. Ambedkar wants to fight Varnashram itself, I cannot be in his camp, because I believe Varnashram to be an integral part of Hinduism.

While this Gandhi-Ambedkar controversy over the temple entry was going on, another great leader, who had been clipped into internment by the British Government at Ratnagiri, flung a pleasant surprise on Ambedkar, inviting him to open a new temple built by Seth Bhagoji Keer in Ratnagiri. Ambedkar replied that he was extremely sorry that he was unable to accept his invitation owing to previous engagements. He further observed in his reply to Veer Savarkar: "I however wish to take this opportunity of conveying to you my appreciation of the work you are doing in the field of social reform. If the untouchables are to be part and parcel of Hindu society, then it is not enough to remove untouchability; for that matter you must destroy chaturvarnya. I am glad that you are one of the very few who have realised this."

Many were surprised that Ambedkar should have drifted to the extreme left when other leaders and forces left the rigid right and made a definite move towards him. It was true that instead of asking his men to co-operate with the movement launched by the caste Hindu reformers, he now turned the eyes of his men to political gains and power. But he did it with reason. Although his name appeared on the Central Board of the Anti-Untouchability League, which was renamed Harijan Sevak Sangh by Gandhi, he had not attended any of its meetings. He had severed his connection with this League when the League made a complete departure from its original aims. The exclusion of Depressed Class leaders and workers from its Executive gradually aroused suspicion of its *bona fides* in the minds of the Depressed Class leaders. Many of them thought that the object of the League was, in effect, not the facilitation of Ambedkar's movement, but the liquidation of his leadership. Not only that, many of them were of the opinion that to Gandhi, removal of untouchability was a platform and not a programme ! In addition to this, there were fundamental differences. It was feared that the poor Untouchables would be immersed in the exultation evoked by the temple entry movement and in the thought of God, and would be diverted from their goal of political and economic equality. Hence this widening split !

What was the reaction of the Press to Ambedkar's statement? Infuriated at the statement of bitter facts made by Ambedkar, the whole hierarchy of the national press relapsed into a campaign of hatred against Ambedkar, and some of them described him as Bhimasur, a devil. A Bombay Marathi daily painted him as a *Brahmadveshta*. According to men of Ambedkar's persuasion, the title was really expressive of the life mission of Ambedkar in the sense that the title. "Father of Indian Unrest", bestowed on Lokamanya Tilak by Chirol, was a real estimation of Tilak's life and mission. In their view Brahmanya or Brahminism meant an ideal of society which was based on the principle of highness and lowness, and was headed by Brahmins. By virtue of being a Brahmadveshta, Ambedkar was against this unjust system based on inequality and injustice. and naturally was more revolutionary, more patriotic, since the mission of a Brahmadveshta was levelling down the caste system, untouchability, highness and lowness, and the exploiters of the lower classes.

Not to speak of the hardened sanatanists, even semi or sanatani social reformers opposed the temple entry Bill of Ranga Iyer. They opposed the Bill and said it should not be decided by a referendum, nor law should be allowed to interfere in religious matters. In a telegraphic outburst Pandit Malaviya urged Gandhi that Ranga Iyer's Bill should be withdrawn as the Pandit was opposed on principle even to a indirect interference by legislature in the management of the temples, and even added that the Bill was not necessarily in accordance with the terms of the Bombay pledge! And the Bombay pledge was nothing more than a ratification of the Poona Pact!

The British rulers on their part suspected foul play in the Gandhi-Rajaji move. They thought that it was their political design to arouse the Depressed Classes against the British Government. Non-intervention in religious matters being their declared policy, they feared that it would add to the bitterness of the people who were already estranged politically. They thought that since the Hindu leaders, who were silent for ages, were now bent upon removing untouchability by law, it meant more than embarrassment to them. But the India Office at last advised the Governor-General to grant permission to the legislators to introduce the Bills. The Viceroy refused permission to Dr. Subbarayan and Narayan Nambiar to introduce their Bills as the problem underlying them was of an all-India character, and so it could not be dealt merely on a provincial basis. He, however, allowed others to introduce their Bills. Except the one introduced by Ranga Iyer, other Bills were dropped.

Ranga Iyer introduced his Bill on March 24, 1933. But with the connivance of the Congress Members and the lack of sympathy on the part of Government for the Bill, the orthodox leaders smothered it by resorting to dilatory methods. The result was that a few months later the Temple Entry Bill dropped dead.

V

After issuing his statement on the Temple Entry Bill, Ambedkar carried on propaganda against the spiritualistic fads and superstitions of his people which had emasculated and devitalised them for ages. He impressed upon their minds that to them bread was better than the worship of God. At a Conference, at Kasara in Thana District he told the Untouchables: "We want equality in Hindu religion. The Chaturvarnya must be rooted out. The principle that privileges for the higher classes and poverty for the lower classes must end now. The British Government is a foreign Government; and so there could not be much advancement in our conditions. Do not allow disunion to grip you. It leads to ruin. Study the situation and surroundings with your own eyes. Do not forget that your fight at Mahad and Nasik won you what political status you are going to get. The news about Nasik satyagraha which appeared in *The Times*, London, every day had interested and instructed the Britishers."

"What you have lost," proceeded he, "others have gained. Your humiliations are a matter of pride with others. You are made to suffer wants, privations and humiliations not because it was pre-ordained by the sins committed in your previous birth, but because of the overpowering tyranny and treachery of those who are above you. You have no lands because others have usurped them; you have no posts because others have monopolised them. Do not believe in fate. Believe in your strength."

At a meeting, at Mazgaon, Bombay, in the last week of February 1933, he declared: "I am in a situation in which Tilak was once placed. As long as the opponents curse me, it is taken for granted that my work for you is on the right lines and is justified. During the last two thousand years never was such an attempt made to annihilate untouchability. The Untouchables are now convinced that the demand for Swaraj and the cause of the Hindus will suffer for want of support from the Depressed Classes. What the Hindus do for you is not by way of charity or mercy. They do it for their own welfare as well. The mission of our movement is to fight out tyranny, injustice and false traditions, and to undo all privileges and release the harassed people from bondage. Our cause has gained recognition because of our ceaseless struggle."

"Give up eating carrion. People ask me then what they should eat. In reply, I ask you to remember the example of a virtuous woman. She will never accept the life of a prostitute for betterment though she falls on evil days. She suffers for self-respect. Learn to live in this world with self-respect. You should always cherish some ambition to do some thing in this world. They alone rise who strive. Some of you nurse the wrong notion that you will not rise in this world. But remember that the age of helplessness is ended. A new epoch has set in. All things are now possible because of your being able to participate in the politics and legislatures of this country."

At another meeting held in Bombay to present him with an address, in the first week of March 1933, he said: "This address is full of superlatives about my work and qualities. It means you are deifying a common man like you. These ideas of hero-worship will bring ruin on you if you do not nip them in the bud. By deifying an individual, you repose faith for your safety and salvation in one single individual with the result that you get into the habit of dependence and grow indifferent to your duty. If you fall a victim to these ideas, your fate will be no better than logs of wood in the national stream of life. Your struggle will come to naught."

"Do not disregard," he continued, "the political rights the new epoch has bestowed upon you. Your whole class was trampled down up till now because you were filled with ideas of helplessness. I may add that these ideas of hero-worship, deification and neglect of duty have ruined Hindu society and are responsible for the degradation of our country." "In other countries," he observed, "during a national calamity and crisis people take united action against the national calamity, ward off the danger, and attain peace and prosperity. But our religion has drummed into our ears that a man does nothing. He is a helpless log. At the appearance of a national calamity God is supposed to descend down and save us from danger! The

result is that instead of taking a united action against their
enemies they await the arrival of an incarnation to do this job
for them."[1]

"You must abolish your slavery yourselves. Do not depend
for its abolition upon God or superman. Your salvation lies in
political powers and not in making pilgrimages and observance
of fasts. Devotion to scriptures would not free you from your
bondage, want and poverty. Your forefathers have been doing
it for generations, but there has been no respite nor even a
slight difference in your miserable life in any way. Like your
forefathers, you wear rags. Like them, you subsist on thrown-
out crumbs; like them, you perish in utter slums and hovels;
and like them, you fall easy victims to diseases with a death
rate that rages among poultry. Your religious fasts, austerities
and penances have not saved you from starvation."

"It is the duty of the Legislature," he concluded, "to provide
for your food, clothes, shelter, education, medicine and all the
means of earning a livelihood. The work of law-making and of
its execution is to be performed with your consent, help and will.
In short, law is the abode of all worldly happiness. You capture
the power of law-making. It is, therefore, your duty to divert
your attention from fast, worship and penance and apply it to
capturing law-making power. That way lies your salvation. That
way will end your starvation. Remember that it is not enough
that a people are numerically in majority. They must be always
watchful, strong, well-educated and self-respecting to attain and
maintain success."

VI

Towards the middle of March 1933, came the announcement
of the British Government in the form of a White Paper
containing proposals for Indian Constitutional Reforms. This
White Paper was to be considered by a Joint Committee of both
the Houses of British Parliament. Jinnah described the White
Paper as a White Hall Rule; Subhas Bose said that it was a serious
breach of peace, and Dr. Moonje said it was a Black Paper.
Jayakar declared that Federation had receded.

---

1. The *Janata*, 11 March 1933.

Just then the Bengal Legislative Council passed a resolution asking for the annulment of the Poona Pact. In a statement issued to *The Times of India* Ambedkar resented the attitude of the Bengal Hindu leaders, and pointed out that the Bengali caste Hindu leaders had taken a very prominent part in negotiating with him the terms of the Poona Pact at Parel and at the office of the Indian Merchants' Chamber, and hence their story that they were not parties to the agreement was false. He then revealed to the public how the British Premier had referred to him a telegram from Sir N.N. Sircar, who said that the Bengal Hindus were unrepresented at the Poona Pact. Ambedkar had replied to the British Premier in these words: "My first submission is that, assuming that the Bengal Hindus were not represented at the Poona settlement, it cannot for that reason alone make it inapplicable to Bengal. Paragraph 4 of the Communal decision of His Majesty's Government was for the whole of British India." Ambedkar further said that although the Poona Pact did not satisfy the Bengal Depressed Class leaders who wanted 50 instead of 30 seats in Bengal, he had forced the terms down their throats. The Depressed Classes in Bombay, Bihar, the Punjab, U.P and Orissa, too, were not satisfied with the terms of the Pact, he concluded.

Immediately after the announcement of the White Paper, the names of the delegates to the Joint Committee were announced. Seventeen men were selected to represent British India, seven to represent the Indian States and thirty-two were from both the Houses of the British Parliament. Ambedkar was invited to work on the Joint Committee along with Sapru, Jayakar, Mirza Ismail, the Aga Khan and Sir Akbar Hydari. Before his departure to London, he went through a crowded programme for two weeks, attending farewell meetings, addressing public meetings and had an important interview with Gandhi at Yeravda Jail.

Although Ambedkar grew in name and fame, the atmosphere in caste Hindu circles had not lost its edge of prejudice, or had shown any appreciable improvement. His Highness the Maharaja of Baroda was to be honoured in Bombay for his great services to the cause of the down-trodden. Ambedkar's name was at first included in the list of members of the reception committee, but it was ultimately dropped, it was said, on account of his untouchability! Ambedkar was now an all-India figure, ranked among men of the highest academic attainments, could talk with and sit by the side of the British Premier and even the King-Emperor, but the semi-reformers in India would not do him that honour as they had not shed their inveterate caste prejudice. After the Yeravda episode, there was a move among the High Court lawyers of Bombay to honour Ambedkar, but the idea had to be given up for want of a suitable place for the function. A Gujarati legal celebrity wanted to invite Ambedkar to the marriage ceremony of his son, but he, too, could not do so on account of his untouchability.[2]

Ambedkar visited the Hostel of the Depressed Class students on April 4, 1933, which was then removed to the Aga Khan's bungalow at Thana. To secure this bungalow Ambedkar had sent a cablegram to the Aga Khan, who with difficulty granted his request. Addressing a meeting of the students, Ambedkar related to them how the Ashram was started at Panvel in the house of a Jew, who took advantage of the helplessness of the Depressed Classes and had enhanced the rent. He asked the students to compare the most insulting and inconvenient environment, in which he himself had studied, with the convenience and surroundings they were now enjoying in the hostel. He then advised them not take part in politics during their school days and asked them to create value and worth for their say. He impressed upon them the importance of self-culture and self-help. He exhorted them to have a purpose in life and to accomplish it by their own industry and perseverance.

Next week Ambedkar addressed a Conference of the Depressed Classes at Sopare. On April 12, he and V.G. Rao, the then Chairman of the Schools Committee, Bombay Municipality, were honoured, the latter for his services to the cause of education of the Depressed Classes. The meeting was held at the maidan behind Damodar Hall. Replying to the address, Ambedkar said that his original plan was to become a professor and lead the life of a student. With that end in view he had sacrificed all pleasures and purchased books in thousands. But fortunately or

---

2. The *Vividha Vritta*, 26 March 1933.

unfortunately he was thrown into the vortex of politics. The same night he was presented with a purse at Kurla near Bombay under the chairmanship of Rao Bahadur S.K. Bole.

In the meantime, Ambedkar decided to sound Gandhi again on the question of the panel and primary elections of the Depressed Class candidates in the light of the coming constitution of India. He was in a hurry to make preparations for his departure to London. Yet he had to attend meetings, to attend courts or dispose of the cases, to make arrangements for domestic affairs, and to select books. Accompanied by More, Shinde, Gaikwad and Chavan, he saw Gandhi on April 23, in Yeravda Jail. Gandhi and Ambedkar sat in chairs under the mango tree and Mahadev Desai sat nearby with a note book and pencil.

At first Ambedkar said that the method of panel would be expensive and told Gandhi that candidates from the Depressed Classes, who would contest the general election, should have secured at least 25 per cent of the votes of the Depressed Classes in the primary election. Gandhi replied that he would give consideration to the matter and would inform him about his reaction to his London address. Gandhi, then, gave a bunch of flowers to Ambedkar and diverted the conversation to the question of removal of untouchability and said that the sanatanists were decrying him (Gandhi) as a devil, Daitya. Ambedkar asked Gandhi what more he expected from the sanatanists, Gandhi caught the thread and said that the leader of the Depressed Classes himself was not pleased with his work. In the end Gandhi asked Ambedkar about the date of his return from London. Ambedkar replied that it would be about August 1933. Gandhi wished Ambedkar *bon voyage* and the interview ended.

On the eve of his departure to London, Ambedkar was given an addr.ss, on April 23, by the Depressed Classes of Poona at the Damodar Hall in Bombay. Addressing the meeting, he said that during the second session of the Round Table Conference he was helpless. He could not estrange the British Government by siding with Gandhi who was not prepared to concede anything to the Depressed Classes. He declared that since his struggle for the rights of the Depressed Classes was nearing success, he would devote his energies to wresting as much power for the country as was possible for him. At the conclusion of the meeting, he appealed to his people not to come to the Ballard Pier to give him a send-off as was their practice. He said they should not do it at the cost of one day's wages.

Ambedkar left for London on April 24, 1933, to attend the session of the Joint Committee and reached London on the 6th May. From London he called for detailed information regarding Gandhi's fresh fast as the London newspapers gave little or no news about Gandhi's fast which he had started on May 8, as a means of purification. From London Ambedkar often asked for detailed news about the movements of Rajbhoj and others.

During these days the leader and organiser in Ambedkar always remained in close touch with his lieutenants, sharing their joys and sorrows and acting as their guide and adviser in the hour of their need. His secretary Shivatkar was promoted to the post of an educational supervisor under the Bombay Municipal Schools Committee. Ambedkar congratulated Shivtarkar on his new appointment. While in London, he tried to help his benefactor Keluskar, who was now an old man. He submitted a representation to the Maharaja of Baroda through his Diwan and appealed to the Maharaja to grant Keluskar a monthly pension. He wrote from London to Bhaskarrao Kadrekar who edited his Weekly *Janata* and looked after the Press. In an appreciative mood he said to Kadrekar: "I quite understand the difficulties you are undergoing and I have always felt, and this is no mere flattery, that we all, and personally myself, owe you a very great debt of gratitude for the way you are slaving yourself for a paltry pittance."

In the same letter he encouraged Kadrekar by pointing to the eternal truth that all movements of the poor and down-trodden had very small beginnings and a very tortuous course, many ups and downs, and he expressed his belief that he had no doubt that the ultimate issue would not be failure but success. Replying to the charge of some of his colleagues that he hid some facts from them, he said: "The whole of my life is open to you all, and I do not know of any other leader who allowed his life to be an open book to every one." He was happy, he added, over the special number of the *Janata* issued by Kadrekar, but he observed that a special issue should never be devoted to one personality entirely, but should mostly be devoted to the different sides and aspects of the cause he represented.

About this time news spread in some circles through Gavai that Ambedkar was to go over to Islam. Subhedar Savadkar wrote to Ambedkar that it was the general opinion of his people that their "Raja" Ambedkar would not take such a hasty step until he had solved their problem. In reply Ambedkar wrote to Savadkar from London that he had a talk with Gavai regarding the issue of conversion and told him among other things that he was determined to leave the fold of Hinduism and embrace some other religion. He had also told him that he would never embrace Islam and that he was at that juncture inclined to Buddhism. He was so much involved, he concluded, in the destiny of his people that he had lost his personal identity and independence, and would not be free until he had solved their problem.

The strain of work had begun to tell upon Ambedkar's health. His eyesight was impaired. He changed his spectacles. Ambedkar would face any disease and suffer any hardship, but he would not tolerate the idea of losing his eyesight. He once wept bitterly like a child at the thought of being a blind Milton. He sobbed that if the eyes were lost, reading would come to an end, and life would not be worth living!

The Indian delegates to the Joint Committee, on their arrival, met in London in formal conference to appoint a Committee to expose the shortcomings in the White Paper. At this Conference, which was attended by Dr. Moonje, Dr. Sachhidanand Sinha, Pandit Nanakchand—who had been there to lead evidence before the Joint Parliamentary Committee—Hari Singh Gour and others, Ambedkar said that he asked for separate electorates because he was driven into a desperate situation. He told the meeting that it was the inhuman attitude of the caste Hindus that drove him to this desperation. If the Hindus made real efforts to achieve complete consolidation of their social order, the Depressed Classes would join them heart and soul. Dr. Moonje appreciated this speech, and offered Ambedkar the presidentship of the Hindu Mahasabha.

By this time, the agitation in India against the Poona Pact reached white heat. Almost all Hindu leaders who had ratified it, now turned out to be its opponents. Their enthusiasm for Gandhi's Harijan Movement had worn out. Tagore, who, had come to Poona on the day following the Poona Pact, floating on the tide of the good news that the British Cabinet had accepted the Pact, and who had buried his face in the clothes on Gandhi's breast, was now singing a different tune. The Hindu Mahasabha leaders, who had ratified the Pact by a special resolution at its Delhi session, felt it necessary to advocate an amendment of the Poona Pact, as regards the Punjab where, they said no Depressed Class problem existed.

The Secretary of State for India told the Hindu delegation that the agreement had the consent of all Hindu leaders, and therefore it stood unaffected. When Sir N.N. Sircar produced a wire from Tagore supporting the cause of the Bengal Hindus, the Assistant Secretary of State for India simply quoted the Secretary of State for India.

When the Joint Committee reopened its session on October 3, 1933, Dr. Jayakar and Sir Manoobhai refused to cross-examine certain British diehards. On October 23 and 24, Winston Churchill was cross-examined. Ambedkar crossed swords with Churchill when he quoted a speech which the latter had made in Parliament, and, asking him questions thereon he floored Churchill. Ambedkar's confidence, fearlessness and fighting spirit proved equal to that of the greatest imperialist of his age.

The Joint Committee completed its work in November 1933. It supported the White Paper and appointed a small committee to draft the constitution in the light of the discussions. Most of the Members returned to India. Ambedkar was then busy in London collecting data for a book on the Indian Army. He had engaged clerks to take down extracts from important Documents of the India Office.

It seems Ambedkar was changing hotels every now and then. At first he wrote letters home from the Imperial Hotel, Russell Square, where he stayed till August; and then from September he wrote from Montagu Hotel, Russell Square; and in October from Palace Hotel, Bloomsburry Street, in the same locality. In one of his letters written from the last place he referred to the controversy between the Mahars and the Chamars. The Mahars are in an overwhelming majority in Maharashtra. The Chamars are a small minority. They accused Ambedkar of partiality for the Mahars. This was hardly fair. Just as Muslims always charged Hindus that the Hindus were in a majority everywhere in Hindustan, so the Chamars said that Ambedkar's organisation was dominated by the Mahars. Ambedkar wrote that he was sick of these small minds and said that this controversy would go on so long as caste remained. The dropping of one man here or neglect of another there would not cure the disease. The bitterness would end with the end of castes.

Ambedkar left London and reached Bombay on January 8, 1934, by the *Victoria*. He was in high spirits and talked gaily with his friends and admirers. In an interview which he gave at the Pier he said that the Joint Committee might modify the proposals made in the White Paper, but, in the main, they would be accepted. "We should accept them and agitate for more. I will not sit with folded hands and do nothing", he added. As regards the agitation of the Hindu leaders for a modification of the Poona Pact, he said that the Joint Committee would not grant their request and further said that it was a shame and disgrace to the Hindus if they were not in a position to respect their words.

Asked about his future political work, he said that just then he was not interested in politics. He was writing a book named *Army in India* and that interested him more than anything else. He could not say when the book would be published, but hoped it would be out shortly. The book was intended to deal purely with the constitutional aspect of the army question. However, it seems, it remained incomplete.

CHAPTER 13

A THUNDERBOLT

THE strenuous work he did during the preceding four years in India and London told upon Ambedkar's health. The continuous study of and discussions on Indian political and constitutional problems, the ceaseless social work, the untiring efforts in the movement for self-respect and the unending struggle for breaking the shackles of slavery spread across a decade would have affected the health of any leader. The untiring frame of his body felt the necessity for rest, the nerves clamoured for relaxation, and he suffered from brainfag. The nervous exhaustion was so great that he sought resort to a secluded place. He went to Bordi for a few days and then to Mahabaleshwar and was under observation of Ayurvedic doctors. At Bordi he had a rest when there was no visitor. There he was engrossed in drawing a plan for a house which he intended to build at Bordi and wrote to Kamalakant Chitre that the latter might laugh at the idea; but it was a wonderful plan. He also informed Chitre that he was going for a swim. "The sea is calling; and it is so near and I must respond."

Great men are like the sea. Their work, thinking and struggling are never at a standstill. When friends visited Ambedkar, he forgot all about the medical advice and entered into conversation. His tongue then ran, like a machine, for hours together without a thought for the indisposed body. It was during these days that, being in an ascetic frame of mind, he looked like a sanyasin with his tonsured head and flowing robe. Pictures of the hermit in this mood appeared in some of the journals in Maharashtra.

After resting for some days, Ambedkar returned to Bombay. There was no urgent problem on hand. He was confident that the age-long suppressed people would rise in status, would have the right of vote and their smothered voice would be freed to have its say in the making of laws and defining liberty of the individual and

243

the nation. They would sit with their heads erect in the Legislative
Assemblies along with the communities who had not allowed them
even to touch those places. Along with them they would have some
chances of bettering their lot. It was a matter of great satisfaction
to him that the Depressed Classes were invested with the right to
vote. This was the first time in their sad history of two thousand
years that they were counted politically. The Bill sponsoring the
draft constitution was about to be placed before the British
Parliament. In the meanwhile what was he to do? He reverted to
the legal profession and acted as a part-time professor in the
Government Law College, Bombay, from June 1934. Truly speaking,
a man of his eminence, erudition and legal experience should have
been appointed Head of the Institution. But it has been the
misfortune of some great men that their merits are not recognised
without their undergoing trials and tribulations for a long time. It
did not flatter the authorities of the college to have a lawyer of
Ambedkar's scholarship, organising capacity and public status as
an ordinary professor in the Law College. But this being the low
water-mark period, he felt like accepting the post and did accept it.

Ambedkar, at this juncture, carried into effect a dream of
his youth. Do you know any man in Asia who has built a bungalow
to house a library? Mark, his name is Ambedkar. He built a house
for books at Hindu Colony, Dadar, Bombay. It was not built in
the normal way in which other houses are built. Like Thomas
Jefferson, the owner of the house bought books on architecture
and studied the subject. So fascinated was Ambedkar with the
idea of raising a convenient and grand structure to his liking
and plan that he caused some parts of the house to be demolished
after they were built, and got them reconstructed. This happened
so often that one of his colleagues remarked that if Ambedkar
had kept insisting on having a window after the model of one
from the grand structure of the London Museum, a door after
the model of the New York Library and the dome and shape of a
palace, the house would have never seen its roof. But at long
last the house was completed, and the library was housed in the
proper way after frequent changes in the arrangement. Now the
scholar was at his best with the ancient and modern scholars
and thinkers, weighing, testing and scraping knowledge derived
from them. The house was named Rajagriha.

The ground floor of the house was used for household purposes, and the simple, pious and religious-minded Ramabai, wife of the Doctor, moved in 'Rajagriha' with strange emotions and some embarrassment. The "Saheb", as he was called by his family and by his people, took his meals in the company of the great thinkers and law-givers of past ages.

The country was drifting to constitutional and constructive work. There was now no enthusiasm left for Gandhian non-violent revolution. And not long before did Gandhi support the revival of the Swaraj Party and declared that he had suspended the struggle. The All-India Congress Committee accepted this new policy and change in May 1934. In the following month Government lifted the ban on the Congress Party, and Congress leaders started reviving their Provincial organizations.

The first thing the Congress leaders did was that they denounced the White Paper and expressed dissatisfaction, at the Communal Award which they considered dangerous and derogatory to the interests and unity of India. They did not stop at this. In order to favour the Muslim League, which was anxious to ratify the Communal Award, and to discourage the vociferous demands put forth by Aney and Malaviya for its annulment, the Congress leaders, at a meeting of the Working Committee in Bombay, in July, declared that the Congress Party neither accepted the Communal Award nor rejected it. This equivocal and nefarious slogan shows how a cankerous growth was developing in the body of India's leading political Party under the leadership of Gandhi.

Just then Government proposed to hold elections to the Central Assembly. On the eve of the elections, Gavai, the Nagpur leader of the Depressed Classes, appealed to Gandhi to declare his attitude towards the Poona Pact, and requested him to ask the Congress Party to adopt five Depressed Class candidates, without imposing any conditions, to contest elections to the Central Assembly, it was held by many Depressed Class leaders that Congressmen would not interfere with the elcctions of the Depressed Classes in view of the undertaking given to them during the negotiations of the Poona Pact. But those Depressed Class leaders who sided with the Congress Party were perhaps not hopeful of their success in the elections independently. So they were anxious to sound the Congress leaders on this point. But Gandhi reiterated his belief in the sanctity of the Poona Pact and rejected the offer of Gavai saying that it would needlessly bring the Depressed Classes, who were carrying on a deadly struggle for their elementary rights with the caste Hindus, into conflict with Government.

Ambedkar was glad to endorse the views of Gandhi, and so he requested him to pass a resolution on the Communal Award at the ensuing session of the Congress Party without affecting the Poona Pact. He congratulated Gandhi on his firm stand and said that those who made such a request did not know what issues were involved in such a step. Ambedkar, the maker and defender of the Poona Pact, up to this moment little dreamt that he would one day be its worst enemy.

Meantime, the Bombay Legislative Council threw out the Removal of Harijan Disabilities Hill moved by R. R. Bakhale. The Government and the opponents of the Bill feared that it would do a great deal of harm, although they all seemingly acknowledged the ideals underlying it.

It was about this time that Ambedkar had been to Daulatabad on a professional visit. There he and his colleagues went to see the old Fort. They took water from a tank to wash themselves. An old Mohammedan ran to them and cried out. "Dheds (Untouchables) have polluted the tank." A big crowd of Muslims collected and the situation became serious. Ambedkar silenced their ringleader by asking them whether they would prevent an Untouchable from taking water from the tank if he became a Muslim, and further asked him whether that was the teaching of his religion. A dangerous situation was averted; but an armed guard thereafter accompanied Ambedkar and his party, so that they might not pollute water anywhere else!

II

Meanwhile, the report of the Joint Committee was out, and on December 19, 1934, the India Bill was introduced in the British Parliament. Expressing his opinion on the Joint Committee's Report, Ambedkar said that the Depressed Classes were opposed not only to the establishment of Second Chambers but also to their composition; for, according to them, the purpose of the Poona

Pact would be defeated and what was more the Depressed Class
candidates stood no chance of success against their influential
caste Hindu rivals in the elections to Second Chambers.

The nationalist press was glad that Ambedkar fell in with
the other political parties in India in condemning the Joint
Committee's Report as retrograde and a hindrance to the
country's progress. Defender as he was of the interests of his
people, Ambedkar kept an eye on every move in the political as
well as constitutional development of India. The least injustice
to the claims of the Depressed Classes would evoke a severe
indictment at his hands. As regards the creation of Second
Chambers in the Provinces, Ambedkar had opposed the idea at
the time of the Simon Commission and at the Round Table
Conference as well.

Debates were going on in the British Parliament on the
India Bill which was based on the Joint Committee's Report. A
notable feature of the debates was that A.W. Goodman, a
Conservative M.P., uttered an impassionate plea for the
Untouchables and protested against the inadequate
representation proposed for them in the Provincial Assemblies
and the Central Assembly. But in India political debates on the
proposed reforms took a worse turn. The Congress leaders
perilously adopted an attitude favourable to the Muslim League
by practising their neither-accept-nor-reject policy in relation to
the Communal Award, and they allowed Jinnah to compel the
Central Assembly to endorse the Communal Award.

Ambedkar, while teaching at the Law College, watched
these developments with keen interest. Owing to the persistent
outcry raised by caste Hindu leaders against the Poona Pact,
he was greatly embittered. He kept silence. His wife was ill.
During the past ten years he could not spare time to look after
the members of his family. Whenever he could get some respite,
he looked into his home affairs. He had once taken his wife for
a change of air to Dharwar; but there was not much
improvement. The result was that though he was blessed with
a good, dutiful and pious wife, there was not much happiness.
He had lost three of his sons and one daughter. Although a
politician with a rougher tongue, iron will and intrepid courage,
he could not bear these grievous shocks and since then he kept
aloof from all family ties.

Ambedkar did his utmost to mitigate his wife's sufferings. Medicine cures curable diseases. It could not cure her wasting disease, and the cruel blow came to him on May 27, 1935, when the last spark of his wife's life flickered out. Ramabai was a symbol of contentment of heart, nobility of mind and purity of character. During the preceding six months she was struggling with her malady. She had grown weaker and weary; her cheeks were sunken and colourless. Her great gift to mind alone enabled her to endure with cool fortitude the hardships and sorrows that fell to her lot in those early friendless days of want and worries. The grandeur and glory attached to Rajagriha could not distract her mind from the realities of life. She had passed the major portion of her life in pinching poverty, spent days and nights in anxiety for her husband's safety and health, observed rigid fasts, on Saturdays took only water and black gram, worshipped God, and invoked his blessings on her Saheb. Her eyes, her hands and her thoughts were devoted to the service of her Saheb. Gentle by temperament and frail by constitution, she was sober in manners, modest in speech, practical in her approach and generous in her dealings.

In her anxious moments she often blamed the conveners of meetings and conferences that gave her husband no respite and created dangerous situations for him. She said that she could not understand why on earth so many conferences were required to teach and preach to the people. One day she had packed her luggage and insisted on her being taken to the conference at which her Saheb was to preside, so that she might not pass her days in his absence in utter restlessness. There was a little violent quarrel, and the Saheb dissipated her fears as arrant nonsense.

Profoundly religious, she had a great longing for making a pilgrimage to Pandharpur where every year lakhs of believing Hindus bow their heads in devotion. But being an untouchable Hindu lady, she would have been required to stand at a certain distance from, the temple and offer her prayers. Self-respecting Ambedkar could not tolerate the idea and consoled her by saying: "What of that Pandharpur which prevents its devotees from seeing the image of God, by our own virtuous life, selfless service

and spotless sacrifice in the cause of the down-trodden humanity
we would create another Pandharpur!"

Another Pandharpur! These words could come from a heart
that was lofty, noble and inspired with the promptings of God. It
was the dawn of humanity when Vishwamitra took a vow to
create a new parallel world. It was two thousand years ago that
Siddhartha Gautama, the greatest Hindu since Lord Krishna,
thought of giving birth to a new order which created new places
of pilgrimage.

Ambedkar had been on a week-end visit to Dr. Sadanand
Galvankar at Bassein. He had returned on the previous night.
Fortunately he was near her death-bed. About 10,000 people,
rich and poor, eminent and common, attended her funeral
procession, Ambedkar walking by with a heavy heart, his eyes
grave, pensive and dry with sorrow. On his return from the
cremation grounds, he kept to his room, a lonely being tortured
with sorrow. For a week he wept bitterly like a child, and it was
difficult for his friends to console him. The goddess of his
prosperity, partner in the cause of humanity, his better-half in
this earthly voyage, had departed this life. Unbeliever and
destroyer of false notions of priesthood, Ambedkar in his divine
love for his wife got all the funeral obsequies performed by his
son in the Hindu tradition at the bidding of a Mahar priest by
name Sambhoo More, who was Ambedkar's colleague since school
days. Some simple, believing men and women said that it was
the promptings of this calamity that had made Saheb, a few days
earlier, put on a hermit's dress and bid farewell to the earthly
joys and happiness. He got his head tonsured. The serious face,
grave and wide eyes, grim surroundings and his saintly saffron
robe presented people the appearance of a hermit with a world-
negating attitude.

The respite for consolation was, however, short-lived. The
Bombay Government appointed him Principal of the Government
Law College from June 1, 1935. He had accepted the post before
the death of his wife. And now he had to look after the
administrative side of the College from the middle of June. This
was a deserving eminence as it was regarded that such a post was
a rung in the ladder of the judicial sphere. In some happy mood
Ambedkar had talked of his ambition in the judicial world, and
the goal was now in sight. Soon after taking up the reigns of office

as Principal, Ambedkar offered a few valuable suggestions to the Government authorities for improving the tone of the college.

In July 1935 news appeared that Ambedkar was going to retire from politics. A journalist wrote in the *Bombay Chronicle* that Ambedkar would become either a judge in the Bombay High Court or a Minister under the new reforms. Since the Civil Disobedience Movement, he observed, entrants into public service had to give an undertaking that they would not participate in political movements. This was the *sine qua non* or the first condition for entering Government service. Being a Government servant by virtue of his office as Principal of the Government Law College, the journalist continued. Ambedkar naturally could not take part in politics, and therefore his retirement from politics was inevitable. The journalist recalled how a proposal to elevate Ambedkar to the Bench fell through during the time of Sir Frederick Sykes' Governorship, and it was expected now that Lord Brabourne would elevate him to the Bench. Ambedkar was promised, he himself afterwards corroborated, that he would be elevated to the bench in course of time if he accepted the post of a district judge which was then offered to him.

Although it is difficult to imagine the state of Ambedkar's mind, one can, from the knowledge of Ambedkar's past activities, safely conclude that his was not a stature to be accommodated in the post of a High Court Judge. It was too small a cage for the lion. Had he accepted such a position, he would have done it to prove that an Untouchable, if given an opportunity, was able to discharge the duties of any higher post in the State and to set an example to his men for emulation and inspiration. What of a judgeship, he had once told his audience that even the mighty Viceroyalty would be unequal to his ambition!

The reported move for retirement from politics might have been a threat held out to bring indirect pressure on his lieutenants to close up their ranks. The India Bill was before the British Parliament, and, as he was determined to work the constitution with a view to deriving benefits for his people, he would do nothing that came in the way of working the constitution. In the meanwhile, he accepted the post of the Principal of the Law College. He would have even accepted the appointment of a judge had it been offered him during this interim period.

III

Then all of a sudden the calm was followed by a storm, unprecedented and unequalled in the history of India. News appeared in the press that Ambedkar was thinking of making a declaration of a change of religion at the Yeola Conference which was scheduled to meet in October 1935. The news was so sudden and shocking that it quickened the palpitation of many a sensible Hindu leader. Friends and admirers of Ambedkar began to inquire of him as to the truth. A letter appealing to the good sense of Ambedkar, promising him a change of heart on the part of caste Hindus, and dissuading him from the proposed announcement, was addressed to him jointly by Kelkar, Bhopatkar, Chitrav and Mate.[1] Prof. S.M. Mate was a sanatani social reformer who had done a great service to the cause of the Untouchables by devoting himself to the cause of their education for years.

For the past ten years Ambedkar had tried in vain to create an opening for his people into Hindu society. He had to fight for securing his people the right of drinking water from public places, for the liberty of wearing good dress and of using metal utensils, and for the right of receiving education. The Mahad struggle had pained him severely. Immediately after the Mahad Conference, the thought of renouncing the Hindu faith had seized his mind. While the Chowdar Tank case was being heard at the Mahad Court, he frequently visited Mahad to arrange for the defence. It was rainy season and a river in flood detained him on the way for two days. As the place where the motor halted had no untouchable locality nearby, Ambedkar had to go without food and shelter; for none would give shelter and food to an Untouchable.

On his return from Mahad, Ambedkar shut himself in great anguish in a room and would not come out. His friends and colleagues accompanied by Bole, with great efforts, pacified his feelings, and he calmed down. At Jalgaon he had, in 1929, advised the Untouchables to embrace any other religion that would

---

1. Kelkar, N.C., *Autobiography* (Marathi), p. 959.

regard them as human beings, give them an opportunity to rise
in the world and enable them to act, eat, walk and live like men.
Consequently, twelve Untouchables had embraced Islam. With
great efforts, great energy and great hope he had launched the
campaign for temple entry, but the caste Hindus showed no sign
of common sense and reasoning. They were impenitent and
relentless as before. They did nothing more than evince a flutter
of emotion. A group of Untouchables from a village near Nasik
had, about this time, decided to embrace Islam, but Ambedkar
advised them to wait for some time and see whether they could
ennoble Hinduism.

It was announced on the eve of the Yeola Conference that it
was convened by the leaders of the Depressed Classes to review
the political and social situation in the light of their ten-year-
aid struggle and the coming reforms. On his way to Yeola,
Ambedkar was entertained at Nasik Road at a tea party by the
Meghwal (sweepers') community, and at an intercaste dinner in
Nasik.

The Conference met, at Yeola on October 13, 1935, and was
attended by about 10,000 Untouchables of all shades of opinion
including representatives from the Hyderabad State and the
Central Provinces. Expressing his pleasure at the great response
and interest evinced by the Depressed Classes in planning their
future, Rankhambe, Chairman of the Reception Committee, said
in his welcome speech that "degenerated Hinduism was rightly
called Brahminism because it benefited only the Brahmin
hierarchy as a class".

In a tremendously feeling speech lasting over an hour
and a half, Ambedkar recounted the plight of the Depressed
Classes in all spheres, economic, social educational and
political, and pointed out the immense sacrifices made by them
to secure the barest human rights as members of the same
community under the aegis of Hinduism. He especially
referred to the Kalaram Temple entry movement wherein
inhuman treatment was meted out to them during the past
five years, and told them how their struggle to secure
elementary right; and equal status in the Hindu society had
come to naught. He said that it gave him a very painful
realisation that the time and money spent on and efforts made
to achieve those objectives had proved utterly fruitless.

He, therefore, expressed his opinion that the time for making a final decision to settle the matter had arrived. The disabilities they were labouring under and the indignities they had to put up with, he added, were the result of their being members of the Hindu community. He inquired if it were not better for them to abjure that fold and embrace some other faith that would give them an equal status, a secure position and rightful treatment.

He, then, with a rise in his voice, exhorted them to sever their connections with Hinduism and seek solace and self-respect in another religion, but warned them to be very careful in choosing the new faith and to see that equality of treatment, status and opportunities was guaranteed to them unreservedly.

Referring to his own personal decision in the matter, Ambedkar said that unfortunately for him he was born a Hindu Untouchable. It was beyond his power to prevent that, but he declared that it was within his power to refuse to live under ignoble and humiliating conditions. "I solemnly assure you that I will not die a Hindu," he thundered. In the end he asked his people to stop the Kalaram Temple satyagraha as the past five years had demonstrated the futility of such agitation against the tyrannical caste Hindus, who had thwarted their attempts and showed impenitent hearts. He exhorted them to conduct themselves in such a way in future as would leave no doubt to the outside world of their decision to be and to remain a separate community outside the Hindu fold, carving out for themselves a future worthy of free citizens.

Accordingly, after a full discussion, the Conference passed, in view of the callous and criminal indifference shown by the caste Hindus to their demand for social equality, a resolution instructing the Depressed Classes to stop the struggle which they had carried on for the past ten years for raising the Untouchables to a status equal with that of the caste Hindus and in the hope of consolidating and strengthening both sections into a great and powerful society. It further exhorted the Untouchables to stop frittering away their energies over fruitless attempts and to devote themselves to securing an honourable status, and an independent position on the basis of equality with the other societies in Hindustan.

The Conference ended, and a new chapter began in the life of Ambedkar. It was a definite, grave departure from the original aims and objects of his movement.

Ambedkar's address rocked all circles, political parties and social institutions to the bottom. Proselytising religions with their topmost missionary zeal pricked up their ears in the hope of hearing the death-rattle of Hinduism in its national home, its birth place! Leaders of Islam cast greedy glances at Ambedkar, and promoters of Christianity turned many a holy thought in their minds at the sight of the prospective recruits who would add strength, power and support to their faith and existence. They all thought that if Ambedkar's threat was translated into action, it would definitely tilt the balance to the permanent crippling of the Hindus. The Sikhs also thought of angling for Ambedkar and of adding to their strength.

A stream of letters and telegrams flowed in Ambedkar's residence in Bombay from all quarters of Hindustan and other parts of the world. Christian and Muslim leaders began to move. The Muslim leader, K.L. Gauba, M.L.A., telegraphed to Ambedkar, stating that all Muslim-India was ready to welcome and honour him and the Untouchables, and promising the fullest equality and rights in every sphere, political, social, economic and religious. He added that if Ambedkar wished to discuss any matter with the Muslims, he should come to the Muslim Conference at Badaun which was to be held on October 20, 1935.

Asked what he thought of Ambedkar's declaration. Bishop Brenton Thoburn Badley of the Methodist Episcopal Church, Bombay, opined that the Christian view of life made it impossible to think that great communities of people involving millions could really become Christians except when they experienced a real change of heart which was called conversion. He further observed that Ambedkar's statement would be welcomed by the Christian Church because it indicated an ambition on the part of the Depressed Classes for the better things in life and it also showed that a new era for them was about to dawn.

Another appealing offer came from the Secretary of the Mahabodhi Society, Banaras in a telegram to Ambedkar saying that Ambedkar with his community was most cordially welcome to embrace Buddhism, which was professed by the greater part of Asia. "Among Buddhists there are no religious or social disabilities. We guarantee equal status to all converts. There is no caste distinction amongst us. We are willing to send workers," concluded the message.[2]

Yet a strange appeal came from a brother community of the Sikhs. Sardar Dalip Singh Doabia, Vice President of the Golden Temple Managing Committee, wired to Ambedkar, stating that the Sikh religion fulfilled the desired requirements regarding the conversion of the Depressed Classes, and he added: "The Sikh religion is monotheistic and all-loving, and provides for equal treatment of all its adherents."

Commenting on the declaration made by Ambedkar, Gandhi styled his decision an unfortunate event especially when untouchability was on its last legs. He said he could understand the anger of a high-souled and highly educated person like Dr. Ambedkar over atrocities such as were committed in Kavitha and other villages, and added: "But religion is not like a house or a cloak, which can be changed at will. It is a more integral part of one's own self than of one's body," "I am convinced," concluded Gandhi, "that a change of faith by him and those who passed the resolution will not serve the cause which they have at their heart, for the millions of unsophisticated, illiterate Harijans will not listen to him and them who have disowned their ancestral faith; especially when it is remembered that their lives for good or for evil are intervolved with those of caste Hindus."

Savarkar, who had ushered in a new era in Maharashtra in respect of the removal of untouchability, warned the Depressed Classes from Ratnagiri, the place of his internment, against taking such a step. On their conversion, he observed, there was no possibility of their receiving treatment of equality under Christianity or Islam in India. He pointed to the prevailing riots between touchable Christians and untouchable Christians in Travancore.

Observing that untouchability was on its wane, Savarkar turned to the rationalistic side of the problem and said in a bold and fervent appeal: "Truly speaking, any Ism in the sense of religion contains something which is not amenable to reason and which is based an belief. Those who hold that the existing

---

2. The *Times of India*, 18 October 1933.

religious opinions are not amenable to reason or logic should not hug irrational prejudices. Ambedkar, therefore, should embrace a religion which is based on principles that are not averse to logic and reason." What they should do, he concluded, was to fight out valiantly for equality by the side of the progressive Hindus and rise in the scale of life.

The Congress President, Dr. Rajendra Prasad, deplored the Yeola resolution; and although he appreciated the resentment which was at the root of the Yeola resolution, he said it was unfortunate that anything should be done to make the work of the reformers more difficult.

Deorukhkar, a Depressed Class leader of Bombay, said that it was no use embracing another religion; instead of being Untouchables in dwindling numbers in Hinduism, they would be Untouchables in another; for inequality was there in one form or the other in almost all religions. Kajrolkar, another leader of the Untouchables in Bombay, was shocked to hear the decision. He added that it broke their hearts to see that especially a leader like Ambedkar, who had given them lead in their moment of despair, should have asked them to commit suicide. He further said that religion was not a matter for business transaction. A Depressed Class leader from Nagpur said that they should strive to secure equal status with the caste Hindus. Ambedkar's colleague, Dr. Solanki, expressed similar views and hoped that the younger generation would improve matters and added that the Depressed Classes should keep up their struggle for their betterment and equality of treatment.

Yet Ambedkar's declaration came as a thunderbolt to a man who was his colleague at the R.T.C. That leader was Srinivasan. He said that conversion to other faiths would weaken the numerical strength of the Depressed Classes and would encourage their aggressors. The best advice, be observed, to be given to the community was that they should keep up their strength and fight for their rights and principles, which would be manly.[3]

IV

No other announcement of Ambedkar got so wide a publicity on a global scale as this. No doubt the decision was the last dreadful scream of a smothered and suppressed people. It was

3. *The Times of India*, 16 October 1935.

the shriek, which the aggrieved soul uttered in a small voice. It gave vent to their untold sufferings, crushing humiliations and dehumanising atmosphere under which they were squeezed out for ages. In a tornado of righteous rage Ambedkar hurled a very powerful weapon at the impenitent Hindu society; and once he was pushed in the arena by the Press, he showed more and more fight and kept it going with his bludgeon.

When, therefore, the Associated Press showed him the comment on his Yeola speech by Gandhi, he asserted that their decision to leave the Hindu fold was a deliberate one since inequality was the very basis of Hindu religion and its ethics were such that the Depressed Classes could not attain their full manhood under it. He agreed with Gandhi that religion was necessary, but did not agree that a man must stick to his ancestral religion even though he found that religion repugnant to his notions of the sort of religion he needed as the standard for the regulation of his own conduct and as a source of inspiration for his advancement and well-being. He had made up his mind, he concluded, to change his religion; and if the people felt that it was good, they would follow him; otherwise they would not follow him and he would not care if the masses followed him or not.

The ruthless and misanthropic orthodox Hindus were unmoved by the decision of the Depressed Classes. Decrepit and decayed as they had grown, they had lost their thinking power and vision. The illiterate non-Brahmins thought that the decision on religious matters was the concern of the Brahmins. Rejoiced at the Yeola decision, the orthodox Hindus heaved a sigh of relief ; and the Nasik orthodox Hindus, who were harassed for the past five years by the temple entry satyagraha, were exceedingly jubilant over the decision of the Depressed Classes to go out of Hindu fold. They applied now to the Collector for the removal of the ban on the Nasik chariot procession in the light of the fresh declaration of the Untouchables. Enlightened and political-minded opinion in the country deplored the Untouchables' decision. The Princes, who had helped their cause, must have been disappointed in the decision taken by the Depressed Class leaders. A Sindhi Hindu wrote a letter in blood and threatened Dr. Ambedkar with death, if he renounced Hinduism.[4]

---

4. The *Vividha Vritta*, 3 November 1935.

On his return to Bombay from Yeola, Ambedkar stayed for about two days with Dr. Sadanand Galvankar at Bassein. There the famous Hindu missionary leader, Masurkar Maharaj, who had reclaimed about ten thousand Christians in Goa to Hinduism, had a three-hour talk with him. Ambedkar told the Hindu Missionary leader that if the Untouchables abjured Hinduism, that would not affect them much. The Missionary leader said that the exodus would not stop at that and it would be the death of the Hindus in the long run. Thereupon Ambedkar said that it mattered little; the history of Hindustan would continue. In that case, observed the Missionary leader, it would not be the history of Hindustan. It would be the history of another Stan such as 'Pakistan'! Ambedkar sadly nodded and admitted that it would be so. He was not happy at the thought and added that it was in the hands of the caste Hindus to avert the tragedy.

When Masurkar asked him about the way out, Ambedkar replied that the caste Hindu leaders should pledge their word that they would extirpate the evil of untouchability within a prescribed period. Masurkar replied that, looking to the magnitude of the problem, it would take some time to do so. In order to enable the caste Hindu leaders to work. Ambedkar must withdraw the declaration or postpone the issue, he added. Ambedkar said that he would wait for five to ten years for a change of heart; but added sarcastically that in the meantime Maharashtrian Brahmins should install K.K. Sakat, a Depressed Class leader, who was, according to the *Kesari* school of thought, an exemplary Hindu, into the Gadi of the Shankaracharya for one year and that a hundred families of Chitpavan Brahmins should fall at the feet of the new Shankaracharya as a token of their change of heart and acceptance of equal status! Ambedkar also asked the Missionary leader to define the term 'Hindu' in exact words.

Shortly afterwards, a deputation, appointed at a public meeting in Nasik, waited on Ambedkar, promising him to agitate for the removal of untouchability in practice, individually and collectively. The lender of the deputation, R.G. Pradhan, assured Ambedkar of a positive result and tried to dissuade him from his decision.

In his characteristic way Ambedkar replied: "Some people think that religion is not essential to society. I do not hold this view. I consider the foundations of religion to be essential to life and practices of society. At the root of Hindu social system lies Dharma as prescribed in the *Manusmriti*. Such being the case, I do not think that it is possible to abolish inequality in Hindu society unless the existing foundation of the Smriti-religion is removed and a better one laid in its place. I, however, despair of Hindu society being able to reconstruct itself on such a better foundation."

As to conversion, he said that it would be done in five years' time and if, in the meanwhile, the caste Hindus assured him by a positive result, he would reconsider the position. He added that he wanted to absorb his community into some powerful community, and he was thinking of embracing Sikhism. Referring to the Muslim religion, he said: "If there are any people with whom religious sentiments and practices make it extremely risky to interfere, they are the Muslims."

According to him, the way out was the emergence of a benevolent dictator in religious and social matters. "India wants a dictator like Kemal Pasha or Mussolini in social and religious matters. Democracy is not suitable for India. My hope that Mr. Gandhi would attain dictatorship in social affairs was dashed to pieces", he declared. In the circumstances it was difficult, he continued, to get such a dictator in social and religious matters, and since he was not hopeful of the younger generation which seemed to be more predisposed to pleasure-seeking and not possessing idealism like Ranade, Gokhale and Tilak, he despaired of the future of India. Concluding his talks with the caste Hindu deputation, he said that he had strong religious sentiments according to his conception of religion, but he had no faith in Hinduism as he hated hypocrisy.[5]

To implement the Yeola resolution, not long after, a conference was convened at Nasik Road, and thousands of leaflets carrying Ambedkar's message were issued to different Depressed Class institutions all over the country. About this time a Lahore vernacular newspaper flashed the news that according to Pir Jamat Ali, Ambedkar and his followers would shortly embrace

---

5. *The Times of India*, 30 November 1935.

Islam. Asked about this, Ambedkar said that it was true that Pir Jamat Ali had seen him in Bombay and discussed the possibility of his embracing Islam, but beyond that nothing had happened.

In the middle of December 1935, Ambedkar addressed a meeting at Foras Road, Bombay, and declared that the issue of conversion would be first decided at a Mahar Conference which he was contemplating. Letters were now pouring in the Press, the majority of them condemning severely Ambedkar, and a minority upholding his stand. Among such letters and articles was a letter written by a semi-social reformer blustering that Ambedkar would be a nonentity, if he went out of the pale of Hinduism; for, according to him, Ambedkar owed his eminence to his untouchability. Ambedkar, in his characteristic thrust, replied that his ability and eminence were the fruit of his patient labour and intellect, and so he would be able to preserve his individuality in any fold or in the company of any literary or political worthies, whether Brahmin or non-Brahmin. He, however, added that he would prefer a life without distinction in any other fold if his down-trodden people prospered in it.

Although engaged in the vital problem of conversion, Ambedkar had not stopped other activities. He presided over a Peasants' Conference at Chari in Kolaba District and impressed upon the poor peasants that their woes had their roots in the joys of the landlords. He urged them to agitate against the serfdom imposed upon them by these self-centred groups. An interesting incident that occurred at the conclusion of the Conference sheds a sidelight on Ambedkar's personality. While his friends and other leaders were discussing some points in the pandal, a scorpion raised its head through the hay spread over the wet ground. There was an uproar and everybody began to call for a stick or a shoe to kill it with. Ambedkar got up and crushed it under his bare foot !

Ambedkar took an interest in the activities and development of the Law College. How the students and staff received him can be seen from the tribute the college magazine paid to the new Principal in its issue of January 1936. Describing Ambedkar as the perfect blend of the lawyer and the scholar, the editorial note observed: "A lawyer of repute, he is a close student of Economics, an authority on constitutional law and a personality known

throughout India and elsewhere. To write more about him is
otiose. Expecting much from our Principal, we shall not
embarrass him now. We prefer to wait and see."

Ambedkar put his radical views on legal education in a
studied article under the title. "Thoughts on the Reform of Legal
Education in the Bombay Presidency." In it he referred to six
classes of legal practitioners in the Presidency and deplored that
there should be such a diversity in the matter of qualifications,
in the matter of examinations and in the matter of status among
persons practising the same profession.

As regards the curriculum for a complete course of legal
education, he said that a lawyer should possess a correct
understanding of the fundamental principles, a grounding in
general knowledge, the art of orderly presentation of the subject
and precision in stating facts, ability to express oneself in dear
language and relevancy of the answers given to the questions
asked. From the educationist's point of view the study of law,
Ambedkar proceeded, requires a study of certain other auxiliary
subjects without which the study of law alone would be an
incomplete equipment for the practice of the profession.
Observing further that a lawyer must have a legal mind, he
quoted Augustine Birrell who said: "A legal mind chiefly displays
itself by illustrating the obvious, explaining the evident and
expatiating on the commonplace."

V

Ambedkar did not leave the main issue of conversion in
the middle. Yet another conference was held at Poona on
January 12 and 13, 1936, under the presidentship of Prof. N.
Shivraj to decide the issue. In his presidential address Shivraj
said: "The only way to get rid of untouchability is that the
Depressed Classes should leave Hindu religion not necessarily
by conversion to another religion already existing but possibly
by starting a new religion, or by reviving the ancient one
practised among the Adi-Dravidas, long before the Aryans
brought to India Hinduism with its various customs."

Addressing the Conference amidst great cheering,
Ambedkar reiterated his declaration on the need for abjuring

Hindu religion. Three things were significant at this
Maharashtra Untouchable Youths Conference. The first thing
was that Dr. Solanki, who had expressed divergent, if not
diametrically opposite, views to those of Ambedkar on the issue
of conversion, turned a some rsault. Supporting now the stand
for conversion, he said that there was only one request he had to
make to Ambedkar and it was that he should not allow the
Untouchables to stay a single moment under the fold of
disorganised Hinduism, but should found a new independent
religion for them. The Depressed Classes needed no saint, or the
Vedas, or the *Geeta*, or any Shankaracharya, or any apostle, but
Ambedkar himself. The second thing was that the Chamar
community began to drift gradually from Ambedkar on the issue
of conversion. The third thing was that, like Gandhi, who had
extended the sphere and time-limit of his fast on the issue of
Guruvayur temple but never undertook it. Ambedkar extended
the time limit of action to an indefinite time and said that he
and his community would welcome that religion which would
give them the fullest equality of status. Just after the Yeola
decision, he had told an interviewer that he was not prepared to
wait for the people to follow him in his footsteps.

Ambedkar, however, warned his people against the
erroneous view that conversion would relieve them from hell and
would lead them to the paradise of equality. He further told them
that under any new religion they would be required to fight for
liberty and equality. "We are fully conscious of the fact," he
observed, "that go anywhere we will, we would have to fight for
our welfare if we took to Christianity, Islam or Sikhism. It is
foolish to suppose that in the event of our conversion to Islam
everybody from amongst us would be a Nawab or would become
the Pope if we went over to Christianity. Go we may anywhere,
fight is inevitable in store for us." He added that his terms for a
compromise with the caste Hindus to keep the struggle for
equality inside the Hindu fold would be never fulfilled by the
Hindus because bread and butter was not the question at issue.
That there was some definite divine purpose behind their
struggle was now beyond doubt; otherwise there could not have
come forward proposals offering them money—it is said from

the Nizam[6]—to the tune of rupees seven crores from conflicting quarters! But for God this would not have been possible, he added. Referring to the Harijan Fund started by Gandhi, he said that its object was to enslave the Untouchables to the camp of caste Hindus. He declared that he was now bent on conversion whether the caste Hindus meant help or hindrance. Even if God were produced before him to dissuade him from leaving the Hindu fold, he would not go back on his resolve.

From the loud and constant applause that punctuated his speech, it seems that his speech was hailed by his supporters and followers as a kick-off in the campaign. The Youths Conference ended with victory for Ambedkar in his own circle; but it positively alienated the sympathy of several supporters and well-wishers of Ambedkar's movement outside, and it alarmed the newspapers and thousands of political-minded Hindus. Excepting leaders of the Mahar community, leaders of most of the untouchable communities declared their unmistakable disapproval of Ambedkar's move, as they held that conversion would riot materially or economically change their fate and would be disastrously disadvantageous.

The brave, sincere and stiffer men from caste Hindu workers and leaders, who had dedicated their lives to the cause of liberation of the Untouchables, were obviously irritated at this repetition of the announcement. Some of them held that never in their history did the Depressed Classes stand in greater danger than at that moment and characterised Ambedkar's attitude as a runaway mentality. They pointed to Ambedkar how the movement for conversion of the Untouchables carried on by the Christians and Muslims for centuries had utterly failed in changing their hellish conditions into heavenly ones. History of the conversion movement did not support, they said, Ambedkar's objective. The ties of tradition and religious customs were so deep-rooted that even the converted Hindus, they stated, observed them unconsciously for decades on. They, therefore, appealed to the Depressed Classes to stand by them, work with them, build with them and fight by their side bravely for the abolition of untouchability as Ambedkar had been doing, and appealed to Ambedkar and others that they should not leave the field like

---

6. Donde, M. V., The *Janata*, 14 April 1951.

cowards. Yet there were a few far-sighted social reformers who assessed the role of Ambedkar's movement from a different angle and more sympathetically. They hailed Ambedkar as a messiah born to reorganize Hindu society and to revitalize Hinduism.

Those who were incapable of assessing the issue described Ambedkar's announcement about conversion as a mere threat, a bluff and a stunt. To say that Ambedkar underrated the difficulties and was under the delusion that there would be paradise before them on conversion was hardly doing justice to Ambedkar. Most of the protagonists on the caste Hindu side viewed the problem from one side and the hot-gospellers of conversion did it from the other. What Ambedkar did was that he pressed the lingering problem of untouchability and accelerated the struggle of his people for human rights in his usual way with his whole heart, with his whole soul, with all his strength and with all his mind to a determined conclusion. Dangerous diseases require drastic remedies. A shock treatment was necessary to knock out the deep-rooted malady, and Ambedkar made the last bid.

It was a fight between Ambedkar the man bred and brought up in an intense religious atmosphere and the iconoclast and expurgator of society. He had said in the early part of his struggle that Hindutva was not the property of the caste Hindus alone. When the news of some Chamar women's conversion to Islam reached him he was greatly perturbed in those days. He had maintained that so long as the caste Hindus called them Hindus, they were entitled to entry into the temples with the caste Hindus. He had even declared that the Untouchables by their struggle would purify Hinduism and wash its stains with their blood. In those days he had even signed the telegraphic Memorandum sent to the Goa Government protesting against the arrests of the Hindu missionaries who had carried the re-conversion movement in Goa.[7] He had insisted in his Memorandum which he submitted to the Minorities Committee to the R.T.C. that the Depressed Classes should be called Protestant Hindus or the Non-conformist Hindus. Above all, he had signed the Poona Pact, and these were gestures large enough

---

7. Kshirasagar, S. D., *The History of Gomantak Shuddhi Movement* (Marathi). Appendix I, p. 32.

to show that he wanted to remain in the Hindu fold.

An important aspect of the Youths Conference, however, remains to be recorded. During the days of the conference, Ambedkar, accompanied by Dr. Solanki, attended the Bhajan programme of the Sikhs at night on January 13, 1936. He was requested by the Sikh leaders to accept the Sikh religion. During the same week two deputations of Muslims waited on him in Poona, appealing to the leader of the Depressed Classes to embrace Islam.

The Youths Conference adopted a resolution unanimously supporting Ambedkar's move at the Yeola Conference and stressed the value of collective action as declared in that resolution.

CHAPTER 14

VERDICT ON HINDUISM

SINCE January 1936 Ambedkar had been preparing an address which he was to deliver to the Jat-Pat-Todak Mandal, at Lahore, at the time of its Annual Conference. The leaders of this anti-caste organization persistently requested Ambedkar to accept their invitation to preside over the Conference. Their representative, Indra Singh, saw Ambedkar in Bombay and persuaded him to accept the invitation. Dr. Gokulchand Narang extended an invitation to Ambedkar in the first week of February to stay with him during the days of the Conference, which was to be held during the Easter days.

Ambedkar received several letters from the opponents and the sympathisers of the address which he had delivered at the Youths Conference in Poona. Some said that Varnashram would remove the ills. Others opined that it was futile to reconstruct society on it and the way out was to destroy castes. Leaders like Malaviya now visited Nasik and other places to sound the intentions of the Untouchables in Maharashtra from where Ambedkar's volcanic proclamations were issued out to the horror of the Hindu leaders.

On March 15 Ambedkar was honoured at the Bombay Theatre, Bombay, by the Chitta Ranjan Theatrical Company which then staged a thrilling play called *Dakhancha Diva*. This play, written by Appasaheb Tipnis, a dramatist of note, dealt with the problem of untouchability and was full of scenes from the history of the Peshwas under whose regime the untouchables were compelled to move about in the streets during certain hours of the day with earthen pots tied to their necks and with a thorny broom hanging from their waists to sweep out the marks of their steps. The news of Ambedkar's acceptance of the invitation to witness the play had drawn a big crowd to the theatre, and it was packed to its capacity.

The main speaker on the occasion was Anantrao Gadre, who was well known for his sincere and burning heart for social reforms on the basis of social equality in Hindu society. Gadre said that the treatment meted out to the Untouchables was so despicable and inhuman that even the actor refused to go out on the stage with a pot hanging from his neck!

At the end of March 1936, the Jat-Pat-Todak Mandal informed Ambedkar that they had postponed their Conference to the middle of May. There was a stir in the Punjab press and the orthodox public had subjected the Mandal to a very bitter criticism for having elected its President a leader like Ambedkar 'who was a declared hater of Hindu religion'. The result was that even the staunch leaders like Bhai Parmanand, Dr. Narang, Mahatma Hans Raj and Raja Narendra Nath, had to disassociate themselves from the Mandal. To give a correct idea to Ambedkar of the situation, the Mandal, whose leading light was Sant Ram, sent Har Bhagwan to Bombay. He saw Ambedkar in Bombay on April 9 and took away the portion of the presidential address which was ready.

The next day Ambedkar also left for Amritsar to attend the Sikh Mission's Conference, which was to meet on April 13 and 14. The Sikh Conference was attended by huge crowds of Sikhs and the Depressed Classes from the Punjab, Kerala, U.P. and C.P. The Conference was presided over by Sardar Bahadur Hukum Singh, a retired District Judge, and the Chairman of the reception committee was Wasakhas Singh. Both the President and the Chairman in their addresses stressed the need for improving the plight of the Depressed Classes by intensive missionary work. Addressing the Conference, Ambedkar expressed his approval of the principles of equality among the Sikhs and added that he had not yet made up his mind, though he had decided to renounce Hinduism. Sir Jogendra Singh, another speaker, stressed the need for missionary work and the creation of a trust for the purpose, and appealed for funds. The main feature of the Conference was the conversion of five prominent Depressed Class leaders of the Thiyya community of Kerala headed by Dr. Kuttir and fifty others from the U.P. and C.P., to Sikhism.

It seems that Ambedkar had not given out a word of his proposed visit to Amritsar in connection with the Sikh Conference to Har Bhagwan, for the latter wrote from Lahore on April 14, to

Ambedkar: "Reaching here, I came to know that you had come to Amritsar. I would have seen you here if I were well enough to go about." Ambedkar's participation in the Sikh Conference worsened the suspicion of the Jat-Pat-Todak Mandal. They therefore informed him to expunge some portions of his printed address which he proposed to deliver at the Jat-Pat-Todak Mandal's Conference and postponed the Conference *sine die*. The portion they wanted to expunge from Ambedkar's printed address related to the *Vedas* and Hindu scriptures. In reply, Ambedkar wrote that he would not change a comma and cancelled the programme. Ambedkar himself was of the opinion that his presence at the Sikh Conference had a good deal to do with the decision of the Committee. As he was engaged in secret talks with the Sikh leaders, and had plainly said in his proposed address that it was the last speech he was going to deliver as a Hindu, the Mandal refused to accept him as their President for the Conference.

About this time Gandhi camp was also disturbed by Ambedkar's activities. Ambedkar was therefore persuaded by Seth Walchand Hirachand to see Gandhi. Accompanied by Walchand, Ambedkar met Gandhi at Wardha and then at Segaon,* but they could not agree on the solution to the problem. Gandhi wrongly thought that there were many influences in India and London acting behind Ambedkar and the problem had been allowed to assume unduly large proportions because of his threats.[1] On his way back from Segaon, Ambedkar was received enthusiastically at Wardha station by the Depressed Classes. Walchand Hirachand and Jamnalal Bajaj, the millionaire supporters of Gandhi, asked Ambedkar why he did not join Gandhi's camp, so that he might have boundless resources at his disposal for the uplift of the Depressed Classes. Ambedkar told them frankly that he vitally differed from Gandhi on many points. Upon this they referred to Nehru and asked him to emulate his example by putting aside his own views. He silenced them by saying that he was not a man to whom Nehru's case would apply and added that he could not sacrifice his conscience for success. The millionaires showed their surprise at the crowds

---

*   Later it was called Sevagram.
1.   Gandhi. M. K., *Letters to Sardar Vdllabhbhai Patel*, p. 115,

of the Depressed Classes that had gathered to receive Ambedkar, and they remarked that although they spent money on their cause the Harijans did not respond to them properly. Ambedkár at once answered that it was the difference between a mother and a nurse.

The Doctor published his undelivered address in the form of a booklet entitled *Annihilation of Caste*, and the posthumous child of the proposed Conference has survived the passage of time as a great thesis on the annihilation of caste. The thesis is, indeed, the work of industrious reading, microscopic observation, and a prognostication of what was revolving in its author's mind. It was logic on fire, pinching and pungent, piercing and fiery, provocative and explosive. It was to the minds of the caste Hindu leaders what silver-nitrate is to a gangrene.

II

According to this thesis, the Hindu society was originally divided into four Varnas—classes. The Varna was based on worth. But as time went on, the Varnas came to be based on birth and thus the four Varnas came to be known as four castes. In Ambedkar's view the caste system is a social division of people of the same race and is not merely a division of labour but also a division of labourers, compelling a man to engage himself in a calling which may not appeal to him. Reorganization of Hindu society on the basis of Chaturvarnya is impossible and harmful because the Varna system has a tendency to degenerate into a caste system. The law of Chaturvarnya prohibited the Shudras from pursuing knowledge, from engaging in economic enterprises, and from bearing arms, with the result that they could never revolt and became ever reconciled to eternal servitude as an inescapable fate. In short, the caste system deadens, paralyzes and cripples the people from helpful activity.

Nor is the caste system, he observes, eugenic in origin. It is a social system which embodies the arrogance and selfishness of a perverse section of the Hindus who were superior enough in social status to set it in fashion and who had the authority to force it on the inferiors. From the standpoint of economy, he adds, it does not result in economic efficiency because callings under the caste system are not followed in accordance with natural aptitude.

Caste has had, he continues, a bad effect on the ethics of the Hindus. It has killed public spirit, destroyed sense of public charity and narrowed down public opinion. It has restricted a man's loyalty to his caste, made virtue and morality caste-ridden. Caste does not appreciate merits in a man from the other caste.

What is more, caste has made Shuddhi—conversion—impracticable because caste is incompatible with conversion, there being no place for a convert. Caste has killed, he adds, the missionary spirit of Hindu religion which was, according to him, a missionary religion in the past. Because there is caste, there is no Shuddhi; and so long as there is no Sanghatan, the Hindus will remain weak and meek, and will tolerate an insult as well as a wrong quite meekly. He then sounds a warning to the Hindus that if they allow without feeling any sense of remorse or repentance the aborigines to remain in primitive state, and if they are reclaimed by non-Hindus and converted to their faiths, they would swell the ranks of the enemies of the Hindus. If this happens, the Hindu will have to thank himself and his caste system.

Although he admits that nowhere is human society one single whole and that groups exist in all societies, he observes that groups in other societies are fundamentally different from the caste groups in Hindu society in point of interplay, intercourse and inclusiveness. In Hindu society each caste, he goes on, lives for itself, and although the Hindus have similarity of customs, beliefs and thoughts, they are not a society nor a nation in the true sense of the term. They are a collection of castes. Caste is the bane of the Hindus. Caste is the cause of the downfall of the Hindus. Owing to caste the Hindu's life has been a life of continuous defeats. Caste has made the Hindus the sick men of India. Caste has ruined the Hindu race and has destroyed, demoralized and devitalized Hindu society.

The real remedy is intermarriage. Inter-dining has not, he says, succeeded in killing the spirit and conscience of caste. Fusion of blood alone can create a feeling of being kith and kin, and unless this feeling of kinship, of being kindred, becomes

paramount, the separatist feeling—the feeling of being aliens—
created by caste will not vanish.

How can that be achieved ? Caste is a notion, a state of
mind. Its destruction means a notional change. The Hindus
observe caste not because they are inhuman and wrong-headed.
They observe caste chiefly because they are deeply religious. They
are not wrong in observing castes. What is wrong is their religion
which inculcates this notion of caste. The real enemy is the
Shastras which teach them this religion of castes. Destroy this
belief in the sanctity of the Shastras—scriptures—destroy the
authority, the sacredness and divinity of the Shastras and the
Vedas, Make every man and woman free from the thraldom to
the Shastras and he or she will intermarry without your telling
him or her to do so.

As a matter of course, the Brahmins, who are the natural
leaders of the Hindus and form the intellectual class, will not
lead the movement to destroy the power and prestige of the
priests; one arm will not fight with the other. So he suggests the
destruction of the idea of hereditary priesthood and
democratization of the profession of priests by the grant of a
sanad to any Hindu who passes a certain test and by narrowing
down the number of priests. You thus kill this Brahminism and
save Hinduism. He also insists that the Hindus should have one
common religious book. The message of Ambedkar's thesis is that
Hindu society stands in need of a moral regeneration and it is
dangerous to postpone it.

This means that a new doctrinal basis must be given to
Hindu society—a basis that will be in consonance with liberty,
equality arid fraternity, in short, with democracy. This means a
complete change in the fundamental notions of life, in the values
of life, in the outlook and in attitude towards men and things.

Ambedkar concludes that the Hindus are the sick men of
India and sounds a warning that "only when Hindu Society
becomes a casteless society, that, it can hope to have strength
enough to defend itself. Without such internal strength, Swaraj
for Hindus may turn out to be only a step towards slavery".

As this cause of the Mandal, he observes, was a national
one he wished the Jat-Pat-Todak Mandal success.

The demand for this thesis was so great that the English edition of the thesis ran out within two months, and it was translated into prominent languages such as Punjabi, Marathi, Tamil, Gujarati and Malayalam.

Ambedkar, however, was not the only man who preached annihilation of caste for the reorganization of Hindu society. Modern leaders such as Swami Shraddhananda, Lajpat Rai, Ram Mohan Roy, Bhai Parmanand, Acharya P. C. Ray, R. C. Dutt, Bepin Chandra Pal, Sir Jadunath Sarkar, Aurobindo Ghose, Ramanand Chatterjee, Lala Har Dayal and Veer Savarkar have condemned the caste system. All have said that the caste has deprived the Hindus of a strong feeling of nationality, of patriotic feeling and of solidarity, "Caste grows by fusion; it is antagonistic to national union," observes the great historian Sarkar. According to him, the solution lies in complete freedom of marriage. Lala Har Dayal observes: "Caste is the curse of India. Caste, in all its forms, has made us a nation of slaves. It is not Islam, it is not England, that has destroyed India, No, our enemy is within us. Priestcraft and caste have slain us. India can never establish and maintain a free State so long as caste rules in our society. You may deliver speeches, pass resolutions, sign Commonwealth Bills *ad infinitum*, but caste Hindu cannot work together, or establish a free State, or create a victorious army."

In short, caste system is the bane of Hindus is the verdict given by India's great and true historians and sociologists, leaders of thought and social reformers. It seems that the remark of some critics that the Europeans pride themselves on racial feelings, the Muslims on religious feelings and the Hindus on caste feelings is not far from truth.

III

Ambedkar was not satisfied with the Untouchable Youths Conference at Poona. In order to have an estimation of the real support of his people for the conversion movement, he decided to hold a conference of the Mahar community from which he sprang. Accordingly the Conference, met on May 30 and 31, 1936, at Dadar, Bombay, in a specially erected pandal. Amongst those that were present by special invitations were Stanley Jones, a

European missionary and B. J. Jadhav. On the platform were a number of Sikh and Muslim leaders and priests eager to catch any direct or indirect hint in the matter of conversion. The object of the Conference was to devise ways and means to implement the resolution passed at Yeola. Revji D. Dolas welcomed the delegates. B.S. Venkatrao, a Depressed Class leader from Hyderabad, presided over the Conference.

Ambedkar then rose to address the Conference. The whole audience listened to him in complete silence. Ambedkar delivered his speech in Marathi which was spread over fifty pages of manuscript. At the outset Ambedkar told the Conference that he had called a Conference of Mahars only, because he wanted to sound the opinion of the Mahar community, and although others, who believed in conversion, were not invited to the Conference, they would do well to support the movement for conversion in their own conferences. Those who were against it, he added, should not mind their being isolated from this Conference.

Describing the numerous and specific disabilities which the Depressed Classes had to undergo, Ambedkar said that so long as they remained in the Hindu fold, there was no salvation for them. They had to go out of the Hindu fold to secure true freedom for their activities such as wearing dress, eating food, securing jobs, receiving education and living in the midst of a civilized society. "You have nothing to lose," he continued, "except your chains and everything to gain by changing your religion." Turning then to the social aspect of the problem, he said that although the problem looked like a struggle for social status, it was essentially a class struggle. Oppressions were a part of that ceaseless struggle which raged between the privileged and the unprivileged. He told the Depressed Classes that they lacked three essential qualities for carrying out their struggle, namely, man-power, money and intellectual power, and so long as they remained in the Hindu fold they would not be able to acquire those powers.

As regards the spiritual aspect of the issue, he observed that the function of a true religion was the uplift of the individual. For that purpose it should teach the virtues of fellow-feeling, equality and liberty. As Hindu religion did not teach these virtues and had failed to provide them a favourable environment, and denied them individual freedom for development without the means of education, wealth and arms, it had become imperative for them, he asserted, to leave the Hindu fold and seek another religion that would offer them better conditions of life.

"Because of untouchability your merits go unrewarded; there is no appreciation of your mental and physical qualities. Because of it you are debarred from entering into the army, police department and navy. Untouchability is a curse that has ruined your worldly existence, honour and name," he thundered.

Ambedkar then in an outspoken way declared that he did not believe in the honesty of the Hindu social reformers who lived in their own caste, married in their own caste and died in it! He declared also that Gandhi had not the courage to take up the cudgels against the caste Hindus on behalf of the Depressed Classes. Some people, he said, asked him what advantages they would gain by changing their religion. His answer was: "What will India gain by Swaraj? Just as Swaraj is necessary for India, so also is change of religion necessary for the Untouchables. The underlying motive in both the movements is the desire for freedom."

As to the political consequences, he said that they would not suffer in any way by changing their religion. They would get the support of the community into which they merged. As for himself, Ambedkar observed vehemently: "I have decided once for all to give up this religion. My religious conversion is not inspired by any material motive. There is hardly anything that I cannot achieve even while remaining an untouchable. There is no other feeling than that of spiritual feeling underlying my religious conversion. Hinduism does not appeal to my conscience. My self-respect cannot assimilate Hinduism. In your case change of religion is imperative for worldly as well as spiritual ends. Do not care for the opinions of those who foolishly ridicule the idea of your conversion for material ends. What avail is the religion that deals with life after death? A rich man's sense may be tickled by this idea in his leisure time. Those who are well-placed and prosperous in this world may pass life in contemplation of life-after-death.

But why should you live under the fold of that religion which has deprived you of honour, money, food and shelter?"

"I tell you, religion is for man and not man for religion. If you want to organize, consolidate and be successful in this world, change this religion. The religion that does not recognize you as human beings, or give you water to drink, or allow you to enter the temples is not worthy to be called a religion. The religion that forbids you to receive education and comes in the way of your material advancement is not worthy of the appellation 'religion'. The religion that does not teach its followers to show humanity in dealing with its co-religionists is nothing but a display of force. The religion that asks its adherents to suffer the touch of animals but not the touch of human beings is not religion but a mockery. That religion which precludes some classes from education, forbids them to accumulate wealth and to bear arms, is not religion but a mockery. The religion that compels the ignorant to be ignorant and the poor to be poor, is not religion but a visitation!"

Concluding his speech with a quotation from the lips of the dying Buddha, he asked his people to seek refuge in reason. The quotation from Buddha led some people to believe that Ambedkar had leanings towards Buddhism. He shrewdly avoided mentioning the name of the religion which he had chosen.

The whole race of historians, thinkers and philosophers such as Max Muller, Emerson, Carlyle, Schlegel, Thoreau, Voltaire, Elliot, Bernard Shaw,[2] Schopenhaur, and others who sang the praise and glory of Hinduism must have turned in their graves. The tearing and burning invective of John Knox, who described the Church of Rome as a prostitute sullied with a thousand abominations, must pale before this volcanic attack by Ambedkar on Hinduism. It was coarse and cutting, yet smashing and dissecting.

The Conference declared by a resolution that they were prepared to change their religion *en masse*, and as a preliminary step towards the change of religion, urged the Mahar Community to refrain thenceforth from worshipping Hindu deities, to put a stop to the observance of Hindu festivals and to stop visiting Hindu places of worship.

---

2. Narang, Dr. Gokulchand, *Real Hinduism*, p. 13.

Immediately after this conference, Ambedkar addressed a meeting of Mahar hermits in the same pandal, and the hermits also decided to renounce Hindu religion. It is a tribute to the forceful appeal of Ambedkar that even the hermits should prepare themselves to burn their old ties with the religion of their forefathers, and they actually made a bonfire of articles which smacked of the symbols of Hinduism. The heavenly denizens, who had adopted a world-negating attitude towards life, became the earthly denizens.

A few days before this, Ambedkar had made a strange gesture towards Sikhism by sending his son and nephew to the Gurudwar Mandir of Amritsar. These youths lived there for about one and a half months in the warm hospitality of the Sikhs who received them with hope.

The declarations reiterated by the leaders of the Depressed Classes made the mouths of the heads of different faiths water, and whetted their appetite. They now began to press Ambedkar to embrace their own religion and win equality and freedom. Some Muslim leaders, probably with the Nizam at their back, were striving their utmost to win Ambedkar to Islam. They tried to contact Ambedkar in Bombay; but Ambedkar spent the whole day in a motor car roaming in the city, and in order to be away from their allurements, he went to a village named Sav, a place of hot springs, near Mahad, and eluded them. Nevertheless, he attended a party held at a Muslim High School in Bombay, but did not make any speech on the pretext of sore-throat and listened to the honeyed speeches of the Muslim spokesmen.

The Buddhists, too, tried in their own way to capture him. One of their Missionaries, an Italian Monk by name Rev, Lokanatha, who was founder of the Lokanath Buddhist Mission, came to Ambedkar's residence at Dadar on June 10, 1936. Clad in the robe of a priest and carrying a bowl and an umbrella, he interviewed Ambedkar and tried to persuade him to embrace Buddhism. After his talk with Ambedkar, the monk, in an interview to the Press, said that the leader of the Depressed Classes seemed to be impressed with the Buddhistic faith and promised to consider the question carefully, but had not given any definite reply. The Saviour—for the monk's original Italian name was Salvatore—said that he had reason to believe that Ambedkar would come round to his view and added that his own ambition was to convert all Harijans to Buddhism. The monk then went to Ceylon on a pilgrimage.

IV

Meantime, Ambedkar consulted his colleagues from different provinces in the matter of choosing the proper religion for conversion. He had now decided to embrace Sikhism. His friends and colleagues felt that Ambedkar should seek the support of the Hindu Sabha leaders in their conversion to Sikhism; for, the Hindu Sabha leaders believed that Sikhism was not an alien'religion. It was an offspring of Hinduism and therefore the Sikhs and the Hindus intermarried, and the Sikhs were allowed to be members of the Hindu Mahasabha.

Accordingly, Dr. Moonje the spokesman of the Hindu Mahasabha, was invited to Bombay. In the presence of two other friends Ambedkar had a talk with Dr. Moonje at Rajagriha, on June 18, 1936, at half past seven that night. Ambedkar cleared all issues and had a free talk with Dr. Moonje. Next day the purport of Ambedkar's views was reduced to a statement and was given to Dr. Moonje, who approved of it personally. After discussing this issue with Dr. M. R. Jayakar and Dr. N. D. Savarkar, Dr. Moonje left Bombay on June 22, to secure the approval of Hindu leaders to the conversion of the untouchable Hindus to Sikhism. He sent a copy of Ambedkar's statement of objects to different Hindu leaders, for their approval. Amongst those who sent their approval in writing were Dr. M. R. Jayakar, Seth Jugal Kishore Birla, Sir C. Vijayaraghavachariyar and Raja Narendra Nath. On June 30 Dr. Moonje wrote to M. C. Rajah, the Harijan leader, who had made a pact with him in 1932. Rajah, who thought that it was a golden opportunity to dislodge Ambedkar, wrote to Gandhi, Rajaji and Malaviya and sought their advice in the matter.

About this time, Pandit Govind Vallabh Pant gave vent to the feelings of Congressmen, saying that the Harijans could not have it both ways. Either they were Hindus and enjoyed the privileges under the Poona Pact or they ceased to be Hindus and forfeited them. Replying to this, Ambedkar said that it was a Congress stunt to frighten him and his party out of contesting the coming elections, and to coerce him and his community into remaining within the Hindu fold. He contended that the Depressed Classes got seats not from the Hindu quota but from the general constituency; and the classification of the Untouchables as the Depressed Classes was not from the religious standpoint but from social and economic standpoints. As long as they had not actually embraced another faith, he added, their declaration that they had lost love for Hinduism, or renounced it should not be construed as conversion to another religion. Saying that his attitude was negative in respect of Hinduism and not yet positive adherence to any other faith, he concluded that he should be called even a *statutory* Hindu.

Referring to the controversy between Govind Ballabh Pant and Ambedkar, the *Sunday Statesma*n observed that Dr. Ambedkar was not a dabbler in constitutional law and was somewhat of an expert. He might at times press a point too hard, the Weekly continued, but had a high intellectual equipment and was ever ready to "argue still". The newspaper gave its verdict by saying: "If by conversion the Scheduled Castes pass into any other community ordinarily recognized as 'General' (Buddhist, Jain or any other), the reserved seats as well as the double elections disappear and they have equal chances with other candidates in the same category. On the other hand, if they become Moslems or Christians (or Sikhs in the Punjab Province only) for whom communal seats are reserved, they can no longer contest the 'General' constituencies. Mass conversions will upset communal proportions in the Award and it will perhaps have to be revised. Of course, the mere expression of disgust with Hinduism (which is quite different from actual conversion) should be no disqualification. The Doctor is right there."

By now Gandhi, Malaviya and Rajagopalachari had replied to Rajah declaring their opposition to the move of Ambedkar and Dr. Moonje. Dr. Moonje had written to Rajah in good faith. But Gandhi urged Rajah to disclose the move publicly, Gandhi wrote to Dr. Moonje asking him to give his consent to the publication of the correspondence between him and Rajah, but the letter could not reach Moonje in time as he was moving from place to

place to secure approval of the Hindu leaders. The object of
Gandhi in making Rajah publish the secret correspondence was
not fair. Gandhi was using the dissatisfied mind of Rajah as a
tool to arouse Muslims, Christians and the Government against
Ambedkar and to dislodge him. So Rajah issued all the
correspondence to the press without the permission of Dr. Moonje.

In his proposal Dr. Moonje said that the Hindu Sabha would
not object to the conversion of the Depressed Classes to Sikhism
and to the inclusion of these neo-Sikhs in the list of the Scheduled
Castes for the enjoyment of the benefits of the Poona Pact if
Ambedkar promised to prefer Sikhism to Islam and Christianity,
to co-operate with the Hindus and the Sikhs in propagating
sincerely to counteract the Muslim movement for drawing the
Depressed Classes into the Muslim fold, and to propagate and
live within the Hindu culture.

Ambedkar's statement, which Dr. Moonje had enclosed with
his letter to Rajah, said that although Islam seemed to give the
Depressed Classes what they needed politically, socially and
economically, although Christianity had boundless resources
available to it from America and England and a Christian
Government behind it, and although Sikhism had few attractions
and was not so helpful to the Depressed Classes socially,
financially and politically compared with Islam and Christianity,
yet he favoured Sikhism in the interests of the Hindus and added
that it was the duty of the Hindus to help the Sikhs in removing
the economic and political difficulties that would lie in the way
of the neo-Sikhs.

Explaining in detail why he chose Sikhism, Ambedkar
further observed: "The second question is, looking at these
alternative faiths purely from the standpoint of the Hindus,
which is the best—Islam, Christianity or Sikhism? Obviously,
Sikhism is the best. If the Depressed Classes join Islam or
Christianity, they not only go out of the Hindu religion, but they
also go out of the Hindu culture. On the other hand, if they
become Sikhs they remain within the Hindu culture. This is by
no means a small advantage to the Hindus."

"What the consequences of conversion will be to the country
as a whole." he continued, "is well worth bearing in mind,
Conversion to Islam or Christianity will denationalize the

Depressed Classes. If they go over to Islam, the number of Muslims would be doubled; and the danger of Muslim domination also becomes real. If they go over to Christianity, the numerical strength of the Christians becomes five to six crores. It will help to strengthen the hold of Britain on the country. On the other hand, if they embrace Sikhism, they will not only not harm the destiny of the country but they will help the destiny of the country. They will not be denationalized. On the contrary, they will be a help in the political advancement of the country. Thus it is in the interests of the country that the Depressed Classes, if they are to change their faith, should go over to Sikhism."[3] Are these not the words of a noble, wise and true son of Bharat ?

Replying to Dr. Moonje, Rajah observed: "We want to remain as a solid community moving of our own accord in the direct progress and this we can best do by not throwing away our birth-right as Hindus but by remaining within Hinduism and changing it so as to make it more comfortable not only to our community but to other Hindu communities. We do not wish to be pawns in the game of communal conflicts and competition."

Rajagopalachari described this move of Ambedkar and Moonje as a diabolical proposal. And he was himself seven years later to propagate the nth degree diabolical proposal for the vivisection of Hindustan! Gandhi endorsed Rajah's views and observed in his usual way that for him the removal of untouchability stood, on a footing of its own. He added that it was a religious question and it could never be a question of barter for him.

Replying to these charges, Ambedkar said that in fairness to Dr. Moonje, Rajah ought not to have released the correspondence to the Press without the permission of Dr. Moonje, and added that if Rajah wanted nothing else except spiritual satisfaction, why should he stress such a material and mundane consideration as reservation of seats in the legislatures for living as a Hindu and dying as a Hindu?

As regards the views expressed by Gandhi and Malaviya, Ambedkar said that, they had now no right to complain as they had utterly failed to carry out the promises which they made at

---

3. *The Times of India*, 24 July 1936.

the time of the Poona Pact for the uplift of the Depressed Classes. Calling Gandhi's language mystic, he said that it did not lie in Gandhi's mouth now to say that the problem could not be a matter for barter; for at the time of the Poona Pact Gandhi himself had treated the whole thing as a barter. Ambedkar then referred to the statement of Rajagopalachari and said that the Hindus who had begun to feel a deep concern regarding their destiny would begin to doubt the sanity of statements made by Rajagopalachari.

Concluding his statement, Ambedkar said with a certain emotion: "The move for conversion to Sikhism has been approved by a number of prominent Hindus, including Shankaracharya Dr. Kurtakoti. In fact, it is they who took the initiative and pressed it on me. If I have gone to the length of considering it an alternative, it is because I felt a certain amount of responsibility for the fate of the Hindus."[4]

Dr. Moonje and Dr. Kurtakoti obviously chose the least evil in supporting Ambedkar in the proposed conversion of the Depressed Classes to Sikhism because they believed, as did all great Hindu leaders of the past and present, that Sikhism was a branch of Hinduism, owning the same culture and principles.

V

Ambedkar, the historian, gave a rude shock to Hindu society, because he knew that conversion of Hindus to other faiths had convulsed Hindustan. It was the converted Hindus who had fought in the past for establishing Muslim suzerainty over the land. Six years after this agitation, Jinnah told Louis Fischer that seventy-five per cent of the Indian Muslims were former Hindus converted to Islam by Mohammedans, and Jawaharlal Nehru improved upon this and put the figure, perhaps with secular pride, at ninety-five per cent.[5] It can be seen, therefore, why Ambedkar's declaration was a thunderbolt to the sensible Hindu leaders who realised that the Hindus were losing national strength through their suicidal apathy and inhuman attitude to the untouchable Hindus.

---

4. *The Times of India*, 8 August 1936.
5. Louis Fischer, *Empire*, p. 27.

What religious conversion of the Hindus, which was neglected by the Congress leaders, who prospered on Hindu strength and support, has done to Travancore, Assam and the Punjab can be seen from the following. It would be then quite clear why Hindu champions like Shivaji, Dayananda, Shraddhananda, Parmanand and Savarkar strove and endlessly strove to reclaim the converted Hindus and stop increasing the number of the anti-nationalists in India. It will be also clear why Dr. Moonje and Dr. Kurtakoti Shankaracharya ran after Ambedkar begging him to prevent the impending colossal calamity from overtaking the land of the Hindus.

In the year 1901 in Assam the proportion of population of Hindus per ten thousand was 5,578, that of Muslims 2,689 and that of Christians 23. In 1941 the Hindus were reduced to 4,129, the Muslims strength rose to 3,373 and the Christians rose to 35. In the Punjab the proportion of the non-Muslims to the total population was 53 per cent while the proportion of the Muslims was 47 per cent. In 1941 the non-Muslims sank down to 47 per cent while the Muslims rose to 53 per cent. In 1920 the Hindus in Travancore were 83 in proportion to the total population and the Christians were 12.4. In 1941 the proportion of the Hindus sank down to 60.5 while the Christians rose to 32.3.

Discussing how to win over more of the Depressed Classes for Christ, Godfrey Edward Phillips in his *Untouchables' Quest* says that the Indian Church was itself to the extent of not less than 70 per cent of Depressed Class origin. He further observes that during the decade ending 1931 the Christian community showed a natural increase of about 5,000 per mensem while there was an increase of 7,000 per mensem by conversion in village groups.

The aim of the Muslim leaders for conversion of the Hindus has been handed over to them from generation to generation. With this end in view the Muslims objected to the Untouchables being recorded as Hindus in the census.[6] With that end in view Maulana Mohamed Ali openly expressed his holy desire from the Presidential seat of the Indian National Congress to divide the Untouchables between Muslims and Hindus!

---

6. Ambedkar, Dr. B. R., *Thoughts on Pakistan*, p. 241.

Ambedkar's thesis, *Annihilation of Caste*, was still being discussed, appreciated or attacked throughout the country. Almost all leaders of thought and action replied to Ambedkar in their own way. A reply came also from Savarkar who held much the same views in respect of the annihilation of caste. But he objected to Ambedkar's remark that the Hindu's life had been a life of continuous defeat and pointed to some of the glorious chapters in history. After expressing his opposition through his letter to Rajah to the conversion of the Untouchables, Gandhi replied to Ambedkar's thesis. In his two articles entitled "Dr. Ambedkar's Indictment", Gandhi in his unique style of damning his enemy with faint praise, said that whatever label Ambedkar wore in future, he was not a man to allow himself to be forgotten. And saying that Dr. Ambedkar was a challenge to Hinduism, Gandhi further observed that Varna taught the Hindus to earn their bread by following the ancestral calling and added that every known religion would fail, if judged by the standard of Ambedkar. Gandhi concluded that a religion that produced Chaitanya, Dnyandeo, Tukaram, Tiruvalluvar, Raja Ram Mohan Roy, Ramkrishna Paramahansa, Devendranath Tagore, Vivekananda and a host of others could not be devoid of merit as made out in Ambedkar's thesis.

Replying to Gandhi, Ambedkar pitied him for making a charge that his motive behind publishing the address was love of publicity, and said that surely those who, like the Mahatmas, live in glass houses should not cast stones at him. He observed that there was no difference between the Chaturvarnya and Gandhi's ideal prescribing pursuit of ancestral calling irrespective of natural aptitude, and he retorted that Gandhi should have preferred scales to law and should not have become half-saint and half-politician. As regards the list of saints quoted by Gandhi, he said that they had not led an agitation against the caste system and added that their pious lives and their noble sermons had no effect upon the life and conduct of the masses as against the teachings of the Shastras. He asked Gandhi why the best were so few and the worst so many! His quarrel with Hinduism and Hindus was not over the imperfection of their social conduct, but over their ideals which were wrong according to his conviction, he ended. Which religion, had produced a galaxy of the best men in successive ages and phases was a point he left alone.

In spite of opposition sponsored by Gandhi and others, Ambedkar took one more step in respect of the conversion movement. He deputed on September 18, 1936, a group of his followers to the Sikh Mission at Amritsar to study the Sikh religion. They were a batch of thirteen men none of whom was a scholar or a first-rate Ambedkarite. In a letter written to one of them, immediately after their arrival at Amritsar, Ambedkar encouraged them, congratulated them on their being the vanguard of the conversion movement, and wished them all success. But it should be noted here that he had not asked them to embrace Sikhism. Ambedkar was now coming into closer contact with the Sikh Mission and its leaders, and there was some understanding between them and the Mission to start a college in Bombay in the interests of the Depressed Classes, who were expected to be converts to Sikhism. It was also rumoured that Ambedkar was to be its head and guide. In an excess of zeal those student-vanguard went over to Sikhism and did what their leader did not mean. They were coldly received back in Bombay, and afterwards they sank into oblivion.

□□□

CHAPTER 15

A NEW PARTY

The year 1936 was drawing to a close, and the year 1937 was to witness the inauguration of the Provincial Autonomy under the Government of India Act, 1935. The coming elections aroused keen interest and contest. Every party was now busy making preparations for fighting the elections. To that end Ambedkar, too, began to lay down his plans. After discussions with his colleagues, he founded a new political party called the Independent Labour Party in August 1936, and drew up a comprehensive programme which answered all the immediate needs and grievances of the landless, poor tenants, agriculturists and workers.

The programme elucidated the following points :

Although the Party recognised that the new constitution fell short of responsible government, it had decided to work the constitution.

The Party believed that the fragmentation of holdings and the pressure of population over them were the causes of the poverty of the agriculturists and the way out was rehabilitation of old industries and starting new ones. In order to raise the efficiency and productive capacity of the people, the Party declared itself in favour of an extensive programme of technical education and the principle of State-management and State-ownership of industries where necessary. The manifesto promised to undertake legislation to protect agricultural tenants from the exactions and evictions by the landlords and to extend the same benefits to them as would be provided for industrial workers, with suitable changes.

For the benefit of industrial workers the Party would endeavour to introduce legislation to control the employment, dismissal and promotion of employees in factories, to fix maximum hours of work, to make provision for adequate wages and for leave with pay and to provide cheap and sanitary dwellings for workers. Unemployment, it observed, would be relieved by introducing schemes of land settlement and by starting public works. It promised the lower middle class adequate protection in matters of house rents in industrial centres and big towns.

As regards social reform, the Party promised help to social reformers, emphasized the need for penalising all forms of orthodoxy and reactionarism, and suggested the use of the surplus from charity funds for such secular purposes as education, it proposed village planning for village sanitation and housing, and to modernise the outlook, of the villages. The Party intended furnishing villages with halls, libraries and rotary cinemas.

Commenting upon this programme, an English Daily said that although it disfavoured multiplication of political parties, the new party which Ambedkar had just organized in the province could be of considerable use in developing the life and moulding the future of the country. Emphasizing that there was both scope and need for such a party, and hoping that it would, together with the Socialists, present a strong defence against the sweeping tide of Communism, it concluded; "Were it not for special electorates and compartmental franchise the new party would probably within a brief period be one of the most powerful political groups in the country." But if, as usual, the scholar in Ambedkar dominated the organizer in him, the expectation of the editor was likely to be belied.

When all the preliminaries for the election work were over, Ambedkar left for Geneva on Wednesday, November 11, 1936, by an Italian steamer for a change of air. But it was said that it was his inner motive to go to London to sound the British statesmen whether the safeguards provided for the Depressed Classes in the new constitution would be available to them even if they went over to Sikhism. It would not be far from truth if one drew the foregoing conclusion from the noiseless hurry with which he left for Europe on the eve of the first general elections to the legislatures under the new constitution.

Prior to his departure, in an interview to a representative of *The Times of India*, he declared that the Congress was a combination of the exploiters and the exploited; it might be necessary for the purpose of achieving political freedom, but it was worse for the purposes of social reconstruction.

As regards his Party, he said that it would endeavour to educate the masses in the methods of democracy, place before them the correct ideology, and organize them for political action through legislation. Almost all his party leaders were present to give him a send-off.

II

Ambedkar's threat of conversion produced widespread repercussions, arousing the social conscience of the caste Hindus to the sense of injustice which they had inflicted for centuries upon the untouchable Hindus. India was now preparing for a giant stride for the removal of untouchability. A few days earlier the Mysore State Government had declared for the first time in its history that the Harijans would take part in the Dasara Durbar celebrations. In the wake of this declaration came out a bold, revolutionary temple entry proclamation by the Travancore State throwing open to the Depressed Classes about 1,600 State-controlled temples. It, indeed, opened a new chapter in the history of Hindustan and Hinduism. The Indian Press rang with tributes to the wisdom and courage of the Maharaja and to the great statesmanship of Sir C. P. Ramaswami Iyer, who was the man behind this great event. The *Manchester Guardian* paid high tributes to Iyer and described the event as an innovating spirit of democracy. M.C. Rajah said that the proclamation fully carried out the aim and spirit of the Poona Pact. The *Hindu*, Madras, described it as a courageous step and a wise act of statesmanship.

The impact of this event was so great that Jawaharlal Nehru, the then Congress President, who never bothered himself whether the Hindus remained in their homeland in a majority or disappeared from the face of the world and who was of the opinion that the ideal solution to the communal trouble was to wall-up[1] all places of worship for two or three generations, too, was moved. Expressing his opinion on the proclamation, he said that although he believed that the whole question was at the basis an economic question of the landless classes, the economic solution itself would be helped by the far-reaching psychological

1. *The Times of India*, 28 October 1941.

consequences and the new atmosphere the proclamation created[2]. The Hindu Mahasabha appealed to the rulers of Gwalior and Indore to emulate the noble example set by the ruler of Travancore.

Even the *Bombay Chronicle* admitted that the proclamation could not be unconnected with the threat of conversion. Newspapers like the *Hindu Herald* plainly said that had the idea of a proclamation been spontaneous, it would have come earlier. The *Hindu Herald* ascribed the causes of the success to the unabating struggle of the Depressed Classes and their ultimatum. In fact, the goodness of the Hindu Prince was made effective by the pressure of one man and it was Ambedkar whose name and credit the Indian Press always bypassed. It was the direct outcome of his threat.

Ambedkar visited Europe, according to him, purely for reasons of health and spent most of the time in Vienna and Berlin. He was in London only for a week. While he was in London, a representative of the Vividha Vritta, a leading Marathi weekly, sent news that Ambedkar had married an English lady and was coming to India with her on January 14, 1937, Looking to the close friendship of the editor with Ambedkar, it could not be said that it was an out-and-out stunt in the world of Journalism. News about the marriage of a great politician thrills the pages of the world press. Men of great powers more often than not act as a magnet to the fair sex. There was a rumour that an English lady was captivated by Ambedkar's great personality and was insisting on marriage. Such a marriage would not have affected his position in any way. He was to the Depressed Classes what the Aga Khan was to his community.

On January 14, 1937, Ambedkar returned to Bombay. When asked in an interview on landing, if he had married, he flatly denied the rumour and dismissed it as entirely baseless. He added that he had no reason to marry stealthily. He said that he had no interviews of a political nature with anyone in London. As regards the change of religion, he affirmed, he held to his decision although he had not made up his mind as to the faith he would embrace. His immediate concern, he concluded, was the ensuing elections to the Bombay Legislative Assembly.

---

2.   The *Hindu Herald*, 26 November 1936.

As usual Ambedkar was accorded a rousing reception at the
Pier. A vast crowd eager to see his European wife thronged the
entire route. But they were surprised to see their Babasaheb
alone!

It would not be merely hazarding a guess if one observes
that the British statesmen, who were deeply engrossed in the
crisis brought about by the proposed marriage of King Edward
VIII, had no time to spend on the stale problem of the conversion
of the Depressed Classes. They must have told Ambedkar that
during the days of the R.T.C. they had heard and done much in
their own way to do justice to the claims of the Depressed Classes
put forth by their leader and as such nothing was then left to be
done in that behalf. Prior to his interviews with the British
statesmen, Ambedkar had consulted some German and other
European jurists of world fame as to the possibility of their
retaining the reserved seats in the Provincial Assemblies if the
Depressed Classes went over to Sikhism; for the Sikhs were
granted reserved seats only in the Punjab. Later the Sikh Mission
authorities and Ambedkar could not hit it off together; and so
they receded from their stand and parted.

III

Ambedkar immediately launched his election campaign. The
election day was drawing very near. A month more and the
elections would be over. His new Party was to face the opposition
from the biggest political party in the land, a Party which was
equipped with men, money and surrounded with the halo of
patriotic sacrifices. It is rather surprising that Ambedkar, who
had presided over the All-India Conferences of the Depressed
Classes and was the voice of the dumb millions, could not create
an All-India Party to fight the elections. His new Party was mostly
confined to the Bombay Province.

Better late than never. Ambedkar started the election
campaign. He had now to make his new role clear to his people.
Why did he found a new Party? His reply was that in the
Provincial Legislative Assembly there were 175 seats out of which
there were only 15 reserved seats. It was obvious that the
strength of fifteen Members was insufficient for an active

opposition. So in consultation with his caste Hindu colleagues, who had stood by him through thick and thin, he decided to set up some more candidates for the general seats. It served two purposes. It preserved the goodwill of his colleagues, strengthened the chances of success for his candidates in the general election in which caste Hindu voters were no less a deciding factor than the Depressed Classes, and it would ultimately help him gain more seats. Ambedkar also supported a few independent candidates. Thus the Party had a broader basis and wider field of influence.

Ambedkar toured all the districts in the Bombay Presidency. He made short speeches at Nasik, Ahmednagar, some places in Khandesh, Sholapur, Satara and Belgaum. During his flying visit to Satara, he placed a wreath on the *samadhi* of his mother with pious tears in his eyes. At Nagar he attended the Nagar District Depressed Classes Conference and exhorted his people to support Roham who was contesting the election on his Party's ticket. He said that the Depressed Classes should not worry about the merits and qualifications of Roham. He assured them that he himself possessed the strength of hundreds of graduates and was there to guide the party inside the legislature and outside. He also addressed meetings at Panvel and Mahad.

Another feature of the election campaign was that Ambedkar extended his support to L. B. Bhopatkar, the leader of the Democratic Swaraj Party. Bhopatkar wrote a letter to Ambedkar in the first week of February 1937, requesting Ambedkar to issue an appeal to his men in Poona to vote for him in the ensuing election. It was not so easy a thing to evoke Ambedkar's sympathy. But though Bhopatkar belonged to a party which was, according to Ambedkar, mostly supported by orthodox reactionaries, he knew well Bhopatkar's sterling qualities and sincerity of purpose. For Bhopatkar had been an unfailing support to the cause of the Depressed Classes. Another factor that weighed with Ambedkar in favour of Bhopatkar was that like Ambedkar's, Bhopatkar's party believed in working the new constitution and for the propagation of this idea of working the constitution, Bhopatkar's colleague, N. C. Kelkar, had borne the brunt of the attack at the hands of his erstwhile Congress colleagues and Congress press for years.

Ambedkar, therefore, with all his heart, supported the candidature of Bhopatkar and wished him success. In his own way Kelkar also supported Ambedkar by issuing a special appeal to the voters of his persuasion in Bombay to vote for Ambedkar. In his statement Kelkar, who always weighed words carefully, paid a long overdue tribute to Ambedkar saying that Ambedkar was the uncrowned king of the Depressed Classes, and that he had attained the top of the ladder by sheer dint of his intellect, singleness of purpose and ceaseless struggle.

Untouchables pledging support to vote for a Poona Brahmin! Politics makes strange bedfellows. Amused at this combination of Ambedkar with the Poona Brahmins, who had the notoriety of having in their fold the most reactionary opponents of social equality, N. M. Joshi, a Bombay Labour leader had a dig at Ambedkar. The proverb he applied to Ambedkar meant that Ambedkar had stinted his spotless ideal and that too for nothing. Ambedkar turned the vulgarity of the saying upon the labour leader by adding one complement to the proverb. On the eve of the election, a piece of sensational news was spread in Sind through Sheikh Masjid Sindhi, a Hindu convert to Islam, that the Harijans were watching whether the Muslims voted for him in the election or not and whether the Muslims respected converts to Islam or not and that after the Sind elections Ambedkar would declare his choice for conversion to Islam. Sir Shah Nawaz Khan Bhutto, who was Sheikh Abdul Masjid's opponent in the election, wired to Ambedkar requesting him to state the facts. Ambedkar said in a telegraphic reply that no such promise was ever given by him to Sheikh Masjid or to anybody else and the statement was a lie.

The Congress Party put up candidates in all Provinces. But in the Bombay Province or perhaps in the whole of India two seats were contested by the Congress Party with all its might, men, materials, ingenuity and tactics. The first was the seat which Ambedkar contested in Bombay, and the second was the one which Bhopatkar contested at Poona. Ambedkar was their bitterest enemy, the hater of their idols and ideals. Bhopatkar was the one-time President of the Maharashtra Provincial Congress Committee and had fearlessly fought along with them against the British. Palvankar, the famous Indian bowler, was the Congress nominee to oppose Ambedkar and Rajbhoj —

afterwards secretary of Ambedkar's Scheduled Castes Federation—and Deorukhar were pushed in the arena to sabotage Ambedkar's chances. The elections took place on February 17, 1937, and when the result was declared, the Congress candidate Palvankar was found to have shown some fight, but the other two were left at the polls undiscovered in the heap of discomfiture and defeat. Ambedkar was elected with a thumping majority. Bhopatkur gave a heroic fight, but lost against heavy odds.

And the first elections under the new constitution proved to be an astounding success for Ambedkar's Independent Labour Party.

Of the seventeen candidates put up by the Party fifteen came out successful. Thinking people now saw ahead a colourful fight between Ambedkar and the Congress Party in the Assembly; for Ambedkar meant terror and battering opposition to the Congress fads and prejudices.

IV

The Depressed Classes in the Bombay Presidency rejoiced in their leader's victory at the polls. Ambedkar was felicitated on his resounding victory at the Maharwada in Sangli immediately after the election results were out. Untouchable Hindus from neighbouring villages and small towns attended the function with great interest and pride.

Yet another victory awaited him to complete Ambedkar's triumph. The protracted case over the use of the water of the Chowdar Tank was decided in favour of the Depressed Classes by the Bombay High Court on March 17, 1937, upholding the decision of the Assistant Judge at Thana, who had decided the case four years earlier.

The Congress scored a triumph at the polls, but was opposed to the acceptance of office.

Ambedkar expressed his views when B.G. Kher, the Congress Party leader, approached him with a request to sign a statement declaring a vote of no-confidence in the Interim Ministry led by Sir Dhanjishah B. Cooper and Jamnadas Mehta. Ambedkar, who had been on a visit to Janjira State, replied from

Janjira that there was no point in the Congress demand but a move to raise its own prestige. His view was that the Governor would have to call the Assembly within six months' time when Congressmen would have an opportunity to have their say in the matter.

Shortly after, at a big meeting held under the auspices of the I.L.P. at the Kamgar Maidan, in Bombay, Ambedkar reiterated his views and expressed his firm determination to work the new constitution for what it was worth in the best interests of the Depressed Classes. Appealing to the Congress Party to play the game and end the deadlock, he sounded a note of warning to the Congress Party and said: "We cannot allow our grievances to continue till the so-called Congress fight against imperialism is over." In the course of his speech he condemned the attitude taken by Congress leaders like Jawaharlal Nehru, who put up menials as candidates to contest the seats with chosen men from the Depressed Classes. He referred to Nehru's servant by name Hari as a case in point. Answering the question why he did not join the interim Ministry, he said that it was no use accepting office in a Ministry which commanded no majority in the Assembly and which was not likely to last long.

At last the Congress leaders prevailed upon themselves and decided to take office on July 19, 1937. The Interim Ministry in Bombay resigned a day before. In the afternoon Members were sworn in. Congressmen took the oath of allegiance to the British King and sat in their places. Ambedkar refused to swear by the *Geeta*, but he took the oath in a dignified manner.

Two leaders, Ambedkar and Jamnadas Mehta, from the opposition parties in the Bombay Assembly, were the best of the lot in the country, and formidable for any Assembly in the world. Whereas they were skilful and renowned debaters, most of the Congress Ministers were then inexperienced. They who had cursed for years participation in the Legislatures as the job of scoundrels now themselves accepted the very job!

CHAPTER 16

LABOUR LEADER

THE Congress leaders formed their Ministry in Bombay. Being routed in the Muslim constituencies, the Congress leaders were in search of Muslim legislators for adoption. There was no need for a coalition. Ambedkar was not a believer in the principle of coalition Ministries which, he said, were to be formed only on rare occasions.

On July 31, 1937, while Ambedkar was on his way to Dhulia on a professional visit, he was accorded a great ovation at dawn by the Depressed Classes at Chalisgaon station. In the morning he reached Dhulia at eight o'clock and was greeted with thunderous applause and amidst shouts of a new slogan—"Who is Ambedkar?" "Ambedkar is our King!" Ambedkar then was taken out in procession to the travellers' bungalow. After the business in the court was over, in the afternoon he was entertained at a tea-party by Barve of Harijan Sevak Sangh. In the evening Ambedkar addressed a meeting at the Vijayanand Theatre. In the course of his speech he said that the main thing to be borne in mind was that the British rulers, who were indifferent to Untouchables, were now replaced by a set of leaders, who belonged to the party of the social oppressors of the Depressed Classes. Those were the days, he continued, of union, organization and precaution from the point of view of the Untouchables. He then pointed out how Brahminism was asserting itself in India through Ministries installed by the Congress. All the Congress Ministries were, he remarked, led by Brahmins while there were no Depressed Class ministers.

Then came off the first general meeting of the Independent Labour Party, It was held at the Neighbourhood House, Nagpada, Bombay, on August 7, 1937. Ambedkar was elected President and treasurer; M. B. Samartha, Bar-at-law, General Secretary; the other Secretaries were K. V. Chitre and S. A. Upasham. K. V. Chitre was the provisional organizer and was rightly called the trusted chief of staff in Ambedkar's personal Cabinet. Addressing the general meeting, Ambedkar said that it did not occur to him to move at the time of the R.T.C. proceedings that the cabinet of every Province should contain a representative of the Depressed Classes. In the third week of August 1937, a Bill proposing salaries for the Ministers at rupees five hundred per mensem plus house and carriage allowances came up for consideration before the Assembly. Ambedkar, who was absent during the general budget discussion, opposed the Bill on many grounds. Criticizing the Bill, he said: "In coming to a decision about the salaries of Ministers, four considerations should govern the principle. "First, it was the social standard; secondly, it was competency; thirdly, democracy; and fourthly, integrity and purity of administration. Of the three arms of the State, he stated, the Executive was the Brain Trust and a salary of rupees five hundred would make competent men turn to other walks of life and in consequence would make those who did not care for money, capture political power.

If salaries were being fixed, he continued, in accordance with the standard of living in the country, then Ministers should draw salaries of rupees seventy-five each as had been suggested. Patriotism, he remarked, was the last refuge of a scoundrel according to Dr. Johnson, but he would add, of a politician as well. Answering the debate, Premier Kher said that the principle underlying the Bill was service of the motherland. Patriotism was the last refuge of scoundrels, but ihe first refuge of honourable men, he added. And then he reminded Ambedkar of his selfless service to the cause of his community and appealed to him to render such selfless service to the country as well.

Ambedkar's propaganda was going on unabated. Early in September 1937, he presided over a District Conference of the Depressed Classes at Masur. In the course of his address he told his audience that it was his confirmed opinion that Gandhi was not the man to look to the interests of the working classes and the poor. Had the Congress been a revolutionary body, he would have joined it. But he was convinced that it was not a revolutionary body. Congress was not courageous enough to proclaim the ideal of social and economic equality, enabling the common man to get leisure and liberty to develop himself according to his liking. That was not possible, he observed, as long as the means of production were controlled by a few individuals in their own interests. According to Gandhism, he said, the farmer would be the third bullock to be harnessed to the plough along with the two natural ones.

As regards the labour movement carried on by the Communists, he added that there was no possibility of his joining them. He declared that he was a confirmed enemy of the Communists, who exploited the labourers for their political ends.

Ambedkar himself was doing his best to promote the interests of the agricultural masses that laboured under unbearable disadvantages. On September 17, 1937, during the Poona Session of the Bombay Assembly, he introduced a Bill to abolish the Khoti system of land tenure in Konkan.

It must be noted that in the first popular Provincial Assemblies Ambedkar was the first legislator in India to introduce a Bill for the abolition of the serfdom of agricultural tenants. By his Bill he aimed at abolishing the tenure with a view to securing occupancy rights to the tenants. He desired abolition of the Khoti tenure and substitution of the ryotwari system, to make provision for payment of reasonable compensation to the Khots for the loss of their rights and to give those inferior holders, who were in actual possession of land, the status of occupants within the meaning of the Land Revenue Code, 1879. But as the Government postponed the issue, Ambedkar could not move the Bill. Ambedkar also introduced a Bill to abolish the Mahar Vatan for which he had been agitating since 1927. It was at last abolished under the Bombay Inferior Village Vatans Abolition Act I of 1959.

A very important defamation case had been going on since March 1937, at the Mazagaon Court, Bombay, in which R. K. Tatnis, editor of the *Vividha Vritta*, a leading Marathi weekly, was charged with defamation by Ali Bahadur Khan, editor of *Hilal*, an Urdu daily. Ambedkar defended his friend, Tatnis, with great interest and skill. He ably argued for over seven hours quoting copiously English and Indian Case Law in support of his defence and pleaded that the article should be read as a whole. The Court held that the accused had proved his defence of good faith, but as he could not prove the imputation regarding the deportation of the complainant he was fined rupees five.

In November 1937, a group of young men belonging to the Depressed Classes congratulated Ambedkar on his great election triumph, on behalf of their Adi-Dravida Youth Sangh, Replying to the address, Ambedkar warned them against joining the Congress. He said that if they did so, none would remain outside to give vent to their grievances. In the last week of the month the Depressed Classes of Bombay felicitated Bhaurao Gaikwad, their Nasik leader, for his ceaseless struggle, sincere social work and the heroic fight he put up for the civic rights of the Depressed Classes. Ambedkar paid his lieutenant a rare tribute for his service, comradeship and sacrifice.

II

On December 30, 1937, Ambedkar left for Pandharpur to preside at the Sholapur District Conference of the Depressed Classes. On his way he was enthusiastically received at dawn at Kurduwadi station. Then he and his party were taken in a special bus to Pandharpur. On their way Ambedkar made a brief halt and made a short speech before Matang Samaj at Karkam village. He advised them to be on their guard against the Congress which, he said, comprised their exploiters, oppressors and bloodsuckers, who professed welfare of the poor under the garb of white dress and cap. At noon he reached Pandharpur where he was taken out in procession to the Travellers' Bungalow. The President of the Pandharpur Municipality met him at the Bungalow, and then they both left for the conference which was held at the Municipal Dharmashala. People from far and near gathered to hear their great leader. More than one thousand women were present.

Ambedkar told the Conference that there were then three problems before them. The first was whether they would be ever given an equal status in Hindu society; the second was whether they would get the proper share of national wealth; and the third was what would be the fate of the self-respect, self-help movement. With regard to the first, he said that it was not possible as long as the caste system existed. As to the second, he expressed strong resentment at the treatment they got from the Congress which was ruled by the capitalists. He observed that as long as the Congress was in the hands of the capitalists, they could not rely on the present Government to do anything for the betterment of their economic condition. It was, therefore, he proceeded, necessary to form a united front against the capitalists, who were out to exploit them. He told them that the time had come for them to win their economic independence. Respecting the third, he said that they should remember one thing that they had nothing to lose and everything to gain by the step. They had only to shed the fear of death.

The Conference supported whole-heartedly the Mahar Vatan Bill introduced in the Assembly by their leader.

Ambedkar was then taken to the Municipal Hall. The members received him cheerfully. The President made a feeling speech on the occasion and garlanded the guest. Ambedkar reciprocated their feelings and thanked them all.

"From Pandharpur Ambedkar went to Sholapur to address the Matang Conference. On his arrival he was presented with a civic address of welcome by the Sholapur Municipality on the morning of January 4, 1938, at the Bhagwat Chitra Mandir. The address was read and presented by Rao Bahadur Dr. V. V Muley, who had helped the cause of the Untouchables at Sholapur in the capacity of the President of the Municipality. In reply Ambedkar made a very important speech, expressing his views on the working of Parliamentary Democracy.

"In the political situation," he declared, "that has grown up in this country, there has grown the habit among the people of paying homage to only one political party, the Congress."

"I am no believer," continued he, "in Democracy as an ideal to be pursued in all circumstances and in all claims; and having regard to the present-day conditions in India, Democracy is a most unsuitable system of Government. At any rate, for some time India needs the strong hand of an enlightened autocrat."

"In this country we have," observed he, "Democracy, but it is a Democracy which has ceased to exercise its intelligence. It has bound itself hand and foot to one organization and only one. It is not prepared to sit in judgment over the doings or thinking of this organization. I consider it the greatest malaise, a disease and a sickness. It has affected all our people. They are intoxicated." "Unfortunately," he added, "the Indian people are by tradition men who have more faith and less wit. Anyone who does anything out of the ordinary, does something so eccentric as to be called in other countries an insane person, acquires in this country the status of a Mahatma or Yogi. And people follow him as the sheep follow the shepherd. . . . . Democracy must learn to give a respectful hearing to all who are worth listening to."[1] "I am glad," he concluded, "that the Sholapur Municipality has set an example in voting an address to me who do not belong to an organization which claims to be the only organization in the country and which all people are in a mood to uphold at present."

The next day Ambedkar made another important speech in Sholapur. The local Christians were eager to hear his views on religion. So he addressed a meeting of the Christians under the presidentship of the Rev. Gangadhar Jadhav. He said in a very sarcastic tone that since the day he declared his intention to abjure Hindu religion, he had become a commodity for bargain or a source of comedy. He referred to the comedy, Vande Bharatam, written by Acharya P. K. Atre, a well-known playwright in Maharashtra, who had ridiculed the idea of conversion in his play. Yet he stated that he was firm in his resolve. From his study of comparative religion he could say that two personalities could captivate him. They were the Buddha and Christ,

He further said that he wanted a religion which instructed people how they should behave with one another and prescribed for man his duty to another and relation with God in the light of equality, fraternity and liberty. He told the Christians that their co-religionists in Southern India observed caste system in churches. Besides they lagged behind politically. If the Mahar boys became Christians they lost their scholarships. Thus there was no economic gain in their being Christians. Moreover, the Indian Christians, he remarked, as a community never fought for the removal of social injustice.[2] Mark here the names of the

1. *The Times of India*, 4 January 1938.
2. The *Janata*, 15 February 1938.

founders of religion which Ambedkar referred to. The love for Sikhism, it seems, had evaporated with his return from London. The speech served both as a rebuke to the Indian Christians and a revelation.

Immediately after his return from Sholapur to Bombay, Ambedkar busied himself with a march, of the peasants which he was to lead to the Council Hall in Bombay. Peasants from outlying Districts such as Thana, Kolabi, Ratnagiri, Satara and Nasik came to Bombay in trains and steamers. With torn clothes on, blankets and bundles on their shoulders, and staffs in their hands, they came to Bombay to voice their grievances. Their sun-burnt faces shone with a certain enthusiasm. They marched on to the Council Hall from three directions in processions; one from Parel, the other from the Alexandra Docks and the third from Chowpatty. Escorted by the police, they walked slowly along the prescribed routes. Police parties were posted at important junctions. The processionists carried posters bearing slogans such as "Down with the Khoti System", "Support Dr. Ambedkar's Bill". The processionists reached the Esplanade Maidan near the Victoria Terminus at half past one in the afternoon. There the police officers held up the processions and allowed twenty leaders to go to interview the Chief Minister who was then called the Premier. Parulekar, S. C. Joshi, D.W. Raut, Indulal Yagnik and A.V. Chitre headed by Ambedkar, saw the Premier.

The first demand presented by the deputationists was the enforcement of the minimum standard of wages for agricultural labourers. The second was that all the arrears of rent should be remitted since the revenue arrears had been also remitted. They urged that immediate legislation should be made to provide with or without compensation for the abolition of the Khoti System and the Inamdar System; and landlordism, which was economically wasteful and socially tyrannous, must go. The last demand was for reduction of fifty per cent of irrigation rates payable by small holders. The Premier told the deputationists that every problem was being tackled by the Ministry in their own way.

The leaders returned to the Esplanade Maidan and addressed a manmoth meeting. Ambedkar made a very powerful speech. He said that the number of books he had read on Communism exceeded the number of books read by all Communist leaders put together.[3] But he was of the opinion that the Communists never looked to the practical side of the question. He observed that there were two classes in the world—the haves and the havenots, the rich and the poor, the exploiters and the exploited ; the third one, the middle-class, was very small. He, therefore, exhorted the peasants and workers to think over the causes of their poverty and told them that they lay in the richness of the exploiters. The way out for them was to organize a labour front without any regard to caste or creed, and to elect to the legislatures those who were their real representatives. If they did so, they would have shelter, clothing, and they who produced the food and wealth of the nation would not die from hunger. The force, logic and sharpness of the speech would put any Communist leader into the shade. His opponents were afraid that Ambedkar would develop into a dangerous leader of the peasants, workers and the landless.

<h1 style="text-align:center">Ill</h1>

While his agitation for the agrarian reforms was going on, Ambedkar had a major clash with the ruling Party. It was a very vital issue from the point of view of the Depressed Classes. One of the clauses of the new Bill aiming at the amendment of the Local Boards Act, defined the Scheduled Castes as Harijans, the people of God. Ambedkar's lieutenant, Bhaurao Gaikwad, moved an amendment begging the House to delete the appellation. In a closely reasoned speech he told the House that the Depressed Classes had through several conferences voiced their opposition to the appellation, and therefore he appealed to the House not to give statutory recognition to the word "Harijan". He told the House that if they did it, they would not do so without raising a protest; and added: "If the untouchable classes were the people of God, were the touchable classes assumed to belong to the monsters ?" "If all the people," he concluded, "were to be called Harijans, we should not object. It is no use only giving the Untouchables a sweet name. Something practical should be done

---

3. The *Janata*, 15 January 1938.

to ameliorate their condition." D. W. Raut supported the amendment. The Hon'ble Mr. L. M. Patil replied that he knew that a mere change of name would not improve the deplorable condition of the Scheduled Castes materially. But there was some odium attached to the word "Untouchable", and they wanted to remove it and to give dignity to that community.

The amendment was put to vote and negatived. The Congress majority forced the appellation "Harijan" down the throats of the Depressed Classes, although the Congress Party had won only two out of the fifteen seats reserved for the Untouchables and Ambedkar had won thirteen out of those fifteen seats. Ambedkar sprang up and said in a firm voice: "1 am very sorry, but I think I cannot help saying that this a matter on which the wishes of the group ought to have prevailed upon Government. Nobody would have been hurt and the interests of the country would not have been injured if the amendment of my Honourable friend Mr. Gaikwad had been accepted. In view of the fact that the Government wished to use its majority in a tyrannical manner, I am afraid we must show our disapproval by walking out in a body and not participating further in the day's proceedings."

The Premier, Mr. Kher, tried to pacify the Members of the Depressed Classes by saying that the word was polite and capable of expressing the desired meaning; and he traced the origin of the word to a song of the Gujarati saint-poet, Narsi Mehta.

Ambedkar replied that all he would say was that he was not in a position to suggest any better name. The ruling party could have discussed the matter with them with a view to finding out some alternative term. Kher's arguments, he added, did not carry conviction to them. He would, therefore, leave the House. And immediately he walked out and all the Members of his Party followed him.

Ambedkar was now fully engrossed in. the promotion of the welfare of the down-trodden. For a time it seems that he was not among his books. He had exchanged books for the masses. He availed himself of every opportunity to hear and study their grievances on the spot, to guide them, and to represent their grievances to the Government. He was the voice of their woes, their views, and their vows. The poor classes of Ahmednagar sought his guidance, and so he addressed a conference of peasants and workers on January 23, 1938, at Ahmednagar.

At Nagar, he was entertained at a tea party in the District Local Board by Bhausaheb Kanawade—a local lawyer, by Sardar Thorat and Tribhuvan, another local pleader. In the evening Ambedkar and his party went in a special lorry to Akola, a small town in the same District, on their way receiving enthusiastic welcomes. He addressed another Conference there for over 90 minutes. The Conference passed resolutions supporting all the Bills that their leader had introduced in the Assembly.

Ambedkar was now bent upon organizing the peasants as well as the railway workers. He now turned his attention to the latter. A big Conference of Untouchable Railway workers was convened at Manmad, on February 12 and 13, 1938. Addressing this Conference of twenty thousand workers, he described vividly how in his boyhood he had carried tiffin-carriers to his relatives in the mills and had gained close knowledge of the problem. He told them that the condition of labour was quite different in those days. Labour leaders did not try to remove the injustice inflicted upon untouchable workers as they feared a split among the workers. He stated that the Conference was the first of its kind. They had hitherto agitated for the removal of social injustice and grievances and had fought out with considerable success. The result was that they got political representation. Now they had taken up the work of the removal of their economic grievances. Hitherto they met as pariahs but now they met as workers. Hitherto he was called the enemy of the nation. He was now called, he added, the enemy of the labour.

According to him, he said, there were two enemies of the working classes in the country and they were Brahminism and Capitalism. "By Brahminism," he stated, "I do not mean the power, privileges and interests of the Brahmins as a community. That is not the sense in which I am using the word. By Brahminism I mean the negation of the spirit of liberty, equality and fraternity. In that sense it is rampant in all classes and is not confined to Brahmins alone though they have been its

originators. The effects of Brahminism were not confined only
to social rights such as interdining and inter-marrying. It denied
them also the civic rights. So omniscient is Brahminism that it
even affects the field of economic opportunities."[4]

Ambedkar then asked the untouchable workers to compare
the opportunities of their class with those of a worker who was
not an Untouchable, and said that the untouchable worker had
less opportunities of obtaining work, securing service or
advancement in his respective occupation. He observed that it
was notorious that there were many appointments from which
a Depressed Class worker was shut out by reason of the fact
that he was an Untouchable. A notorious case in point was that
of the textile industry. In the railways it was their lot to work
as gangmen. Not to speak of other posts, they were not even
appointed porters because porters were used as domestic
servants by the station masters, and being Untouchables, they
were dropped out. The same condition prevailed in the railway
workshops. He asked his critics how they would consolidate the
working classes when they did not remove such glaring injustice
and partiality which was wrong in principle and injurious to
the principle of solidarity. In other words, he told the workers
that they must uproot Brahminism, the spirit of inequality from
among the workers, if the ranks of labour were to be united.
He then referred to trade unionism in India and said that it
was in a sorry state. It was a stagnant and stinking pool, because
its leadership was either timid, selfish or misguided. The
warfare between different unions was far more deadly than
what existed, if any at all, between workers and owners. The
communists had misused the power which they had once
secured.

He was surprised to note that M. N. Roy opposed the
existence of a separate party of labour inside or outside the
Congress. He said that Roy was a puzzle to many as he was to
him. A communist and opposed to separate political organization
of labour! A terrible contradiction in terms! A point of view which
must have made Lenin turn in his grave ! It might be, he added,
that Roy looked upon the destruction of imperialism as the first
and foremost aim of Indian politics. But if, he proceeded, after

---

4. *The Times of India,* 14 February 1938.

the disappearance of imperialism, labour would require to fight
the landlords, millowners and money-lenders who would remain
in India to bleed the people, it should have its own organization
from the moment to fight capitalism as much as imperialism.

Ambedkar had also to address a very important Conference
of the Depressed Class youths in the same pandal. After the
Chairman of the Reception Committee, Murlidhar Pagare, made
his welcome speech, Ambedkar delivered a very instructive,
inspiring and thrilling speech. The rule in life, he said, they
should keep in mind, was that they must cherish a noble ideal.
Whatever might be one's ideal either of national progress or of
self-development, he continued, one should patiently exert
oneself to reach it. He observed that all great things in the world
were achieved by patient industry and by undergoing toil and
tribulations. He further said that one should concentrate one's
mind and might on one's goal. Man must eat to live and should
live and work for the well-being of society.

Turning then to the problem of education, Ambedkar said
that education was a sword and being a double-edged weapon,
was dangerous to wield. An educated man without character
and humility was more dangerous than a beast. If his education
was detrimental to the welfare of the poor, he remarked, the
educated man was a curse to society. "Fie upon such an educated
man !" "Character is more important," he emphasized, "than
education. It pains me to see youths growing indifferent to
religion. Religion is not an opium as it is held by some. What
good things I have in me or whatever have been the benefits of
my education to society, I owe them to the religious feelings in
me. I want religion but I do not want hypocrisy in the name of
religion." The conference was a great success. It showed that,
given a chance, the Depressed Class leaders also could organize
the masses.

IV

On his arrival in Bombay, a small purse was presented to
Ambedkar on March 19, 1938, by R. K. Tatnis, editor of the
Vividha Vritta, on behalf of the Depressed Classes, at Tadwadi,
Bombay. Replying to the address, Ambedkar urged his people to

join the I.L.P. He said that his health was not good; and he was advised by his doctors to observe complete fast for two days a week, Saturday and Sunday, He was even forbidden to take water and he broke his fast every Monday at noon. He further said that people observed fasts either for fulfilling their vows to God or in expectation of a fulfilment of their prayers. But his was a fast, he concluded, undertaken as a remedy for digestive troubles. His fast, however, had its reverberations in the Bombay Assembly when he had a sip of water while making a vigorous speech in which he attacked the Home Minister for having suspended the sentences of two convict-gamblers. A Congress Member asked the speaker whether drink was allowed in the House. Ambedkar offered his explanation as mentioned above.

Encouraged by the success in the Assembly elections, Ambedkar now turned his attention to the Local Board elections. He visited Islampur and urged the Depressed Classes to vote for his Party candidates, who were contesting elections to the Satara District Local Board. There he advised the Marathas to organize a separate political party independent of the Congress; for, the Congress which was dominated by the Capitalists and Brahmins, he asserted, would not promote the interests of the peasants and middle classes. After visiting Satara and Poona, he returned to Bombay.

In the same month a very important Bill was on the Legislative anvil. It related to the Primary Education Amendment Act. During the discussion there were frequent passages-at-arms between Ambedkar and Munshi, the then Home Minister, who was a brilliant lawyer and a skilful debator. It seems that these two men differed temperamentally and fundamentally, and opposed each other bitterly.

When during the course of a discussion on the Bill, Ambedkar attacked the Wardha Scheme of Education fathered by Gandhi and nurtured by Gandhian ideology. Munshi rose and said that Ambedkar was not the competent authority to judge the scheme, and declared that most of the legislators who were not educationists would not be able, to judge the scheme in its proper perspective. Infuriated at this insult thrown at the Legislative body, Ambedkar sprang up and said: "You may dismiss the Legislature altogether."

Munshi   : The Hon'ble Member has neither the ability
                    nor the insight to distinguish between the
                    general principles of legislation and
                    technical departmental details. Every rule
                    that Government will make will have the
                    imprimatur of the majority of the Members.

Ambedkar   : Does my Hon'ble friend wish to say that the
                    opposition should have no voice?

The Hon'ble Mr. Kher (Premier) : After all when you were
                    under a Government which you could not
                    remove, impress or induce according to your
                    wishes in any public manner. . . .

Ambedkar (*rather indignantly*) : Is it different now ?

The Speaker : "Order, order."

One thing is to be noted. Ambedkar was not only an
authority on education but also the Principal of a Law College,
whereas Munshi was a lawyer and was himself no better judge
than Ambedkar, who had moved and worked in the world of
education and studied the problems of education.

Another vital issue of national importance was discussed
in the Bombay Assembly in the first week of April 1938. It was
the demand of Karnatak for its separation from the Bombay
Province. Speaking on the resolution, Ambedkar expressed his
fears that if Karnatak was created a separate Province, it would
be a Province of Lingayats against any body. Against the
background of such divisions he expressed his gratitude to British
rule for its two gifts—one in the form of a common law code and
the other a common central government. He declared that the
common goal was the building up of a feeling that they were all
Indians, and he warned the House and the country in these
words: "The feeling that we are Indians is still in embryo, and is
only beginning to ripen, and to allow other loyalties, feelings of
culture, feelings of nationality to grow simultaneously — I say
deliberately—is the greatest crime that we can commit and I for
myself, will not be a party to it. I strongly, very strongly, oppose
the resolution." (Applause.) Ten years earlier he had opposed
the separation of Karnatak on the same ground in his separate
report to the Simon Commission.

There was another important Bill introduced in the Bombay Assembly. It aimed at amending the Bombay City Police Act. No other Bill was more hotly discussed and more vehemently attacked. All the opposition leaders tried to see that the measures proposed in the Bill should be applied only to the rioters. Moving an important amendment to the Bill, Ambedkar agreed, that the people were being molested by dangerous characters and consequently the danger to their lives was a real one. He told the House that he had lived for over twenty-two years in the underworld of Bombay and knew more than anybody in the House or even more than the Police Commissioner, how the poor people were molested by what were called the *Mavalis* and *Dadas*, and how utterly impossible it was for those victims to obtain any redress because they themselves, for fear of further molestation, would not go to a court of law and seek to get them convicted.

Referring to the history of communal riots, he said that all agreed that those annual bloodbaths must be stopped effectively; but at the same time, there should be some safeguards laid down in order to see that arbitrary power should not be misused by the Commissioner of Police. He, therefore, told the House that there should be no lacuna or loophole left for the executive to use the provision of the section for any other purpose than those for which it was intended.

The Bill provided some interesting moments for the House. Jamnadas Mehta, who opposed the first reading of the Bill said that even the gangster should be given the right of defending himself. Upon this Ambedkar asked him whether it was an ideal. Jamnadas remarked that even in the U.S.A. they had not thought it fit to curtail the liberty of the subject like this. A few minutes later Ambedkar said: "I am myself more anxious than Jamnadas Mehta is that this measure should not be extended to labour disputes."

Jamnadas Mehta : As anxious, not more.

Ambedkar   : If you will allow me to say, I am more anxious.

Ambedkar then asked the Home Member to define the word community in the Bill.

Early in May 1938, Ambedkar visited Nagpur to conduct a case concerning the affairs of the head of the Satnamis. At the

Nagpur station he was accorded a grand reception. After the court business was over, at night people thronged to hear him in spite of storm, rain and lightning. Next morning he addressed a students' meeting, visited Kamtee where he made a speech and returned to Bombay.

Although the Congress Party ruled over the Province, Ambedkar still continued as the Principal of the Government Law College, Bombay. He resigned in May 1938 and, in the words of the College Magazine, the college "undoubtedly lost in him a Principal who was greatly respected by the students for his learning and ability. His lectures were always known to be prepared with great industry and care and were listened to with rapt attention." The Magazine mentioned gratefully the enrichment of the Library during his tenure and said he had radical views on legal education.

V

Immediately on May 13, he made a tour of Konkan Districts. He went to Kankavli via Kolhapur. He presided over a conference of the Depressed Classes at Kankavli in a pandal named Ambedkar Nagar. A. V. Chitre, the driving force behind the agrarian movement in Konkan, was present. Kowly, Pradhan and Tipnis were also present at the Conference. The little town first saw in its life the use of a loud-speaker at this Conference. Ambedkar in his exhortations to the Conference said that out of two million Mahars in Maharashtra a few should struggle endlessly to win their rights and a living of self-respect for their community. They should give up the nasty habit of begging and of living on the leavings. They should watch the work of their representatives in the Assembly. He declared that he was determined to end their serfdom by abolishing the Khoti system, and if the Bill which he had introduced failed, they should be prepared to launch passive resistance.

The next day Ambedkar visited Devrukh and Aravali, making brief halts and short speeches before crowds of Depressed Classes and reached Chiplun at night on May 16. Next morning he went to Guhagar, addressed a meeting and returned to Chiplun to address another meeting. He told his audience that Gandhi's so-called mesmerism could not capture him. Jawaharlal

Nehru and Subhas Bose yielded to Gandhi, but he would never do so, and if he ever entered the Congress he would shine out there by dint of his merits, he added. He further said that the Congress Party was postponing for the past ten months the Khoti Abolition Bill introduced by him. If it failed for want of support, they should start a no-tax campaign; and he would be the first man to court jail on that issue. He told the farmers that he wanted to see a man from amongst the peasants, who formed 80 per cent of the population, occupying the Gadi of the Premier of the Province.

After addressing meetings at Khed and Dapoli, he reached Mahad, the battlefield, where he gave the first battle to the orthodox Hindus and the reactionary forces in Konkan. He made a thrilling speech at Mahad before a vast audience expressing disappointment at the policy of the existing Government. He returned to Bombay on May 21, after travelling about a thousand miles. The continuous strain of speeches affected his voice, and at the last meeting he could not utter even a single word.

On his arrival in Bombay, in the course of an interview, Ambedkar expressed great satisfaction at the growing support of the people to his Party and their grateful appreciation of his efforts towards abolishing their serfdom. He said that in its own way his I.L.P. was striving to redeem its election pledges, but if the Congress Ministry refused to give relief through constitutional methods, and if people's faith in it was thus lost, the alternative was obvious. He, however, was surprised at the attitude of the Socialists, who, he said, had been all those years shouting for the confiscation of all Zamindari lands and the abolition of the capitalist system, but were now inactive when a concrete Bill was brought forward to put an end to the Khoti system.

By now a crisis had brewed in the working of the Congress Ministry in the Central Provinces. The Congress bosses dethroned Dr. Khare, the Premier, for his rebellious spirit. He then explained to the people his position at several places in regard to democracy.

One such meeting was held at the R. M. Bhat High School, Bombay, in the first week of August 1938. Three things drew a huge crowd. One was the Mahatma's denial of his having himself corrected the draft of Dr. Khare's resignation; the second was the exposure of that false denial by Dr. Khare; and the third was the Mahatma's opposition to Khare's taking up in his new Ministry a Harijan Member. These points gave a deep colour to the background of the whole tragedy. At that meeting Dr. Moonje, Jamnadas Mehta and Dr. Ambedkar made speeches upholding Dr. Khare's viewpoint that being the leader of the House, Dr. Khare was justified in forming a new Ministry of his choice. Dr. Khare was a Member of the Working Committee of the Harijan Sevak Sangh and Gandhi had made a tour of C.P. along with Dr. Khare to give an impetus to the uplift of Harijans. And yet Gandhi would not allow Dr. Khare to include a Harijan Member in his Ministry!

During those days, if somebody praised Gandhi as a holy man, Ambedkar replied that Gandhi was owly and described his conduct at the R.T.C. as an act of treachery! In an interview for a Marathi weekly he said that if a man with God's name on his tongue and a sword under his armpit deserved the appellation of a Mahatma, then Mohandas K. Gandhi was a Mahatma![5] No other leader in Indian politics had a rougher tongue! No revolutionary speaks a soft language and marches without raising dust and smoke.

In the last week of October, Ambedkar visited Bavla, a little town thirty miles from Ahmedabad, where he was presented with an address in the Depressed Class locality. Moved at the pitiable sight of their faces, he asked the Untouchables to take heart and develop confidence in themselves as their brethren in Maharashtra had done. On his return be addressed a meeting at the Premabhai Hall, in Ahmedabad. He admitted that he was opposed to Gandhi in politics. It was because he had no faith in Gandhi; he did not believe that Gandhi would do good to the Depressed Classes. He said if Gandhi was sincere why should he not ask the Premiers of Bombay and C.P. to include representatives of the Depressed Classes in their ministries? He maintained that the Congress Government of Bombay was not reducing the land revenue, nor was it prepared to tax the rich. The former Government had recommended the grant of waste lands to the Depressed Classes for cultivation, recruitment of

---

5. Kelkar, N. C., *Autobiography* (Marathi), p. 734.

the Depressed Classes in the police services and a certain
percentage of reservation in Government Departments for the
Depressed Classes. But the Congress Government did not care
for them. On the last day of the month, he visited Nipani to
preside over a conference convened by the Belgaum District I.L.P.
On his arrival at Nipani, a mammoth crowd gave him a
thunderous applause, and he was taken out in a mile-long
procession wherein he was made to sit in a chariot drawn by
fifty bullocks.

VI

Meanwhile, the consideration of the Industrial Disputes
Bill was taken up in September 1938 by the Bombay
Legislative Assembly. Ambedkar and Jamnadas Mehta
opposed the Bill tooth and nail. Ambedkar described the Bill
as bad, bloody and bloodthirsty inasmuch as it made a strike
under certain circumstances illegal and affected the right of
the labourer to strike. Moreover, it did not ask the employer
to disclose his budget and sought to use police force against
the workers.

Ambedkar stated that according to him strike was a civil
wrong and not a crime, and making a man serve against his will
was nothing less than making him a slave. To penalise him was
to make a worker slave and as defined in the constitution of the
United States, he proceeded, slavery was nothing less than
involuntary servitude. He then observed that a strike was
nothing else than the right to freedom of one's services on any
terms that one wanted to obtain. If the Congressmen accepted
that the right to freedom was a divine right, then, he contended
that the right to strike was also a divine right.

The Bill, he continued, ought to have been called 'the
Workers' Civil Liberties Suspension Act'. Being retrograde and
reactionary, it restricted the right of the labourer to strike and
made strike illegal and impossible; and, therefore, its author, he
said, was a far greater Tory than the author of the Trade Disputes
Act of 1929. The last hit led to a wordy warfare between Munshi
and Ambedkar, and the last reply in the series was as follows:

Munshi　　　: That would have been, slavery for the wage earner.

Ambedkar　　: You have enough, and you should, not have been abashed for going a step further in thc Bill (interruption).

The Speaker : "Order, Order."

Ambedkar then teased the Government by saying that it was a Government which claimed to be elected on labour votes; but it did not stand by its election pledges. It was a democracy, he added, that was enslaving the working class, and therefore it was a mockery of democracy. Ambedkar and Jamnadas, the two labour leaders, with their great power of debate and superior intellect so much belaboured and hammered the Bill that the Treasury benches were pushed into hot water. But the Congress Ministry was determined to pass the Bill, which they ultimately did.

That indifferent attitude created a big tide of opposition outside the Legislative Assembly in the industrial towns and cities which voiced disapproval of the Bill. A one-day strike was declared by the I.L.P. and the B.P.T.U.C. for Monday, 7th November 1938. A whirlwind propaganda was carried on in the city of Bombay preparatory to the strike on the one hand, and for the frustration of the strike move on the other hand.

Sixty different unions sent out their calls to workers. A meeting of the Council of Action of the T.U.C. was held under the Chairmanship of Jamnadas Mehta on November 6, at 8 a.m. to give final touches to their programme for November 7. Ambedkar, Parulekar, Mirajkar, Dange, Nimbkar and others were present. The Council planned a procession and decided to launch peaceful picketing in front of all mills and factories, and sent forth an appeal to workers in industrial towns to express their indignation at the Bill.

Ambedkar summoned his party M.L.A.s to a meeting of the Council of Action of his Party, and chalked out an elaborate programme for making the strike a success. Jamnadas Mehta, too, was present at this meeting. The Party men were assigned special localities to work and to enthuse the workers. The Congress Socialists, whom M. N. Roy then described as inverted

Gandhites, refused their support as they thought that Ambedkar
was using the strike to strengthen his Party. S.K. Patil, the
steam-roller of the Congress, arranged for anti-strike meetings
and addressed one himself at Cotton Green.

The Government of Bombay summoned about 300 armed
Reserve Police with twelve officers from the bordering districts
of Bombay and placed them at strategic points near the mill gates
in the city. The mainspring of action was the I.L.P., which had
distributed among the workers thousands of hand-bills through
its volunteers. Thus the two sides stood for action.

A labour rally was held at Kamgar Maidan on the evening
of November 6, and was attended, in the words of the Congress
papers, by no less than 80,000 labourers. Jamnadas Mehta
presided over the meeting. Jamnadas made a scathing attack on
the Congress Ministry, and other labour leaders made vigorous
speeches condemning the Bill. Indulal Yagnik asked the workers
to break the bonds of the Black Bill. Dange lashed at the
ridiculous psychology of the Congress leaders. Ambedkar
condemned the Congress Ministry on different counts, and said
it was the duty of the workers to make the strike a success.

The rally over, a huge procession started from the Kamgar
Maidan and wending its course through Parel. Lalbaug and
DeLisle Road, it ended in the Jambori Maidan at Worli.

At night, a chief supervising committee was formed with
Jamnadas as its Chairman and Ambedkar, Dange, Nimkar,
Mirajkar and Pradhan as its members. Out of twenty-five
hundred volunteers engaged in this propaganda 90 per cent
belonged to Ambedkar's Party.

Morning came Police officials took their posts in the
various nerve-centres of strike at half past five in the morning.
The Home Minister, Munshi, had apprehended the seriousness
of the situation and instructed the Police Commissioner to
leave no loopholes in the arrangement for prevention of any
breach of peace. The strike commenced in an atmosphere
which was quite peaceful. A spectacular feature of the
propaganda was the tour in the mill areas by the two great
labour leaders, Ambedkar and Jamnadas Mehta, sitting side

by side, in a lorry decorated with red flags and carrying a loud-speaker equipment by means of which they exhorted the workers, who lined the streets to make the strike programme a success. Almost all the textile mills as also the Municipal workshops closed down. A few mills worked partially.

It was the first successful strike launched against a popular Government by labour leaders in the teeth of opposition from the interested parties. Manned and maintained by men of Congress persuasion and capitalists, most of the newspapers sided with the Government; and the Anglo-Indian newspapers, which wanted the Congress to remain in office, were hostile to the move for the strike. They all published fabricated reports with a view to minimising the importance of the strike and Ambedkar's growing influence upon the working classes.

DeLisle Road, the nerve-centre of the mill area, was the storm-centre. As a result of stone-throwing there, some people were injured. One police officer and some constables were injured and the police opened fire to disperse the crowd, when two persons were wounded. There was an unpleasant incident at Parel Road about eleven in the morning when the car of Munshi was attacked by a man who smashed the window screen and the glass to pieces. Sardar Patel, Mathuradas Trikamji and Bhavanji Khimji, who were in the car of the Minister, were not hurt. In all seventy-two persons were injured, eleven severely wounded, and thirty-five were arrested during the day. The demonstration was in full swing all throughout the day.

In response to the labour leaders' call there was also a partial strike on that day in other districts where industrial concerns flourished. In those parts, too, processions were taken out, and pickets were active at many places in cities like Ahmedabad, Amalner, Jalgaon, Chalisgaon, Poona and Dhulia.

As a finale to the one-day strike, a gigantic rally of workers was held at Kamgar Maidan, Bombay, under the presidentship of Jamnadas Mehta in the evening, at which Ranadive, Pradhan, Nimkar, Dange and Mirajkar, the cream of Communist leaders, opened their batteries of attack on the Government for the Black Bill. An effigy of the Bill, and it is said of the Home Minister also, were set on fire at the end of the meeting. Ambedkar made a very fiery speech. At the outset, he congratulated the workers on their having staged a successful strike; and he denounced the evening papers which had depicted the strike as a failure, as the hirelings of the Government and Mill owners. He said that the strike was a grand success; but he told them that their duty did not end by simply attending meetings, crying themselves hoarse and expressing their opposition to the Bill. He stressed the need for capturing political power by electing their own represent-atives. Concluding his speech, Ambedkar said that he would join the Congress if it really started a genuine fight against British Imperialism.

Sardar Patel issued a statement saying that the labour leaders had used coercive methods. In reply to this, Ambedkar said that Sardar Patel's statement was from beginning to end a tissue of untruths.

Two things emerged from this strike. It was proved on all counts that Ambedkar could dominate the labour field also. His organization played a very important role and proved supreme. His reputation as a labour leader was established; and it prepared a background for his future relationship with the all-India Labour Problems. Ambedkar and the Communists made a united front on the issue of Labour welfare. Ambedkar, however, had shrewdly kept his Party and organization intact and aloof from those of the Communists and yet could effectively dominate the field.

So great was this event that Swami Sahajanand, the Peasant leader from U.P., saw Ambedkar at his residence in Bombay on December 25, 1938, and had a talk with him about the labour problem in Bombay and the agrarian reforms in general. He tried to persuade Ambedkar to join the Congress to form a united front against imperialism. Ambedkar replied that he would be glad to liquidate the I.L.P. and join the Congress Party if the Congress decided to fight imperialism. But he said that the Congress was using the constitutional machinery to advance the interests of the capitalists and other vested interests by sacrificing the interests, of peasants and workers, and therefore he could not join such an organization.[6]

---

6. The *Janata*, 31 December, 1938.

In the last week of December 1938, Ambedkar presided over the Aurangabad District Depressed Classes Conference at Aurangabad. It was the first Conference of the Untouchables in the Hyderabad State. The Chairman of the reception committee gave a graphic description of how the people were persecuted and converted to Islam by force and how the Brahmins with the help of the Muslims flouted their attempts to take water from the public tanks and to enter temples. In his message to the Hyderabad Depressed Classes Ambedkar stressed the importance of the Self-respect Movement.

CHAPTER 17

ON FEDERATION AND PAKISTSAN

On January 6, 1939, Ambedkar addressed a big meeting of agriculturists at Mahad when he impressed upon the audience that the Congress Ministry had failed to mitigate their woes. He said that Premier Kher was simply a figurehead; and he described the other Ministers of the Provincial Government as dogs at the door of Sardar Patel. Referring to the boastful statement of Sardar Patel, which he had made at a reception given to Kher in Gujarat, to the effect that they welcomed liner as a devotee of Gandhi and not as Premier Kher, otherwise they would have sent him back unceremoniously, Ambedkar said that he would wreak vengeance on Patel for this dire insult inflicted upon a Maharashtrian. If Patel dared insult him in this manner, he added, he would thrash him. This was not a soliloquy; this was a public speech! It was a natural outburst of anger sprung from a strong mind which was consistent with its contempt for the Congress leaders' rude mentality, and determined to show its superiority.

On his return to Bombay, Ambedkar paid a glowing tribute to the quality of service and sense of responsibility of the volunteers of the I.L.P. at the annual parade held at Parel, on January 8, 1939. He recalled to them how both Sardar Patel and Premier Kher had extolled the Dal for its work and discipline.

By now the question of the inauguration of the proposed Federation had assumed first class political importance in India. The Viceroy's return from London, after consultations with the British statesmen, was construed as a step for the early inauguration of Federation. The British statesmen now favoured participation of the Indian States in the Federation without democratization of their States Governments. Briefly told, the right wing of the Congress was struggling for a majority in the proposed Federal Assembly through the help of the States representatives, and hence it agitated for installing responsible

Governments in the States. The Congress President, Subhas Bose, was against the acceptance of Federation. Muslims opposed it tooth and nail. The Hindu Mahasabha wanted to bring it into effect with a view to frustrating the fissiparous tendencies of the Muslims and unifying India.

Ambedkar was deadly against the kind of the proposed Federation. He had declared his views once or twice at public meetings in December 1938. He now decided to raise his voice as loudly as possible against the Federal scheme. Such an opportunity came when he was invited to Poona by the Gokhale Education Society's School of Politics and Economics to deliver an address. In his two hour speech on January 29, 1939, he explained how Federation far from leading the country to Independence would block its way permanently. The reason, he said, was that the British Indian representatives would be free men while the States representatives would be bondmen in the hands of the British bureaucrats, who would dictate to the Princes the selection of their representatives.

The proposed Federation did not forge, continued he, a common citizenship as the people in the States remained States subjects and the Federal Government could not deal with them directly. Although he was not opposed, he stated, to the Federal scheme, he was in favour of Unitary Government as nationalism was compatible with the latter form of Government, which was the need of India. Further, he said that Federation would not help to unite India as it was not open to all States to join it; nor would it give responsible Government as the powers of the Federation did not extend to Defence and Foreign attairs. It would help to destroy democracy in British India, he concluded.

In the course of his speech Ambedkar compared the age of Ranade with the age of Gandhi. The age of Ranade was honest and more enlightened. In the age of Ranade the leaders struggled to modernize India. The leaders took care to be well-clad. A politician who was not a student was treated as an intolerable nuisance. In that age people engaged themselves in studying and examining the facts of life, and moulded their lives and character in accordance with the light they found as a result of their research. In the age of Gandhi leaders took pride in being half-clad and were making India a living specimen of antiquity. Learning was not deemed to be a necessary qualification for a politician, and people ceased to read and examine the facts of life. So his verdict was that Gandhi age was the dark age of India.[1]

In February Ambedkar squarely attacked the Budget in the Bombay Assembly. From the point of revenue he said that the budget was reckless and from the point of expenditure, it was senseless as it included an increase in stamp duty against the declared opposition of the Congress Party to it, increased the duty on the consumption of electricity and encouraged indirectly the consumption of kerosene oil, which was injurious to public health.

Pointing to the other problems on which Government wasted Rs. 125 lakhs for no other purpose than to wipe out a deficit arising from what they called the Prohibition policy, he observed: "The issue is narrowed down and that issue is this. Is drink a problem and if drink is a problem, is it an urgent problem? There is no question that drinking is an evil and it does have a very bad consequence, but to admit that drink is an evil is not to admit that drink is a problem, much less is it an admission that it is an urgent problem." Then he quoted figures with regard to the total excise revenue derived in various countries such as Great Britain, Australia, Canada, Irish Free State, Denmark and Norway, and said that it was not a problem in the Bombay Province when the total excise revenue was Rs. 325 lakhs on a total population of 180 lakhs.

He further referred to the United States of America and quoted the opinions from the book *Prohibition* by Feldman. His contention, therefore, was that it was wrong on the part of the Ministry to say that this was a problem which they ought to deal with. "It cannot be a problem," he proceeded, "in our part of the country and for two very good reasons. One good reason is that all religions in India agree in imposing an injunction upon the people that drink is a sin. Religion may have done many mischievous things; but certainly there can be no doubt that the one good thing that the Indian religions have done, Hindu, Mohammedan and Zoroastrian religions, is that they do impose such an injunction, which has been so directly obeyed by a large

---

1.   Ambedkar, Dr. B. R., Federation Versus freedom, p. 155.

part of our people." The second distinguishing feature which marked out, he explained, our country from other countries and which could not create a problem so far as drink was concerned was that drink traffic was in the hands of Government. In the end he asked Government whether it was such an urgent problem that they should keep aside everything else and deal with it first. In short, Ambedkar appealed to Government to abandon their prohibition policy in the larger interests of the province and evolve a proper order of priorities.

II

The echoes of the 7th November strike were still reverberating in the Assembly. Government had instituted a committee to inquire into the firing of the 7th November. In its report the Committee blamed the Communists and Ambedkar for the disorder, and justified the firing by the police. When the Committee's report came up before the Assembly for discussion, it produced unprecedented heat. Jamnadas Mehta described the report as one-sided and added that they were not findings but they were found for the Committee! Making a very fighting speech in self-defence. Ambedkar thundered: "Speaking for myself, inasmuch as I was connected with this Council of Action, I am prepared to take my trial. Let any man who has the courage, who has the confidence, who believes in this evidence, come forward and prosecute me. The Committee has said that the firing was justified, and that there were reasons for the firing." "The only question," he observed, "is this, whether, in maintaining peace and order, we shall not have regard for freedom, and for liberty. And if Home Rule means nothing else—as I think, it can mean nothing else—than that our Minister can shoot our own people and the rest of us merely laugh at the whole show or rise to support him because he happens to belong to a particular party, then I say Home Rule has been a curse and not a benefit to all India." (Applause.)

Replying to the debate, Munshi, the Home Minister of Bombay, said that Ambedkar had not come before the Committee to state the facts and added that at eleven o'clock on the day of the strike Ambedkar was conducting a case in the court and then joined the meeting in the evening. With an air of ridicule he then stated that they were familiar with the pompous, bombast and imprudent challenge which Ambedkar threw out in ten minutes of his fleeting presence with which he graced the debate. Munshi roared that he would prosecute him and make him a martyr if he made actionable speeches and did many more things to deserve the martyrdom. He, however, withdrew the word imprudent on a point of order from Sir A.M.K. Dehlavi. Ambedkar intervened and asked Munshi why he did not prosecute, on the basis of evidence at his disposal, the workers who were alleged to have battered on the strike day the heads of the millhands. Upon this Jamnadas Mehta said: "Do not believe it! "

If Ambedkar was over-powering and unyielding in his arguments, the Ministers used another weapon against him and that was reminding him of his late coming and fleeting visits to the Assembly. And yet Premier Kher paid tributes to Ambedkar some years after describing Ambedkar as a leader from the opposition who had made helpful, constructive criticism and suggestions, and pointed out defects. But to have a correct perspective of the conditions under which Ambedkar performed his duty in the Assembly one should turn to a speech made by Jamnadas Mehta in the Assembly as regards the Congress Ministers' attitude to the Opposition in the Assembly. Mehta observed: "If we oppose Government point-blank, then it is complained that we are opposing for the sake of opposition; if we support the principle and then show the difficulties, then it is said that this is no support at all. I wish that that kind of attitude should be reduced to a minimum."

Since February 1939, trouble had been brewing in the Rajkot State where a strong agitation was going on for political reforms. Defeated and disappointed by Subhas Bose's election to the Presidentship of the Congress, Gandhi hurried to Rajkot apparently to settle the State problem, but with an inward desire to create a crisis just at the time of the Tripuri Congress Session over which Subhas Bose was to preside. Ambedkar was urgently called by the local Depressed Classes to intervene in the dispute regarding their non-inclusion in the Reforms Committee of the State. He, therefore, left by air for Rajkot and on the evening of April 18, saw the ruler, the Thakor Saheb, and at night addressed a meeting of the Depressed Classes, urging them to carry on their struggle for political rights.

The next morning he had a talk with Gandhi for forty-five minutes on the question of representation for the Harijans on the Reforms Committee. He stated in an interview at Rajkot that he could not discuss in detail all the points with Gandhi, as the Mahatma had a sudden temperature. He, however, revealed that the suggestion that his alternative proposal should be submitted to a constitutional expert like Sir Tej Bahadur Sapru was not acceptable to Gandhi. At last Gandhi failed in his attempt to effect a change of heart by his non-violent methods and resorted to coercive methods by appealing to the Viceroy to intervene. Gandhi, the apostle of the principle of change of heart and non-violence, himself publicly confessed that his non-violence had not yet been developed to the fullest power, and so he left Rajkot, to quote his words, with hopes cremated and body shattered.

Accordingly, a few days thereafter Sir Maurice Gwyer, the Chief Justice of the Federal Court, gave an Award on the disputes in the State of Rajkot. Ambedkar challenged the interpretation of the word " recommend" given by Sir Maurice Gwyer. He stated that Gwyer had given his decision on the footing that "There is no conclusive precedent for the purposes of the present reference." Ambedkar quoted two authorities in support of his assertion, *Knolt* vs. *Cottee*, and *Johnson* vs. *Rowlands*.

In the first week of July 1939, Ambedkar attended a meeting organised by the Chamar community under the aegis of the Rohidas Education Committee at the R. M. Bhat High School Hall, Bombay. His presence at this meeting was significant since almost all the Chamar community leaders were estranged from him on the problem of conversion. They had broken with him at the time of the general elections gone by as, according to them, Ambedkar had refused to set up candidates from their community on the ground that they had not supported his conversion policy. Addressing the meeting, Ambedkar said that he had started his uplift work for the whole of the Depressed Classes. He never favoured sectional or sectarian ideas or policy in his uplift work.

He told them that he favoured the abolition of sub-castes among the Depressed Classes and honestly worked to that end. He further said that the question of marriage was not one that could be settled by force. It was not that a Mahar girl, he observed, and a Chamar boy or a Mang boy should be married perforce as if by waving a magic wand. It was upto them to encourage those men who showed courage to perform such marriages. Referring to the political problem, he said that the Congress leaders were shrewdly bringing about a rift among the Depressed Classes by encouraging some Depressed Class leaders against his Party. He appealed to them not to fall a prey to the Congress false propaganda. Congress leaders were cajoling the Harijan leaders, he added, because he was not there in the Congress camp. He stated that it was a fact that the I.L.P. drew its major following from the Mahars. But it was, he explained, not his fault that the Mahars had a majority in the Depressed Classes.[2] In his concluding remarks, however, he did not fail to reiterate his old slogan that to get rid of those sectional feelings the only way out was to embrace another religion.

A few days later, Ambedkar was entertained at a tea-party by the authorities of Hansraj P. Thackersey College at Nasik. Replying to questions that were put to him in writing at that function, Ambedkar said that the money the Government was raising in the form of taxes must be utilised to relieve the farmers of their debts, to fight poverty and to impart education; but he said that it could not be done if prohibition was given a priority or a preference over these urgent problems. Asked whether he agreed to the zonal scheme sponsored by Sir Sikander Hyat Khan in respect of a division of India, he replied that he did not approve of the seven zones and suspected that it was a step in the direction of establishment of Pakistan. As regards British rule, he expressed his view that apart from all other defects or disabilities, it had conferred two benefits on Indians, namely, one common Central Government, and a feeling among the people belonging to different religions that they were part of one Government.

About this time, Ambedkar chastised the Treasury Benches while speaking on the Finance Act Second Amendment Bill in the Bombay Legislative Assembly. He expressed his sense of surprise that a Government which included no less than five eminent lawyers should have thought it fit to bring a Bill with a penalty which had got a retrospective character.

---

2.   The *Janata*, 8 July 1939.

Ill

Just then World War II broke out in Europe over the question of the safety of Poland. India was committed to the war with Germany by a proclamation of the British Viceroy. Different Indian leaders viewed the global war differently. The Indian Liberal leaders favoured unconditional help to Government in their war efforts, but the chief Muslim organisation led by Jinnah stated that the British should create a sense of security and salvation in the minds of the Indian Muslims. At first the Congress leaders including Sardar Patel, and Jawaharlal Nehru, who was on his way back from his invigorating visit to Chiang Kai-shek's China, favoured unconditional help as they said they were not out to bargain at such a juncture.

Gandhi broke down before the British Viceroy at the very thought of the destruction of the British House of Parliament and Westminster Abbey. Savarkar declared that Britain's claim that she had entered the war to safeguard the vital principles affecting human freedom would be regarded as a political stunt so long as she continued to hold India in political bondage.

An event of great significance took place on September 11. The Viceroy announced that although Federation was the ultimate objective of the Government, under the existing conditions they had no choice but to hold it in suspension. Jinnah was beside himself with joy at this declaration.

Ambedkar, the leader of the I.L.P., issued a statement, declaring that there was not much virtue on the side of Poland, especially in her treatment of the Jews. He said that the Polish issue was only an incident in the war and Germany's claim to impose her will upon those who disagreed with her was a menace to all nations. He disagreed with those who held that England's difficulty was India's opportunity and added that Indians should not go in for new masters.

He declared that it was unfair to India that it should have no voice in her foreign policy in declaring war and in the making of peace. India should remain within the British Commonwealth of nations and strive to achieve the status of equal partnership therein. Appealing then to Government to take steps in preparing

Indians for the defence of their country, he reminded the British Government how they had agreed at the Round Table Conference that the defence of India was to be treated as the responsibility of India. Concluding his statement, he stated that the duty of Britain towards India was to reassure her of the status she would occupy in the British Empire after the war was over, and that India could not willingly and heartily fight for principles if she was not assured that the benefits of those principles would be extended to her when the war was won.

On September 14 the Congress leaders changed their attitude. They declared that a free democratic India would gladly associate herself with the free nations for mutual defence and asked the British Government to declare their war aims in regard to democracy and imperialism, and particularly to India.

A few days later, a joint statement was issued by seven leaders Savarkar, Kelkar, Jamnadas, Ambedkar, Sir Chimanlal Setalvad, Sir Cowasji Jehangir and Sir V. N. Chandavarkar, declaring that Gandhi's claim that the Congress was an all-representative body, was a fascist one and would prove a deathblow to Indian democracy.

Lord Linlithgow, the Viceroy of India, had interviews in the first and second weeks of October with about fifty-two Indian leaders, representing different interests and parties such as Gandhi, Jinnah, Nehru, Savarkar, Patel, Rajendra Prasad, Subhas Bose, Ambedkar and others. Ambedkar's interview took place on October 9. In the course of his interview Ambedkar impressed upon the Governor-General the viewpoint of his community *vis-a-vis* the constitutional advance of India and complained that the working of the Poona Pact had been far from satisfactory, and so he intended to raise the question at the next revision of the constitution.

After discussions with the Indian leaders, the Viceroy issued a statement clarifying the position of the British Government with regard to their hopes and objectives for India. The important part of the statement was that at the end of the war the Government of India Act would be revised in consultation with all the leading parties in India, and that no substantial political advance would be made without the consent of the minorities.

He added that a consultative committee would be formed during the war on which all parties would be represented. The Working Committee of the Congress declared the Viceroy's statement to be wholly unsatisfactory and as any help to Britain would amount to an endorsement of her imperial policy, they called upon all Provincial Ministries to tender their resignations thus, in fact, enabling the British Government to pursue more conveniently a policy which the Congress leaders themselves hated.

Ambedkar issued a statement from Delhi stating that the minorities problem would never be solved unless Gandhi and the Congress gave up their egoistic and insolent attitude towards persons and parties outside the Congress. He added that patriotism was not a monopoly of Congressmen, and, therefore, persons holding views divergent from the Congress had a perfectly legitimate right to exist and be recognised. Referring to the Muslim problem, he said that he did not believe in the allegations made by the Muslims that they were being tyrannised or terrorised in the Provinces ruled by the Congress. What they wanted along with other minorities, he affirmed, was a share in the Government. Lastly, he warned that if the demand of the Muslim League for a division of India was allowed to hold the Muslim masses, there would be no hope for a united India and that the responsibility of driving the Depressed Classes to another fold would lie with the Congress.

It seems that the Congress leaders were disturbed by the aforesaid joint statement of the seven leaders and the joint statement of non-Congress leaders from Southern India both of which were signed by the leaders of the Depressed Classes. With a view to acquainting himself with the claims of the Depressed Classes, Jawaharlal Nehru, the Chairman of the War sub-Committee ot the Congress, had talks for two days in the third week of October with Ambedkar in Bombay.[3] This was the first meeting of Ambedkar with Nehru whom the former, in his private talks had described as a fourth standard boy. It was Kher who took Ambedkar to Nehru. Immediately after this talk, discussions were held between the Congress leaders and Ambedkar for three or four days at the residence of Bhulabhai Desai, President of the Bombay Provincial Congress Committee and Member of the

---

3. *The Times of India*. 30 October 1939.

Congress Working Committee. The talks were held in the presence of Gandhi's secretary, Mahadeo Desai, who had specially come from Wardha for the purpose. He was to communicate the views of Ambedkar to Gandhi and the Congress. The talks were confined to the relinquishment of office by the Congress Ministry of Bombay.

The Congress Ministries introduced the war resolution in all Provincial Assemblies on the eve of their resignations. The Bombay Ministry introduced the resolution amidst grave atmosphere. It declared that the British Government had made India a participant in the war between Britain and Germany without the consent of the people of India, and "have further in complete disregard of Indian opinion passed laws and adopted measures curtailing the powers and activities of the Provincial Governments".

Moving an amendment to delete the words "and have further in ... Provincial Governments", Ambedkar blamed the Prime Minister for nor having tabled the demands in the name of the country but in obedience to the Congress High Command. He reiterated his statement on war policy and declared that the Untouchables would never accept a political status that would make them political Shudras. He said he would not tolerate it if to the social dominance, the economic dominance and the religious dominance which the Hindus exercised over them, was added the political dominance. He then reminded the House of the fate of the Spanish American colonies separated from the Spanish Empire which had referred to Jeremy Bentham of Britain to frame their own constitution, and how Bentham shipped documents from England and how the constitution had failed in those countries, and was publicly burnt. He said that a constitution, like, a suit, must fit.

Ambedkar then described how the majority were denying liberty, equality and fraternity for the growth of the Untouchables. He told the House that out of one hundred Mamlatdars, only one was from the Depressed Classes; out of 34 Mahalkaries, none was from them; out of 246 Head Clerks none was from them;, out of the total 2,444 revenue clerks, only 30 were from his class; out of 829 Public Works Department clerks, only 7 were from the scheduled classes; in the Excise Department

3 out of 189; out of 538 police inspectors only 2; out of 33 Deputy Collectors only one, was from the Scheduled Class.

In a very appealing and powerful tone Ambedkar further declared: "I know my position has not been understood properly in the country. It has often been misunderstood. Let me, therefore, take this opportunity to clarify my position. Sir, I say that whenever there has been a conflict between my personal interests and the interests of the country as a whole, I have always placed the claims of the country above my personal claims. I have never pursued the path of private gain. If I had played my cards well, as others do, I might have been in some other place. I do not want to say about it, but I did not do it. There were colleagues with me at the Round Table Conference who, I am sure, would support what I say—that so far as the demands of the country are concerned, I have never lagged behind. Many European Members who were at the Conference rather felt embarrassed that I was the *enfant terrible* of the Conference."

"But I will also," he thundered, "leave no doubt in the minds of the people of this country that I have another loyalty to which I am bound and which I can never forsake. That loyalty is the community of Untouchables, in which I am born, to which I belong, and which I hope I shall never desert. And I say this to this House as strongly as I possibly can, that whenever there is any conflict of interests between the country and the Untouchables, so far as I am concerned, the Untouchables' interests will take precedence over the interests of the country. I am not going to support a tyrannising majority simply because it happens to speak in the name of the country. I am not going to support a party because it happens to speak in the name of the country. I shall not do that. Let everybody here and everywhere understand that that is my position. As between the country and myself, the country will have precedence, as between the country and the Depressed Classes, the Depressed Classes will have precedence—the country will have no precedence. That is all that I wanted to say with regard to these two amendments of mine."

In conclusion Ambedkar asked the Premier of the Province why he required his sanction for his going out. He said it was for the party caucus to decide. Ambedkar took an hour and a half and the Speaker said that the other Members would curtail their speeches. Upon this Ambedkar said: "I apologise, Sir."

IV

The Congress Ministries eventually resigned in obedience to the mandate of their High Command in the first week of November 1939. So hilarious was Jinnah at this exit of the Congress that he announced that the Muslim India heaved a sigh of relief and appealed to his community to observe a "Day of Deliverance". A large number of Parsees who were affected by the prohibition policy of the Congress expressed joy over this exit; and they promised in their individual capacity to join the 'Day of Deliverance'. Ambedkar declared that he would like to join Jinnah in celebrating the Deliverance Day and observed: "I read Mr. Jinnah's statement and I felt ashamed to have allowed him to steal a march over me and rob me of the language and the sentiment which I, more than Mr. Jinnah, was entitled to use." He said that if Mr. Jinnah proved 5 out of 100 cases of alleged oppression, he would prove 100 out of 100 cases before any impartial tribunal. He, however, explained that it was not an anti-Hindu move; it was anti-Congress and, therefore, purely political. He concluded by saying that if the Hindus construed it as an attack on themselves, it meant that the Congress was a Hindu body and that they should thank themselves for the consequences.

The most significant feature of the celebration of the "Deliverance Day" was that these two eminent opponents of Gandhi and Congress shook hands at the "Deliverance Day" meeting at Bhendi Bazaar, Bombay, and belched fire on the Congress leadership!

One problem, in the meantime, was coming to a head which engaged Ambedkar's mind for a considerable period. The Bombay Government levied additional taxes on the Mahar Vatans. Ambedkar had been fighting that problem since 1927. But now instead of relieving the poor from the serfdom, the Government added salt to their injuries by the levy of additional taxes. The Mahars, Mangs and Vethias, in Maharashtra and Karnatak met in Conference at Haregaon in the middle of December 1939, to voice their grievances under the presidentship of Ambedkar. Addressing the Conference of 20,000 Mahars, Mangs and Vethias, Ambedkar warned Government that if Government did not abrogate the harassing orders, and relieve those poor people within six months from the date of the conference from the extortion of work which they were forced to do without any remuneration, there would be no alternative for those people but to refuse the services as a protest against the harassment. He appealed to Government to see that the Vatandars were paid as were the State servants and demanded abolition of their serfdom.

On March 19, which the Depressed Classes observed as their Independence day—for on that day in 1927 at Mahad their struggle for emancipation began—Ambedkar addressed a rally of 10,000 people at Mahad. In the course of his speech he observed that it was entirely wrong for the Indians to concentrate all their attention on political independence of the country and forget the foremost social and economic problems. He said that it was high time that Hindu society were organised on modern lines breaking down its age-long framework. At night an address of welcome was presented to Ambedkar by the Mahad Municipality.

Meanwhile, the political situation assumed a very serious tempo. The Congress, at its annual session held in April 1940 at Ramgarh, repudiated any attempt to divide India or split up her manhood. Simultaneously the Muslim League at its annual session at Lahore passed a resolution demanding the creation of Independent States in the North-Western and Eastern parts of India where Muslims were in a majority. Jinnah, the angel of unity and peace, had now decided to be the destroyer of the unity of the land.

Ambedkar was watching and studying these developments in Indian politics. He was also guiding his people. He founded the Mahar Panchayat and addressed a conference under the auspices of the Panchayat at Bandra, Bombay, in May 1940.

Just then Hitler overran the low countries, and the war took a serious turn for Britain and her allies. Congress leaders abandoned Gandhi's leadership, and offered co-operation in war efforts, provided a fully representative National Government was formed at the centre. This offer was reiterated by them at Poona and came to be known as the Poona offer. Jinnah opposed it, saying that it would mean a permanent Hindu majority at the centre. The Viceroy announced a new proposal for the expansion of his Executive Council and the establishment of a war advisoiy committee for the conduct of the war. The Congress rejected this proposal as being wholly opposed to the best interests of India.

At this time Subhas Bose, who was dethroned from the Congress Presidentship, was growing restless. He was trying to rally the Indian forces against the British power that was engaged in a life-and-death struggle in Europe. He came to Bombay and saw Jinnah, Ambedkar and Savarkar on July 22, 1940. Subhas Bose was deadly against the acceptance of the proposed Federation; and because Ambedkar was opposed to it he must have considered it a rallying point between them. After their discussion on the issue of Federation, Ambedkar asked Subhas Bose whether he would put up his candidates in the elections against the Congress. He replied in the negative. Ambedkar then asked Subhas Bose what the positive attitude of his party would be to the problem of Untouchables. Bose had no convincing reply and the interview ended. It seems Savarkar's inspiring talk changed Subhas Bose's mind; and he began to ponder over the possibility of fighting a war of Independence against the British power from outside.

The Congress now switched over again to Gandhi's dictatorship for a struggle. Gandhi inaugurated individual civil disobedience movement in October 1940, preaching non-participation in the war on the grounds of non-violence. As a result, almost all Congress leaders were thrown into prison. Criticising this move of Gandhi, Ambedkar said that Gandhi's new performance in preaching against supplying men or money to the war efforts meant civil disobedience of the Defence of India Act. "It can be beyond Gandhi," he observed, "to appreciate that while all thinking men must hate the use of force, a distinction has to be made between the use of force to put down force and to use the victory obtained by force to impose ignoble and unjust terms upon the vanquished." "It seems to me," he went on, "that the root of the evil is not in the use of force but in the misuse of victory. Mr. Gandhi and all pacifists and believers in non-violence will do a lasting service to humanity if they went on a fast unto death when peace is announced, if the terms of peace offered to the vanquished are ignoble and unjust. The pacifist, it seems to me, has misunderstood his mission. His fight must be against a base peace and not against force. By calling upon people to abjure the use of force, the pacifist is only helping those who will insist on using force to victory." Quoting then Rajagopalachari who was reported to have said in his speech that if he were a Viceroy he would continue the old order, Ambedkar declared: "That the Congress is fighting for the cause of the country is humbug. The Congress is fighting to obtain the keys of power in its hands, Why did Gandhi not start civil disobedience immediately after the Defence of India Act was passed a year ago ? "

The year 1940 was coming to an end when Ambedkar's *magnum opus, Thoughts on Pakistan*, was published. Written at a psychological moment, it fell like a bombshell on the heated atmosphere of the day. India's man of great learning, great constitutional pundit and politician of varied experience gave out his reflections on the political problem of India. The refrain of the book was the division of India into Hindustan and Pakistan for the prosperity, peace and salvation of the Hindus to whom the book was mainly addressed.

That the Muslims, the book argues, are a nation must be accepted without cavil. It advises the Hindus to have no fear for want of a nationally safe frontier in the event of the birth of Pakistan because geographical conditions are not decisive in modern world and modern technique. As the resources of Hindustan are far greater than those of Pakistan, the creation of Pakistan will not leave Hindustan in a weakened condition. It also impresses upon the Hindus that it is better to have Muslims whose loyalty to India is always doubtful, without and against, rather than within and against. A safe army rid of the Muslim preponderance is better than a safe border.

The book is not without its antidote to the poison of Pakistan. It prescribes a sovereign remedy for securing peace and homogeneity by arranging for a total exchange of population, Hindus from Pakistan and Muslims from Hindustan, as did Turkey, Greece and Bulgaria to solve their internecine wars.

But unlike M. N. Roy's *Historical Role of Islam*, this historic book castigates the anti-reformist tendency of the Muslims. It observes that the dominating influence with the Muslims is not democracy. The predominant interest of Muslims is religion, their politics being essentially clerical. The Muslims are opposed to social reform, and are an unprogressive people all over the world. To the Muslims, the book states, Islam is a world religion, suitable for all peoples for all times and for all conditions. The brotherhood of Islam is not the universal brotherhood of man. It is the brotherhood of Muslims for Muslims only. For non-Muslims there is nothing but contempt and enmity. The Muslim has allegiance to a nation which is ruled by a Muslim; a land not ruled by a Muslim is his enemy land. The book, therefore, concludes that Islam can never allow a true Muslim to adopt India as his Motherland and regard a Hindu as his kith and kin. The spirit of aggression is a Muslim's natural endowment. He takes advantage of the weakness of the Hindus and follows gangsterism.

Some penetrating and caustic paragraphs describing the regressive bent of the Muslim mind, however, were deleted, it is said, at the instance of Ambedkar's close admirers. Otherwise the author of *Thoughts on Pakistan* would have experienced what H. G. Wells experienced at the hands of Muslims in London!

The book then asserts that the Muslims are now awakened to a new life. They will to be a nation. The were up till now calling themselves a minority, a community; but they have now discovered their destiny. The book observes that a Muslim must be very stupid if he is not attracted by the glamour of this new destiny. According to the book, it is a new destiny, a new vision, the sun of their destiny in full glow!

After giving philosophic justification for Pakistan, interpreting to the Muslims their inspiring destiny and putting forth arguments before the Hindus, the book asks the Hindus whether integral India is an ideal worth fighting for. Coercion is no remedy. It you agree to partition, it will liberate both the Hindus and the Muslims from the fear of enslavement and of encroachment upon each other. You should profit by a deeper study of Turkey, Greece and other nations; and avert the catastrophe by agreeing to partition India into Hindustan and Pakistan. To avoid ship-wreck in mid-ocean, you must lighten the draught by throwing overboard all superfluous cargo. Divide

India to have a strong central Government. Otherwise the consequences will be terrible. Forced union will hinder progress, There will be frustration of all her hopes of freedom; complete frustration of her destiny will be her fate if it is insisted that India shall remain an integral whole. United India will never be an organic whole. Nor will it solve the problem of the third party, the British. The virus of dualism will surge up. India will be an anaemic and sickly State, a living corpse, dead though not buried. Compare with the dark vista, the vista that opens out if India is divided into Pakistan and Hindustan. The partition opens a way to the fulfilment of the destiny each may fix up for itself, whether dominion or independence, concludes the book.

After the publication of this great book, the author of *Thoughts On Pakistan*, however, described Rajagopalachari in these words: "Mr. Rajagopalachari's political exploits are too fresh to be forgotten. Suddenly he enrolled himself as a soldier of the Muslim League and proclaimed a war on his own kin and former friends and for what? Not for their failure to grant the reasonable demands of the Muslim but for their not conceding the most extravagant one, namely Pakistan!"[4] It may be recalled here that Ambedkar was highly praised for his patriotic and rationalistic report which he submitted to the Simon Commission. In it he had attacked, exposed and held to ridicule the demand of the Muslims for separate electorate; but now he supported and justified a separate nation for the same Muslims!

With the cool intelligence of a doctor he viewed and examined the malady of India. A book by a vigorous man is unlikely to be dispassionate. The subject was dealt with candour, competence, knowledge, courage and excellence. *Thoughts On Pakistan* is a masterpiece in which learning and thinking are blended and displayed at their highest order. It is entrancing in its magic, intriguing in its construction, terse in its style, and provocative in its manner. It is a model in scientific propagation!

Ambedkar's political favourite was Burke whose political philosophy echoed in his speeches and writings. Burke wrote his *Thoughts On The Cause Of The Present Discontents*. Burke supported enthusiastically in his speech, on Conciliation with

---

4.   Ambedkar, *Mr. Gandhi And The Emancipation Of The Untouchables*, pp. 60-61.

America the stand taken by the American colonies which were
hundreds of miles away from England. It was not the question
of Scotland's Home Rule. Ambedkar favoured the vivisection of
one living entity. Burke committed a glaring miscalculation by
throwing aspersions and making an onslaught upon the French
Revolution in his *Reflections on the Revolution in France.*
Similarly, future historians may think about Ambedkar's
Thoughts On Pakistan ! Historians may borrow the remark
Ambedkar passed on Rajagopalachari's role, and fling it at the
author of *Thoughts On Pakistan.*

The effect of this book was terrible. It shattered the brains
of many Hindu politicians. It was applauded as an epitome of
the political and social history of India; and it rocked Indian
politics for over a decade. The Muslims rejoiced at this support
to their ideal. The Congressmen, who were bred and brought
up in the sordid philosophy of neither-reject-nor-accept, winked
at one another. It gave an impetus to the Pakistan propaganda
of Rajagopalachari. Some of the leaders of Hindu Mahasabha,
who were the stoutest opponents of Pakistan on national and
rational grounds, were confused; but their leader Savarkar
staked his all at the altar of the integrity of India and stoutly
refuted the theory of vivisection of India. He said that it was
not bravery or statesmanship to run away from danger, to
abandon the fight, and yield to the aggressor. Aggressors were
never pacified or appeased. He warned the Hindus that partition
would strengthen the hands of the avowed enemies of India,
and the hoards would invade India. Partition, said Savarkar,
would be a standing menace to the peace, security, liberty and
prosperity of India.

But it is also pathetically true that no front-rank Hindu
leader issued a counter treatise refuting Ambedkar's arguments
with equal force, scholarship, courage and brilliance. An author
of Mahasabha persuasion from Poona and an editor of a Bombay
Weekly of Congress persuasion replied to Ambedkar, but their
books were written in Marathi and were mere commentaries
evoked by *Thoughts On Pakistan*, Dr. Rajendrat Prasad later
published a volume full of moonshine. But books are not read in
the moonlight! Restless at the arguments of Ambedkar, Dr.
Moonje wrote to N. C. Kelkar, stressing the urgent need for a

reply to Ambedkar.[5] Many will agree that Kelkar's judicious but wavering genius was quite unsuited to this purpose. It was the duty of the Hindu Mahasabha, the bulwark of fighters for undivided India to do so; but nothing ever came out in time from the Mahasabha!

During this period of labour leadership, the question of conversion had receded in the background. Ambedkar used to pay courtesy calls, often with his friends, on a certain Miss Dressler who resided at Byculla in Bombay. She belonged to some American Church Mission and had also established an American Indian Mission. Ambedkar sometimes had his meals with the lady. She was drawn to him intellectually and was his admirer. Whenever Dr. Ambedkar published a new book or any article, he would send it over to her. After Ambedkar's appointment as Labour Member, his visits to her became few and far between.

◻◻◻

---

5.   Kelkar, N.C., Correspondence, p. 33.

CHAPTER 18

FROM DUST TO DOYEN

DURING the first quarter of 1941, Ambedkar was busy with the problem of recruitment of the Untouchables, especially the Mahars who are famous for their fighting qualities. He saw the Governor of Bombay and voiced his grievances against the militarisation policy of the Government which excluded the Mahars on the basis of a senseless distinction between martial and non-martial classes. He explained to him the role played by the Mahars under the East India Company, how afterwards they were prohibited from admission into the military forces and how the Mahar battalion was revived at the end of World War I but was disbanded not long afterwards on the excuse of economy. He, therefore, appealed to the Government to raise a battalion of Mahars now for the combatant corps.

Thereupon Government decided to raise a Mahar battalion, and Ambedkar issued an appeal to the Mahars to seize the opportunity both for their own sake and for the sake of the country. Soon after a battalion was established, and several men from the Mahar community were enlisted while a number of them were appointed recruiting officers, one of them being Ambedkar's lieutenant, Jadhav *alias* Madakebuva who had a genius for organization. Savarkar, who wished the Hindus to be reborn into a martial race, expressed his hope that under the able guidance of Ambedkar the Mahar brethren would be re-animated with the military qualities and their military uplift would contribute to the consolidation of the Hindus.

In the last week of July 1941, the Viceroy expanded his Executive Council by including eight representative Indians and established a Defence Advisory Committee. Ambedkar was appointed on the Defence Advisory Committee along with Jamnadas Mehta, Ramrao Deshmukh, M. C. Rajah and other well-known Indians and Indian Princes. The Sikhs and the Depressed Classes resented their non-inclusion in the Executive Council.

Ambedkar protested against the injustice done to the claims of the Depressed Classes. He sent a cablegram to Amery, the Secretary of State for India, informing him that the non-inclusion of their representative was regarded by them as an outrage and a breach of trust. Savarkar upheld Ambedkar's demand and wired to the Viceroy to include Ambedkar in the Executive Council.

As Government failed to respond to the appeal made by the Mahar Conference at Haregaon, another conference was called at Sinnar in the middle of August 1941. Ambedkar told the Conference that he had addressed a Memorandum to the Government and complained how similar Vatan holders like Deshpandes and Deshmukhs were relieved of their duties and yet were enjoying their Vatan property even to that day. Exasperated by the adamant attitude of the Government, the Mahars were driven to adopt an extreme measure of no-tax campaign. The Conference gave a message to the aggrieved Mahars to resort to non-co-operation with Government till Government abandoned the demand for the additional levy.

Returning to Bombay, Ambedkar called on the Governor, Sir Lawrence Roger Lumley, in the morning at the Government House. Ambedkar's Sinnar speech was flashed in the evening newspapers by I. A. Ezekiel, a front-rank journalist, who unfailingly supported Ambedkar and his movement for years in the world of journalism. Lord Linlithgow, the Governor-General, who was then in Bombay, happened to read the speech in the newspapers. He remonstrated with the Governor of Bombay for having alienated the Depressed Classes and for having driven them in the opposite camp. Shortly after this, the Bombay Government revoked its unjust orders and Ambedkar won the day!

Two weeks later Ambedkar addressed some meetings, stressing the need for joining the military forces. In a stirring appeal at one such meeting in Bombay, he said that although the Central Government had denied representation to the Depressed Classes in the Executive Council, he regretted that those who felt that the Government should not be helped, had lost the sense of proportion and relative value of things. He replied to them that if the Nazis overran the country, there would not be much of an Expanded Council left to fight for. He added that he was not prepared for a change of rulers and to start the struggle once again for self-government right from the beginning. He concluded his speech by urging the Mahar youths to suspend their studies and qualify themselves for military commissions and preserve their high martial traditions.

Ambedkar took keen interest in the militarisation movement, and he attended the second session of the National Defence Council in the first week of December 1941. The third session of the Defence Council was held in February 1942. He was present at the meeting.

About this time Ambedkar was working on a book entitled "What The Hindus Have Done To Us ".[1] It seems he began writing it on February 13, 1942, and an American firm had talks with him in the matter of its publication. It was then in the air that plans were under consideration for further reshuffling and strengthening the personnel of the Viceroy's Executive Council.

The political deadlock was yet unresolved. Congress leaders were in jail. Their generalissimo, Gandhi, was outside. Some politicians thought that Gandhi would start a fast unto death for Hindu-Muslim unity; for the Muslims had started Pakistani riots and Jinnah said that only a change of heart would ease the tension. Gandhi, however, clearly realised the historical mistake and futility of his slogan which had drummed into the people for over twenty years that freedom would not come without Hindu-Muslim unity. Without Muslim support he was now on the eve of a 'do or die struggle'!

II

In the middle of February 1942, there were discussions held at the spring lectures series at Wagle Hall, Bombay. Three days were reserved for the discussion on *Thoughts On Pakistan.* Ambedkar was present at the time of the discussion. Acharya M. V. Donde presided over the meeting. At the express request by Donde, his friend, colleague and an eminent educationist in the Province, Ambedkar rose to reply to the debate. He said at the outset that he would not waste his words on those who thought that Pakistan was not a debatable subject at all. If it was thought

---

1.   It was subsequently published under the title. *What Congress And Gandhi Have Done To The Untouchables.*

that the demand was unjust, then the coming of Pakistan would be a terrible thing for them. It was wrong, he said, to tell the people to forget history. "They cannot make history," he continued, "who forget history. To bring down the preponderance of the Muslims in the Indian army and to make, the army safe, it is wise to let out the hostile element. We will defend our land. Do not be under the false impression that Pakistan would be able to spread its Muslim empire over India. The Hindus will make it lick the dust. I confess I have my quarrel with the caste Hindus over some points, but I take a vow before you that I shall lay down my life in defence of our land."[2] A thunder of applause greeted his speech.

About this time Sir Stafford Cripps returned to England from his successful mission to Russia; and it was declared that he would be entrusted with solving the deadlock in India, Ambedkar put forth his scheme on the eve of the visit of Sir Stafford Cripps. Referring to Chiang Kai-shek's recommendation that Britain should give India immediately real political power, Ambedkar said that the Chinese leader did not give a solution to the difficulties in the way of that consummation. He further stated that the British Government should promise to raise India to a Dominion Status within three years from the date of peace; and if the Indian parties failed to produce an agreed solution within one year from the date of the signing of the armistice, the Indian dispute should be submitted to the International Tribunal for decision; and Britain should declare that she would undertake to give effect to it as a part of the Dominion Constitution for India.

He, however, described Jinnah's demand for 50 per cent representation as monstrous, and, congratulating Lord Linlithgow on having turned it down, said that no National Government should be established as an interim measure, if it meant conceding to Jinnah his claim for 50 per cent seats for the Muslims.

Those who criticised this Scheme said that they were surprised that the historian and constitutionalist in Ambedkar should have expected the Muslim League to consent to a decision of the International Tribunal.

---

2.   The *Lokamanya*, 20 February 1942.

Meanwhile, the British lost Singapore to Japan. The sun on the British Empire was now setting; the Empire was cracking. Impelled by these reverses in the eastern theatre of war and pressed by the U.S.A. and China, the British Government decided to end the Indian political deadlock. Sir Stafford Cripps came plane-haste to India in the third week of March 1942 to settle the Indian political problem on the basis of a scheme. He held consultations with the representatives of the Congress, the Muslim League, the Hindu Mahasabha, the Sikhs' Organization and the Princes' Chamber and put before them the proposals. Ambedkar, accompanied by M. C. Rajah, met Cripps on March 30. According to the Cripps proposals, a Constituent Assembly was to be convened immediately after the cessation of hostilities. It was to draft the constitution in co-operation with the Indian States, but the right of joining or staying out of the Indian Union was given to Provinces and the Constituent Assembly was to enter into a treaty with the British Government.

Gandhi described the Cripps offer as a post-dated cheque. Savarkar rejected it *in toto* condemning it as a scheme designed to balkanize India. The Liberals termed it a travesty of self determination. The Muslim League rejected it as it did not contain a definite or unequivocal announcement in favour of Pakistan although it favoured its ideal by implication. The Congress leaders, who were more keen on the immediate transfer of power than the balkanisation of India, swallowed the pill of the division of India, but were straining at the gnat of the Defence Portfolio.

After a full discussion with the other provincial leaders of the Depressed Classes, Ambedkar, too, rejected the scheme as it was calculated to do, according to the leaders of the Depressed Classes, the greatest harm to the Depressed Classes as it bound them hand and foot to a Hindu rule and would lead them, they feared, to the black days of their ancient past. They asked Sir Stafford Cripps to convey to His Majesty's Government that the Depressed Classes would look upon it as a breach of faith, if the British Government decided to force upon them a constitution to which they did not give their consent.

In another statement Ambedkar described the attitude of the British Government to the Depressed Classes as a Munich mentality, the essence of which was to save oneself by sacrificing others. He further stated that the Cripps proposal had distinctly given to the League the right to create Pakistan. According to him, the proposals were the result of a loss of nerve and of a sense of principle, a breach of faith and a sudden *volte-face!*

III

The new policy of Britain in regard to the Depressed Classes compelled Ambedkar to make a departure from his new role as a labour leader. During the interview Cripps asked Ambedkar whether he represented the labour or the Depressed Classes and asked him also about the strength of his Party. That gave a turn to his role; and once again Ambedkar thought it wise to resume the leadership of the Depressed Classes in the interest of his people for whom he had been fighting all along the past twenty-five years. He, therefore, convened on March 30 and 31, 1942, a conference of the leaders of the Depressed Classes who were present in Delhi and held consultations with them on the Cripps proposals. M. C. Rajah, who had up to that time opposed Ambedkar, was now reconciled with Ambedkar. Rajbhoj had already joined him. It was decided, after a gap of ten years, to hold an All-India Depressed Classes Conference at Nagpur, in July 1942, with a view to creating an All-India organization with distinct aims and purposes in co-operation with all the inter-provincial forces.

The fiftieth birthday of Ambedkar fell on April 14, 1942. To mark the occasion the I. L. Party and forty-five other public institutions in Bombay and suburbs organised a nine-day celebration consisting of flag salutations, processions and public meetings. The celebrations began on April 12 in all the wards of Bombay City and its suburbs.

At Poona processions were taken out through prominent streets and Cantonment, and felicitations were showered on Ambedkar for his selfless services to the cause of the Untouchables at a public meeting, at the Shaniwarwada, addressed by M. C. Rajah and P. N. Rajbhoj under the presidentship of Prof. S. M. Mate. The meeting wished their leader a long and happy life. A big meeting was held in the

Assembly Hall of the Poona Municipality under the chairmanship of Ganpatrao Nalavade. President of the Municipality, and tributes were paid to the great leader of the Untouchables. Dr. Mohile, Popatlal Shah, Chavan and R. R. Bhole spoke highly about the ability and achievements of the great leader. There was another important function held to celebrate the birthday of Ambedkar. Amidst great excitement and jubilation, Aute, the President of the District Local Board, Poona, unveiled a portrait of Ambedkar and said that the Board was proud to have the portrait of Ambedkar who was not only a great leader of the Depressed Classes but also one of the great leaders of India. He added that Ambedkar by his selfless sacrifice had secured a place in the heart of the nation. Keshavrao Jedhe and Bapusaheb Gupte also made speeches paying their meed of tributes to Ambedkar.

On the morning of April 19, Ambedkar performed the open ing ceremony of the women's branch of the Rohidas Tarun Sudharak Sangh. Addressing the meeting of the Sangh in the local cinema house at Kalyan, he exhorted the youth not to accept help from Hindu institutions and patrons, so that they might not sacrifice their spirit of independence for caste Hindu patronage. He also asked them to emulate the spirit of Kacha, a mythological hero, in not deviating from the purpose of life. It was characteristic of Ambedkar that whenever he spoke before his people he cited inspiring anecdotes from the *Mahabharata* such as the love of self-respect of Dronacharya, the story of Yayati and the devotion of Kacha.

The main function in the series of the Golden Jubilee Celebrations was held at Chowpatty, Bombay, on April 19, at which Dr. M. R. Jayakar presided. Processions from all quarters of the city ended in a mammoth meeting. Acharya Donde, Chairman of the Jubilee Committee, said that Ambedkar was one of the greatest men of India who had ushered in an epoch in history. Addressing the meeting, Jayakar paid a glowing tribute to the long years of service rendered by Ambedkar to the cause of the Depressed Classes. He told the vast audience how Dr. Ambedkar's independent line of thinking and action had brought about a phenomenal change in the status of Depressed Classes and how it had infused confidence in them and awakened the caste Hindus. Jayakar commended the work done by Ambedkar at the R.T.C. and also at the time of the Poona Pact, and appealed to the Depressed Classes to afford their loyal support to their great leader. M. R. A. Baig, Sheriff of Bombay, characterised Ambedkar as a great leader. N.M. Joshi, who also addressed the meeting, felt proud that his former pupil, whom he had taught in Standard IV, had attained such eminence, and added that Ambedkar had been a bright and forward student.[3]

On April 21 almost all leading newspapers, especially in Maharashtra, expressed their appreciation of the services and scholarship of Ambedkar, and offered him felicitations. Stating that the Depressed Classes owed much of the small amelioration in their existing status to Ambedkar's vigorous advocacy. The Times of India, Bombay, observed: "Without political and economic power, the Harijans will find it hard to attain social equality, and Dr. Ambedkar has done well in realising this fact." "He brings to his difficult task," concluded the editorial, "considerable acumen and a gift for pungent, often barbed utterance. Since the removal of untouchability must strengthen the Hindu social structure, and also make for the general advancement of Indian people. Dr. Ambedkar's efforts on behalf of the Harijans deserve wide support."

The Bombay Chronicle paid tributes to the worthy service of Ambedkar to his community and said that Ambedkar brooded day in and day out over the unending inhumanity to his community and it was no wonder therefore that his devotion to the Harijans was equalled, if not exceeded, by his bitterness against their tormentors. The Maharashtra of Nagpur said that Ambedkar was one of the few Maharashtrian leaders who came to the forefront in Indian politics by the sheer force of their personality, struggle, sacrifice and scholarship. It added that the Depressed Classes owed their present political status to his ceaseless struggle.

The Dnyanaprakash of Poona paid glowing tributes to his fearless and selfless mind with which he attacked both the Government and the political leaders. The Paper added that Ambedkar's life was an example to the down-trodden; he was an

---

3. *The Times of India*, 20 April 1942.

exemplary man who never sacrificed his conscience for success. The *Kal*, a Marathi Daily of Poona, said that Ambedkar was a representative leader of Maharashtra, and, like other great Maharashtrian leaders, he was not only a leader of ability and intelligence but also a man of letters, of selfless heart and of integrity. The *Prabhat*, a Marathi Daily of Bombay, hailed Ambedkar as a revolutionary leader of modern India, and added that without meaning any disrespect to Dayanand, Gandhi and Savarkar, Ambedkar's services to the Untouchables ranked higher.

The most, important tribute full of appreciation and estimation came from Savarkar. A political and social revolutionary was estimating the work of another revolutionary! Offering his hearty felicitations to Ambedkar on his Golden Jubilee, Savarkar observed: "Ambedkar's personality, erudition and capacity to lead and organise would have by themselves marked him out as an outstanding asset to our Nation. But in addition to that the inestimable services he has rendered to our Motherland in trying to stamp out untouchability and the results he has achieved in instilling a manly spirit of self-confidence in millions of the Depressed Classes, constitute an abiding, patriotic as well as humanitarian achievement. The very fact of the birth of such a towering personality among the so-called untouchable castes could not but liberate their souls from self-depression and animate them to challenge the supererogatory claim of the so-called touchables."[4] "With great admiration for the man and his work," Savarkar concluded, "I wish Dr. Ambedkar a long, healthy and eventful life."

The Bombay Provincial Hindu Sabha, by a special resolution, felicitated Ambedkar on his Golden Jubilee.

B. G. Horniman, the editor of the *Bombay Sentinel*, said that Ambedkar's great intellectual qualities and his service to the country and his community had put him in the front-rank of great men of India. He added that his work would command the respect and gratitude of all those concerned for the achievement of human freedom throughout the world generally and India particularly.

The last meeting organized by the Jubilee Committee was held at Kamgar Maidan, Parel, Bombay, under the presidentship of Acharya Donde, the chairman of the Celebration Committee, when Ambedkar was presented with a purse of Rs. 880. In reply

4.   Quoted in full by Bhide Guruji in *Free Hindustan*, 14 April 1946.

Ambedkar asked the mammoth gathering to discontinue the habit of celebrating his birthday; for, according to him, a society which idolised and raised a mere man to the level of God was set well on the path of destruction. No one, he observed, was endowed with superhuman and divine attributes and one rose and fell through one's own efforts.

Reviewing the progress of the Depressed Classes, he said that there was considerable improvement in their political, social and economic conditions. He declared that willingly or unwillingly the Depressed Classes formed a limb of Hindu society and added that he had staged the Mahad and Nasik struggles to make the Hindus accept the Depressed Classes on terms of equality; but the desired effect was not achieved. He then sounded a note of warning to the British that any Scheme which did not recognize their legitimate aspirations and rights would be resisted by them with every means in their power. To Hindus he said that if they accommodated them, the Depressed Classes would fight their battles shoulder to shoulder with them.

IV

News came in the third week of June 1942 that the Viceroy was about to expand his Executive Council. Among the probable names were Sir C. P. Ramaswami Iyer. Sir Muhammad Usman, Dr. Ambedkar, Sir J. P. Srivastava, Sir Jogendra Singh, M. N. Roy, Jamnadas Mehta and Sir Shanmukham Chetty. On July 2 names were announced and excepting the last three all were included in the Executive Council making the strength of Indians 14 as against 5 Europeans.

Ambedkar's appointment did not become a subject of hostile criticism. The Congress papers criticised it softly saying that it might bring in good for the labour. The *Sunday Standard* of Bombay said that it was an ideal portfolio for a man who had spent his lifetime championing the cause of the underdog and fighting for labour's rights. If the independent Dr. Ambedkar, added the paper, did not become a thorn in the side of the Government, he would not become a. rubber-stamp either. *The Times of India* Bombay, observed that it was the first time in the history of the country that an untouchable Hindu was appointed a Member in the Executive Council of the Government of India.

And indeed it was an unprecedented event. Never before in the history of India a member of the Depressed Classes held such a high office in the governance of the country except one untouchable who went over to Islam in the last quarter of the fourteenth century, assumed the name of Khoosro, became a Sardar of the Khilji King of Delhi, seized the throne of Delhi, returned to Hinduism, proclaimed a Hindu Raj, and harassed the Muslims. Yet Ambedkar's appointment was unique from another point of view. He was the first mass leader to be appointed to the Viceroy's Executive Council. Another important point was that the Depressed Classes had clamoured for the appointment and brought pressure upon Government. Besides, he was equipped as few Indians of that rank, were in the past. His study of the world labour movement and the problems and legislation about them in his own country, in Europe and in America, was profound. Above all he was the first social rebel to be enthroned in the office of the Chief Executive Council of India.

A few years earlier, Ambedkar had an opportunity to create a record by becoming a Judge of the High Court where he could have weighed the winning arguments from those persons who had turned up their noses at him in the High Court. But he let it off.

Steersman of his own destiny, Ambedkar thus raised himself from dust to doyen. By his great gifts, force of character, long patient industry, the love of service, the spirit of sacrifice and the quality of moral heroism, a poor untouchable boy rose to the top of the ladder. He could build a dynamic personality that exercised a tremendous influence over the Indian social and political world of thought and wielded an irresistible power over a section of humanity in Hindustan.

Ambedkar received hundreds of congratulatory letters and telegrams from prominent and leading public men such as Swatantryaveer Savarkar, Sir Tej Bahadur Sapru, Lokanayak Aney, Sir Sultan Ahmed, the Maharaja of Bikaner, the Chief Justice of Bombay, Sir Chimanlal Setalvad, Rao Bahadur M. C. Rajah and several other admirers.

Ambedkar immediately left for Delhi on July 5, to attend a meeting of the National Defence Council and returned to Bombay on July 11.

On his return, Ambedkar attended a dinner given by his friends and admirers at the Radio Club, Bombay. Speaking on the occasion, Acharya M. V. Donde referred to the years of patient labour through which they stood by him, and hoped that the leader would end the slavery of his people and succeed in ameliorating the conditions of the labouring masses of India. Ambedkar said in reply that he was born of the poor, was brought up among them, lived among them, had slept like them on the damp floor covered with sack-cloth, and shared the sorrow of his people. He promised to remain absolutely unchanged in his attitude to his friends and to the rest of the world, and added that the doors of his house in New Delhi would always remain open to his friends.

The next day the Independent Labour Party and the Bombay Municipal Labour Union held a meeting to congratulate their leader. He told the labourers that although the main task before the Executive was the defence of the country, much of what he would accomplish would depend upon the colleagues in the Council. At another meeting held at R. M. Bhat High School, Bombay, by the peasants of Konkan Districts and States, Ambedkar declared that he would never surrender in the battle he would have to wage for protecting and advancing the interests of the working classes in India; but added that he would not at the same time threaten his colleagues in the Cabinet with his resignation at every point of minor difference. Replying to a charge that a separate organisation for the Depressed Classes was prejudicial to the interests and solidarity of the Labour Classes in general, he observed that the struggle which comprised the lowest strata of society was bound to help in the amelioration of all other sections of the working class because when the bottom-most stone in a structure was shifted from its place, those above it were bound to be shaken out of their positions. He pointed out that the caste Hindu labourers had not outgrown their prejudice against the Depressed Class labourers. Anantrao Chitre, who presided over the function, urged Ambedkar to extend the field of his influence and activity of labour movement so as to include the non-Depressed Class labouring classes and assume the leadership of the entire toiling masses of India.

At a reception given by the Mahar Panchayat, Ambedkar related vividly how he had planned in his boyhood to run away from Satara to Bombay to become a mill-worker aud how his plan to steal the purse of his aunt had failed. He then impressed upon his audience that it was true as some of the speakers before him had said that the pressure from the Depressed Classes compelled Government to take him up, but he asked them to bear in mind another fact that Government would not have been able to meet their demand if they had not among them one with the requisite training and qualifications for the post.

The All India Depressed Classes Conference was scheduled to meet on July 18 and 19. Ambedkar along with N. Shivraj, the President-elect of the All-India Conference of the Depressed Classes, reached Nagpur at 9 on the morning of July 18. A mammoth crowd of 40,000 people gave a thundering ovation to their chosen leader and to the President-elect. Leaders from the Punjab, Bengal and Madras had come to attend it. The conference began its session at Mohan Park in Nagpur in a very spacious pandal.

N. Shivraj, President of the conference, at the outset congratulated Ambedkar on behalf of the Depressed Classes on his elevation to the Cabinet and said that this office opened a new avenue for service to the people.

As Ambedkar rose to speak, he was cheered vociferously by the vast conference of 70,000 persons. He reviewed the situation in reference to the claims of the Depressed Classes from the days of the R.T.C. to the Cripps proposals and described the Cripps proposals as a great betrayal of the Depressed Classes.

Referring to the demand of the Muslim League for Pakistan, he said that when Jinnah called his community a minority, the other minorities derived strength from each other; but now that Jinnah called his community a nation, his breakaway meant that they were left alone to carry on the fight. It might be, he added, that the Muslims might turn out to be the very people against whom they might have to raise the standard of revolt!

"It is a matter of immense satisfaction," he declared, "that the Untouchables have made great strides along all sides." He was happy to announce that they had acquired a great degree of political consciousness which few communities in India had acquired. They had made considerable progress in education and secured a foothold in the institutions of public service of the country. Above all the progress made by the untouchable women was encouraging and astonishing. It was a record of progress of which they should be legitimately proud. It was not the result of Hindu charity. It was an achievement which was entirely the result of his own labour. The basis of his politics lay in the proposition that the Untouchables were not a sub-section of the Hindus, but a distinct element in the national life of India, as separate and distinct as the Muslims. Therefore he wanted separate political rights as against the Hindus. Gandhi, he declared, was their greatest opponent. A seat for the Depressed Classes in the Executive Council, he said, was a death-blow to Brahminism.

He offered unconditional support to the war. It was a war, he observed, between dictatorship and democracy, a dictatorship based on not any moral order but on racial arrogance. Nazism was a menace to the future of Man, and so it was their duty to see that Democracy did not vanish from the face of the earth as a governing principle of human relationship. They should, therefore, strive along with other democratic countries to maintain the basis of democratic civilization. "If democracy dies," he observed, "it will be their doom."

"My final words," he concluded, "of advice to you is educate, agitate and organize; have faith in yourself. With justice on our side, I do not see how we can lose our battle. The battle to me is a matter of joy. The battle is in the fullest sense spiritual. There is nothing material or social in it. For ours is a battle, not for wealth or for power. It is a battle for freedom. It is a battle for the reclamation of human personality."

The conference declared the formation of the All-India Scheduled Castes Federation and put forth their demand for the establishment of separate village settlements at the cost of Government. At the end of the conference, Ambedkar made a moving speech protesting against the charges to the effect that he was indifferent to society and lived among books. He replied that he had no ill-feeling against anybody and he never meant any insult to anybody. He had to achieve maximum progress in minimum time. "Many Hindus regard me as their enemy. But I have personal friends from even the Brahmin community. Situated as I am, it has fallen to my lot to lash the antisocial actions of the Brahmins who treat my people worse than dogs and cats and impede their progress," he concluded. Appreciating the viewpoint of Ambedkar, the *Hindu*, Madras, asked him to bestow thought on his demands for separate settlements and although it might be agreeable from the point of better housing and hygienic conditions, the newspaper added, it might perpetuate untouchability.

Ambedkar addressed two more conferences at Nagpur in the same pandal. The one was the Depressed Classes Women's Conference which was held under the presidentship of Mrs. Sulochanabai Dongre of Amraoti. He was a believer, Ambedkar said, in women's organization. He knew what they would do to improve society if they were convinced. In the eradication of social evils they had rendered great services. He measured the progress of a community by the degree of progress which women had achieved. He was both happy and convinced that they had made progress. Learn to be clean. Keep from vices. Give education to your children. Instil ambition into them. Inculcate in their minds that they are destined to be great. Remove from them all inferiority complex. Do not be in a hurry to marry. Marriage is a liability. You should not impose it upon your children unless they are financially able to meet the liabilities arising from marriage. Those who will marry will have to keep in mind that to have too many children is a crime. The paternal duty lies in giving each child a better start than its parents had. Above all, let every girl who marries stand by her husband, claim to be her husband's friend and equal, and refuse to be his slave. I am sure if you follow this advice, you will bring honour and glory to yourselves," he concluded.

The Conference was an indication of the extent of awakening among the women of these down-trodden classes and was a tribute to its leaders like Mrs. Indirabai Patil and Mrs. Kirtibai Patil. The Women's Conference demanded abolition of polygamy and urged institution of pensions and leave with pay for women workers. Addressing the Samata Sainik Dal Conference which was held under the presidentship of Sardar Gopalsing, O.B. Ambedkar observed that he had love for the principle of non-violence, but he differentiated non-violence from abject surrender. He told the volunteers that it did not befit a man to live a life of surrender, servitude and helplessness. He declared that he believed with the saint Tukaram that destruction of the wicked was also a form of non-violence. Although love and kindness towards all creatures was a part of the principle of non-violence, to destroy all evil doers was the principal element in the doctrine of *ahimsa*. Without that, *ahimsa* was an empty shell, a beatitude. *Shakti* (strength) and *shila* (character) should be their ideal.

During his stay in the city, he was entertained at a tea party by Lala Jainarayan. At Nagpur, a regal messenger from Delhi saw Ambedkar and according to the message, Ambedkar telegraphically took over the charge of the Labour Portfolio on the morning of July 20, 1942, from Nagpur. But such was the indifference and hatred cultivated by men of the so-called higher classes that when the messenger from Delhi inquired of the people at Nagpur station and outside about the venue of the Depressed Classes Conference, the messenger was greeted with indifferent looks or words.

On his return from Nagpur, Ambedkar attended the last of the series of receptions held by the Depressed Class women of Bombay under the presidentship of Mrs. Donde, He advised educated girls not to go in for marriage with the young men of higher classes. In the end, he expressed satisfaction that the women of the Depressed Classes, especially the Mahar ladies, were more advanced from the viewpoint of politics than the Maratha, Bhandari or Agari women.

CHAPTER 19

LABOUR MEMBER

PRIOR to his departure for Delhi, on the evening of July 27, 1942, Ambedkar gave an interview to a representative of *The Times of India*, Bombay, when he described Gandhi's all-out open rebellion as both irresponsible and insane, a bankruptcy of statesmanship and a measure to retrieve the Congress prestige that had gone down since the war started. It would be madness, he proceeded, to weaken law and order at a time when the barbarians were at the gates of India for the mastery of India. The British *vis-a-vis* Indians were in the last ditch; and if democracy won, no one could stand in the way of India's independence. Later he also called Gandhi an old man in a hurry.

The Congress papers bitterly criticized this statement and added that Ambedkar was justifying the British Government's policy as a return gift for the Labour Membership.

Ambedkar, however, was not alone in opposing the move of Gandhi. The Muslim League leaders warned the Muslims to keep aloof from the proposed struggle of the Congress. Savarkar declared that the Hindu Mahasabha would join it if the Congress, before its contemplated struggle, solemnly guaranteed that it would irrevocably stand by the unity and integrity of India. Savarkar, however, foretold that Gandhi, as was his wont, would agree not only to one Pakistan but to many.

Arabedkar was now hardly a week in New Delhi in his new place when the Congress August struggle started. The Viceroy's Executive met immediately and resolved that the decision of the Congress was a challenge, plunging India into confusion and anarchy, insensibly paralysing her efforts in the cause of human freedom.

The Congress leaders all over the country were arrested and put in detention. As a result of their arrests, popular discontent, mass disturbances and their rigorous suppression by Government plunged the country into turmoil. The Muslims

354

remained aloof from this struggle. So did the Hindusabhaites. The Ambedkarites kept aloof from the struggle and concentrated their efforts on militarisation.

Ambedkar gave expression to his pent-up thoughts in Delhi when he spoke at a reception given in his honour by the Depressed Classes Welfare Association on August 23. He declared that he had no love for office and would be glad to go back to his work if he found that his efforts to improve the lot of the masses were unsuccessful. He pointed out that in the Executive Council the representation given to the Muslims was three times greater than that given to the Depressed Classes, who were almost equal in population strength to the Muslims. He declared that the Depressed Classes resented this.

Though Ambedkar was now in power, he had his carking anxieties. He had no news from his son and nephew, who were in Bombay where violent political disturbances had taken place. He tried to contact them on phone, but in vain. So he wrote them an express letter asking them to take the utmost care of themselves as he feared that they would be marked out on his account as the targets.

Next month there was a discussion in the Central Assembly on the political situation in India since the August disturbances. Replying to the debate, Ambedkar said that from what he had studied during the last two or three years there was a landslide in the principle of non violence. As regards the veto which was vested in the Secretary of State for India, he said that it should have been vested in the legislatures; but since there were no fresh elections, the existing legislatures could not be regarded as sufficiently representative.

The Labour Member made a very thought-provoking speech on "Indian Labour And War" on November 13, 1942, from the Bombay Station of All-India Radio, This was, he observed, not altogether a war for the division of the world's territories but also for a revolution which demanded a fundamental change in the terms of associated life between man and man and between nation and nation. It was a revolution which called for the revision of the terms of associated life—a replanning of the society. So labour must fight for victory over Nazism, which, if successful, would end in Nazi order under which liberty would be found to be suppressed, equality denied, and fraternity expunged as a pernicious doctrine. The fruits of victory, he continued, would be independence and a new social order. But independence was not enough. The worth of independence depended upon the kind of Government and the kind of society that were built up. So labour ought to place more emphasis on 'New India' and less on 'Quit India'. Peace obtained by surrender to forces of violence was no peace. It was an act of suicide and a sacrifice of all that was noble and necessary for maintaining a worthy human life to the forces of savagery and barbarism. "War cannot be abolished," he concluded, "by merely refusing to fight when attacked. To abolish war, you must win war and establish a just peace."

In December 1942 Ambedkar wrote in response to an invitation by the authorities of the Pacific Relations Committee a Paper on the problem of the Untouchables in India for the session of the Conference to be held in December 1942 at Quebec. N. Shivraj read it at the Conference. In it Ambedkar lamented that although slavery, serfdom and villanage had vanished in different countries, untouchability existed in India. The Paper appealed in the end to the American people not to be misled by the Congress Hindu propaganda and asked them to get themselves satisfied that the Hindu war of freedom would not be the enemy of the freedom of millions of men who were regarded as Untouchables in the land.

On January 17, 1943, Ambedkar paid a visit to Surat where he addressed a Civil Pioneer Rally, Stressing the need for military training, he told the rally that when Indians would get Independence it would be the trained soldiers and civil pioneers who would help to defend the Independence against aggressors.

From Surat Ambedkar came down to Bombay; and in the evening he was given a reception by the Maratha and allied communities at the R. M. Bhatt High School. In the course of his speech he traced the causes that led to the downfall of the non-Brahmin Parties which were in power in Bombay and Madras for full twenty years. He said that the first cause was that the non-Brahmin Parties prostituted their positions of power for providing jobs for their men and nothing more. They had no broad policy, no broad measures, that benefited the masses of their followers, the peasants and labourers who were their main support. What was equally tragic was that those men who were given jobs by the non-Brahmin Parties, when put into the saddle, forgot the class from which they came and became as insolent and arrogant as any foreigner. Democracy failed in its full purpose in the West because it was in Tory hands. The same would be the position in this country if the Brahmin minority came to power. He then told his audience that three things were essential to making a political party powerful. The first was that its leader must be so great as to be a match for the leaders of other parties. The second essential was a disciplined organization; and the third was a clear-cut programme. These requisites should be fulfilled if Democracy was to succeed in India and to be rescued from the hands of the Tories.

Ambedkar was invited to Poona to address a meeting on January 19, 1943, on the occasion of the birth anniversary of Ranade, India's patriot and reformer. Ambedkar went to Poona and delivered one of the most important speeches in his life. At the outset he discussed three different theories of estimating the greatness of a man. He observed that the Augustine theory that history was only an unfolding of a divine plan in which mankind was to continue through war and suffering until that divine plan was completed on the day of judgement, was now a belief only with the theologians. The theory of Buckle that history was made by Geography and Physics, and the theory of Karl Marx that history was the result of economic forces, he observed, did not represent the whole truth. They were quite wrong in holding that impersonal forces were everything and that man was not a factor in the making of history. Man was necessary to rub two pieces of flint to make fire.

Military heroes left their nations smaller than they found them and did not affect society. In defining the greatness of a man, Ambedkar proceeded, Carlyle laid emphasis on his sincerity. According to Rosebery a Great Man was launched into the world as a great natural or super-natural force, as a scourge and scavenger born to cleanse. Ambedkar remarked that all these tests were partial and none was complete. Summarising his discussion, he opined that a Great Man must be motivated by the dynamics of a social purpose and must act as the scourge and scavenger of society. Applying this test to Ranade, Ambedkar held that Ranade was a Great Man not only by the standards of his time, but was a Great Man according to any standard. Ranade's life was nothing but a relentless struggle against social injustice, social evils and for social reforms. Ranade struggled to create rights, to vitalise the conscience of Hindu society which had become moribund and morbid, and to create a social democracy.

Ambedkar compared Ranade with Gandhi and Jinnah, and opined that it would be difficult to find two persons who would rival Gandhi and Jinnah for their colossal egotism. To them personal ascendancy was everything and the cause of the country a mere counter on the table; and fawned upon by flunkeys, they claimed infallibility for themselves.

He then observed that Indian journalism was once a profession, but it had then become a trade. He, therefore, denounced the writings of the Congress journals as the writings done by drum boys to glorify their heroes.

In the end he said that hero-worship in the sense of expressing one's unbounded admiration was one thing; to obey the hero blindly was a totally different thing.

This speech was published in a book form entitled *Ranade, Gandhi and Jinnah*, and Ambedkar said in the preface that no one could hope to make any effective mark upon his time and bring the aid that was worth bringing to great principles and struggling causes if he was not strong in his love and hatred. "I hate," he continued, "injustice, tyranny, pompousness and humbug, and my hatred embraces all those who are guilty of them. I want to tell my critics that I regard my feelings of hatred as a real force. They are the reflex of the love I bear for the causes I believe in and I am in no wise ashamed of it." He hoped that his countrymen would some day learn that the country is greater than an individual.

The principle of hate Ambedkar had not imbibed from Buddhism. The phase of Buddhism was yet to come in his life. It was Buddha's eternal rule that hatred never ceases by hatred, but by love. Ambedkar loved the principle of absolute non-violence as an end and believed in relative violence as a means. He was of the opinion that Gandhi's non-violence was derived

from jainism and not from the Buddha, who never stretched it
to the extreme view of Jainism.[1]

II

The ill-prepared and ill-ordered August Revolution came
to an end after a few weeks of violent disorder, mass lawlessness
and mob violence.

Realising the fiasco, Gandhi started a twenty-one-day fast
on February 10, 1943. which was a tactical move to force his
release from the Aga Khan Palace. The fast rocked the whole
nation, and the Indian sky was filled with cries of "Release
Gandhi". Pressure was brought upon the Members of the
Executive Council to resign. Ambedkar and Srivastava remained
unmoved. Aney, Modi and Sarkar resigned under nervous
pressure. Their resignation created a faint smile on the face of
the fasting Mahatma. But this had nothing to do much with
Ambedkar's popularity or prestige as a few days after the end of
the fast Sir Chimanlal Setalvad paid Ambedkar a glowing tribute
on his 51st birthday saying that Ambedkar was an outstanding
example of natural intelligence, perseverance and courage.

Ambedkar was now deeply engrossed in the welfare of the
labouring classes. He knew their wants, vices, virtues and
sufferings. The third meeting of the Standing Labour Committee,
set up during the term of his predecessor. Sir Firoz Khan Noon,
by the Tripartite Labour Conference, met at the Bombay
Secretariat on May 7, 1943, under the presidentship of Ambedkar.
One of the important proposals that came up for consideration
was the question of setting up Joint Labour Management
Committees at least in factories and industrial units employed
in war work. Such Committees were established in the U.S.A.
and the United Kingdom. The second question was the
establishment of an Employment Exchange. This was to be done
in the interests of labourers, so that the skilled and semi-skilled
labour technicians that were being trained out under different
schemes should not be thrown out in the streets; they should
find avenues of employment.

---

1.   Desai, H. V., *Mothyanchya Mtilakhati* (Marathi), p. 24.

On May 10, 1943, the Bombay Presidency Committee of the Indian Federation of Labour gave in Bombay a tea-party in honour of the Labour Member, Dr. Ambedkar. In a critical examination of the aims and diffused strength of the Labour organizations, he deplored the unfortunate split in the ranks of Labour movement and observed that in his opinion Indian Labour movement was hollow and most superfluous. He, therefore, appealed to them to seek out defects and to remedy them. In the end he said that his frank opinion was that Labour ought to work for the establishment of Labour Government in India. It was not enough, he concluded, that India should get Swaraj; it was more important in whose hands that Swaraj would be.

On the same day he addressed the Maharashtra Chamber of Commerce, Bombay. In the course of his address he said that the world was sick of war and suffered from three diseases. The first was imperialism of one nation over another; the second was the colour bar which must be tackled and solved in some manner, so that peace might not be disturbed any more; the third was poverty. The way out to equalise the position between nations was to make a weaker country strong. Recalling then how the representatives of the English and European nations humbled themselves before the Peshwas, he remarked that the reason why the European nations adopted an attitude of superiority towards the Oriental nations was, in his judgment, their potential economic and industrial strength. He, therefore, held that India's economic and industrial strength would resolve the problem of imperialism and the problem of colour.

As to the problem of poverty, he expressed horror at the thought of the sky-soaring daily expenditure the nations incurred in destroying the civilisation of Man. He said he could not understand why Britain who spent fourteen crores per day and the U.S.A. who expended about the same amount as also India in her way enormously, should not spend half of it on liquidation of poverty in peace time, to better the lot of the suffering humanity. "The world will have," he concluded, "to make amends, will have to surrender and give up some of the cherished privileges in order that poverty may be abolished."

Just at this time discussions were going on in the newspapers on a scheme put forth by Ambedkar to solve the political deadlock. The scheme contemplated an Act of the British Parliament for the setting up of a Delimitation Committee and the holding of two plebiscites. According to the first plebiscite, the Muslims were to determine whether they wanted Pakistan and the second was to decide whether the non-Muslims in the proposed Pakistan wanted to stay in Pakistan or not. If the non-Muslims preferred to stay in Pakistan, the scheme suggested no change in the existing boundaries. If they declared their opposition to be in Pakistan, a boundary commission was to be appointed to demarcate the predominantly populated Muslim Districts, and at the end of two years it was to be decided whether the Muslims wanted separation or not.

The second session of the Tripartite Labour Conference under the presidentship of the Labour Minister, Dr. Ambedkar, was held at New Delhi on the 6th and 7th September 1943, when in a very impressive and appealing speech Ambedkar defined the demands of the labour for food, clothing, shelter, education, cultural amenities and health resources. A resolution to set up a machinery to investigate questions of wages and earnings and to collect material on which to plan a policy of social security for labour, was adopted.

In the same month Ambedkar gave an interview regarding the proposals put forth by Curtin for an Imperial Consultative Council. Ambedkar stated that it was in the interest of the Dominions to make India a willing partner in the British Commonwealth; but at the same time declared that Indians had no love for the empire because the empire recognised Indians as subjects and not as citizens of equal status.

In the next month the Central Assembly passed an important resolution moved by Pyarelal Kuril Talib, a Member for the Depressed Classes from U.P., for the removal of restrictions on the Depressed Class men in the military forces against holding post of officers.

Ambedkar had now some satisfaction that he could add to the representation of the Depressed Classes in the Central Assembly as well as in the Council of States. Enumerating the benefits he had secured since his taking office, he told in November 1943, in New Delhi, the leaders and workers of the Depressed Classes that he had secured 8¼ percent appointments in Government posts, reserved seats for technical education of the Depressed Class students in London and one more seat in the Central Assembly and got one created in the Council of States.

Ambedkar's insistence on securing a fixed percentage of Government posts for Depressed Classes sprang from two reasons. He was absolutely convinced that but for caste Hindu predominance in Government services it would have been well-nigh impossible for the caste Hindus to perpetuate tyranny over the Depressed Classes. Secondly, Government jobs increased the possibility of their getting justice in Government dealings in addition to raising their economic status.

A South Indian officer serving in Delhi once taunted Ambedkar by saying that his politics was a hunt for jobs! Ambedkar answered back: "If it is so, why do you hold 90 per cent of the jobs? Why don't you get out from the jobs which you treat with contempt, and make room for us ?"

The Standing Labour Committee met again at Lucknow on January 26, 1944, under the chairmanship of Ambedkar. From there Ambedkar proceeded to Kanpur where the annual session of the Scheduled Castes Federation was held on January 29.

N. Shivraj, the President, said that the Depressed Classes were not against the transfer of power provided the demands of the Depressed Classes set forth at the Nagpur Session in July 1942 were conceded.

In his address to the mammoth gathering Ambedkar declared that the Government of India must be shared by the Hindus, Muslims and Untouchables; and if the Depressed Classes did not get a proper share in the conduct of the national Government, they would launch a struggle to achieve that object. He advised the students to take the fullest advantage of the facilities offered by Government for studies in technical and higher fields and appealed to the young leaders not to misunderstand the old leaders who had been fighting with invincible courage, unflagging energy and unswerving faith.

In April 1944, Ambedkar took another step towards bettering the lot of labourers. He moved an amending Bill proposing holidays with pay for industrial workers employed in perennial factories.

A few days after this, Gandhi was released on health grounds from internment in the Aga Khan Palace in Poona. He went to Panchgani from where Rajagopalachari declared that he had sent a new offer to Jinnah which had been approved of by Gandhi during his fast in internment. The nationalist press kept a guilty silence over the treacherous offer. The Liberal leaders described the offer as a danger to India's security, and Savarkar declared that Rajagopalachari alone was not the villain of the tragedy.

III

Ambedkar, who looked at this grim tragedy with the eyes of a constitutional expert, regarded this action of Rajagopalachari as a return to sanity which action he had condemned a little earlier, in his paper to the Pacific Relations Committee! Ambedkar welcomed Gandhi's acceptance of the principle of vivisection ; but felt that it would have been better had the offer been made by Gandhi himself and if it had been an unconditional one. He further said he could not understand why Jinnah turned down the offer; there were risks in a plebiscite, but at any rate people must be the final judges.

Ambedkar was sorry that Gandhi took such a long time to come to the conclusion. In order to have a dig at the Congressites he said he was sorry that Gandhi should have thrown overboard his friends, who, believing that Gandhi was firmly opposed to Pakistan went on opposing it and were now made to look small. Ambedkar added that the Hindu-owned press could be depended upon to suppress the voice of the Hindu Mahasabha. He was right. The Hindu Sabha was the last haven of those who were wedded to the integrity of India and what Ambedkar said about the press came out true. It suppressed the voice of the Hindu Mahasabha. But it is very strange that in his second edition of *Thoughts On Pakistan* Ambedkar described this very scheme as a snare which did not offer any solution!

Seeing Gandhi's growing gestures to the League Lord, Ambedkar, too, held out the olive branch to Gandhi and thought that the Mahatma would be in a mood to compromise with the leader of the Untouchables. In his letter to Gandhi he observed that in addition to the settlement of the Hindu-Muslim problem, the settlement of the problem of the Hindu-Untouchables was necessary if the Indian political goal was to be achieved, and added that on his own part he was willing to formulate points on which a settlement was necessary. In his letter dated the 6th August 1944, Gandhi replied that with him the question of the Depressed Classes was of a religious and social reform. Although he knew, he concluded, Ambedkar's ability, and "would love to own you as my colleague and co-worker, I know to my cost that you and I hold different views on this very important question". Licks to those who are aggressive and kicks to those who are feeble. As a politician, Gandhi was no exception to this.

At the end of August 1944, Ambedkar visited Calcutta. There he was presented with an address by a number of Scheduled Castes organisations. Replying to the address; Ambedkar said that the new constitution would make India a Dominion. He told the audience that victory was in sight and what he wanted from them was unity. He declared that it was good on the part of the Viceroy to tell Gandhi that for the transfer of power a tripartite agreement was necessary among the Hindus, Muslims and the Depressed Classes. In the end he said if the Hindu Mahasabha conceded his demands, he would join the Hindu Mahasabha; and if the Congress did so, he would join the Congress.

Referring to his Calcutta speech, Dr. Moonje wrote a letter to the leader of the Depressed Classes just after his Calcutta speech and asked him to put forth his demands; but he received no reply. The Mahasabhaites had never opposed the demands of the Depressed Classes.

Ambedkar then visited Hyderabad, Deccan. Speaking at a meeting there, he forcibly reiterated his new stand that the Depressed Classes were a separate element. He declared that the Depressed Classes also did not lag behind in their love for India's freedom; but they wanted the Independence of their community along with the independence of the country.

Ambedkar then proceeded to Madras. On his arrival in Madras, he received a Memorandum from the Tamil Nad Depressed Class Christian Association. It stated that since they were drawn from the Depressed Classes, their social and economic position was the same as that of their brethren from the Hindu fold. It further observed that the caste Christians continued to retain their castes even after conversion and ill treated the Depressed Class Christians. The Missionaries did not in any way try to curb the attitude of the caste Christians. The Memorandum, therefore, appealed to Ambedkar to redeem them from the slavery at the hands of caste Christians and other communities.

On September 22, 1944, Ambedkar was presented with an address by the Madras Municipal Corporation at the Rippon Building. Members of the Congress Municipal Party were conspicuous by their absence. Replying to the address, Ambedkar said that he was not opposed to a National Government or Swaraj or Independence. He, however, added that history did not warrant the assumption that once a Parliamentary Government was established on adult suffrage, it would end all human sufferings. If the National Government fell in the hands of the governing class which believed in one community and one class being entitled to education and prosperity and that the people of other communities were born to live and die in servility, then a National Government in the hands of that class would not be better than the existing one.

In the evening Ambedkar was presented with an address by the Andhra Chamber of Commerce. The address was glad to note that Ambedkar had given a new orientation to the attitude of the Government towards labour and added that its main feature was the development of mutual understanding of the viewpoints of the employees and the workers and the Government. Immediately after this function, the Labour Member, Dr. Ambedkar, was entertained at a tea-party by Kumararaja Sir Muthiah Chettiar on the lawns of " Chettinad House ".

Next evening the M. & S. M. Railway employees, belonging to both the Scheduled Castes and non-Scheduled Castes, presented the Labour Member with addresses. In reply Ambedkar said that he was happy to see that in Madras for the first time workers of both the sections had joined together in a meeting and told them that they must stand together to put an end to their poverty. He further observed that the capture of political power was far more important than organizing trade unions.

On the morning of September 24, he addressed a public meeting held under the auspices of the Madras Rational Society at the Prabhat Talkies. In the course of his speech he said that no country in the ancient past had such a tremendous and dynamic political life as the ancient Indians. India had been a land of revolutions in comparison to which the French Revolution would be only a 'Bagatelle' and nothing more. The fundamental fact, observed Ambedkar, was that there had been in ancient India a great struggle between Buddhism, which had ushered in a revolution, and Brahminism, which had launched a counter-revolution. The quarrel was on one issue and that was "What is truth?" Buddha said that truth was something to which any one of the 'Dasha Indriyas' could bear witness. The Brahmins said that it was something which was declared by the *Vedas*. And analysing some aspects of the *Vedas*, Ambedkar further said that certain portions of the *Vedas* were a forgery introduced at a later stage. He was surprised, he added, that so clever a people as the ancient Brahmins should have insisted upon fastening such tremendous sanctity and authority on such books as contained nothing but tomfoolery. "Today we are in the grip of counter-revolutionaries, and unless we do something very quickly," he concluded, "we may bring greater disaster to this country."[2]

In the afternoon Ambedkar spoke at a luncheon party given in his honour by P. Balasubramanya Mudaliar at Hotel Connemara. Analysing the causes of the downfall of the non-Brahmin Party, he said that many of them tried to become second class Brahmins and it occurred to him that they had not abandoned Brahminism which they were slavishly aping, and holding to its ideal. He stressed the need for a good leader, good organization and a clear-cut ideology for the non-Brahmin Party.

In the evening Ambedkar was presented with addresses at the Memorial Hall, Park Town, by different Scheduled Castes Federations and the South Indian Buddhists' Association. Replying to the addresses, he strongly defended the Viceroy's declaration on the Communities' position in the national life of India. He then turned to certain remarks made by Srinivas Sastri that Ambedkar's presence at the international peace gathering would be inimical to the general interests of the country. Ambedkar frankly said that there was nothing disgraceful in the record of his own public life that would make it a shame for

---

2. *The Free Press Journal*, 26 September 1944.

him to be seated at any international gathering on India's behalf. He added that Sastri was the lap dog of the British Government; and if he had achieved anything great or international popularity, it was particularly due to the fact 'that the British Government was pleased to make him a snow-boy.[3] And recalling some events from the proceedings of the R.T. Conferences, he declared that if India had been let down at the R.T.C., it was not by him or the Scheduled Castes but by Gandhi, Sastri and others. Although the Depressed Classes had, he proceeded, a thousand excuses to adopt the attitude that Sir Edward Carson had adopted saying "Damn your safeguards", they were large-hearted enough to support the demand for Home Rule with a small condition attached to it, namely reasonable safeguards. In spite of the Brahmmical rule under which the Depressed Classes suffered for the past two thousand years, they were patriotic enough to ask for only just demands. He, therefore, appealed to the Hindu brethren to reverse their mentality and said: "Let us come to terms, and settle the question".

During his stay in Madras, he had a long discussion with E.V. Ramaswami, leader of the Justice Party, on the political problems in Madras. Ambedkar then went to Ellore where he was presented with addresses by the District Scheduled Castes Federation, Christian Federation, the West Godavari District Board and the Ellore Municipal Council.

Replying to the Municipal address, Ambedkar said that one of the defects which he had noticed in Gandhi was his complete lack of vision, and the founders of the Congress must never have dreamt that just at the time when India was about to reach her destiny, she would be cut into parts. Turning to the problem of minorities, he said that Gandhi's attitude to the problem was the same as Lincoln had adopted towards the Negro problem. Passionately devoted to the Union, Lincoln issued the Proclamation of Freedom for the slaves in 1862 to win the help of the Negroes[4] for the Northern States. Similarly, Gandhi wanted freedom but also Chaturvarnya Dharma. He added that if a constitution accepted by all Parties could be drafted, Gandhi could see the British Prime Minister as the single and solitary representative of India.

---

3. *The Free Press Journal*, 26 September 1944.
4. *The Hindu*, 29 September 1944.

Since the departure of Cripps, Ambedkar worked furiously to impress upon the country and the British Government that the Depressed Classes were an important element and demanded a recognised place in the social, economic and political structure of Indian society. That was the long and short of his whirlwind propaganda; and his arguments won the Viceroy over.

Describing this growing struggle of the Depressed Classes, *The Times of India* in a balanced and brilliant editorial said: "Gandhi's country-wide demonstration of friendliness with the Depressed Classes were more spectacular than real.[5] Experience unfortunately proved that the temporary flood of goodwill was more a demonstration of regard for the Congress leader than an expression of genuine concern." The editorial added that reforms like temple entry, opening of wells and common cremation grounds barely touched the fringe of the problem and any attempt to sidetrack the issue would in the long run prove disastrous to the country's interest.

In the last week of November, Ambedkar attended in Poona a function held in his honour by Rajbhoj. Speaking at the function, Ambedkar said that every religious book written in olden times was also a political book; and the *Geeta* must be considered a political book aimed at upholding the teachings of the *Vedas* and raising Brahminism to a supreme position.

During this period the Sapru Committee was busy preparing proposals to solve the Indian deadlock. Ambedkar refused to co-operate with it as some of the members of the Committee did not inspire any confidence in him.

In the first week of January 1945, Ambedkar visited Calcutta. Performing there the inaugural ceremony of the *People's Herald*, a weekly organ of the Scheduled Castes, he said that the Congress after Gandhi's death would be blown to pieces. He stressed the importance of the Scheduled Castes Federation and added that it would be an eternal party in the country from the political and moral point of view, and because elevation of the Scheduled Castes was the noblest work a leader could find in India, he had devoted himself to it.

During his stay at Calcutta, Ambedkar dined at D. G. Jadhav's place; the next morning the cook and all servants of

---

5. *The Times of India*, 26 September 1944.

this Railway Conciliation Officer, who himself hailed from an untouchable caste, refused to serve at his place as Ambedkar, an Untouchable, had dined with him! And yet Ambedkar was the Hon'ble Labour Member of the Chief Executive Council of India!

Lord Wavell, the Viceroy, flew to London in March 1945 to discuss the Parity proposals contained in the Pact made between Bhulabhai Desai and Liaquat Ali Khan. The Pact was later supported by the Sapru Committee whose findings were cabled to Lord Wavell in London.

IV

Meanwhile, Ambedkar took out the second edition of his book *Thoughts On Pakistan* under a new title *Pakistan or Partition of India*, adding one more chapter to the book. Although he admitted the cultural and geographical unity of India and stated how two or more than two nations lived under one constitution in Canada, Switzerland and South Africa, he said that Pakistan should be conceded for a sure defence of free India and for the sentiments of the Muslims who wanted to be a nation.

Vigorous attempts were now being made to solve the political deadlock. There were about nine schemes outlined by different leaders of note as alternatives to Pakistan. They were: the Cripps proposals, Prof. Reginald Coupland's regional scheme, Sir Ardeshir Dalal's plan, M. N, Roy's scheme, Dr. Radhakumud Mukherjee's plan and Sir Sultan Ahmed's scheme and others.

Ambedkar, too, unfolded his plan on Sunday, May 6, 1945, when he addressed the annual session of the Scheduled Castes Federation at Parel in Bombay. Declaring that the majority rule was untenable in theory and unjustifiable in practice, he proposed weightages to be given to the minority communities in their representation in the legislatures and asked the Hindus to be satisfied with a relative majority. Although his plan ensured a united India, he appealed to the Muslims to accept his plan as it promised them better security, a continuance of weightage and relieved them from the fear of Hindu domination. The most prominent feature of the plan was that the Depressed Classes were to hold the balance of power; and the aboriginals were not to get any representation as, according to Ambedkar, they were devoid of political sense. The plan regarded the proposal for a Constituent Assembly as absolutely superfluous, an act of supererogation and a dangerous proposition that might involve the country in a civil war. Much of the Constitution was ready under the 1935 Act. The plan brushed aside the Sapru Committee's report.

The plan was severely criticized by the Press. *The Times of India*, notorious for its partiality for non-Hindus, said that although the plan might appear to be a poetical justice to an outsider, it suffered from extremism, and described it as one raising the Depressed Classes to the status almost of a new herrenvolk. Ambedkar's plan surpassed the Sapru proposals in its blow to the Hindus on one move count. It proposed that the Prime Minister and other caste Hindu Ministers should be elected by the representatives of the Minorities while the representatives of the Minorities in the Ministry were to be ejected by Minorities themselves. The consensus of opinion among the Hindu journals was that Ambedkar aimed at a minority rule over India! Had Ambedkar been a caste Hindu leader, he would have blown up this scheme. But unfortunately he was on the other side. Nowhere in the history of the world a national majority had ever been subjected to such humiliation, they added.

Thakkar attacked Ambedkar for denying representation to the aboriginals, and Ambedkar said in reply: "I have never claimed to be a universal leader of suffering humanity. The problem of Untouchables is quite enough for my slender strength. ... I do not say that other causes are not equally noble. But knowing that life is short, one can only serve one cause and I have never aspired to do more than serve the Untouchables." He added that he did not include the aboriginals in the scheme because they had not as yet developed the political capacity which was necessary to exercise political power for one's own good. These very arguments were used by the higher classes when they opposed the enfranchisement of the lower and especially the Depressed Classes !

The Hon'ble Labour Member was entertained at a party given in his honour by a group of friends at 'Cafe Model', Bombay, on May 20. Speaking on the occasion, he said that it was better for India to prefer Dominion Status to Independence if they could not retain it. Dominion Status, according to International Law, meant perfect sovereignty, he added.

In June 1945 another major work by Ambedkar appeared in the market. Its title was *What Congress And Gandhi Have Done To The Untouchables*. Polemic in its violence, vigorous in its style, powerful in its appeal, replete with a wealth of convincing statistics and an array of forceful arguments, the book burst upon the Congress Party like a bombshell. The main thesis of the book was that the advertised Harijan uplift work of the Congress Party, since the Congress adopted it in 1917 as one of its planks, was actuated more by the desire to prevent the Depressed Classes from appealing as a separate element in the national life than by the desire for the actual removal of disabilities of the Untouchables. Criticizing the work of Gandhi, Ambedkar paid a rare tribute in this book to Swami Shrad-dhanand by praising him as the greatest champion of the Untouchables.

In the most important part of the book Ambedkar warned the Depressed Classes to beware of Gandhi and Gandhism. According to him, Gandhism was nothing but a return to the village life, a return to nature, to animal life and anathema to the modern age of machine. Having no passion for economic equality, it was a reactionary philosophy from both the social and economic points of view, blazing on its banner the call for return to antiquity. If there was any ism, he further observed, which had made full use of religion as an opiate to lull the people into false beliefs and false security, it was Gandhism. So he warned the Untouchables to be on their guard against the inroads of Gandhism.

In the end the book uttered a warning to the radicals in America and Britain to beware of the Indian Tories who were misusing the slogan of liberty to befool and befog the world. It declared that to Gandhi removal of Untouchability was a platform and not a programme of action, and so Gandhi was not the liberator or emancipator of the Untouchables. The book is dedicated to an English lady with whom the author, Ambedkar, had studied the Bible during his London days.

The book evoked a bitter controversy. The Deputy Gandhi, Rajagopalachari, tried his hand; but his reply to the book was what penknife is to a hammer. A better reply came from Santhanam but without scholarship, originality and statistics; and thus Ambedkar's book remained undemolished.

Ambedkar's violent opposition to Gandhism on rationalistic basis was not a new phase. Ten years earlier he had told an American official who grew lyrical about Gandhism that the American was either a hypocrite or a lunatic and asked him why the Americans did not scrap their army and navy and pull down factories and skyscrapers, and go back to primitive times. He further told the American official that men like him did not believe in Gandhism and only succeeded in misleading both the Indians and the Americans.

After a stay of nine weeks in London, Lord Wavell returned to India in the first week of June with the so-called Wavell Plan. He released the Congress leaders from jails and convened a conference at Simla in the last week of June 1945.

The pity of it was that the Congress represented the caste Hindus through its Muslim President Maulana Azad, the Muslims were represented by Jinnah, the Scheduled Castes by N. Shivraj and the Sikhs by the Sikh representative, and all the ex-Premiers of Provincial Governments attended the Conference. The Hindu Mahasabha was dropped out as an inconvenient body. Ambedkar, being a Member of the Executive, could not take part in it. But he was preparing the case for the Scheduled Castes. His contention was that the Scheduled Castes should have three seats in the Central Executive on the basis of population if the Muslims had five. The Conference broke on the question of the personnel of the interim Ministry, the Congress insisting on Muslim nominees of its own.

V

In July Britain went to polls and there was a landslide against the Tories and Labour came to power. Japan also surrendered. Ambedkar appreciated the courage shown by the British electorate in destroying the lead of the governing classes.

The Labour Member was back in Bombay for a while. During his stay he addressed the Students' Union of the Tata Institute of Social Sciences in the last week of July 1945. He declared that the compulsory conciliation or arbitration was a great advantage . to Labour and hoped to make that principle a permanent feature of the Labour Code. He added that he hoped to retain all the Technical Training Schools started by the Government of India as part of the educational system of the country.

In the last week of August, the Standing Labour Committee met at New Delhi and discussed rules for the Industrial housing, employer's responsibility and holidays with pay. Ambedfcar presided over the deliberations.

Meantime, Lord Wavell again went to London in the latter part of August 1945 to take counsel. He returned to India after the middle of September and announced general elections.

All the Parties entered the election arena. The Congress, backed by a gigantic purse and giant election machinery, entered with the "Quit India" slogan; Jinnah, backed by the Pakistan purse, entered with the "Pakistan or Perish" slogan; the Hindu Mahasabha with "Independence and Integrity of India"; and Ambedkar's Scheduled Castes Federation with no electioneering machinery or funds. On October 4, Ambedkar started the election propaganda at a meeting in Poona where he stressed three points. He emphasized that the Depressed Classes should not believe in the lead of the Congress which was full of surrenders; it was a tool in the hands of the capitalists and those socially indifferent; it never strove to remove their disabilities, and to redress their grievances. The remedy lay in their hands and therefore they should capture the political power which was their life-blood. They should develop into a ruling race and guard their rights; otherwise they would remain on paper. He enumerated the benefits and rights he had secured for them during his short term of office. In the end he said that the coming elections were a matter of life and death to them; and more so, because the Constitution-making body was likely to be elected by the provincial legislatures.

Ambedkar returned to New Delhi. There he presided over the Seventh Indian Labour Conference which met on November 27, 1945. In his presidential address he observed: "Labour may ask the moneyed classes a pertinent question saying 'if you do not mind paying taxes to meet the expenditure on war, why do you object to raising funds when their purpose is to raise labour standard?' How many uneducated persons could have been educated and how many sick persons could have been restored to health, if the money spent on war had been spent on public welfare?"

The election propaganda was now launched by the Scheduled Castes Federation with greater vigour. To give an impetus to their election work, they held a Provincial Conference at Ahmedabad on November 29 and 30, 1945. Govind Parmar presided. Ambedkar went to attend the conference. Leaders of M. N. Roy's Radical Democratic Party, the Communists and the Hindu Sabha also met him at the station. All mills were closed. Addressing the conference in a spacious pandal called Buddhanagar on the bank of the Sabarmati, Ambedkar told the vast crowd that whatever benefits they were enjoying had been secured by him and not by Gandhi who had sought the help of the Muslims to oppose their demands.

On November 30 the Ahmedabad Municipality presented him with an address. Replying to the address, he declared that if drastic action had not been taken by Government in August 1942, India would have been overrun by the Japanese and the Germans. He thanked the Municipality for the honour it had done him and said the treatment it had given him on the occasion stood in glaring contrast—he would not say cruel contrast—to that of his own Bombay City Corporation which had refused to include in its agenda a resolution for presenting an address to him.

Ambedkar inaugurated the Conference of the regional Labour Commissioners at the Bombay Secretariat in the first week of December 1945. In his inaugural address he said that three things were necessary to mitigate or prevent industrial disorder, namely, a machinery for conciliation; secondly, an amendment of the Trade Disputes Act; and thirdly, minimum wage legislation. He said that the first was already in operation, and he hoped to put forth proposals for the remaining two before long.

Giving his views on the possibilities of achieving industrial peace, he observed that industrial peace on the basis of power was no longer a possibility. On the basis of law, it was possible, but not certain. Based on social justice, he continued, it was a hopeful proposition. It evolved a triangular approach which must start with the workers who must recognise on their part the duty to work, which was the same as elimination of shirking. The employer on his part must pay reasonable wages which was another name for elimination of exploitation and provide comfortable conditions of work which was another name for labour welfare; and thirdly the State and the society must realise that the maintenance of proper industrial relations was a public affair and not a mere matter of a contract between the employer and the employee. S. C. Joshi, Chief Labour Commissioner, said in his welcome address that the industrial relations machinery was neither the advocate nor the opponent of any of the two parties to the Industry—the employer and the employees.

VI

Ambedkar immediately went to Manmad to address a conference of the Scheduled Castes Federation. There he declared that his efforts in securing an agreement with the Congress for several years on the rights of his people had failed and there was no alternative but to capture all seats reserved of them. He then addressed a meeting at Akola and proceeded to Nagpur where at a public meeting, on December 13, he demanded a blueprint from the Congress about the self-government that was to be ushered in. He explained how the Congress campaign for the removal of Untouchability had proved an utter failure and cited how during his recent visit he could have only a distant view of the famous Jagannath temple at Puri from the terrace of a neighbouring house.

Ambedkar then made a tour of Southern India to give a fillip to the election work of his Party in that Province. At Madras he described the Congress election Manifesto as a humbug as it said nothing about the future constitution. He next visited Madura and made an election speech. Proceeding to Coimbatore, he declared at a public meeting there that the coming elections would determine the constitution of the country, and reiterated his demands for guaranteed representation in the legislatures and executive services, for sufficient money for education and provision of lands in villages. Some newspapers and leaders criticized Ambedkar for abusing his position as Member of the Executive to further the cause of his Party at public expense.

On his way back, Ambedkar addressed a gathering of the South Indian Liberal Federation at the Memorial Hall, Park Town, Madras. In the course of his speech he traced the growth and power of the Congress Party and said that the Liberal Party led by Gokhale was regarded by the people as an ineffective organization. The Revolutionary Party could capture the imagination of the people, but few people were prepared to sacrifice like them. The strength of the Congress Party lay in the fact that it had Gandhi as its leader, who appealed to the political-minded as well as to the religious-minded people. He advised the Justice Party to have a leader, a programme and discipline for the success of their Party.

He then inaugurated the Second Annual Conference of the non-Brahmin Lawyers' Association in the same Hall. In the course of his speech he made a violent attack on the *Manusmriti* and other Hindu scriptures. This speech evoked a furious storm among the caste Hindus in Southern India, and angry Hindus showered on him letters which were full of filthy abuse, unmentionable and unprintable, and full of dire threats to his life.

Immediately after his Madras speech, he returned to New Delhi, In the first week of January 1946 arrived in New Delhi the British Parliamentary delegation of ten members. During their stay in New Delhi they interviewed Ambedkar, Jinnah and Nehru on January 10. Their talks with Jinnah lasted two hours. Two hours after their talk with Jinnah eight members of the delegation had a 90-minute talk with Ambedkar. Then came the turn of Jawaharlal Nehru. The delegation had important talks with other leading politicians in the country. They visited some places, surveyed India in their own way for four weeks, and returned home on February 10, 1946.

Immediately after this interview with the British Delegation, Ambedkar returned to Bombay on January 13, 1946, and left for Sholapur. There he was presented with an address by the District Local Board and the Municipality. He thanked both the institutions for their good work for the uplift of the Scheduled Castes and made a touching reference to Dr. Muley, the ex-President of the Municipality, 'with whose co-operation he had started his public career twenty years ago'. It may be recalled here that Dr. Muley had helped him to conduct a hostel at Sholapur for the Depressed Class students. Addressing a public meeting at the place, Ambedkar declared vehemently that if the Scheduled Castes Federation candidates were not returned, he would surrender to the Congress, wear a white cap and work, under the Congress!

At the end of January Ambedkar returned to his Delhi Headquarters. On February 4, he made a speech before the Delhi Scheduled Castes Provincial Federation and said that the constitution which did not receive their approval would not be binding on them. He then left Delhi and addressed several meetings at Satara, Belgaum and other places urging his people to elect the S.C.F. candidates. He sounded a warning to the Congress leaders that if they would make it impossible for them to hold their meetings, they would also make it impossible for them to hold their meetings peacefully.

On his return to Bombay, he was presented with a purse by the Scheduled Castes of Bombay. Admission to the meeting was by tickets. In the course of his speech he urged his people to see that in a free India they also were citizens. The Scheduled Castes, he stated, were not asking for a territorial division like the Muslims. What they wanted was equal rights and no patronage. If the Congress felt that their demands were not just then let the matter be referred to an impartial International Tribunal. He said he was prepared to abide by the verdict of the Tribunal.

Just before this speech of Ambedkar, Sardar Vallabhbhai Patel had declared that the first concern of the Congress Ministries would be to destroy the very roots of untouchability by force of law. He said that Ambedkar's aspirations for his community, were legitimate, but his ways were wrong. Though the Harijans, he concluded, had been benefited by the Poona Pact, Ambedkar continued abusing the Congress Party and Gandhi.

There was a series of letters in the Press by educated men from the Scheduled Castes in reply to Sardar Patel, stating how the Poona Pact had proved a curse to them.

Working for a fortnight in his Delhi office, Ambedkar attended a conference convened by the U.P. Scheduled Castes

Federation at Agra on March 10, under the presidentship of N. Shivraj. Ambedkar declared at the conference that if Swaraj meant conducting Government by majority with the co-operation and consent of the minorities, he would welcome such a Swaraj.

The Provincial elections were held. The Scheduled Castes went on foot to the polling booths as advised by their Babasaheb. They stood in queues from early dawn and voted up to the last minute. But the Congress easily outnumbered the votes of the Federation with the help of the vast number of caste Hindu votes. It was all over with Ambedkar's Scheduled Castes Federation. His party was utterly routed. Absence of and indifference to the co-operation of caste Hindu votes and lack of organization made Ambedkar eat his words which he had uttered at Sholapur. This was a stunning blow to his prestige as a leader, which drove him to desperation and his bitter mind began to think of drastic methods. Congress defeated both Ambedkar and Hindu Mahasabha, but the Muslim voters pricked the bubble of the Congress prestige and their nationalism. They routed the Congress!

The patriotic upsurge emanated from the I.N.A. Revolt and their Trials, the Revolt raised by the Royal Indian Naval Ratings and the Royal Indian Air Force seemed to break down the imperial structure. It was a clear indication that the Indian army was feeling and experiencing the pangs of freedom. Politics and nationalism had reached their ranks and magnetized their hearts. The Britishers knew that it was no longer possible for them to keep India in bondage. So on March 15, the British Prime Minister, Clement Attlee, acknowledged India's right to attain full independence within or even without the British Commonwealth and said that they would not allow a minority to place their veto on the advance of the majority.

The British Premier sent out a delegation of three Cabinet Ministers, Sir Stafford Cripps, A. V. Alexander and Lord Pethick Lawrence who was then the Secretary of State for India, to discuss with Indian party leaders on the spot the question of resolving the political deadlock. The British Cabinet delegation reached New Delhi on March 24, 1946. Numerous interviews, high level discussions and delicate deliberations took place in the Viceregal Lodge. Nehru, Patel, Gandhi, Jinnah, and Dr. Shyama Prasad Mukherjec were interviewed. But the outstanding feature of the political scene was that Maulana Abul Kalam Azad represented the Congress Party; Mohammed Ali Jinnah, the Muslim League; and the Nawab of Bhopal, the Princely India. Thus the whole of India was represented by three Muslim leaders.

Amidst this atmosphere two representatives of the Minority communities were interviewed by the Mission on April 5. They were Ambedkar and Master Tara Singh. The failure at the elections had made Ambedkar's position shaky. He was almost throttled. Authorised by the Scheduled Castes Federation as its sole spokesman for the Scheduled Castes, he expounded in his interview the views and claims of the Scheduled Castes. It was reported that Ambedkar pleaded his case forcefully and repudiated the accusation that the Scheduled Castes were putting a veto on India's political advancement. He placed a memorandum before the Mission asking for a provision to be made in the constitution for the election of the Scheduled Castes through separate electorates. He also stressed the importance of a new settlement, emphasized the need for the appointment of a settlement commission, demanded adequate representation in the Central and Provincial Legislatures as also in the Central and Provincial Executives, in the public services and on the public service commissions, Federal as well as Provincial, and urged for earmarked sums for their education. The main feature of the memorandum was that it demanded the inclusion of these safeguards in the new constitution.

The Mission declared on May 16, 1946, their decision in the form of a State Paper according to which they contemplated a feeble and formal union with three groups of Provinces, the formation of a Constituent Assembly and an interim Government. There was no reference to the demands of the Scheduled Castes in the "State Paper".

As it was now almost decided by the British Government to set up a new Government with the representatives of the successful Parties, the Viceroy now made it clear, to his Cabinet colleagues that they were to go. Ambedkar left New Delhi and came down to Bombay in the last week of May 1946.

□□□

CHAPTER 20

SPELL ON CONSTITUENT ASSEMBLY

ON his arrival in Bombay, Ambedkar found the atmosphere tense with excitement. There were disturbances in the City between his adherents and the Caste Hindu Congressmen. As a result of this clash, the Bharat Bhushan Printing Press conducted by his son had been burnt down. He was apprised of the occurrences by the Secretary and other members of the Federation, Ambedkar called a meeting of the Working Committee of the S.C. Federation at Rajagriha, Bombay, in the first week of June 1946. By a resolution it denounced the British proposals of 16th May as mischievous and threatened to resort to direct action if the wrong done to the Scheduled Castes was not rectified. It condemned the heinous acts perpetrated by the goondas of the Congress persuasion on persons of Scheduled Castes as a result of which the Printing Press of Ambedkar was burnt down. He then went back to New Delhi. The Viceroy was to set up a caretaker Government; so the Members of the Executive Council bade goodbye to the Viceroy in the third week of June 1946. It may be noted here that Ambedkar had proved himself an efficient and purposeful Labour Member.

But amidst this uncertain atmosphere came to reality one of the dreams of Ambedkar, which he had cherished since September 13, 1945. It was his dream to found an ideal educational institution with modern scientific apparatus and with a staff of proved merit, with a view to promoting higher education among the lower middle classes and especially among the Scheduled Castes. He founded the People's Education Society which started a college on June 20, 1946, and it has proved to be one of the leading colleges in India. The fears and prophecies of friends failed, and he succeeded in collecting funds and attracting a group of capable and willing workers on the staff. The name of the college is Siddharth which is one of the names of Lord Buddha.

Ambedkar returned to Bombay on June 25 when the Scheduled Castes gave a great ovation to their leader at the

Bombay Central Station. Ambedkar now gave a clarion call to his people to give battle for the cause of justice and humanity and to expose the machinations and conspiracy hatched against the rights of his people. He knew this was the last opportunity to assert the lights and the will of his people; for he feared that a free India might revert to the old traditions, and his people would be impoverished, neglected and ostracized from society and public services.

On June 29, a caretaker Government was announced, and the British Mission left for London, leaving other details to be settled by the Viceroy.

The Scheduled Castes agitation started with a march to the meeting of the All-India Congress Committee which was held in Bombay. The Scheduled Castes leaders and workers made a black flag demonstration in front of the Congress Pandal and demanded an explanation from the Congress leaders as to their rights and representation in a free India. Rajbhoj interviewed Gandhi in Poona and told him that the Congress Harijan leaders were not the representatives of the Scheduled Castes. And the battle started on July 15, 1946, at Poona, synchronizing with the opening of the Poona session of the Bombay Assembly.

The fight was evidently against the Congress which had usurped their claim to speak, voice and represent the grievances of the Untouchables. Contingents of volunteers poured in Poona. They defied the order of the District Magistrate who had banned processions and meetings. They were arrested one batch after another before the Council Hall. Ambedkar was in Bombay when the non-violent battle began at Poona. In an interview before his departure to Poona on July 17, he stated that they had launched the campaign against the Cabinet Mission's proposals and declared that, although it was not necessary for a general to be on the battlefield, if the developments necessitated his participation in the struggle, he would court imprisonment. Ambedkar received messages from some leaders supporting his stand, but the General Secretary of Gandhi's Harijan Sevak Sangh threatened him with a counter satyagraha movement if he did not withdraw the struggle. The Federation simultaneously started satyagraha campaigns at Kanpur and Lucknow.

Just then Members were elected by the Provincial
Legislatures to go to the Constituent Assembly which was to meet
at New Delhi in accordance with the provisions of the Mission's
Plan. The Congress elected its men. The majority of them were
elected not because they knew much of constitution-making but
because they had suffered imprisonment in the patriotic struggle.
Ambedkar had no men in the Bombay Assembly to support his
candidature, and so his name was put up through the Scheduled
Castes representatives in the Bengal Assembly. There with the
backing of Muslim League, he was elected to the Constituent
Assembly. In his otherwise war-like career there was a certain
unfailing chord of adaptability for catching the right moment to
show his mettle, his worth, his power. His vision was ever fresh
and his perception quite correct.

On July 19 Premier Kher, true to his Gandhian
characteristic, declared that he did not know the root cause of
the offer of satyagraha by the Scheduled Castes Federation. "One
does not know," he added sarcastically, "whether their grievance
is against the Cabinet Mission's failure to give them what they
want or against the defeat of Dr. Ambedkar and his party in the
recent election, or whether it is due to a general sense of
frustration."

Replying to all these charges and threats, on July 21
Ambedkar stated in a press interview in Poona that the British
had decided to quit India and their powers were to be inherited
by the caste Hindus and the Muslims, and hence the Scheduled
Castes were entitled to demand a blueprint from the Congress
regarding the rights and interests of 60,000,000. Untouchables
in the future Constitution of India. He said that the satyagraha
started in Poona was only the beginning of a countrywide struggle
to secure for the Scheduled Castes their just political rights. He
claimed that the Poona satyagraha was carried on on a higher
moral plane, and the non-violent behaviour of the whole mass of
volunteers provided a lesson to Gandhi who regarded himself as
a graduate in satyagraha. Referring to the Poona Pact, he said
that as it prevented the real representatives of the Scheduled
Castes from being elected to the Legislatures, it must go. It was
a virtual disfranchisement of the Scheduled Castes. In the end
he issued a warning that if moral resources were exhausted, they
would look for other means to register their protest.

At a big meeting in Poona, he exhorted his men to carry on the struggle to the bitter end. The Congress Harijan leaders, who always reaped the fruit of Ambedkar's labour and struggle, spoke against Ambedkar's agitation and supported those who always opposed Harijans' demands. It was like barking at one's own benefactor.

Gandhi, referring to this satyagraha, wrote in *Harijan* that there was a parody of satyagraha in the show staged by Ambedkar; and if the means were non-violent the cause was certainly vague.[1]

The satyagraha movement went on unabated for a fortnight, and its pressure forced the Government to abrogate their Poona Assembly session. The Congress leaders felt the need for a rapprochement with Ambedkar. So S. K. Patil, Chief of the Bombay Provincial Congress Committee, saw Ambedkar at the Siddharth College; and they both, accompanied by, N. M. Joshi, met Sardar Patel on July 27. The talks continued for an hour or so in connection with the representation of the Scheduled Castes on the Constituent Assembly and the Poona satyagraha. It seems they could not come to a settlement as on August 8 a Scheduled Caste procession led by prominent leaders of the Scheduled Castes such as Gaikwad and Rajbhoj, marched to the meeting of the All-India Congress Committee which was holding its session at Wardha.

Some time later, Ambedkar wrote to Sardar Patel that he considered the country greater than any individual howsoever great he might be. He also said that one could be a great nationalist without being a Congressman and added that he was a greater nationalist than any Congress leader.

On August 24 the names of the Members of the Interim Ministry were announced. Along with Nehru, Patel, Azad, Rajagopalachari and Sarat Chandra Bose appeared the name of Jagjivan Ram, who was a leader of the Untouchables from Bihar. The Muslim League did not co-operate; the Muslim posts were filled by other Muslim leaders, one of whom was fatally stabbed by a Muslim fanatic.

That day Ambedkar was in Poona where the Working Committee of the Scheduled Castes Federation was reviewing

---

1. *Harijan*, 9 August 1946.

the political situation. The announcement of the Viceroy was a
terrific disappointment for Ambedkar and his Party. He expressed
sharp dissatisfaction at the inadequate representation given to
the Scheduled Castes in the newly constituted Cabinet at the
Centre and demanded one more seat for the Scheduled Castes
in the Cabinet. He was surprised to see Jagjivan Ram's name in
the list as he had supported the claim of the Scheduled Castes
for increased representation in the Executive when Ambedkar
had sent a cablegram to the British Prime Minister protesting
against the inadequacy of the representation. The Working
Committee of the Scheduled Castes Federation appealed to
Jagjivan Ram not to accept the post, declared that the new
Government was not entitled to their respect and asked the
Scheduled Caste leaders to renounce the titles conferred upon
them by the British Government.

In the first week of September, the Scheduled Castes
Federation started satyagraha at Nagpur, and in a very short
time nearly eight hundred persons were arrested.

II

Ambedkar realised now that although the protestations and
demonstrations had their limited result, he must make a final
attempt himself in Britain and effect a change if he could. With
that end in view he started on his political mission on October
15 via Karachi. In a Press interview at Karachi, he told the Press
that he was going to London; but he refused to be drawn into
any discussion or to clarify the details of his mission. On his
arrival in London, he declared that the Labour Party had let
down the Untouchables and betrayed their cause. When asked
about his reaction to the situation at Delhi since the Muslim
League joined the Interim Government, Ambedkar said that it
was a Government of one country by two nations. He plainly
told the press that India was in the midst of a civil war, He,
therefore, suggested to the British Government to enforce the
1935 Act and hand over to the Indian Parties a United India
after a period of ten years.

He immediately got his Memorandum printed in London
and approached the political bosses of England. Asked by Reuter's

political correspondent, whether he had asked the Depressed Classes to go over to Islam, he said he had not given advice to that effect.

Ambedkar was facing a political paralysis, and it was a very severe blow to the life-long efforts which he had made towards the cause of the Untouchables. His only point was that the Scheduled Castes should be given due representation in the Executives and Legislatures. He was working desperately to achieve that end. He admitted that he was depressed, and his friends, too, said he was terribly pulled down in health. One thing had taken the wind out of his sails. The Muslim League, which joined the Interim Cabinet on October 26, 1946, had taken up Jogendranath Mandal as Law Minister in the Interim Government. The Scheduled Castes had now two seats in the Central Cabinet. Moreover, Jogendranath Mandal was a Member of the Working Committee of the Scheduled Castes Federation!

On the last day of October 1946, Ambedkar had talks with some leading British politicians connected with India. He discussed his Memorandum with Prime Minister Attlee and the Secretary of State for India. He saw Churchill and Lord Templewood—formerly known as Sir Samuel Hoare—who was once the Secretary of State for India—and others. On November 5 he addressed a meeting of the Conservative-Indian Committee in the House of Commons which was attended by some Labour M.P.s also. The Press was not allowed. The meeting lasted for about an hour. Ambedkar placed facts and figures before them. But there seemed no hope for him to gain his points. There was lip sympathy and a nod of assent here and there. The close interruption of the Labour Members showed that they were not willing to rake up the communal question at the last stage. Ambedkar was advised to adjust himself to the changed situation and to try his luck in the Constituent Assembly. So in an utterly depressing mood he had to leave London.

Shortly after his arrival in Bombay, in an interview with the representative of the Globe Agency, he observed that although it was a vain hope, the Untouchables were ready for the assimilation or absorption of their classes into Hindu society in the real and substantial sense of the term on the basis of inter-marriage and inter-dining. But another aspect of the same

question, he added, was that their merger into Hindu society
would become easier only when the Untouchables rose to the
social status of the caste Hindus. He expressed a feeble hope
that Hinduism in the course of time might so reform itself that
it would become acceptable; and therefore they were prepared
to stay on where they were as it was not possible to uproot
humanity and transplant it from one soil to another.

As regards conversion of the Untouchables to Christianity
as suggested by the Rev. Livingston, he said: "Religion among
Christians, as well as non-Christians, is a mere matter of
inheritance. The Christian inherits his father's property and
along with it his father's religion. He never stops to contrast
Christianity with other religions and to make his own judgment
as to its spiritual value."

At this juncture Ambedkar's book *Who Were The Shudras*?
was published. The book is dedicated to Mahatma Jotiba Phooley
whom he regarded as one of the greatest reformers. This is a
book of great erudition. A work of long patient industry and
research, it presents an impressive method of arranging a
catalogue of facts, and a brilliant illuminating exposition. It is
the thesis of Ambedkar that, the Shudras were Kshatriyas. They
were Dasas and Dasyus. They were one of the communities
belonging to the solar race. But they were degraded as the result
of a violent conflict between the Brahmins and the Kshatriyas.
The Brahmins refused to perform thread ceremonies of these
Kshatriyas and degraded them to the fourth Varna which
previously did not exist.

During the last week of November, Jogendranath Mandal,
Law Member in the Interim Government, visited Bombay. In an
interview he said that he was satisfied with the result of
Ambedkar's mission to London and added that he had Ambedkar's
full support for his joining the Interim Government.

Although it was boycotted by the Muslim League, the
Constituent Assembly met on December 9, 1946, as scheduled.
It elected Dr. Rajendra Prasad its President, appointed a
Committee for framing the rules of procedure, and on December
13, Pandit Nehru laid the foundation of its work by moving a
resolution on the Declaration of Objectives in a magnificent
speech. Ordinarily a good speaker, and a serious, sincere and

visionary leader, Nehru rose to his full stature at this momentous hour of the nation and of his life, and captivated the House, by the panoramic sweep of his speech. Nehru declared India's objective as an Independent Sovereign Republic. Purushottamdas Tandon, who seconded the resolution, delivered a powerful speech.

On December 15, 1946, India's legal luminary. Dr. M. R. Jayakar, known for his gift of peace-making, moved an amendment to Nehru's resolution, seeking postponement of the passing of the resolution until the Muslim League and Indian States representatives came into the Constituent Assembly. And he did it in good faith. But this irritated the Congress bosses, and voices rose from the Congress groups heckling Dr. Jayakar as an obstructionist. The sweet, flowing, persuasive Jayakar sat down never to rise again in that House. His amendment now became a battle royal. M. R. Masani supported Nehru's resolution as a democratic socialist. Frank Anthony supported Dr. Jayakar's amendment on legal and technical grounds although he accepted the solemn character of the main resolution. Dr. S. P. Mookerjee, Hindu Mahasabha leader, saw no point in deferring a decision as he feared that the postponement would encourage the Muslim League to stay out and block the progress.

And then the President of the Constituent Assembly unexpectedly called upon a Member to have his say. In response to the call a massive figure with a long head, a stubborn chin and an oval face rose from his seat to support Jayakar's amendment. It was Ambedkar, the avowed enemy of the Congress, who had lashed their ideology and scoffed at their leader privately and publicly. The House was all attention. Ambedkar took a view of the House. Everybody now thought that Ambedkar, by playing such a dangerous role, would go under with the mover of the amendment. To rise against the will and objectives of the Congress bosses, who were the nation's most powerful leaders, was to meet one's Waterloo! The Congress Members were ready with their hands raised to smash their avowed enemy and throw him down.

Ambedkar saw himself surrounded by great political leaders. The majority of the white-clad elite had never heard him although they had heard big things about him. In a grave manner, with an unlimited command of language and supreme courage he began his speech. He said that he considered the first part of Pandit Nehru's resolution to be controversial and the later part, which set out the objectives of the future constitution, to be non-controversial, although that too was pedantic in that it enunciated only rights without prescribing remedies open to the injured parties. The Congress Members were now breathless. But to put himself with the psychology of the House he switched over, in the twinkling of an eye, to the important point, the crux of the amendment.

"I know," he said, "today we are divided politically, socially and economically. We are in warring camps and I am probably one of the leaders of a warring camp. But with all this I am convinced that, given time and circumstances, nothing in the world will prevent this country from becoming one, and, with all our castes and creeds, I have not the slightest hesitation in saying that we shall in some form be a united people.

"I have no hesitation in saying that, notwithstanding the agitation of the League for the partition of India, some day enough light will dawn upon the Muslims themselves, and they, too, will begin to think that a United India is better for everybody," he proceeded.

Blaming the Congress Party for having consented to the dismantling of a strong centre, Ambedkar said he would not ask whether the House had the right to pass such a resolution. It might be it had the right. "The question I am asking is," he asserted with a glow in his eyes, "is it prudent for you to do it? Is it wise to do it? Power is one thing and wisdom and prudence quite a different thing." He, therefore, made a fervent appeal to the Congress Members to make yet another attempt to bring about a conciliation and said: "In deciding the destinies of a people, the dignity of the leaders or men or parties ought to count for nothing."

In the end he referred to three ways by which the issue could be decided; the permanent surrender of one party to the other, a negotiated peace or war. He confessed that he was appalled at the idea of war, and uttered a warning that it would be a war on the Muslims or what was probably worse, a war on the combination of the British and the Muslims. Quoting Burke's famous passage in favour of reconciliation with America, Ambedkar observed in a moving tone: "If anybody has it in his mind that this problem can be solved by war, or that the Muslims may be subjugated and made to surrender to a constitution that might be prepared without their knowledge and consent, this country would be involved in perpetually conquering them. As Burke said: 'It is easy to give power, but difficult to give wisdom.' Let us prove by our conduct that we have not only the power but also the wisdom to carry with us all sections of the country and to make them march on that road which is bound to lead us to unity."

So forceful was the passionate appeal that it produced an excellent impression upon the Constituent Assembly. He was frequently cheered by the Congress Members. Dr. Jayakar's speech containing the same appeal aroused resentment while Ambedkar's fine oration evoked a sense of co-operation in their minds, and the hands that were itching to smash him rang with approbation! It was a red-letter day in the amazing life of Ambedkar. The sacrileger had become now a counsel, the scoffer had become a friend who cast a spell on the Congressmen. Few speeches have given such a turn to the life of a speaker. The consideration of the resolution was postponed to another session which was to meet in January, and it was passed on January 20, 1947.

Ambedkar returned to Bombay to look after the People's Education Society. The conflict between his men and the Congress-minded men had not yet ceased. Deorukhakar, a Bombay Depressed Class leader, was stabbed to death early in January 1947 and when someone told Ambedkar at the Siddharth College, Bombay, that he should not go to his house which was surrounded by hooligans, he furiously frowned upon him and said he would not save his own life when his son and nephew and his books that were as dear to him as life itself, were in danger. At the risk of his life he returned to his residence.

On February 21, 1947, Ambedkar assisted by M. B. Samarth, G. J. Mane and P. T. Borale, defended 38 accused at a General Court martial held at Deolali. The accused were soldiers belonging to the untouchable communities from Bihar,

III

Meanwhile, the British Government announced that it would hand over by June 1948 the Government of India either

390   DR. AMBEDKAR : LIFE AND MISSION

to some form of Central Governmeni for Bititsh India or to the
existing Provincial Governments in India. It called back Lord
Wavell who used his only eye to see things from the Muslim angle
of vision.

Ambedkar, who read the times correctly, realised that the
time was ripe,for him to put before the Constituent Assembly
his constitutional views. He therefore prepared a Memorandum
in March 1947 in which he proposed that the Scheduled Castes
should have a separate electorate only in those constituencies in
which seats were reserved for them and in others they were to
vote jointly.

The Memorandum was published in the form of a brochure
under the title *States and Minorities*. It is a draft of the
constitution which he had prepared for the Indian Union. It is
interesting and instructive to study his political philosophy and
so it is given below in a nutshell.

To Ambedkar Democracy was essentially a form of society.
It involves unmistakably two things. The first is an attitude of
mind, an attitude of respect and equality towards one's
fellowmen. The second is a social organization free from rigid
social barriers. Democracy is incomplete and inconsistent with
isolation and exclusiveness, resulting in the distinction between
the privileged and unprivileged—privileges for a few and
disabilities for the vast majority.[2]

A democratic society must assure a life of leisure to each of
the citizens. Therefore the slogan of a democratic society must
be machinery, more machinery and civilization. He, therefore,
welcomes the machine age. The fact that machinery and modern
civilization have produced many evils may be admitted. But these
evils are no argument against them. They are due to a wrong
social organization which has made private property and pursuit
of personal gain matters of absolute sanctity. If machinery and
civilization have not benefited everybody, the remedy is not to
condemn machinery and civilization, but to alter the organization
of society, so that the benefits will not be usurped by the few but
will accrue to all.

Man occupies the highest place in the scheme of animal
existence. The ultimate goal of brute's life is reached once his

2. Ambedkar. Dr. B. R., *Ranade, Gandhi And Jinnah*, pp. 36-37.

physical appetites are satisfied. The goal of man's life is not reached unless and until he has fully cultivated his mind. In short, what divides the brute from man is culture. That being so the aim of human society must be to enable every person to lead a life of culture which means the cultivation of mind as distinguished from the satisfaction of mere physical wants. A life of culture can be made possible where there is sufficient leisure for a man to devote himself to a life of culture. Leisure is quite impossible unless some means are found whereby the toil required for producing goods necessary to satisfy human needs is lessened. That can happen only when machine takes the place of man.[3]

That is why he opposed Gandhism that hated the machine. According to him, Gandhism was the doom of the common man, and had no passion for economic equality.

Ambedkar hated the orthodox Marxist who quoted Marx and Engels on every occasion. He liked new ideas, new approaches. He said that one could not lay down an ideal by a stroke of the pen. Society should always be in an experimental stage. According to him, Marx's philosophy was the satisfying philosophy to the lower order.[4] It was a direction, not a dogma. Once he described Russian Communism as a fraud.[5]

He was a believer in State socialism. "State socialism is essential to the rapid industrialization of India. Private enterprise cannot do it; and if it did, it would produce these inequalities of wealth which private capitalism has produced in Europe which should serve as a warning to Indians. Consolidation of holdings and tenancy legislation are worse than useless. They cannot bring about prosperity in agriculture. Neither consolidation nor tenancy legislation can be of any help to the 60 millions of Untouchables who are just landless labourers. Only collective farms can help them."

Observing that basic industries should be owned by the State, he said: "Insurance shall be a monopoly of the State. Agriculture shall be a State industry. Land will belong to the State and shall be let out to villagers without distinction of caste or creed and in such a manner that there will be no landlord, no tenant and no landless labourer."

---

3. Ambedkar, Dr. B. R., *What Congress And Gandhi Have Done To The Untouchables*, pp. 283-284.
4. Desai, H. V., *Mothyancha Mulakati* (Marathi), p. 26.
5. The *Navayug's* Ambedkar Special Nnmber, 13 April 1947.

He, however, wanted to establish State socialism by the law of the constitution and thus make it unalterable by any act of the legislature or the executive. State socialism should be practised through Parliamentary Democracy which was a proper form of Government for a free society. It was only by this method that one could achieve the triple object, namely, to establish socialism, retain parliamentary democracy and avoid dictatorship.

"But if democracy is to live up to its principle of one man, one value," he added, "the laws of the constitution should not only prescribe the shape and form of the political structure but also must prescribe the shape and form of the economic structure of society."

But did Ambedkar fall in with the Indian Socialists? He desired to invite the attention of the Indian Socialist' to the social problem. He observed that "economic motive is not the only motive by which man is actuated. That economic power is the only kind of power no student of human society can accept. That religion is the source of power is amply illustrated by the history of this country." He cited an example from the history of the Plebians, who gave up material gain rather than their religion for which they had fought so hard.

The fallacy of the Socialists, he asserted, lay in supposing that, "because in the present stage of the European society property as a source of power is predominant, the same is true of India or that the same was true of Europe in the past. Religion, social status and property are all sources of power and authority."

He, therefore, disagreed with the Socialist view that equalisation of property was the only real reform and that it must precede everything else. He asked the Socialists whether they could have economic reform without first bringing about a reform of the social order. "If Socialists are not to be content with the mouthing of find phrases," he warned, " if they wish to make Socialism a definite reality, then they must recognise that the problem of social reform is fundamental and that for them there is no escape from it. Unless they do so, they cannot achieve their revolution. They will be compelled, to take account of caste after revolution, if not before revolution."[6]

---

6. Ambedkar, Dr. B. R., *Annihilation of Caste*, pp. 17-19.

IV

The nebulous British policy, the atrocities committed by the Muslims and the Congress leaders' incapacity to rise to the occasion threw the Hindus on the defensive, and now they thought it wise to demand a partition of the Punjab and Bengal. Speaking of this new move, Ambedkar said in an interview at New Delhi that he must know what the caste Hindus wanted to do with the Untouchables who would shift and how they would be rehabilitated. Ambedkar attended the third session of the Constituent Assembly which met in April 1947. The reports of the Advisory Committee and the Fundamental Rights Committee were adopted by the Constituent Assembly.

And on April 29, 1947, the Constituent Assembly declared to the world: " Untouchability in any form is abolished and the imposition of any disability on that account shall be an offence." It was the good fortune of Sardar Patel to move the Clause. It was a glorious day in the history of India when the ruling power in India declared its will to wash out the stigma of untouchability. The world Press described this event as the freedom of the Untouchables, the day of emancipation of the outcastes, a historic act outlawing untouchability and a victory for human freedom! The *New York Times* said: "The advance toward wiping out their ancient stigma has been matched in modern times only by our own abolition of slavery and the freeing of the Russian serfs." The *News Chronicle*, London, praised it as one of the greatest acts of history. The *New York Herald Tribune* described it as one of the fresh and dean beams of light in the post-war world.

The whole foreign Press rang with praise for Gandhi for this great achievement of India. Apparently it was the Congress Party that was declaring the abolition of untouchability. And Mahatma Gandhi was the uncrowned King of the Congress Party. No foreign journal mentioned Ambedkar's name whose motive-power had driven the nation to perform the deed. They all described 'Hamlet' without a reference to the Prince of Denmark! When this was the case of Ambedkar, there was no possibility of the names of Jotirao Phooley, Dayananda. Shraddhanand and Savarkar being mentioned with any grateful appreciation.

❑❑❑

CHAPTER 21

A MODERN MANU

THE new Viceroy, Lord Mountbatten, studied the situation and went to London. He returned to India and declared his plan on June 3, 1947. The Plan announced two Central Governments, two Constituent Assemblies and plebiscites for Sylhet and the North-Western Province. Gandhi and Nehru threw their whole weight and forced the All-India Congress Committee to accept the vivisection of the country. The truthseeker in Gandhi, who had considered Pakistan a sin, a patent untruth and had solemnly asked the protagonists of partition to "vivisect me before you vivisect India", was dominated by the politician in him and he drove the last nail in the coffin of the integrity of India. The Socialists were culpably neutral. The Hindu Sabhaites rattled in vain.

At this juncture Travancore and Hyderabad States declared that they would be independent when India became a Dominion on August 15, 1947. Expressing his views on this move, Ambedkar advised the States to merge their sovereignty in the Indian Union and warned them that to be independent and to hope to get recognition and protection from the United Nations Organisation was to live in one's paradise.

In the first week of July, Ambedkar gave his opinion on the new India Bill and said that Berar would revert to the Nizam as the treaty by which it was ceded to the British would lapse.

Ambedkar returned to Bombay on July 3, 1947. As he was a Member of the Flag Committee of the Constituent Assembly, some Maratha leaders and leaders of the Bombay Provincial Hindu Sabha saw him at his residence. He promised that he would try to put in a word in favour of the Geruva flag if there was sufficient pressure and agitation from responsible quarters. On July 10 Ambedkar was given a send-off at the aerodrome by different leaders of the Marathas and the City Hindu Sabha leaders who handed over a Geruva flag to him when he was about to take his seat in the aeroplane. Ambedkar promised support if there was agitation for the establishment of that flag and with a hearty laugh asked S. K. Bole, Anantrao Gadre and others whether they expected the son of a Mahar to unfurl the Geruva flag on the Constituent Assembly.

The Constituent Assembly adopted on July 22 the Tri-colour flag with the Ashoka Chakra on it as the National Flag, It is said that Ambedkar put in a word, but as there was no agitation from outside for the adoption of the Geruva flag he threw his weight in favour of the Ashoka Chakra. Savarkar also had appealed to Dr. Rajendra Prasad, the Chairman of the Flag Committee, to substitute Chakra for Charkha, the Gandhian emblem. The adoption of Chakra instead of Charkha terribly pained Gandhi, who declared that he had nothing to do with the flag if the basic character of the flag had lost its Khaddar and the Charkha.

From New Delhi Ambedkar rivetted the attention of the Indian Government on the work of the boundary commission and said; "If my fears come true and the boundary drawn by the commission is not a natural one, it needs no prophet to say that its maintenance will cost the Government of India very dearly and it will put the safety and security of the people of India in great jeopardy. I hope, therefore, that late as it is, the Defence Department will bestir itself and do its duty before it is too late." This shows the heart of a patriot and the vigilance of a statesman. And yet the author of *Thoughts On Pakistan* had preached that geographical conditions were not decisive in modern world technique!

The British Parliament passed the Act of Indian Independence on July 15. Now the Constituent Assembly became a sovereign body. It was originally meant for the whole of India; but now it was meant for a mutilated India. Bengal was partitioned, and so many of its Members lost their seats in the Constituent Assembly. So did Dr. Ambedkar who owed his seat to Bengal. He was now chosen by the Bombay Legislative Congress Party to fill the vacancy in the Constituent Assembly caused by the resignation of Dr. M. R. Jayakar.

In the last week of July, the names of the Ministers of the first Cabinet of free India were in the air. In the list the name of Muniswami Pillay of Madras appeared in the Press although Ambedkar's name was scented in it as early as June. Ambedkar

was at that time in New Delhi. Destiny was working a miracle.
Congress bosses Patel and Patil had a talk on the phone about
Ambedkar's inclusion in the Cabinet. The preliminaries over, Nehru
called Ambedkar to his chambers and asked him whether he would
join the new Cabinet of Free India as Minister for Law. He was
promised that at a later stage he would be given the portfolio of
Planning or Development. Ambedkar agreed. Nehru went to the
Bhangi Colony to present the final list of nominees to Gandhi. He,
too, nodded his assent. The Congress leaders, who were to inherit
power from the Britishers, now desired rapprochement with
Ambedkar and, were in a conciliatory and appreciative mood. Hither
to they had neglected to utilize Ambedkar's gifts. Now they decided
to utilize them for the solidification of freedom. Ambedkar, too, on
his part forgot the past bickerings and agreed to welcome the olive
branch. Dr. Mookerjee the Mahasabha leader, too, was invited to
join the Cabinet.

On August 3 the names of the Cabinet Ministers were
announced among which Ambedkar's name appeared. That day
he was in Bombay and addressed a meeting at Chembur, Bombay,
under the auspices of the Bombay Municipal Kamgar Sangh. He
was presented with a purse of rupees two hundred towards the
construction of a central building which he had been
contemplating since 1932.

As soon as it was known that Ambedkar was to be the Law
Minister of New India, his friends, admirers and the Press
showered their good wishes and congratulations upon his success
that was a feat from dust to doyen. For the first time in history
an Untouchable Hindu became a popular Minister in the Central
Cabinet of India; and the man who was decried as a stooge of the
Britishers was now eulogised as a statesman by his erstwhile
opponents. He was honoured in Bombay on August 6 as a Member
of the Cabinet of Free India on behalf of the Bar Association.
Ambedkar had now jumped beyond their bar.

A great day dawned in the history of the world on August
15, 1947, when India became a free nation. A great force was
released in Asia in the form of Indian Independence. But its
happiness was marred in one respect. It was mutilated and bled
and out of its ribs was taken out Pakistan, the greatest Muslim
State under the sun.

In the wake of this success followed a development which led Ambedkar to the top of the ladder of eminence. On August 29, the Constituent Assembly appointed a Drafting Committee with N. Madhava Rao, Syed M. Saadullah, Sir Alladi Krishnamachari, T. T. Krishnamachari and two others as members and Ambedkar as its Chairman. An Untouchable who was kicked out from carts and segregated in schools in his boyhood, who was insulted as a professor, and ousted from hotels, hostels, saloons and temples in his youth as a despicable Mahar, and who was cursed as a British stooge, despised as a heartless politician and devil, hated as a reviler of the Mahatma and decried as an Executive Councillor, became now the first Law Minister of a free nation and the chief architect of the Constitution to define the will, aim and vision of India! It was a great achievement and a wonder in the history of India. India chose, in amends for her age-long sin of Untouchability, her Law-giver, new Manu, and new *Smritikar* from among a caste which had been dehumanized, demoralized and devitalized for ages. New India entrusted the work of framing her new laws to a man who had a few years before burnt the *Manusmriti* the Code of the Hindus! Was it the goddess of Nemesis that played the trick ? Or was it a whirligig of time ?

Although now Law Minister, Ambedkar kept a close contact with the development of Siddharth College, his child educational institution. On September 25 he inaugurated the Parliamentary Institution of his college. In his thought-provoking speech he impressed upon the budding youths the need for cultivating the art of speaking. In a Parliamentary Institution, he observed, success went to the man who had the capacity to possess the house in a gentle or strong logical and instructive manner. In order to develop that power students must equip themselves with many things. They must enlarge their minds, their vision, their capacity to think and their ability to solve the actual problems which the people had to face. He then dealt with the various aspects of parliamentary democracy and said that Government meant decision. Government by compromise was no Government, because they got a decision which was neither fish nor fowl, he concluded.

On September 1 the Congress Party, which was in power in the Bombay Municipal Corporation, resolved to present civic addresses to Pandit Nehru, Sardar Palel, Dr. Rajendra Prasad and Maulana Azad who were due to visit Bombay. Members from the Opposition demanded that addresses should be given to the entire Union Cabinet including Members from Bombay like Ambedkar, Gadgil and Bhaba. But S. K. Patil, Chief of the Bombay Congress Party, said that the four leaders whom they were seeking to honour were men of outstanding calibre and were in a class by themselves. The Bombay Congressmen, it seems, were not yet fully reconciled and willing to regard Ambedkar as the equal of their political bosses. Old prejudices die hard. Later the Bombay Corporation resolved to give an address to Ambedkar; but he did not even reply to the letter of the Mayor!

In the first week of October, Ambedkar addressed a meeting of the Scheduled Castes youths in Bombay. He told them that independence had come so suddenly that he did not have any clear line of action before him at that moment. He stressed the need for keeping the S.C. Federation intact under whatever circumstances and appealed to them to take to organization seriously.

II

Meanwhile, the horrible consequences of the partition of India gave terrible shocks to the whole nation. The disturbances in Delhi, Ambedkar said in one of his letters to Kamalakant Chitre, could hardly be described as riots. It might be easily called a rebellion. "The number of wounded and murdered," he said, "is for a city like Delhi colossal. There was complete stoppage of life for the last few days." Ambedkar had proposed partition with complete transfer of population of the Muslims and Hindus from their respective zones in order to avert a civil war and its attendant massacres. Like Lincoln, Savarkar was prepared to face a civil war for a while in order to preserve the unity of India. But the Congress leaders in whose hands the destiny of the country had fallen ultimately accepted partition plus massacres and with secular zest ridiculed the idea of transfer of population as they had done with the idea of Pakistan till the dawn of Pakistan. Their policy only worsened, as usual, the fate of Hindus who were in the zone of Pakistan. Thus Ambedkar's prophecy and fears were both borne out to a letter !

Millions were uprooted in the holocaust; lakhs were butchered. Children and women were molested, kidnapped or forcibly converted to Islam. Streets were flooded with broken skulls and mutilated corpses, and they echoed with the agonies of dying men, children and women. The Untouchables being Hindus had to share the same fate. Jogendranath Mandal, Law and Labour Member of Pakistan, who had asked the Scheduled Castes in Pakistan to look upon Jinnah as their saviour and had even asked them to wear a badge blatantly suggestive of Islamic associations, was now rudely shaken from his dream. He grieved at the way things had shaped in Pakistan.

Ambedkar was terribly upset, and he issued a statement denouncing the Pakistan Government. He complained that the Scheduled Castes were not allowed to come to Hindustan and that they were being forcibly converted to Islam. He further said that in the Hyderabad State, too, they were being forcibly converted to Islam in order to increase the strength of the Muslim population in the Hyderabad State. He, therefore, advised his people: "I would like to tell the Scheduled Castes who happen today to be impounded inside Pakistan to come over to India by such means as may be available to them. The second thing I want to say is that it would be fatal for the Scheduled Castes, whether in Pakistan or in Hyderabad, to put their faith in Muslims or the Muslim League. It has become a habit with the Scheduled Castes to look upon the Muslims as their friends simply because they dislike the Hindus. This is a mistaken view."

Ambedkar further asked the Scheduled Castes in Pakistan and Hyderabad not to succumb to conversion to Islam as an easy way of escape; and to all those who were forcibly converted to Islam he pledged his word that he would see that they were received back into the fold and treated as brethren in the same manner in which they were treated before their conversion. Whatever the tyranny and oppression which the Hindus practised on them, he asserted, it should not warp their vision and swerve them from their duty. He warned the Scheduled Castes in Hyderabad not to side with the Nizam and bring disgrace upon the community by siding with one who was the enemy of India.[1] He also appealed to Prime Minister Nehru to take speedy steps in evacuating the Scheduled Castes from Pakistan.

The whole nationalist press rang with praise for Ambedkar. The change in his attitude was highly appreciated by all. The

---

1. The *Free Press Journal*, 28 November 1947.

Hindu, Madras, said that it was glad that Ambedkar no longer thought that the Harijans would be justified in abjuring Hinduism because they had been treated badly by caste Hindus in the past. That showed the passionate attachment of the Harijans to the faith of their forefathers and the tenacity with which they clung to it despite all attempts to wean them from Hindu sciety, it added.

During the past two months the Congress Ministry of Bombay had made a considerable headway in removing social injustice respecting the temple entry of the Harijans. It passed the Temple Entry Bill in September and as the result of this Act and the popular pressure, the famous temple of Vithoba at Pandharpur, tbe Dnyaneshwar temple at Alandi, and the Kalaram Temple at Nasik were thrown open to the Scheduled Caste Hindus. This was no mean achievement for which the Depressed Classes had launched a struggle fifteen years earlier. It washed away the ugly blot and cleared and purified the atmosphere declaring the arrival of a new era.

By this time the Constituent Assembly had begun to operate as the legislature. It is important to note that in one of her speeches the Health Minister, Rajkumari Amrit Kaur, admitted that although there were acts in almost every State for the removal of disabilities of the Scheduled Castes, it was common knowledge that those were observed more in the breach than in practice!

Ambedkar arranged, about this time, for the publication of the book *The Essence of Buddhism*[2] by Prof. P. Lakshmi Narasu. He thought that it was the best book on Buddhism that had appeared till then; and a text complete in its treatment and lucid in its exposition. He praised Narasu as a social reformer and an iconoclast.

Ambedkar was now engrossed in the work of drafting the Constitution. He was working almost singly and furiously, concentrating his hand, heart and head on the work entrusted to him in spite of his deteriorating health. How he worked and why he was called the chief architect of the Constitution can be seen from the speech of T.T. Krishnamachari which he made on

---

2. Thacker & Co. Ltd., Bombay.

November 5, 1948, in the Constituent Assembly. He invited the
attention of the House saying: "The House is perhaps aware that
of the seven Members nominated by you, one had resigned from
the House and was replaced. One died and was not replaced.
One was away in America and his place was not filled up and
another person was engaged in State affairs and there was void
to that extent. One or two people were far away from Delhi and
perhaps reasons of health did not permit them to attend. So it
happened ultimately that the burden of drafting the Constitution
fell on Dr. Ambedkar and I have no doubt that we are grateful to
him for having achieved this task in a manner which is
undoubtedly commendable." The picture will be complete when
it is noted that only Ambedkar and his Secretary were present
at some of the meetings of the Drafting Committee! And the
historic work was now nearing completion.

In the middle of January 1948, Ambedkar returned to
Bombay. During his stay he addressed a meeting of the
Elocution Prize Distribution Ceremony of the Dhobi Talao Night
School, which held its function at the Siddharth College
premises. He impressed upon the boys that the art of speaking
in public could be developed with great efforts. He told them
how the great speaker G. K. Gokhale was disconcerted while
making his maiden speech, how Phirozeshah Mehta developed
his powers by reciting his speeches in a room fitted with mirrors
where he could watch how his expressions changed and how
his hands moved. He said that Mehta took great care to see
that his dress and appearance were neat and impressive. He
added that Churchill, the great orator, never delivered any
speech without preparation.

The terrific shocks of partition were coming one after
another, Nehru confessed that the nation had to wade
through an ocean of blood and tears. People showed profound
disbelief in Gandhism. The Congress leaders were also
chilled in their beliefs. Tandon declared at one meeting that
the Gandhian doctrine of absolute non-violence was greatly
responsible for the partition of India. Twenty-four hours
before the dawn of freedom people had stoned Mahatma
Gandhi's residence in Calcutta.

And the crisis was capped by Gandhi's famous fast which
he started on January 13, 1948, for the reinstatement of the

Muslims in their houses in Delhi, for the restoration of some Mosques to their former use and for five other reasons; and as a sequel, the Government of India was forced to pay Pakistan a sum of rupees fifty-five crores which had been loudly decried and refused.

And in the midst of such an extreme gloom, confusion and disaster, Nathuram Godse shot Mahatma Gandhi on January 30, 1948.

The whole world was shocked with horror at the tragic disappearance of one of the greatest men of all times. But Ambedkar, a queer combination of softness and hard-heartedness, did not react. Hard facts mentioned above had galled him, and his old bitterness, too, had not cooled down. He did not utter publicly a syllable on this tragedy; nor did he issue any statement. He joined the funeral procession for a while and retired to his study. Perhaps he thought that the mighty personality in Gandhi had choked the free passage of Indian democracy. It was said that he was put in mind of the pithy remarks of Cicero who had exclaimed at the news of Caesar's murder that the dawn of liberation had come!

In the last week of February 1948, Ambedkar completed the Draft Constitution and submitted it to the President of the Constituent Assembly. The Draft Constitution was plated before the country for opinion. Ambedkar now wanted to propose an amendment substituting the word 'State' for the word 'Republic' in the preamble of the draft. His object in so doing was to see that nothing in the Constitution brought about an automatic and instantaneous severance between India and the British Commonwealth. The word 'State' was more neutral and was accepted by the Constitution of Ireland and South Africa. But most of the Indian leaders and Journals did not like this idea.

III

After the completion of the drafting work, Ambedkar badly needed rest. He came to Bombay for treatment. He felt now the need for a companion who would attend on him in his old age. In the hospital he came across Dr. Miss Sharda Kabir. Since August 1947, he had been showing grave anxiety about his health which

he said was on the down-grade. For the last fifteen days, he wrote
in August 1947, he had not had a wink of sleep. The nights were
a night-mare to him. A neurotic pain always came at midnight
and continued throughout the night. He was then taking insulin
as well as homoeopathic medicine. Neither seemed to give him
relief. He said he must now learn to endure what appeared
beyond cure. So in August 1947 he was anxious to see "what our
doctors have to say".

In January 1948, he complained that the pain in the leg
started at four in the evening and went on the whole day.
Exactly after a month, he wrote to Chitre that his health had
suddenly gone down and that he was facing a relapse. He
passed four nights without a wink of sleep with most
excruciating pain in both the legs; and his servants had to
keep awake and had to nurse him the whole night. "I have
been examined," he further observed, "by two most eminent
doctors who say that if my condition does not improve
immediately the trouble in the legs may become chronic and
incurable. I am now thinking of your suggestion of having
someone to look after my health more sympathetically than I
was prepared to do before. I have decided to marry Dr. Kabir.
She is the best match I can find. Right or wrong the decision
is made." He then called for Chitre's observations, if any.

He informed Bhaurao Gaikwad, his chief lieutenant, of his
proposed marriage. Although after the death of his first wife, he
observed, he had resolved not to marry again, he had decided
now to marry. He wanted an educated lady who knew cooking
and was a medical practitioner. As it was quite impossible to
find such a lady among the members of the Scheduled Castes,
he chose a Saraswat Brahmin lady.[3]

He wrote to Chitre with great sorrow that one of his close
colleagues was sowing seeds of ill-feeling between his son
Yashwant and his fiancee. He added that as he feared that
postponement would open a field for wider publicity and greater
opportunity for evil tongues to wag, he had decided that the event
should irrevocably take place on April 15, 1948. Desiring Chitre
to attend the marriage function, he concluded: "I feel no moral
turpitude in what I am doing. Nobody, can have any ground for

3. Kharat, S.R., *Doctor Babasaheb Ambedkaranchi Patren* (Marathi), p. 266.

complaint, not even Yashwant. To the latter I have given about Rs. 30,000 and in addition a house which is today worth at least Rs. 80,000. I am sure no father can do more for his son than I have done." The marriage was settled, and Dr. Miss Sharda Kabir flew to New Delhi. On the morning of April 15, 1948, the second day of his fifty-sixth year, Ambedkar married Dr. Miss Sharda Kabir, a Saraswat Brahmin by caste, at his residence at No. 1, Hardinge Avenue, New Delhi. The marriage was celebrated under the Civil Marriages Act by the Deputy Commissioner of Delhi in the presence of a few personal friends of Ambedkar, who later entertained them to a luncheon. *The New York Times* described the marriage as more significant than the wedding of a royalty to a commoner.

During the previous four years, the thought of engaging his son in some business was gnawing at Ambedkar's mind. He wrote to his friend Naval Bhathena to draw a plan of any industry he would like to suggest for his son and nephew, so that the boys might have an honest calling as a means of living, and he might die peacefully. He pleaded to Bhathena to take the same interest which a father does in his sons and to teach them some stable business. Some business was started, but to the father in Ambedkar it proved to be a sore disappointment.

His birthday was celebrated as usual with splendour. The Chief Minister of Bombay, B. G. Kher, paid glowing tributes to Ambedkar. Describing him as one of the most learned men among the political leaders of the country, he said that Babasaheb was not only their leader but was also the leader of India. Addressing a meeting at Sewri, Bombay, S. K. Patil told his audience that Ambedkar was a great servant and a great power, and his gifts were such that he could alone run the Central Government. Describing Ambedkar as a great architect of future India, the Bombay boss of the Congress prayed to God that the great son of India be spared for another twenty-five years for the conduct of national affairs. The *National Standard* of Bombay said that Ambedkar's conception of reform embraced the entire field of Hindu regeneration and described him as a leader gifted with a rare political acumen. The paper observed that he was a fighter who fought for principles and his idealism ensured the abolition

of social injustices and the uplift of the underdog. As Law
Minister, it added, he was a tower of strength to his colleagues.

In the last week of April 1948, Ambedkar addressed the
United Provincial Scheduled Castes Conference. In the course
of his speech he said that political power was the key to all social
progress, and the Scheduled Castes could achieve their salvation
if they captured the power by organizing themselves into a third
party and held the balance of power between the rival political
parties, the Congress and the Socialists.

He said he had joined the Central Government and not the
Congress Party. The Congress Party was a burning house; and
he would not be surprised if it was completely ruined in a couple
of years. If he joined the Congress, he would be unaffected like a
stone in water; but if his followers would join it they would, like
clods, be dissolved. He therefore warned them to keep their
organization intact. This speech brought hornets' nest about his
ears. "There is a furore," he wrote to Chitre, "over my speech.
There has been somewhat heated controversy between myself
and Patel and Pandit. I told that if they feel embarrassed I am
prepared to resign. The issue may be settled in the next few days
one way or the other," He, however, issued a statement from New
Delhi, stating that his speech was *ex tempore* and was
misreported. He added that he had joined the Cabinet because
the invitation was free from any condition, that he thought that
the interests of the Scheduled Castes would be better served by
joining the Cabinet and that he hated the principle of opposition
for opposition's sake. But this fire was smouldering till August
1948. He had to cancel his visit to Bombay "as there are political
happenings which may raise their head and cause a crash to the
Government."

Ambedkar, who had once planned a book *Army in India*
discussed with great interest the subject with G. M. Jadhav from
Baroda. Jadhav had a very large collection of books on military
science and the Defence Problem of India. Ambedkar wanted to
start a class for boys desirous of studying military science and
wanted Jadhav to teach the class. So much impressed he was
with the idea that he wrote to Chitre at this juncture: "I think
the college ought to make teaching military science its speciality.
Thereby it will be doing a great national service and also service

to the Scheduled Castes." The idea did not materialise, but some books were purchased from Jadhav by his college.

About this time the Central Government set up a Linguistic Commission to report on the demands for Linguistic Provinces. Prominent among those who gave evidence before the Commission on behalf of Maharashtra was Ambedkar. He prepared a Memorandum with his usual care and study for being placed before the Commission.

In the Memorandum which he submitted to the Commission in Bombay on October 14, 1948, he stated: "A Linguistic Province produces what democracy needs, namely, social homogeneity, and makes democracy work better than it would in a mixed Province. There is no danger in creating Linguistic Provinces. Danger lies in creating Linguistic Provinces with the language of each Province as its official language." The latter would lead to the creation of Provincial nationalities. For the use of Provincial Languages as official languages would lead Provincial cultures to be isolated, crystallised, hardened and solidified. That would lead to a break-up of India and instead of remaining united, India might end in becoming Europe.

It may be recalled here that he had expressed his valuable opinion on the question of the official language of India on April 19, 1947, in the Constituent Assembly in a minute of dissent. He had presented an irrefutable case for a single official language for the Centre and the States. But the Constituent Assembly proposed it differently and the warning went unheeded!

Further, Ambedkar visualised a unitary Maharashtra Province and observed in his Memorandum to the Linguistic Commission that it would not merely be a viable Province but a strong Province in point of area, population and revenue. He also said: "Maharashtra and Bombay are not merely interdependent; they are really one and integral. Bombay and Maharashtra are tied together by God, to use a Biblical phrase. As regards arbitration in this case it is as absurd as the suggestion to refer a matrimonial cause to arbitration. Maharashtra should not be denied the right to claim Bombay because it is an emporium for the whole of India. Every port serves a much larger area than the region it belongs to. Will Calcutta be separated from the Bengal Province because the

Bengalis are in a minority in Calcutta and they do not own the trade and industry of Calcutta? Do the coal mines of Bihar belong to the Bihar Province or to the coal-owners who are the Gujaratis, Kathiawaris or Europeans? The trade and industry of Bombay was built up by Europeans chiefly on the labour of Maharashtra. Maharashtrians are not actuated by any bad motive. They are not a commercial community. Unlike other communities, the Maharashtrians have no nose for money, and I am one of those who believe that it is one of the greatest virtues. Money has never been their god. It is no part of their culture." That is why, he concluded, they had allowed all other communities coming from outside Maharashtra to monopolize the trade and industry of Maharashtra.

In the same month Ambedkar's great book, *The Untouchables*, was published. With great erudition and force the author has expressed the view that the Untouchables were Broken Men and because those poor men could not give up beef-eating and Buddhism, they were treated as Untouchables. He traces the origin of untouchability to a time about 400 A.D. and with his profound scholarship maintains that it is born out of the struggle for supremacy between Buddhism and Brahminism. He tells his readers that the Brahmins gave up beef-eating and adopted Buddhistic ways and means to regain their prestige and power which they had lost owing to the rise of Buddhism.

It may be noted here that Col. Alcott in his book *The Poor Pariah* and Babu Nagendranath Basu in his *Modern Buddhism and Its Followers in Orissa* had some years before propounded the theory that the Untouchables were Buddhists who had refused to join the renaissance in Hinduism.

This book, as all his writings, shows that, like Dr. Johnson, Ambedkar had the power of language and strength of thought and wielded a powerful pen. His writings had a peculiar fragrance of simplicity and directness. His style was pointed, logical and judicial and it often rose to an eloquence, sober and impassioned, hiding its intriguing lawyership beneath its construction. His style abounded in epigrams, provocative phrases and picturesque expressions.

Ambedkar's knowledge was extensive, varied, profound and encyclopaedic. His learning instructed and his thoughts provoked thinking. He wrote for the writers and thinkers. Yet he used words not as an artist but like a fighter. He wrote books not for literary fame, but for great causes. As such, as a historian his writings might be, according to some critics, open to the charge of harshness. The man of mission dominated the historian in Ambedkar and was not satisfied with the defeat of rival arguments. He lacerated his opponent till the latter swooned. That was unavoidable, for dissection is always associated with blood. The critics said that the theory was novel but convincing.

The Draft Constitution was before the public for six months. At last the day dawned when Ambedkar introduced on November 4, 1948, the Draft Constitution in the Constituent Assembly. The Draft Constitution contained 315 articles and 8 schedules. Describing the Draft as a formidable document, he brought out in a grand, lucid and elaborate speech its salient and special features, the whole Assembly listening to him as one man. He brushed aside all criticism which was based on misunderstanding and inadequate understanding of the articles.

Explaining first the form of Government which the Draft Constitution visualised, he said: "The American form of Government is called the Presidential system of Government. Under the Presidential system the President is the Chief Head of the Executive. Under the Draft Constitution the President occupies the same position as the King under the English Constitution. He is the Head of the State but not of the Executive. He represents the nation, but does not rule the nation."

As regards the Executive, he observed: "The American Executive is a non-Parliamentary Executive which means that it is not dependent for its existence upon a majority in the Congress, whereas the British system is a Parliamentary Executive, which depends upon a majority in Parliament. Being a non-Pailiamentary Executive, the Congress of the U.S.A. cannot disown the Executive and it tends to be less responsible to the Legislature whereas Parliamentary Executive tends to be more responsible. The Draft Constitution preferred more responsibility."

Pointing to the other salient features of the Draft Constitution, Ambedkar said: "The Draft Constitution, though a dual polity, has a single citizenship for the whole of India with a single integrated judiciary having jurisdiction and providing remedies in all cases arising under constitutional law, the civil law, or the criminal law and has a common all-India civil service to man important posts whereas under the Constitution of the U.S.A. there is a dual citizenship—a citizenship of the U.S.A. and a citizenship of the States;, there is a Federal judiciary and a State judiciary and there is also a Federal Civil Service and a State Civil Service." "Subject to the maintenance of the republican form of Government," Ambedkar continued, "each State in the U.S.A. is free to make its own constitution whereas the constitution of the Indian Union and of the States is a single frame from which neither can get out and within which they must work." As regards the point of rigidity he maintained that it had been assuaged by giving power to Parliament to legislate on exclusively provincial subjects in normal times and by making provision for facility with which the constitution could be amended. "So its distinguishing feature is that it is a flexible Federation," he added.

Replying then to the charges that there was nothing new in the Constitution, he said: "More than a hundred years have rolled by since the first written constitution was drafted. It has been followed by many countries reducing their constitutions to writing. What the scope of a constitution should be has long been settled. Similarly, what the fundamentals of a constitution are, are recognised all over the world. Given these facts, all constitutions in their main provisions must look similar. The only new things, if there can be any, in a constitution framed so late in the day. are the variations made to remove the faults and to accommodate it to the needs of the country. That the constitution has produced a good part of the provisions of the Government of India Act of 1935, I make no apologies. There is nothing to be ashamed of in borrowing. It involves no plagiarism. Nobody holds any patent rights in the fundamental ideas of a constitution."

Dealing with the suggestions for village Governments, Ambedkar said that the village was a sink of localism, a den of ignorance, narrow-mindedness and communalism and added that the village republics had been the ruination of India. He was glad, he proceeded, that the Draft Constitution had discarded the village and adopted the individual as its unit.

"I feel," he concluded, "that the constitution is workable; it is flexible and it is strong enough to hold the country together both in peace time and in war time. Indeed, if I may say so, if things go wrong under the new Constitution the reason will not be that we had a bad Constitution. What we will have to say is that Man was vile. Sir, I move."

IV

The whole Constituent Assembly was illuminated by the grand commentary, and speaker after speaker paid glowing tributes to Ambedkar for his lucid, able, symmetrical speech and the brilliant analysis of the Constitution. Prof. K.T. Shah, Pandit Lakshmikant Maitra, and T. T. Krishnamachari who was a Member of the Drafting Committee, paid him high compliments. Dr. Punjabrao Deshmukh expressed satisfaction at the excellent performance and the impressive commentary of Ambedkar on the Constitution, and said that Ambedkar would have perhaps shaped the Constitution differently if he had the scope to do so.

Kazi Syed Kamruddin congratulated him on the introduction of the Constitution and said that he was sure that Ambedkar was bound to go to posterity as a great constitution-maker.

The articles of the Constitution were then discussed and adopted one by one. On November 29, 1948, Article 11 was adopted declaring abolition of untouchability amidst great acclamation.

Ambedkar returned to Bombay on December 18, 1948, and addressed a gathering of the workers and leaders of the Scheduled Castes Federation. At Manmad, he was presented with a purse on January 15, 1949. Speaking on the occasion, he declared that his people would establish real socialism in the land under the rule of peasants and workers. He also impressed upon his audience that the progress of a community always depended upon how they advanced in education. Ambedkar then stayed for some days at Hyderabad in connection with the college he proposed to start at Aurangabad. During his stay there he visited the excavations in the neighbouring places, and, attending a meeting of his Party in the third week of January, he went back to New Delhi, In March and May 1949 he twice visited Bombay. These frequent flying arrivals in and departures; from Bombay were in connection with the work of the People's Education Society and for medical advice.

On May 26 the Constituent Assembly resumed its work and adjourned on June 10. On July 7 Ambedkar returned to Bombay. By now the strike launched by the Bombay Municipal Kamgar Sangh had reached a critical stage, and being its President, Ambedkar was in a quandary. "It is learnt that when the Hon'ble Dr. Ambedkar expressed his desire to intervene with a view to settling the dispute, he was offered the ultimatum of resigning either the presidentship of the Municipal Kamgar Sangh or his seat in the Cabinet. The Hon'ble Dr. Ambedkar had to be persuaded not to quit his seat in the Cabinet which position was more beneficial to the general interests of the Scheduled Castes in India."[4]

A battle royal was fought on the question of the national language, and Hindi with Nagari script was declared to be the national language of India by a majority of one vote only.

As Chairman of the Drafting Committee, Ambedkar had to explain in the Constituent Assembly many knotty points and the niceties of law. Dealing with the powers of the Centre, he warned that its strength must be commensurate with its weight; it would be folly to make it so strong that it might fall by its own weight.

He described the article 32 which defines the powers of Parliament and the Supreme Court in respect of the fundamental rights, as the very soul of the Constitution and the very heart of it.

As regards the powers of the President of the Indian Union, he observed: "The President of the Indian Union will be generally bound by the advice of his Ministers. He can do nothing contrary to their advice, nor can he do anything without their advice."[5] According to him, the President has no discretionary functions but will have certain prerogatives.

---

4. Statement by the Secretary of the All-India Municipal Workers' Federation.
5. Pylee, M. V., *India's Constitution*, pp. 169, 172.

From July 30 the Constituent Assembly sat in a long session till October 17 with a break for a fortnight in September 1949 when Ambedkar had a little rest at Srinagar and returned to Delhi on October 3, 1949. In September M S. Golwalkar, the R.S.S. Chief, met him in New Delhi. During this session the Constituent Assembly concluded the second reading of the Constitution. Ambedkar was working hard despite ill-health, moving practically every article, elucidating points and replying to the debates.

In the first week of November 1949, Ambedkar returned to Bombay for medical advice and treatment and left for New Delhi on November 10. The Constituent Assembly began the third reading of the Constitution from November 14. On that day Ambedkar moved: "The Constitution as settled by the Assembly be passed." Members cheered him in the expectation of a speech, but Ambedkar decided to let other Members have their say first. Muniswami Pillay said that his Harijan Community had produced a Nandanar, a great devotee; a Tiru Panalwar, a great Vaishnavite saint; and a Tiruvalluvar, a great philosopher; and now it has produced Ambedkar who showed to the world that the Scheduled Castes also could rise to the heights and render service to the world. The Deputy Speaker congratulated Ambedkar on framing the Constitution and on reciprocating the goodwill shown to him by the Members. Pandit Thakurdas Bhargava invited Ambedkar, who had now found a place in the hearts of Congressmen, to join the Congress Party and become a leader of the whole nation.

It was not that all the Members were pleased with the form of the Constitution. There were a few dissenting voices. A Member said that the Constitution was worthless as the Provinces were reduced to the status of Municipalities. Another bewailed that the Constitution-maker had discarded the idea of decentralization favoured by Gandhi. Yet a third one felt sorry that the Constitution did not provide for a ban on cow-slaughter. Some described it as a mixture of the constitutions of the world and a lawyer's paradise, and added that although a grand document, it did not implement Gandhi's social and economic ideals. All these arguments were forestalled and refuted by Ambedkar in his introductory speech.

One speech was important in this respect. M. Sadulla, a Member of the Drafting Committee, revealed that the Drafting Committee was not a free agent and was handicapped by various circumstances. He added that many provisions which went against a sense of democracy had to be incorporated by the Committee because of superior forces that were operating.

And amidst loud applause rose the Chief Architect of the Constitution on November 25, 1949, to reply to the debate on the third reading of the Constitution. At the outset Ambedkar told the House that he had entered the Constituent Assembly to safeguard the rights of the Scheduled Castes. He was surprised when the Constituent Assembly elected him to the Drafting Committee; he was more than surprised when the Drafting Committee elected him to be its Chairman. He, therefore, expressed his gratitude to the Constituent Assembly and to the Drafting Committee for reposing in him so much trust and confidence and for choosing him as their instrument and giving him that opportunity for serving the country. He expressed warm appreciation of the co-operation of Sir B. N. Rau and the secretarial staff, and of the lively interest shown by H. V. Kamath, Dr. Panjabrao Deshmukh, Saxena, K. T. Shah, Pandit Thakurdas, R. K. Sidhva and H. N. Kunzru in the proceedings.

As regards the merits of the Constitution, he said that the principles embodied therein were the views of the present generation, or if this was an overstatement, the views of the Members of the House. And however good a constitution might be, he observed, it was sure to turn out bad if those who were called to work it, happened to be a bad lot; it would turn out to be good if those who were called to work it, happened to be a good lot.

Looking to the future of the country, he showed his anxiety and observed: "What perturbs me greatly is the fact that India has not only once before lost her independence but she lost it by the infidelity and treachery of her own people. In the invasion of Sindh by Mahommed-Bin-Kasim, the military commanders of King Dahir, accepted bribes from the agents of Mahommed-Bin-Kasim and refused to fight on the side of their king. It was Jaichand who invited Mahomed Ghori to invade India and to fight against Prithviraj and promised him the help of himself and the Solanki Kings. When Shivaji was fighting for the liberation of the Hindus, the other Maratha noblemen and the Rajput kings were fighting battles on the side of the Moghul emperors. When the British were fighting the Sikh rulers, their principal commander sat silent and did not help to save the Sikh kingdom. In 1857 when a large part of India had declared a war of independence against the British, the Sikhs stood and watched the event as silent spectators."

"Will history repeat itself?" he asked, the House. His anxiety was deepened, he proceeded, by the realization of the fact that in addition to their old enemies in the form of castes and creeds people had too many parties with diverse opposing creeds. He, therefore, urged the people of India to resolutely guard against the eventuality of parties placing their creed above the country or else "our independence will be put in jeopardy a second time and probably be lost for ever. We must be determined to defend our independence till the last drop of our blood." (Cheers.)

He then turned to the ways of maintaining democracy. He said that the first thing they must do was to hold fast to the constitutional methods of achieving their social and economic objectives and abandon the methods of civil disobedience, non-co-operation and satyagraha, for those methods were nothing but the grammar of anarchy.

Another danger, he felt, arose from hero-worship. He quoted from John Stuart Mill, who warned the defenders of democracy not to lay their liberties at the feet of even a great man, or trust him with powers which enabled him to subvert their institution. Striking a note of warning against the spirit of irrational blind hero-worship which prevailed in the country, he observed: "There is nothing wrong in being grateful to great men who have rendered life-long service to the country; but there are limits to gratefulness. As has been well said by the Irish patriot Daniel O'Connell, 'No man can be grateful at the cost of his honour; no woman can be grateful at the cost of her chastity; and no nation can be grateful at the cost of its liberty.' This caution is far more necessary in the case of India than in the case of any other country. For, in India *Bhakti* plays a part in politics unequalled in magnitude than the part it plays in the politics of any other country in the world. *Bhakti* may be a road to the salvation of the soul; but, in politics *Bhakti* or hero-worship is a sure road to degradation and eventual dictatorship."

The third thing people must do to safeguard the Indian Democracy, he said, was that they must not be content with mere political democracy but that they should make the political democracy a social and economic democracy. He added that political democracy could not last unless there lay at the base of it social democracy which recognised liberty, equality and fraternity as the principles of life. They formed an inseparable trinity. Without equality, liberty would produce the supremacy of the few over the many. Equality, without liberty would kill individual initiative. Without fraternity, liberty and equality could not become a natural course of things. They must acknowledge, he continued, the fact that there was complete absence of two things in Indian society: equality in social and equality in economic life.

Sounding a grave warning, Ambedkar said with great fervency: "On January 26, 1950, we are going to enter into a life of contradictions. In politics we will have equality and in social and economic life we will have inequality. .. . We must remove this contradiction at the earliest moment, or else those who suffer from inequality will blow up the structure of political democracy which this Assembly has so laboriously built up."

In the end he appealed to the Indians to be a nation in the social and psychological sense of the word by discarding castes which brought about separation in social life and created jealousy and antipathy between caste and caste.

The House listened to his forty-minute lucid, eloquent and prophetic speech spell-bound, punctuating it with cheers. Members later described it as a graphic and realistic appraisal of the political conditions prevailing in India. The next day newspapers published his speech; with great joy and pride, and showered eulogies on his words of wisdom and warning.

On November 26, 1949, the Constituent Assembly, in the name of the people of India, adopted the Constitution with its 395 articles and 8 schedules. In his concluding speech Dr. Rajendra Prasad, the President of the Constituent Assembly, said: "Sitting in the chair and watching the proceedings from day to day, I have realised as nobody else could have, with what zeal and devotion the Members of the Drafting Committee and especially its Chairman Dr. Ambedkar in spite of his indifferent health, have worked. (Cheers). We could never make a decision,which was or could be ever so right as when we put him on the Drafting Committee and made him its Chairman. He has not only justified his selection but has added lustre to the work which he has done."

The Constituent Assembly worked strenuously for two years eleven months and seventeen days. There were over 7600 amendments to the Draft Constitution, but of these 2473 were moved and disposed of.

A weekly of Gandhian persuasion compared Dr. Ambedkar with Upali who was chosen to rehearse the *Vinaya* to the Buddhists convocation that met three months after the *Mahaparinirvana*[6] of the Buddha.

The main feature of the Constitution is that sovereignty resides in the people, and Parliament as the representative of the people carries that sovereignty. The directive principles lay down that our ideal is social and economic democracy; and as observed by K. C. Wheare in his *Modern Constitutions*[7] the Indian Constitution strikes a good balance in respect of the amending process.

❑❑❑

---

6. Total extinction of personality.
7. P. 143.

CHAPTER 22

SHADOW OF BUDDHISM

AFTER his great triumph in the Constituent Assembly, Ambedkar returned to Bombay by air on January 2, 1950. He was lustily greeted by his lieutenants and prominent citizens at the aerodrome.

The Constitution was complete; but Ambedkar had now brought with him a new battle cry! It was the Hindu Code Bill which he had revised and submitted to the Constituent Assembly (Legislative) in October 1948. The work of revising and codifying the Hindu Law had been going on for the past ten years. The Government of India had set up in 1941 a Committee under the Chairmanship of Sir B. N. Rau. The Committee toured the country, heard various views and drafted the Hindu Code Bill. The Bill had been in and out of the Central Assembly since 1946. Ambedkar transformed it and parts of the Code Bill relating to joint family and women's property became a nightmare to most of the Members of the Select Committee. It gave a great shock to its reactionary opponents.

As soon as Ambedkar touched the Code and became its spokesman, the Hindu intelligentsia was driven all over India into two camps, raising loud denunciations and singing loud praises. Traditions and modern times were at loggerheads, sanctimoniousness was at grips with social progress, and learning was pitted against revolutionary intellect. The authority of the Shastras was invoked on both sides. On one side was Manu; and on the other was Ambedkar. Those who hated the change opposed the Code on different grounds. Some argued that the Code should be taken up for consideration after the first general elections. Some shouted that it should be put before the people of the merged areas and others cried out that it was a complete abrogation of the Hindu customs and traditions. Some pointed to the fundamental rights in the Constitution.

Ambedkar started the war on January 11, 1950, when he addressed the second session of the Siddharth College Parliament in Bombay. He declared that it would be wrong to describe the Hindu Code Bill as either radical or revolutionary. He said that the Bill, while according sanction to the new ways of progress, did not oppose the orthodox practices. He further stated that the new Republican Constitution of India had given a positive direction that Government should endeavour to prepare a Civil Code for the benefit of the country as a whole. The purpose of the Hindu Code Bill was, he explained, to codify and modify certain branches of the Hindu Law. Dwelling upon its significance, he said that it was beneficial from the point of the country's oneness that the same set of laws should govern the Hindu social and religious life. He further told his audience that the Hindu laws were being revised not because the Hindus were a weak people to resistance revival but for uniformity's sake. The Hindu Code was a right step towards a Civil Code. The laws should be easily understandable and be applied to all society irrespective of regional barriers. Moreover, a Hindu was free to adopt anybody from the Hindu society and he could make a will denying inheritance to his daughter.

As regards the authority under which the Code was drafted, he said that the modifications proposed were based on the Hindu Shastras and Smritis. The property was governed by Dayabhag system; the child belonged to the caste of the father under Pitrisavarnya; divorce was supported by Kautilya and Parashara Smriti; and women's rights to property were supported by Brihaspati Smriti, he concluded.

On the evening of 11th January 1950, Ambedkar was presented with a golden casket containing a copy of India's Constitution at a meeting at Parel, Bombay, which was convened by the Bombay Scheduled Castes Federation. Ambedkar said in reply that he had entered the Constituent Assembly with the object of safeguarding the interests of the Scheduled Castes and not with the ambition of drafting the Constitution. However, through some circumstances the responsibility for drafting the Constitution fell on his shoulders, and he was proud that his name had been associated with the framers of the Constitution, because one got such a unique opportunity once in one's life time.

He said he had been branded for the last twenty years as a pro-Muslim and pro-British leader. He hoped now that his work for India's Constitution would help Hindus to understand him and also show them how the accusations hurled at him were utterly untrue.

Exhilarated in his hopes, he asked his people to shed narrow outlook and think in terms of the welfare and prosperity of the nation as a whole.[1] He stated that so far the country's future had not occupied any place in their thought; but now the time had come to think in terms of the wider interests of the nation as a whole. He, therefore, urged his people not to maintain their separate entity and asked them to win sympathies of all the political parties in the country. The vast meeting, he said, had falsified the charge that the sand had been swept from under his feet and showed that the ground was much more firm and solid than before.

Ambedkar was also honoured, on January 29, by Maharashtrian institutions in New Delhi. Replying to the address, he said that the Maharashtrians were more sincere, more conscious of their duties to the nation and were ever willing to sacrifice for the cause of the nation. He was proud that two Maharashtrians were in the Central Cabinet and the Governor of the Reserve Bank, too, was a Maharashtrian. In politics, in learning and in the cause of sacrifice, Maharashtrians were far ahead, he concluded.

Ambedkar was now at the zenith of popularity. It was natural that his birthday was celebrated in April on a nationwide scale, and functions in connection with it were attended by eminent men like the Chief Justice Chagla of the Bombay High Court. Presiding over a birthday celebration meeting at Naigaon, Bombay, Justice Chagla said that every Bharatiya citizen would remember gratefully the name of Ambedkar when he enjoyed his rights. He said that he attended the function not merely because Ambedkar was the leader of the Scheduled Castes, but because he considered him a leader belonging to the whole nation. India's eminent and popular Justice recalled with pride how Ambedkar and he had studied at the same time for the Bar in England, how they had started practice at the same time, and

---

1. *The Times of India*, 12 January 1950.

how both of them had taught classes in the Law College, Bombay. He observed that Ambedkar was now a name well known throughout the world as a great authority on Constitutional Law and added that Ambedkar was also an authority on politics.[2]

Addressing Ambedkar's birthday meeting at New Delhi, K. Hanumanthaiya, an M.P., said that Ambedkar would go down to posterity as a saviour, a constitutional authority, and a day would dawn when the people would find Ambedkar at the helm of the nation as the Premier of India. R. K. Sidhva, another Member of Parliament, said that truly speaking. Gandhi was influenced by Ambedkar to do something for the political rights of the Untouchables. Sidhva further declared that Ambedkar was the liberator of the down trodden and was a great seer as well.

II

Ambedkar now reassumed his old role of an iconoclast. Speaking at a meeting, on the occasion of the Buddha anniversary, in New Delhi, he attacked the Godmen in Hinduism. He said that the Buddha's religion was based on morality. It was based on ethics and the Buddha acted as a guide and not as a god whereas Krishna said that he was the god of gods; Christ said he was God's son and Mohammad Paigamber said that he was the last messenger of God. Except the Buddha all founders of religions claimed for themselves the role of *Mokshadata* (Saviour) and claimed infallibility for themselves, while the Buddha was satisfied with the role of *Margadata* (Guide). The religion of the Buddha was morality. In place of God in Buddhism there was morality. The Buddha propounded a most revolutionary meaning of the word "*Dharma*". *Dharma* to Brahmins was Yajnas and sacrifices to God. In place of *Karma* the Buddha substituted morality as the essence of *Dharma*. The social gospel of Hinduism was inequality whereas Buddhism was for equality. The *Geeta* upheld Chaturvarnya, he added.

In his article entitled "Buddha and the Future of his Religion", which he contributed to the *Mahabodhi Society Journal* for its May number, Ambedkar summarised his thoughts on Buddhism as follows: "(1) The society must have either the

---

2.   The *Janata*, 22 April 1950.

sanction of law or the sanction of morality to hold it together. Without either the society is sure to go to pieces. (2) Religion, if it is to function, must be in accord with reason which is another name for science. (3) It is not enough for religion to consist of a moral code, but its moral code must recognise the fundamental tenets of liberty, equality and fraternity. (4) Religion must not sanctify or ennoble poverty."

According to him Buddhism fulfilled these requirements and so among the existing religions Buddhism was the only religion which the world could have. He felt that the propagation of Buddhism needed a Bible and opined that the majority of the Bhikkhus of the day had neither learning nor service in them.

After this stormy speech in New Delhi, Ambedkar came to Bombay on May 5, 1950. Asked whether he was initiated into the Buddhist fold, he told a representative of the *Janata*, a weekly conducted and edited by his son, Yashwantrao Ambedkar, that he was definitely inclined to Buddhism because the principles of Buddhism were abiding and were based on equality. He, however, made it clear that he had not embraced Buddhism, nor had he given any message to his followers to do so.

On May 19 Ambedkar went to Hyderabad in connection with the college which he was about to start at Aurangabad. During his stay in Hyderabad he declared that he had been invited to the Buddhist Conference at Colombo convened by the Young Men's Buddhist Association. While in Hyderabad, he addressed a meeting at the Boat Club where he said that secularism did not mean abolition of religion.

Accompanied by his wife and his Party Secretary Rajbhoj, Ambedkar reached Colombo by air on May 25, 1950. On his arrival at Colombo, he told the pressmen that he had come there to observe Buddhistic ceremonials and rituals, and to find out to what extent the religion of Buddha was a live thing.

At Kandy, Ambedkar declined to address the Conference in its representative capacity and even showed disapproval of some of the resolutions passed by the Conference. He, however, urged a declaration on the part of the Buddhistic Conference stating that they were determined not merely to have a fellowship but that they would propagate the religion and make sacrifices for it. As regards himself, he said: "Even though I have not declared myself to be a member of the fellowship. I have a much deeper purpose in the visit I have undertaken."

Ambedkar addressed the delegates of the Young Men's Buddhist Association at Colombo 'on the rise and fall of Buddhism in India'. Repudiating all suggestions that Buddhism had disappeared from India, he said: "Buddhism in its material form had disappeared. I agree. But as a spiritual force it still exists." As regards Hinduism, he said that it went through three stages: the Vedic Religion, Brahminism and Hinduism. It was during the period of Brahiminism that Buddhism was born. Brahminism preached inequality. Buddhism preached equality. It was not true, he observed, that after the days of Shankaracharya Buddhism was dead in India. It was going on for years together. In fact the Shankaracharya and his teacher were both Buddhists, he added.

Turning to the causes that led to the decline and downfall of Buddhism in India, he said that he was digging for materials on the subject, but in his view they were: the adoption of some rituals and practices from Buddhism by the Vaishnava and Shaiva cults which were vociferous in their propaganda against Buddhism. During the invasion by Allauddin Khilji thousands of Buddhist priests in Bihar were massacred, and consequently some of them fled for their lives to Tibet, China and Nepal. In the meanwhile, the majority of Buddhists went over to Hinduism. The third cause was that Buddhism was difficult to practise while Hinduism was not. The fourth cause was that the political atmosphere in India had been unfavourable to the advancement of Buddhism, he concluded.[3]

But according to Hindu scholars, thinkers and some foreign scholars the fall of Buddhism was due to many causes. Owing to its universalistic ambition its spread was everywhere but it had geographical centre nowhere. It discarded all national gods and god men and acclaimed Buddha the greatest of all gods. The drunken hero-worship against which the Buddha revolted was practised with a vengeance by the Buddha's followers by taking out processions of his tooth, hair and ashes! As long as it reacted as a reformative flank in India, Buddhism gained ground but when it began to act against the Vedic Religion, which was the national religion of the majority, Buddhism lost sympathy in

3. The *Janata*, 10 June 1950.

India. The Vedic Hindus fought the Muslims bravely and did not fly to any other country. But the Buddhists, having a centre nowhere, fled to different countries and even, it is said acclaimed the invasion of India by non-Hindus with the ringing of bells. Besides its godlessness, its over-emphasis on redemption, its sad tone, its unconcern with the world, and neglect of family, checked rather than fostered enterprise. The Hindu leaders therefore warned the Scheduled Caste Hindus that if they went over to Buddhism in the hope that the outer Buddhistic world would exert influence to improve their destiny in India, no blunder or miscalculation could be greater. Because of its extra-territorial sympathies Buddhism lost its support and sympathy in India,

Ambedkar then addressed a meeting in the town hall at Colombo and appealed to the Untouchables there to embrace Buddhism. He told them that there was no necessity of their having a separate organization. He also urged Buddhists in Ceylon to accept the Depressed Classes in Ceylon and look after their interests with paternal care.

The Conference over, Ambedkar visited, on his way back, Trivandrum and Madras. Addressing a meeting at the Legislative Chamber at Trivandrum, he declared that constitutional morality was far more important than the constitution, and added that if democracy was to succeed in India, both the people and the Governments should observe certain moralities or conventions. Dealing with the point of impartial administration, he pointed to Britain and remarked that in India there were many instances of the Party in power showing special favours.

Ambedkar then discussed general principles of the Hindu Code Bill at the State Guest House with the Chief Minister, Advocate-General, eminent lawyers and retired judges from Kerala. During his stay in Trivandrum Ambedkar was taken round some of the temples in the city and after observing minutely everything about temples and the Brahmin priests he exclaimed: "O what a waste of wealth and food!"

On his arrival in Bombay, Ambedkar addressed a meeting on July 25, under the auspices of the Bombay Branch of the Royal Asiatic Society. In the course of his speech he refuted the charges that he was an opportunist with regard to his views on Buddhism. He said that he had been interested in Buddhism ever since his

boyhood. At the same meeting Dr. V. M. Kaikini said that modern
Hinduism was nothing but a branch of Mahayana Buddhism with
some special beliefs, rituals and caste system added to it. The
meeting was presided over by Prof. N. K. Bhagwat.

Ambedkar returned to his headquarters at New Delhi. In
the middle of August and September he visited Bombay for eye
treatment. During the September visit he made a speech at the
Buddha Temple, Worli, on September 29. In the course of his
speech he said that in order to end their hardships people should
embrace Buddhism and added that the present Hinduism was
the same about a thousand years earlier. It was nothing but
Buddhism, but after the Mohammedan invasion and on account
of other causes it lost its purity and was mixed up with dross. In
the end he declared that he would devote the rest of his life to
the revival and spread of Buddhism in India.

Regretting Ambedkar's decision to renounce politics. *The
Times of India*, Bombay, said that those who knew the economic
and social views of the erudite scholar and doughty fighter were
under no delusion that he would don the politician mantle and
take the lead in forming a progressive party, and it attributed
his new bent to the disgust of politics. The *Shankar's Weekly,* in
a sarcastic tone, said that Ambedkar was nothing more than an
Indian to whom renunciation appealed more than jobs and power.
The *Weekly* suggested that Ambedkar should be regretfully
handed over to Aldous Huxleys and Aurobindos and should be
called Bhikku Bhimrao.

Ambedkar went back to Delhi. He had concentrated his
tremendous energies on the Hindu Code Bill which was on the
anvil. Here lay a golden and unique opportunity to change under
law the basic framework of Hindu society on more liberal patterns
suited to modern conditions and times. For some months he had
been inspired by the one single and thrilling idea, the idea of a
Mahar reorganising the basic framework of Hindu society. The
preparation of the Bill had involved extensive studies in the
scriptures, long discussions with a host of pundits and jurists,
and a vast collection of materials, books and manuscripts with
which a whole room was filled. He was working indefatigably,
neglecting his health and impairing his eyes although he was
prohibited from reading and writing by his doctors.

Ambedkar returned to Bombay at the end of October for medical treatment. In November he returned to Delhi and circularized among the Members of Parliament a 39-page booklet containing the nature and scope of the changes in the Hindu Code Bill which was revised by the Law Ministry in the light of representations from various Hindu organizations in the country. It was then hoped that the consideration of the Hindu Code Bill would be taken up sooner but even in December 1950 it was not taken up. In December the Law Minister introduced in Parliament the 'Representation of the People (Number Two) Bill, 1950', to provide for the qualifications and disqualifications for membership of Parliament and State Legislatures, the conduct of elections and for other cognate matters.

On December 22 Parliament adjourned till February 5, 1951, and Ambedkar returned to Bombay. In those days most of his visits to Bombay were either in connection with the work of the People's Education Society or for health reasons. On January 14 he made a speech before the Buddha Vihar, at Worli, Bombay. He stated that Buddhism flourished for over 1,200 years in India. During the same week, he was to have been presented with a purse by the Dock workers in Bombay. But he could not attend that function as be was suffering from pain in his leg. The purse was received by R. R. Bhole on behalf of the leader.

□□□

CHAPTER 23

BACK TO OPPOSITION

THE day for the battle on the Hindu Code Bill dawned, and all opponents rallied. The Bill had aroused widespread and bitter controversy. Social reactionaries raised a hue and cry in the name of religion. Political opponents of the Congress drummed that there was no mandate from the people on the issue and, therefore, it was unwise on the part of Government to rattle the Bill through Parliament. Others opposed the Bill on the plea that the times were inopportune to press forward that controversial legislation while there were some who foresaw the break-up of Hindu society if the Bill was passed in that form. The political opponents of the Congress argued that the Congress manifesto of 1945 contained no mention of the Hindu Code Bill; nor could that Parliament, elected indirectly by the States legislatures, possess popular authority on the issue; nor could a Government which styled itself a caretaker Government do so. They further argued that secularism did not mean that the Hindu Society could have no say in a matter affecting its social structure.

The Congress Party, too, was ramified into sections over this issue. Premier Nehru had vehemently declared, on his return from America, that his Government would resign if the Hindu Code Bill was not passed by Parliament. Another boss of the Congress Party, Sardar Patel, had declared his unmistakable opposition to the Bill and said that it would not be taken into consideration at all. Up to now Nehru seemed to throw his weight in favour of the Bill; and Sardar Patel and Dr. Rajendra Prasad were against it. Veer Savarkar, the Hindusabha leader, said that Congress leaders should take up the Hindu Code Bill if it really helped the nation. They should not take it up or drop it with an eye to elections, he added.

Amid such atmosphere Ambedkar introduced the Hindu Code Bill on February 5, 1951. Speaking on the Bill, Pandit Thakurdas Bhargava said that the Punjab should be exempted from its purview. Sardar Hukum Singh, the Sikh spokesman, regarded the Bill as a dubious attempt on the part of the Hindus to absorb the Sikh community. Another Member said that the legislators had no mandate from the people.

Replying to these objections, Ambedkar said that the Hindu Code would be uniform throughout India. As regards the Sikh objection, he replied that "the application of the Hindu Code to the Sikhs, Buddhists and Jains was a historical development and it would be too late, sociologically, to object to it. When the Buddha differed from the Vedic Brahmins he did so only in matters of creed, but left the Hindu legal framework intact. He did not propound a separate law for his followers. The same was the case with Mahavir and the ten Sikh Gurus. The Privy Council had as early as 1850 laid down that the Sikhs were governed by the Hindu Law."[1] To those who asked for a Civil Code he said that he was surprised to see the opponents of the Bill turn overnight the protagonists of a Civil Code, and added that he suspected their serious intention and pious purpose for having a good law for the country. Referring to the point of secularism, he said that the idea of a secular State in the Constitution did not mean that they could abolish religion. It meant that Government could not thrust any particular religion on the people. The suggestion for referendum he rejected on the ground that Parliament was sovereign. Parliament competent to make and unmake laws.

The debate continued for three days, and the consideration of the Bill was postponed to the next session which was to meet in September 1951.

About this time Dr. Ambedkar wrote an exhaustive article 'The Rise and Fall of the Hindu Women' in the journal. *The Maha Bodhi*, Calcutta. It was a reply to an article in the *Eve's Weekly* in which the writer had charged the Buddha with being the man responsible for the downfall of women in India. Ambedkar vehemently attacked the article and said this was an oft-repeated, grave and vile charge levelled against the Buddha.

According to Ambedkar, the passage on which the writer had based his conclusions was a later interpolation by the Bhikkus who were Brahmins. The Buddha did not shun women

---

1. *The Times of India.* 7 February 1951.

or express any disdain for them. Before the advent of the Buddha,
woman was denied the right to acquire knowledge which is the
birth-right of every human being, and she was denied the right
to realize her spiritual potentiality. This was a cruel deal for
women. By admitting woman to the life of *parivrajaka* (an
ascetic), the Buddha, by one stroke, removed both these wrongs.
He gave them the right to knowledge and the right to realize
their spiritual potentialities along with men. It was both a
revolution and liberation of women in India which allowed them
liberty and dignity. Manu, the greatest opponent of Buddhism,
wanted to protect the house against the invasion by Buddhism;
so he put women under restraint and heaped many inequalities
on them. Thus it was Manu and not the Buddha, he concluded,
who was responsible for the decline and fall of women in India.[2]

Ambedkar, outside his library, was a beehive of opposition
and storms. While laying the foundation stone of Ambedkar
Bhavan in New Delhi, he made a violent attack, in the middle of
April 1951, on the Central Government, accusing the Government
of apathy towards the rights of the Scheduled Castes. This was
a bitter broadside, and it rocked the thinking world of India.
The Congress Party was deeply perturbed at this, and even
Premier Nehru conveyed to Dr. Ambedkar his sense of
displeasure against his remarks. Some of the Congress leaders
murmured that Ambedkar should not be allowed to continue as
a Member of the Cabinet with whose policies he was in
disagreement. While the Law Minister's supporters said that he
was misreported, the non-Congress Party leaders said that
Ambedkar had every right to exercise his freedom of expression
at least in respect of problems affecting his own community. Some
of the newspapers inquired whether the Cabinet observed the
principle of joint or individual responsibility.

Two days after, when Ambedkar introduced the
Representation of the People (Amendment) Bill, his Sunday
punch had repercussions in Parliament. J. R. Kapoor acidly
described the Bill as "an election stunt on the part of Ambedkar
who wanted to extract the fullest advantage by casting himself
in the role of a saviour of the Scheduled castes". Upon this
Ambedkar protested saying that the Bill had been introduced

2.   The *Maha Bodhi*, May and June 1951.

before he had delivered his Sunday punch, and he was stung to remark: "You can go ahead, Mr. Kapoor, I have borne all this for twenty-five years." Then Kapoor went on to say that Ambedkar was "a bold and audacious man who levelled accusations against his Cabinet colleagues and fellow M.P.s". The bitterness was increasing, and it was even said that Nehru was to submit his resignation to the President at the end of the current session of Parliament in order to permit himself to reform and reorganize his Cabinet and even had asked Ambedkar to resign if he was not prepared to retract his charge. Things had, indeed, come to such a pass. When Ambedkar returned to Bombay at the end of April 1951, circles close to him said that the only reason why he remained in Government was his passionate desire to pilot the Hindu Code Bill through Parliament before the general elections.

After returning to New Delhi in May, the Law Minister presented the Representation of the People Bill to Parliament. During the course of his 90-minute speech he resolved doubts and disputes with a patient explanation or disconcerting repartee. While discussing the qualifications for membership of Parliament, he observed that Parliament could not be allowed to degenerate into an association of "chorus girls", always dutifully crying "ditto" to Government. The serious business in the House had its humorous interludes. The serious scholarly exposition was enlivened, now and then, with flashes of humour. The M.P. who wanted to become both a Parliamentarian and a permit-holder would have to choose either of the two, said Ambedkar. Lakshmikant Maitra of Bengal interrupted, saying "whichever is more profitable!"

In the course of the debate Dr. Parmar asked Ambedkar whether the Princes should be debarred from being Members of Parliament. The Law Minister answered: "Dr. Johnson, the author of the first English Dictionary, defined a political pensioner as a slave of the Government but he himself subsequently accepted a pension from the Government. It is no use being too logical." Thereupon Dr. Parmar asked: "Are political pensioners debarred from the House of Commons ?" Ambedkar flashed back: "No, only Lords and lunatics as they used to say!" And the House burst into a resounding laughter.

Meanwhile, some decisions of the High Courts and an important decision of the Supreme Court raised some vital points in connection with the Article 15(i) and Article 29(2). The Supreme Court invalidated the Madras State Government's communal order on admission of students to colleges and services. A series of court decisions nullified the Article 19(2) and Article 31 in respect of freedom of speech and property. So the Union Government moved the Constitution Amendment Bill in Parliament stating that the Bill sought no other changes, but brought out what was implicit in the Constitution and gave effect to the intentions of that charter. Ambedkar rose in an expectant House to defend the Amendment. "Then slowly and deliberately," observed the special correspondent of *The Times of India*, Bombay, "but with all the weighty almost inevitable decision of the steam-roller in motion, Dr. Ambedkar expanded its real purpose and meaning, and crushed much of the criticism, which when he rose to speak, seemed to have decimated Prime Minister Nehru's original statement when he initiated the discussion."

Turning to the Supreme Court judgment, which had invalidated the Communal Order of the Madras State Government on the ground that it involved discrimination between castes, Ambedfcar remarked that "it was utterly unsatisfactory and was not in consonance with the Articles of the Constitution". This remark created a storm in the House. When it died down, Ambedkar explained that the Supreme Court had overlooked the operative word "only" in Article 29(2)—"No citizen shall be denied admission into any educational institution on grounds only of religion, race and caste." He further stated that Article 46 directed the State to protect the interests of weaker classes. If then Article 46 was to be fulfilled, he added, the Articles 16(4) and 29(2) must be amended. The Amendment to Article 19(2) involved the addition of three more heads of restrictions to the freedom of speech and expression, public order and incitement to an offence and friendly relations with foreign states. This part of the Amendment also he supported.

The result was that the motion was approved and the Bill was referred to a Select Committee. The overwhelming decision in favour of the motion was largely the result of a very eloquent and impressive speech delivered by Dr. Ambedkar. "His peroration for its incisiveness and lucidity of exposition concerning difficult and delicate constitutional and legal issues must rank as one of the most outstanding debating performances ever witnessed in this Parliament," concluded the correspondent of *The Times of India*.[3]

The Press, however, attacked Government for its undignified haste and said that the champions of the freedom of speech and expression having settled down in the seats of power, were now themselves imposing rigid restrictions upon them. Some doubted the competency of the then Parliament to pass the amendment of the Constitution, and even criticized Ambedkar for defending the amendment.

II

In May again Ambedkar delivered another broadside against Hinduism on the occasion of the Buddha Jayanti Celebrations in New Delhi. In the course of his speech he attributed all the vices of the Hindus such as violence, immorality and corruption in Government offices, to deterioration in Hinduism and declared that real salvation for India would come when the people embraced Buddhism. This meeting was presided over by the Ambassador of France; and it was attended by almost all Ambassadors in Delhi. His critics said that it was very strange that Ambedkar, who was striving his best to codify the Hindu Law, and, in fact, was pulling on with the Government with that end in view, should antagonise the caste Hindus on every occasion. This speech evoked bitter remarks against Ambedkar in newspapers which said that historically Ambedkar's charge was untrue. On eminent Hindu leaders this speech had no effect; they seemed to think, that repeated thunders excited no more terror than the noise of a mill.

In July and August Ambedkar was busy with his educational activities. He had started a new college at Aurangabad, and the foundation-stone of the new building for the college at Aurangabad was laid a few days later, on September 1, by the President of the Indian Republic, Dr. Rajendra Prasad, who paid a glowing tribute to Ambedkar for his erudition and for his zeal in spreading education among the poor classes. He commended highly the aims and ideals of the People's Education Society.

---

3. *The Times of India*, 19 May 1951.

Ambedkar now looked tired. He wrote on August 10, 1951, to Prime Minister Nehru that his health was causing anxiety to him and to his doctors, and before he put himself into the hands of his doctors, he was anxious that the Hindu Code Bill should be disposed of. He, therefore, asked Pandit Nehru for a higher priority by taking it up in Parliament for consideration on August 16, so that it would be completed by September 1. He further observed that the Prime Minister knew that he attached greater importance to that measure and would be prepared to undergo any strain on his health, to get the Bill through. Prime Minister Nehru wrote in reply on the same day that he should take things easy and as there was opposition inside and outside to the Hindu Code Bill, the Cabinet had decided that it should be taken up at the beginning of September 1951.

Accordingly, Nehru himself urged in the first week, of September at the meeting of the Congress Parliamentary Party for a speedy disposal of the Hindu Code Bill. It was the last session of Parliament. The majority in the Congress Parliamentary Party were against the measure and wanted to put off the consideration till the new Parliament. They, therefore gave freedom of vote to their party members in Parliament. The Bill was not taken up in the first week of September. Just then it was decided at the Congress Party meeting that one part of Hindu Code Bill, the Marriage and Divorce, should be taken up on September 17, and the other clauses relating to property would be taken up later if time permitted.

September 17 dawned. Strong police pickets posted round the Parliament buildings were fully engaged with rival groups of excited women demonstrators in the morning when Parliament began consideration of the long awaited Hindu Code Bill.

The guns from the other side began to boom! Dr. Mookerjee said that the Hindu Code Bill would shatter the magnificent structure of Hindu culture and stultify a dynamic and catholic way of life that had wonderfully adapted itself to the changes for centuries. He, however, suggested that the principle should be applied to the members of all religions on the basis of human law and taunted that there was an opportunity to implement secularism. N. V. Gadgil made a spirited speech in defence of the Bill saying that the Bill was necessary to bring the law into line with the existing public morality. Sardar Bhopendra Singh Mann termed the Code a conversion law and added that the new Manu of Ambedkarian religion should not be imposed upon him. Pandit Kunzru supported the Bill in his characteristic sober speech. Pandit Malaviya warned the Government not to demolish the fabric of respect for law. The women Members described the Bill as a testament of their faith in the Constitution.

While discussions were going on in Parliament on the Hindu Code Bill, Nehru lost his grit and suggested a compromise that the Divorce and Marriage part of the Bill should be treated as a separate Bill. So, on September 19, Ambedkar announced in Parliament that since the exigencies of time would not permit the House to legislate on any more than Part II of the Hindu Code Bill during that session, the second part would stand as a self-contained Marriage and Divorce Bill.

This truncated Bill the opponents hotly debated. They were determined to talk it out. There was no pressure from the whip. There was no time-limit on speeches. At this critical stage of the Bill, the Law Minister himself added fuel to the fire of the opponents of the Bill. Desperately disappointed at the slow progress and extraordinarily long discussion lasting four days during this session and three days during the last one on the second clause, Ambedkar made a fighting speech on September 20, in which he referred to the story of Rama and Sita which created an uproar in the House and alienated public opinion. It wounded the religious susceptibilities of some Hindu Members one of whom rose excitedly and shouted: "We stand for progress and are prepared to vote for the Bill without listening to the Minister's abuse and invective against Hindu religion." The Law Minister replied that had the Members done so his speech would have been redundant. He, however, said that he had not even remotely intended to wound anybody's feelings and if he had done so inadvertently, he apologised. On a request from another Member he expressed his willingness to have the passage deleted from the records.

Replying to the debate, the Law Minister said that Dr. Mookerjee's remarks were not worth serious consideration as he had not opposed the Code while he was in the Cabinet but opposed it now for the sake of opposition. He asserted that "the previous enactment amending the Hindu Law had always been made applicable to the Sikhs and the law had all along assumed that Sikhs, for purposes of law, were Hindus". As regards the speech of Sardar Bhopendra Singh Mann, he said that it was repugnant and there was again uproar in the House there being cries of "Your speech is repugnant to the whole House".

The uncalled for attack on Rama and Sita and the pungent desperate tone worsened the situation and alienated more than most Members. Ambedkar brought hornets' nest around his ears and some of the bees stung Nehru who lost his grit completely and in confusion asked Ambedkar to drop the Bill. Describing Nehru's state of mind at this juncture one journalist quoted Garrick's famous epitaph on Goldsmith: "He wrote like an angel and spoke like poor Poll."

On September 22 the debate on clause 4 came to an end. On September 24 the debate was resumed. Ramnarayan said that Dr. Ambedkar was likened to Manu, but Manu Mahashay was accepted by all; he was not guarded by the police while making laws. On September 25 clause 4 of the Hindu Code Bill was adopted by the House without enthusiasm or protest and the galleries ebbed out as other Bills came up for consideration. Even the Marriage and Divorce Part of the Hindu Code Bill could not be complete. The Bill was let down in a tragic manner and in the words of Ambedkar "it was killed and buried, unwept and unsung after four clauses were passed". A few months before this incident. Justice Gajendragadkar of the Bombay High Court, a famous jurist and Sanskrit scholar, in the course of his speech on the Hindu Code Bill before the students of Karnatak University, had said: "If Dr. Ambedkar gives us Hindus our Code, his achievement would go down in history as a very eloquent piece of poetic justice indeed." Destiny, however, seemed unwilling to concede to the Law Minister the full laurels of a modern Manu!

Ambedkar's disappointment was sore. He was gruff and grinning. The news of his resignation flashed in the newspapers. He resigned his seat from the Cabinet on September 27. In his letter of resignation he wrote to the Prime Minister: " For a long time I have been thinking of resigning my seat from the Cabinet. The only thing that had held me back from giving effect to my

intention was the hope that it would be possible to give effect to
the Hindu Code Bill before the life of the present Parliament
came to an end. I even agreed to break up the Bill and restricted
it to Marriage and Divorce in the fond hope that at least this
much of our labour may bear fruit. But even that part of the Bill
has been killed, I see no purpose in my continuing to be a Member
of your Cabinet."

He, however, as a matter of civility to the Prime Minister
and to the Cabinet, expressed his willingness to continue till the
Bills and motions standing in his name were finished for which
he pleaded priority. Nehru appreciated his hard labour at the
Bill and said that the Fates and the rules of procedure were
against the Bill. He agreed to accept his resignation from the
last date of the current session, and asked for a copy of his speech
in advance. In reply Ambedkar informed the Premier on October
4 that if he prepared a speech he would give him a copy and
stated that he had obtained permission of the Deputy Speaker
to make his statement on October 11, after the business standing
in his name was finished.

Ambedkar continued in office till after the Dasara Holidays.
Parliament resumed work on October 11, 1951. There was no
question hour on that day. The Delimitation Orders were taken
first. After that work the Deputy Speaker called on H. K. Mahatab
to move the Industries Development and Regulation Bill. It was
at this juncture that Ambedkar rose to submit that he should be
heard first. But he was surprised when he was told by the Deputy
Speaker that he would have been allowed to speak then if he
had earlier submitted a copy of his statement to the Chair. The
Deputy Speaker added that be should, however, make his speech
at 6 p.m. Upon this Kunzru and Kamath inquired if it did not
amount to pre-censorship. In answer to a query the Deputy
Speaker said that as he was the custodian of the rights and
privileges of Parliament, it was necessary for him to see that the
statement contained nothing irrelevant or libellous. He then
turned to Ambedkar and continued: "Hon'ble Minister...." But
he was cut off by Ambedkar who retorted that he was no longer
a Minister and he did not intend to submit to that kind of dictate.
He collected his papers and left the House in protest. Thus the
Chief Architect of the Constitution was made to leave the House
as soon as he resigned his seat from the Ministry!

Most Members were unhappy at this turn of events. They were very anxious to hear Ambedkar. They applauded him as he went out. Section 128 of the rules of procedure does not specially mention that the Speaker should be in possession of an advance copy of the statement of a Minister who resigns and wants to make a statement. The Deputy Speaker said at 6 p.m. that he would have permitted Dr. Ambedkar to read his statement even if he had still chosen not to submit a copy of his statement in advance for scrutiny. Members, however, were at a loss to understand how pre-censorship, if necessary at 10.15 a.m., became unnecessary at 6 p.m. The next day the House welcomed Ambedkar back to its fold as "leader of the opposition".

Ambedkar gave his statement to the newspapers immediately after his walk-out. In it he stated five points on which he differed from the Cabinet. He explained how Nehru left him out of every Cabinet Committee although he had promised Ambedkar the Planning Department, when he offered him Law Ministry. The second point was the charge levelled against Government that it had apathy towards the Scheduled Castes uplift. He differed from Government policy over Kashmir and said : "The right solution for the Kashmir issue is to partition the State. Give the Hindu and Buddhist parts to India and the Muslim part to Pakistan as we did in the case of India." The fourth point was the wrong foreign policy of India which increased enemies rather than friends. Owing to that wrong foreign policy India had spend Rs. 108 crores out of Rs. 350 crores of her revenue on Army. He added that that colossal expenditure India had to foot because India had no friends on whom she could depend for help in any emergency that might arise. The last point was Nehru's lukewarm policy towards the Hindu Code Bill and it was his impression that Prime Minister Nehru, though sincere, had not the earnestness and determination required to get the Hindu Code Bill through. It was thus clear, he said, that he went out not as a sick man but a very disappointed man; for, he said, he was the last man to abandon his duty because of illness.

III

The reaction of the Press and people to Ambedkar's resignation was very favourable. *The Times of India* said in its editorial: "Bereft of the crown of Manu, Dr. Ambedkar none the less leaves the Government with a considerable record of achievement behind him. The Cabinet is not overburdened with talent, and the departure of this discerning scholar and industrious student of public affairs cannot but dim its limited lustre." "Political memories, it is true," added the editorial, "are short but in shedding old prejudices Dr. Ambedkar showed himself capable of rising to the height of new responsibilities and occasions." "India can ill-afford," continued the editorial, "to lose the service of this able politician and it would be little short of tragedy, personal and national, if Dr. Ambedkar were to relinquish the national stage and relapse to communal politics." "A formidable ally," concluded the editorial. "Dr. Ambedkar is also a foeman worthy of one's steel. The last few years have seen him harnessing his outstandiag ability to constructive purposes and both the country and his community stand to gain if he continues in that path."

The *National Standard*, Bombay, observed: "There are few men in the country so well equipped as Dr. Ambedkar to take charge of Planning, or of Finance, or of Commerce and Industry. What the Government loses the country hopes to gain by his constructive association with the Opposition." The *Free Press Journal*, Bombay, was sorry that a Minister of Ambedkar's eminence should have been forced to make his exit from the Cabinet in so unhappy a manner. Writing on the ruling of the Deputy Speaker, the journal said: "The Deputy Speaker in his wisdom has thought otherwise. In doing so, he even cast aspersions on the Minister by saying that the Chair had power to stop 'irrelevant, libellous and improper statements'. This is hard on the Minister who certainly did not deserve that treatment. The Minister ought to have been permitted to make his statement as scheduled."

For some months negotiations had been going on for electoral alliances between the leaders of the Peasants and Workers Party in Maharashtra and the leaders of the S.C.F. on the one hand, and the Socialist leaders and the S.C.F. leaders on the other. Jayaprakash Narayan and Ashok Mehta contacted Ambedkar through Acharya Donde who saw him at Delhi. It was Ambedkar's confirmed opinion that the P. & W.P. led by

Shankarrao More was allied to Russian ideology besides being a
prominently Maratha organisation of a communal nature. He,
therefore, refused to have anything to do with the P. & W.P., and
Jayaprakash Narayan also told him that More was in favour of
the Communists.[4]

The Executive Body of the Scheduled Castes Federation met
in the first week of October 1951 at New Delhi to consider the
election manifesto meticulously drafted by their leader
Ambedkar. The S.C.F. declared that it would have no truck with
the Congress, the Hindu Mahasabha or the Reds in elections.
The reaction of the Radical Democrats was notable. Mrs. Maniben
Kara told Acharya Donde that M. N. Roy greatly appreciated
the manifesto; and Roy was in full agreement with Ambedkar on
the Kashmir issue.

Ambedkar was now free to make his move and reappear on
the political party platform. He addressed a meeting at Jullunder
in the last week of October. There he declared that there was no
place for the Scheduled Castes in the heart of the Congress Party
and added that Nehru suffered from Muslim mania and his heart
was pitiless to the Scheduled Castes. A few days later Ambedkar
addressed a meeting of Lucknow University students and warned
the country against indifference to the backward classes and said
that if they were frustrated in attempts to rise to the status of
equality, the Scheduled Castes Federation might prefer the
Communist system and the fate of the country would be doomed.
In regard to the Kashmir issue, he said: "If we cannot save the
whole of Kashmir, at least let us save our kith and kin. It is a
plain analysis of the fact which cannot be denied."

Ambedkar then returned to his permanent abode in Bombay
on November 18. When he arrived in Bombay, he was given a
joint reception by the S.C.F. and Socialist Party at the Victoria
Terminus. After this colourful reception, he was taken in
procession to Siddharth College which was his residence during
his stay in Bombay. On his arrival, he took to organizing his
party for election purposes. He immediately opened an election
front against the Congress Party and at a meeting at Chowpaty,
Bombay, declared that it was Subhas Bose who won Independence

---

4.   Kharat, S. R., *Doctor Ambedkaranchi Patren* (Marathi), p. 280.

for India and not the Congress Party. Next evening he addressed a meeting held under the joint auspices of the S.C.F. and the Socialist Party in the Sir Cowasji Jehangir Hall, where he declared that the Congress Ministries had failed to give people pure administration, and expressed his sore disapproval of the statement of Nehru, who, as the President of the Congress had declared that Corruption in India was not such a great evil as should demand great attention. Referring to the Congress criticism that Ambedkar was ungrateful to the Congress Party, he quoted a citation from an Irish philosopher who said, "No man can be grateful at the cost of his honour; no nation can be grateful at the cost of its liberty; and no woman can be grateful at the cost of her chastity."

Replying to another question, he said that it was not true that he got into the Cabinet through the efforts of S. K. Patil. He told his audience that it was one of the greatest surprises in his life how he got into the Cabinet particularly when the Congress was deadly against his entry into the Constituent Assembly. He, however, said that it was Nehru who called him in his chambers and gave him an offer of Ministership. After all, this was election propaganda. There was, however, much truth in the statement that Sardar Patel, Patil and Acharya Donde had discussed the question of his entry into the Cabinet.

Ambedkar addressed a meeting at Nare Park, Bombay, and told his people that the Congress was not looking into the welfare of the Scheduled Castes and Backward Classes. At a mass meeting attended by about two lakhs of people at Shivaji Park, Bombay, on November 25, he asked Nehru to join the Socialist Party and lead the country. He impressed upon the mammoth audience the need for an Opposition Party to build the nascent Democracy in India and keep the ruling party in check.

In his whirlwind election tour, Nehru visited Bombay and Madras and in the course of his speeches at these places he denounced the alliance of the Socialists with the S.C.F. as unholy and said that it was very surprising and strange that Ambedkar did not oppose his foreign policy in the Cabinet meetings, though he had been a Minister for nearly four years. Ambedkar must have remembered his reply to Dr. Mookerjee on the Hindu Code Bill.

Ambedkar, in his vehemence against the Congress Party, made a speech before the Muslims of Bombay, impressing upon their minds the importance of separate electorates. This speech was lamented by many of his sympathisers who said that it was unbecoming of the Father of the Constitution.

The Congress Party was the oldest and the best organised party in the country. Their election preparations had been going on for months together methodically and energetically. Besides it was a ruling Party, Ambedkar could not do much·in the direction of organizing his Party, and owing to his failing health could not go outside Bombay for election propaganda. For the past ten years he was not in close touch with his organization, as he had to stay in Delhi as Labour Member and Law Minister. He had no correct idea of the strength and efficiency of his Party and that of the Socialist Party. The elections to Parliament and to the State Assemblies were held in the month of January 1952. The election tide flowed with Nehru, and Ambedkar together with the Socialist Party was swept away at the polls, Ambedkar getting 1,23,576 votes as against the Congress nominee, N. S. Kajrolkar, who secured 1,37,950 votes. More than 50,000 votes, which were to be cast for the reserved seat, were purposely wasted.

It was a colossal failure, and Ambedkar fell like a rocket. It proved once again that there is no gratitude in politics. The nation which had conferred so much glory on him seemed now unwilling to show him gratitude. The advocacy for the partition of Kashmir, his speech before the Bombay Muslims on separate electorates for the Muslims, lack of positive speeches before the people and above all the weakness of his disorganized Party resulted in the rout. During the entire election campaign, said a paper while writing on his defeat, he laid emphasis on the defects of the Congress Government, but did not lay stress on his alternative constructive programme. His vociferous lieutenant Rajbhoj who was elected to Parliament, and his young lieutenant B. C. Kamble who was elected to the Bombay Legislative Assembly, were the only survivors in the Election debacle.

Immediately after the polling, Ambedar had left for Delhi. In a statement which he issued from Delhi, on January 5, he said: " How the overwhelming support of the public of Bombay could have been belied so grossly is really a matter for inquiry by the Election Commissioner." The Socialist leader, Jayaprakash Narayan, issued a statement from Calcutta and said that, like Dr. Ambedkar, he, too, was at a loss to understand the debacle because from all accounts there was an overwhelming support for the Socialists in Bombay.

Ambedkar was in Delhi when the results of the Bombay elections to the House of People were declared. The political atmosphere was sad and full of surprise at Ambedkar's defeat. He said he was not unprepared for it, and that is why he had not taken it tragically. He felt that his defeat was due to the machinations of S. A. Dange.

IV

Although defeated at the polls, Ambedkar had not lost hope of a way out to public life, and so he asked Kamalakant Chitre to sound the persons and parties concerned about his election to the Council of States. Ambedkar's wife wrote to Kamalakant Chitre that Ambedkar's partymen should do for him what Congressmen were doing for Morarji Desai. In an appealing letter to Chitre she observed that politics was Doctor's very existence, the best tonic for his mental and physical health and that Parliamentary work he enjoyed most. Stating that his physical ailment was more of a psychic nature, she added with great vivacity and earnestness: "I dare say he will start running about if (and a very big if though) he were to be the Prime Minister of India. That is the desire of his and let us pray some day it will be fulfilled." Although he had borne well the present defeat, she continued, political events had affected in the past his health curve. He had planned so many things to be done when returned to Parliament which was the only place for a man of Doctor's height and stature. "It is here," she wrote in a moving tone, "that your role as the trusted lieutenant comes in." She was confident, she concluded, that he would move in the matter and there would be no disappointment.

Accordingly, things were arranged, and Ambedkar filed towards the middle of March 1952 his nomination to one of the 17 seats allotted to the Bombay State in the Council of States and he was declared elected at the end of the month. In April his birthday was celebrated as usual by his people. Literate people, who had a grudge against Ambedkar for his caustic speeches against the Congress Party and Hinduism, told his ignorant people in the villages that the great Doctor was done up, and had now receded back from Delhi to Bombay; but there too, he could not hold his own and was routed! He had run out his role, they told his people mischievously; and the poor people snarled at these cheap calumniators.

Ambedkar had many things to do in connection with his educational activities. He went to Aurangabad to attend a meeting of the People's Education Society concerning the college at Aurangabad. There he said in an interview that the step of converting Osmania University into a Hindi University was ill-advised and added that the Central Government could have picked out one of the Universities in North India.

He them went to Delhi to attend the session of the Council of States which opened in the last week of May 1952. There in an explosive speech on the Budget he described the defence budget as being the greatest stumbling block in the path of the progress of the country and said: "The army is eating into the vitals of the funds that are necessary for the well-being of the country." If the defence budget were reduced by Rs. 50 crores, he said, it would do much good to the country. If India's foreign policy aimed at maintenance of friendship and peace, who were the enemies against whom it was necessary to maintain a huge army? he asked.

At this juncture Ambedkar appeared in the Supreme Court on behalf of the Zamindars of U.P. in connection with the U.P. Zamindari Abolition and Land Reforms Act. Ambedkar's argument was that there was lack of legislative competence and public purpose in enacting the law. The Supreme Court, howewer, rejected the appeal.

Then came the news that Ambedkar was to receive the Doctorate of Laws at Columbia University convocation on June 5. Learning commands universal respect.

In fact he was to have received the Degree at the hands of General Eisenhower, who was then President of the University, but Cabinet responsibilities, and, later, electioneering, came in the way of the trip. It was said that the University was reluctant to confer it *in absentia*. Ambedkar said that his wife was not accompanying him to New York for lack of adequate foreign exchange.

From New Delhi he returned to Bombay on Saturday, May 31. At night he was felicitated at a dinner party at the Cricket Club of India, Bombay, by Dr. V. S. Patankar, Principal, and K. V. Chitre, Registrar of Siddharth College. Dr. Patankar said that it was an irony that none of the Indian Universities had yet thought of honouring Dr, Ambedkar who was the Chief Architect of the Indian Constitution. Not even Bombay University of which he had been a student had taken the initiative and it was left to a foreign University to honour him, he added. Ambedkar replied that although he was said to possess vitriolic temperament and had on many occasions conflicts with those in authority, no one should be under an apprehension that he would say anything harsh there about India. He had not on a single occasion been a traitor to the country and always had the interests of the country at heart. Even at the Round Table Conference he had been two hundred miles ahead of Gandhi so far as the interests of the country were concerned, he added.

Ambedkar left Bombay for New York by a T.W.A. flight on June 1, 1952. A large gathering of his followers and admirers gave him a send-off at the Santa Cruz airport. On June 5 the Convocation was held. Columbia University conferred on six persons the honorary degree of Doctor of Laws. While awarding him an honorary degree of Doctor of Laws, at its 198th Commencement exercises, the University hailed Ambedkar "as a framer of the Constitution, Member of the Cabinet and of the Council of States, one of India's leading citizens, a great social reformer and a valiant upholder of human rights". Ambedkar received the degree before a large crowd assembled to watch 6,848 graduates of Columbia's 17 schools and colleges receiving their degrees. Among those who also received honorary degrees were Lester B. Pearson, Canadian Secretary of State for Foreign Affairs and M. Daniel Mornet, the noted French literary historian.

Ambedkar returned to Bombay on June 14. The next day in an interview to the press he said that it was his impression that

the American public was favourably inclined towards Pakistan.
On inquiries he was told in America that this happened because
Pakistan always took great care in the selection of her foreign
representatives and ambassadors while India sent abroad
inexperienced men to represent her. He added that it was the
opinion of the American professors who visited India that Indian
students received education of an inferior grade and could not
derive sufficient guidance and knowledge from it, nor did they
derive any inspiration for research and independent thinking.

V

A few days later Ambedkar and Asoka Mehta, the Socialist
leader, filed election petitions pleading that the propaganda
aimed at influencing the electorate to cast both votes in a double-
member constituency in favour of the same candidate amounted
to a corrupt election practice and hence these elections should
be held invalid. The respondents against these petitions were
S. A. Dange, Dr. Deshmukh, Dr. V. B. Gandhi, Kajrolkar and
others.

The hearing of the election pleas of Ambedkar and Asoka
Mehta commenced in Bombay before the Election Tribunal in
the first week of October 1952. Ambedkar appeared in person
and said that the propaganda for wastage of votes was illegal
and that it was a gross perversion of law to arouse communal
feeling among the electorates. The appeal, however, was
dismissed.

On September 28 Ambedkar addressed a meeting of the
Scheduled Castes organizations at Nare Park, Bombay, when he
publicly criticized the organizers of the Building Fund and asked
the organizers to submit accounts immediately. He said to his
people that he had lost faith in the educated men of his
community and pinned his faith on the illiterate. He was in an
angry mood so much so that when in his ten-minute speech
someone whispered on the rostrum, he roared: "I will not tolerate
this. Give me the accounts tomorrow." This speech caused a
flutter among his lieutenants. The Building Fund was started in
1931, and the collection was then incomplete.

Ambedkar left for New Delhi in the first week of November
and returned to Bombay in December. On December 16, 1952,

he addressed the students' annual gathering at Elphinstone College on "the problems of modern students". He appealed to the students to reorganize university education to meet the requirements of the modern world, and to make the University a place for knowledge and not a centre for training clerks.

In December 1952, the members of the Poona District Law Library invited Ambedkar to unveil the portrait of L. R. Gokhale and declare open the collections of the books donated to the library. Ambedkar unveiled the portrait and declared open the new sections of the library on December 22, 1952, at Poona, and addressed the gathering on the "Conditions Precedent for the Successful Working of Democracy". In this important speech he observed that "Democracy is always changing its form, that it is not always the same in the same country and that it undergoes changes in purpose". According to him, he said, the purpose of modern democracy was not so much to put a curb on an autocratic King but to bring about the welfare of the people. Referring to the definition of Walter Bagehot that Democracy was government by discussion and that of Abraham Lincoln that 'a government of the people, by the people, for the people', Ambedkar said that his own definition was "a form and a method of government whereby revolutionary changes in the economic and social life of the people are brought about without bloodshed".

He then dealt extensively with the subject and said that the first thing required for the successful working of Democracy was that there must be no glaring inequalities and there must be neither an oppressed class nor a suppressed class. The second thing required was the existence of opposition to show whether the Government was going wrong. The third thing was equality before law and in administration. The fourth was the observance of constitutional morality. The fifth point was that the successful working of Democracy required the functioning of moral order in society; for moral order was taken for granted in Democracy. The last thing was the requirement of public conscience, he concluded. This thought-provoking speech became a topic for discussion for many days in the newspapers.

Ambedkar left for Kolhapur, and on December 24, 1952, addressed the annual gathering of the students of the Rajaram College. In the course of his speech he observed: "Knowledge is the foundation of a man's life and every effort must be made to maintain the intellectual stamina of a student and arouse his intellect." He asked the students to develop their thinking power and make use of the knowledge they had gained. Dr. (Mrs.) Savita Ambedkar distributed the prizes.

Women of Kolhapur gathered in their thousands to present an address to Dr. Ambedkar. Replying to their address, Ambedkar referred to the Hindu Code Bill and said that none of the prominent Indian women leaders were really interested in the social progress of women and stated that the Hindu Code Bill was now just like milk spoiled by mixture with a bitter acid. He added that if they wanted to have the Hindu Code Bill passed, they should find two fat women to fast! Addressing a rally of 50,000 people under the auspices of the Belgaum District Branch of the Scheduled Castes Federation, Ambedkar sounded a note of warning to the ruling party that if the lot of the Scheduled Castes was not improved by the next election, the Scheduled Castes Federation would be forced to take stern measures which might upset the chariot of the Government and anarchy might follow. He recalled the dreadful results of the French and Russian revolutions in the past and thundered: "I shall wait for another couple of years or even till the next elections, for the alleviation of the misery of my people and if a new deal is not forthcoming through negotiations, I shall be forced to take recourse to stern measures."[5] The speech raised the whole issue of the future of the Scheduled Castes.

All newspapers again criticized his speech and although some of them realised the depth and gravity of his restlessness, many said that his threats might be dismissed without much ado since he had been issuing threats at intervals. To them he was a by-word for threats!

On January 12, 1953, Osmania University, Hyderabad-Deccan, conferred on Ambedkar the degree of Doctor of Literature *honoris causa*, in recognition of his eminent position and attainments. To this University alone in the whole of India went the honour of recognising the eminence and excellence of the scholar and Chief Architect of the Constitution of India.

---

5.   *The Times of India*, 29 December 1952.

In February 1953, Ambedkar was present at a reception given in New Delhi by Rajbhoj in honour of M. R. Murti, Vice-President of the Indo-Japanese Cultural Association in Japan. Speaking on the occasion, Ambedkar said that he had come to the conclusion that the present generation or future generations would have ultimately to choose between the gospel of the Buddha and the gospel of Karl Marx.[6] He added that the East had already become more important than the West, but he feared that if the Buddhist Gospel was not adopted, the history of conflict in Europe would be repeated in Asia.

The threats were not going in vain. In April Parliament rang with clamours for steps towards the removal of untouchability and passed a resolution calling for the enactment of a comprehensive law to deal with the problem. Some Members of Parliament, who participated in the debate, complained untouchability was abolished on paper but not in practice. A need for drastic measures for penalizing untouchability offences was felt all the more urgent. A Harijan Member told the House how a hotel-keeper had kicked off the cups which he and a Harijan M.L.A. had used, how a Harijan Minister of Hyderabad on trying to enter a temple was threatened with lathis and how in Delhi a barber refused to shave a Harijan Member of Parliament. And yet the caste Hindu leaders grumble that Ambedkar was still bitter and did not forget the past!

In May Ambedkar delivered in Bombay a grand eulogoy on Buddhism, and reiterated his faith in and dedication to the propagation of Buddhism. A few days later he gave an interview to Crowley for his transmission series in which the leader of the Scheduled Castes told him that if the social structure were not altered, the present system was likely to collapse soon, and added that the alternative, if democracy did not work in India, was something of Communism.[7]

Ambedkar was fully engaged in the work of his colleges in July and August. For most of the days in July and August, he stayed in Aurangabad. There he addressed a meeting of the Hyderabad Scheduled Castes Federation workers and leaders in which he said that politics was not the be-all and end-all of the nation's life. He urged them to study diligently the Indian

6. The *Free Press Journal*, 16 Febnucy 1953.
7. The *Illustrated Weekly of India*, 12 July 1951.

Problem in all its aspects, political, social, religious and economic, and then fight with one accord for the salvation of the down-trodden. At this meeting he sounded a note of warning to his people that he would ex-communicate those who would make pilgrimages to Hindu places of worship. He said it did not do them any good.

While in Aurangabad, he told the press in an interview that whatever be the effects of Linguistic States once the Andhra State came into being, other Linguistic States were bound to come into existence. He said that he would favour two Marathi-speaking States if it facilitated the administration of two States. Referring to the events in Kashmir, he observed that Indians had every right to ask the Kashmiris when they had spent crores of rupees for the safety of Kashmiris, whether they were ready to merge with India or not. During his stay at Aurangabad he did not see his visitors unless they had qualified themselves by planting a tree each in the vast barren compound of the College and as a result hundreds of trees were planted. He had once himself cleared the compound of a hostel at Mahad by leading a host of lieutenants and leaders with axes, hoes and picks on their shoulders.

❑❑❑

CHAPTER 24

GOVERNMENT ON THE ANVIL

THEN all of a sudden the calm was disturbed by a storm. It burst over the Andhra State Bill aiming to create a new Andhra State. While speaking on the Bill in the Council of States on September 2, 1953, Dr. Ambedkar criticized Government for its vacillating policy on the formation of linguistic states. He strongly repudiated the view that linguistic reorganization would lead to the disintegration of India. Potti Sriramalu, he observed, had to sacrifice his life for the sake of creating Andhra. If, he added, in any other country a person had to die in order to invoke a principle that had already been accepted, it was possible that the Government of that country would have been lynched.

Ambedkar blamed Home Minister Katju for having made no provisions in the Bill to safeguard the rights of the Scheduled Castes against the tyranny, oppression, and communalism of the majority. He regretted the lack of a provision in the Constitution investing the Governors of the States with special powers for the protection of the interests of minorities. "We have," he observed, "inherited a tradition. People always keep on saying to me, 'Oh you are the maker of the Constitution.' My answer is I was a hack. What I was asked to do, I did much against my will."

At this there were serious interruptions which added to the heat and acerbity of the debate; and tempers ran high. One Member fanned the fire in Dr. Ambedkar, taunting him with the statement that Ambedkar had himself defended the Constitution; and Home Member Katju stirred the embers by saying that Dr. Ambedkar himself had drafted the Constitution. To the first charge he replied: "We lawyers defend many things." Referring to the second, he said, "You want to accuse me of your blemishes." Then he burst out explosively: "Sir, my friends tell me that I made the Constitution. But I am quite prepared to say that I shall be the first person to burn it out. I do not want it. It does not suit any body. But whatever that may be, if our people want to carry on, they must remember that there are majorities and there are minorities; and they simply cannot ignore the minorities by saying: 'Oh, no, to recognize you is to harm democracy.' I should say that the greatest harm will come by injuring the minorities. I fear sometimes that if the minorities are treated in the way in which they are being treated in our Bombay State—I do not want to be parochial, I do not know what will ultimately happen—I do not even like to call myself a Maharashtrian; I am fond of Hindi, but the only trouble is that Hindi-speaking people are enemies of Hindi."

The last two disconcerting sentences show that the tempest of anger had, that day blown off the sails; the ship was violently tossing about! The chairman called Dr. Ambedkar to order, saying, "Dr. Ambedkar, it is an aside! And Dr. Ambedkar said, "It is an aside."

Ambedkar's was indeed a virulent attack on the Constitution. He had made the attack and volleyed his thunder in a spirit of utter desperation and frustration. It was restlessness capped by righteous anger. The newspaper world felt sorry for his angry reaction and reminded him of the glorious speech he had made during the third reading of the Constitution. Criticizing Ambedkar's plea for more constitutional safeguards for minorities, P. Kodanda Rao said: "It was very sad that our modern Manu should style himself an Untouchable." Some likened Ambedkar to a mother who denounced her own child and invited all and sundry to tear it from limb to limb.

Ambedkar, however, seemed to be retrieving his position when next week Government itself unassumingly made incursions on the Constitution. He severely criticized the Government for resorting to Article 356 of the Constitution to continue President's rule in Pepsu and said that such action would besmear the name of the Government. He remarked that it was a wrong thing, and it ought not to be done. In the same speech he attacked the Government for installing Rajagopala-chari and Morarji Desai as Chief Ministers in two States. Rajagopalachari was a Member of the Legislative Council, and Morarji Desai had been defeated in the general elections. He decried their promotion as two instances of the most violent kind of assaults on the Constitution by the Government.

Shortly after, the Special Marriage Bill came up for discussion. The method of dealing piecemeal with the Hindu Law was a dangerous thing and it would create more chaos than reform. Ambedkar warned, while speaking on the Special Marriage Bill in the Council of States. The Act of 1872 should have been amended by an Amending Bill instead of repealing it. Hindu society, he concluded, was orthodox, and therefore it was the duty of the Government to take time by the forelock and make changes which appeared to be supported by society.

Speaking on the Estate Duty Bill on September 18, 1953, in the Council of States, he warned the Government of India that the yield from Estate Duty might not be commensurate with the cost of collection and administration of the Estate Duty law. He further said that India was running amuck because some other countries had done some thing. He added that India should not blindly follow Europe. What was good for Europe could not be good for India. Before India adopted such measures, Indians should reach the standards which the European people had reached.

It would have been a different matter, he sarcastically remarked, if India was a communist country; and he had no doubt that India would soon become a communist country. But so long as India did not adopt the Russian system, she should not take steps that might retard capital formation. He said he was not opposing the Bill, but be wanted the distinction made between capitalists, whom people hated in India, and capital. Therefore he was not making a case for the capitalists.

Ambedkar withdrew in the third week of November 1953 the satyagraha launched by the Scheduled Castes Federation for securing waste lands in Marathwada. He did this in view of the good response to its demands for land. About 1,700 satya-grahis were arrested, and 1,100 were released unconditionally. Ambedkar, however, expressed his regret for the action of some of the satyagrahis who had cut down trees during the agitation.

The bitter attacks on Government by Ambedkar had the desired effect, and it published in the last week of December 1953, a Bill entitled "The Untouchability (Offences) Act, 1953" and later introduced it in March 1954. The Bill aimed at rooting out untouchability and declared that the practice would be punished with jail, fine, forfeiture of the licence for a trade, profession or employment, extending its jurisdiction over citizens who were not Hindus. There was a general welcome and support for Government's proposed Bill, and Dr. Ambedkar spoke on it a few days after, making various suggestions to Government on the Bill.

II

Ambedkar's health again deteriorated, and for over two months he was under close treatment at Hotel Mirabelle in Bombay. Although bedridden, he performed the inaugural ceremony of Atre Pictures' Marathi offering. 'Mahatma Phooley' at the Famous Studios in Bombay on Sunday, January 4, 1954. Wishing success to the producer, Acharya P.K. Atre, he said: "Today everybody is after politics and films, but social service has a greater value because it builds up character. Atre's picture will reive the memory of Jotiba Phooley who was one of the greatest of our social reformers." Acharya Atre, a myriad-sided personality and winner of the President's gold medal for his film *Shyamchi Aai*, produced a brilliant picture, depicting vivid scenes in the life of Phooley and won the President's silver medal for his momentous, historic and laborious task.

On the previous Sunday, Ambedkar had inaugurated the convention of the All-India Sai Devotees at the St. Xavier's College grounds, Bombay. In his inaugural speech he said: "Our religion today has neither God nor morality. I have no doubt that this is a very degenerated state of human mind; and it is a task for the future generation to restore religion in the purer and nobler form." He added that in his day in India there was no religion except the worship of idols, whether they were of Sadhus, saints or miracle-makers. He said that in its original form religion was a matter of personal salvation of man's soul, and in its second stage it meant the maintenance of human brotherhood based on moral rules governing the conduct of human beings towards each other. In its third stage, men worshipped those personalities who satisfied the wants of their lives; and in its last stage they worshipped a person who performed miracles. The money collected in the name of saints should be utilized, he concluded, for hospitals, education, establishment of small-scale industries for the helpless, and the widows. At the outset he declared that he was not a follower of Sai Baba; nor had he any opportunity of meeting him.

In the middle of March 1954, he went to Delhi to attend the session of the Council of States. But he soon came down to Nagpur in the last week of April 1954 to contest the reserved seat in a by-election to the House of the People from the Bhandara Constituency. During his election campaign he said that because the country was going to ruin he was fighting the election so that he might give the people the other point of view from the Opposition. It would not have been difficult, he said, for him to be in Parliament if he was prepared to make a compromise with the Congress. He made a frontal attack on the Nehru Government and the leadership of Nehru. He said that Nehru's foreign policy had made India a friendless country, that Nehru had bungled the Kashmir issue and had sheltered men who were dishonest, and that India was encircled by a kind of United States of Islam on one side and on the other side there were Russia and China in a combination for the conquest of Asia to bring it under Communism.

"If you want to be effective," Dr. Ambedkar added. "then you must have guns and not mere soft speech. You must make up your mind. Do you want Parliamentary Government? This is the crux of the whole situation. If you want it, then you must be friendly with those who have Parliamentary Government and are trying to protect it against the attacks. If you do not want it, let us join with Russia and China tomorrow and make friends with them." It was, therefore, the bounden duty of the people to replace the Government which could not solve any problem although it was given a long time to prove its mettle, he concluded.

Ambedkar had been disillusioned by the rout of the Socialist candidates in the previous elections who, he said, had no roots anywhere. There were chances of their growth in the cities; but they had, in his opinion, little chance in the rural areas. And "a Party," he observed, "which has no support in rural areas has no future." The socialist programme was so unrelated to the needs of the rural people, so disturbing to the lower middle class that he could not see from where they were going to get their support. So he wanted an independent candidate to run with him for the general seat in the by-election. However, he supported Asoka Mehta's candidature as he was a better candidate. In the first week of May 1954 the by-election took place; and although Ambedkar got 1,32,483 votes he lost his seat by 8,381 votes to the Congress Harijan candidate. Asoka Mehta was, however, elected to Parliament against the Congress candidate.

On the eve of the results of this by-election, Ambedkar left by plane for Rangoon to attend Buddha Jayanti Celebrations. Before leaving Delhi for Rangoon, he wrote to his trusted colleague, K. V. Chitre: "Reports from other sources reaching here speak of my being eliminated in the by-election. This is not impossible, and I am quite prepared for it." He read the news of his defeat in a Rangoon newspaper. After staying there for nearly a fortnight, he returned to Delhi.

Ambedkar's health was no better. Still he attended the session of the Council of States. On August 26, 1954, he made a very thought-provoking speech on foreign policy and reminded the Members of the cartoon by Low in which foreign ministers of Europe were depicted as dancing and singing 'Oh ! give us peace without principles.' He said he was glad that the Prime Minister had certain principles on which he was proceeding. He observed that the foreign policy of Nehru was based on three props—one was peace; the second was co-existence between Communism and free Democracy, and the third was opposition to SEATO. And when Ambedkar said that Russia had swallowed ten European States and had annexed some territories of China, Manchuria and Korea, there was heckling by a Communist Member. Peace was being purchased, he observed, by what might be called partitioning and dismembering of countries in the world.

Referring to Russia, Ambedkar observed: "Here you have a vast country endlessly occupied in destroying other people, absorbing them within its fold on the theory that it is liberating them. The Russian liberation, so far as I can understand, is liberation followed by servitude: it is not liberation followed by freedom." "You are," he proceeded, "by this kind of peace, doing nothing more, but feeding the giant every time the giant opens his jaw and wants something."

Ambedkar, therefore, warned that Indians should bear in mind and not forget or overlook the question whether the Russians would not turn to India! He expressed his opinion that the theory that Communism and free Democracy would live together was to him, at any rate, utterly absurd; for Communism "is like a forest fire; it goes on burning and consuming anything and everything that comes in its way." Countries living in the vicinity of the forest fire stood in danger. He also pointed out that one must not forget that in the foreign policy of a country the geographical factor was one of the most important. Each country's foreign policy must vary with its geographical location. What was good for England might not be good for India. "Therefore, the co-existence," he added, "seems to me a principle which has been adopted without much thought on the part of the Prime Minister." He reminded the House how Churchill repented that they had done a great mistake, and a great wrong, in sacrificing the liberty of so many nations for the sake of winning victory against Hitler. It was the duty of the U.S.A. and Britain to liberate them; but neither country had the will or moral stamina to engage itself in such a stupendous task.

They were planning the SEATO, he said, to prevent Russia and China from making further aggression and occupying any further part of the free world. According to Ambedkar, the SEATO was not an organization for committing aggression on any country; it was an organization for the purpose of preventing further aggression on free countries. Repugnance to SEATO, he added, seemed to flow from some sort of estrangement between Nehru and the U.S.A., and also from the fear of what Russia would think if India joined the SEATO. He drew the attention of the House to the fact that India had been completely encircled on the one side by Pakistan and the other Muslim countries; and on the other side by allowing China to take possession of Lhasa. "The Prime Minister," Ambedkar continued, "has practically helped the Chinese to bring their border down to the Indian border. Looking at all these things it seems to me that it would be an act of levity not to believe that India, if it is not exposed to aggression right now, is exposed to aggression and that aggression might well be committed by people who always are in the habit of committing aggression."

The Prime Minister, Ambedkar proceeded, should not depend upon the Panchsheel accepted by Mao and recorded in the Tibet treaty of non-aggression. If Mao had any faith in the Panchsheel, which was the essential part of Buddhist religion, he certainly would treat the Buddhist in his own country in a very different way. "There is no room for Panchsheel" he observed "in politics; and secondly, not in the politics of the Communist country. The Communist countries have two well-known principles on which they always act. One is that morality is always in a flux; there is no morality. Today's morality is not tomorrow's morality. ... . Asia has been the cock-pit of war. More than half of Asia is Communist. It has adopted a different principle of life and a different principle of Government. It is therefore, better to align ourselves with what we call free nations if we believe in freedom."

"The key note of our foreign policy," he bitingly remarked, "is to solve the problems of other countries and not to solve the problems of our own country."

As regards Goa, he said that it could be annexed or purchased, or India could take Goa on lease. He was sure that a small police action on the part of the Government of India would have been quite sufficient to enable the Indians to get possession of Goa, but Nehru was only shouting against the Portuguese and doing nothing. Concluding his speech, he warned Nehru not to disregard the consequences of Chamberlain's policy of appeasement.

III

On September 6, 1954, while speaking on the report of the Commissioner for Scheduled Castes and Scheduled Tribes, Ambedkar launched a bitter attack on the Government's policy towards the Untouchables and the attitude of the caste Hindus. He was opposed to the amendment of the Constitution 'every Saturday', but he suggested amending it to bring all waste lands within the purview of the Central Government He fervently pleaded for re-imposition of the salt tax and the creation of a Gandhi Trust Fund for the uplift of the Untouchables. The fund could be utilized for resettling the Scheduled Castes on waste lands. Government should do it either by limiting land holdings and taking over excess land or through financing the purchase of land by the Scheduled Castes. The revenue from the salt tax would amount to Rs. 20 crores. "The abolition of salt tax," he observed, "was done in memory of Mr. Gandhi. I respect him. After all, Untouchables, according to all of us, were nearest and dearest to him. There is no reason why Mr. Gandhi may not bless this project from heaven."

Ambedkar, however, reiterated his charge that Nehru seemed to be not only apathetic but anti-untouchables. He added that Nehru was against organizing a conference by the Congressite Harijans; and that the Government propaganda for removal of untouchabtlity was a waste. He also pointed out to the House how C. Rajagopalachari, who had a knack of giving a pious look to an impious act, had abolished the system of sending scheduled caste students to foreign lands when he became the Education Minister in the Central Government. Dr. Katju, the Home Minister, intervened to say that probably Ambedkar was not aware that Scheduled Caste students were at that very time being sent abroad on foreign scholarships.

It seems Ambedkar was making amends for his provoked outburst against the Constitution. So whenever the Government laid its heretical hands on it, he availed himself of every opportunity to retrieve his position and to defend its stability and sanctity. At this juncture the Government moved the Constitution (Third Amendment) Bill seeking to alter an item in the legislative lists in the Seventh Schedule. The Bill sought to give legal powers to the Commerce and Industry Ministry to control production.

Ambedkar carpingly criticized the manner in which the Government was amending the Constitution from time to time without any mandate from the people. The Constitution, he observed, was four years and some months old; but within that period it had been amended twice; and that was the third amendment. He did not know of any constitution in the world which had been amended so rapidly and so rashly by the Government in office. Simply because, he charged, the Government had obtained a majority, it assumed that it had not only the power to make any law, but it also had the power to amend the Constitution without notifying their intention to the people. He said he had been noticing the great contempt and low regard and respect which the Government had for the Constitution. He wanted the Government to realize, he growled, the essential difference between constitution and law. They should treat the Constitution in a more respectful manner. This time Ambedkar hit the nail on the head squarely. His stand was upheld by leading newspapers in the country. He felt the agonies of a mother when he saw the infant Constitution being tortured and twisted to suit the passing moods, policies, plans and projects of the ruling party.

While speaking on the Untouchability Offences Bill on September 16, 1954, Ambedkar said that the evil could not be eradicated unless a minimum sentence of imprisonment was provided. He also pleaded for punishment against social boycott, which, because of their economic power, enabled the high castes in villages to prevent the exercise of their constitutional rights by the Scheduled Castes. He said that power should have been used to modify a number of State laws such as the Punjab Law which were discriminating against the Scheduled Castes and which prevented the Scheduled Caste and the lower classes even from having permanent homes. He charged the Home Ministry and the Law Ministry with laziness and said that they had neither the zeal nor the urge to move in the matter; and no idealism either. The Bill should have been named, he concluded his powerful one-hour speech, the "Civil Rights (Untouchables Protection) Act," and it would have been better if the Home Minister had specifically stated in the Bill itself that it sought to remove any kind of bar against the exercise of civil and constitutional rights by the Scheduled Castes.

On October 3, 1954, All-India Radio broadcast a speech of Dr. Ambedkar in the series "My personal philosophy." "Every man," he observed, "should have a philosophy of life, for everyone must have a standard by which to measure his conduct. And philosophy is nothing but a standard by which to measure." "Negatively, "he went on, "I reject the Hindu social philosophy propounded in the *Bhagwad Geeta* based as it is, on the *Triguna* of the Sankhya philosophy which is in my judgement a cruel perversion of the philosophy of Kapila, and which had made the caste system and the system of graded inequality the law of Hindu social life."

"Positively, my social philosophy," he continued, "may be said to be enshrined in three words: liberty, equality and fraternity. Let no one however say that I have borrowed my philosophy from the French Revolution. I have not. My philosophy has roots in religion and not in political science. I have derived them from the teachings of my master, the Buddha." In his philosophy, liberty and equality had a place; but he added that unlimited liberty destroyed equality, and absolute equality left no room for liberty. In his philosophy, law had a place only as a safeguard against the breaches of liberty and equality; but he did not believe that law can be a guarantee for breaches of liberty or equality. He gave the highest place to fraternity as the only real safeguard against the denial of liberty or equality or fraternity—which was another name for brotherhood or humanity, which was again another name for religion.

"Law is secular," he proceeded, "which anybody may break while fraternity or religion is sacred which everybody must respect. My philosophy has a mission. I have to do the work of conversion; for, I have to make the followers of Triguna theory to give it up and accept mine. Indians today are governed by two different ideologies. Their political ideal set out in the preamble to the Constitution affirms a life of liberty, equality and fraternity. Their social ideal embodied in their religion denies them." He profoundly believed that what was political ideal for most Indians would become a social ideal for all. A Muslim graduate of Aligarh University, appreciating his speech, praised him for pointing out the contradiction in the social and religious philosophy of the majority of the people.

On October 29, 1954, Ambedkar was presented with a purse for Rs, 1,18,000 by members of the Bombay City Scheduled Castes Federation. It had sometime back formed a committee to make preparations for the celebration of his Diamond Jubilee, which should have been celebrated on April 14, 1951. The presentation was made by R. D. Bhandare, President of the Scheduled Castes Federation, Bombay.

Dr. Ambedkar promised his men that he would utilize the money to meet the cost of a building which was being built at Dadar to house a hall and a library. He declared that he would soon write his autobiography and said he believed in humility, character and knowledge. He was proud to have been born an untouchable; and whatever he had achieved was entirely due to the strength of his community.

❏❏❏

CHAPTER 25

OLD AGE

AMBEDKAR was now sixty-three. His weak constitution could not cope with the rebellious surge in his brains to wrest and wring from the Constitution the good he expected for his people who were landless, shirtless, shoeless and hungry. He was painfully conscious of the fact that his hopes about a better future for his people remained largely unfulfilled. Opinions may differ on his frequent volcanic attacks, but it would be unrealistic to say that Ambedkar was crying wolf too often. The gravamen of his charges against the Government was that it did not show initiative and imagination in social and economic matters pertaining to the landless people; nor did it foresee the seriousness of the threat to national peace and Indian democracy which their problem implied.

What did Ambedkar achieve for the Untouchables? The story of the past life of the Scheduled Caste Hindus was pitch dark. The fate of those sixty million people was more insufferable than that of the Negroes in that the Negroes were not regarded as Untouchables. At least the Negroes could be servants in the whitemen's houses. It is no exaggeration to say that the fate of the Israelites in Egypt, or the life of the Negroes in America or the condition of the Jews in Germany was better than the life of Scheduled Castes in India, their own land.

It was for the first time in the history of the past twenty-five hundred years that the sun of a better future arose on their horizon. Ambedkar, the son of their soil, their kith and kin, focussed the world attention on their civic, social and political rights and liberties, made untouchability a burning topic of the day, raised it to an international importance, and gave it a global publicity. His ceaseless hard struggle and his merciless hammer forced an opening for them, and inaugurated an era of light and liberty. He awakened in them a sense of human dignity, a feeling of self-respect and a burning hatred of untouchability that was worse than slavery. He pulled them out of slough and exorcised

461

despondency and despair from their minds. He infused courage and new life into their demoralized and dehumanized cells. He gave them their soul and reimbued them with a spirit which enabled them to voice their grievances, and to stand up for justice, equality and liberty. Before the rise of his leadership they were treated worse than animals. His heroic struggle raised them to political equality with other communities in India. What is more, his volcanic struggle shattered the hopes of Missionaries and Moulavies, barring the Communists from organizing these poverty-stricken masses for their own political ends. This is what he did for the Untouchables.

The night of shame and despair in India had passed. Old dilapidated walls were crumbling down. A new India was dawning at the foot of the Himalayas. The Untouchables were emerging from the dust. Their men were being gradually planted in administration, the police, courts, army, navy and the air force. Their progress over these past few years was not less encouraging. In their own way they also improved their habiliments, habits and sanitary conditions. Politically they were now fully conscious. They did not depend upon others for guidance and leadership. Their organizers conducted big conferences and vast meetings, and their leaders have established institutions of considerable importance. But it was unfortunate that most of those men who rose from amongst the Scheduled Castes turned their back upon them. They tried to become second-class Brahmins.

Yet it was an indisputable fact that the Scheduled Castes still suffered social and economic hardships and land and legal impediments in rural areas. These lowest of the low felt that the Government, which flooded the world with delegations and missions, had not taken seriously to the problem to remove their ills in villages, to redeem their life from village serfdom and economic morass, and to rehabilitate them as normal human beings. They wanted all the State Governments to adopt a bold and radical agrarian policy. Sensible men felt that land should be given to these landless people, the sons of the soil, on the basis of assessment. They must find boarding and lodging in Hindu hotels and hostels, and any breach on this count should be treated as a crime, so that the owners of those hotels and hostels might not shun them on excuses of their invention. They should be provided with drinking-water facilities in villages. Lack of water was one of the most painful things in their life in villages.

Research scholars observed that their housing conditions- their small huts made of tin or coconut leaves and mud were crowded with families—had a direct bearing on their morals and health. Their separate localities should be abolished and families should be accommodated in city plots. Although all public services should go according to merit, promotions in mills, factories and railways should not be denied to them under any pretext. The reservation of percentage in services prescribed for them by the Constitution should be rigidly implemented by Government. In villages and cities they suffered from desperate poverty. Grinding poverty dragged them into the ranks of beggars. It made them vulnerable to the feelings of decency, self-respect and possible victims to conversion. When they had no rags to cover their shame with and had no clothes to wash, men enjoying all material benefits of civilization strangely enough murmured of their dirty clothes!

The disease, however, was being cured. It was disappearing gradually. But no sensible Hindu would pretend that the Untouchable was out of it. Caste, of which untouchability was the perverted outcome, was decaying, but it was not dead. Those who indifferently shelved the problem and shrank from responsibilities would do well to remember the words of a Negro girl, who, when asked to suggest a fitting punishment for Hitler, replied: "Make him black and make him live in America!" The one leader in a liberated India who unceasingly cried for the speedy abolition of untouchability was Veer Savarkar. He was continually warning the Hindus that if they did not bury the gasping untouchability and lift the curse, it would reappear and ruin the land. To him abolition of untouchability was more than winning a major war for the country.

The view expressed by Ambedkar's opponents that the economic problem of the Scheduled Castes was bound up with the larger issue of poverty and employment was not fair. It was dangerous to postpone the issue assuming that once poverty was abolished untouchability would disappear. It was also felt that to bury the ghost of untouchability both economic and social regeneration programme must be taken up simultaneously. The Government should even inflict a punitive tax upon villages which would not act up to its laws in this respect. Government should help the social reformers materially and substantially.

The Indian Government should take a cue from a speech of Dr. J. H. Holmes of the U.S.A. who once said in Bombay: "We have our own untouchables exactly as you have them here. They number over 14 millions." And slavery was said to have been abolished under the Constitution of the U.S.A. some decades ago! The Indian Government should have taken a lesson from the appeal made by Clarence Mitchel, Director of a Negro Institution, to the Secretary of Defence of the U.S.A., demanding an end of segregation of Negro children in schools on army posts. The rebuffs and rebukes by Malan were too illustrative. It was a great pity, the leaders of the Scheduled Castes maintained that the rulers who filled their imaginations with the pictures of world affairs, were not giving a moment's thought to the condition of the down-trodden who numbered about 60 million in their own country. They rightly felt that the Government should lighten their age-long burden instead of lighting the towns and sub-towns.

II

The mission of Ambedkar's life was the establishment of human dignity, development of self-respect among the downtrodden classes, and attainment of self-salvation. In a word, it was man-making! Ambedkar was a great teacher who taught the common man to have belief in his potential power, to rouse it up, to develop it, and to stand on his own feet. Man should not think that he was a mere nobody, that he was good for nothing and that he was a helpless log.

His advice to the down-trodden classes, and especially to young men, was exemplary. He asked them to rely on their self, on their own efforts, to trust and exercise their own intelligence and to seek refuge in reason. To him nothing was more sacred than learning. Nature made none a slave. No man was born a dullard. He recalled to students the glorious traditions and untiring industry, high aims and high sense of public life of Ranade, Tilak and Gokhale. He related to his people the story from the Greek mythology of the Godless Demeter who tried to develop superman's power in a child by keeping it on fire every day.

His message to his people was that they should strive endlessly, sacrifice the present pleasures for a great future and should go through the ordeal of fire and sacrifice till they attained their goal. "You must have a firm belief in the sacredness of your goal. Noble is your aim and sublime and glorious is your mission. Blessed are those who are awakened to their duty to those among whom they are born. Glory to those who devote their time, talents and their all to the annihilation of slavery. Glory to those who would keep on their struggle for the liberation of the enslaved in spite of heavy odds, carping humiliations, storms, and dangers till the down-trodden secure their human rights."

Ambedkar, therefore, did not like that his hungry men should envelop themselves in the coils of *Bhakti*, the cult of devotion, the opium of helplessness. He asked the common man not to resign himself to his fate and accept his position as a divine dispensation. The ignorant people believed that their fate was pre-appointed and irretrievable. Ambedkar wanted to root out this disease from their minds. Like Vivekananda, he told them that it was sentimental nonsense which made them impotent. For *Bhakti* made their nerves soft, delicate and yielding.

Ambedkar tried to divert the minds of the down trodden from the thought of life after death to their present life of degradation. He wanted them to enjoy material amenities and to bring themselves up to the cultural level of the majority. This was an antidote to the demoralized and dehumanized minds of the Scheduled Castes people who had been made to accept their position as a divine dispensation. At the same time, to the more advanced men and societies he softly warned that material comfort is by no means the solvent of all human ills. Man does not live by bread alone. He is a cultural being.

That is why thinking people regarded the life of Ambedkar, who was one of the greatest Protestant Hindu leaders of modern India, as a phase in the renaissance of Hinduism and in the reorganization of Hindu social order. The first renaissance of Hinduism was inaugurated by the Upanishads with their stream of new thoughts when the gods, priests and sacrifices receded into the background. With the resurgence of orthodox priests and ideas of sacrifices, decadence set in again with added vigour. At this time the Buddha came forward to rejuvenate and reorganize the social and religious systems of the Hindus. He attacked the priestcraft, the institution of sacrifice and stood for the abolition of the ramifications in society.

With the rise of Shankaracharya Hinduism slyly absorbed Buddhistic principles, but tightened its hold on the caste system and karmakand. Then came another revival with the spiritual teachings of Ramanuja, Chakradhar, Kabir, Ramanand, Nanak, Chaitanya, Namdeo and other saint-poets of Maharashtra. The fourth phase began with the rise of Ram Mohan Roy, Phooley, Ranade, Dayananda and Vivekananda carried forward by Savarkar on a rationalistic basis. Gandhi's contribution was more of a humanitarian nature than a social one.

Ambedkar's movement saw the fifth phase of the renaissance of Hinduism and reorganization of the Hindu social order. His revolt against Hinduism and Hindu society was volcanic, and varies from the revolts inaugurated by revolutionaries from the Buddha to Veer Savarkar; for Ambedkar was the first great revolutionary leader who rose for the first time from among the oppressed people during the history of over two thousand years of their slavery. He started not only a war against Hinduism and Hindu social order but also a mental revolution unprecedented in the history of Hinduism, to purify and revolutionize Hinduism, to reorganize and revitalize Hindu society and to save it from decadence and degradation. His contribution, therefore, to Hinduism and to Hindustan will be considered greater than that of most of the modern Hindu leaders like Ram Mohan Roy, Dayananda and Vivekananda; for, unlike them, he has contributed to the constitutional and political thought and development of this country.

Ambedkar wanted reorganization of the Hindu social order on the basis of liberty, equality and fraternity. In other words, on the basis of social equality and democracy. He demanded liberation of Hindu society from casteism and priestcraft. If the Hindus acted up to his principles, they would be a free people, a living, movable race, a moving society. According to his social philosophy, every Hindu must have the liberty to associate in all

legitimate ways with his co-religionists. The Hindus must build
a common Social Code. If they had the freedom to marry among
themselves, to dine together, to work together in all spheres of
life, they would become a united people, and would have the
ability to grow and to assimilate new members in their fold.
Ambedkar was for one national language, the Hindi: one common
script, the Nagari. He expected all classes to do their own
thinking. It was not good for them to leave thinking to a certain
section of the society which called itself the custodian of
knowledge. They should develop the ability to think over the
problems which affected their destiny, religion and country.

Thus his social philosophy appealed to the Hindus to liberate
Hinduism and solidify Hindu society, and to revitalize the Hindu
thought and abolish the caste system and the touch-me-not-ism.
Indeed his emphasis on the abolition of the caste system was so
great that like Karf Marx, who sent the expression class struggle
resounding throughout the world, Ambedkar sent the expression
caste system reverberating throughout the world. It is, therefore,
clear that his was the cause of Hindu society, the cause of the
country, the cause of humanity. The service rendered to the
Scheduled Caste Hindus was service rendered to the cause of
the poorest of the poor in the world.

Ill

The evening of life added lustre to the serenity and grandeur
of Ambedkar s personality. Solid, massive, grave and dynamic,
Ambedkar was a thick-set man with an oval face having a fierce
air round it and a bald dome. He was five feet seven inches tall
and weighed about one hundred and eighty pounds. His majestic
forehead was an index to the height of his ambition for which
even the highest position in the land, he said, would be unequal.
His protruding, defying chin indicated the superb courage that
saw a task through even though the heavens fell. It had a will to
suspend the whole hate of bell on its bend. The challenging nose
stood like a rudder to the ship of a stormy life. His eyes were
penetrating and animated, but had a certain look of scepticism.
But when he was enraged, through his penetrating eyes looked
the bitterness of all ages and through his lips passed the embers
of an Untouchable's hate. He was a Jamadagni. Yet when he was

in a brighter mood, his face shone like a light-house. They who
have light in themselves do not revolve as satellites.

By temperament Ambedkar was cyclonic. At the least
provocation he flew into anger. A slight change in the order
of his books on the table irritated him, and he would roar :
"Where are the papers, the books? Who has removed them?"
The Doctor wife and his servants took fright. Then somebody,
entered the room slowly and asked him what he meant by
papers. "Is it a book or a note-book? What colour is it and
what size?" Then a running search followed till the book or
the note-book was found, and when it was produced before
him, he would ejaculate: "Oh! that is it. Where was it?"' The
next moment his anger cooled down.

It will not be far from truth if one says that Ambedkar was
not a man of the family. He called himself *asang*, unfit for
familiarity. Constant tours, continuous study and public
appointments keep a great leader engrossed all the time.
Naturally to his family also he comes to be a leader. Ambedkar,
too, came to be a leader to his son and nephew; so much so that
he did not attend the marriage ceremony of his only son. His
wife, Mrs. Savita Ambedkar, however, graciously attended it.

The fierce air around Ambedkar's face and his
industrious life were unfavourable for familiarity. There
might be none around him who did not suffer rebukes at his
hands at some time or other. Some eminent men described
him as a British Bulldog, and Sarojini Naidu called him
Mussolini. His ability, integrity, great learning and untold
sacrifice inspired devotion and confidence. Yet his imperious
life was like an empire which had lost many cities under the
debris of forgetfulness and neglect.

No doubt Ambedkar manifested interest in the welfare of
those who stood by him or were loyal to his cause; but he did not
show enthusiastic familiarity with or admiration for anybody.
His opponents were never generous to him although they showed
a sort of *rapprochement;* so he also was not generous to them.

His truthfulness was shattering. He was harsh like truth.
Like all great men, he was a dynamo of energy and used time
sparingly. He had the vision of the Buddha; but humility was
not conspicuous among his merits. No one had ever accused him

of it. His proud self-confidence often verged on boastfulness. But the opinion he expressed about his merits he justified by the great service he rendered to the nation. No wonder then that he responded to the new way of expressing greeting introduced by his followers, by repeating 'Jai Bhim' to their salutation at the end of his letters.

It is said that the higher one rises, the more isolated one becomes. Although this was true of Ambedkar, in his relaxed mood he talked endlessly. His talks gave his visitors both entertainment and arguments. He laughed the loudest when he had a dig at somebody, and his laughter drowned even the retort of his victim. Clad in a lungi and a shirt, he then radiated joy and laughter. Besides a strong sense of humour, he had an irresistible taste for country jokes and country idioms. They were all hard, rude, crude, grinding and rollicking. The hearers held their sides and revelled in his quips. His humour was caustic, and often verged on rudeness which might be a legacy of the underworld in which he passed his early life. And the relieving feature of it was that one got more jokes from him in one hour than one got from all other politicians in five years. But there were lightnings more often than sunshine.

That jovial and communicative mood was gradually wearing out with his delicate health. In the evening of life he had assumed the grandeur of a colourful potentate. Before he came out to meet the visitors announcements were made that he was ready. He wore sometimes tight pyjamas and a kurta with embroidery on it; he reclining in a chair, his attendants busy adjusting cushions on which he rested his legs, and the waiting crowd whispering outside.

The sweetest nuts are in the hardest shells. Though grave and fierce in appearance, Ambedkar was a fountain of emotions. The pathos of a picture made him abandon a show in the middle. When his pet dog fell ill, he inquired after its health, personally visiting the hospital twice a day; and when news came to him that the poor dog had laid its bones, he rolled in his chair like a bereaved mother, the messenger curbing his laughter with much difficulty! Once a poor woman knocked his door at two in the morning and bewailed that for nearly twelve hours she had tried to get her dying husband admitted to a certain hospital, but to no purpose. Ambedkar took her into his car, drove to the hospital and got him admitted. Then at four in the morning he shouted at his friend Acharya M. V. Donde, who resided near the hospital, and called for tea. He gave advice free on several occasions and conducted free of charge several cases wherein the interests of the poor were at stake.

When his youngest son died. Ambedkar was so much overwhelmed with grief that he would not part with the dead body; and for days together he would not enter the room wherein his son had breathed his last. When his first wife went the way all life must go, his grief knew no bounds. He writhed with grief. He once suffered terribly from eyesore and burst into tears at the thought of losing his sight which, he said, would make life impossible for him. At the last glimpse of the dead body of a colleague be wept piteously at the cremation grounds.

In his otherwise busy, engrossed and stormy life, Ambedkar found time in his old age to hear music for which he had a liking. It was his opinion that every man should love harmony in music and beauty in art. In the evening of his life he took lessons in playing the violin. Like Prime Minister Churchill, he drew pictures and was tickled when the servants told him that the drawings were full of life! But the artist and painter in Ambedkar had to be shrewdly wooed into that mood by his servants when the Doctor wife and they thought that the Saheb was not leaving books for days together. Nice pictures and beautiful specimen of architecture had an attraction for him. He complained that in India appreciation of art was confined to casteism. A man must be born into a caste which followed a certain art. Art suffered, he observed, because man could not follow his bent.

Ambedkar's house was not a detached villa that gave you an appearance of seclusion. His vast library, his rich clothes, his enormous pens, his grand car, the numerous varieties of shoes and boots and the rare collection of pictures were not a mere expression of diversion, but were the living marks of his conquering personality that marched on removing all obstacles till he felt he had secured all that he was capable of winning in the world in which he lived. Those fine, rich and rare articles illustrated not the disinterestedness but the march of a great mind determined to show its superiority;

splendour, power and knowledge. They were the marks left behind on the path of life by a man who had for many years lived under a starvation line and in squalor, and who was shown out of saloons, was kicked out of carts, was ousted from hotels and was ostracized in colleges, courts and offices and yet had vowed to sleep in the shade of bank notes.

Big and varied types of fountain pens had an irresistible fascination for Ambedkar. Rich dress and the best cut interested him. It seemed he took a secret joy in making himself as large as possible. Yet in all other aspects of life, thrift, which was the child of hard early life, had a strange control over him. He did not smoke. He was a thorough teetotaller.

The bookworm in Ambedkar had no time for social life. Once in a great while he went to the pictures. *Uncle Tom* he saw in the company of his first wife. *Achhyut Kanya*, a film based on the life of Untouchables, he witnessed with peculiar emotion in his eyes. In the company of his Doctor wife he saw *Oliver Twist.* The life of the underdog, the poor, the suppressed gave him a throb. In his boyhood he played cricket and when his first wife had been to Dharwar for a change of air, there he played cricket with the boys of the hostel which he was then conducting for the students of Depressed Classes. In the early twenties he enjoyed the game of cards and sometimes had a round of bridge with great interest, and had a daily bathe in the sea, both as a diversion and an exercise.

Though an expert cook, Ambedkar never insisted on any particular dish. At times he took his meal in his library. When he was angry with the members of his family, he remained still like a statue, without words, without food. He then murmured that he was not a man to be associated with. Long years of strenuous struggle, the cares of the down-trodden, the maladies he suffered from and the perils which beset his way, did not leave their marks on his radiant face. He suffered for some time from appendicitis and had blood pressure. But in his declining years diabetes marred his health. His body seemed to have yielded to it; but his will was unbent. His wonderful faculties were very little impaired. Early in 1954 he underwent an electric treatment for his legs which were now unable to prop the heavy burden. With the support of a walking stick, or throwing his arm on the shoulder of his private honorary secretary or bearer, he trudged on.

His handwriting had an elegant style which indicated firmness, clarity and display. He loved fine dogs and would bring one from the farthest corner of the country if his eyes fell on a charming breed.

To visit Ambedkar was to visit a speaking museum. His conversation was illuminating, enhancing, vigorous and communicative. His talk ranged over many subjects which were stored in his prodigious mental museum. He gave his listener a ride through the dark ages with the lamp of history, and took him to the Pamir, the roof of the world, where his listener got a bird's-eye-view of the world. Ambedkar gave him an interpretation of the past, revealed the significance of mythology and explained the ancient and modern philosophies, creeds and doctrines. The fascination was simply unfailing. The listener enjoyed the contact with one of the greatest minds of our age.

Before his appointment as Labour Member, Ambedkar did not have a regular routine. In those days he got up early in the morning, or after reading the whole night, he slept from dawn to morning and took a little exercise, his bath and then breakfast. After the newspaper reading, he took his meal and went to the court in his car, looking hurriedly into a new book which came by the morning post. Sometimes he ate lunch at noon in a hotel if he had a case in the court. After the court business was over, he had a round in book-stalls and returned home with a heap of new books; or on his way back rarely he visited the house of an acquaintance from whom he wanted to seize a rare book. Then dinner in a nook with a book; and then followed the endless reading.

When Ambedkar was engrossed in reading he had no time to talk with his visitor, or to take his dinner if he had not taken it, or to get angry with anybody. He would have a glance at his visitor and would lose himself in the book. The visitor waited, felt embarrassed and realised that it was a sin to disturb his deep concentration and profound contemplation. So he would come downstairs and leave the place. Alexandre Dumas, the author of *The Three Musketeers*, held out his hand in greeting a friend who dropped in but went on scribbling

with his right hand! Ambedkar did no such thing. At such a
time he did not move even his eyelid. Before retiring he took
a glass of milk. After his second marriage, his Doctor wife
tried to enforce rigid regularity in his routine; but she must
have found the case almost impossible.

The time factor was a legend that revolved round
Ambedkar's name. None could encroach upon his time. To
Napoleon time was everything. To a business magnate time is
money, but to Ambedkar time was knowledge. Two great Indians
of our age utilized every moment of their life as life's greatest
treasure. They were Gandhi and Ambedkar. They knew the
meaning of a moment. To them time was a precious gold mine.
Ambedkar was one of those few men of our age who with resolute
purpose, patient industry and careful economy of time acquired
knowledge and developed capacity for work for which ordinary
men would require ten births. To Ambedkar love of books was
the greatest means of education and self-development, and the
highest type of recreation and enjoyment. Ambedkar never read
for amusement. "What instructs me," he observed, " amuses me."

Company of books gave Ambedkar supreme joy of life and
serious aloofness. As stated above, the reading continued after
dinner. Night disappeared, morning arrived, buzzing in the half-
awakened buildings nearby began; still the scholar was at one
with the world's great minds and the great thinkers of all ages,
who were his spiritual ancestors. The dog Peter went to his feet
to receive his morning palling, and the scholar knew that it was
morning. Ambedkar the scholar desired to be away from the clang
of the bell, clatter of the carts, stroke of the hammer and
splulterings of the cars. His motto was *ancora Imparo*. His thirst
for knowledge was that of an empire. His ultimate hope was to
sit conversing with the great thinkers and law givers of all ages
in a library built in a dense forest! Was this a search for divine
light or for probing the secrets of human heart, pride, justice
and selfishness?

Jefferson said that his first love was literary pursuits. Tilak,
the first mass leader of modern India, too, said that he would be
a professor of Mathematics in a free India. Great men are
sometimes pushed into the vortex of politics by their sense of
justice and love of liberty; and at the first opportunity they turn

their back upon the tumult of the daily life and seek refuge in knowledge. The cause of the Indian Independence pushed Tilak into politics. The cause of the Untouchables drove Ambedkar into politics. Otherwise Ambedkar would not have cared to see the inside of a Legislative Assembly. He would have been a savant, a seer, a Dnyaneshwar. Thanks to the Baroda officers and peons who inflicted insults on Ambedkar; otherwise Indian politics and the world problem of slavery would have been deprived of a mighty and colourful personality and a saviour.

Goethe said we know accurately when we know little; for with knowledge our doubts increase. Ambedkar knew accurately only when he knew more. He had no flash of a Savarkar or of a Nehru. But when he proved his point, he quoted one after another all the great thinkers on that particular topic to support his point, and he became supreme, irresistible and invincible. Johnson seldom went through a book from cover to cover; neither did he believe that anyone did it. But Ambedkar could recollect and describe the colour and the chapter of a book that he had read. Ambedkar's thirst for books was ever growing and flowing like the ever-flowing Ganges, He had purchased thousands of books and had collected some rare books. Pandit M. Malaviya, had once offered him two lakhs of rupees for his library. Ambedkar declined the offer saying that if he lost his library he would lose his life. But like Dr. Johnson, Dr. Ambedkar was not a good man, it was said, to lend books to.

Nobody was allowed to touch any book in Ambedkar's library. He once said that if ever owing to any misfortune a bailiff came to take possession of his library, he would kill him on the spot before he touched the first book. Books were the breath of his life. Cicero said he would give up all to live among books. Gibbon said he would not exchange his book-love for the treasures of India. Macaulay said he would not be a king if he would not be allowed to read books. Sir Walter Scott burst into tears as he bade his lifelong friends on the bookshelves a sorrowful farewell. Ambedkar bitterly wept at the thought of losing his eyesight; for then life would be meaningless. He said that he would put an end to his life if he lost his eyesight.

Great was his joy whenever he wrote a book. When he saw his thoughts printed in a book, he got heavenly joy. A new book born of his brains gave him greater joy than the birth of four children. Jefferson sold his library to the U.S. Government to be able to pay his debts. Ambedkar parted with his magniftcient library for the use of Siddharth College, on irresistible appeals from the People's Education Society which paid him almost half the price Birla had offered for the priceless collection. Thereafter the purchase of books went on as usual, and another library sprang up at 26 Alipore Road, Delhi.

IV

All that is great in men comes through labour. "You have no idea of my sufferings and labour; you would have been wiped out," said Ambedkar to one journalist. Pursuit of an ideal gives a man driving power and a splendid moral heroism. All his life Ambedkar laboured to develop his powers and devoted them to the release of his people from bondage. It was the breath of his nostrils and the fire in his blood. To that end he directed all his knowledge, all his capacity, all his happiness and all his exertions. He was a queer combination of a thinker who loved action, and a profound scholar who was a man of affairs. Action without knowledge is blind. But Ambedkar was a man of reflection as well as action. He made a stir in the world of letters and politics as well. He possessed a wonderful store of knowledge and had a vast field of experience and observation.

Three personalities influenced the life and actions of this great man. Besides the stories from the *Mahabharata* and *Ramayana*, which he heard with rapt attention in his childhood, the life of the Buddha, the teachings of Kabir and the struggle of Phooley contributed tremendously to the building of his personality. These personalities gave him his soul force, and Western education gave him his weapons.

By the combination of idealism and practical life, by knowledge and experience, Ambedkar belonged to the race of Ranade, Bhandarkar, Tilak and Telang who unfurled the Indian flag of learning in the world of learning and research. They were leaders in whom learning was happily blended with life. Tagore's *Gitanjali*, Raman's Rays, Prafulla Chandra Ray's researchers into Science, Bose's researches into Plant Physiology and

Radhakrishnan's Philosophy adorned the world and made it richer. But that was a different order. Ambedkar was the last link of the batch of the scholar-politician, the type that was living out in India and making politics poorer. The lawyer-politician type of Sapru, Jayakar and Sastri held for a time its own; but now the action-politicians in alliance with the dividend-politicians were capturing the field.

Yet Ambedkar had one more advantage over the scholar-politicians save Tilak. Ambedkar led a stormy political life, launched political struggles and passive resistance movements and was in the firing line when it was necessary. To him life did not consist in recklessly running into fire. He faced cruel attacks and returned merciless blows. But when? When he was forced out; when he felt that the cause of the Scheduled Castes was likely to go by default and when he was baited out from his books. When he was awakened from his eternal talk with the great ones of the world, ancient and modern, and compelled to art, in a moment he knew how to begin the fight and he thundered and, like the Colossus Bheem, threw thunderbolts into the camps of his opponents. That is why he was rated among the best brains, was regarded as one of the dozen most astonishing men and one of the bravest sons of India. Some rated him among the best brains of the world. Indeed, he was a giant, a Gulliver among Lilliputians. When one thought of Ambedkar, one thought of a Colossus and an enormous repository of knowledge! He was the son of India who would equal any mighty man of his age in learning and politics. Those who boasted of their erudition and acquirement in politics returned humbled and bowed, after one visit to Rajgriha, measuring the light of their lamp in the light of the eternal *Dnyana Yadnya*.

Ambedkar was a powerful speaker both on the platform and in Parliament. Galvanic and embarrassingly brutal to a fault in his speech, he showered a fusillade of pistol shots at his opponents. He had not the oratory of Burke. Simple, direct and trenchant, his speech had a charm of its own. Its fearlessness was sharpened by a vast confidence and experience which he had attained by his ceaseless study. What he told he believed, was gospel truth and those whom it hit decried its vehemence and violence as insolence par excellence.

Like all positive men of character and mission, Ambedkar had his idolaters and detractors. He had a reputation for great personal integrity and fearless intellectual honesty. Yet it was a fact that he paid bills stintingly. Whenever a party approached him to settle up the accounts, he would complain that the payment had already been made. Sometimes there was some truth in what he said; more often than not, the fault lying either with the manner of payment or the surroundings. Though he led an immaculate public life, he had his detractors. Every iconoclast breaks the idols of the previous generations and sits in the temple himself. The Buddha was an iconoclast, and he was afterwards idolized and worshipped as an incarnation. Ambedkar's word was law to his people. To them his words were gospel truth. They idolized him and every year they took out processions with his pictures in palanquins on the occasion of his birthday. His birthday was celebrated with devotion and belief like the anniversaries of Rama, Krishna, the Buddha, Tilak, Gandhi, Savarkar and Nehru.

Ambedkar's hold over his people was unshakable. One example will bear out this remark. When he prohibited his people from worshipping Hindu gods, for a time they obeyed him literally. But custom and tradition are ingrained in blood and are not easily uprooted. Ignorance aggravates the fears of the people. So after a while the fear of God got the upper hand, and a majority of them stealthily reverted to their old forms of worship. An old devout man went to his 'Babasaheb' and entreated him to allow him to bring the image of Ganapati, the Hindu god, so that he might fulfil his vow which he had made to God. Ambedkar smiled at the guileless heart of the old man and said to him in a loud voice: "Who told you that I do not believe in God? " "Go! do as you like," was the reply. And then the old man fulfilled his vow. Another example. A Congress Minister provided one of Ambedkar's followers with the post of a watchman. The son of the job-seeker scolded his father for having gone over to the opponents of Babasaheb for bread and shelter. The old man went to the minister and with a break in his voice told him about his inability to accept the job as, according to him, acceptance of a post in that begging attitude would mean disloyalty to their "Raja" Ambedkar.

One striking feature about Ambedkar was his marvellous combination of obstinacy and resilience and his ability to seize an opportunity by the forelock which quality succeeds in politics. It was resilience and not expediency that made him shed his obstinacy without compromising his stand or conscience. He was shrewd enough to know that dawn does not come twice to awaken a man. He had the gift of catching the ball as it bounced. In his early twenties he impressed upon the mind of his father's friend the importance of Shakespeare's immortal lines: "There is a tide in the affairs of men, which, taken at the flood, leads on to fortune." His co-operation with the Simon Commission brought out the star in him in the political sky. His tremendous conscientious work at the R.T.C. in the constitution-making brought forth the constitutionalist in him. The Executive Councillorship gave him a chance to show his abiding interest in the betterment of the conditions of labour problem, and he gained varied experience as an administrator; lastly, the labour he undertook and the ability which he showed as the Chief Architect of the Constitution of India crowned his work as a constitutional authority of world fame, showing what an untouchable Hindu could do and how he could vie with the best brains of the world. Self-made and self-raised Ambedkar's morning of life was dusty, noon bright and evening golden as a matter of course.

Ambedkar did not accept the Geeta at all. To him it was an irresponsible book on ethics, a compromise of all errors. He believed in the necessity for religion. He said that a poor man mad with hunger did not resort to theft not because he feared the legal consequences, but because of the healthy pressure his religion exercised over his mind. He held that religion had a direct connection with the heart; and laws, with reason. In life, emotion played a predominant part. Hence the importance of religion in the building of man. He often said that whatever good points he had in him they were the fruit of religion.

He believed in God in the sense that some unknown power might be influencing the human destiny. This faith in the unknown power he expressed on many occasions. One day while passing over a bridge in the countryside, his motor car was about to fall into the river below. The front wheels were hanging in the air above the water, and the hind wheels were stopped by a large stone underneath and the car itself was swinging like a pendulum. Quick as flash Ambedkar and his driver rushed out of the car and stood outside stupified! Ambedkar prayed to the heavens for his rescue. On his return home in Bombay, he called his son and nephew and held them to his bosom and said it was a freak of destiny and the blessings of heavens that had saved his life. And he wept like a child! He was sceptical of the sincerity of the man who boasted that he had no faith in God and no belief in religion. This was a paradox for the Socialists who were toadying him in politics and a poser to the followers of godless Buddhism. This faith in God he, however, unified, since he took active interest in the revival of Buddhism, with the worship of the image of the Buddha before which he knelt and said prayers morning and evening. Some times he devoutly said that he would say his prayers to the Buddha if things took shape as he wished.

As a frontrank leader, Ambedkar kept himself away from the controversies over provincialism. But when points came up for discussion, he proudly said in his characteristic frankness that Maharashtrians never acted as traitors to the country and cited the exemplary behaviour of the patriotic Maharashtrian students in London. In that vein he also said that Maharashtrians would be the last people to be frightened by the threat of the proposed Pakistan because they had once in their living past routed the Muslim forces in battlefield after battlefield. None was so emphatic as Ambedkar over the question of a separate Maharashtra State with Bombay as its inseparable part; and he asked Maharashtrians not to budge an inch from that stand.

Ambedkar was a leader of the masses. The Liberal statesmen influenced the upper classes. Tilak was the first leader of modern India who influenced the middle class and spread his influence over the masses. Gandhi moved the masses and Ambedkar moved the lower strata of society. Ambedkar had travelled endlessly throughout the land, and like Tilak, Gandhi, Nehru, Savarkar and Subhas Bose, had his say before the people. Ambedkar belonged to the type of men who are born with a mission. He represented more a cause than an organization. He said a leader should not pander to the whims of the people. He was a leader who placed courageously before the people the true path of salvation.

Such a type of leadership generates magnetism, but is more related to the cause than to the organization.

Ambedkar did not try to organize his political party on modern lines. He had no taste for individual organization. There were no regular annual conferences, or general meetings of the organizations with which he was connected. Where and when he sat was the venue of conference and the time for decision. The President or the Secretary or the Working Committee had to fall in line with his arrangement. His followers were attracted to him by his integrity, ability, sacrifice and learning. The formation of caucuses, the manufactured eulogies of the Press and the craftiness of playing one leader against another had no appeal for him. When he wanted his people to assemble under his hammer, he simply gave them a clarion call, and the organisation sprang up like the crop in the rainy season. In summer there would be nothing in the field; the banner resting in his study corner and the people at home.

◻◻◻

CHAPTER 26

REVIVAL OF BUDDHISM

So in the last phase of his life, Dr. Ambedkar made a great resolve to raise the banner of Buddhism and bring back to his motherland the Buddha who had suffered an exile for over twelve hundred years. He unfurled the banner, and his people marched. Thus began the last phase of the war.

In the early days of December 1954, Ambedkar went to Rangoon to attend the third Buddhist World Conference. His wife and his personal attendant S. V. Savadkar accompanied him. His health had not improved; still he addressed the Conference. A few minutes before his speech, he was seen visibly moved; tears streamed down his cheeks. He was moved intellectually, psychologically and spiritually. But as his speech proceeded, his face brightened. He cast a spell on the Conference with his thought-provoking views on the mission and propagation of Buddhism. He said that Ceylon and Burma were in the forefront of Buddhist countries. He felt, however, that a lot of money was squandered on decoration during celebrations of Buddhist religious festivities. Grandeur had no place in Buddhism. The Burmese and Ceylonese Buddhists should spend that money on the revival and propagation of Buddhism in other countries. Ambedkar, a man of provocative learning, challenged opponents of Buddhism to hold discussions with him, and he was confident that he would defeat all pandits. Buddhism had far-reaching effects on Hinduism, and cow protection was a victory of the Buddhist principle of non-violence, he added.

Ambedkar also declared that he would propagate Buddhism in India when equipped with proper means for the task. As maker of the Constitution, he had already achieved several things to that end. He described the provision for the study of Pali made in the Constitution, the inscription of a Buddhistic aphorism on the frontage of the imposing Rashtrapati Bhavan in New Delhi, and the acceptance of the Ashoka Chakra by Bharat as her symbol, as his personal achievements. The Government of India had declared Buddha Jayanti a holiday mainly through his efforts. He had effected this wonderful change, he proudly stated, without any opposition; so lucid and effective was his exposition in Parliament. None of the eighteen nations, he observed, that attended the Rangoon Conference had made such progress in these matters. Besides, he had established two Colleges, one at Bombay and the other at Aurangabad, where about 3,400 students were studying and where he could encourage the study of Buddhism. He pointed sadly to the fact that Buddhism had disappeared from the place of its birth. If sufficient funds came forth, it would be possible to spread Buddhism in India, for which the ground was prepared. He would achieve his goal with or without help.

Soon after, Ambedkar unveiled an image of the Buddha in a newly constructed Buddha Vihara at Dehu Road near Poona. He had brought the image from Rangoon. On that occasion he said that the honour of establishing the image of Bhagwan Buddha twelve hundred years after the fall of Buddhism, went to his people. It was a great event, and without doubt it would be recorded in history. He declared that he would dedicate himself to the propagation of the Buddhist faith in India. He told the gathering of 20,000 men and women that he was writing a book on Buddhism explaining its tenets in simple language to the common man. A year might be needed to complete the book; on its completion he would embrace Buddhism.

Ambedkar also told his audience that the image of the god Vithoba at Pandharpur was in reality the image of the Buddha. He intended writing a thesis on the subject, and after completing it he would read it before the Bharatiya Itihas Sanshodhan Mandal at Poona. The name of the god Pandurang, he observed, was derived from Pundalik. Pundalik meant lotus, and a lotus was called Pandurang in Pali. So Pandurang was none other than the Buddha.

In this speech Ambedkar referred to an article by Laxman Shastri Joshi in which it was stated that the mission of Ambedkar had come to an end. Ambedkar was sorry that a pandit like Joshi should have expressed such views and added that the mission of his life would soon begin in right earnest.

Ambedkar started writing his thesis in March 1955 at Lonavla; but it seems he wrote only about five pages.

The new year 1955 opened with the news that Ambedkar was going to embrace Buddhism. D. Valinsinha, General Secretary of the Maha Bodhi Society of India, Calcutta, extended hearty congratulations to Ambedkar on his decision to embrace Buddhism in May 1956. He observed that Ambedkar's name would go down in history as one of the greatest benefactors of humanity. If six crores of people in India, he concluded, accepted Buddhism, it would bring new life to the country and enable her to progress very rapidly.

As Ambedkar now boldly came out as a champion of Buddhism, he received several invitations from different parts of the country to address Buddhist Institutions which were stirred at the news of his decision. A Christian missionary, who had heard in Europe about Ambedkar's work and personality and was immensely charmed by the sincerity and frankness of his book *What Congress and Gandhi Have Done To The Untouchables*, sent forth an appeal to Ambedkar to give serious thought to the purity and radiancy of the doctrine of Christ.

Ambedkar now stepped up his campaign for the propagation of Buddhism. He wrote to D. Valinsinha that he had prepared a formula of certain rites called 'Dhamma Diksha Ceremony', which everyone embracing Buddhism would be required to undergo; for it was his confirmed belief that conversion of the laity was no conversion at all; it was only a nominal thing. Buddhism disappeared from India because of the wavering attitude of the laity which worshipped along with the Buddha many other gods and goddesses set up by Brahmins to destroy Buddhism. So there should be a ceremony for initiation into the Dhamma.

It seems he was patiently collecting, about this time, rules of grant-in-aid to colleges, prevalent in different States, with a view to making a comprehensive study of these rules. He was contacting all States Governments and requesting them to furnish him with information on the subject. No one can raise himself to eminent usefulness except by dint of persevering application, study and energy! That was Ambedkar.

Another announcement made in the early part of the year by Dr. Ambedkar was regarding the starting of a Buddhist Seminary at Bangalore to train preachers for propagating the faith in India. A plot of five acres of land was donated by the

Maharaja of Mysore when Dr. Ambedkar had met him at
Bangalore early in June 1954. This was the result of his two
visits to Burma. The World Buddhist Council and the Buddha
Sasana Council had promised him financial and technical help.
He would shortly set out, he said, with the begging bowl for public
contributions. The Seminary would be provided with temples and
class-rooms; and furnished with a large library, a dormitory for
teachers, students and research scholars, and a press to print
books written by eminent scholars from all over the world
commissioned to write books on Buddhism.

Prior to this announcement, Ambedkar was in
correspondence with Dr. Felix Valyi who was in Tokyo. He desired
Ambedkar to take part in the Round Table Conferences on the
origin of Indian thought with special reference to Buddhism and
Jainism. These conferences were held at Tokyo under the
auspices of the Society for International Cultural Relations—
Kokusai Banka Shinkokie—sponsored by the Government of
Japan. "It is of immense significance," wrote Dr. Felix Valyi, "to
have you participating in our Round Table Conference. Your name
is well known in Japan as a Buddhist leader in India, and your
world-fame would give to our work world-wide importance." Dr.
Felix Valyi wrote to Ambedkar to know whether the American
lady, who had offered money to Dr. Ambedkar for Buddhist
purposes, would allow the use of the money for the plan of an
Institute of Comparative Studies in Cultural History, Philosophy
and Religion at Bangalore. He also made inquiries whether
Ambedkar was able to secure the plot of land, mentioned above,
from the Maharaja of Mysore.

The Japanese Consul-General in Bombay, at the instance
of the Foreign Ministry of Japan, wrote to Ambedkar inquiring
about the possibility of exchanging scholars between Japan and
India, whose expenses would be borne at the other end by the
International Cultural Institution of Japan and at this end by
the proposed Indo-Japanese Cultural Institute at Bangalore, with
Ambedkar's collaboration. The Consul-General in his next letter
asked Dr. Ambedkar to help Dr. Felix Valyi to pay his hotel bills
and for his passage back to India. Ambedkar replied that he was
hardly in a position to help Dr. Felix Valyi; nor did he know
anybody who would do it as there were so few devout Buddhists
in the country.

Dr. Ambedkar informed Dr. Felix that the American lady was not a Buddhist; nor was she interested in Buddhism. Thereupon Dr. Felix suggested that Ambedkar should contact Ratanchand Hirachand who repeatedly proposed Poona as the centre for the Institute. But Poona, Dr. Felix feared, was the seat of the reactionary Brahmins and therefore unfit for the purpose. He aimed at establishing an Indo-Japanese Institute in India as they had done in Tokyo. He had written to Premier Nehru and Dr. Radhakrishnan on the subject.

Hisato Ichinada, Governor of the Bank of Japan and President of the Indo-Japanese Association in Tokyo, wrote to Dr. Felix stating that his Association was happy to know that the Prime Minister of India was considering the return of the Japanese assets, confiscated by the British during World War II, to their Japanese owners on condition that a part of those properties would be used for the promotion of closer cultural relations between India and Japan. Dr. Ambedkar, replying to Dr. Felix, said that India was inhospitable to the Buddha as she had been in the past.

Dr. Felix, in company with two Japanese eminent litterateurs, came to India in April 1955 and met Dr. Ambedkar. There is one important incident associated with Dr. Felix's visit to Bombay. When he lectured on Buddhism to the students of Siddharth College, Bombay, Dr. Felix made some statements on which Dr. Keny, Professor of History, in his vote of thanks to the guest, casually passed some critical remarks. Dr. Keny got the sack from Dr. Ambedkar, the Chairman of the People's Education Society which conducted the College. Whether a breach of decorum committed by the professor, or the Chairman's utter dislike of the critics of Buddhism led to the unceremonious removal of the professor was a moot point.

There was a wordy duel between Govind Ballabh Pant, the Home Minister, and Dr. Ambedkar in the Council of States over the Constitution Amendment Bill which aimed at restoring the distinction between the police powers and the powers of the eminent domain, regarding acquisition of land.

Dr. Ambedkar described the Bill as trivial and insignificant and suggested that rather than encroach upon the fundamental rights in this manner, the Government should clothe Parliament once for all with the right to determine compensation, by enacting

a suitable Land Acquisition Act in place of the present statute.
Frequent changes in the Constitution, he observed, were bad
because they tended to create uncertainty and disturbed social
values. He told the House that Article 31 was not the product of
the Drafting Committee, but a result of the compromise made
by the three leading personalities, Patel, Nehru and Pant. The
first favoured full compensation; the second opposed it; and the
third took a middle position.

Pant, citing extracts from Dr. Ambedkar's speech made on
the occasion of the first Amendment Bill to the Constitution, said
pungently that he preferred to err with Dr. Ambedkar the Law
Minister than with the Dr. Ambedkar who sat on the opposition
bench. Pant expressed satisfaction at the vigour which Ambedkar
had brought to bear upon the proposition and felt assured about
his physical recovery, bitingly remarking that "in other respects
too he will be healed in no time."

Since May 1955, Ambedkar's health deteriorated further
and faster. On medical advice his teeth had been extracted long
before. While getting up and moving about in the house, he would
require support. He had also trouble in breathing. An oxygen
cylinder was purchased, and he was given oxygen off and on.
But this was kept a secret as Dr. Ambedkar himself feared that
his followers would take fright at this news. Later he was given
oxygen twice a week. In winter his body was given warmth by a
heating apparatus. Sometimes he was also given an electric bath.
In the earlier stages nobody knew, except his wife and Dr.
Malvankar, that he was being given oxygen. His private secretary
and some close devotees were aware of the condition of his health.
Though Ambedkar resisted, he was persuaded to take a nip of
brandy in winter and some beer in summer with his evening
meals. This was done on medical advice for the restoration of
his health.

Western type of food was also tried for his health, but it
was not to his taste; and the arrangements for having such food
prepared for him had to be discontinued. He was terribly reduced
in weight. His majestic stature now looked shrunk, with the
result that his woollen clothes and suits had to be altered. A
keen desire expressed by his close colleagues for setting up a
medical board to examine him remained largely unfulfilled.

While Ambedkar was in this mental and physical condition, he pulled down cruelly the last pillar of his long association, Kamalakant Chitre, who had been his trusted colleague for over thirty years. Devoted to the mission and his master, Chitre had loyally and unselfishly served him through thick and thin, day and night. With some colleagues already estranged, others mercilessly driven into the opposition, and with the exit of Chitre, chief of his staff, Ambedkar broke the last link with his old and loyal associates. During his illness and last days Ambedkar was almost shut in by the ambitious and contriving influences around him and Chitre was victimized. To be the wife of a great man is an ordeal enough: to be the secretary of a great man is certainly a great trial. He is either tormented or misunderstood more often than not he suffers both the punishments.

Despite Ambedkar's ill-health he was all the while worried about the finance required for the running of his colleagues and different activities. He wrote on August 5, 1955, from Bombay, where he had been brought for treatment, to Prime Minister Nehru, to sign an appeal for funds required by his Society. Nehru had sent a message; but Ambedkar appealed to him to re-write it by adding one paragraph to his original message as suggested by him. In the same letter Ambedkar congratulated Nehru on his safe return from Russia. Ambedkar also wrote in November 1955 to Dr. B. G. Gokhale, a former professor of his college and a scholar of Buddhism, who was then in America, to contact some trusts there seeking help for his institutions. "I have found it," he said, " very difficult to persuade the various American trusts to come to our help. Perhaps your personal talks would be more fruitful." He was staying for some days at Aurangabad, It may be noted here that owing to illness he could not attend the session of the Council of States. On his application he was granted leave from March 29, 1955, till the end of the ninth session.

The Working Committee of the Scheduled Castes Federation under its president Dr. Ambedkar expressed itself by a resolution, on August 27, 1955, in favour of abolition of reservation of seats for Scheduled Castes in the Central and State Legislatures and District Local Boards throughout the country, as it believed that the time had come for its abolition, and there was no need now for such a provision. Its rout in the elections had dismayed the

Scheduled Castes Federation; the mice of the Congress Harijan candidates had beaten hollow the lions of the Scheduled Castes Federation in their dens!

The Scheduled Castes Federation supported Goa's merger with India. It also adopted a new constitution and appointed Rajabhau Khobragade its secretary; the vociferous Rajbhoj left his master after ten years of untiring work in his own way protesting against his dictatorial demeanour and decrying him for usurping the powers of the President unconstitutionally! Rajbhoj complained that Dr. Ambedkar was estranged from his Federation leaders since his marriage; and N. Shivraj, too, grumbled that in spite of his loyalty to Dr. Ambedkar he was thrown overboard.

II

In the early part of the year 1956, the great book on the Buddha and Buddhism was almost completed. Ambedkar had started writing the book in November 1951. Along with this book he had started writing two other books, *Revolution and Counter Revolution in India*, and *Buddha and Karl Marx*, for a proper understanding of his main work. Upto March 1956 *Buddha and Karl Marx*, was incomplete. It needed one more chapter, and the other book required some more chapters to bring out its full significance. But these two books were left incomplete; and the one on Buddha and Buddhism was brought to completion. In the third week of December 1954, he had started writing another, *The Riddle of Hinduism*, in which he described how Dr. Rajendra Prasad, the President of India, washed the feet of Brahmin priests on the banks of the holy Ganges.

The type-script of the book on Buddha and Buddhism was corrected and recorrected several times. The paragraphs were arranged and rearranged, numbered and renumbered several times; and cut away and pasted at their proper places. Sometimes a whole chapter was recast. It was a tremendous task, which his honorary private secretary Nanak Chand Rattu and his colleague Parkash Chand had to perform for months, Rattu never having his meals before midnight.

The book on Buddha and Buddhism was printed at last, for private circulation, under the title *The Buddha and His Gospel*, and about 50 copies were circulated for private opinion. In February 1956 two new chapters were added to it: 'There is no god' 'There is no soul'.

Despite his ill-health, Ambedkar was making the best of the situation. He would sit for hours together, writing at his table. On a Saturday in March 1956 he asked Rattu to come early the next morning. It seems he was writing the preface and the introduction to the book which he had completed in February 1956. Rattu came as instructed to his master's residence. But he was surprised to see Babasaheb absorbed in writing, sitting in the same chair which he had occupied the previous night. For nearly five minutes he stood by his chair; still his master remained deeply engrossed in his work. In order to attract his attention Rattu then displaced some book on his table. At this, Ambedkar raised his head and asked Rattu whether he had not gone home yet. Rattu said he had spent the Saturday night at home; it was Sunday morning, and so he had come to begin work early. "I thought you were still here and not gone home. I did not know that the day had dawned. I kept writing and did not move," said the scholar-sage. He then paid his morning devotions before the image of Lord Buddha, took a little exercise at the iron bar, drank some tea and resumed work.

On March 15, 1956, Ambedkar wrote the Preface to his book in his own handwriting and dictated it to Rattu.

Simultaneously the political hammer was banging in the Council of States as well. Ambedkar made a fighting speech over the linguistic problem on May 1, 1956. He told the House that Bombay had become the storm centre of the debate on the Bill. The premier city of India, which had taught politics and civic affairs to the rest of the country, was reduced to the status of the Andamans and was turned into a Union territory. Bombay belonged to Maharashtra, its original inhabitants being the Kolis. It belonged to Dowager Lakshmi Bai from whom the Portuguese took it on lease and later took it over. He said he differed from other Maharashtrians who wanted Bombay to be included in Maharashtra, whereas he was against United Maharashtra. After making this speech he said it would not please all. A fortnight later he came out with another scheme suggesting two Maharashtra States divided by the lines of the Sahyadris. He, however, suggested that Aurangabad should be the capital of United Maharashtra instead of Poona or Nagpur.

A talk by Dr. Ambedkar was broadcast in May 1956 from the British Broadcasting Corporation, London, on "Why I like Buddhism and how it is useful to the world in its present circumstances. "I prefer Buddhism," he observed, "because it gives three principles in combination which no other religion does. Buddhism teaches *prajna* (understanding as against superstition and supernaturalism), *karuna* (love), and *samata* (equality). This is what man wants for a good and happy life. Neither god nor soul can save society. Marxism and Communism have shaken the religious systems of all the countries."He claimed that Buddhism was a complete answer to Marx and his Communism and observed: " Buddhistic countries that have gone over to Communism do not understand what communism is. Communism of the Russian type aims at bringing it about by a bloody revolution. The Buddhist communism brings it about by a bloodless revolution. The South-East Asians should beware of jumping into the Russian net. All that is necessary for them is to give political form to Buddha's teaching. Poverty there is and there will always be. Even in Russia there is poverty. But poverty cannot be an excuse for sacrificing human freedom. Once it is realised that Buddhism is a social gospel, its revival would be an everlasting event."

In his talk given at this juncture for the Voice of America, Ambedkar dealt with the prospects of Democracy in India. He said that Democracy could not be equated either with Republic or Parliamentary Government. The roots of Democracy lay not in the form of Government, parliamentary or otherwise. "A Democracy," he observed, 'is a mode of associated living. The roots of Democracy are to be searched in the social relationship, in terms of the associated life between the people who form the society," Indian society was based on castes which were exclusive in their life. The voting and setting up of candidates was guided by castes. In industry, castemen of the industrialist occupied topmost posts; the commercial house was a camp of one caste; charity was communal. The caste system was a descending scale of contempt. Caste and class differed in the fact that in the class system there was no complete isolation as there was in the caste system.

"If you give education," he concluded, "to the lower strata of the Indian society, which is interested in blowing up the caste system, the caste system will be blown up. At the moment the indiscriminate help given to education by the Indian Government and American Foundations is going to strengthen the caste system. Giving education to those who want to blow up caste system will improve the prospect of Democracy in India and put Democracy in safer hands."

Ambedkar was going to start soon a political party called the Republican Party. He said he would move in the matter when he felt better. He wrote to S. S. Rege, Librarian of the Siddharth College, Bombay, on May 5, 1956. "There is one urgent matter, which I want you to attend to and that is the publication of my book *The Buddha And His Dhamma*." He said he wanted to publish his book, and the model for and the size of the book was to be that of Jeanyee Wong's *Buddha His Life And Teachings*. He asked Rege to show it to Messrs. G. Claridge and Company and to get an estimate from them. " I am," observed the ailing man, " in a great hurry and I want the book to be published by September the latest, I am ready to hand over the book to the printer as soon as he is ready to proceed with it. Let me know by wire what is their quotation. I want about 2,000 copies.'

The printing of *The Buddha And His Dhamma* began under the supervision of Rege. Ambedkar was now busy correcting the proofs. These were corrected, but sometimes some lines were recast and returned for recomposing. Rege had to perform a great task. The trustees of Sir Dorabji Tata Trust, Bombay, sanctioned a grant of Rs. 3,000 towards the publication of this book.

In order to invigorate the democratic forces in India and to bring new blood to his proposed Republican Party, Ambedkar decided to establish a Training School for entrance to politics. With that end in view he was busy making arrangements and preparations with the help of S. S. Rege. The school was meant for those who cherished the ambition of joining the legislature. The school was to be the first of its kind in the country. For that school he wanted a suitable person for the post of principal. According to him, to be a principal, a person must have a personality; to be a teacher one must be well versed in one's subjects, must have a good delivery and an attractive personality. The reputation of a school, he said, would depend greatly upon the ability and speaking capacity of its teachers. The school, with S. S. Rege as its registrar, worked with 15 students on its roll from July 1, 1956, to Maich 1957. But, as luck would have it, its founder and director Dr. Ambedkar never had an opportunity to visit the school. It naturally died an orphan's death.

Early in May 1956, Arabedkar came down to Bombay, and on May 24, at Nare Park, he declared on the day of Buddha Jayanti Celebrations that he would embrace Buddhism in October 1956. In his speech he made a vitriolic attack on Veer Savarkar who had written a series of articles on the non-violence preached by Buddhism. Ambedkar with a snort of rage said he would reply to Savarkar if he knew precisely what Savarkar had to say. Savarkar's articles were, as all his writings are, reasoned, forceful and thought-provoking; and his views were the views of a leader of thought. Ambedkar was stung by his cringing flatterers into saying something in reply to Savarkar when he started for the meeting and even on the dais. It seemed as if there was again a fierce debate between the leaders of Hinduism and those of Buddhism. Those alone, Ambedkar roared, who aimed at uplifting them were entitled to criticize them. He said his critics should leave him alone; let him and his people have the freedom to fall into a ditch. Ambedkar stated frankly that his people were his sheep, and he was their shepherd. There was no theologian as great as he. They should follow him, and they would get knowledge by and by.

To him Buddhism differed from Hinduism. He further observed: "Hinduism believes in God. Buddhism has no God. Hinduism believes in soul. According to Buddhism there is no soul. Hinduism believes in Chaturvarnya and the caste system. Buddhism has no place for the caste system and chaturvarnya." He told his followers that his book on Buddhism would be published soon. He had closed all the breaches in the organization of Buddhism and would now consolidate it; so the tide of Buddhism would never recede in India. The communist should study Buddhism, so that they might know how to remove the ills of humanity.

During his speech Ambedkar compared himself with Moses who had led his people from Egypt to Palestine, the land of freedom. According to him, there were three causes for the decline of any religion. Lack of abiding principles in it; lack of versatile and conquering orators; and lack of easily understandable principles. He also declared that he was going to build a magnificient temple of Buddha. Thus ended his last speech in Bombay.

Ambedkar, a devoted student of the *Bible*, who possessed a huge collection of Biblical literature, was led to compare himself to Moses. And aptly so. Moses wanted to relieve the Israelites from forced labour and their unending servitude. Moses was brought up and educated by a Princess. Ambedkar was provided with educational facilities by a Prince. Moses learnt at the University Temple of On, then a famous centre of learning. Ambedkar received his education at three world famous universities with an inquiring, searching and acquisitive mind. Like Moses, he was strong, determined and courageous. But Moses was humbled by his respect for and worship of God. Ambedkar was learning this attribute at the feet of his man-god, the Buddha, Both led their people out of bondage, gave them their religion and law and brought them to the doorsteps of the Promised Land. Moses was eighty when he liberated his people, and Ambedkar was sixty-five. Like Moses, Ambedkar catalogued, expanded and interpreted the code of the laws of a nation.

Ill

From June to October 1956, Ambedkar stayed at his Delhi residence, 26 Alipore Road. In June and July he was very depressed, almost heart-stricken. His legs could not bear the weight of his body. His eyesight was now fast failing. He could not move in the house by himself; nor could he go out in that condition. For over ten years he had not been in normal health. Drug-taking is a pernicious habit and it overpowered him. Endlessly and desperately, he tried to get medicine from this friend or that or from any other source. On receiving such medicines or herbs, his doctor-wife might not have thought it advisable to allow him to take these medicines. He had lost all hope of life.

A French lady doctor desired to try her treatment based on the principle of cosmic radiation, to tone up the degenerated tissues of his legs and the spine; but was pooh-poohed by his wife, she herself being a noted physician. At times Ambedkar got angry with his wife and shouted, "Why should you object to others giving treatment to me, when your doctors could not cure me for these eight years?" Then he would not have his meal or medicine, and the help of his honorary private secretary or some devotee was sought to cajole him into taking his meal and medicine.

He was lame, crippled, and sad at heart; and as he thought that he could not fulfil his mission, he sadly and bitterly wept. He wanted to make his people a governing class in his lifetime. But he was now prostrated by illness. What he had achieved was enjoyed by the educated few from the Depressed Classes; the vast illiterate masses in the villages remained almost unchanged economically. He wanted to do something for them. But life seemed to be short, and there was, he thought, no other depressed class leader who would rise to the occasion and shoulder the responsibility. Most of his lieutenants, he said sadly, fought among themselves for leadership and power.

The thought of being helpless to complete the books he had planned distressed him terribly. *The Buddha And Karl Marx, Revolution And Counter Revolution in India and The Riddle of Hinduism* were to be completed and published. And nobody after him would be able to complete those books. He wanted to do more for his country, but in the existing set-up, he observed, it was difficult to maintain one's interest in its affairs when the people were not prepared to give a hearing to any view which did not agree with that of the Prime Minister. "It is a sin," he sighed," to take birth in such a country whose people are so prejudiced. Anyhow I have done a lot in spite of the words of abuse hurled at me from all sides. I will continue to do so till my death." So saying, he burst into tears. "Tell my people" he said one day to Rattu, his honorary private secretary, " whatever I have done, I have been able to do after passing through crushing miseries and endless trouble all my life and fighting with my opponents. With great difficulty I have brought this caravan where it is seen today. Let the caravan march on despite the hurdles that may come in its way. If my lieutenants are not able to take the caravan ahead they should leave it there, but in no circumstances should they allow the caravan to go back. This is the message to my people." Unbearable sorrow and bitter anguish wrung this soliloquy. In tears he would lie in his bed with no heart for eating.

So prostrate was Ambedkar that eminent politicians who saw him said that death was hovering over his face. They wondered at his will power. Corroded by and crushed under diabetes his body was totally crippled. Yet spurred as it was by the power of his will, his spirit was resurging and moving like the electric fan which rotates for a while even after the switch is turned off.

October 14, 1956, the day appointed for Ambedkar's going over to Buddhism was fast approaching. His devoted lieutenants often anxiously discussed the matter with him. In the first week of August, Ambedkar had a talk with Shankaranand Shastri, a lieutenant of unbounded devotion to Babasaheb. He told him that he would hold his conversion ceremony at Bombay, Sarnath or Nagpur. He himself preferred Nagpur, which was a historic town where the Buddhist Nagas flourished in ancient times. He would set the wheel of the Buddha's Dhamma in motion once again, spreading the message of his Master to all the corners of the world. A disciple expressed his fear to Ambedkar that if his followers did not follow him *en bloc*, it would be a shock, smashing and damaging. The leader replied gravely that he had thought over the problem for a pretty long time and had somehow been deferring the issue of conversion. Day by day, he said with a sigh, his health was sinking fast, and he thought he was approaching his end. So this time he would not defer his conversion any longer. Those who wished to join him were most welcome; those who did not favour conversion were free to go anywhere else they liked.

Accordingly, he called W. M. Godbole to Delhi. Godbole was secretary of the Bharatiya Bouddha Jana Samiti established not long earlier by Ambedkar himself. Ambedkar discussed with him the arrangements to be made at Nagpur; for he wanted to make the ceremony a grand success. A general appeal to the Depressed class people was issued by the B.B.J. Samiti directing them to come in large numbers dressed in white, for the initiation ceremony.

On September 23 Ambedkar issued a press note announcing that his conversion to Buddhism would take place at Nagpur on the Dassara day, October 14, 1956, between 9 and 11 a.m.

Ambedkar invited the Rev. Bhikkhu Chandramani, of Kushi-nara, Gorakhpur District, to Nagpur, to initiate him into Buddhism on October 14. "It is our great wish," he added, " that you should officiate at the ceremony. You being the oldest monk in India we think it would be appropriate to have the ceremony performed by you." He expressed his desire to provide the priest with an air or train passage, and added that he would send someone to bring him from Kushinara to Nagpur.

Ambedkar then reserved an air passage for himself, his wife and Rattu for the 11th October. He wrote to D. Valisinha expressing his desire that Mahabodhi Society of India should participate in the function. He informed him that he had no idea of exactly what rituals there were. Apart from the customary rituals, he himself had framed an important formula of a series of vows to be administered at the time of Dhamma Diksha Ceremony either by a Bikkhu or by some Buddhist layman. He pressed him to attend the ceremony and asked him whether it was possible to get some contribution from his friends and interested persons. He again wrote to Valisinha on October 5, saying that if there were some differences between Valisinha and himself over the initiation ceremony, he would resolve them if he came a little earlier to Nagpur.

Describing the near-at-hand conversion, the *Maha Bodhi*, the famous Buddhist journal in India, excited with joy, observed: " When on the coming Vijaya Dashmi day the lion-hearted leader and his followers make that momentous step forward, a threefold shout of ' Sadhu ! ! !' will surely rise from every part of the Buddhist world and would be taken up by the Devas-celestial beings and echoed from heaven to heaven until finally it reaches the foot of the throne of the enlightenment, and there who labour in the heat of the day in the field of Buddhist revival in India, hearing that shout, will pause for a moment in their work, and know, with joy in their hearts that at last the tide has turned." Quite a Hindu way of expressing heavenly joy!

Ambedkar with his wife and Rattu left Delhi by air on the morning of October 11 and reached Nagpur at noon. Arrangements for their stay in Nagpur were made at Sham Hotel Vast throngs of people wanted to touch the feet of their saviour, but they were content with applying the dust from his footprints to their foreheads.

IV

For a week prior to this appointed day thousands of men, women and children of the Depressed Classes, especially the Mahars, had been hourly pouring into Nagpur from the Marathi-speaking areas of Central Provinces and Berar and Bombay by trains and in buses; poor people selling their trinkets for the transport and for white sarees and white shirts, the dress prescribed by their leader. Thousands who could not find easy transport trekked hundreds of miles shouting slogans "Bhagwan Buddha ki jay, Babasaheb ki jay." They were happy like travellers going towards their homes. They were accommodated in school houses. A huge volunteer corps guided them properly. Some ate in hotels; others cooked their food in the open. The whole atmosphere was surcharged with Buddhist piousness. Nagpur sanctified in the olden times by the residence of Nagarjun, the great scholar-leader of Buddhism, was now transformed into a holy place of great significance, historical, cultural and religious. The vast throngs of visitors as they moved on to their destination raised skyrending slogans. "Babasaheb gives a clarion call, embrace Buddhism all"; "Move heaven and earth and switch over to Buddhism."

An expansive open ground of 14 acres near the Vaccine Institute at Shradhanand Peth was turned into an enclosure. At the northern end of it stood a huge dais lined with white cloth and surrounded by a replica of the Sanchi stupa, facing two specially erected pandals on either side—one for men and the other for women. Buddhist flags consisting of blue, red and green stripes fluttered everywhere. All approaches and streets leading to the place were decorated with bunting.

On the evening of October 13, Ambedkar held a press conference. He told newsmen that his Buddhism would cling to the tenets of the faith as preached by Lord Buddha himself without involving his people in differences which had arisen on account of Hinayana and Mahayan.

His Buddhism would be a sort of neo-Buddhism or Navayana. When asked why he was embracing Buddhism, he said angrily "Why cannot you ask this question to yourself and to your forefathers as to why I am getting out of the Hindu fold and embracing Buddhism?" He asked newsmen why they wanted his men to remain Harijans to enjoy only such 'benefits' as those of reservation. He asked them whether the Brahmins were prepared to be Untouchables to enjoy these privileges. He said that they were making efforts to reach manhood. He also declared that he had once told Mahatma Gandhi that though he differed from him on the issue of untouchability, when the time came, "I will choose only the least harmful way for the country. And that is the greatest benefit I am conferring on the country by embracing Buddhism; for Buddhism is a part and parcel of Bharatiya culture. I have taken care that my conversion will not harm the tradition of the culture and history of this land."

He predicted with a glow in his eyes that in the next ten or fifteen years the wave of mass conversion would spread all over the country, and India would become a Buddhist country. Brahmins would be the last to follow, and let them be the last! He reminded the newsmen of the conversion of the lowest folk to Christianity during the fall of the Roman Empire. He admitted that his followers were ignorant. He would inculcate in them the principles of Buddhism through his books and sermons. They preferred honour to bread; yet they would make great efforts to improve their own economic condition.

Ambedkar also said that before the next election he wanted to form a political party called the Republican Party. This would be open to all who accepted its three guiding principles-liberty, equality and fraternity. He added that he would contest election to the Lok Sabha from some suitable constituency. He would fight for putting an end to the new bilingual State of Bombay which combined Gujarat and Maharashtra. With that end in view he extended his wholehearted support to the Samyukta

Maharashtra Samiti which was fighting for a united Maharashtra.

He gave one more interview that evening. Men of Ambedkar's imperious characteristics are seldom a success at press conferences. At times during this interview he got excited, and argument became impossible. He said that the press men had been dogging his footsteps for long, but had not been able to do any harm to him.

On the night of October 13, there was some discussion between Ambedkar and some of his chosen lieutenants as to whether their conversion could not be put off till after the coming general elections. There was a division of opinion, and Ambedkar was terribly upset. He threatened them with dire consequences if they prevaricated and faltered. They left the hotel like bleating lambs.

On the morning of October 14, 1956, Ambedkar woke up early. He asked Rattu to arrange for a hot bath and then to make sure that arrangements at the pandal were perfect. Rattu made inquiries and returned.

Since early morning a sea of humanity had been flowing towards the *Deeksha* Bhoomi. The sweepers had swept the street leading to it at day-break as they deemed it their fortune to sweep a street along which their saviour was to pass. The skies were filled with the resounding 'jais' to Buddha and Babasaheb.

Dressed in silk white dhoti and white coat, Dr. Ambedkar left the hotel at eight-thirty in the morning in a car with Rattu and his wife Mrs. Savita Ambedkar. She also had put on a white saree. By now all the arrangements proved inadequate and collapsed. The huge crowds enthusiastically cheered their saviour as he reached the pandal and was taken up on the dais. He stood on the dais with a staff in one hand and the other hand on the shoulders of Rattu. There was thunderous applause. It was now a quarter past nine in the morning. Cameramen were busy taking photographs; newsmen writing reports. On the dais there stood on a table a bronze statuette of the Buddha flanked hy two tigers and incense burning before it. Sitting on the dais were D. Valisinha, Ven. M. Sanghratna Thera, Ven. H. Sadda Tissa Thera and Ven. Pannanand Thera.

The ceremony commenced with a Marathi song sung by a lady in praise of Dr. Ambedkar. The vast gathering stood up for

a minute and observed silence in memory of the death
anniversary of Dr. Ambedkar's father. Then the actual ceremony
began. Scores of photographers rushed towards the dais. The
vast humanity of over three lakhs of men and women from all
parts of the State watched the ceremony eagerly as the eighty-
three-year-old Mahasthaveer Chandramani of Kushinara and his
four saffron-robbed Bhikkhus administered in Pali to Dr.
Ambedkar and his wife, who were both bowing before the image
of Buddha, the three *Sarans* under Buddha, Dhamma and Sangh
and Panchsheel of five precepts of abstention from killing,
stealing, telling lies, wrongful sex life, and drink. They repeated
the Pali mantras in Marathi. Then they bowed down thrice with
clasped hands before the Buddha statuette and made offerings
of white lotuses before it. With this, Ambedkar's entry into the
Buddhistic fold was announced, and the vast concourse gave full-
throated cries of 'Babasaheb Ambedkar ki jay and Bhagwan
Buddha ki jay.' The whole ceremony was filmed. It was now a
quarter to ten in the morning.

On his conversion Ambedkar was profusely garlanded by
his closest devotees. D. Valisinha presented Dr. Ambedkar and
Mrs. Savita Ambedkar with an image of Lord Buddha. Dr.
Ambedkar then declared: "By discarding my ancient religion
which stood for inequality and oppression today I am reborn.. I
have no faith in the philosophy of incarnation; and it is wrong
and mischievous to say that Buddha was an incarnation of
Vishnu. I am no more a devotee of any Hindu god or goddess. I
will not perform Shraddha. I will strictly follow the eightfold
path of Buddha. Buddhism is a true religion and I will lead a life
guided by the three principles of knowledge, right path and
compassion."

Once or twice, when he repeated the pledges to renounce
the worship of the Hindu god and when he declared, "I renounce
Hinduism," the great leader seemed deeply moved; his voice
choked visibly as he spoke. These pledges, framed by himself,
were twenty-two in number. He denounced Hinduism, its customs
and traditions and declared that from that moment onwards he
would strive for the spread of equality among human beings.

Now a Buddhist, Dr. Ambedkar called upon those who
wanted to embrace Buddhism to stand up. The entire gathering

rose up, and he administered the three refuges and five precepts
and different pledges to the vast gathering. They repeated in
loud and joyous tones the precepts and pledges. Nearly three
lakhs of his followers embraced Buddhism, and, to use his own
analogy of shepherd, he flocked them into Buddhism. He had
always taunted both Christians and non-Christians, saying that
to them religion was a matter of inheritance. They inherited
religion along with their father's property. In fact, few religious
people have studied comparative religion and hardly any have
attained belief as a result of such a study. Among those who
embraced Buddhism with Dr. Ambedkar, were Dr. M. B. Niyogi,
former Chief Justice of the Nagpur High Court, and Dr.
Ambedkar's leading Maharashtrian lieutenants. Dr. Niyogi,
however, said that denunciation of Hinduism as was done by Dr.
Ambedkar while embracing Buddhism had no place in the
original Buddhist rituals. The ceremony was over by ten to eleven
in the morning.

Messages welcoming the great leader and his followers to
Buddhism were sent by U Ba Sway, Prime Minister of Burma, U
Nu, former Burmese Premier, Dr. Arvind Barua of Calcutta and
H. W. Amarsuriya from Colombo. It is very important lo note
that no message from any great Indian leader such as Nehru,
Dr. Radhakrishnan, C. Rajagopalachari or Dr. Rajendra Prasad
was received on the occasion, not to speak of Veer Savarkar.
Nehru believed that there was nothing inconsistent between
Indian philosophy, religion and democracy. Hindu religion, he
pointed out, had within itself an impressive universalism. It could
adjust itself to change; it was large enough to encompass different
and even conflicting beliefs. According to Nehru, it might take a
little time, but religion in India would undergo whatever
reorientation was necessary to have it reflect the general welfare
of the people. Many times before Hinduism had digested great
changes. After Buddhism came to India, Hinduism did not set
itself up in competition with Buddhism; it absorbed it.[1]
Radhakrishnan believed that the Buddha had attempted to
achieve a purer Hinduism.[2]

The next day Ambedkar initiated another vast crowd of his
followers into Buddhism at the same place and said that the

1.   Norman Cousins, *Talks with Nehru*, pp. 10-11.
2.   *The Times of India*, 7 February 1956.

Scheduled Castes would not lose their rights with the change of faith. The privileges enjoyed by the Scheduled Castes under the Constitution, he observed, were the fruits of his labour, and he was capable of retaining them for his people. He reminded them of his vow taken in 1935 that "even though I am a Hindu born, I will not die a Hindu". He had fulfilled his vow and had divine satisfaction that he had come at last out of the hell of Hinduism. He did not believe in hurried action; and therefore he took more than twenty years to think and arrive at a mature decision.

Referring to Marx's philosophy, Dr. Ambedkar observed: "Man cannot live by bread alone. He has a mind which needs food for thought. Religion instills hope in Man and drives him to activity. Hindu religion has watered down the enthusiasm of the down-trodden. And I found it necessary to change my faith and embrace Buddhism." Buddhism was independent of time and place and could flourish in any land. He would have no truck with a country whose people preferred bread to culture of the mind. If Hinduism had given the Scheduled Castes freedom of weapons, the country would not have been enslaved at any time, he added.

He then seriously warned his people that a great responsibility had fallen on their shoulders in connection with the upholding of Buddhism; and if they would not follow rigidly and nobly the principles of Buddhism, it would mean that the Mahars reduced it to a miserable state. No other person under the sun was burdened with such unparalleled responsibility as he was, he concluded.

While in Nagpur, Ambedkar addressed a meeting of his partymen at Shyam Hotel. He said his partymen were interested more in politics than in religion, while he himself was interested more in religion than in politics. The Scheduled Castes Federation had created self-respect among the Depressed Classes; but it had also raised a barricade between them and the other classes. Matters had come to such a pass that other people did not vote for the Scheduled class candidates; nor did they themselves vote for the candidates of other parties. So they would have to form a party with the help of those who had sympathy for their grievances; and they should try to do work with the leaders of other communities.

A time had rome, he concluded, for reviewing the whole situation. This was his last political speech. This realisation came upon him 14 years after the Independent Labour Party was dissolved. He seldom encouraged his partymen or followers to mix with other communities, except on one occasion when he asked them to shed the narrow outlook and think in terms of the welfare and prosperity of the nation as a whole. This happened when the glory and laurels of the Chief Architect of the Constitution were quite fresh!

Although the great leaders of the country were indifferent to Dr. Ambedkar's going over to Buddhism, leading newspapers reviewed it with seriousness and anxiety. Congratulating Dr. Ambedkar on his becoming a good *Dwija* by his religious rebirth, the Indian Express, Bombay, observed: "One is glad, however, that even while recoiling from the traditional Hindu social order, he chose another essentially Indian way which, like Sikhims; Brahmonism and the Arya Samaj, is only a variant of Hinduism." Depicting the conversion as the most significant development during the present century, the *Hitawad*. Nagpur, said: "Paradoxically enough, Dr. Ambedkar, a highly rationalistic and scientific thinker stands in line with Emperor Ashok and others of historic memory, as the High Prophet of Buddhist faith." It added that the Harijans' conversion at Nagpur was a warning to the Hindu reformers.

Veer Savarkar, who defined a Hindu as one whose fatherland and holyland is India, described the conversion of Dr. Ambedkar as a sure jump into the fold of Hinduism and declared that the Buddhist Ambedkar was Hindu Ambedkar. He had embraced a non-vedic but Indian religious system within the orbit of Hindutva, and according to him it was not a change of faith. Change of religious system would not resolve their problem, Savarkar concluded. It may be noted here that a leaflet issued on this occasion by Mahasthavir Chandramani and other Bhikkhus said that Hinduism and Buddhism are branches of the same tree.

According to the Buddhist view, the great conversion constituted a new chapter in the history of modern India. "Conversion was not a happy term to describe the changes because force and temptation are associated with conversion",

observed a Buddhist writer. It was self-conversion and not
conversion that had come to mean giving up one's own faith and
embracing something foreign, he added. Other Buddhists said
that the Dhamma Chakra was set revolving by the intrepid
leader; and it was the greatest religious revolution which India
had witnessed in modern times.

V

Next day, October 15, Dr. Ambedkar was presented with an
address of welcome by the Nagpur Municipal Corporation at the
Town Hall, where he said that the Congress had made a mess of
politics. If the ruling party remained in power for long the country
would be in flames. He said as the maker of the Constitution he
was always thinking how it was working and whether it would
lead to the establishment of real democracy in the country. He
called himself the maker of the Constitution not out of any sense
of pride; for there were many learned men in the country who
could have framed the Constitution, he added. He vehemently
criticized Nehru whom, he said, he had observed from close
quarters. The educated women were going astray, he pointed out,
and would go to any extent to obtain tickets to fight elections.
The Corporation was glad to receive a "social reformer,
philosopher and erudite constitutionalist of the stature of
Babasaheb." On October 16, 1956. Ambedkar attended a
conversion ceremony at Chanda, where the vast gathering of the
Depressed Class people repealed the pledges which he gave.

Dr. Ambedkar then left Chanda by train for Delhi, listening
to the reports read by Rattu that had appeared on the mass
conversion in different newspapers. On reaching Nagpur,
however, he and his party returned to Delhi by air. Although he
looked tired and exhausted, he was in high spirits. Taking a
complete rest for three days, he felt fresh and invigorated and
sang songs very loudly. One of these was from Kabir. There was
heard the musical tone of His Master's song on the radiogram.
Though his health was poor, his face was beaming with pride
and joy. He was, indeed, the author of an epoch-making event.
He had the divine satisfaction of having accomplished a great

deed, and set in motion the wheel of Dhamma once again, thus establishing the revival of Buddhism in India. He had fulfilled the prediction of Sir William Hunter who had said as early as 1881 that "the revival of Buddhism is, I repeat, one of the possibilities in India."[3] Gurudev Tagore, too, had sent forth a call, eagerly awaiting the arrival of the Buddha, singing:

Bring to this country once again
    the blessed name
which made the land of thy birth sacred
    to all distant lands!
Let thy great awakening under the Bodhi Tree
    be fulfilled. ...
Let open the doors that are barred,
    and the resounding conch shell
Proclaim thy arrival at Bharat's gate.
Let, through innumerable voices,
    the gospel of an unmcasurable love
    announce thy call."[4]

□□□

---

3. Hunter, W. W., *Ancient India*, p. 175.
4. *Buddhadev*. p. 17.

CHAPTER 27

THE LAST JOURNEY

IN an exhilarating state of mind, Ambedkar showed the photographers taken at the conversion ceremony to persons close to him. He expressed his desire that he would carry out conversion programmes in Delhi, Uttar Pradesh, the Punjab and Bombay. He narrated the story of the conversion ceremony to his admirers with keen and colourful interest.

At this juncture the Principal of Elphintone College, Bombay, wrote to Dr. Ambedkar requesting him to contribute a paper on a subject of his choice to be included in a volume which the college was going to publish on the occasion of its centenary celebrations. Dr. Ambedkar accepted the invitation and informed him that he would like to speak on "What is Democracy and what are its prospects in India?" He was not sure that he would be able to address the gathering, he said, as his eye-sight was poor and he was ailing. He also signed an appeal for funds for the college. He, however, wondered whether his signature would be an asset. He said if the college authorities insisted that he should be present he would have to make a special journey from Delhi.

He wrote on October 30, 1956, to D. Valisinha in reply to his letter dated October 25, 1956, that "it was a great event and the crowd that came forward for conversion was beyond my expectation. Thank Buddha, it all went well." "We," he added, "have to consider ways and means of imparting the knowledge of Buddhism to the masses who have accepted His Dhamma and will accept it on my word. I am afraid the Sangha will have to modify its outlook; and instead of becoming recluses, Bhikkhus should become, like the Christian missionaries, social workers and social preachers."

It was then enthusiastically arranged by the circle close to Ambedkar that he should attend, although his health was poor, the World Buddhist Conference at Khatmandu in Nepal. The arrangement for his stay in Nepal was made through M. Jyoti, of

Calcutta. Dr. Malvankar, the physician in charge of his health, was called from Bombay to Delhi to accompany him to Khatmandu. Ambedkar took some of the manuscripts of his incomplete books to work on them during his journey. But before proceeding to Patna from where he was to fly to Khatmandu, he had to face some financial difficulties. A suit was filed against him in the Bombay High Court for non-payment of a big sum claimed by the contractors in connection with the extension of Rajgriha, his former residence in Bombay. He went to a friend in Delhi and got some money, and the remaining amount was arranged in Bombay making up Rs. 40,000 which he had to deposit in the High Court. Mrs. Ambedkar came to Bombay, deposited the required amount and went back to Delhi. Then Ambedkar and his party flew to Khatmandu on November 14, 1956, from Patna. M. B. Chitnis Principal of the Milind Mahavidyalaya, Aurangabad, and B. H. Varale also accompanied him.

The Fourth Conference of the World Fellowship of Buddhists met at Khatmandu. It was inaugurated by King Mahendra of Nepal in the Singha Darbar Gallery Hall on the afternoon of November 15, 1956. The Government of Nepal, a Hindu State, declared a holiday on November 15, 1956, and true to its Hindu tradition of overgenerosity to other faiths, banned the exhibition of an Indian film on the life of Shankaracharya, the mighty Hindu leader, who liquidated Buddhism in India. It was alleged that it contained certain anti-Buddhist scenes. And as if to counteract the traditionally tolerant view taken by the King, the priests in Khatmandu withdrew the recently-conceded right of Buddhists to enter the temple of Pashupatinath. This declaration, curiously enough, coincided with Ambedkar's presence among the Buddhist delegates.

Speaking on this occasion. Dr. Ambedkar said that he had come to attend the Conference to declare to the world that he found Buddhism the greatest of all religions, as it was not merely a religion but a great social doctrine. As he rose to speak at this inaugural session, the entire Congress gave Dr. Ambedkar a tremendous ovation.

Dr. Malalasekara, President of the Conference, described Dr. Ambedkar's one-month-old conversion with half a million of his followers as the greatest-ever religious conversion. On

November 20 Dr. Ambedkar was requested to make a speech on "Ahimsa in Buddhism", but the majority of the delegates pressed him to speak, on "Buddha and Karl Marx". Accepting this subject, Ambedkar expressed concern over the fate of Buddhist youngsters in Buddhist countries who looked upon Karl Marx as the only prophet for worship. He stated that the goal of Buddha and of Karl Marx was the same. Marx said that private property was the root cause of sorrow. It resulted in exploitation, suffering and enslavement. Buddha also wanted to abolish *Dukhha* (sorrow) and the expression sorrow was used in the Buddhist literature in the sense of property. According to Buddha, everything was impermanent, and so there was no struggle for property. The Bhikkhus were not allowed to own private property. Buddha did not lay the foundations of his religion on God or soul. So Buddha would not stand in the path of abolition of private property, if the principle of the denial of private property was applied to society.

But Buddhism, he continued, and Communism violently differed from each other in their means to achieve their goal. Communism adopted violent methods to abolish private property. Buddhism adopted non-violent means to achieve the goal. Marx's method gave quick results. Buddha's method, though tedious, was non-violent; yet it was the surest way. The world could not be reformed except by the reformation of the mind of man and the mind of the world. There was no trouble once the mind was converted; the achievement became permanent. The Marxist way was based on force. If the Dictatorship in Russia failed, Ambedkar predicted, there would be bloody warfare among the Russian people for appropriating the property of the State. Moreover, the Buddhist system was a Democratic system, whereas the Communist system was based on Dictatorship. Therefore, the Buddhist method was the safest and soundest. The Buddhist monks should copy some of the methods of Christians in order to propagate religion among the Buddhist people, he concluded.

It is impossible, observed George Washington, to rightly govern the world without God and the Bible. According to Dr. Ambedkar, it is impossible for humanity to live peacefully and righteously without the Buddha and His Dhamma.

The suit filed against Ambedkar by the contractors in the High Court was defended by his lawyer, K. J, Kale, in Bombay, and Rattu passed on the telegram received from the lawyer to his master at Khatmandu. On his return journey Ambedkar made speeches at Benaras Hindu University and the Kashi Vidyapith in his usual challenging vein. He intensely believed in intellectual conquest; and he thought that he would achieve now for Buddhism what Shankaracharya had done for Hinduism. In the Benaras Hindu University Hall he spoke on Shankaracharya's philosophy as expounded in the aphorism: "Brahma Satyam Jagan Mithya". Ambedkar said that if the Brahman pervaded all, a Brahman and an Untouchable were equal. But Shankara did not apply the doctrine to social organization and kept the discussion on a vedantic level. Had he applied it on a social level and preached social equality, his proposition would have been profound and worth consideration, apart from his erroneous belief that the world was an illusion.

Ambedkar, therefore, asked the students whether they would follow Hindu scriptures which supported the graded inequality propounded by the Purusha Sukta and give religious sanction to social inequality or whether they would stand by the principles liberty, equality and fraternity propounded in the Constitution and refute the graded inequality preached by Hindu scriptures. Ambedkar then completed his second round of visits to the Buddhist holy places. He returned from Kushinagar and reached Delhi by air on November 30,1956. While coming from the aerodrome to his residence, the first question he put to Rattu was about the health of his dog who had been admitted to hospital a few days before, and then he inquired about the civil suit.

On his arrival, he was found sad, worried and depressed. Mrs Ambedkar's father, brother and Dr. Malvankar were staying with the Ambedkar family. As he was terribly exhausted, he asked Rattu to stay at his place for the night, which he did On the morning of December 1, Ambedkar got up at 7-15 a.m. had a cup of tea and felt refreshed. In the evening he paid a visit to an exhibition held at Mathura Road, saw with greal interest the Buddhist Art Gallery, came out and sat in the car outside the exhibition. Asked by a close admirer of his why the statues of the Buddha from different countries differed in features, he replied that till 600 years after the Mahaparinirvana of the Buddha, there was no picture or statue of the Buddha. Someone thereafter made a statue of the Buddha from his own imagination, and then in all Buddhist countries statues were made in accordance with the standard of beauty prevailing in those lands.

On his away home, Ambedkar paid a visit also to a bookshop at Connaught Place to have a look at the new arrivals and ordered some books to be sent to his residence.

On December 2 Ambedkar attended a function held at Ashok Vihar in honour of the Dalai Lama who had come to India to attend the winter celebrations of the 2500th Buddha Mahaparinirvana to be held at Boudh Gaya. In the evening, sitting in a chair on the lawn in his compound, Ambedkar had a chat with some of his devotees and had his supper on the lawn. After 10-30 p.m. he retired and in a short while he was fast asleep. Next evening he felt tired and asked his attendants to keep chairs on the lawn when a group photograph was taken by Mrs. Ambedkar's brother, Balu Kabir. Sitting in the group were Mrs. Ambedkar, Dr. Ambedkar, Mrs. Ambedkar's father K. V. Kabir, and Dr. Malvankar.

After nightfall, with a staff in one hand and the other on the shoulder of Rattu, he went to inquire after the health of his *mali* who had been ill with fever for over three days. The old man had fever and cough; his poor wife was standing by his bedside. The *mali* feared that he would lose his job, and if he died in his extreme old age, his wife would be thrown on the streets. Lying in his bed with his face upwards, he greeted his master with a smile and folded hands; and then he was all tears. He was overwhelmed by his master's kindness. He sighed, sobbed, and said: "Bhagwan Himself has blessed me with a visit. But Sir, there is no hope for my life; my wife will have to.. ." and he again sobbed piteously. Soothing him, his master said: "Stop crying. Everybody is going to die some day or other. I am also to die some day. Take courage. Take medicine I am sending you and you will be all right. .. ." "Just see," he said to Rattu, "the poor man is afraid of death. ... I am not. ... Let him come at any moment !" Was Death, who had been shadowing him these two years, listening to this exclanation?

Ambedkar asked Rattu to make inquiries at the Railway booking office about the reservation of some tickets for December

14 as he was to carry out a programme of conversion of his followers at Bombay on December 16, 1956. He took out from his library Marx's *Das Kapital*, completed the last chapter of his book. *The Buddha And Karl Marx* and gave it for typing. On Tuesday, December 4, Ambedkar was present for a while in the Council of States and was seen in the lobby engaged in casual discussion. None thought that this would prove to be his last visit. In the evening he dictated two important letters; one to Acharya P. K. Atre, and the other to S. M. Joshi, both among the top leaders in opposition to the Congress Party in Maharashtra and front rank leaders in Samyukta Maharashtra agitation. The object of his writing these letters was to persuade the two leaders to join his proposed Republican Party. He also dictated a letter to M. B. Samartha, Bar-at-Law, asking him whether his brother's bungalow would be available for his stay in Bombay.

Although Ambedkar and his party were to start for Bombay on December 14, 1956, the arrangement was changed; and Mrs. Ambedkar's father, her brother and one Jadhav left by the evening train for Bombay on December 4. Ambedkar decided to go to Bombay by air on December 14 as he would not be able to stand the journey by train. Rattu did the typing work till half past one in the early morning and retired at his master's place. On the morning of December 5, Rattu got up early and saw his master asleep. The master got up at a quarter to nine in the morning. Rattu took leave of him and went to his office on bicycle having his meal at a hotel on his way to the office.

II

Mrs. Ambedkar left home at half past one in the afternoon to do some shopping with her guest Dr. Malvankar. Much later the master rang the bell two or three times and inquired about his wife, but she had not returned. The cook put on the light and took him to the bathroom. Then Ambedkar had some tea. Again he rang the bell and his face suddenly flamed red. Rattu came at 5.30 in the evening and found his master terribly upset. He gave Rattu some typing work. Just then Mrs. Ambedkar returned with Dr. Malvankar. She peeped in and Ambedkar, in an angry mood, hurled fire and brimstone at her. She asked Rattu to pacify his master.

By eight o'clock at night the fire had burned low. A deputation of Jain leaders came to meet him by previous appointment. Ambedkar was thinking of calling them the next day; but since they had come, he said, he should have a talk with them. After about twenty minutes he went to the bathroom. With his hand on the shoulder of Rattu he then came out of the drawing room, flung himself into the sofa and sat with his eyes closed.

The Jain leaders stood up us a mark of respect and then sat down. There was complete silence for some minutes, the Jain leaders gazing on his face intently. Then raising his head a little, he asked them the purpose of their visit. They casually inquired after his health and he replied, "It is going on." Then they discussed for few minutes questions concerning Buddhism and Jainism. They seemed well impressed and presented Dr. Ambedkar with a copy of the book *Jain aur Buddha*. They pressed him to attend a function the next morning and discuss some points with their Muni. He agreed to attend if his health permitted. And the last visitors left his residence. While he was talking to the Jain visitors, his last guest Dr. Malvankar also left his residence and went to Bombay by the night plane.

Rattu was pressing his master's legs. Ambedkar asked him to anoint his head with oil. He did so. The master felt a little relaxed. Suddenly a gentle, pleasant, musical tone was heard; and it took little time for Rattu to know that his master was, with his eyes shut, singing a song, the fingers of his right hand striking the arm of the sofa. Slowly the song became distinct and louder. Its lines became firm and 'Buddham Saranam Gachhami' became clearer. Ambedkar asked Rattu to play this favourite song of his on the radiogram; and with devotion the master accompanied the recorded song.

Just at this moment his cook Sudama came out and said that supper was ready. His master said he would have simply a little rice and nothing else. He was still under the spell of the song. The servant came a second time and Ambedkar rose up to go to the dining room. While walking with his hand on the shoulder of Rattu, he took out some books from different *almirahs*. He had a look at other books there and asked Rattu to keep them on his table near his bed. He cast another longing glance at his books, the great and real friends of his lifetime, and went in. With the help of Rattu he sat in the chair facing the kitchen. He ate little food and asked Rattu to massage his head. Then he got up with the help of a staff in his hand, singing a song from Kabir, "Chal Kabir tera bhav sagar dera." Singing in this way, he entered the bedroom adjacent to the kitchen.

As soon as he sat down, he took up the books one by one which he had picked from the library some twenty minutes earlier, looked into them and kept them on the table.

He lay down in his bed and asked Rattu to press his legs softly. It was now 11·15 p.m. Rattu had not gone home the previous night. He felt like going home as he saw that sleep seemed heavy on his master's eyes. Just to arrest his attention he shifted the books on his table a little. He looked up. He took his master's leave and brought out his bicycle to go; for he was now hungry and tired, and he knew that his wife was probably waiting for his return. Scarcely did he reach the gate when Sudama came running and said that Babasaheb was calling him back. The master asked Rattu to bring from his *almirah* the typescripts of the Preface and the Introduction to *The Buddha And His Dhamma* and the typed letters to Acharya Atre and S. M. Joshi and also the letter to the Burma Government, and to keep them on his table. Rattu kept all these letters, the Introduction and Preface, on the table near his master's bed and went home. Ambedkar said he would go through the Preface and Introduction in the night, and also read the letters to Atre, Joshi and the Burma Government; for they were to be despatched the next day. Near the bed of his master Sudama kept as usual a thermos containing coffee and a dish of sweets. Neither his doctor-wife, who had striven hard to save his life for the past eight years, nor his attendants had the faintest idea that Death was hiding behind his bed.

On the morning of December 6, 1956, Mrs. Savita Ambedkar got up as usual. About 6.30 a.m. when she had a look at the bed of her husband she saw his leg resting on a cushion. After taking a round as usual in the garden, she went to wake him up according to her routine. She tried to wake him up. She was terribly shocked to discover that her husband was no more a denizen of this world. She sent her car for Rattu and he came. On his arrival Mrs. Ambedkar collapsed in the sofa crying that

Babasaheb had departed this world. Rattu could not bear the thought, and with a trembling voice he exclaimed, "What! Babasaheb had departed this world." Rattu could not bear. They attempted to stimulate heart action in the mortal remains by massaging his limbs, moving his arms and legs, pressing upward the diaphragm and putting in his mouth a spoonful of brandy; but they failed to stimulate respiration. He had passed away in sleep. Ambedkar had been suffering severely from diabetic neurosis; his heart, which had grown weaker during the previous two years, had stopped healing.

Mrs. Ambedkar now loudly mourned her husband and Rattu wept bitterly over the dead body of his master, crying "Oh! Babasaheb. I have come, give me work". One Chamanlal Shah, who was on intimate terms with Ambedkar on account of his yogic and mystic studies, was staying at Ambedkar's residence.

Long before this, in 1946, Ambedkar had said that it was his belief that his life would be prolonged so long as it was necessary for the welfare of the Depressed Classes. This faith carried him through disappointments and disorders of health. He prayed to God that he should bless him with a span of life that was necessary for his work, if not more. It may be he thought that a great man passes away when his mission is fulfilled. Four years earlier he had written to his chief lieutenant Bhaurao Gaikwad that he would not live long, and so Bhaurao Gaikwad should prepare his mind for the event.

III

Rattu then broke the shocking news to circles closest to Babasaheb and then to Ministers of the Central Government. The news spread like wildfire throughout Delhi.

All of his admirers and lieutenants and devotees ran to 26 Alipore Road, and soon a throng of mourners collected outside his residence to have a last glimpse of the great man. The Bombay associates of the leader were intimated through Siddharth College, and they were also informed that the body was being flown to Bombay that night.

Premier Nehru, who used to take pride in introducing Ambedkar to foreigners as the jewel of his Cabinet and to

inquire most cordially after the health of Babasaheb whenever
he came across him in the lobby or at any function, called at
Ambedkar's residence and made kind and anxious inquiries of
Mrs. Ambedkar. He also inquired about the arrangements his
followers desired to make about the funeral. Home Minister
Pant, Jagjivan Ram, Minister for Communications, and the
Deputy Chairman of the Council of States called at his residence
to pay their respects to the departed leader. When apprised of
the situation, Jagjivan Ram arranged for a plane to transport
the body to Bombay.

By now thousands of people thronged Alipore Road, and all
the traffic came to a standstill in the neighbouring area. The
body was put on a platform in a truck and with cries of
"Babasaheb Amar Rahe" the funeral procession started in Delhi,
passing through streets lined with thousands of people bowing
their heads in reverence to the great leader. The procession took
five hours to reach the airport. It was now 9 p.m. Nehru sent a
wreath through a special messenger. The Secretaries of the Lok
Sabha and the Rajya Sabha garlanded the great parliamentarian.
Several Members of Parliament, leading lawyers and eminent
scholars paid their homage to the great scholar-statesman. The
plane took off at 9·30 p.m. Shankaranand Shastri, Bhikkhu
Anand Kausalyayan, Mrs. Ambedkar, Rattu, Sudama, Shankarlal
Shastri and few others accompanied the body.

The body was received at the Santa Cruz airport at 3 a.m.
by thousands of people who, in a post-midnight silent procession
took the body to Rajagriha, Ambedkar's former residence at
Dadar in Bombay. Lakhs of people had gathered to have a last
glimpse of their saviour, and had stood in queues for over ten
hours. Several political party leaders and trade union leaders
called at Rajagriha to pay their homage to the great leader. Grief
had enveloped Bombay; and on the morning of December 7,
factories, docks, railway workshops and textile mills in Bombay
closed. The Bombay Municipal conservancy staff stayed away
from work. Schools, colleges and cinemas were closed. There were
spontaneous *hartals* and processions in different cities like
Sholapur and Nagpur in Maharashtra. The Ahmedabad textile
mills were closed. The shock had unnerved many; and nearly a
score of persons fainted.

At noon the arrangements for the funeral procession were complete. The body was kept on a truck full of flowers and wreaths. Near the head of the body stood a statuette of Lord Buddha. Around the body were placed lighted candle-sticks, and in four corners incense was burning. The procession started at 1·30 p.m. at snail's pace through Vincent Road, since renamed Dr. Babasaheb Ambedkar Road, Poibavdi, Elphinstone Bridge, Sayani Road and Gokhale Road for the Dadar Hindu crematorium. For over five hours traffic came to a standstill in North Bombay. Dense crowds lined the entire route, people even perching on tree-tops to have a last glimpse of the great man. Hundreds of people, who had come from the neighbouring districts, had joined the two-mile-long procession. As the cortege passed, people showered petals and garlands over the body, and the heaps had to be removed constantly to enable the people to have a glimpse of the dead leader. State Ministers and Congress Party leaders offered floral tributes while the procession was on its way.

And thus came to its destination, after four hours, the greatest funeral procession in the living memory of Bombay. Hundreds of policemen were posted at the Dadar Hindu crematorium to maintain order, and top rank police officers personally supervised the police arrangement. More than half a million people witnessed the last rites performed by Buddhist priests. Over a lakh of people embraced Buddhism at the crematorium in order to fulfil the last wish of their departed leader. And as the pyre was lit by his son Yashwantrao at 7·30 p.m. the crowd wept bitterly. The city police honoured the departed leader by sounding the "last post", an honour given for the first time in Bombay to a non-official person.

Speaking near the pyre, Bhikkhu Anand Kausalyayan said that Dr. Ambedkar was a great leader; he had served the country and had attained nirvana. Bhikkhus from Malaya and Ceylon paid their homage to the deceased leader. Acharya P. K. Atre, speaking on the occasion, said with his voice like an ocean tide that Dr. Ambedkar had suffered and struggled for the rights of the Depressed Classes. Atre's thundering speech moved the half a million people to sobs and tears. Atre added that Ambedkar fought injustice, oppression and inequality; and he did not revolt against Hinduism but tried to reform it.

S.L. Silam, Speaker of the Bombay Assembly, the Chief
Secretary of the Bombay Government, Mrs. Savita Ambedkar,
Mukundrao Ambedkar, Rao Bahadur Bole, Ambedkar's
lieutenants B. S. Gaikwad, R. D. Bhandare, B. C. Kamble, P. T.
Borale and Ambedkar's colleague Acharya M. V. Donde were
present at the cemetery. It was a great coincidence that Ambedkar's earthly remains should vanish on December 7, 1956, the
day on which the eight-day celebrations of the 2500th Buddha
Jayanti concluded at Sanchi.

IV

The nation mourned the death of Ambedkar. All parties said
that in his death one of the greatest sons of India had passed
away. His death removed from the political scene a figure which
had prominently played for over thirty years a varied, vital and
valiant role in the affairs of the nation. Democracy in the world
had grown poorer by his death. Democratic thought had lost its
great champion. Recalling Ambedkar's great services to the
nation in constitution-making and Hindu law, Prime Minister
Nehru said in the Lok Sabha that Dr. Ambedkar would be
remembered mostly as the symbol of revolt against all the
oppressing features of Hindu society. His virulent opposition to
these oppressive features had kept people's minds awake.
Although he was a highly controversial figure, he played a very
constructive and very important role in the Government
activities. He revolted against something which everybody should
revolt against. And as Nehru considered that Dr. Ambedkar
belonged to the category of outstanding personages, he requested
the House to adjourn for the whole day.

Veer Savarkar said that India had lost in Dr. Ambedkar a
truly great man. The acting Chief Justice of Bombay Coyajee
said that Dr. Ambedkar led a purposeful life and held high his
mission in life to support the oppressed and that mission he
carried out to the end. Dr. Rajendra Prasad, President of the
Indian Republic, said that Ambedkar was the architect of our
Constitution and his services in various capacities, particularly
for the uplift of the Depressed Classes, could not be exaggerated.

C. Rajagopalachari said that Ambedkar's last demonstration of anger was his so-called conversion to Buddhism which unfortunately was more anti-Hinduism than an acceptance of the doctrine of compassion and rectitude that Buddhism was. Describing Ambedkar as a thoroughly upright person and a man with a keen jurist sense, a proud and irreconcilable heart, great learning, and when approached in the right spirit, full of friendliness, Rajagopalachari added that such a one had found peace after life's fitful work.

The newspaper world described him as a doughty, valiant and relentless champion of the Depressed Classes. All agreed that he was a great son of India, a great scholar, a jurist and constitutionalist of the world repute and a great parliamentarian; but the majority of them said that Ambedkar was bitter, belligerent, and irreconcilable and that he over-looked the great strides that India had taken both socially and legally in doing away with the disgrace of untouchability. *The Times of India* said that he was an able, gifted and versatile man who in different circumstances might have rendered even greater services to his country and community. "If the Ambedkars," warned the *Tribune*, Ambala, "who take up the cause are left, for the most part, to fight it alone, they cannot be expected to avoid giving expression to the desperation and frustration which consumes their innermost beings." *The Hindustan Times* observed thoughtfully: "What will remain is a recollection of his great services to the country and the impression left on his contemporaries of a vivid and versatile personality." The *Free Press Journal* said that the country would long remember him as one who righteously revolted against wrongs.

Depicting his career as the struggle of the intellect and will, the *Statesman*, Calcutta, observed that his deep erudition and experience in fields so diverse as law, economics, sociology, labour and politics would, in more propitious circumstances, have enabled him to make an even more impressive contribution to the world of letters. The *Amrita Bazar Patrika*, speaking highly of the amazing career of Dr. Ambedkar and describing him as a militant spirit bent upon the destruction of the old order which was based on injustice and denial of human rights, observed that his sudden demise reminded his countrymen once again of the great qualities and great patriotism that made him a worthy son of this continent.

The *New York Times* said that Ambedkar was known and honoured throughout the world chiefly as a champion of the Untouchables. "What is," it added, "perhaps not so well known is that he put a profound impress upon India's major legal structures." *The Times*, London, said that his name would figure prominently in any history of the socio-political evolution of India in the closing years of British rule. The determination, it went on, and courage of this thick-set, spectacled man were writ large upon his features, but he gave little evidence in manner and address of the wide scholarship gained by assiduous study in three continents; for he failed to acquire polish.

Yet the last tribute was paid by U. Nu, Premier of Burma. He said that Ambedkar was without dispute one of the illustrious figures that played a historic part in the annals of the great country, India, at a time when changing trends and conditions were making a significant impression on the life and social structure of the nation. He was, the Burmese Premier remarked, one of those who helped to accelerate the process of social change in the country, a process in the case of which hundreds of thousands, even millions, had been enabled to look forward to a better life and a happier life.[1]

On the eleventh day, after Ambedkar's death, his followers held a mammoth meeting in Delhi requesting the Government of India to make full investigations into the circumstances of Ambedkar's death. A deputation met Prime Minister Nehru, Home Minister Pant and Dr. Rajendra Prasad, President of Indian Republic, requesting them to make inquiries into the matter. His son also lodged a complaint with the Police in Delhi. So the Government ordered an inquiry into the circumstances of Ambedkar's death. And on November 26, 1957, Pant, as Home Minister, informed the Lok Sabha that the late Dr. Ambedkar had died a natural death according to an inquiry made by the Deputy Inspector-General of Police, Delhi.

The world does not know that the great jurist in Dr. Ambedkar had, in his Preface to *The Buddha And His Dhamma*, acknowledged a certain debt gratefully: "During the five years

1. The *Maha Bodhi*, January 1958.

there were many ups and downs in my health. At some stage my
condition had become so critical that doctors talked of me as a
dying flame. The successful rekindling of this dying flame is due
to the medical skill of my wife and Dr. Malvankar the physician
who has been attending me. To them I am immensely grateful.
They alone have helped me to complete the work." Why this
Preface, particularly this portion, has not appeared in the book
is a mystery.

Ambedkar had said at Khatmandu in his speech on Buddha
and Karl Marx that *Dukkha* was called property in Buddhist
scriptures. He always said that he would not suffer the fate of
Tilak as he was confident that his heirs would never go to Court.
His hopes were, however, belied. His son and his wife went to
Court for their respective share in the property. And at long last
his wife and son reached a compromise in the Court.

After Ambedkar's death some events of note closely
associated with his life took place. Yashwantrao Chavan, Chief
Minister of Maharashtra State, reputed for his judicious and
balanced policy responded to the popular appeal and declared
Ambedkar's birthday a public holiday. Government also gave over
to the Buddhist societies concerned for erecting memorials upon,
eleven acres of land at Nagpur where the historic *Diksha*
ceremony took place on October 14, 1956, and a small piece of
land at the Dadar Hindu Crematory where the saviour of a
suppressed people was cremated. A statue was erected at a
prominent place near the old Secretariat, Bombay, and in 1968 a
grand stoopa (pagoda) was erected on the *Chaitya-Bhoomi* at
the Dadar Chaupaty, Bombay.

In conformity with the directions of Dr. Ambedkar the
Republican Party was formed; but it was a mere conversion of
the Scheduled Castes Federation into the Republican Party. The
Party, however, split into two factions after the formation of
Maharashtra State. One co-operated with the Samyukta
Maharashtra Samiti dominated by the Red parties; the other co-
operated with the Praja Socialist Party with which Dr. Ambedkar
himself had co-operated. No great leader worth the name joined
the Republican Party. So it proved to be a change in the name of
the Party and nothing more.

Ambedkar's monumental work, *The Buddha And His Dhamma*, was posthumously published. It provides the interpretation Ambedkar has put on Buddhism or states what he means by Buddhism. The book is somewhat subjective, direct and a good model. The language is pithy. It is a prodigious commentary glistening with reasoned arguments. A great book always reflects the personality of its author. *The Buddha And His Dhamma* is, indeed, a fusion of the personality of Ambedkar and philosophy of the Buddha; just as the *Geeta-Rahasya* is a fusion of Tilak and the *Geeta*.

The *Maha Bodhi*, a famous Buddhist journal in India, however, opined that *The Buddha And His Dhamma* was a dangerous book; Ambedkar's interpretation of the theory of Karma, the theory of Ahimsa and his theory that Buddhism was merely a social system, constituted not the correct interpretation of Buddhism but a new orientation. Indeed, the whole of the book, observed the reviewer, explained the hatred and aggressiveness the neo-Buddhist nourished and displayed. "Ambedkar's Buddhism," added the reviewer, "is based on hatred, the Buddha's on compassion. It would seem more important to be careful what we accept in Ambedkar's book as being the word of the Buddha."

The title, pleaded this reviewer, should be changed from *The Buddha And His Dhamma* to that of *Ambedkar And His Dhamma*; for Ambedkar preached non-Dhamma as Dhamma for motives of political and social reform.[2]

The Light of the Dhamma, Rangoon, observed that although this was a book by a great man, unfortunately and how unfortunately, it was not a great book which the author with all his manifold virtues was not fit to write. The reviewer pointed out that the great Doctor tampered with the texts and whenever he found views in Buddhism, inconvenient to his own, denounced them as later accretions made by monks. The author was, nevertheless, a great and good man; the tragedy was that it was neither a great book nor a good book, concluded the reviewer.[3]

Whatever the critics may say, the Buddhism of Ambedkar would be a reformist plank in India as have been the, Brahmo

---

2. The *Maha Bodhi*, December 1959.
3. *The Light of Dhamma*, January 1959.

Samaj, the Satyashodhak Samaj, the Arya Samaj and the Prarthana Samaj. There is Zen Buddhism. There is Burmese Buddhism with its indigenous *nat* worship. There is Mahayana Buddhism and there is Hinayana Buddhism. Ambedkar wanted Protestant Hinduism. You may call his Buddhism Ambedkarayan or Buddhist New Testament, which would emerge as a strangely indigenous form of Neo-Buddhism paying homage to the Buddha and clinging to ritualistic practices and traditions woven into the fibre of the Indian mind. Hinduism and Buddhism are the branches of the same tree; just as the Catholic church and Protestant church are the branches of the same tree, Christianity. So those who worship the Buddha in India would do well to remember the words of Dr. Rhys Davids who observes: "We should never forget that Gautama was born and brought up a Hindu and lived and died a Hindu. His teaching, far-reaching and original as it was, and really subversive of the religion of the day, was Indian throughout. .... He was the greatest and wisest and best of the Hindus."[4]

Ambedkar found a peculiar charm and magnetism in the appellation Bharat. He had named one of his weeklies *Bahishkrit Bharat*. The name of his printing press was Bharat Bhushan Printing Press. His fight for temple entry and his battle for codifying the Hindu laws speak volumes for his inner struggle. You might believe the conversion of Lord Halifax, but not of Ambedkar, if conversion implies embracing a foreign faith. Ambedkar had insisted at the Round Table Conference that the Depressed Classes should be styled Protestant Hindus or non-Conformist Hindus. For one must not forget his memorable words which echoed the feelings of the innermost recesses of his heart. "Had my mind been seized with hatred and revenge. I would have brought disaster upon this land in less than five years."

His anxiety to live in Hindu culture, his avowal of embracing a religion that would neither denationalise the Depressed Classes nor harm the ancient culture of this land, all point to the fact that his religion has something to do with the culture, history and tradition of this land. His religion and politics went hand in hand. This is why Buddhist critics say that the Dhamma preached by Ambedkar is not Buddhism but Ambedkarism. And rightly

---

4.   Davids. Dr. Rhys, *Buddhism*, pp. 116-17.

so. *His Dhamma* preaches the necessity to kill if there is need to do so, and his message to India is that Indians should be determined to defend the independence of this land to the last drop of their blood.

The story of the life of Dr. Ambedkar was thus the struggle of a champion for human rights. It passed before the eyes of the people as the condolence meetings were being held all over the country. All agreed that he was a fighter for the dignity of man and the saviour of a suppressed people. No man in this country, or perhaps in any other country, could equal Ambedkar in his career which was exciting, varying, romantic and wonderful. To be born on a dunghill, to begin life as an Untouchable, to be treated in one's boyhood as a leper, and to have passed one's youth barred and bolted from society, which showed one out of hairdressing saloons, hotels, hostels, cars, temple: and offices, is a shocking experience in life. To have acted as a tiffin-carrier boy, to study while starving to obtain the highest degrees from world famous universities, to devote one's time to study, to have made one's way fighting every step forward, now with a surgical scalpel, now with a bludgeon, favoured neither by a family fortune, nor by political adoption, and to have faced perils and bitter political opposition, is creditable, courageous and remarkable enough.

And yet to have grown in name, fame and national prominence without being lifted by a party press or party caucuses, to have served on important committees relating to the development of Franchise, Economics and Constitution of a nation, to have been Labour Member of the Executive Council of a Government, to have been the first Law Minister of a free nation, to have been the Chief Architect of the Constitution of a nation that trampled one in one's boyhood, and to have released a suppressed people from the stigma, shackles and slavery under which they had groaned for ages, is surely an unequalled achievement in the whole experience of mankind! And so this son of an untouchable Hindu stands out in the history of this ancient land as an educationist, economist, author, professor, lawyer, leader, fighter, law-giver, law-maker, leveller and liberator.

Ambedkar edited newspapers. He wrote books on economics and sociology, history and politics. He conducted hostels and reading rooms. He was Principal of a Law College. He presided over hundreds of political and social conferences. A mass leader, he led social, political and labour movements. He founded political parties and colleges. He displayed the wisdom of a statesman, the qualities of a leader, the courage of a hero, the endurance of a martyr and the erudition of a savant. He adorned high public offices enriching them with his wisdom, democratic mind and love of human dignity. That in such a span of life the son of an Untouchable could crowd such varied interests, distinctions and scholarship is an unparalleled achievement in the modern world.

Great men have sprung from palaces as well as from cottages. They have sprung from the homes of shoemakers, tailors, butchers, bricklayers and blacksmiths. But Ambedkar had the unique distinction of springing from the dust. He came of a family whose hundred forefathers were treated in this land worse than dogs, whose touch was regarded as a pollution and whose shadow a sacrilege.

Ambedkars name, therefore, will be imperishably linked with the history of India. Most of his ideals have been incorporated into the Constitution. He rebelled against Manu and dethroned him from his high pedestal. This was a victory unequalled in the history of this ancient land. Ambedkar thus achieved what was above the ambition and attainment and beyond the dream of men of his community. He belongs to the men of first eminence of our age. He belongs to the line of those who have been saviours of the suppressed and oppressed. He shaped the life of sixty million people. He made his mark on the times. He wrote his name on the future of this country and in the history of human freedom.

Ambedkar's life constituted a proof that the strength in the seed to rise is not dead among the suppressed castes in India. It is a solid evidence of the survival of their manhood, virility and virtues. His life provides an example and an inspiration to the down-trodden masses of humanity that no bar of class, no bar of caste, no bar of privilege, no bar of riches, can prevent the full attainment and growth of an individual who is determined to build his personality on patient labour, burning sincerity, supreme courage and selfless sacrifice. He dealt a shattering blow to the arrogance of those who held that individual elevation and attainment were the monopoly of, the privileged few. We will not see the like of Ambedkar. Nature breaks, Emerson observes, the mould of a Great Man as soon as he is born.

"If I fail to do away with the abominable thraldom and inhuman injustice under which the class, into which I was born, has been groaning, I will put an end to my life with a bullet. This was the glorious vow taken by Ambedkar. Untouchability was abolished under the Constitution of free Bharat The vow was fulfilled, the dream realized, and the ambition materialized. The bondage ended. He said it. He did it.

Thus the unique life of Bharat Bhushan Ambedkar has become a new source of learning and a new source of inspiration for devotees. From it has emerged a new deity, and the lamp that will be burning in its temple in this land of temples will be seen from all sides of the nation and from distant corners of the world. A new academy of knowledge, a new inspiration for poetry, a new place of pilgrimage and a new opportunity for literature have sprung up!

WORKS OF
DR. BABASAHEB AMBEDKAR

1. 'Administration and Finance of the East India Company.' (Thesis for M. A. Degree Submitted to Columbia University, New York on May 15, 1915).

2. 'National Dividend of India - A Historical and Analytical Study' (Thesis for Ph. D. submitted to Columbia University in June 1916). Subsequently published by P. S. King & Co, London under the title 'The Evolution of Provincial Finance in British India'.

3. 'Castes in India : Their Mechanism, Genesis and Development' (A paper read in Prof. Goldenweiser's Anthropological Seminar on May 9, 1916, which was later published in the Indian Antiquary, May 1917).

4. A Review of Bertrand Russell's 'Principles of Social Reconstruction' (Published in Journal of Indian Economic Society, Vol. I, no.1 of March 1918).

5. Small Holdings in India and their Remedies (Published in the Journal of the Indian Economic Society Vol. I, 1918).

6. Provincial Decentralisation of Imperial Finance in British India (Thesis for Master of Science (M. Sc.) accepted by London University and M. Sc. Degree conferred on Dr. Ambedkar on June 20, 1921).

7. 'Problem of the Rupee' (Thesis for Doctor of Science (D. Sc.) submitted to London University in 1922. Later published in 1925 and subsequently reprinted in May 1947 under the title 'History of Indian Currency and Banking').

8. 'Annihilation of Castes' (Dr. Ambedkar published on May 15, 1936 his undelivered Presidential address - prepared for the annual conference of 'Jatpattodak Mandal' to be held at Lahore - in the form of book).

9.   'Federation Versus Freedom' (Lecture delivered by him before the Gokhale Institute of Economics, Pune on January 29, 1939. First published in 1939).

10.   'Thoughts on Pakistan' (Published in 1940 and revised edition was published under the title 'Pakistan or the Partition of India' in 1945).

11.   'Ranade, Gandhi and Jinnah' (address delivered on the 101st Birth Celebration of Mahadev Govind 'Ranade held on January 18, 1943 in Gokhale Memorial Hall, Poona. First published in book form in 1943).

12.   'What Congress and Gandhi have done to the Untouchables' - (Published in June 1945).

13.   'Communal Deadlock and a Way to Solve it' (Address delivered at the Session of the All India Scheduled Castes Federation held in Bombay on May 6, 1945. Published in 1945).

14.   'Who were the Shudras?' (Published in 1946 by Thacker and Co. Bombay).

15.   'States and Minorities: What are their rights and how to secure them in the constitution of Free (Memorandum on the safeguards for Scheduled Castes submitted and the Constituent Assembly on All India Schedule Castes Federation, published in 1947).

16.   'The Untouchables' (Published in October 1948, Amrit Book Co. New Delhi).

17.   'Maharashtra as a Linguistic Province' (A statement submitted to the Linguistic Province Commission. Published by Thacker & Co. Bombay in 1948).

18.   'The Buddha and His Dhamma' His magnum opus, in which he presented life and teachings of Buddha from a rational point of view. Published in 1957 after his death.

19.   'Buddha Pooja Path' (in Marathi, 1956).

20   Ambedkar in the Bombay Legislature, with the Simon Commission and at the Round Table Conferences, 1927–1939.

21 Ambedkar as member of the Governor General's Executive Council, 1942–46.

22 Unpublished writings; Ancient Indian commerce; Notes on laws; Waiting for a Visa ; Miscellaneous notes, etc.

23 Ambedkar as the principal architect of the Constitution of India.

24 Dr. Ambedkar and The Hindu Code Bill (Part 1 and 2).

25 Ambedkar as free India's first Law Minister and member of opposition in Indian Parliament (1947–1956).

26 Ambedkar and his Egalitarian Revolution – Struggle for Human Rights. Events starting from March 1927 to 17 November 1956 in the chronological order; Ambedkar and his Egalitarian Revolution – Socio-political and religious activities. Events starting from November 1929 to 8 May 1956 in the chronological order; Ambedkar and his Egalitarian Revolution – Speeches. Events starting from 1 January to 20 November 1956 in the chronological order.

27. Dr. Ambedkar's unpublished books published by Government of Maharashtra.

i   Philosophy of Hinduism (Dr. Babasaheb Ambedkar writings and speeches: Vol. 3. Published in 1987).

ii   India and Pre-Requisite of Communism (- do -).

iii   Revolution and Counter Revolution in ancient India (- do -).

iv   Buddha or Karl Marx (- do -).

v   Riddles in Hinduism (- do -).

vi   Untouchables or the Children of India's Ghetto (Dr. Babasaheb Ambedkar Writings and Speeches: Vol. 5. Published in 1989).

vii   Pali Grammar (Dr. Babasaheb Ambedkar Writings and Speeches: Vol. 16. Published in 1998).

viii   Pali Dictionary.

INDEX

534

□□□